Victorian Women Poets

BLACKWELL ANTHOLOGIES

Editorial Advisers

Rosemary Ashton, University of London; Gillian Beer, University of Cambridge; Gordon Campbell, University of Leicester; Terry Castle, Stanford University; Margaret A. Doody, Vanderbilt University; Jerome J. McGann, University of Virginia; David Norbrook, University of Oxford; Tom Paulin, University of Oxford; Michael Payne, Bucknell University; Elaine Showalter, Princeton University; John Sutherland, University of London.

Blackwell Anthologies are a series of extensive and comprehensive volumes designed to address the numerous issues raised by recent debates regarding the literary canon, value, text, context, gender, genre, and period. While providing the reader with key canonical writings in their entirety, the series is also ambitious in its coverage of hitherto marginalised texts, and flexible in the overall variety of its approaches to periods and movements. Each volume has been thoroughly researched to meet the current needs of teachers and students.

Chaucer to Spenser: An Anthology
edited by Derek Pearsall

Renaissance Literature: An Anthology
edited by Michael Payne

Sense and Sensibility: An Anthology of British Literature 1640–1789
edited by Robert DeMaria

Romanticism: an Anthology
edited by Duncan Wu

The Victorians: An Anthology
edited by Valentine Cunningham

Victorian Women Poets: An Anthology
edited by Angela Leighton and Margaret Reynolds

Nineteenth-century American Women Writers: An Anthology
edited by Karen L. Kilcup

VICTORIAN WOMEN POETS

AN ANTHOLOGY

EDITED BY

**ANGELA LEIGHTON &
MARGARET REYNOLDS**

BLACKWELL
Oxford UK & Cambridge USA

Copyright © Blackwell Publishers Ltd 1995
Arrangement and editorial apparatus copyright ©
Angela Leighton and Margaret Reynolds 1995

First published 1995

2 4 6 8 10 9 7 5 3 1

Blackwell Publishers Ltd
108 Cowley Road
Oxford OX4 1JF
UK

Blackwell Publishers Inc.
238 Main Street
Cambridge, Massachusetts 02142
USA

British Library Cataloguing in Publication Data

A CIP catalogue record for this book is available from the British Library.

Library of Congress Cataloging-in-Publication Data

Victorian women poets: an anthology / edited by Angela Leighton and Margaret
Reynolds.
p.   cm. — (Blackwell anthologies)
Includes bibliographical references (p.   ) and index.
ISBN 0–631–17608–X. — ISBN 0–631–17609–8
1. English poetry—Women authors. 2. English poetry—19th century.
3. Women—Poetry. I. Reynolds, Margaret, 1957–   . II. Leighton, Angela,
1954–   . III. Series.
PR1177.V53   1995   95–2697
821'.80809287—dc20   CIP
0-631-17609-8
Cover illustration: Lord Frederic Leighton, *Greek Girls Picking up Pebbles by the
Sea*, exhibited 1871, oil on canvas, 84 × 129.5cms.
Private Collection.
Typeset in $9\frac{1}{2}/11$pt
by Pure Tech India Ltd, Pondicherry
Printed in Great Britain by T. J. Press Ltd, Padstow, Cornwall
This book is printed on acid-free paper

Contents

List of Poets

Preface

The title 'Victorian Women Poets' is intentionally broad, covering, as it does, poetry written from the 1820s to the 1920s. We thus use the term 'Victorian' in its ideological–aesthetic rather than strictly historical sense, to define a cultural movement rather than a delimited period. Felicia Hemans, we would argue, is much closer in spirit to Barrett Browning than to Dorothy Wordsworth, and Charlotte Mew closer to Michael Field than to H.D. or Amy Lowell. The raggedness at the beginnings and ends of literary movements reflects the awkward realities of human lives and artistic developments, which do not necessarily follow the larger shifts of history or culture. We would argue that the poets included in this collection are essentially Victorian in their attitudes, themes and ideas, rather than Romantic or modernist. At the same time, we hope that this collection will help to push out the very meaning of the term 'Victorian', which has often carried unwarranted connotations of narrowness, naivety and homeliness.

In our choice of poets and poems we have looked, firstly, for literary merit rather than ideological 'fit'. Thus the major poets, as we see them, receive considerably more space than the minor ones, who may be represented by a few poems only. However, we have also tried to bring out the sense of a tradition, in which individual poets influence each other and certain characteristic themes and forms recur. We have also, wherever possible, reproduced long poems in their entirety, thus correcting the tendency of most anthologies to emphasize the short lyric at the expense of other, more ambitious forms. It is this tendency which is largely to blame for diminishing the scope and variety of Victorian women's poetry, both in their own time and in ours.

In the end, we have aimed for a collection which will be both evaluative and representative, both distinctive and comprehensive, while remaining true to the 'Victorian' spirit of the age as well as to the surprising, diverse and original voices of its women poets.

Acknowledgements

Among the many people who have offered help, advice and support in the compiling of this anthology we would particularly like to thank: Gillian Beer, James Booth, Julia Briggs, Marilyn Butler, Kate Challis, Heather Ingman, Julie Lockley, Jerome J. McGann, Harriet Marland, Clemency Moore, Richard Pugh, David Shaw, Marion Shaw, Neil Sinyard, Bob Smeaton, Patsy Stoneman, Jane Thomas and Jeanette Winterson.

In addition, thanks to all the women in the Inter-Library Loans office at Hull University Library, and to the staff of the British Library and of the Bodleian Library.

Extracts from the letters of Alice Meynell to Katharine Tynan are reproduced by courtesy of the Director and Librarian of the John Rylands Library, University of Manchester. For permission to quote from the letters of Michael Field and Constance Naden, we are grateful to the Librarian of Western Manuscripts at the Bodleian Library, Oxford. Extracts from the unpublished journals of Michael Field are reproduced by courtesy of the Manuscripts Librarian at the British Library. Extracts from Elizabeth Barrett Browning's letters to Isa Blagden are reproduced by kind permission of the Syndics of the Fitzwilliam Museum, Cambridge and the Henry W. and Albert A. Berg Collection, the New York Public Library. Poems by Christina Rossetti are reproduced, with permission, from *The Complete Poems of Christina Rossetti: A Variorum Edition*, vols I–III, edited by R. W. Crump, Copyright © 1979, 1986 and 1990 by Louisiana State University Press. Poems by Elizabeth Siddal are reproduced from *Poems and Drawings of Elizabeth Siddal*, eds Roger C. Lewis and Mark Samuels Lasner, Wolfville, Nova Scotia, The Wombat Press, 1978. Poems by Anne Brontë are reproduced, with permission, from *The Poems of Anne Brontë: A New Text and Commentary*, ed. Edward Chitham, Macmillan Press Ltd, © 1979. Poems by Charlotte Brontë are reproduced, with permission, from *The Poems of Charlotte Brontë: A New Annotated and Enlarged Edition of the Shakespeare Head Brontë*, ed. Tom Winnifrith, © Tom Winnifrith and the Shakespeare Head Press, 1984. Emily Brontë's poems are reproduced, with permission, from *The Poems of Emily Brontë*, ed. Barbara Lloyd-Evans, Batsford, © 1992, Barbara Lloyd-Evans and B. T. Batsford. Extracts from Elizabeth Barrett Browning's *Aurora Leigh* are reproduced, with permission, from *Aurora Leigh*, ed. Margaret Reynolds, Ohio University Press, © 1992. Extracts from Elizabeth Barrett Browning's *Casa Guidi*

Windows are reproduced, with kind permission from the Browning Institute and John Murray, from *Casa Guidi Windows* ed. Julia Markus, The Browning Institute, New York, © 1977. Poems by Eliza Ogilvy are reproduced, with kind permission from the Provost and Fellows, Eton College, from *Elizabeth Barrett Browning's Letters to Mrs. David Ogilvy* ed. Peter N. Heydon and Philip Kelley, John Murray, © 1974.

We have endeavoured to trace all holders of copyright material. If, however, we have failed to find any, the editors would be grateful to hear from them.

Lastly, profound thanks to Andrew McNeillie, our editor at Blackwell, for his unflagging encouragement and support, and to Alison Truefitt, our copy-editor, for her truly exacting, expert sifting of the mountain of our typescript. We thank our meticulous proof-reader and compositors as well.

Introduction I

'I wonder', said Lydgate, leafing through a copy of *The Keepsake*, 'which would turn out to be the silliest – the engravings or the writing here'. The scene, of course, takes place in the Vincys' drawing room in George Eliot's *Middlemarch*. Lydgate points derisively to a picture of a 'smirking' bridegroom coming out of church. The adorable Rosamund, anxious always to display the very best taste, suggests that Lydgate is a 'Goth'. 'I suspect you know nothing about Lady Blessington and L.E.L.', she says. Rosamund's provincial suitor poor Ned Plymdale, his addresses spurned, his gift disparaged, attempts to defend *The Keepsake*'s writing and engravings by pointing out that no less a personage than Sir Walter Scott contributes to the volume.[1]

The characters and the conversation may be fictitious, but the historical reference and context are exact. Though *Middlemarch* was published in the 1870s, it is set in the age of the Reform Bill and the volume of *The Keepsake* described in Chapter 27 is that for the year 1832. The frontispiece is an engraving of Mrs Stanhope looking playfully over her shoulder, ribbons flying. Ned attempts a compliment by suggesting that 'the Honourable Mrs S. is something like you'. But Rosamund dismisses him with the rejoinder, 'Her back is very large; she seems to have sat for that'. Rosamund may not have meant any satire, but the criticism is accurate and very funny when compared with the original. The engraving of the bridegroom which so amused Lydgate illustrates a (pretty silly) story about mistaken identity called 'The Wedding' and written by the Hon. Charles Phipps. Otherwise, the contents of the 1832 *Keepsake* include a short story by Mary Shelley, two poems by L.E.L. and two by the Countess of Blessington, an article about London by Lord John Russell, an account of an ascent of Mont Blanc, and engravings by Clarkson Stanfield and John Martin. Sir Walter Scott's contribution is 'A Highland Anecdote'.

Ned brought Rosamund *The Keepsake* because he shared her social ambitions, and the annual represented everything that was elegant and fashionable. Lydgate despised it because, to a man of science, *The Keepsake* represented everything that was trivial,

---

[1] George Eliot (1871) *Middlemarch*, chapter 27.

sentimental and effeminate. What neither of these views allows for, though George Eliot herself knew it very well, is that *The Keepsake*, like the many other annuals and albums published in the early part of the nineteenth century created a forum which helped to establish and professionalize the work of women writers, particularly the poets.

The annuals of the early nineteenth century grew out of the eighteenth-century vogue for pocket-books, calendars and almanacs. These were issued at Christmas, and so the annuals too were offered for sale as gifts and remembrancers, tokens to be presented to friends. Their very names – the *Forget Me Not*, *The Keepsake*, the *Amulet*, the *Literary Souvenir*, the *Gem* – suggest their sentimental purpose.

If sentiment was the main commodity of the annuals, their chief selling-point was social snobbery. At first, literary contributions to the annuals were anonymous, but while Frederic Mansel Reynolds was editor of *The Keepsake* (1829–35) he solicited for work by many famous names and it became the custom for publishers to seek out well-known society hostesses to edit their volumes as if the contents of the annual itself mimicked a select fashionable gathering.[2] This is why so many women predominated as editors of the annuals. The Countess of Blessington and Marguerite Power edited *The Keepsake* (1841–50 and 1851–7), Mrs S. C. Hall and Mary Russell Mitford edited *Findens' Tableaux* (1837 and 1838–41), the Countess of Blessington edited *Heath's Book of Beauty*, and *Fisher's Drawing Room Scrap-Book* was edited successively by L.E.L., Mary Howitt, Mrs Sarah Stickney Ellis and Caroline Norton. All of these writers published in each others' volumes and formed a part of a close literary circle. Mary Russell Mitford's Prefaces to *Findens' Tableaux*, for example, invariably included acknowledgement and thanks for the contributions of her friends.

Which is not to say that any of these poets or editors considered the annuals to be an easy publishing option. The Preface to the first edition of *The Keepsake* (1828) declares that 'the principal object [of this new undertaking] will be, to render the union of literary merit with all the beauty and elegance of art as complete as possible'.[3] The technical production of the annuals was high quality. The engravings were superbly reproduced, the paper was heavy, the type exquisitely clean. As far as 'literary merit' is concerned however, it became usual later in the nineteenth century to denigrate the annuals and Lydgate was certainly not the first of the accusers. 'The worst poems by the best writers' was the criticism generally levelled against them.[4] The twentieth century has simply forgotten that they ever existed.

In retrospect it is possible to see that the annuals had two roles, one that they played in the lives of readers, and another in the lives of their producers. The writers and editors working in the annuals industry took them very seriously, not so much for what they were, as for what they made possible. In professional and financial terms the annuals were of immense significance in the lives of Hemans and L.E.L. and many other women writers because they provided, for the first time for women, a reliable source of income, a practical working world, a professional status, and a framework of supportive literary friendships. For the woman writer the annuals meant real work and were valued for that. For the woman reader, however, they were about leisure, decoration, lifestyle.

---

[2] Alison Adburgham (1972) *Women in Print: Writing Women and Women's Magazines from the Restoration to the Accession of Victoria*, London, George Allen and Unwin, pp. 236–42.

[3] *The Keepsake* (1828) p. vi.
[4] Adburgham (1972) p. 236.

Today the annuals look like girls' stuff. *The Keepsake* is wrapped in crimson watered silk. *Findens' Tableaux* is large format, impossible to read anywhere but spread out on a display table, and its cover is green leather elaborately tooled and gilded with twining flowers and fat cherubs. Pictures appear at regular intervals, some illustrate the poem or story, some, especially the pictures of aristocratic society ladies, are just there for embellishment. On the positive side, they do clearly encourage a female audience and suggest that it is perfectly proper for women to participate in an artistic life; the half title for *The Keepsake* of 1828 shows two women in classical drapery, one with palette and brushes, the other bearing pen and notebook, and both presided over by the image of Athene in the clouds. The presence of the pictures encouraged an imaginative life, for they promoted a visually heightened poetry, and allowed for suggestive interplay between the text and the illustration. Similarly, in terms of literary content, the annuals are more intelligent than may at first appear. They have their fair share of trite poems about angels, but they also contain poems which are politically critical (L.E.L.'s 'The African' a protest poem about slavery in *Fisher's Drawing Room Scrap-Book*, 1832), and poems which challenged gender stereotypes (Elizabeth Barrett Browning's 'The Romaunt of the Page' in *Findens' Tableaux*, 1839). The message given out could be distinctly double-edged.

Whatever their effect upon their readers, the effect of the annuals upon the marketplace was clear. From the 1820s to the 1850s they proliferated. As new titles appeared, preface after preface made clear that publishers found this a lucrative and enduring formula. And it was the poetry, particularly the women's poetry, which made the volumes so popular. In 1848 three anthologies devoted exclusively to the work of women poets capitalized upon this public demand. The first was Frederic Rowton's *The Female Poets of Great Britain, Chronologically Arranged with Copious Selections and Critical Remarks* (London, 1848). 'The fact', he writes, 'that this is almost the first book expressly devoted to the poetical productions of the British Female mind, tends strongly to prove that woman's intellect has been overlooked, if not despised, by us hitherto: and that it is high time we should awake to a sense of our folly and injustice.'[5] His supplying of this 'want' begins with selections from Juliana Berners (in the fifteenth century) and Ann Boleyn (in the sixteenth) and comes up to date with Hemans, L.E.L., Norton, Howitt, Butler (Frances Kemble) and Barrett Browning. As might be expected, Rowton subscribes to theories of the 'separate spheres'; 'Man is bold, enterprising and strong: woman cautious, prudent and stedfast. Man is self-relying and self-possessed; woman timid, clinging and dependent' he declares.[6] But his account of why and how women's poetry has been neglected includes such considerations as the narrowness of women's education, condescension in patronage, and simple sexual prejudice, and altogether reads like a nineteenth-century version of Joanna Russ's *How to Suppress Women's Writing*.[7] His conclusion that 'such a word as Poetess' should be struck from the vocabulary is telling.[8]

The other two anthologies of 1848, published as companion volumes by Lindsay and Blakiston of Philadelphia, were not quite so forward thinking. *The British Female Poets* edited by George Bethune also gives selections from some sixty poets from Berners to Barrett Browning, but its tone leads back to the refined world of the annuals. The

---

[5] Frederic Rowton ed. (1848) *The Female Poets of Great Britain*, London, p. xvii.

[6] Rowton (1848) pp. xxiv–xxv.

[7] Joanna Russ (1984) *How to Suppress Women's Writing*, London, The Women's Press.

[8] Rowton (1848) p. xix.

frontispiece is an engraving of Caroline Norton negligently dressed, wearing a 'Corinne'-style band in her hair, and leaning pensively over an open book. The title page displays a picture of a house in hilly countryside and bears the legend 'Rhyllon Near St. Asaph, The Residence of Mrs. Hemans'. If this were not enough, Bethune owns that his volume 'contains the Editor's gatherings during a leisurely excursion through a most pleasant department of English Literature' and that his '... only merit, is having furnished the string which binds the flowers together'. Quite. But then, Bethune is a gentleman, and if readers find him 'too lenient in his criticisms' then he begs us to remember that 'Finding fault is ever an unwelcome office, but especially distasteful to an American when a lady is the subject'.[9]

American ladies seem to have been similarly polite. Caroline May was the editor of Lindsay and Blakiston's other volume, *The American Female Poets* (1848). May solicited her living contributors for biographical information but did not press for it if it was not forthcoming: 'No women of refinement, however worthy of distinction – and the most worthy are always the most modest – like to have the holy privacy of their personal movements invaded. To say where they were born seems quite enough while they are alive. Thus, several of our correspondents declared their fancies to be their only facts; others that they had done nothing all their lives; and some – with a modesty most extreme – that they had not lived at all'.[10] Definitely an anthologist of the old school, May's volume mirrors Bethune's in its variations on the frontispiece theme. There is a picture of Frances S. Osgood in contemplative mode, while the title page depicts a winding path to a cottage door, a stream running by, roses round the door, and smoke billowing from the chimney. Its title is 'The Poet's Home'.

In spite of the notable advances in women's education which took place so much earlier in the United States than comparable developments in Britain, the Americans seem to have retained a taste for the prettified image of the woman poet. Certainly there must have been a market for it, because both May's and Rowton's anthologies were reprinted by American publishers. May's appeared again in 1871 deliciously re-named as *Pearls from the American Female Poets*, beautifully bound in purple leather with gold stamping, and sumptuously embellished with engravings ('Innocence' is the frontispiece) which bear no relation whatsoever to the poems.[11] Rowton's was re-issued in the 1870s as *The Cyclopaedia of Female Poets* 'with additions by an American Editor' in two fat volumes and with the apparently obligatory engravings of Eastern maids, medieval scenes and children in country paths, all stuck in haphazardly and irrelevant to the poems.[12]

These publications were still working with an aesthetic of women's poetry which, for most thinking women, had become distinctly old-fashioned by the end of the nineteenth century. This would not have mattered much if it was only a question of prettification, but it extended also to the pernicious assumption that women's poetry was always about personal experience and that its true subjects were home and the heart. This was taken for granted in May's introduction: '... poetry, which is the language of the affections, has been freely employed among us to express the emotions of woman's heart ... the themes which have suggested the greater part of the following

---

[9] George Bethune ed. (1848) *The British Female Poets*, Philadelphia, pp. iii, vi, vi.

[10] Caroline May ed. (1848) *The American Female Poets*, Philadelphia, p. vii.

[11] Caroline May ed. (1871) *Pearls from the American Female Poets*, New York, Allen Brothers.

[12] Rowton ed. (c.1875) *The Cyclopaedia of Female Poets*, Philadelphia, J. B. Lippincott and Co.

poems have been derived from the incidents and associations of every-day life. And home, with its quiet joys, its deep pure sympathies, and its secret sorrows, with which a stranger must not intermeddle, is a sphere by no means limited for a woman whose inspiration lies more in her heart than her head.'[13] The same theory had been proposed by an interesting and influential book which was published in London in 1842. Mary Ann Stodart's *Female Writers: Thoughts on Their Proper Sphere and on Their Powers of Usefulness* reveals its agenda in its title. In her chapter on 'Poetry and Poetesses' she begins by personifying poetry as female because of its identification with feeling ('The domain of poetry is wide; her power over the human heart is immense . . .') and she goes on to argue that women writers therefore should be good at poetry because they too are more heart than head: 'We have struck on the point where lies the true poetic power of woman, it is in the heart – over the head – and especially in the peculiarities of her own heart'.[14]

The power of these two parallel commonplaces – the gender construction of woman as instinctive, feeling, personal, and the consequent genderizing of poetry which appeared to be about the same things – had far-reaching consequences which stretch well beyond the nineteenth century. Even today there is a sneaking suspicion among the general public that poetry is rather wet and effeminate, and a related expectation that when women write poetry they will write about themselves and their feelings. Connected to this is the sense that they will pay dearly for their genius in being frustrated and unhappy, if not downright mad. Mary Ann Stodart's last two chapters are entitled 'Social Disadvantages of Literary Women' and 'Dangers to the Moral and Religious Character'. To be a woman and a poet was, perhaps still is, a risky business. But its riskiest aspect lies in the demeaning assumptions made about women and about poetry, rather than in the realities of literary practice.

This is what Barrett Browning perceived when she wrote her much-quoted line 'I look everywhere for grandmothers and see none'. It's a rallying cry. She might have written it specially for all latter-day feminist critics seeking a matrilineal descent with all the power born of yearning for a lost home. But look again at Barrett Browning's two letters on the subject, and they tell quite a different story. When she said that she longed for 'grandmothers' Barrett Browning didn't mean that she couldn't find any women poets. She could think of plenty, and she lists them (Marie of Brittany, Vittoria Colonna, Lady Winchelsea, the Duchess of Newcastle, the author of 'Auld Robin Gray', Joanna Baillie, L.E.L., Felicia Hemans). But of all these only Joanna Baillie, she says, is in the very highest sense a true poet. The rest are 'versifiers'.[15]

Obviously Barrett Browning was making a space for herself much as Virginia Woolf made a space for herself when she wrote her 1919 essay on 'Modern Novels' and announced that contemporary writing wasn't up to scratch.[16] But Barrett Browning is also saying something very serious about what had happened to women's poetry and to critical attitudes to women's poetry in the first half of the nineteenth century. The annuals and the anthologies were good for women poets because they made a

[13]   May (1848) p. vi.
[14]   M[ary] A[nn] Stodart (1842) *Female Writers: Thoughts on Their Proper Sphere and on Their Powers of Usefulness*, London, pp. 87–91.
[15]   Elizabeth Barrett to H. F. Chorley, 3 January 1845 and 7 January 1845, in Philip Kelley and Scott

Lewis eds (1992) *The Brownings' Correspondence*, Winfield Kan., Wedgestone Press, vol. 10, pp. 3–5 and 13–15.
[16]   Virginia Woolf (1925) [1919] 'Modern Fiction' in *The Common Reader*, First Series, London, The Hogarth Press, pp. 184–95.

community and a professional circle for these writers. But the annuals and anthologies were also bad for women writers because they seemed to promote a small and trivialized style of poetry in which women were presumed to specialize. Barrett Browning knew all about both these good and bad sides. In the 1840s she quarrelled with Robert Browning over the value of the annuals, defending them for their professional purposes, deprecating them for their compromising content. In the 1850s she wrote those two sides into her story of the professional woman poet. Aurora Leigh strives to get beyond the 'cyclopaedias, magazines, / And weekly papers', beyond carving 'many an article on cherry-stones / To suit light readers' (*Aurora Leigh*, III, 310–11 and III, 318–19), but she none the less appreciates the financial freedom this work gives her, and she is not ungrateful to receive a request from 'Blanche Ord, the writer in the "Lady's Fan"' (*Aurora Leigh*, III, 51).

Of the poets included in this collection, Felicia Hemans, Mary Howitt, Maria Jewsbury, L.E.L., Elizabeth Barrett Browning, Helen Dufferin, Caroline Norton, Adelaide Procter, Christina Rossetti, Frances Kemble, Eliza Cook, Henrietta Tindal, Jean Ingelow and Menella Smedley were all published in the annuals. That the women in this collection valued them for this reason is clear, whether one cites the Brontës' reading and making notes on *Friendship's Offering* for 1829,[17] or Barrett Browning appreciating Theodosia Garrow's poems in the *Book of Beauty* for 1838.[18] Even George Eliot's close reading of *The Keepsake* (did she remember it, or did she look it up?) is evidence of how and why these writers used the annuals. This constant looking at each others' work, valuing and assessing each others' talent, marks not only the personal experience of the Victorian women poets, but spills over into their poetry too. There are numerous poems addressed by one poet to another as if carrying on a conversation with one another. Hemans's 'The Last Song of Sappho', our first poem, is an obvious example, but there are many others: L.E.L.'s 'Stanzas on the Death of Mrs. Hemans', Barrett Browning's 'L.E.L.'s Last Question', Kemble's 'To Mrs. Norton', Charlotte Brontë's two poems to her sisters, Blagden's 'To George Sand on her Interview with Elizabeth Barrett Browning', Dora Greenwell's poems to Barrett Browning, Parkes's 'For Adelaide', Rossetti's 'L.E.L.', Amy Levy's 'To Vernon Lee' and Michael Field's 'To Christina Rossetti'.

Among the poets the sense of a professional sisterhood remained consistent, starting early in the century and continuing to the end. It began as a practical and personal network, but gradually changes took place both in attitudes to women, and in the publishing world, which gave this solidarity a more political aspect. This change began in the 1850s. Of course the old school of critical views on women's poetry continued. There were, as we have seen, those late re-issues of the saccharined anthologies; there were also the late sentimental male critics such as Edmund Gosse ('It is no new theory that women, in order to succeed in poetry, must be brief, personal and concentrated.' 1882)[19] and Eric Robertson ('What woman would not have been Niobe rather than the artist who carved the Niobe? It is a very old-fashioned doctrine this, that children are the best poems Providence meant women to produce, but it is not therefore any the

---

[17] Elizabeth Gaskell (1975) [1857] *The Life of Charlotte Brontë*, Harmondsworth, Penguin, p. 118.

[18] Elizabeth Barrett to Mary Russell Mitford, 23 November 1838, in Philip Kelley and Ronald Hudson

(1986) *The Brownings' Correspondence*, Winfield Kan., Wedgestone Press, vol. 4, p. 105.

[19] Edmund Gosse (1882) 'Christina Rossetti' in *Critical Kit-Kats* (1896), p. 136.

worse.' 1883).[20] Old-fashioned is right. After all they had both had their answer long since in Barrett Browning's *Aurora Leigh* (1857).

During the time that she was working on *Aurora Leigh*, Barrett Browning met, and raged with, the feminist activist Bessie Rayner Parkes. She signed her petition for the Married Women's Property Bill and she encouraged Parkes in her plan to found a new journal for women. The day of the annual was over. In the 1840s and 1850s all the famous names disappeared: *Findens' Tableaux* in 1841, *Friendship's Offering* in 1844, *Forget Me Not* in 1847, *Fisher's Drawing Room Scrap-Book* in 1851 and *The Keepsake*, last survivor after all, in 1857. Their demise was partly commercial. Technical advances in printing meant that the market was now flooded with new magazines, cheaply produced and cheaply sold, and this wiped out the profit on the sale prices of the luxurious and expensive annuals. But their going out of fashion also had a great deal to do with the fact that the new 'strong-minded woman' needed a new publication to read and a new type of publication to work for.

The aims of the *English Woman's Journal* set up in 1858 by Parkes and Barbara Bodichon appealed to Barrett Browning. It was run by women for women and focused on encouraging women's writing, offering profiles of successful women as role models and promoting opportunities for the employment of women. But this was work for a new generation, and the names of those involved in the *English Woman's Journal* are still linked with the history of progress in education, in women's rights, in the campaign for suffrage. Emily Davies, founder of Girton College Cambridge, was, for a short while, an editor of the *Journal*; Elizabeth Garrett Anderson, England's first woman doctor, was a contributor; Jessie Boucherett founded the Society for Promoting the Employment of Women which shared offices with the *Journal*; and when the activist Emily Faithfull established the Victoria Press in 1860 to train women to work as compositors, the Press took over the printing of the *English Woman's Journal*.

Professional, political, practical and workwomanlike, the *Journal* most certainly was not ornamental. The first issue in March 1858 included a factual article on 'The Profession of Teacher' by Parkes which drew on the annual reports of the Governesses Benevolent Institute, an account of a visit to the London Diocesan Penitentiary for Women at Highgate, a piece on the eighteenth-century Methodist preacher Miss Bosanquet, a jokey tale by Amelia B. Edwards called 'Bradshaw the Betrayer' where a weary traveller (male) fulminates over the unreliability of the railway Guide to Europe, an article on the Married Women's Property Bill, and Notice of Books (including Coventry Patmore's *Angel in the House* which the reviewer deems 'too conventional', and two children's books called *How to Choose a Wife* and *How to Choose a Husband*). 'Notes on Passing Events' ranges from speeches in the Houses of Parliament to remarks on the Indian Mutiny of 1857. There is only one poem. It's 'Grief' by Adelaide Procter, and it is published anonymously.

But poetry was still important to the women who worked on the *Journal* and at the Victoria Press. The Press's first production was a showcase anthology called *Victoria Regia* (1860) which was edited by Adelaide Procter with a Preface by Emily Faithfull. *Victoria Regia* is, in some ways, the last of the annuals. They might have been activists and agitators, but all the women who worked on *Victoria Regia* had been brought up on the annuals and so they adopted that style. Bound in blue leather, stamped and

---

[20] Eric Robertson (1883) *English Poetesses* A Series of Critical Biographies, with Illustrative Extracts, p. xiv.

gilded, each poem or story is embellished with engravings of flowers or religious symbols. The frontispiece is a picture of the huge African water lily which was named Victoria Regia for the Queen, and the first poem in the volume is a dedication to the Queen written by Bessie Rayner Parkes. Adelaide Procter, Isa Blagden, Mary Howitt and Caroline Norton, all contributed to *Victoria Regia*.

The *Journal* only continued until 1864 but it marked the beginning of a new kind of publication for women, one which reflected the character of the times. It was succeeded by the *Alexandra Magazine* which ran for only one year, and then by the *Englishwoman's Review* edited by Jessie Boucherett and then by the suffragists Caroline Ashurst Biggs and Helen Blackburn. The last editor was Antoinette Mackenzie who ran the *Review* on the funds which Boucherett had provided right up until 1910.[21]

Another publication which carried on the *English Woman's Journal* style of mixing stories and poems with politics and women's issues, was Emily Faithfull's *Victoria Magazine* (1863–80). Its first issue in May 1863 included a poem on the Queen, an article on social life in the United States, a chapter from Trollope's *Lindisfarne Chase*, Christina Rossetti's poem on L.E.L., an article on the spirits and another on the careers of Englishwomen in India. The list of 'Literature of the Month' included mention of books on *Profitable Gardening*, *Elementary Hydrostatics*, and an issue of Barrett Browning's *Greek and Early Christian Poets*.

For the most part, however, towards the end of the century, women's journals became more specialized, dividing sharply into those which were large-circulation ladies' magazines devoted to the domestic and the fashionable, and those which were feminist and political (Lydia Backer's *Women's Suffrage Journal*, and Louisa M. Hubbard's *Work and Leisure*).

The tone of women's anthologies also changed. Elizabeth A. Sharp's 1887 anthology of women poets was a collection for a new era. More comprehensive and representative than its predecessors, she called it *Women's Voices* (not just 'pearls' and flowers, but snakes and toads are spoken here too), and the title page carried two dedications: 'To All Women' and 'To My Mother'. Most of the poets appearing in the present selection are included in Sharp's, although our choice of poems is often different. She says that 'The idea of making this anthology arose primarily from the conviction that our women-poets had never been collectively represented with anything like adequate justice; that the works of many are not so widely known as they deserve to be ...' Interestingly she decided to put her selection in chronological order because she found '... as I trust others may, that the collection thus made pointed to a steady develop-ment of intellectual power'.[22]

In making the present selection, we have also opted for a chronological arrangement. But our reasons for doing so have more to do with practical questions of influence, interpretation and revision, than any supposed 'development' in 'intellectual power'. Indeed we would argue for something quite different and suggest that Sharp was, here, being misdirected by considerations to do with subject matter. For us it is quite clear that the intellectual address of the woman poet to her subject and her form, is and remains intense, sustained and sophisticated from the beginning of the century to the

[21] Janet Horowitz Murray and Myra Stark (1980) Introduction to the facsimile edition of *The English-woman's Review*, New York, Garland Publishing, p. viii.

[22] *Women's Voices* (1887) An Anthology of the Most Characteristic Poems by English, Scotch, and Irish Women. Selected, Arranged and Edited by Mrs. William Sharp, London, pp. viii–ix, ix.

end. What does change, and the distinction is marked, is what it is that women poets write about.

By the time that Alfred Miles compiled his large retrospective anthology *The Poets and the Poetry of the Century* (1891–7), it seemed natural and appropriate to put the women in one volume, on the grounds that 'The work of the Women Poets of the nineteenth century is a characteristic feature of its literature. As such it has been thought well to separate it from the general body of the poetry of the period and present it in a form calculated to show its progress and development. It is hoped that the result will be found of sufficient interest to justify this special treatment.'[23] An aspiration modest enough, but then Miles was a man of his time.

Elizabeth Sharp, however, was rather more advanced. In 1890 when she published a revised edition of her anthology as *Women Poets of the Victorian Era*, it was dedicated to a feminist activist: 'To my friend Mona Caird, the most loyal and devoted advocate of the cause of Woman'. And Sharp's new Preface included a passionate call to arms:

> It is easy to generalise what women have been and are – what they have done and are yet doing: . . . but who shall predict what women will do in the future? Daily, yearly, prejudices are being broken down, fetters are falling off; women are released into knowledge and to experiences of life through wider doors; legitimate freedom is now partly theirs, and before long will be theirs wholly as it belongs to men. Who, therefore, can predict exactly what will or will not be the outcome of these possibilities? The promise of today is so manifold that the morrow which is at hand can hardly but be one of lofty aim and accomplishment.[24]

Sharp was, of course, right about those legal and political possibilities. But she was wrong about her women poets. For much of the twentieth century, they have simply disappeared from literary history.

And why? Partly because of the experiments of modernism, partly because of a new feminist sensibility, partly because of a critical value placed on the dry, the intellectual, the dispassionate, early twentieth-century writers, readers and critics were embarrassed by their Victorian 'grandmothers'. Convinced by the 'Pearls from . . .' presentation, convinced by the apparently 'natural' relation between women and feeling and poetry, the Victorian women poets seemed too effusive, too wayward, too flimsy and altogether too womanly to be claimed by writers such as Woolf, H. D. or Stein as a literature of their own.

Another scene from *Middlemarch*. Will and Dorothea have met in Rome and are holding a conversation about poetry. 'To be a Poet', says Will, 'is to have a soul so quick to discern, that no shade of quality escapes it, and so quick to feel, that discernment is but a hand playing with finely ordered variety on the chords of emotion . . .' Dorothea objects. 'But you leave out the poems . . . I think they are wanted to complete the poet. I understand what you mean . . . But I am sure I could never produce a poem'. Will is quick with his compliment and the narrating voice of George Eliot is audibly sceptical, if amused, 'You *are* a poem', he says.[25]

---

[23] Alfred H. Miles (1891–7) *The Poets and the Poetry of the Century*, London, vol. 7, Joanna Baillie to Mathilde Blind, p. v.

[24] Elizabeth Sharp (1890) *Women Poets of the Victorian Era*, London, p. xxxii–xxxiii.

[25] George Eliot (1871–2) *Middlemarch* chapter 22.

This is the problem. If the woman is the poem, then you 'leave out' the work. Little wonder then that Victorian women's poetry has been neglected for so long. The purpose of this anthology is to provide the poems which are necessary 'to complete the poet'.

M.R.

Introduction II

In 1824, Byron, the 'last man' of Romanticism, died. That same year, L. E. L. published her immensely popular long poem, *The Improvisatrice*, in which a woman poet tells a series of sad tales about betrayed heroines and herself dies of a broken heart. The twilight years between Romanticism and Victorianism proper, between about 1824 and 1837, could be said to belong to women. The rise of the popular annual at this time both supported and testified to a widespread feminization of literature at all levels – a feminization, as Tennyson's own early 'magazine' poetry shows, not restricted to women, but affecting the whole development of Victorian verse. These highly decorative journals provided both a realistic income and a willingly unrealistic female readership for new poets, while helping to generate certain myths and expectations which would influence poetry for the rest of the century. As the risqué, literary effeminateness of the male Romantics gave way to the literal femininity of their successors, and as the solitary bardic wanderer became a Sappho, Corinne, Properzia Rossi or Eulalie, the idea of the poet underwent a crucial change. While the source of the male Romantic's angst tended to be obscurely metaphysical or aesthetic, a torment of the spirit without cause or cure, the source of the female poet's alienation was likely to be familiarly domestic.

The word which sums up this shift of sensibility during the 1820s and 30s is 'home'. After the cosmopolitan ambitions of Romanticism, its restlessness and sexual adventure, the idea of home came to represent national, domestic and gender stability. As England settled into a Queenly peace and prosperity (at least for some), and cut itself off from continuing revolution on the continent, home, with its connotations of rightful property and legitimate family, could be idealized as the thing for which England had won the war with revolutionary France. However, it is interesting that, in the literature of the period, home becomes the domain of deep anxiety, regret, distrust and longing. Even Felicia Hemans, who might be credited with making the shift from a Romantic ethic of nature to a Victorian ethic of the home almost single-handed, is usually uncertain of its whereabouts. In many of her poems, home is either empty of its main figurehead, the father, or else home is somewhere else: in Italy, in the south – paradoxically, in one of those places still subject to the convulsions of political change. One thing that can be said about Victorian women poets in general is that they are rarely 'at home'. From Hemans to Mew, home is either an ideal that is yearned for, or else it is a prison-house from which to escape. Hemans's 'The Chamois Hunter's Love', Rossetti's 'At Home', Levy's 'The Old House', Mary Coleridge's 'The Witch', Nesbit's 'Haunted', Mew's 'The Farmer's Bride', for example, all pivot on the double meaning of home which runs through women's poetry: home may be unhomely, the woman's place may have shut her out, it may not be the woman's place at all. Related to this are the various 'convent' poems (by Rossetti, Procter, Naden, Mew) which play on the tricky threshold between being in and out, between safety and the world, vocation and desire. The threshold, both external and internal, is a crucial moral, sexual as well as imaginative location for Victorian women.

The catalyst for this new poetic confidence in the 1820s and 30s was, as Ellen Moers has shown, Madame de Staël's *Corinne* (1807), the story of the passionate woman from the south, whose genius frightens and ultimately repels her male suitor. *Corinne* popularized the myth of the woman poet as a creature of self-destructive contradiction for generations to come. While Tennyson and Browning, D. G. Rossetti and Swinburne generally continue in the Romantic tradition of internalizing self-destruction as an anti-social, criminal or Faustian drive, dealing death or despair from within, their female contemporaries tend to externalize it as a social incompatibility: between love and ambition, the hearth and the stage, woman and fame. The repercussions of de Staël's highly influential, enabling but also disabling myth, can be felt for the rest of the century, most obviously in its grand rewriting in Barrett Browning's *Aurora Leigh*, but also, for instance, in George Eliot's *Armgart*, Levy's 'A Minor Poet', and Naden's 'Love Versus Learning'.

However, the problem with the Corinne model of creativity is that it can lead to bad faith (the suicidal gesture as emotional blackmail) or to a merely repetitive melancholy (yet another waving-and-drowning 'last song'). Unfortunately, many nineteenth-century reviewers assumed that the pose of heartfelt despair was the natural one for women, thus perpetuating the notion that women's verse was essentially melancholy, easy and lyrical. Such an assumption, as this anthology shows, is far from true. The figure of the woman poet who dies as she sings, or who must die because she has dared to sing (apology and punishment being closely linked), largely disappears by the middle of the century, when it is transmuted into something else. Rossetti, for instance, reproduces the Sappho story in many of her poems, but her protagonists usually sing *after* death, in a twilight landscape beyond apology and punishment. Michael Field then takes the whole myth back to its more authentic classical origins, making Sappho, not a poet of death at all, but of sensuous lesbian love. Paradoxically, it is they who also demythologize the subject of woman's death by writing overtly autobiographical poems about their own dying of cancer. If the figure of the woman poet starts as one of stylized emotional reproach and poetic apology, it develops into something much more varied, assertive and surprising.

Three recurring images hint at the difficulties women encountered in identifying themselves as poets in a society which, on the one hand, cast them in an unremittingly sentimental mould, and, on the other, was astonished at their mere existence. The first of these is the mask. In L. E. L. it is used to probe the differences between outer and inner self, the face and the heart. Many of her verses are about the secrets women must keep in order to survive as social beings. Barrett Browning's 'The Mask', Rossetti's 'Winter: My Secret', Mary Coleridge's 'True to myself' and Mew's 'Fame' then develop the idea of subjectivity as a performance which conceals as much as it reveals. As the nature of the woman's poetic self is imagined and invented in the course of the century, almost from nothing, its essentialism is at once paraded and questioned. The mask provides a teasing figure for this contradiction.

The second image is the picture. The annuals first set the fashion for picture poems, which were often written to accompany visual illustrations. Both Hemans and L. E. L. wrote verses which either describe a picture – the poem thus remaining at two removes from the reality – or themselves present pictured tableaux of women in heroic or tragic poses. There are dangers to this method, of course, not least that of turning the woman into a self-conscious sexual object and the reader into a voyeur. It is interesting to notice, however, how the picture poem later develops through the use of irony and self-distance. The famous garden scene in *Aurora Leigh* Book II, for instance, turns the tables against the admiring male onlooker, whose 'picture' Aurora refuses to be. Other poems, like Siddal's 'The Lust of the Eyes', Rossetti's 'In an Artist's Studio' and ' "Reflection" ' and Probyn's 'The Model', all end by framing the male framer, by setting up another perspective, either inside the poem (the model herself does the looking) or outside (the reader is the ultimate observer and artist), which undermines his. Each of these poems thus goes in search of the unpicturable, secret female self, against the fixed or famished needs of the idealizing male gaze. By contrast, Michael Field's picture poems ('A Portrait', "A Girl", 'A Picture') have the curious effect of investing sexual potential and authoritative choice in the woman who is pictured (by another woman of course), thus bringing the whole tradition to its natural conclusion.

The third, recurring and related image is that of the mirror. Interestingly, this predominates in the second half of the century, as if the implicit male observer of the earlier picturesque mode has been dispensed with, and, in his place, the woman observes herself. The mirror functions to bring the divided subject and object together, in a meeting which may be either a reassertion of identity or a traumatic mis-match. Webster's three dramatic monologues, 'By the Looking-Glass', 'Faded' and 'A Cast-away', all focus on the difference between self and face, as each woman searches for some inner explanation of her socially determined identity. Here the mirror gives back a story which is both true and untrue, both fixed and arbitrary, both public and private. Mary Coleridge's 'The Other Side of a Mirror' and Lindsay's 'To My Own Face', as well as such variations on the theme as Smedley's 'A Face from the Past', Procter's 'A Legend of Provence', Levy's 'The Old House' and Meynell's 'A Letter from a Girl', summon up a visual self-image which is strange, lost, different or horrifying. Certainly, the many forms of self-encounter in Victorian women's poetry suggest a deep-rooted split in the very nature of the female self, as the poem tries to put together what the age has ideologically simplified or fragmented.

The search for self may also take the form of a strange meeting with the other, usually figured as a fallen woman. These meetings, which transgress the social and moral divides between the pure and the impure, are common from the mid-century, when the problem of prostitution was brought to public attention. Greenwell's 'Christina' (1851), with its titular suggestion of a new female Christ, was one of the first, but it was soon followed by Barrett Browning's *Aurora Leigh* (1857) and Rossetti's *Goblin Market* (1862), both of which turn the idea of philanthropic rescue-work into something much more like a love story between women. In all three the actual meetings between 'sisters' are charged with emotional and physical significance, as if the sistering gesture permitted the expression of all sorts of desire, maternal, religious, political as well as sexual. The unexpected eroticism of some of these encounters perhaps explains the relatively relaxed reception given later in the century to Michael Field's lesbian love poems. A poetic tradition of physical love between women had already been established – a tradition which is, in many senses, freer in its language and attitudes than the heavily brocaded one of heterosexual desire.

Not only is sisterhood a crucial theme and goal of Victorian women's poetry, so too is motherhood. Babies, for some reason, have never been regarded as a serious subject for poetry, perhaps because they have seemed so exclusively a woman's theme. Death, traditionally, is more poetic than birth. Yet for centuries, for women, the two were related. The figures for maternal and child mortality remained high for much of the nineteenth century, and certainly the dangers and fears of giving birth are reflected in many of the baby poems included here – a body of work which is probably the most neglected area of Victorian women's writing. Clive, Tindal, King, Ogilvy, Webster, Meynell, Nesbit and Sigerson all write movingly about motherhood, rarely separating its delights from its griefs. Sigerson's 'The Mother', for instance, is a powerful reminder, in the high sentimental manner, of the tragic side of motherhood, as the two women, one now childless, face each other through the separating glass of the funeral cortège. Like many others, this is a poem which exploits the dramatic power of sentimentality as a way of bringing 'home' the wider emotional facts. The deaths of children, whether one's own or another's, whether at birth or later, must always have shadowed the joys of motherhood.

Mothering could also provide poets with a metaphor for other forms of love or creativity. Michael Field and Mew, for instance, both write love poems in which mothers and lovers are ambiguously confused (' "A Girl" ' and 'The Forest Road', for instance), while sister relationships readily turn into mother–daughter relationships (Greenwell's 'Christina' and Rossetti's *Goblin Market*). It is also tempting to detect some more literary, matrilineal yearning in the many poems about mothers, mourned or celebrated, by Victorian women. The crimes of motherhood, on the other hand, are largely absent from these poems, with two powerful exceptions: the unnervingly cool infanticide of Barrett Browning's 'The Runaway Slave', and the eerily implicit infanticide of Marriott Watson's 'A Ballad of the Were-Wolf'.

It was not only in the domestic sphere that women poets resorted to a sentimental rhetoric for poetic effect. Most of the protest poems in this volume, and there are many (by Howitt, Barrett Browning, Norton, Cook, Greenwell, Procter, Johnston, Bevington), use a register of emotionally heightened rhetoric to convey 'to the heart' the sense of an injustice perpetrated against the weak. Whether the subject is the exploitation of children in factories, of slaves, of the insane, of women on the streets or animals in scientific laboratories (the RSPCA and Anti-Vivisection League being active from the 1870s onwards), one way of reaching a wide audience was to write in a compulsively sentimental style, which personally implicates each reader. Romney's accusation in *Aurora Leigh* that women poets could only write about social evils as domestic dramas: 'as if / Your father were a negro, and your son / A spinner in the mills', might be turned to their poetic advantage. Not only were women, through their philanthropic activities, in some ways more in touch with social problems than their middle-class male counterparts, but the ability to see the political as the personal might also become a source of imaginative sympathy across the barriers of class, morality or nationality. The low legal status of women from all classes probably gave them a natural sense of identity with other dispossessed creatures under the rule of 'man'.

In addition to this crusading social conscience, Victorian women's poetry shows a surprising diversity and unorthodoxy in its religious positions. There are, of course, the famous hymns and carols: Alexander's, Havergal's and Rossetti's. The latter must be accounted one of the great religious poets of all time, the mysterious yearning of 'A Christmas Carol' and the lacerating doubt of 'A Better Resurrection' and 'An Old-World Thicket' are unparalleled. While Rossetti remained staunchly within the established church, it is interesting how many other poets left it. The immense attraction of Roman Catholicism for women was noted as early as 1855 by Mrs Jameson who, in her pamphlet on *Sisters of Charity*, concluded that it was the greater availability of vocational work in the Catholic church which drew so many women to its ranks. Undoubtedly, too, as the century wore on, and Christianity came under attack from many quarters, the authoritarian as well as richly decorative atmosphere of Catholicism provided a 'home' for the sceptical, aesthetic imagination – a home which had the advantage of still not being part of the English establishment, associated, as Catholicism always was, with foreigners, Italy, the Irish and the poor.

However, the assumption that Victorian women's poetry is characteristically pious and sweet – an assumption held by contemporary reviewers and anthologists as well as by the twentieth century – must be disproved by the number of poets who were in fact either agnostic or atheist, and whose poems express their dissent. The tremendous popularity of Ingelow, Havergal and Greenwell in their own day has tended to obscure the fact that others (L. E. L., Emily Brontë, George Eliot, Naden, Bevington, Blind, Webster, Michael Field, Kendall, Levy and Mew, to name but some) were writing from implicitly or overtly unorthodox positions. The anarchist atheism of Bevington or the scientific atheism of Naden are only more extreme versions of a pervasive questioning of belief in this body of poetry. It could be argued that the characteristic 'When I am dead' motif, which was perfected and immortalized by Rossetti (after Hemans's and L. E. L.'s more obviously Sapphic use of it), gives to later poets (Naden, Michael Field and Mew for instance) a specifically agnostic or atheist theme, of death as a return to the natural processes of decay and evolution – an implication which is already half-present in Rossetti. Thus, at a time when 'woman' was being hailed as the last bastion of the values of domesticity, chastity, religious faith, sincerity and true feeling, women poets, it would appear, were actually writing about homelessness, sexual desire, unbelief, the self as a masked or mirrored secret, as well as the subversive new sciences.

Evolutionary theory itself seems sometimes to have had the pull of an alternative faith. Although still largely excluded from the main centres of higher education, women were, perhaps for that very reason, drawn to more unorthodox sources of learning – the sciences remaining outside the traditional classical and theological emphases of Oxford and Cambridge. Many of these poets read Darwin and Spencer with enthusiasm, and several found in Darwinism an inspiring creed of revolutionary change. Perhaps, once again, women's affiliation with the natural world and with animals made the 'link', for them, not so humiliatingly horrifying. The subject of science, as poems by Blind, Naden, Kendall, Probyn, Robinson, Bevington and Michael Field suggest, often had the effect of recharging poetry with a new, idiomatic contemporariness, with a feeling for the vast, impersonal perspectives of nature, as well as with the keen thrill of the subversive. Certainly the writings of Darwin and Spencer brought a whole new language of nature into play, a language which often carries strong connotations of inevitable social improvement and of free sexual desire. It is noticeable that most of these poets confront Darwinian theory with cheerful acceptance rather than Tennysonian regret.

In particular, the subject of science inspired something for which Victorian women have almost never been praised: a sense of humour. In spite of the streak of melancholy suicidalism in the Sappho–Corinne myth, a great deal of women's poetry of the nineteenth century is humorous, whether consciously entertaining and light (Naden, Smedley, Probyn and Kendall), or else wry, quirky, ironic, sardonic or bizarre. The many 'fairy' poems (see Sara Coleridge, Ingelow, Rossetti, Violet Fane and Mary Coleridge) often covertly poke fun at serious institutions like love, marriage and sexual sin, childhood fantasy here freeing even the most dutiful imagination from moral responsibility. The use of folklore, myth and legend similarly provides a useful screen through which to puppet the values of the contemporary world. Women's uneasy access to the classics no doubt also gave an added spice of the forbidden to their invocations of the pagan gods. Altogether, the strain of sentimental melodrama in Victorian women's verse is more than matched by its humour, wit and playful provocation.

In the end, however, it is the sheer variety of this poetry, in verse form as well as subject matter, which makes it worthy of recovery and reassessment. This is a body of writing which has been largely lost to literary history – the numbers of poetic addresses from one poet to another suggesting just how strong and self-aware a tradition it was. Even the few voices which have survived this neglect or have recently been revived – Emily Brontë, Barrett Browning, Rossetti and Mew, for instance – gain from being re-read in the company of their contemporaries. They too are part of that communal, uncertain self-mythologizing and self-inventing which is the mainspring of this forgotten tradition of verse. It is the range and energy of Victorian women's poetry which make it still, today, worth being read, wept over, laughed at and enjoyed.

A.L.

Note on the Text

The text for most of the poems in this collection is the first volume publication. Many of the poets included here published first in volume form and were never reprinted so that the first edition is the only edition. In a few cases, where a poem has only ever appeared in a magazine, that version is the text. If a poem was printed in magazine but subsequently published in volume form seen through the press by the author, then the first volume version is used.

Where an authoritative collected edition is available, either overseen by the author, or prepared for the press by a literary executor or a relative soon after the poet's death, the text of that edition has been preferred.

In the few cases (some of Barrett Browning's works, the Brontës, Rossetti) where a modern scholarly critical edition exists, that edition has been used for the text of the poems and appropriate credit lines appear in the Acknowledgements.

Following the notes for each individual poet is a list of references. This gives, first, the works of the poet from which the copy-text for the poems is taken, with those of her other works which are referred to in the notes, and second, a list of biographical and critical sources. At the end of the book there is a fuller bibliography of each poet's published works, and a bibliography of anthologies and criticism.

As this is not a critical edition but a reading text for the poems, no corrections or emendations have been made to the copy text, except for obvious misprints or transcription errors which have been silently corrected.

Felicia Hemans (1793–1835)

Felicia Hemans was one of six children born to George Browne, a Liverpool merchant, and Felicity Wagner. In 1800 financial difficulties forced the family to move to North Wales. There, under the encouragement of her mother, the fourteen-year-old Felicia published her first volume of poems. It may have been at about this time that her father left home for Quebec, from where he never returned. The financial and emotional burdens of rearing a family thus fell on his wife and poetical daughter. In 1812 Felicia married Captain Alfred Hemans, and after one year away, the couple returned to the family home in Wales. Over the next six years Felicia gave birth to five sons. Then, in 1818, not waiting for the birth of his fifth child, Captain Hemans took a trip to Italy, ostensibly for the benefit of his health. Like Felicia's father, he also disappeared for good. Although she continued to correspond with her husband, this second desertion must have reinforced the poet's sense of women's domestic responsibilities in the face of the unreliable vagaries of men. It also reinforced her need to make a commercial success of her poetry. Between 1818 and her death in 1835 Hemans published more than fourteen volumes of verse and became one of the most popular and loved poets of the day.

The main tragedy of her life was the death of her mother in 1827. Felicia wrote to a friend that 'the death-bed scene of my beloved and excellent mother is still as mournfully distinct as the week when that bereavement occurred, which threw me to struggle upon a harsh and bitter world' (1839: I, 294). This banishment from the Eden of her mother's care, which many of her poems re-enact, was both emotional and practical. 'I am now for the first time in my life holding the *reins of government*, independent, managing a household myself; and I never liked any thing less' (Chorley 1836: I, 228), she lamented. When she visited Wordsworth in 1830, Felicia's apparent carelessness of 'household economy' (Wordsworth 1940–9: 461) scandalized her host. The poet who, in her work, repeatedly extolled the ideals of 'hearth and home' seems to have been, in life, a reluctant if not incompetent housewife. Wordsworth, none the less, was impressed by her good nature and especially by her emotional loyalty to 'an unfeeling husband' (1940–9: IV, 461). He consistently praised her writings, and in his 'Extempore Effusion' set her in the august company of his Romantic contemporaries: Hogg, Scott, Coleridge, Lamb and Crabbe. Byron was altogether less sympathetic, once expostulating to his publisher: 'no *more modern* poesy – I pray – neither Mrs. Hewoman's – nor any female or male Tadpole of Poet Turdsworth –' (1973–82: VII, 158).

When she died in 1835, Felicia was worn out, not only by the long years of writing and providing for a family, but also by that very fame which, she claimed, destroyed her domestic privacy and her peace of mind. 'I wish I could give you the least idea of what *kindness* is to me – how much more, how far dearer than *fame*' (Chorley 1836: I, 212–13) was one of her repeated cries. Yet her poetry is obsessed by fame, both its cost and its attraction to women. Hemans's own reputation remained high for much of the first half of the century. She was widely read by all classes, but particularly by the increasingly large class of women readers whose appetite for poetry was fed by the many illustrated annuals of light verse which flourished at the time. Elizabeth Gaskell, in *Wives and Daughters*, recalls this immense popularity when she informs her (woman) reader of the 1860s that 'To be nearly as good as Mrs Hemans' was saying as much to the young ladies of that day, as saying that poetry is nearly as good as Tennyson's would be in this' (1986: 97). By the 1890s, however, her reputation had waned and Alfred Miles, in his anthology of nineteenth-century poetry, had to urge his readers not 'to judge her too harshly' (1891–7: VII, 53).

For all her disclaimers, Hemans inevitably came to exemplify the very thing she deprecated: the successful, professional woman poet. Her interest in the contradictions of power and womanliness, fame and modesty, self-expression and self-denial, also gave to later generations a characteristic topos for women's poetry. The fact that death is frequently invoked as the extreme solution to these contradictions only highlights their tension. The story of Sappho, who, according to legend, threw herself into the sea out of unrequited love, is one which Hemans popularizes as the central drama of creativity for women.

Her legacy, however, was not unequivocal. Barrett Browning, who expressed her admiration in public (see 'Felicia Hemans'), also expressed certain reservations in private. To Miss Mitford she wrote that her predecessor 'was too conventionally a *lady*, to be a great poetess – she was bound fast in satin riband. Her delicacy restrained her sense of Beauty – and she had no reverence for Humanity' (1983: II, 425). The effect of 'satin riband' in Hemans is indeed a problem for later poets. There is a safe and saccharine sentiment in her work which unfortunately was often hailed as the voice of true womanhood. Whether her 'delicacy' stems from real limitation or from some over-compensation for the notionally unrespectable nature of her profession is difficult to say. At its worst her poetry is pious and facile. It repeats certain stock consolatory sentiments of women's domestic faithfulness and enduring loyalty in love, while the very predictable regularity of the metre can sound comically routine. Of these faults she herself may have been aware. 'It has ever been one of my regrets', she wrote, 'that the constant necessity of providing sums of money to meet the exigencies of the boys' education has obliged me to waste my mind in what I consider mere desultory effusions' (Williams 1861: 473–4). At its best, however, her poetry is memorable, rousing and accessible. It was much recited in schools, particularly girls' schools, and set to music in drawing-rooms. Behind its apparent acceptance of the sad lot of women there can also be heard, in its militant rhythms, a passionate protest on their behalf. If Hemans's sentiments are those of resignation and victimization, her metres often tell another tale of rallying female solidarity and defiance.

One of her best volumes is *Records of Woman* (1828). It was published the year after her mother's death, and was dedicated to another literary 'mother': the poet and playwright Joanna Baillie. This collection of stories about heroic women from history and mythology expresses one of Hemans's main preoccupations: the split between woman's capacity for heroism and her yearning for domesticity. The famous model for this split, which she, like many other women writers, acclaimed as the story of her own life, was Madame de Staël's *Corinne*. Poems like 'Corinne at the Capitol', 'Properzia Rossi', 'Woman and Fame' and 'The Grave of a Poetess' all present women's artistic success in terms of lost security in love. Yet the rhetoric of fame is often stronger and more purposeful than the tacked-on ethic of domesticity. Hemans, when she writes about creative women, often writes against the grain of her own regret. Other poems about motherhood frequently associate mothers with a southern landscape, an Edenic, all-female homeland, from which daughters have been exiled. This strain of matrilineal longing is both autobiographical and literary. Hemans, like Barrett Browning after her, seems to be casting for lost mothers and grandmothers of verse. Their unanswering invisibility, with the exception of Baillie and Mary Tighe (the object of 'The Grave of a Poetess'), is perhaps the reason why she starts to draw the first maps of that 'other country' of the imagination, that place of fruitful nurturing and satisfied desires, which many later poets will explore.

Altogether, Hemans deserves to be read beyond the few notorious anthology pieces, like 'Casabianca' and 'Evening Prayer, at a Girls' School', for which she is still (satirically) remembered. Even these, with their urgent, coercive oratory and fated sense of gender, invite reassessment. The duties of suffering mothers and the laws of absent fathers (see Armstrong 1993: 330–1) might, after all, be terrifying, inhuman forces without their coating of sentimentality. It is interesting how often in this verse a pioneering masculinity is set against home-loving femininity (see 'Song of Emigration' and 'The Chamois Hunter's Love'), to suggest a world deeply and perhaps insolubly divided into gender oppositions.

Hemans's place is undoubtedly (in spite of her pre-Victorian dates) at the head of a Victorian tradition of women's poetry. For all her faults, she bequeaths to it certain central and recurrent preoccupations: the theme of the heroic suicide, the Sappho–Corinne drama of divided love and creativity, the idea of the woman's lost mother-land in the south and the recurrent conflict between public and private spheres. The unequivocally gendered voice of her poetry gives to later poets a platform, however ritualized and sentimentalized, from which to speak. It is as if her cry to 'think of me!' ('A Parting Song') rings on down the generations, as successive poets reiterate its anxious bid to be heard (L. E. L., Barrett Browning, Rossetti), while certainly remembering in their turn the poet who first made the woman's voice so memorably and crusadingly audible.

A. L.

Hemans, Felicia (1839) *Works*, With a Memoir of her Life by her Sister, 7 vols, Edinburgh.

Armstrong, Isobel (1993) *Victorian Poetry*, London, Routledge, pp. 320–32.
Barrett Browning, Elizabeth (1983) *The Letters of Elizabeth Barrett Browning to Mary Russell Mitford: 1836–1854*, 3 vols, eds Meredith B. Raymond and Mary Rose Sullivan, Winfield, Kan., Wedgestone Press.
Byron, Lord (1973–82) *Letters and Journals*, 12 vols, ed. Leslie A. Marchand, London, John Murray.
Chorley, Henry F. (1836) *Memorials of Mrs. Hemans*, 2 vols, London.
Clarke, Norma (1990) *Ambitious Heights: Writing, Friendship, Love: The Jewsbury Sisters, Felicia Hemans and Jane Carlyle*, London and New York, Routledge.
Gaskell, Elizabeth (1864–6; 1986) *Wives and Daughters*, Harmondsworth, Penguin.
Leighton, Angela (1992) *Victorian Women's Poetry: Writing Against the Heart*, Hemel Hempstead, Harvester, pp. 8–44.
Lootens, Tricia (1994) 'Hemans and Home: Victorianism, Feminine "Internal Enemies", and the Domestication of National Identity', *Publications of the Modern Language Association of America*, 109 no. 2 (1994), 238–53.
Mack, Anne, Rome, J. J. and Manneje, George (1993) 'Literary History, Romanticism, and Felicia Hemans', *Modern Language Quarterly*, 54 no. 2 (1993), 215–35.
Mellor, Anne K. (1993) *Romanticism & Gender*, New York & London, Routledge, pp. 123–43.
Miles, Alfred H. (ed.) (1891–7) *The Poets and the Poetry of the Century*, 10 vols, London.
Ross, Marlon B. (1989) *The Contours of Masculine Desire: Romanticism and the Rise of Women's Poetry*, New York, Oxford University Press.

Stephenson, Glennis (1993) 'Poet Construction: Mrs Hemans, L. E. L., and the Image of the Nineteenth-Century Woman Poet', in *ReImagining Women: Representations of Women in Culture*, eds Shirley Neuman and Glennis Stephenson, Toronto, University of Toronto Press, pp. 61–73.

Sweet, Nan (1994) 'History, Imperialism, and the Aesthetics of the Beautiful: Hemans and the Post-Napoleonic Moment', in *At the Limits of Romanticism: Essays in Cultural, Feminist, and Materialist Criticism*, eds Mary A. Favret and Nicola J. Watson, Bloomington and Indianapolis, Indiana University Press, pp. 170–84.

Williams, Jane (1861) *The Literary Women of England*, London.

Wordsworth, William (1940–9) *Poetical Works*, 5 vols, eds E. de Selincourt and Helen Darbishire, Oxford, Clarendon Press.

The Last Song of Sappho

Suggested by a beautiful sketch, the design of the younger Westmacott. It represents Sappho sitting on a rock above the sea, with her lyre cast at her feet. There is a desolate grace about the whole figure, which seems penetrated with the feeling of utter abandonment.

Sound on, thou dark unslumbering sea!
  My dirge is in thy moan;
My spirit finds response in thee,
To its own ceaseless cry – 'Alone, alone!'

Yet send me back one other word,   5
  Ye tones that never cease!
Oh! let your secret caves be stirr'd,
And say, dark waters! will ye give me *peace?*

Away! my weary soul hath sought
  In vain one echoing sigh,   10
One answer to consuming thought
In human hearts – and will the *wave* reply?

Sound on, thou dark unslumbering sea!
  Sound in thy scorn and pride!
I ask not, alien world, from thee,   15
What my own kindred earth hath still denied.

And yet I loved that earth so well,
  With all its lovely things!
– Was it for this the death-wind fell
On my rich lyre, and quench'd its living strings?   20

– Let them lie silent at my feet!
  Since broken even as they,
The heart whose music made them sweet,
Hath pour'd on desert-sands its wealth away,

Yet glory's light hath touch'd my name,   25
   The laurel-wreath is mine –
– With a lone heart, a weary frame –
O restless deep! I come to make them thine!

Give to that crown, that burning crown,
   Place in thy darkest hold!   30
Bury my anguish, my renown,
With hidden wrecks, lost gems, and wasted gold.

Thou sea-bird on the billow's crest,
   Thou hast thy love, thy home;
They wait thee in the quiet nest,   35
And I, th' unsought, unwatch'd-for – I too come!

I, with this winged nature fraught,
   These visions wildly free,
This boundless love, this fiery thought –
– *Alone* I come – oh! give me peace, dark sea!   40

Corinne at the Capitol

Les femmes doivent penser qu'il est dans cette carrière bien peu de sorte qui puissent valoir la plus obscure vie d'une femme aimée et d'une mère heureuse.[1]

Madame de Staël

Daughter of th' Italian heaven!
Thou, to whom its fires are given,
Joyously thy car hath roll'd
Where the conqueror's pass'd of old;
And the festal sun that shone,   5
O'er three hundred triumphs gone,[2]
Makes thy day of glory bright,
With a shower of golden light.

Now thou tread'st th' ascending road,
Freedom's foot so proudly trode;   10
While, from tombs of heroes borne,
From the dust of empire shorn,
Flowers upon thy graceful head,
Chaplets of all hues, are shed,
In a soft and rosy rain,   15
Touch'd with many a gem-like stain.

---

[1] Women must think there is very little in this career as worthy as the most obscure life of a loved woman and of a happy mother.   [2] The trebly hundred triumphs. Byron

Thou hast gain'd the summit now!
Music hails thee from below;
Music, whose rich notes might stir
Ashes of the sepulchre;   20
Shaking with victorious notes
All the bright air as it floats.
Well may woman's heart beat high
Unto that proud harmony!

Now afar it rolls – it dies –   25
And thy voice is heard to rise
With a low and lovely tone
In its thrilling power alone;
And thy lyre's deep silvery string,
Touch'd as by a breeze's wing,   30
Murmurs tremblingly at first,
Ere the tide of rapture burst.

All the spirit of thy sky
Now hath lit thy large dark eye,
And thy cheek a flush hath caught   35
From the joy of kindled thought;
And the burning words of song
From thy lip flow fast and strong,
With a rushing stream's delight
In the freedom of its might.   40

Radiant daughter of the sun!
Now thy living wreath is won.
Crown'd of Rome! – Oh! art thou not
Happy in that glorious lot? –
Happier, happier far than thou,   45
With the laurel on thy brow,
She that makes the humblest hearth
Lovely but to one on earth!

To a Wandering Female Singer

Thou hast loved and thou hast suffer'd!
    Unto feeling deep and strong,
Thou hast trembled like a harp's frail string –
    I know it by thy song!

Thou hast loved – it may be vainly –   5
    But well – oh! but too well –
Thou hast suffer'd all that woman's breast
    May bear – but must not tell.

Thou hast wept and thou hast parted,
  Thou hast been forsaken long,   10
Thou hast watch'd for steps that came not back —
  I know it by thy song!

By the low clear silvery gushing
  Of its music from thy breast,
By the quivering of its flute-like swell —   15
  A sound of the heart's unrest.

By its fond and plaintive lingering,
  On each word of grief so long,
Oh! thou hast loved and suffer'd much —
  I know it by thy song!   20

Woman and Fame

Thou hast a charmed cup, O Fame!
  A draught that mantles high,
And seems to lift this earthly frame
  Above mortality.
Away! to me — a woman — bring   5
Sweet waters from affection's spring.

Thou hast green laurel leaves, that twine
  Into so proud a wreath;
For that resplendent gift of thine,
  Heroes have smiled in death: 10
Give *me* from some kind hand a flower,
The record of one happy hour!

Thou hast a voice, whose thrilling tone
  Can bid each life-pulse beat
As when a trumpet's note hath blown,   15
  Calling the brave to meet:
But mine, let mine — a woman's breast,
By words of home-born love be bless'd.

A hollow sound is in thy song,
  A mockery in thine eye,   20
To the sick heart that doth but long
  For aid, for sympathy —
For kindly looks to cheer it on,
For tender accents that are gone.

Fame, Fame! thou canst not be the stay   25
  Unto the drooping reed,

The cool fresh fountain in the day
  Of the soul's feverish need:
Where must the lone one turn or flee? –
Not unto thee – oh! not to thee!   30

Properzia Rossi

Properzia Rossi, a celebrated female sculptor of Bologna, possessed also of talents for poetry and music, died in consequence of an unrequited attachment. A painting, by Ducis, represents her showing her last work, a basso-relievo of Ariadne, to a Roman knight, the object of her affection, who regards it with indifference.

> *Tell me no more, no more*
> *Of my soul's lofty gifts! Are they not vain*
> *To quench its haunting thirst for happiness?*
> *Have I not loved, and striven, and fail'd to bind*
> *One true heart unto me, whereon my own*   5
> *Might find a resting-place, a home for all*
> *Its burden of affections? I depart,*
> *Unknown, though Fame goes with me; I must leave*
> *The earth unknown. Yet it may be that death*
> *Shall give my name a power to win such tears*   10
> *As would have made life precious.*

I

One dream of passion and of beauty more!
And in its bright fulfilment let me pour
My soul away! Let earth retain a trace
Of that which lit my being, though its race   15
Might have been loftier far. Yet one more dream!
From my deep spirit one victorious gleam
Ere I depart! For thee alone, for thee!
May this last work, this farewell triumph be –
Thou, loved so vainly! I would leave enshrined   20
Something immortal of my heart and mind,
That yet may speak to thee when I am gone,
Shaking thine inmost bosom with a tone
Of lost affection; – something that may prove
What she hath been, whose melancholy love   25
On thee was lavish'd; silent pang and tear,
And fervent song, that gush'd when none were near,
And dream by night, and weary thought by day,
Stealing the brightness from her life away –
While thou—Awake! not yet within me die!   30
Under the burden and the agony

Of this vain tenderness – my spirit, wake!
Even for thy sorrowful affection's sake,
Live! in thy work breathe out! – that he may yet,
Feeling sad mastery there, perchance regret   35
Thine unrequited gift.

II

                    It comes – the power
Within me born flows back – my fruitless dower
That could not win me love. Yet once again
I greet it proudly, with its rushing train
Of glorious images: – they throng – they press –   40
A sudden joy lights up my loneliness –
I shall not perish all!
                  The bright work grows
Beneath my hand, unfolding, as a rose,
Leaf after leaf, to beauty; line by line,
I fix my thought, heart, soul, to burn, to shine,   45
Through the pale marble's veins. It grows! – and now
I give my own life's history to thy brow,
Forsaken Ariadne! thou shalt wear
My form, my lineaments; but oh! more fair,
Touch'd into lovelier being by the glow   50
  Which in me dwells, as by the summer light
All things are glorified. From thee my woe
  Shall yet look beautiful to meet his sight,
When I am pass'd away. Thou art the mould,
Wherein I pour the fervent thoughts, th' untold,   55
The self-consuming! Speak to him of me,
Thou, the deserted by the lonely sea,
With the soft sadness of thine earnest eye –
Speak to him, lorn one! deeply, mournfully,
Of all my love and grief! Oh! could I throw   60
Into thy frame a voice, a sweet, and low,
And thrilling voice of song! when he came nigh,
To send the passion of its melody
Through his pierced bosom – on its tones to bear
My life's deep feeling, as the southern air   65
Wafts the faint myrtle's breath – to rise, to swell,
To sink away in accents of farewell,
Winning but one, *one* gush of tears, whose flow
Surely my parted spirit yet might know,
If love be strong as death!

III

Now fair thou art,   70
Thou form, whose life is of my burning heart
Yet all the vision that within me wrought,
   I cannot make thee! Oh! I might have given
Birth to creations of far nobler thought;
   I might have kindled, with the fire of heaven,   75
Things not of such as die! But I have been
Too much alone; – a heart whereon to lean,
With all these deep affections that o'erflow
My aching soul and find no shore below;
An eye to be my star; a voice to bring   80
Hope o'er my path like sounds that breathe of spring:
These are denied me – dreamt of still in vain –
Therefore my brief aspirings from the chain,
Are ever but as some wild fitful song,
Rising triumphantly, to die erelong   85
In dirge-like echoes.

IV

Yet the world will see
Little of this, my parting work, in thee –
   Thou shalt have fame! – Oh, mockery! give the reed
From storms a shelter – give the drooping vine
Something round which its tendrils may entwine –   90
   Give the parch'd flower a rain-drop, and the meed
Of love's kind words to woman! Worthless fame!
That in *his* bosom wins not for my name
Th' abiding place it ask'd! Yet how my heart,
In its own fairy world of song and art,   95
Once beat for praise! Are those high longings o'er?
That which I have been can I be no more?
Never! oh, never more! though still thy sky
Be blue as then, my glorious Italy!
And though the music, whose rich breathings fill   100
Thine air with soul, be wandering past me still;
And though the mantle of thy sunlight streams,
Unchanged on forms, instinct with poet-dreams:
Never! oh, never more! Where'er I move,
The shadow of this broken-hearted love   105
Is on me and around! Too well *they* know,
   Whose life is all within, too soon and well,
When there the blight hath settled! – but I go
   Under the silent wings of peace to dwell;
From the slow wasting, from the lonely pain,   110

The inward burning of those words – '*in vain*,'
   Sear'd on the heart – I go. 'Twill soon be past,
Sunshine, and song, and bright Italian heaven,
   And thou, Oh! thou, on whom my spirit cast
Unvalued wealth – who know'st not what was given   115
In that devotedness – the sad, and deep,
And unrepaid – farewell! If I could weep
Once, only once, beloved one! on thy breast,
Pouring my heart forth ere I sink to rest!
But that were happiness, and unto me   120
Earth's gift is *fame*. Yet I was form'd to be
So richly bless'd! With thee to watch the sky,
Speaking not, feeling but that thou wert nigh:
With thee to listen, while the tones of song
Swept even as part of our sweet air along –   125
To listen silently: with thee to gaze
On forms, the deified of olden days –
This had been joy enough; and hour by hour,
From its glad well-springs drinking life and power,
How had my spirit soar'd, and made its fame   130
   A glory for thy brow! Dreams, dreams! – the fire
Burns faint within me. Yet I leave my name –
   As a deep thrill may linger on the lyre
When its full chords are hush'd – awhile to live,
And one day haply in thy heart revive   135
Sad thoughts of me: – I leave it, with a sound,
A spell o'er memory, mournfully profound –
I leave it, on my country's air to dwell –
Say proudly yet – '*'Twas hers who loved me well!*'

The Grave of a Poetess[1]

Ne me plaignez pas – si vous saviez[2]
Combien de peines ce tombeau m'a epargnées!

I stood beside thy lowly grave;
   Spring odours breathed around,
And music, in the river wave,
   Pass'd with a lulling sound.

All happy things that love the sun,   5
   In the bright air glanced by,

---

[1] Extrinsic interest has lately attached to the fine scenery of Woodstock, near Kilkenny, on account of its having been the last residence of the author of *Psyche*. Her grave is one of many in the churchyard of the village. The river runs smoothly by. The ruins of an ancient abbey, that have been partially converted into a church, reverently throw their mantle of tender shadow over it. *Tales by the O'Hara Family*

[2] [Do not grieve — if you knew How much pain this grave has spared me!]

And a glad murmur seem'd to run
  Through the soft azure sky.

Fresh leaves were on the ivy bough
  That fringed the ruins near;   10
Young voices were abroad, but thou
  Their sweetness couldst not hear.

And mournful grew my heart for thee,
  Thou in whose woman's mind
The ray that brightens earth and sea,   15
  The light of song was shrined.

Mournful, that thou wert slumbering low,
  With a dread curtain drawn
Between thee and the golden glow
  Of this world's vernal dawn.   20

Parted from all the song and bloom
  Thou wouldst have loved so well,
To thee the sunshine round thy tomb
  Was but a broken spell.

The bird, the insect on the wing,   25
  In their bright reckless play,
Might feel the flush and life of spring –
  And thou wert pass'd away.

But then, e'en then, a nobler thought
  O'er my vain sadness came;   30
Th' immortal spirit woke, and wrought
  Within my thrilling frame.

Surely on lovelier things, I said,
  Thou must have look'd ere now,
Than all that round our pathway shed   35
  Odours and hues below.

The shadows of the tomb are here,
  Yet beautiful is earth!
What see'st thou then, where no dim fear,
  No haunting dream hath birth?   40

Here a vain love to passing flowers
  Thou gav'st – but where thou art,
The sway is not with changeful hours,
  There love and death must part.

Thou hast left sorrow in thy song, 45
   A voice not loud but deep!
The glorious bowers of earth among –
   How often didst thou weep?

Where couldst thou fix on mortal ground
   Thy tender thoughts and high? 50
Now peace the woman's heart hath found,
   And joy the poet's eye.

Evening Prayer, at a Girls' School

Now in thy youth, beseech of Him
   Who giveth, upbraiding not;
That his light in thy heart become not dim,
   And his love be unforgot;
And thy God, in the darkest of days, will be,
Greenness, and beauty, and strength to thee.
              Bernard Barton

Hush! 'tis a holy hour – the quiet room
   Seems like a temple, while yon soft lamp sheds
A faint and starry radiance, through the gloom
   And the sweet stillness, down on fair young heads,
With all their clust'ring locks, untouch'd by care, 5
And bow'd, as flowers are bow'd with night, in prayer.

Gaze on – 'tis lovely! – Childhood's lip and cheek,
   Mantling beneath its earnest brow of thought –
Gaze – yet what seest thou in those fair, and meek,
   And fragile things, as but for sunshine wrought? – 10
Thou seest what grief must nurture for the sky,
What death must fashion for eternity!

O! joyous creatures! that will sink to rest,
   Lightly, when those pure orisons are done,
As birds with slumber's honey-dew opprest, 15
   'Midst the dim folded leaves, at set of sun –
Lift up your hearts! though yet no sorrow lies
Dark in the summer-heaven of those clear eyes.

Though fresh within your breasts th' untroubled springs
   Of hope make melody where'er ye tread, 20
And o'er your sleep bright shadows, from the wings
   Of spirits visiting but youth, be spread;
Yet in those flute-like voices, mingling low,
Is woman's tenderness – how soon her woe!

Her lot is on you – silent tears to weep,   25
   And patient smiles to wear through suffering's hour,
And sumless riches, from affection's deep,
   To pour on broken reeds – a wasted shower!
And to make idols, and to find them clay,
And to bewail that worship – therefore pray!   30

Her lot is on you – to be found untired,
   Watching the stars out by the bed of pain,
With a pale cheek, and yet a brow inspired,
   And a true heart of hope, though hope be vain;
Meekly to bear with wrong, to cheer decay,   35
And, oh! to love through all things – therefore pray!

And take the thought of this calm vesper time,
   With its low murmuring sounds and silvery light,
On through the dark days fading from their prime,
   As a sweet dew to keep your souls from blight!   40
Earth will forsake – O! happy to have given
Th' unbroken heart's first fragrance unto Heaven.

The Image in Lava[1]

Thou thing of years departed!
   What ages have gone by,
Since here the mournful seal was set
   By love and agony?

Temple and tower have moulder'd,   5
   Empires from earth have pass'd,
And woman's heart hath left a trace
   Those glories to outlast!

And childhood's fragile image,
   Thus fearfully enshrined,   10
Survives the proud memorials rear'd
   By conquerors of mankind.

Babe! wert thou brightly slumbering
   Upon thy mother's breast,
When suddenly the fiery tomb   15
   Shut round each gentle guest?

---

[1] The impression of a woman's form, with an infant
clasped to the bosom, found at the uncovering of
Herculaneum.

A strange, dark fate o'ertook you,
　　Fair babe and loving heart!
One moment of a thousand pangs –
　　Yet better than to part!　　　　　　　　　20

Haply of that fond bosom
　　On ashes here impress'd,
Thou wert the only treasure, child!
　　Whereon a hope might rest.

Perchance all vainly lavish'd　　　　　　　　25
　　Its other love had been,
And where it trusted, nought remain'd
　　But thorns on which to lean.

Far better, then, to perish,
　　Thy form within its clasp,　　　　　　　　30
Than live and lose thee, precious one!
　　From that impassion'd grasp.

Oh! I could pass all relics
　　Left by the pomps of old,
To gaze on this rude monument　　　　　　　35
　　Cast in affection's mould.

Love, human love! what art thou?
　　Thy print upon the dust
Outlives the cities of renown
　　Wherein the mighty trust!　　　　　　　　40

Immortal, oh! immortal
　　Thou art, whose earthly glow
Hath given these ashes holiness –
　　It must, it *must* be so!

Casabianca[1]

The boy stood on the burning deck
　　Whence all but he had fled;
The flame that lit the battle's wreck,
　　Shone round him o'er the dead.

Yet beautiful and bright he stood,　　　　　　5
　　As born to rule the storm;

---

[1]　Young Casabianca, a boy about thirteen years old, son to the Admiral of the Orient, remained at his post (in the Battle of the Nile) after the ship had taken fire, and all the guns had been abandoned; and perished in the explosion of the vessel, when the flames had reached the powder.

A creature of heroic blood,
  A proud, though child-like form.

The flames roll'd on – he would not go
  Without his Father's word;   10
That Father, faint in death below,
  His voice no longer heard.

He call'd aloud: – 'Say, Father, say
  If yet my task is done?'
He knew not that the chieftain lay   15
  Unconscious of his son.

'Speak, Father!' once again he cried,
  'If I may yet be gone!'
And but the booming shots replied,
  And fast the flames roll'd on.   20

Upon his brow he felt their breath,
  And in his waving hair,
And look'd from that lone post of death,
  In still, yet brave despair.

And shouted but once more aloud,   25
  'My Father! must I stay?'
While o'er him fast, through sail and shroud,
  The wreathing fires made way.

They wrapt the ship in splendour wild,
  They caught the flag on high,   30
And stream'd above the gallant child,
  Like banners in the sky.

There came a burst of thunder sound –
  The boy – oh! where was he?
Ask of the winds that far around   35
  With fragments strew'd the sea! –

With mast, and helm, and pennon fair,
  That well had borne their part –
But the noblest thing which perish'd there
  Was that young faithful heart!   40

Song of Emigration

There was heard a song on the chiming sea,
A mingled breathing of grief and glee;

Man's voice, unbroken by sighs, was there,
Filling with triumph the sunny air;
Of fresh green lands, and of pastures new,   5
It sang, while the bark through the surges flew.

    But ever and anon
      A murmur of farewell
    Told, by its plaintive tone,
      That from woman's lip it fell.   10

'Away, away o'er the foaming main!'
This was the free and the joyous strain,
'There are clearer skies than ours, afar,
We will shape our course by a brighter star;
There are plains whose verdure no foot hath press'd,   15
And whose wealth is all for the first brave guest.'

    'But, alas! that we should go,'
    Sang the farewell voices then,
    'From the homesteads, warm and low,
    By the brook and in the glen!'   20

'We will rear new homes under trees that glow,
As if gems were the fruitage of every bough;
O'er our white walls we will train the vine,
And sit in its shadow at day's decline;
And watch our herds, as they range at will   25
Through the green savannas, all bright and still.'

    'But woe for that sweet shade
      Of the flowering orchard-trees,
    Where first our children play'd
      'Midst the birds and honey-bees!'   30

'All, all our own shall the forests be,
As to the bound of the roebuck free!
None shall say, "Hither, no further pass!"
We will track each step through the wavy grass;
We will chase the elk in his speed and might,   35
And bring proud spoils to the hearth at night.'

    'But, oh! the grey church-tower,
      And the sound of Sabbath-bell,
    And the shelter'd garden-bower,
      We have bid them all farewell!'   40

'We will give the names of our fearless race
To each bright river whose course we trace;

We will leave our memory with mounts and floods,
And the path of our daring in boundless woods!
And our works unto many a lake's green shore,   45
Where the Indian's graves lay, alone, before.'

   'But who shall teach the flowers,
     Which our children loved, to dwell
In a soil that is not ours?
    – Home, home and friends, farewell!'   50

The Chamois Hunter's Love

For all his wildness and proud phantasies,
I love him!
                Croly

Thy heart is in the upper world, where fleet the chamois bounds,
Thy heart is where the mountain-fir shakes to the torrent-sounds;
And where the snow-peaks gleam like stars, through the stillness of the air,
And where the Lauwine's[1] peal is heard – Hunter! thy heart is there!

I know thou lov'st me well, dear friend! but better, better far,   5
Thou lov'st that high and haughty life, with rocks and storms at war;
In the green sunny vales with me, thy spirit would but pine,
And yet I will be thine, my love! and yet I will be thine!

And I will not seek to woo thee down from those thy native heights,
With the sweet song, our land's own song, of pastoral delights;   10
For thou must live as eagles live, thy path is not as mine,
And yet I will be thine, my love! and yet I will be thine.

And I will leave my blessed home, my father's joyous hearth,
With all the voices meeting there in tenderness and mirth,
With all the kind and laughing eyes, that in its firelight shine,   15
To sit forsaken in thy hut, yet know that thou art mine!

It is my youth, it is my bloom, it is my glad free heart,
That I cast away for thee – for thee, all reckless as thou art!
With tremblings and with vigils lone, I bind myself to dwell,
Yet, yet I would not change that lot, oh no! I love too well!   20

A mournful thing is love which grows to one so wild as thou,
With that bright restlessness of eye, that tameless fire of brow!
Mournful! – but dearer far I call its mingled fear and pride,
And the trouble of its happiness, than aught on earth beside.

---

[1] *Lauwine*, the avalanche.

To listen for thy step in vain, to start at every breath,   25
To watch through long long nights of storm, to sleep and dream of death,
To wake in doubt and loneliness – this doom I know is mine,
And yet I will be thine, my love! and yet I will be thine!

That I may greet thee from thine Alps, when thence thou comest at last,
That I may hear thy thrilling voice tell o'er each danger past,   30
That I may kneel and pray for thee, and win thee aid divine,
For this I will be thine, my love! for this I will be thine!

The Stranger's Heart

The stranger's heart! Oh! wound it not!
A yearning anguish is its lot;
In the green shadow of thy tree,
The stranger finds no rest with thee.

Thou think'st the vine's low rustling leaves   5
Glad music round thy household eaves;
To him that sound hath sorrow's tone –
The stranger's heart is with his own.

Thou think'st thy children's laughing play
A lovely sight at fall of day; –   10
Then are the stranger's thoughts oppress'd –
His mother's voice comes o'er his breast.

Thou think'st it sweet when friend with friend
Beneath one roof in prayer may blend;
Then doth the stranger's eye grow dim –   15
Far, far are those who pray'd with him.

Thy hearth, thy home, thy vintage-land –
The voices of thy kindred band –
Oh! 'midst them all when bless'd thou art,
Deal gently with the stranger's heart!   20

A Parting Song

Oh! mes Amis, rappellez vous quelquefois mes vers; mon âme y est empreinte.[1]
Corinne

When will ye think of me, my friends?
        When will ye think of me? –

---

[1]   O my friends, sometimes remember my poems;
my soul is printed on them.

When the last red light, the farewell of day,
From the rock and the river is passing away –
When the air with a deep'ning hush is fraught,   5
And the heart grows burden'd with tender thought –
      Then let it be!

When will ye think of me, kind friends?
      When will ye think of me? –
When the rose of the rich midsummer time   10
Is fill'd with the hues of its glorious prime –
When ye gather its bloom, as in bright hours fled,
From the walks where my footsteps no more may tread –
      Then let it be!

When will ye think of me, sweet friends?   15
      When will ye think of me? –
When the sudden tears o'erflow your eye
At the sound of some olden melody –
When ye hear the voice of a mountain stream,
When ye feel the charm of a poet's dream –   20
      Then let it be!

Thus let my memory be with you, friends!
      Thus ever think of me!
Kindly and gently, but as of one
For whom 'tis well to be fled and gone –   25
As of a bird from a chain unbound,
As of a wanderer whose home is found –
      So let it be.

Mary Howitt (1799–1888)

Mary Botham was the daughter of a landsurveyor who worked in Staffordshire. She
was brought up in the country 'in a picturesque, old fashioned part of England, remote
from books and from the world, and under circumstances of almost conventual
seclusion' (Howitt 1847: v). Her family were strict Quakers and few books were
available to Mary though she did go to school from the age of nine where her strange
manner of dress was a source of amusement to the other children. The most important
influence on her early imaginative life was a servant.

> . . . an old domestic, with every requisite for a German Märchen-Frau, who had
> a memory stored with ballads, old songs, and legends, inflamed my youthful
> imagination by her wild chaunts and recitations, and caused it to take very early
> flights into the regions of romance (Howitt 1847: v).

This same singular person seems to have taught Mary the most un-Quaker like occupations
of whist, strong oaths and a taste for scandal.

Mary married William Howitt in 1821. He was also a Quaker, but much less strict than her own family and he encouraged and shared her interest in literature. With his guidance, she began to choose her own reading and started with Percy's *Reliques of English Poetry* which she had heard of, but never seen. Happily devoting herself to poetry Mary spent fifteen years reading and writing in collaboration with William from their home in Nottingham. Together they produced a volume of poems called *The Forest Minstrel* in 1823, and a daughter called Anna in 1824. Remembering the story ballads which she had loved as a child, Mary began to write in this vein and successfully published in many of the annuals 'to bring in a little cash' (Howitt 1889: 69). As a professional woman poet working in the marketplace she made many friends in similar circumstances. Felicia Hemans and Mary Russell Mitford were two women whom she knew both privately and professionally. Anna Jameson, the art critic, and L. E. L. were also friends, and the latter included a portrait of Mary in her novel *Romance and Reality* (1831). Later, Mary and William augmented their income with *Howitt's Journal* and both Elizabeth Gaskell and Eliza Meteyard were first published there.

Mary published a series of dramatic sketches *The Seven Temptations* (1834) and followed it with village stories in *Wood Leighton: or A Year in the Country* (1836). But, as Barrett Browning rightly judged, she couldn't write prose, and it was only when she returned to the 'simplicity and sweetness' of her *Ballads and Other Poems* (1847) that she regained her popularity with the reading public. Barrett Browning admired her gift for stories in verse and said that 'I like Mary Howitt's lyrical poetry – ballad poetry, I should say distinctively, – and I once thought, – before I had read the 'Seven Temptations', that I would prefer having her genius to work with, than either Mrs Hemans's & [sic] Miss Landon's . . .' (Barrett Browning 1983: II, 109). If Barrett Browning could not collect other women's 'genius', she could collect their autographs, and possessing a 'bump of veneration' she applied to Mary Russell Mitford, for some assistance: 'I have autographs of your own (a few) but I want Mrs Hemans's & Mrs. Howitt's . . .' (Barrett Browning 1983: II, 319)

In the 1830s the Howitts moved south. They spent three years abroad and Mary lamented to her sister that 'Were it not for the tie children are of necessity, and the obligation they impose upon us to have a fixed home, I could like to turn gypsy and lead the life of a wild Indian, and have no home or hardly any country, except such as chance and circumstance gave us. At least, such a life I should very much like to try.' However, she added 'I am not going to do any wild thing' (Howitt 1889: I, 232) and after some time in Heidelberg they settled in Clapton where they kept up a range of literary friendships with Leigh Hunt, Tennyson, Barbara Leigh Smith, Bessie Parkes, and the Rossettis. They earned their living solely by writing and Mary wrote a certain number of pages every day no matter what, even the death of her young son causing little interruption:

> Tomorrow I intend again to commence my regular avocation. Poor dear Claude! At this very moment I see the unfinished translation lying before me which was broken off by his death. Alas! I could have shed burning tears over this. How often did he beg and pray of me to put aside my translation just for that one day, that I might sit by him and talk or read to him? I never thinking how near his end was – said 'Oh, no! I must go on yet a page or two' (Belloc 1895: 81).

Mary, having been born a Quaker, later became a Unitarian, but by the 1850s she was much interested in spiritualism. In later life she lived in Italy and the Tyrol on the Civil List pension which she received after William's death in 1879. In 1882, at the age of eighty-three she became a Roman Catholic. When she died in Rome special permission was given for her to be buried in the Protestant cemetery beside her husband.

Howitt took up many causes in her long life, anti-slavery, Catholic emancipation, women's rights and anti-vivisection. Her poems on the abuses of the factories were well known and compare with the work of Norton ('A Voice from the Factories') and Barrett Browning ('The Cry of the Children'). The fretful voice in 'The Dying Child' has a compassionate honesty which distinguishes the more sickly and elevated versions of children's speech offered, say, by Cook in ' "Our Father" '. It is significant however that all of these poems make a point of giving the actual speaking voice of the oppressed subject whether or not they attempt to make it authentic.

M.R.

Howitt, Mary (1847) *Ballads and Other Poems*, London.
—— (1889) *Mary Howitt: An Autobiography*, ed. Margaret Howitt, London.
—— (1900) *The Cry of the Animals. A Poem*, London, Church Extension Association.
Barrett Browning, Elizabeth (1983) *The Letters of Elizabeth Barrett Browning to Mary Russell Mitford: 1836–1854*, 3 vols, eds Meredith B. Raymond and Mary Rose Sullivan, Winfield, Kan., Wedgestone Press.
Belloc, Bessie Rayner Parkes (1895) *In a Walled Garden* [Miscellaneous Essays], London.
Woodring, Carl (1952) *Victorian Samplers: William and Mary Howitt*, Lawrence, Kan., University of Kansas Press.

The Dying Child

My heart is very faint and low;
My thoughts, like spectres, come and go;
I feel a numbing sense of woe:
Until to-day it was not so,
   I know not what this change may be.   5

The unseen Angel of Death

It is my voice within, that calls;
It is my shadow, child, that falls
Upon thy spirit, and appals,
That hems thee in like dungeon walls;
   My presence that o'ershadoweth thee.   10

Oh, mother, leave me not alone!
I am a-feared; my heart's like stone;
A dull pain cleaveth brain and bone;
I feel a pang till now unknown –
   Stay with me for one little hour!   15
Oh! soothe me with thy low replies;

I cannot bear the children's cries;
And, when I hear their voices rise,
Impatient tears o'erflow my eyes;
  My will seems not within my power.   20

Poor Johnny brought me flowers last night,
The blue-bell and the violet white,
Then they were pleasant to my sight;
But now they give me no delight,
  And yet I crave for something still.   25
Reach me the merry bulfinch here,
He knows my voice; I think 'twill cheer
My heart, his piping song to hear.
— Ah! I forgot that bird so dear
  Was sold to pay the baker's bill.   30

Oh! why was Mary sent away?
I only asked that she might stay
Beside me for one little day;
I thought not to be answered nay,
  Just once — I would have asked no more.   35
— Forgive me if I'm hard to please —
Mother, weep not! Oh, give me ease!
Raise me, and lay me on thy knees!
I know not what new pangs are these;
  I never felt the like before.   40

It is so stifling in this room —
Can it be closer in the tomb?
I feel encompassed by a gloom.
O father, father, leave the loom,
  It makes me dizzy like the mill.   45
Father, I feel thy hot tears fall;
If thou hast thought my patience small
Forgive me! Fain would I recall
Each hasty word — I love you all:
  I will be patient, will be still.   50

The unseen Angel of Death

Be still! My pinions o'er thee spread;
A duller, heavier weight than lead
Benumbs thee, and the life hath fled.
Child, thou hast passed the portals dread,
  Thou now art of the earth no more.   55
Arise, thy spiritual wings unfold:
Poor slave of hunger, want, and cold,
Thou now hast wealth surpassing gold,

Hast bliss no poet's tongue hath told;
Rejoice! all pain, all fear is o'er.   60

The Cry of the Animals

Oh, that they had pity, the men we serve so truly!
    Oh, that they had kindness, the men we love so well!
They call us dull and stupid, and vicious, and unruly,
    And think not we can suffer, but only would rebel.

They brand us, and they beat us; they spill our blood like water;   5
    We die that they may live, a million in a day!
Oh, that they had mercy! for in their dens of slaughter
    They afflict us and affright us, and do far worse than slay.

We are made to be their servants – we know it and complain not;
    We bow our necks in meekness the galling yoke to bear;   10
Their heaviest toil we lighten, the meanest we disdain not;
    In all their sweat and labour we take a willing share.

We know that GOD intended for us but servile stations,
    To toil, to bear man's burdens, to watch beside his door;
They are of earth the masters, we are their poor relations,   15
    Who grudge them not their greatness, but help to make it more.

We have a sense they know not, or else dulled by learning –
    They call it instinct only, a thing of rule and plan;
But oft when reason fails them, our clear, direct discerning,
    And the love that is written within us, have saved the life of man.   20

And in return we ask but that they would kindly use us
    For the purposes of service, for that for which we're made;
That they should teach their children to love and not abuse us,
    So each might face the other, and neither be afraid.

If they would but love us, would learn our strength and weakness,   25
    If only with our sufferings their hearts would sympathise,
Then they would know what truth is, what patience is and meekness
    And read our hearts devotion in the softness of our eyes!

If they would but teach their children to treat the subject creatures.
    As humble friends, as servants who strive their love to win,   30
Then would they see how joyous, how kindly are our natures,
    And a second day of Eden would on the earth begin.

Maria Jane Jewsbury (1800–1833)

Maria Jane Jewsbury was one of the first of those formidable nineteenth-century poets who were also ambitious women. To her friend Felicia Hemans she explained:

> The passion for literary distinction consumed me from nine years old... The ambition of writing a book, being praised publicly, and associating with authors, seized me as a vague longing. As I grew older it took permanence and led to effort. I sat up at night, dreamed dreams and schemed schemes... (Clarke 1990: 15).

That Maria retained these plans, and saw them through, is a tribute to her tenacity. Maria was the eldest of the seven children of Maria Smith and Thomas Jewsbury, a mill owner in the Derbyshire village of Measham. Maria received what she described as 'commonplace instruction' at home and at Miss Adams's school in Shenstone up to the age of fourteen. She also read widely according to her own inclination and acquired 'the isolating consciousness of intellectual superiority' (Williams 1861: 378–9). In 1818 Thomas's mill seems to have failed and the family moved to Manchester where he set up in a modest way as a cotton and insurance agent. When her mother died shortly after the birth of a baby in 1819 Maria had to take over the care of her younger brothers and sisters, among them the novelist Geraldine Jewsbury who was born in 1812. With six young children to care for and the running of a smooth household to consider, Maria had little time to pursue her youthful plans or her new determination to improve her own education. To Mrs Alaric Watts Maria described her situation:

> ... you are on your sofa in a state of enviable serenity of body and mind. How different is my condition at this present! Three dear children are catechizing me at the rate of ten questions every five minutes. I am within hearing of one servant stoning a kitchen floor; and of another practising a hymn; and of a very turbulent child and unsympathetic nurse next door. I think I could make a decent paper descriptive of the miseries of combining literary tastes with domestic duties (Jewsbury 1932: xvii–xviii).

Recalling those early days, Maria said to Felicia Hemans, 'My life after eighteen became so painful, laboriously domestic, that it was an absolute duty to crush intellectual tastes... I could neither write nor read legitimately till the day was over...' (Chorley 1836: 164–73). So that is exactly what Maria did; educated toddlers, made gruel for the ailing; ordered dinners and restrained servants with consummate efficiency all day, and sat up until the early hours to think and read and write. As Norma Clarke argues, if her life as a spinster matron was hard, it at least meant that beyond her chores, the government of her *manner* of life was her own. In the 1820s when 'facility and audacity went hand in hand' Maria wrote furiously (in both senses) and contributed to the *Manchester Gazette* where her work attracted the attention of Alaric Watts. He arranged for the publication of a collection of her prose and verse and *Phantasmagoria* appeared in 1825 with a dedication to William Wordsworth. On receiving the earliest copy of the first volume Maria promptly packaged it up and sent it, with an effusive letter, to the great man himself. It worked. Wordsworth replied with a little thoughtful criticism (he preferred her prose to her verse) and some advice.

'... let me caution you', he wrote, 'who are probably young, not to rest your hopes or happiness on Authorship. I am aware that nothing can be done in literature without enthusiasm ... – but of even successful Authors how few have become happier Men ... Why should this be?' Then remembering himself, and that he addressed a young woman he added, '... & yet I cannot but feel persuaded that it is so with our sex, & your's is, I think, full as much exposed to evils that beset the condition ...' (Jewsbury 1932: xxii). William then helpfully sent the volume on to Robert Southey for review. But the Poet Laureate, possibly offended by her all-too-accurate parody of his discursive reviewing style ('First Efforts in Criticism', Jewsbury 1825: 8–18), declined, declaring that 'the best service he could render to the misguided young person was to leave her wholly unnoticed'. In view of Southey's attitudes to women and writing, later expressed so devastatingly to Charlotte Brontë, Maria might have been grateful that he did.

A happier outcome was an invitation to visit Rydal Mount where Maria's domestic efficiency and cheerfulness made her hugely popular with the male and female members of the household alike. It probably also helped that Maria happily played out the role of pretty disciple venerating every syllable uttered by the master. Sometimes, anyway. When she later spent a holiday at Kent's Bank with the Wordsworth family, Maria recorded a little story under the heading 'Philosophic Remark':

> The following has been transmitted to us from authority which it would be impossible to dispute, and will, we think, gratify our readers ... a celebrated Belle made a lively remark upon a well-known gentleman's susceptibility. 'You are too severe on the gentleman,' said an illustrious poet with an emphasis which showed him sensible of the Worth of Words. 'You ladies are often infinitely more susceptible. Your hearts very often resemble looking-glasses, not in their capability of being broken, but in that of receiving every impression and retaining none' (Jewsbury 1932: xxvii).

If Maria was wickedly sceptical, William was constitutionally inadequate, and the lasting friendship which resulted from these days was with William's daughter Dora who remained close to Maria up till her death. But the image of the successful and authoritative male poet had done damage, and Maria's youthful 'fury' was never to be recovered. In 1829 she wrote to Dora about Felicia Hemans, herself, and women and writing:

> You cannot think how often and how fondly I look back to Kent's Bank and your father's conversations there – when in Wales I repeated some of his opinions on the pains and penalties of female authorship, and Mrs Hemans agreed to them, in the sober sadness that I do. Her fame has gilded *her* chain, but it has not lost its clank. I cannot conceive how, unless a necessity be laid upon her, any woman of acute sensibility, and refined imagination can brook the fever strife of authorship. Do you remember your father's simile about women and flowers – growing in their native bed and transplanted to a drawing room chimney place? I wish I could forget it (Clarke 1990, Dove Cottage papers: 68).

Clearly Maria never could forget it. When she returned home to Manchester, she fell violently ill. The reasons are mysterious. She speaks of a weakness in the spine; she speaks also of a rebellious stomach; whatever it was, it was serious, debilitating, long lasting and depressing. The fight had gone out of her. Her strange and miserable poem

'A Farewell to the Muse' was written in the October after she returned home from her happy time with the Wordsworths, and a copy was sent back to the family to show that she really had learnt the womanly qualities of renunciation, self-abasement and humility. This is a classic poem of the kind discerned by Gilbert and Gubar as gendered by 'anxiety of authorship'. As a woman, Maria knew that she was always to be excluded. Intercourse with the true fount of real poetry had shown her that she had no gift and would not be endowed. He was on the inside, she was outside, looking in.

For nearly two long years Maria stayed ill. She spent some time at Leamington Spa, keeping away from the old demanding domestic routine and the equally demanding requirements of her new local Manchester fame as the author of *Phantasmagoria*. Writing to Dora, she described herself as a 'misguided being', and said that her miseries lay not 'in the hour of disappointment and of chagrin – it was in the moment of full unalloyed success that she was most wretched'. Her only prayer now was to keep just 'well enough to fulfil my home *duties*' (Clarke 1990, Dove Cottage papers: 69). In this mood of despair and self-castigation, Maria wrote and published a series of letters to her sister Geraldine, *Letters to the Young* (1828) which draws upon an earlier tradition of eighteenth-century 'conduct books' while it points toward the female didacticism of Sarah Stickney Ellis and her kind. The general tone of *Letters to the Young* can be gauged from Maria's birthday message to the sixteen-year-old Geraldine: 'The wreath of fame is often a fiery crown, burning the brows that wear it – I do my dear love wish you all *good* things on your birthday – and amongst them moderated expectations of life' (Clarke 1990, Jewsbury papers: 70).

Interestingly, if there is any subversive message in *Letters to the Young* – and, for the most part it is about the dangers of literary aspiration for young women – it lies in the suggestion that sickness is one route which may allow control of one's intellectual environment because it means opting out of the real world of domesticity and the marriage market. While Maria was ill, she wrote copiously and published a great deal in the annuals, even exceeding the amount published there by either Hemans or L.E.L. However dispirited, this new success and attention were clearly restorative for Maria. But the most important factor in her recovery was her strengthening friendship with Felicia Hemans, and in this the woman did not let her down. Felicia and Maria had discovered shared interests through their correspondence and in June 1827 Maria took her two younger brothers and her sister Geraldine to Rhyllon in Wales to stay with Felicia and her family. The children – seven boys counting Felicia's five – got on well together and roamed the countryside, unchecked, while for a whole four months the two writers talked and argued and agreed and differed while Maria regained her health and spirit. For the first time a sympathetic woman friend of like mind and ambition was showing to Maria the paths she had recently been forbidden. A substantial result of her intimacy with Felicia Hemans was that Maria produced a volume of poems *Lays of Leisure Hours* (1829) which she dedicated to Mrs Hemans. Out of this new relation she also wrote *The Three Histories* (1830) which consists of three tales, 'The History of an Enthusiast', 'The History of a Nonchalant', and 'The History of a Realist'. In the 'Nonchalant' Maria tells of a young man on tour in Italy who falls in love with Egeria, a poetess. For this version of the Corinne myth, Maria took Felicia Hemans as her model:

Egeria was totally different from any other woman I had ever seen ... She did not dazzle; she subdued me ... Her gladness was like a burst of sunlight; and if in her depression she resembled night, it was night wearing her stars ... she was a muse, a grace, a variable child, a dependant woman – the Italy of human beings (Jewsbury 1830: 187–9).

All the same, the old doubts about the writing woman are there. The 'nonchalant's' father disapproves of the connection and disinherits him. This puts the hero into a difficult position but he forcefully rejects Egeria's suggestion that they live on her earnings; '. . . live upon the money earned by a woman – that woman my wife – and that wife Egeria! – I could far sooner have died than permitted such a reversal of the order of nature, such a desecration of my dignity and her softness!' (Jewsbury 1830: 193). The problem is resolved when Egeria conveniently dies. But in her 'History of an Enthusiast' Maria presents another, more subversive solution. Julia, the heroine, is a writing woman, part Maria herself, part Felicia Hemans, part Corinne. She achieves fame and literary success in spite of homely warnings ('Genius [is] the smallpox of the soul') that these are not fit aims for a woman. Living alone in London, fêted, but very much alone, Julia's mind is presented as one suffering always from doubt, and frenzied, unhealthy intellectual ambition. Her erstwhile lover refuses to marry her. 'I should not like a lioness for a wife' he says, 'because it interferes with . . . implanted and imbibed ideas of domestic life and womanly duty' (Jewsbury 1830: 124). Maria's own earlier poem 'To My Own Heart' makes clear that she was indeed the 'enthusiast' who tortured herself with inappropriate 'energies'. But in that poem Maria uses an image of herself, alone certainly, but cut off from human fellowship 'like a ship' which leaves 'the world' behind. And this is what happens to Julia; for she decides at the end of the tale to leave England and wander Europe, acknowledging – and it's a double-edged claim – that 'I *am* a woman belonging to nobody' (Jewsbury 1830: 151).

In 1830 Maria was a successful woman. She had an income from writing, she was admired, sought out, invited. She had the companionship of other women writers – L.E.L. was now one of her correspondents – and she was independent. She travelled to Edinburgh where she met Sir Walter Scott, and she lived in London to be nearer her work, which, among other things, included writing articles on women and on proto-feminist topics for *The Athenaeum*. And then, she decided to marry. *Why* is the question, though one can cite her age, her anxiety over her career, her boredom with her family life, her wish for emotional support. In spite of difficulties (Thomas Jewsbury objected) Maria married William Kew Fletcher in 1832, one friend relating that 'I must do her the justice to recount that she uttered the terrible "*obey*", with edifying distinctness' (Jewsbury 1932: lix). In September the couple set out for India where William had obtained a post as Chaplain to the East India Company, and eventually they arrived in Bombay 'alias biscuit-oven, alias brick-kiln, alias burning Babel, alias Pandemonium, alias everything hot, horrid, glaring, barren, dissonant, and detestable . . .' Maria wrote. Travelling on to William's post, Maria suffered an attack of cholera in June 1833. She recovered enough to attempt a return to Karnai where the climate was cooler, but she died at Poona in October and there she was buried. William soon married again. Felicia Hemans wore mourning.

Jewsbury's poetry is sprightly and accomplished, and her talent for imitation and parody is sure. In this vein she was also an ironic writer, and her two parodies of Cowper and Burns included here amusingly translate their original masculine speakers from noble solitude to domestic trial and affliction. Otherwise, Jewsbury's poems are important because they play out some of her own miserable anxieties over her right to the role of author. 'A Farewell to the Muse' most obviously works on the theme in setting masculine images ('the sons of song') and allusions (Moses smiting 'the rock of song') against the feeble feminine versions ('idle toys') which are all that she fears she can manage. The same theme appears in 'To My Own Heart', but its conclusion hints at subversion. 'Leaving the world behind' could mean the usual feminine solution to a failed life, i.e., death. But it might also mean shrugging off the world and its expectations, thus releasing the woman poet into a new freedom, and looking forward to the similar imaginative recognition of death which is employed by Christina Rossetti. However, for the most part, Jewsbury's poetry is only a sign of what might have been. In her life she regretted her own failure; '*I have done nothing to live*,' she wrote to Hemans, 'and what I have done must pass away with a thousand other blossoms, the growth, the beauty, the oblivion of a day'. Later writers recognized the loss, Mary Russell Mitford and Barrett Browning among them:

> The sister Jewsbury was a woman of more comprehensiveness of mind & of higher logical faculty than are commonly found among women – but it is true, what you observe, that she has done little, if anything. Her life was an aspiration: noble indeed in its kind, & affecting (to my thoughts,) as a remembrance – but no more! – Those letters of hers in Mr. Chorley's memoir of Mrs Hemans were strikingly superior to the poetess's, – ... It was impossible to help recognizing in them a *working-power*... though no worthy work was left behind! Hand and mallet fell together – but once they were upraised – & nothing is more affecting to me than a course half run... (EBB to MRM, 21 June 1845: Barrett Browning 1983: III, 118–19).

M.R.

Jewsbury, Maria Jane (1825) *Phantasmagoria, or Sketches of Life and Literature*, London, Hurst Robinson and Co.
—— (1828) *Letters to the Young*, London, J. Hatchard and Son.
—— (1829) *Lays of Leisure Hours*, London, J. Hatchard and Son.
—— (1830) *The Three Histories*, London, F. Westley.
—— (1932) *Occasional Papers, selected with a Memoir*, by Eric Gillett, London, Oxford University Press.

Barrett Browning, Elizabeth (1983) *The Letters of Elizabeth Barrett Browning to Mary Russell Mitford: 1836–1854*, 3 vols, eds Meredith B. Raymond and Mary Rose Sullivan, Winfield, Kan., Wedgestone Press.
Chorley, H. F. (1836) *Memorials of Mrs. Hemans*, London, Saunders and Otley.
Clarke, Norma (1990) *Ambitious Heights: Writing, Friendship, Love: The Jewsbury Sisters, Felicia Hemans and Jane Carlyle*, London and New York, Routledge.
Fryckstedt, Monica (1984) 'The hidden rill: the life and career of Maria Jane Jewsbury', *Bulletin of the John Rylands University Library of Manchester*, vol. 66, no. 2, Spring 1984, and vol. 67, no. 1, Autumn 1984.
Williams, Jane (1861) *The Literary Women of England*, London, Saunders and Otley.

To My Own Heart

I am a little world made cunningly.
Donne

Come, let me sound thy depths, unquiet sea
Of thought and passion; let thy wild waves be
Calm for a moment. Thou mysterious mind –
No human eye may see, no fetters bind;
Within me, ever near me as a friend   5
That whilst I know I fail to comprehend;
Fountain, whence sweet and bitter waters flow,
The source of happiness, the cause of woe, –
Of all that spreads o'er life enchantment's spell,
Or binds it by anticipated hell; –   10
Come let me talk with thee, allotted part
Of immortality – my own deep heart!

Yes, deep and hidden now, but soon unsealed,
Must thou thy deepest thoughts and secrets yield:
Like the old sea, put off the shrouding gloom   15
That makes thee now a prison-house and tomb;
Spectres and sins that undisturbed have lain,
Must hear the judgement-voice and live again.
Then woe or bliss for thee: – thy ocean-mate,
Material only in its birth and fate,   20
Its rage rebuked, its captive hosts set free,
And homage paid, shall shrink away, and be
With all the mutinous billows o'er it hurled,
Less than a dew-drop on a rose impearled!
But thou – but thou – or darker, or more fair   25
The sentence and the doom that waits thee there.
No rock will hide thee in its friendly breast,
No death dismiss thee to eternal rest;
The solid earth thrilled by the trumpet's call,
Like a sere leaf shall tremble ere it fall, –   30

From heaven to hell on EYE extend and shine,
That can forgotten deeds and thoughts divine –
How wilt thou brook that day, that glance, frail heart of mine?

Spirit within me, speak; and through the veil
That hides thee from my vision, tell thy tale;   35
That so the present and the past may be
Guardians and prophets to futurity.
Spirit by which I live, thou art not dumb,
I hear thy voice; I called and thou art come;

I hear thy still and whispering voice of thought   40
Thus speak, with memories and musings fraught: –
'Mortal, Immortal, would desires like these
Had claimed thy prime, employed thine hours of ease!
But then, within thee burned th' enthusiast's fire,
Wild love of freedom, longings for thy lyre; –   45
And ardent visions of romantic youth,
Too fair for time, and oh! too frail for truth!
Aspirings nurst by solitude and pride,
Worlds to the dreamer, dreams to all beside;
Bright vague imaginings of bliss to be,   50
None ever saw, yet none despaired to see,
And aimless energies that bade the mind
Launch like a ship and leave the world behind.
But duty disregarded, reason spurned,
Knowledge despised, and wisdom all unlearned,   55
Punished the rebel who refused to bow,
And stamped SELF-TORTURER on th' enthusiast's brow.

'No earthly happiness exists for such,
They shrink like insects from the gentlest touch:
A breath can raise them, but a breath can kill,   60
And such wert thou – how sad the memory still!
Without a single real grief to own,
Yet ever mourning fancied joys o'erthrown; –
Viewing mankind with delicate disdain,
Unshared their pleasures, unrelieved their pain;   65
Self, thy sole object, interest, aim, end, view,
The circle's centre, oft the circle too.

' 'Tis past! 'tis past! – and never more may rise
The wasted hours I now have learned to prize;
Youth, like a summer sun, hath sunk to rest,   70
But left no glory lingering in its west.
Maturer life hath real sorrows brought,
And made me blush for those that such once thought;
Fancy is bankrupt for her golden schemes,
Tried in the world they proved but glittering dreams;   75
Remembrance views with unavailing tears,
the accusing phantoms of departed years,
While Hope too often lays her anchor by,
Or only lifts to heaven a troubled eye;
Too oft forebodings agonize the soul,   80
As lamentation filled the prophet's roll.
'Why do I speak of this? though sad, though true,
I know a calmer mood, a brighter view:
The restless ocean hath its hours of rest,
And sleep may visit those by pain opprest;   85

More shade than sunlight o'er his heart may sweep,
Who yet is cheerful, nay, may seldom weep;
And he may learn, though late, and by degrees,
To love his neighbour and desire to please;
Rejoice o'er those who never go astray,   90
And those who do, assist to find their way:
Life he may look on with a sobered eye,
And how to live, think less than how to die;
Love all that's fair on earth, or near or far,
Yet deem the fairest but a shooting star,   95
And strive to point his spirit's inward sight,
To orb for ever fixed, for ever bright;
Mourn countless sins, yet trust to be forgiven,
And feel a hesitating hope of heaven!'

A Farewell to the Muse

Not in envy, ire, or grief
Bid I now the Muse farewell;
'T is no childish fancy brief,
Lured away by newer spell;
As of earthly good the chief,   5
I have sought her long and well.

Not in anger; – inward joys
Have been mine, and meed of praise, –
Payment vast for idle toys,
Fleeting, unsubstantial lays;   10
Sandy columns wind destroys,
And that wind again can raise.

No, – nor yet in grief we part –
Never unto bard like me,
Gave the Muse a broken heart;   15
'T is to nobler votaries, she
Doth that awful gift impart –
Pledge of immortality!

Not in envy; – though around
Like the stars, a radiant throng,   20
In their several orbits found,
I behold the sons of song, –
Every brow with laurel bound,
And a few as giants strong.

Not in envy; – though I know   25
Neither wreath nor radiance mine;

I will yet pay homage low
Pilgrim-like, at every shrine;
Seek where buds and blossoms grow,
And for others garlands twine.   30

Never hath my Muse bereaved me,
Song hath lightened hours of pain;
Never Poet yet deceived me,
Truer friend I scarce could gain;
Ne'er among the things that grieved me,   35
Ranked the minstrel lute and strain.

Yet I bid the art adieu,
It may be, adieu for ever;
I abjure the syren too,
Vain, I own, my best endeavour;   40
Weak to grasp, though keen to view
Climbing alway – rising never.

Though I smite the rock of song,
At my stroke no stream will flow, –
At my spell no spirits strong   45
Bidden come, or mastered go;
Nor the world of passion throng
With its wild waves to and fro.

Farewell Muse! – vouchsafing never
But dim glance and veiled brow;   50
Farewell Lute! – a rude toy ever,
Broken, stringless, soon art thou;
Farewell Song! – thy last notes quiver, –
Muse, – Lute, – Music, – farewell now!

A Summer Eve's Vision

Thought from the bosom's inmost cell,
  By magic tints made visible.
                    Montgomery

I heard last night a lovely lute,
  I heard it in the sunset hour,
When every jarring sound was mute,
  And golden light bathed field and flower.

I saw the hills in bright repose,   5
  And far away a silent sea,
Whilst nearer hamlet-homes arose,
  Each sheltered by its guardian tree.

O'er all was spread a soft blue sky,
　　And where the distant waters rolled,　　　　　　　　10
Type of the blest abodes on high
　　Swept the sun's path of pearl and gold.

I turned me from a gentle throng,
　　Night stilled the lute and quenched the beam,
But sunset and the voice of song　　　　　　　　　　15
　　Pursued me – and I slept to dream.

I dreamt that I again was young,
　　With merry heart and frolic will,
That hopes around my spirit clung,
　　As morning mists enwreathe the hill.　　　　　　　20

I saw ambition's heights arise,
　　Fame's pathway o'er it spread sublime,
And sprang all bird-like to the skies,
　　Nor feared the coming night of time.

Unwearied up the steep I prest,　　　　　　　　　　25
　　And vainly deemed my home would be
'Mid the bright bowers where crowned ones rest,
　　Amid the glorious and the free.

But soon came on a darker mood,
　　Fame's lingering sunbeam ceased to glow,　　　　30
The heights grew barren where I stood,
　　And Death's wide Ocean roared below.

Then waking from that troubled dream,
　　This lesson did my heart imbue,
In every earthly hope and scheme,　　　　　　　　　35
　　How far the seeming from the true!

Verses

Supposed to be written by an invalid during his solitary abode in Bed: a parody on Cowper's 'Alexander Selkirk'.

I

I am monarch of troubles a host,
　　With my power there is none may compete
From the pillow all down to the post,
　　I am lord of the blanket and sheet.
O sickness! but where are the charms　　　　　　　5

That doctors can see in thy face,
Better dwell in the midst of alarms
　　Than reign in this horrible place.

2

I am far from the dining room baits,
　　I must finish my fasting alone,　　　　　　　　　　10
Never hear the sweet clatter of plates,
　　I have not even one of my own.
My nurses go downstairs to carve
　　The dishes that I may not see;
They are so unaccustomed to starve,　　　　　　　　15
　　They think starving is nothing to me.

3

Pig – Ven'son – and Poultry – all juice
　　So divine when bestowed within men,
O had I the wings of a Goose
　　How soon would I taste them again!　　　　　　　20
My sorrows I then might assuage
　　With apple sauce sweet to the eye;
Might feast on the onions and sage,
　　And be cheered by a pudding or pie.

4

(*Not parodied.* [*i.e., as in Cowper*])

5

Ye winds as ye kitchen-wards swell,　　　　　　　　25
　　Convey through the chinks of my door,
Some cordial and savoury smell
　　Of the dishes I carve at no more.
My friends – is there one asks to send
　　Some nice little tid-bit to me?　　　　　　　　　30
O tell me I have such a friend
　　Though the tid-bit I never may see.

6

How poor is a drink from the well
　　Compared with a glass of good beer;

But water is all that may dwell   35
  With the white-labelled pill-boxes here.
When I think of a London beef steak,
  I seem to be eating one there;
But alas, in a moment I wake
  To find toast and water my fare.   40

7

But the doctor is gone to his nest,
  The nurse is asleep in her chair;
Even here is a season of rest,
  And I for my pillow prepare.
There is hunger in every place,   45
  And if hunger – encouraging thought!
But give to my figure fresh grace
  'Twill reconcile me to my lot.

'My heart's in the kitchen, my heart is not here'[1]

My heart's in the kitchen, my heart is not here,
My heart's in the kitchen, though following the *dear*,
Thinking on the roast meat, and musing on the fry,
My heart's in the kitchen whatever I spy.

Caroline Clive ('V') (1801–1873)

Caroline Clive was the daughter of Anna Maria Meysey, heiress and owner of the estate at Shakenhurst where the family lived, and Edmund Wigley, a barrister and MP for Worcester. At the age of three she contracted infantile paralysis which left her permanently lame in one foot. She was an ugly child, squint-eyed and heavy-jowled, and as a result tended to be melancholy and solitary. In later life her appearance continued to provoke comment. Barrett Browning, who met her in 1854, thought her 'a very peculiar person as to looks' (1983: III, 402). Caroline's appetite for literary melodrama may have been nourished by the accidental early deaths of her two brothers, one of whom left her with a complicated insurance case to fight in the courts. Some notes towards an unwritten novel give a hint of this early taste for the sensational. The heroine bears an illegitimate child and rears her in a brothel. Years later, the child's son comes 'in search of adventures', is virtuously resisted by his mother, but gets the grandmother instead. The liaison leads to marriage, when all is revealed: 'One more kiss my Jack – Impossible (never) Madam, – I have married my grandmother' (1949: 22).

In her youth Caroline was inclined 'to fall into the most violent friendships' with women, one of the 'strongest' (1949: 55–6) being for Mrs Gore, the novelist, whom she visited in Paris in 1838. On this first trip abroad she enjoyed scandalizing onlookers

---

[1] A parody of Robert Burns' 'My heart's in the highlands'.

by dining with her maid, visiting a mesmerist and going to the theatre on her own. On her return to England, in 1840, she published *IX Poems by V*, which was singled out by the *Quarterly* as the most promising work by a contemporary woman poet – a fact which may explain the coolness between herself and Barrett Browning, one of whose early volumes was also reviewed. By this time Caroline had fallen in love with the Revd Archer Clive, the Rector of the local parish. It seems that, disappointed in love for another, he first became a close friend – it was he who gave her the nickname Vigolina (probably a Latinate version of Wigley, hence her pseudonym 'V') – and then, in 1840, against all the prevailing mores of the time, joined her for a six-week tour of the continent. On their return they married. She was thirty-nine.

Thus began what was, evidently, an extraordinarily harmonious and happy relationship. Caroline, who never expected to marry, expressed her surprise and gratitude to the end of her life. When Archer was away from home she suffered a recurring nightmare, 'the old bad dream . . . about not being his wife' (1949: 237). Onlookers, too, seem to have been impressed by their domestic and intellectual companionship. Florence Nightingale once gleefully informed a friend, who had exclaimed in pity at the poet's unattractive lameness: 'Dear me, to think of the creature having a heart but no legs!' that Caroline was indeed, contrary to all presuppositions, a happy wife and mother. She particularly admired Archer 'for disproving the general proposition that we are to be treated as furniture or a piece of fine clothes for the man's vanity, while they may be as ugly as they please and no one is to wonder at anybody's marrying them' (1949: 269). During 1841 Caroline kept detailed notes of her first pregnancy which, her editor in the 1940s claimed, were 'too indelicate to be printed' (1949: 133). She subsequently bore a boy and later a girl.

In 1855 she published the novel which was to make her famous: *Paul Ferroll*, a sensational tale about a man who murders his hateful wife in order to marry his true love. Three more novels in the same vein followed, though these never achieved the notoriety of the first. Meanwhile, Caroline continued to add to her small output of poems.

At the age of sixty-four she suffered a paralytic stroke which left her severely incapacitated, unable to walk and able to write only slowly with her left hand. She died eight years later, when a stray spark from the library fire caught a pile of newspapers at her feet. The more delicate (or perhaps punitive) version, put about by nineteenth-century commentators, that she died when her own books and papers caught fire in her boudoir, is untrue.

Clive's prose has a certain rollicking gusto, but her poetry tends to be anaemically conventional. Most of her verses are slight, melancholy affairs, lacking the wit and earthiness of the diary entries or the risqué melodrama of the novels. They suggest the extent to which poetry could be worn by Victorian women writers as a sort of 'best dress', a formal, tailor-made mood, to be put on and taken off at will. Here and there, however, something of Clive's own voice and experience breaks through. 'The Mother', which was written after her first pregnancy, is a rare poem on the woman's fear of miscarriage – thus touching on that implicitly 'indelicate' topic of the female body. 'Old Age' is similarly about a relatively unconventional subject (see Webster's 'Faded'), which the poet evokes with a knowing and unregretful sense of acceptance.

A.L.

Clive, Caroline ('V') (1872) *Poems by 'V', the Author of 'Paul Ferroll'* London.
—— (1949) *From the Diary and Family Papers of Mrs. Archer Clive*, ed. Mary Clive, London, Bodley Head.

Barrett Browning, Elizabeth (1983) *The Letters of Elizabeth Barrett Browning to Mary Russell Mitford: 1836–1854*, 3 vols, eds Meredith B. Raymond and Mary Rose Sullivan, Winfield, Kan., Wedgestone Press.

The Mother

I feel within myself a life
That holds 'gainst death a feeble strife;
They say 'tis destined that the womb
Shall be its birthplace and its tomb.
O child! if it be so, and thou   5
Thy native world must never know,
Thy Mother's tears will mourn the day
   When she must kiss thy Death-born face.
But oh! how lightly thou wilt pay
   The forfeit due from Adam's race!   10
Thou wilt have lived, but not have wept,
   Have died, and yet have known no pain;
And sin's dark presence will have swept
   Across thy soul, yet left no stain.
Mine is thy life; my breath thy breath: 15
   I only feel the dread, the woe;
And in thy sickness or thy death,
   Thy Mother bears the pain, not thou.

Life nothing means for thee, but still
It is a living thing, I feel;   20
A sex, a shape, a growth are thine,
A form and human face divine;
A heart with passions wrapp'd therein,
A nature doom'd, alas! to sin;
A mind endow'd with latent fire,   25
To glow, unfold, expand, aspire;
Some likeness from thy father caught,
Or by remoter kindred taught;
Some faultiness of mind or frame,
To wake the bitter sense of shame;   30
Some noble passions to unroll,
   The generous deed, the human tear;
Some feelings which thy Mother's soul
   Has pour'd on thine, while dwelling near.
All this must pass unbloom'd away   35
To worlds remote from earthly day;
Worlds whither we by paths less brief,
Are journeying on through joy and grief,
And where thy Mother, now forlorn,
May learn to know her child unborn;   40

Oh, yes! created thing, I trust
Thou too wilt rise with Adam's dust.

Old Age

Thou hast been wrong'd, I think old age;
    Thy sovereign reign comes not in wrath,
Thou call'st us home from pilgrimage,
    Spreadest the seat and clear'st the hearth.

The hopes and fears that shook our youth,   5
    By thee are turn'd to certainty;
I see my boy become a man,
    I hold my girl's girl on my knee.

Whate'er of good has been, dost thou
    In the departed past make sure;   10
Whate'er has changed from weal to woe,
    Thy comrade Death stands nigh to cure.

And once or twice in age there shines
    Brief gladness, as when winter weaves
In frosty days o'er naked trees,   15
    A sudden splendour of white leaves.

The past revives, and thoughts return,
    Which kindled once the youthful breast;
They light us, though no more they burn,
    Then turn to grey and are at rest.   20

L.E.L. (Letitia Elizabeth Landon) (1802–1838)

The daughter of an army agent who lost much of his wealth in speculation, Letitia Elizabeth Landon, like Hemans, was forced to turn her poetic gifts prematurely to economic use. She began to publish in *The Literary Gazette*, a forerunner of the popular annuals, when she was sixteen. In 1824 her long poem, *The Improvisatrice*, gained its 22-year-old author instantaneous renown and a command of the increasingly lucrative market for light verse. When, in 1825, her beloved father died, Letitia was able to contribute considerably towards the maintenance of her mother as well as her brother's education at Oxford. She published six volumes of verse between 1821 and 1830 and undertook vast quantities of casual writing, both poetry and prose, for the annuals. The alluring initials of L.E.L. or L. became a sure selling-point in such annuals as the *Book of Beauty* and the *Drawing Room Scrap-Book*. Unlike Hemans, however, L.E.L. did not compensate for this economic independence by assiduously cultivating an ethic of domesticity. Quite the opposite. In her own life she moved out of the family home, rented an attic room in London and wrote poems, à la Corinne, about orphaned, creative women whom the world, and especially men, reject. This independence was probably the cause of her social downfall.

Thrown into the limelight of London literary life, befriended by such 'free' women as Lady Caroline Lamb and Lady Blessington, L.E.L. soon became the subject of scandalous gossip. In time, the names of three men became associated with hers: William Jerdan, who first published her poems in the *Gazette*, William Maginn, an Irish journalist whose wife allegedly found a love letter of Letitia's in his pocket, and Bulwer Lytton, with whom she was observed to flirt openly. The truth of the accusations is impossible to substantiate. Letitia herself vehemently denied any impropriety, pointing, instead, to the double standards applied to women of the aristocracy and those of her own class. 'It is only because I am poor, unprotected, and dependant [sic] on popularity' she once expostulated, 'that I am a mark for all the gratuitous insolence and malice of idleness and ill-nature' (Blanchard 1841: I, 54). Elsewhere, generalizing from her own experience, she proclaimed that 'envy, malice, and all uncharitableness, – these are the fruits of a successful literary career for a woman' (Hall 1871: 264). To be an 'unprotected' woman poet in Regency London was very different from being a Corinne in an imaginary Italy. In the end, L.E.L. paid dearly for her success. As a result of continuing rumours about an adulterous affair, she was forced to break off her engagement to John Forster, the future biographer of Dickens, and in the end she married a man whose unsuitability must soon have become apparent. Captain George McLean was Governor of Cape Coast Castle in West Africa, a notorious slave-trading post. In the summer of 1838 Letitia left England for good.

At first, she seems to have been quite cheerful. But soon the loneliness of the place, the surly temper of her husband and, it seems, his refusal to let her have a room of her own in which to write, began to weigh on her spirits. 'He expects me to cook, wash, and iron; in short, to do the work of a servant' (Hall: 278), she lamented to friends at home. Two months after landing she was found dead on the floor of her bedroom, a bottle of prussic acid in her hand. Inevitably, news of her death stirred up old gossip at home. It was recalled that Captain McLean was said to have had a native mistress at the castle, and the idea of 'a horrible spirit of female vengeance' (Blanchard: I, 217) was publicly aired by L.E.L.'s biographer. The possibility of an accident (Letitia was taking prussic acid for an ailment) was also mooted. But the likelihood that it was suicide – a theme which runs through her poetry – seems the most plausible explanation. The effect of this mysterious and much publicized death was to give the Sappho–Corinne myth of so many of her poems a tawdry, real-life colouring in the public eye. L.E.L.'s suicide could easily be made to prove the moral disreputableness of professional women writers in general.

To later poets, L.E.L. became an object of mixed pity and admiration. Barrett Browning's poem, 'L.E.L.'s Last Question', mourns the untimely death of her pre-decessor, but also criticizes the narcissism of her verse. 'The Romance of the Swan's Nest' may also be a comment on L.E.L.'s unsexualized, childish imagination. Barrett Browning once complained that her 'passion was pasteboard', but added perceptively that, when death cut her off, 'she was rising into light & power & knowledge' (1983: I, 252). For Rossetti, L.E.L. offered a more enduring and seductive model of the poèt (see 'L.E.L.') – a model which she herself embraced and rehearsed in her poetry. The drama of the lovelorn heroine, singing as she is about to die, is one which Rossetti makes peculiarly her own. L.E.L.'s contribution to the history of women's poetry in the nineteenth century thus lies in her development of the myth which Hemans originates: that of the poet as a heroic but doomed Sappho.

This model depends on two connected ideas: that the woman poet is a public improviser, performing for a specifically female audience, and that she is inevitably therefore rejected in love, by an equally specific male betrayer. There is a strong element of self-advertisement, on the one hand, and of accusation, on the other, in these poems. However, unlike Hemans, there are few correcting domestic morals. In 'Sappho's Song' and 'A History of the Lyre', the heroines sing, love and die with exhibitionist fluency. They flaunt their sensibilities before the world and tell their unhappy stories with voluble enthusiasm. If the quality of the verse is sometimes thin, it also has a hypnotic, free-wheeling energy which is curiously gripping. In particular, the dramatic monologue form of 'A History' seems calculated to put the woman's voice, as well as the woman's very visible body, centre stage. The motif of improvisation – of the woman poet as an impromptu 'singer', uninhibited and unashamed – encourages an association between writing and the body, text and sex, verse and voice, which suggestively points towards contemporary theories of *écriture féminine*. It is as if L.E.L. takes many of Hemans's motifs: woman's creativity, her mythical southern heritage, her unrequited passions and heroic suicide, but writes about them in a place outside the home, where they remain undomesticated and unsafe, as well as from within the unmoralized, close-up 'I' of the woman's suffering subjectivity.

There is also a streak of weary scepticism in L.E.L. which is not present in Hemans. She rarely offers religious solutions to life's problems (compare 'A Girl at Her Devotions' with Hemans's 'Evening Prayer'), and she occasionally shows an awareness of class differences ('The Dying Child' and 'The Poor'), which the older poet glosses over in broad generalizations of Woman. Most notably, the late *Fragments* (ten of which are reprinted here), which served as epigraphs to her society novel *Ethel Churchill* (1837), reveal a sharp-edged realism and disillusionment which suggest a genuine development from the mellifluous, effortless-sounding flow of the early work. These fragments tell of lessons of experience learned too late, of darker, moral secrets in the soul, of social hypocrisy and emotional distrust and, most movingly of all, of poetic 'Gifts Misused'.

L.E.L. may have become aware, too late, that she had sold herself to the market. Yet to give her her dues, she had little choice. Both her own and others' survival depended on her writing. If she caught the fashions of the moment and exploited the vein of the pathetic and the mournful which the age expected of women, she also helped to realize, in her life as well as her work, the newly emerging idea of the woman poet as a successful, if suffering, professional. She herself paid the high price of that success, in tragic corroboration of the drama of many of her own poems.

A.L.

L.E.L. (1839) *Poetical Works*, 4 vols, London.
—— (1873) *Poetical Works*, ed. William B. Scott, London.

Barrett Browning, Elizabeth (1983) *The Letters of Elizabeth Barrett Browning to Mary Russell Mitford: 1836–1854*, 3 vols, eds Meredith B. Raymond and Mary Rose Sullivan, Winfield, Kan., Wedgestone Press.
Blain, Virginia (1995) 'Letitia Elizabeth Landon, Eliza Mary Hamilton, and the Genealogy of the Victorian Poetess', *Victorian Poetry*, 33 (1995).
Blanchard, Laman (1841) *Life and Literary Remains of L.E.L*, 2 vols, London.

Curran, Stuart (1988) 'Romantic Poetry: The I Altered', in *Romanticism and Feminism*, ed. Anne K. Mellor, Bloomington and Indianapolis, Indiana University Press, pp. 185–207.

Hall, S. C. (1871) *A Book of Memories of Great Men and Women of the Age*, London.

Leighton, Angela (1992) *Victorian Women Poets*, Hemel Hempstead, Harvester, pp. 45–77.

Mellor, Anne K. (1993) *Romanticism & Gender*, New York and London, Routledge, pp. 110–23.

Stephenson, Glennis (1992) 'Letitia Landon and the Victorian Improvisatrice: The Construction of L. E. L.', *Victorian Poetry*, 30 (1992), 1–17.

—— (1993) 'Poet Construction: Mrs Hemans, L. E. L., and the Image of the Nineteenth-Century Woman Poet', in *ReImagining Women: Representations of Women in Culture*, ed. Shirley Neuman and Glennis Stephenson, Toronto, University of Toronto Press, pp. 61–73.

Stevenson, Lionel (1947) 'Miss Landon: "The Milk-and-Watery-Moon of our Darkness", 1824–30', *Modern Language Quarterly*, 8 (1947), 355–63.

from The Improvisatrice

Sappho's Song

Farewell, my lute! – and would that I
    Had never waked thy burning chords!
Poison has been upon thy sigh,
    And fever has breathed in thy words.

Yet wherefore, wherefore should I blame   5
    Thy power, thy spell, my gentlest lute?
I should have been the wretch I am,
    Had every chord of thine been mute.

It was my evil star above,
    Not my sweet lute, that wrought me wrong;   10
It was not song that taught me love,
    But it was love that taught me song.

If song be past, and hope undone,
    And pulse, and head, and heart, are flame;
It is thy work, thou faithless one!   15
    But, no! – I will not name thy name!

Sun-god! lute, wreath are vowed to thee!
    Long be their light upon my grave –
My glorious grave – you deep blue sea:
    I shall sleep calm beneath its wave!   20

Stanzas on the Death of Mrs. Hemans

The rose – the glorious rose is gone.
Lays of Many Lands

Bring flowers to crown the cup and lute, –
    Bring flowers, – the bride is near;
Bring flowers to soothe the captive's cell,
    Bring flowers to strew the bier!
Bring flowers! thus said the lovely song;   5
    And shall they not be brought
To her who linked the offering
    With feeling and with thought?

Bring flowers, – the perfumed and the pure, –
    Those with the morning dew,   10
A sigh in every fragrant leaf,
    A tear on every hue.
So pure, so sweet thy life has been,
    So filling earth and air
With odours and with loveliness,   15
    Till common scenes grew fair.

Thy song around our daily path
    Flung beauty born of dreams,
And scattered o'er the actual world
    The spirit's sunny gleams.   20
Mysterious influence, that to earth
    Brings down the heaven above,
And fills the universal heart
    With universal love.

Such gifts were thine, – as from the block,   25
    The unformed and the cold,
The sculptor calls to breathing life
    Some shape of perfect mould,
So thou from common thoughts and things
    Didst call a charmed song,   30
Which on a sweet and swelling tide
    Bore the full soul along.

And thou from far and foreign lands
    Didst bring back many a tone,
And given such new music still,   35
    A music of thine own.
A lofty strain of generous thoughts,
    And yet subdued and sweet, –

An angel's song, who sings of earth,
 Whose cares are at his feet.   40

And yet thy song is sorrowful,
 Its beauty is not bloom;
The hopes of which it breathes, are hopes
 That look beyond the tomb.
Thy song is sorrowful as winds   45
 That wander o'er the plain,
And ask for summer's vanish'd flowers,
 And ask for them in vain.

Ah! dearly purchased is the gift,
 The gift of song like thine;   50
A fated doom is her's who stands
 The priestess of the shrine.
The crowd – they only see the crown,
 They only hear the hymn; –
They mark not that the cheek is pale,   55
 And that the eye is dim.

Wound to a pitch too exquisite,
 The soul's fine chords are wrung;
With misery and melody
 They are too highly strung.   60
The heart is made too sensitive
 Life's daily pain to bear;
It beats in music, but it beats
 Beneath a deep despair.

It never meets the love it paints,   65
 The love for which it pines;
Too much of Heaven is in the faith
 That such a heart enshrines.
The meteor-wreath the poet wears
 Must make a lonely lot;   70
It dazzles, only to divide
 From those who wear it not.

Didst thou not tremble at thy fame,
 And loathe its bitter prize,
While what to others triumph seemed,   75
 To thee was sacrifice?
Oh, Flower brought from Paradise
 To this cold world of ours,
Shadows of beauty such as thine
 Recall thy native bowers.   80

Let others thank thee – 'twas for them
　　Thy soft leaves thou didst wreathe;
The red rose wastes itself in sighs
　　Whose sweetness others breathe!
And they have thanked thee – many a lip　　　85
　　Has asked of thine for words,
When thoughts, life's finer thoughts, have touched
　　The spirit's inmost chords.

How many loved and honoured thee
　　Who only knew thy name;　　　　　　　　90
Which o'er the weary working world
　　Like starry music came!
With what still hours of calm delight
　　Thy songs and image blend;
I cannot choose but think thou wert　　　　　95
　　An old familiar friend.

The charm that dwelt in songs of thine
　　My inmost spirit moved;
And yet I feel as thou hadst been
　　Not half enough beloved.　　　　　　　　100
They say that thou wert faint, and worn
　　With suffering and with care;
What music must have filled the soul
　　That had so much to spare!

Oh, weary One! since thou art laid　　　　　105
　　Within thy mother's breast –
The green, the quiet mother-earth –
　　Thrice blessed be thy rest!
Thy heart is left within our hearts,
　　Although life's pang is o'er;　　　　　　110
But the quick tears are in my eyes,
　　And I can write no more.

A History of the Lyre

Sketches indeed, from that most passionate page,
A woman's heart, of feelings, thoughts, that make
The atmosphere in which her spirit moves;
But, like all other earthly elements,
O'ercast with clouds, now dark, now touch'd with light,　　5
With rainbows, sunshine, showers, moonlight, stars,
Chasing each other's change. I fain would trace
Its brightness and its blackness; and these lines

Are consecrate to annals such as those,
That count the pulses of the beating heart.   10

'Tis strange how much is mark'd on memory,
In which we may have interest, but no part;
How circumstance will bring together links
In destinies the most dissimilar.
This face, whose rudely-pencill'd sketch you hold,   15
Recalls to me a host of pleasant thoughts,
And some more serious. – This is EULALIE,
Once the delight of Rome for that fine skill
With which she woke the lute when answering
With its sweet echoes her melodious words.   20
She had the rich perfection of that gift,
Her Italy's own ready song, which seems
The poetry caught from a thousand flowers;
The diamond sunshine, and the lulling air,
So pure, yet full of perfume; fountains tuned   25
Like natural lutes, from whispering green leaves;
The low peculiar murmur of the pines:
From pictured saints, that look their native heaven –
Statues whose grace is a familiar thing;
The ruin'd shrine of mournful loveliness;   30
The stately church, awfully beautiful;
Their climate, and their language, whose least word
Is melody – these overfill the heart
Till, fountain-like, the lips o'erflow with song,
And music is to them an element.   35
– I saw EULALIA: all was in the scene
Graceful association, slight surprise,
That are so much in youth. It was in June,
Night, but such night as only is not day, –
For moonlight, even when most clear, is sad: 40
We cannot but contrast its still repose
With the unceasing turmoil in ourselves.
   – We stood beside a cypress, whose green spire
Rose like a funeral column o'er the dead.
Near was a fallen palace – stain'd and gray   45
The marble show'd amid the tender leaves
Of ivy but just shooting; yet there stood
Pillars unbroken, two or three vast halls,
Entire enough to cast a deep black shade;
And a few statues, beautiful but cold, –   50
White shadows, pale and motionless, that seem
To mock the change in which they had no part, –
Fit images of the dead. Pensive enough,
Whatever aspect desolation wears;
But this, the wrecking work of yesterday,   55

Hath somewhat still more touching; here we trace
The waste of man too much. When years have past
Over the fallen arch, the ruin'd hall,
It seems but course of time, the one great doom,
Whose influence is alike upon us all;   60
The gray tints soften, and the ivy wreath
And wild flowers breathe life's freshness round: but here
We stand before decay; scarce have the walls
Lost music left by human step and voice;
The lonely hearth, the household desolate,   65
Some noble race gone to the dust in blood;
Man shames of his own deeds, and there we gaze,
Watching the progress not of time, but death.
– Low music floated on the midnight wind,
A mournful murmur, such as opes the heart   70
With memory's key, recalling other times,
And gone by hopes and feelings, till they have
An echo sorrowful, but very sweet.
'Hush!' said my comrade, – 'it is EULALIE;
'Now you may gaze upon the loneliness   75
'Which is her inspiration.' Soft we pass'd
Behind a fragment of the shadowy wall.
– I never saw more perfect loveliness.
It ask'd, it had no aid from dress: her robe
Was white, and simply gather'd in such folds   80
As suit a statue: neck and arms were bare;
The black hair was unbound, and like a veil
Hung even to her feet; she held a lute,
And, as she paced the ancient gallery, waked
A few wild chords, and murmur'd low sweet words.   85
But scarcely audible, as if she thought
Rather than spoke: – the night, the solitude,
Fill'd the young Pythoness with poetry.
– Her eyes were like the moonlight, clear and soft,
That shadowy brightness which is born of tears,   90
And raised towards the sky, as if they sought
Companionship with their own heaven; her cheek, –
Emotion made it colourless, that pure
And delicate white which speaks so much of thought,
Yet flushes in a moment into rose;   95
And tears like pearls lay on it, those which come
When the heart wants a language; but she pass'd,
And left the place to me a haunted shrine,
Hallow'd by genius in its holiest mood.
– At Count ZARIN's palazzo the next night   100
We were to meet, and expectation wore
Itself with fancies, – all of them were vain.
I could not image aught so wholly changed.

Her robe was Indian red, and work'd with gold,
And gold the queen-like girdle round her waist.   105
Her hair was gather'd up in grape-like curls;
An emerald wreath, shaped into vine leaves, made
Its graceful coronal. Leant on a couch
The centre of a group, whose converse light
Made a fit element, in which her wit   110
Flash'd like the lightning: – on her cheek the rose
Burnt like a festal lamp; the sunniest smiles
Wander'd upon her face. – I only knew
EULALIA by her touching voice again.
– They had been praying her to wake the lute: 115
She would not, wayward in her mood that night;
When some one bade her mark a little sketch
I brought from England of my father's hall;
Himself was outlined leaning by an oak,
A greyhound at his feet. 'And is this dog   120
Your father's sole companion?' – with these words
She touch'd the strings: – that melancholy song,
I never may forget its sweet reproach.
– She ask'd me how I had the heart to leave
The old man in his age; she told how lorn   125
Is solitude; she spoke of the young heart
Left in its loneliness, where it had known
No kindness but from strangers, forced to be
Wayfarer in this bleak and bitter world,
And looking to the grave as to a home.   130
– The numbers died in tears, but no one sought
To stay her as she pass'd with veiled face
From the hush'd hall. – One gently whisper'd me.
EULALIA is an orphan! * * *
Yet still our meetings were mid festival.   135
Night after night. It was both sad and strange.
To see that fine mind waste itself away,
Too like some noble stream, which, unconfined.
Makes fertile its rich banks, and glads the face
Of nature round; but not so when its wave   140
Is lost in artificial waterfalls,
And sparkling eddies; or coop'd up to make
The useless fountain of a palace hall.
– One day I spoke of this; her eager soul
Was in its most unearthly element.   145
We had been speaking of the immortal dead.
The light flash'd in her eyes. ''Tis this which makes
The best assurance of our promised heaven:
This triumph intellect has over death –
Our words yet live on others' lips; our thoughts   150
Actuate others. Can that man be dead

Whose spiritual influence is upon his kind?
He lives in glory; and such speaking dust
Has more of life than half its breathing moulds.
Welcome a grave with memories such as these,   155
Making the sunshine of our mortal world!'
'This proud reward you see, and yet can leave:
Your songs sink on the ear, and there they die,
A flower's sweetness, but a flower's life.
An evening's homage is your only fame;   160
Tis vanity, EULALIA.' – Mournfully
She shook the raven tresses from her brow,
As if she felt their darkness omen-like.
'Speak not of this to me, nor bid me think;
It is such pain to dwell upon myself;   165
And know how different I am from all
I once dream'd I could be. Fame! stirring fame!
I work no longer miracles for thee.
I am as one who sought at early dawn
To climb with fiery speed some lofty hill: 170
His feet are strong in eagerness and youth;
His limbs are braced by the fresh morning air,
And all seems possible: – this cannot last.
The way grows steeper, obstacles arise,
And unkind thwartings from companions near.   175
The height is truer measured, having traced
Part of its heavy length; his sweet hopes droop.
Like prison'd birds that know their cage has bars,
The body wearies, and the mind is worn –
That worst of lassitude: – hot noon comes on;   180
There is no freshness in the sultry air,
There is no rest upon the toilsome road;
There is the summit, which he may not reach,
And round him are a thousand obstacles.
    'I am a woman: – tell me not of fame.   185
The eagle's wing may sweep the stormy path,
And fling back arrows, where the dove would die.
Look on those flowers near yon acacia tree –
The lily of the valley – mark how pure
The snowy blossoms, – and how soft a breath   190
Is almost hidden by the large dark leaves.
Not only have those delicate flowers a gift
Of sweetness and of beauty, but the root –
A healing power dwells there; fragrant and fair,
But dwelling still in some beloved shade.   195
Is not this woman's emblem? – she whose smile
Should only make the loveliness of home –
Who seeks support and shelter from man's heart,
And pays it with affection quiet, deep, –

And in his sickness – sorrow – with an aid   200
He did not deem in aught so fragile dwelt.
Alas! this has not been my destiny.
Again I'll borrow Summer's eloquence.
Yon Eastern tulip – that is emblem mine;
Ay! it has radiant colours – every leaf   205
Is as a gem from its own country's mines.
'Tis redolent with sunshine; but with noon
It has begun to wither: – look within,
It has a wasted bloom, a burning heart;
It has dwelt too much in the open day,   210
And so have I; and both must droop and die!
I did not choose my gift: – too soon my heart,
Watch-like, had pointed to a later hour
Than time had reach'd: and as my years pass'd on,
Shadows and floating visions grew to thoughts,   215
And thoughts found words, the passionate words of song,
And all to me was poetry. The face,
Whose radiance glided past me in the dance,
Awoke a thousand fantasies to make
Some history of her passing smile or sigh.   220
The flowers were full of song: – upon the rose
I read the crimson annals of true love;
The violet flung me back on old romance;
All was association with some link
Whose fine electric throb was in the mind.   225
I paid my price for this – 'twas happiness.
My wings have melted in their eager flight,
And gleams of heaven have only made me feel
Its distance from our earth more forcibly.
My feelings grow less fresh, my thoughts less kind: 230
My youth has been too lonely, too much left
To struggle for itself; and this world is
A northern clime, where ev'ry thing is chill'd.
I speak of my own feelings – I can judge
Of others but by outward show, and that   235
Is falser than the actor's studied part.
We dress our words and looks in borrow'd robes:
The mind is as the face – for who goes forth
In public walks without a veil at least?
'Tis this constraint makes half life's misery.   240
'Tis a false rule: we do too much regard
Others' opinions, but neglect their feelings;
Thrice happy if such order were reversed.
Oh why do we make sorrow for ourselves,
And, not content with the great wretchedness   245
Which is our native heritage – those ills
We have no mastery over – sickness, toil,

Death, and the natural grief which comrades death –
Are not all these enough, that we must add
Mutual and moral torment, and inflict   250
Ingenious tortures we must first contrive?
I am distrustful – I have been deceived
And disappointed – I have hoped in vain.
I am vain – praise is opium, and the lip
Cannot resist the fascinating draught,   255
Though knowing its excitement is a fraud –
Delirious – a mockery of fame.
I may not image the deep solitude
In which my spirit dwells. My days are past
Among the cold, the careless, and the false.   260
What part have I in them. or they in me?
Yet I would be beloved; I would be kind;
I would share others' sorrows, others' joys;
I would fence in a happiness with friends.
I cannot do this: – is the fault mine own?   265
Can I love those who but repay my love
With half caprice, half flattery; or trust,
When I have full internal consciousness
They are deceiving me? I may be kind,
And meet with kindness, yet be lonely still;   270
For gratitude is not companionship. –
We have proud words that speak of intellect;
We talk of mind that magnifies the world,
And makes it glorious: much of this is true, –
All time attests the miracles of man: 275
The very elements, whose nature seems
To mock dominion, yet have worn his yoke.
His way has been upon the pathless sea;
The earth's dark bosom search'd; bodiless air
Works as his servant; and from his own mind   280
What rich stores he has won, the sage, the bard,
The painter, these have made their nature proud:
And yet how life goes on, its great outline
How noble and ennobling! – but within
How mean, how poor, how pitiful, how mix'd   285
With base alloy; how Disappointment tracks
The steps of Hope; how Envy dogs success;
How every victor's crown is lined with thorns,
And worn mid scoffs! Trace the young poet's fate:
Fresh from his solitude, the child of dreams,   290
His heart upon his lips, he seeks the world,
To find him fame and fortune, as if life
Were like a fairy tale. His song has led
The way before him; flatteries fill his ear,
His presence courted, and his words are caught;   295

And he seems happy in so many friends.
What marvel if he somewhat overrate
His talents and his state? These scenes soon change.
The vain, who sought to mix their name with his;
The curious, who but live for some new sight;   300
The idle, – all these have been gratified,
And now neglect stings even more than scorn.
Envy has spoken, felt more bitterly,
For that it was not dream'd of; worldliness
Has crept upon his spirit unaware;   305
Vanity craves for its accustom'd food;
He has turn'd sceptic to the truth which made
His feelings poetry; and discontent
Hangs heavily on the lute, which wakes no more
Its early music: – social life is fill'd   310
With doubts and vain aspirings; solitude,
When the imagination is dethroned,
Is turn'd to weariness. What can he do
But hang his lute on some lone tree, and die?
    'Methinks we must have known some former state   315
More glorious than our present, and the heart
Is haunted with dim memories, shadows left
By past magnificence; and hence we pine
With vain aspirings, hopes that fill the eyes
With bitter tears for their own vanity.   320
Remembrance makes the poet; 'tis the past
Lingering within him, with a keener sense
Than is upon the thoughts of common men
Of what has been, that fills the actual world
With unreal likenesses of lovely shapes,   325
That were and are not; and the fairer they,
The more their contrast with existing things,
The more his power, the greater is his grief.
– Are we then fallen from some noble star,
Whose consciousness is as an unknown curse,   330
And we feel capable of happiness
Only to know it is not of our sphere?
    'I have sung passionate songs of beating hearts;
Perhaps it had been better they had drawn
Their inspiration from an inward source.   335
Had I known even an unhappy love,
It would have flung an interest round life
Mine never knew. This is an empty wish;
Our feelings are not fires to light at will
Our nature's fine and subtle mysteries;   340
We may control them, but may not create,
And love less than its fellows. I have fed
Perhaps too much upon the lotos fruits

Imagination yields, – fruits which unfit
The palate for the more substantial food   345
Of our own land – reality. I made
My heart too like a temple for a home;
My thoughts were birds of paradise, that breathed
The airs of heaven, but died on touching earth.
– The knight whose deeds were stainless as his crest,   350
Who made my name his watchword in the field;
The poet with immortal words, whose heart
I shared with beauty; or the patriot,
Whose eloquence was power, who made my smile
His recompense amid the toil which shaped   355
A nation's destiny: these, such as these,
The glorified – the passionate – the brave –
In these I might have found the head and heart
I could have worshipp'd. Where are such as these?
– Not mid gay cavaliers, who make the dance   360
Pleasant with graceful flatteries; whose words
A passing moment might light up my cheek,
But haunted not my solitude. The fault
Has been my own; perhaps I ask'd too much: –
Yet let me say, what firmly I believe,   365
Love can be – ay, and is. I held that Love
Which chooseth from a thousand only one,
To be the object of that tenderness
Natural to every heart; which can resign
Its own best happiness for one dear sake;   370
Can bear with absence; hath no part in Hope, –
For Hope is somewhat selfish, Love is not, –
And doth prefer another to itself.
Unchangeable and generous, what, like Love,
Can melt away the dross of worldliness;   375
Can elevate, refine, and make the heart
Of that pure gold which is the fitting shrine
For fire, as sacred as e'er came from Heaven?
No more of this: – one word may read my heart,
And that one word is utter weariness!   380
Yet sometimes I look round with vain regret,
And think I will restring my lute, and nerve
My woman's hand for nobler enterprise;
But the day never comes. Alas! we make
A ladder of our thoughts, where angels step,   385
But sleep ourselves at the foot: our high resolves
Look down upon our slumbering acts.'
    I soon left Italy: it is well worth
A year of wandering, were it but to feel
How much our England does outweigh the world.   390
A clear cold April morning was it, when I first

Rode up the avenue of ancient oaks,
A hundred years upon each stately head.
The park was bright with sunshine, and the deer
Went bounding by; freshness was on the wind,   395
Till every nerve was braced; and once the air
Came with Arabian sweetness on its wing, –
It was the earliest growth of violets.
A fairy foot had left its trace beside, –
Ah, EMILY had nursed my favourite flowers.   400
Nearer I came, I heard familiar sounds –
They are the heart's best music; saw the blaze
Through the wide windows of the dear old hall.
One moment more, my eager footsteps stood
Within my father's home, beside his hearth.   405
– Three times those early violets had fill'd
Their urns with April dew, when the changed cheek
Of EMILY wore signs of young decay.
The rose was too inconstant, and the light
Too clear in those blue eyes; but southern skies   410
Might nurse a flower too delicate to bear
The winds of March, unless in Italy.
I need not tell thee how the soothing air
Brought tranquil bloom that fed not on itself
To EMILY'S sweet face; but soon again   415
We talk'd of winter by our own wood fire,
With cheerful words, that had no tears to hide.
– We pass'd through Rome on our return, and there
Sought out EULALIA. Graceful as her wont
Her welcome to my bride; but oh, so changed!   420
Her cheek was colourless as snow; she wore
The beauty of a statue, or a spirit
With large and radiant eyes: – her thrilling voice
Had lost its power, but still its sweetness kept.
One night, while seated in her favourite hall,   425
The silken curtains all flung back for air,
She mark'd my EMILY, whose idle gaze
Was fix'd on that fair garden. 'Will you come
And wander in the moonlight? – our soft dew
Will wash no colour from thine island cheek.'   430
She led the way by many a bed, whose hues
Vied with the rainbow, – through sweet-scented groves
Golden with oranges: at length the path
Grew shadowy with darker, older trees,
And led us to a little lonely spot.   435
There were no blossoming shrubs, but sweeping pines
Guarded the solitude; and laurel boughs
Made fitting mirrors for the lovely moon,
With their bright shining leaves; the ivy lay

And trail'd upon the ground; and in the midst   440
A large old cypress stood, beneath whose shade
There was a sculptured form; the feet were placed
Upon a finely-carved rose wreath; the arms
Were raised to Heaven, as if to clasp the stars
EULALIA leant beside; 'twas hard to say   445
Which was the actual marble: when she spoke,
You started, scarce it seem'd a human sound;
But the eyes' lustre told life linger'd still;
And now the moonlight seem'd to fill their depths.
'You see,' she said, 'my cemetery here: –   450
Here, only here, shall be my quiet grave.
Yon statue is my emblem: see, its grasp
Is raised to Heaven, forgetful that the while
Its step has crush'd the fairest of earth's flowers
With its neglect.' –   455
                    Her prophecy was sooth:
No change of leaf had that green valley known,
When EULALIE lay there in her last sleep.

   Peace to the weary and the beating heart,
That fed upon itself!   460

A Girl at Her Devotions

She was just risen from her bended knee,
But yet peace seem'd not with her piety;
For there was paleness upon her young cheek,
And thoughts upon the lips which never speak,
But wring the heart that at the last they break.   5
Alas! how much of misery may be read
In that wan forehead, and that bow'd down head: –
Her eye is on a picture, woe that ever
Love should thus struggle with a vain endeavour
Against itself: it is a common tale,   10
And ever will be while earth soils prevail
Over earth's happiness; it tells she strove
With silent, secret, unrequited love.

   It matters not its history; love has wings
Like lightning, swift and fatal, and it springs   15
Like a wild flower where it is least expected,
Existing whether cherish'd or rejected;
Living with only but to be content,
Hopeless, for love is its own element, –
Requiring nothing so that it may be   20
The martyr of its fond fidelity.
A mystery art thou, thou mighty one!

We speak thy name in beauty, yet we shun
To own thee, Love, a guest; the poet's songs
Are sweetest when their voice to thee belongs,   25
And hope, sweet opiate, tenderness, delight,
Are terms which are thy own peculiar right;
Yet all deny their master, – who will own
His breast thy footstool, and his heart thy throne?

'Tis strange to think if we could fling aside   30
The masque and mantle that love wears from pride,
How much would be, we now so little guess,
Deep in each heart's undream'd, unsought recess.
The careless smile, like a gay banner borne,
The laugh of merriment, the lip of scorn, –   35
And for a cloak what is there that can be
So difficult to pierce as gaiety?
Too dazzling to be scann'd, the haughty brow
Seems to hide something it would not avow;
But rainbow words, light laugh, and thoughtless jest,   40
These are the bars, the curtain to the breast,
That shuns a scrutiny: and she, whose form
Now bends in grief beneath the bosom's storm,
Has hidden well her wound, – now none are nigh
To mock with curious or with careless eye,   45
(For love seeks sympathy, a chilling yes,
Strikes at the root of its best happiness,
And mockery is worm-wood), she may dwell
On feelings which that picture may not tell.

The Dying Child

The woman was in abject misery – that worst of poverty which is haunted by shame – the only relic left by better days. She shrunk from all efforts at recovery, refused to administer the medicines, and spoke of the child's death but as a blessing.

My God! and is the daily page of life
Darken'd with wretchedness like this?

Her cheek is flush'd with fever red;
    Her little hand burns in my own;
Alas! and does pain rack her sleep?
    Speak! for I cannot bear that moan.

Yet sleep, I do not wish to look   5
    Again within those languid eyes;
Sleep, though again the heavy lash
    May never from their beauty rise.

– Aid, hope for me? – now hold they peace,
    And take that healing cup away: 10
Life, length of life, to that poor child! –
    It is not life for which I pray.

Why should she live for pain, for toil,
    For wasted frame, and broken heart;
Till life has only left, in death,   15
    With its base fear of death to part!

How could I bear to see her youth
    Bow'd to the dust by abject toil,
Till misery urge the soul to guilt,
    From which its nature would recoil?   20

The bitterness of poverty,
    The shame that adds the worst to woe, –
I think upon the life I've known,
    Upon the life that I shall know.

Look through yon street, – a hundred lamps   25
    Are lighting up the revels there, –
Hark! you can hear the distant laugh
    Blending with music on the air.

The rich dwell there, who know not want;
    Who loathe that wretchedness whose name   30
Is there an unfamiliar sound: –
    Why is not my estate the same?

I may have sinn'd, and punishment
    For that most ignorant sin incur;
But be the curse upon my head, –   35
    Oh, let it not descend to her!

Sleep, dear one! 'tis a weary world;
    Sleep the sweet slumber of the grave!
Vex me no more with thy vain words:
    What worth is that you seek to save?   40

Tears – tears – I shame that I should weep;
    I thought my heart had nerved my eye: –
I should be thankful, and I will, –
    There, there, my child, lie down and die!

from *Fragments*

Secrets

Life has dark secrets; and the hearts are few
That treasure not some sorrow from the world –
A sorrow silent, gloomy, and unknown,
Yet colouring the future from the past.
We see the eye subdued, the practised smile,   5
The word well weighed before it pass the lip,
And know not of the misery within:
Yet there it works incessantly, and fears
The time to come; for time is terrible,
Avenging, and betraying.   10

Small Miseries

Life's smallest miseries are, perhaps, its worst:
Great sufferings have great strength: there is a pride
In the bold energy that braves the worst,
And bears proud in the bearing; but the heart
Consumes with those small sorrows, and small shames,   5
Which crave, yet cannot ask for sympathy.
They blush that they exist, and yet how keen
The pang that they inflict!

The Marriage Vow

The altar, 'tis of death! for there are laid
The sacrifice of all youth's sweetest hopes.
It is a dreadful thing for woman's lip
To swear the heart away; yet know that heart
Annuls the vow while speaking, and shrinks back   5
From the dark future that it dares not face.
The service read above the open grave
Is far less terrible than that which seals
The vow that binds the victim, not the will:
For in the grave is rest.   10

Gifts Misused

Oh, what a waste of feeling and of thought
Have been the imprints on my roll of life!
What worthless hours! to what use have I turned
The golden gifts which are my hope and pride!
My power of song, unto how base a use   5
Has it been put! with its pure ore I made

An idol, living only on the breath
Of idol worshippers. Alas! that ever
Praise should have been what praise has been to me –
The opiate of the mind!   10

The Poor

Few, save the poor, feel for the poor:
    The rich know not how hard
It is to be of needful food
    And needful rest debarred.

Their paths are paths of plenteousness,   5
    They sleep on silk and down;
And never think how heavily
    The weary head lies down.

They know not of the scanty meal,
    With small pale faces round;   10
No fire upon the cold damp hearth
    When snow is on the ground.

They never by the window lean,
    And see the gay pass by;
Then take their weary task again,   15
    But with a sadder eye.

Stern Truth

Life is made up of vanities – so small,
So mean, the common history of the day, –
That mockery seems the sole philosophy.
Then some stern truth starts up – cold, sudden, strange;
And we are taught what life is by despair: –   5
The toys, the trifles, and the petty cares,
Melt into nothingness – we know their worth;
The heart avenges every careless thought,
And makes us feel that fate is terrible.

The Mask of Gaiety

'Tis strange to think, if we could fling aside
The mask and mantle many wear from pride,
How much would be, we now so little guess,
Deep in each heart's undream'd, unsought recess!

The careless smile, like a bright banner borne;   5
The laughlike merriment; the lip of scorn;
And for a cloak, what is there that can be
So difficult to pierce as gaiety?

Too dazzling to be scanned, the gloomy brow
Seems to hide something it would not avow;   10
But mocking words, light laugh, and ready jest,
These are the bars, the curtains to the breast.

The Power of Words

'Tis a strange mystery, the power of words!
Life is in them, and death. A word can send
The crimson colour hurrying to the cheek.
Hurrying with many meanings; or can turn
The current cold and deadly to the heart.   5
Anger and fear are in them; grief and joy
Are on their sound; yet slight, impalpable: –
A word is but a breath of passing air.

The Farewell

Farewell!
Shadows and scenes that have, for many hours,
Been my companions; I part from ye like friends –
Dear and familiar ones – with deep sad thoughts,
And hopes, almost misgivings!   5

Song

Farewell! – and never think of me
  In lighted hall or lady's bower!
Farewell! – and never think of me
  In spring sunshine or summer hour! –
But when you see a lonely grave,   5
  Just where a broken heart might be,
With not one mourner by its sod,
  Then – and then only – THINK OF ME!

Sara Coleridge (1802–1852)

Sara Coleridge had the misfortune of being the daughter of a famous poet. She was the third child of Samuel Taylor Coleridge and Sarah Fricker. For most of her childhood her father lived with the Wordsworths, near his beloved Sarah Hutchinson, William Wordsworth's sister-in-law. In her Memoir Sara notes that her birth was entered in the family bible in her mother's, not her father's hand, which seemed like 'an omen' of her 'separation' from him (1873: I, 2).

Her account of childhood visits to the Wordsworths then hints at an unpleasant emotional manipulativeness in her father. He refused to caress her when she arrived dressed in bright colours (he liked girls to wear white for 'delicacy and purity' (I, 21)); he regaled her with admiring praise of Sarah Hutchinson and, when she expressed a longing for her own mother, he reproached her and 'contrasted [her] coldness with the childish caresses of the little Wordsworths' (I, 19). Altogether, these visits must have been miserable affairs for the timid, sickly girl, who confusedly internalized her father's guilt as her own. 'The sense that you have done very wrong, or at least given great offence, you know not how or why – that you are dunned for some payment of love or feeling which you know not how to produce or to demonstrate on a sudden, chills the heart, and fills it with perplexity and bitterness' (I, 18–19), she once wrote. At night, she slept in her father's bed and listened, sometimes terrified, to the fairy stories he told her.

In her teens, Sara translated and published a three-volume work from the Latin, which gained her father's high praise. It also gained her a small income, originally intended to defray a brother's college expenses in the face of continuing paternal irregularities. Aberrant fathers and expensive brothers or sons often lurk behind the story of women's writing in the nineteenth century. In the event, Sara kept the money for herself. In 1829 she married her cousin, Henry Coleridge. When her father died in 1834, she embarked with her husband on the lifelong task of editing and annotating his works. Her intelligence, learning and scholarship have been recognized by many later editors as the foundation for their own work. She also bore two children, whom she educated at home and for whom she wrote *Pretty Lessons in Verse for Good Children* (1834). After the death of her husband in 1843, Sara continued to work on her father's manuscripts, thus, as one contemporary put it, 'expending in this desultory form an amount of original thought and an affluence of learning which, differently and more prominently presented, would have made her famous' (*Dictionary of National Biography*). As Virginia Woolf feelingly observed: 'A whole day's work would result in one erasure' (1942: 75). Sara herself explained to a friend, on the publication in 1847 of her edition of the *Biographia Literaria*: 'the trouble I have taken with this book is ridiculous to think of . . .' but added: 'I have done the thing *con amore*' (1873: II, 40). Evidently she worked her difficult childhood relationship with her father into a kind of intellectual love for him after his death. When she herself died of breast cancer in 1852, she had published only one original work of verse apart from the *Pretty Lessons*: her fairytale narrative, *Phantasmion* (1837). One uncollected fragment, ' "Father! no amaranths . . ." ' movingly accepts the role of daughterly subservience she embraced throughout her life.

Phantasmion is a delightful piece of children's fantasy, in which the eponymous hero, endowed with magical powers, sets out on a love quest through various exotic lands to win the heart of the princess Ialine. The prose narrative is interwoven with short, poignant lyrics, written somewhat in the mode of Hemans and L.E.L. Coleridge once admitted that Hemans's 'Evening Prayer, at a Girls' School' was one of her favourite poems (I, 152). Interestingly, the majority of these lyrics are sung by women, and express the woman's distrust of love. The plethora of female names and voices (Ialine, Malderyl, Zalia, Leucoia, Feydeleen) also suggests, as do the tales of L.E.L., a backdrop of female solidarity in the face of the disruptive love quest. The lovely song 'Blest is the tarn...' is sung by one of these female voices, as Phantasmion drifts across a lake in 'a mother-of-pearl boat... drawn by a team of swans' (1837: 258). It is noticeable that the verse reproduces a scene of female reciprocity and inspiration, between the unconscious tarn and the queen moon, which is in danger of some brutal invasion or molestation. Against the male quest of the prose narrative, poetry, in this work, seems aligned to the female principle.

A.L.

Coleridge, Sara (1837) *Phantasmion*, London.
—— (1873) *Memoirs and Letters*, 2 vols, ed. by her daughter, London.

Mudge, Bradford K. (1989) *Sara Coleridge: A Victorian Daughter*, New Haven, Yale University Press.
Woolf, Viriginia (1942) 'Sara Coleridge', in *The Death of the Moth and other Essays*, London, Hogarth Press, pp. 73–7.

' "Father! no amaranths e'er shall wreathe my brow" '

'Father! no amaranths e'er shall wreathe my brow;
Enough that round thy grave they flourish now!
But Love his roses 'mid my young locks braided,
And what cared I for flowers of richer bloom?
Those too seemed deathless – here they never faded,   5
But, drenched and shattered, dropt into the tomb.'

'Blest is the tarn which towering cliffs o'ershade'

Blest is the tarn which towering cliffs o'ershade,
Which, cradled deep within the mountain's breast
Nor voices loud, nor dashing oars invade:
Yet e'en the tarn enjoys no perfect rest,
For oft the angry skies her peace molest,   5
With them she frowns, gives back the lightning's glare,
Then rages wildly in the troubled air.

This calmer lake, which potent spells protect,
Lies dimly slumbering through the fires of day,
And when yon skies, with chaste resplendence decked,   10
Shine forth in all their stateliest array,
O then she wakes to glitter bright as they,
And view the face of heaven's benignant queen
Still looking down on hers with smile serene!

What cruel cares the maiden's heart assail,   15
Who loves, but fears no deep-felt love to gain,
Or, having gain'd it, fears that love will fail!
My power can soothe to rest her wakeful pain,
Till none but calm delicious dreams remain,
And, while sweet tears her easy pillow steep,   20
She yields that dream of bliss to ever welcome sleep.

Elizabeth Barrett Browning (1806–1861)

Elizabeth Barrett was the oldest of eleven children born to Edward and Mary Moulton Barrett. Her father owned sugar plantations in Jamaica, though after the abolition of the slave trade in 1834 the income from them decreased dramatically, and the family moved from a large country house in Herefordshire to Wimpole Street in London. Elizabeth, who was a precocious and active child, seems to have suffered some physical or emotional crisis in her teens which left her, conveniently enough, a confirmed invalid, unable to take on any domestic responsibilities. She lived till the age of forty in her father's house, writing poetry, seeing few visitors outside the family circle, but keeping, none the less, an eager eye on the affairs of the world outside. After the death of his wife in 1828 Mr Barrett had become neurotically anxious to keep the family together and forbade any of his children to marry. Elizabeth, whose love for him was profound and complex (he was the first to encourage her writing and she dedicated all her early volumes to him), suffered his rule for as long as she could.

In 1840 the main tragedy of her life occurred. She had been sent to Torquay to recuperate from an illness and insisted, against her father's wishes, that her favourite brother, Bro, remain with her. On a day when they had parted on unfriendly terms, Bro went sailing, his boat capsized and he drowned. For the rest of her life Elizabeth bore the guilt of this accident, which inspired some haunting poems: 'Grief', 'The Mask', 'I lift my heavy heart up solemnly' (*Sonnets from the Portuguese*, no. V) and parts of the quest for Marian in *Aurora Leigh* Book VI. On returning to London, she found some solace in a long, affectionate correspondence with Mary Russell Mitford, who encouraged her to publish ballads in the popular annuals, and who gave her a companion to cheer her solitude: the spaniel Flush (see 'Flush or Faunus'). In these intimate, witty letters, Elizabeth confides her new-found enthusiasm for George Sand (see the two sonnets 'To George Sand'), of whose emancipated habits she dared not tell her father, she discusses her own poetic aspirations, grumbles about her family, particularly her narrow-minded brothers, and relates bits of literary and family gossip. Although a recluse, she was far from unworldly. Her political poems, though often written in the face of disapproval from her family, bear witness to a passionate commitment to social and political issues. 'The Cry of the Children', which appeared in *Blackwood's* in 1843, helped prepare the way for Shaftesbury's 'Ten Hours' Amendment Bill, while 'The Runaway Slave', published in 1848 in a Boston anti-slavery journal, added its powerfully dramatic but also personally guilt-ridden voice to the growing chorus of opposition to slavery.

In 1844, Barrett Browning published a two-volume edition of her poems which was to make her name in the literary world as well as directly affect the course of her life.

This volume came to the attention of Robert Browning and inspired him to write a letter to its author which began: 'I love your verses with all my heart, dear Miss Barrett,' rounding up, for good measure, with 'and I love you too' (1969: I, 3). The edgy, effusive correspondence which followed led first to secret meetings in Elizabeth's room and eventually to a proposal of marriage. In spite of her years of invalidism and a fearful loyalty to her father, Elizabeth agreed to a secret elopement. She risked disinheritance, but a private income meant that she was able to support her penniless husband. In September 1846 the couple were married and left England for Italy. They settled in Casa Guidi in Florence.

Elizabeth's subsequent life forcefully dispels the romantic image of the sheltered poet of Wimpole Street. In Italy (now real, not mythical, as *Casa Guidi* insists) she travelled, wrote, *walked* a little and became a keen supporter of the political movement for unification. After a number of miscarriages she also bore a child, Penini or, appropriately enough, Pen – the daughter she longed for never came. In 1852 she met her idol George Sand in Paris, and was overcome with emotion when the novelist kissed her on the lips in welcome. The release of energy which marriage and travel provided are evident in the creative output of these years, in particular the great epic story of the woman poet, *Aurora Leigh* (1857), which is Barrett Browning's version of the *Corinne* myth. Projected years before as a new kind of 'novel–poem' which would challenge 'conventions' and rush 'into drawing-rooms' (1969: I, 31), she wrote it out of the charge of imaginative excitement which Italy, motherhood and her new-found freedom gave her. She also wrote it, however, out of the griefs which she could not lay: Bro's death, and also, now, her father's refusal to see or write to her, in spite of pleading letters and strategically renewed visits to London. What she had gained would always be measured, in her imagination, against what she had lost.

There were also some tensions in the marriage. Elizabeth's perhaps understandable interest in spiritualism – 'How the spiritual world gets thronged to us with familiar faces' (1897: II, 401) she once wrote, after a series of bereavements – was a source of annoyance to Robert, while her stubborn faith in the good intentions of Louis Napoleon remained a subject of dispute between them, till 1859, when, against his own promises of support for unification, he made an ignoble peace with occupying Austria – 'not a line have I written since the peace' (1929: 317), Elizabeth mourned. The disappointment and weariness which mark her later poems ('My Heart and I', 'The Best Thing in the World', 'Mother and Poet') suggest how far her poetic and emotional energies had been used up by the political turmoil of these years. When, in 1860, she heard that a sister had died of cancer, leaving young children behind, she seems to have given up altogether. A year later she herself died, quietly and unexpectedly, after a short illness, in Robert's arms.

Barrett Browning's career as a poet is representative of the struggle faced by many women poets of the time. The story of that struggle, against the sentimental, picturesque mode of Hemans and L. E. L., with their idealized emotional staginess, is indirectly told in Book II of *Aurora Leigh*. Barrett Browning's own early poems ('Felicia Hemans' and 'L. E. L.'s Last Question') already betray both her debt to, and her disagreement with, these poetic mothers. As she moved away from their womanly-virtuous mannerisms, she began to write ballads which, although retaining the courtly atmosphere of their writings, also subtly undermine the consolations of romantic love. In 'The Romance of the Swan's Nest', some hidden, perhaps sexual knowledge spoils the bookish daydreaming of the child-narrator. In the political poems, Barrett Browning turns the weapon of sentimentality against the vicious injustices of the contemporary world. 'The Cry of the Children' and 'The Runaway Slave' both expose an intriguing network of power relations in the family systems they describe – systems which are also strongly and suggestively gendered. The voice of the *woman* poet consciously aligns itself in these works with the voices of the exploited children or the raped slave. The sheer explicit force of the latter poem, which openly describes rape, torture and infanticide, must to some extent refute the charge (repeated by Romney in *Aurora Leigh* Book II) that all Victorian women's poetry is self-indulgently personal.

Even when Barrett Browning does write personal love poems, her *Sonnets from the Portuguese* for instance, these are not expressions of ill-used virtue and suicidal melancholy, but of active sexual demands and dangers. A certain baroque wit runs through these sonnets, reminding the reader, not only of the literary tradition they revive (this is practically the first love sonnet sequence in English since the Renaissance), but also of the crucial overturning of sex roles involved. By being both poet and muse, invisible lover and visible beloved, both subject and object, Barrett Browning enters into some ingenious, even acrobatic, reversals of the courtly tradition. There is an energy of desire in these poems which is, as Sonnet V seems to hint, positively inflammatory.

However, the culmination of Barrett Browning's development as a poet is *Aurora Leigh*. This ambitious epic, written in the low style of a sensation novel, with its energetic, eloquent narrator and panoramic sweep of events, is unparalleled in literature. In a sense, this is the old Corinne story of the artistic heroine betrayed in love, but with a new twist: here, it is Aurora who does the rejecting and who gets, for her reward, both love and art at the end. Furthermore, although recalling the romance plot of *Jane Eyre*, the importance of other women in *Aurora Leigh*, whether aristocratic or working class, diffuses the heterosexual bind of romance and creates some intriguingly new configurations of desire. The relationship between Aurora and Marian in Book VI has an intensity of feeling which almost rivals the abruptly concluded love story between Aurora and Romney. Above all, as in much of her best poetry, Barrett Browning keeps her epic tale of art and love focused on the political structures of race, class and family lineage. Aurora's long quest for success and self-respect, for which she has to forego an easy crowning in the garden, is not an idealized supra-social event, but one constantly grappling with the realities of money, inheritance, patrilineage and sexual power. For all the implausibilities of the plot, the imagery of *Aurora Leigh* keeps it rooted in the socio-economic facts of the real world. The woman's story, Barrett Browning seems to argue, cannot be told apart from those facts: the woman poet must meet her raped sister, and the love story must meet the other story of sexual brutality and violation.

For all her faults, Barrett Browning remains one of the major women poets of the nineteenth century. She can be verbose, extravagant and garrulous. But even these failings are a sign of the extent to which she has rejected, at least in her later work, the nostalgic archaisms of much Victorian verse. In her best work she finds a voice which belongs, noisily, exuberantly and provocatively, to the contemporary world of her age – and discovers it to be, not accidentally, a woman's world.

A.L.

Barrett Browning, Elizabeth (1900) *Complete Works*, 6 vols, eds Charlotte Porter and Helen A. Clarke, New York, Crowell.

Barrett Browning, Elizabeth (1897) *The Letters of Elizabeth Barrett Browning*, 2 vols, ed. Frederick G. Kenyon, London.

—— (1929) *Letters to her Sister, 1846–1859*, ed. Leonard Huxley, London, John Murray.

—— (1969) *Letters of Robert Browning and Elizabeth Barrett, 1845–1846*, 2 vols, ed. Elvan Kintner, Cambridge, Mass., Harvard University Press.

—— (1977) *Casa Guidi Windows*, ed. Julia Markus, New York, The Browning Institute.

—— (1983) *The Letters of Elizabeth Barrett Browning to Mary Russell Mitford: 1836–1854*, 3 vols eds Meredith B. Raymond and Mary Rose Sullivan, Winfield, Kan., Wedgestone Press.

—— (1992) *Aurora Leigh*, ed. Margaret Reynolds, Athens, Ohio, Ohio University Press.

Case, Alison (1991) 'Gender and Narration in *Aurora Leigh*', *Victorian Poetry*, 29 (1991), 17–32.

Cooper, Helen (1988) *Elizabeth Barrett Browning, Woman and Artist*, Chapel Hill and London, University of North Carolina Press.

David, Deirdre (1987) *Intellectual Women and Victorian Patriarchy: Harriet Martineau, Elizabeth Barrett Browning, George Eliot*, London, Macmillan.

Forster, Margaret (1988) *Elizabeth Barrett Browning*, London, Chatto and Windus.

Gelpi, Barbara Charlesworth (1981) '*Aurora Leigh*: The Vocation of the Woman Poet', *Victorian Poetry*, 19 (1981), 35–48.

Gilbert, Sandra M. (1984) 'From *Patria* to *Matria*: Elizabeth Barrett Browning's Risorgimento', *PMLA*, 99 (1984), 194–209.

Hayter, Alethea (1962) *Mrs Browning: A Poet's Work and its Setting*, London, Faber.

Hickok, Kathleen (1984) *Representations of Women: Nineteenth-Century British Women's Poetry*, Westport, Conn. and London, Greenwood Press, pp. 171–96.

Kaplan, Cora (1978) Introduction to *Aurora Leigh and Other Poems*, London, Women's Press.

—— (1986) 'Wicked Fathers: A Family Romance', in *Sea Changes: Essays in Culture and Feminism*, London, Verso, pp. 191–211.

Leighton, Angela (1986) *Elizabeth Barrett Browning*, Brighton, Harvester.

—— (1987/8) ' "Stirring a dust of figures": Elizabeth Barrett Browning and Love', *Browning Society Notes*, 17 (1987/8), 11–24.

—— (1992) *Victorian Women Poets*, Hemel Hempstead, Harvester, pp. 78–117.

Mermin, Dorothy (1981) 'The Female Poet and the Embarrassed Reader: Elizabeth Barrett Browning's *Sonnets from the Portuguese*', *English Literary History*, 48 (1981), 351–67.

—— (1989) *Elizabeth Barrett Browning: The Origins of a New Poetry*, Chicago and London, University of Chicago Press.

Riede, David G. (1994) 'Elizabeth Barrett: The Poet as Angel', *Victorian Poetry*, 32 (1994), 121–39.

Reynolds, Margaret (1987/8) '*Aurora Leigh*: "Writing her story for her better self" ', *Browning Society Notes*, 17 (1987/8), 5–11.

Rosenblum, Dolores (1986) 'Face to Face: Elizabeth Barrett Browning's *Aurora Leigh* and Nineteenth-Century Poetry', *Victorian Studies*, 26 (1983), 321–38.

Steinmetz, Virginia V. (1983) 'Images of "Mother-Want" in Elizabeth Barrett Browning's *Aurora Leigh*', *Victorian Poetry*, 21 (1983), 351–67.

Taplin, Gardner B. (1957) *The Life of Elizabeth Barrett Browning*, London, John Murray.

Woolf, Virginia (1932) 'Aurora Leigh', in *The Common Reader*, Second Series, London, Hogarth Press, pp. 202–13.

Felicia Hemans

To L.E.L.,
Referring to her Monody on the Poetess[1]

I

Thou bay-crowned living One that o'er the bay-crowned Dead art bowing,
And o'er the shadeless moveless brow the vital shadow throwing,
And o'er the sighless songless lips the wail and music wedding,
And dropping o'er the tranquil eyes the tears not of their shedding! –

II

Take music from the silent Dead whose meaning is completer, 5
Reserve thy tears for living brows where all such tears are meeter,
And leave the violets in the grass to brighten where thou treadest,
No flowers for her! no need of flowers, albeit 'bring flowers!' thou saidest.

III

Yes, flowers, to crown the 'cup and lute,' since both may come to breaking,
Or flowers, to greet the 'bride' – the heart's own beating works its aching; 10
Or flowers, to soothe the 'captive's' sight, from earth's free bosom gathered,
Reminding of his earthly hope, then withering as it withered:

IV

But bring not near the solemn corse a type of human seeming,
Lay only dust's stern verity upon the dust undreaming:
And while the calm perpetual stars shall look upon it solely, 15
Her spherèd soul shall look on *them* with eyes more bright and holy.

V

Nor mourn, O living One, because her part in life was mourning:
Would she have lost the poet's fire for anguish of the burning?
The minstrel harp, for the strained string? the tripod, for the afflated
Woe? or the vision, for those tears in which it shone dilated? 20

---

[1] See L.E.L.'s 'Stanzas on the Death of Mrs Hemans'.

VI

Perhaps she shuddered while the world's cold hand her brow was wreathing,
But never wronged that mystic breath which breathed in all her breathing,
Which drew, from rocky earth and man, abstractions high and moving,
Beauty, if not the beautiful, and love, if not the loving.

VII

Such visionings have paled in sight; the Saviour she descrieth,
And little recks *who* wreathed the brow which on His bosom lieth:
The whiteness of His innocence o'er all her garments, flowing,
There learneth she the sweet "new song" she will not mourn in knowing.

VIII

Be happy, crowned and living One! and as thy dust decayeth
May thine own England say for thee what now for Her it sayeth —
'Albeit softly in our ears her silver song was ringing,
The foot-fall of her parting soul is softer than her singing.'

L.E.L.'s Last Question

Do you think of me as I think of you?
From her poem written during the voyage to the Cape

I

'Do you think of me as I think of you,
My friends, my friends?' — She said it from the sea,
The English minstrel in her minstrelsy,
While, under brighter skies than erst she knew,
Her heart grew dark, and groped there as the blind   5
To reach across the waves friends left behind —
'Do you think of me as I think of you?'

II

It seemed not much to ask — 'as *I* of *you?*'
We all do ask the same; no eyelids cover
Within the meekest eyes that question over: 10
And little in the world the Loving do

But sit (among the rocks?) and listen for
The echo of their own love evermore –
'Do you think of me as I think of you?'

III

Love-learnèd she had sung of love and love, –   15
And like a child that, sleeping with dropt head
Upon the fairy-book he lately read,
Whatever household noises round him move,
Hears in his dream some elfin turbulence, –
Even so suggestive to her inward sense,   20
All sounds of life assumed one tune of love.

IV

And when the glory of her dream withdrew,
When knightly gestes and courtly pageantries
Were broken in her visionary eyes
By tears the solemn seas attested true, –   25
Forgetting that sweet lute beside her hand,
She asked not, – 'Do you praise me, O my land?'
But, – 'Think ye of me, friends, as I of you?'

V

Hers was the hand that played for many a year
Love's silver phrase for England, smooth and well.   30
Would God her heart's more inward oracle
In that lone moment might confirm her dear!
For when her questioned friends in agony
Made passionate response, 'We think of thee,'
Her place was in the dust, too deep to hear.   35

VI

Could she not wait to catch their answering breath?
Was she content, content with ocean's sound
Which dashed its mocking infinite around
One thirsty for a little love? – beneath
Those stars content, where last her song had gone, –   40
They mute and cold in radiant life, as soon
Their singer was to be, in darksome death?

VII

Bring your vain answers – cry, 'We think of thee!'
How think ye of her? warm in long ago
Delights? or crowned with budding bays? Not so.   45
None smile and none are crowned where lieth she,
With all her visions unfulfilled save one,
Her childhood's, of the palm-trees in the sun –
And lo! their shadow on her sepulchre!

VIII

'Do ye think of me as I think of you?' –   50
O friends, O kindred, O dear brotherhood
Of all the world! what are we that we should
For covenants of long affection sue?
Why press so near each other when the touch
Is barred by graves? Not much, and yet too much   55
Is this 'Think of me as I think of you.'

IX

But while on mortal lips I shape anew
A sigh to mortal issues, verily
Above the unshaken stars that see us die,
A vocal pathos rolls; and HE who drew   60
All life from dust, and for all tasted death,
By death and life and love appealing, saith
Do you think of me as I think of you?

The Romance of the Swan's Nest

So the dreams depart,
So the fading phantoms flee,
And the sharp reality
Now must act its part.
        Westwood *Beads from a Rosary*

I

Little Ellie sits alone
    'Mid the beeches of a meadow,
        By a stream-side on the grass,
And the trees are showering down

Doubles of their leaves in shadow   5
On her shining hair and face.

II

She has thrown her bonnet by,
And her feet she has been dipping
In the shallow water's flow:
Now she holds them nakedly   10
In her hands, all sleek and dripping,
While she rocketh to and fro.

III

Little Ellie sits alone,
And the smile she softly uses
Fills the silence like a speech,   15
While she thinks what shall be done,
And the sweetest pleasure chooses
For her future within reach.

IV

Little Ellie in her smile
Chooses – 'I will have a lover   20
Riding on a steed of steeds:
He shall love me without guile,
And to *him* I will discover
The swan's nest among the reeds.

V

'And the steed shall be red-roan,   25
And the lover shall be noble,
With an eye that takes the breath:
And the lute he plays upon
Shall strike ladies into trouble,
As his sword strikes men to death.   30

VI

'And the steed it shall be shod
All in silver, housed in azure,
And the mane shall swim the wind;

And the hoofs along the sod
  Shall flash onward and keep measure,   35
    Till the shepherds look behind.

VII

'But my lover will not prize
  All the glory that he rides in,
    When he gazes in my face:
He will say, "O Love, thine eyes   40
  Build the shrine my soul abides in,
    And I kneel here for thy grace!"

VIII

'Then, ay, then he shall kneel low,
  With the red-roan steed anear him
    Which shall seem to understand,   45
Till I answer, "Rise and go!
  For the world must love and fear him
    Whom I gift with heart and hand."

IX

'Then he will arise so pale,
  I shall feel my own lips tremble   50
    With a *yes* I must not say,
Nathless maiden-brave, "Farewell,"
  I will utter, and dissemble –
    "Light to-morrow with to-day!"

X

'Then he'll ride among the hills   55
  To the wide world past the river,
    There to put away all wrong;
To make straight distorted wills,
  And to empty the broad quiver
    Which the wicked bear along.   60

XI

'Three times shall a young foot-page
  Swim the stream and climb the mountain
    And kneel down beside my feet –

"Lo, my master sends this gage,
   Lady, for thy pity's counting!   65
      What wilt thou exchange for it?"

XII

'And the first time I will send
   A white rosebud for a guerdon,
      And the second time, a glove;
But the third time – I may bend   70
   From my pride, and answer – "Pardon
      If he comes to take my love."

XIII

'Then the young foot-page will run,
   Then my lover will ride faster,
      Till he kneeleth at my knee: 75
"I am a duke's eldest son,
   Thousand serfs do call me master,
      But, O Love, I love but *thee!*'

XIV

'He will kiss me on the mouth
   Then, and lead me as a lover   80
      Through the crowds that praise his deeds;
And when soul-tied by one troth,
   Unto *him* I will discover
      That swan's nest among the reeds.'

XV

Little Ellie, with her smile   85
   Not yet ended, rose up gaily,
      Tied the bonnet, donned the shoe,
And went homeward, round a mile,
   Just to see, as she did daily,
      What more eggs were with the two.   90

XVI

Pushing through the elm-tree copse,
   Winding up the stream, light-hearted,
      Where the osier pathway leads,

Past the boughs she stoops – and stops.
  Lo, the wild swan had deserted,   95
    And a rat had gnawed the reeds!

XVII

Ellie went home sad and slow.
  If she found the lover ever,
    With his red-roan steed of steeds,
Sooth I know not; but I know   100
  She could never show him – never,
    That swan's nest among the reeds!

Grief

I tell you, hopeless grief is passionless;
That only men incredulous of despair,
Half-taught in anguish, through the midnight air
Beat upward to God's throne in loud access
Of shrieking and reproach. Full desertness,   5
In souls as countries, lieth silent-bare
Under the blanching, vertical eye-glare
Of the absolute Heavens. Deep-hearted man, express
Grief for thy Dead in silence like to death –
Most like a monumental statue set   10
In everlasting watch and moveless woe
Till itself crumble to the dust beneath.
Touch it; the marble eyelids are not wet:
If it could weep, it could arise and go.

To George Sand

A Desire

Thou large-brained woman and large-hearted man,
Self-called George Sand! whose soul, amid the lions
Of thy tumultuous senses, moans defiance
And answers roar for roar, as spirits can:
I would some mild miraculous thunder ran   5
Above the applauded circus, in appliance
Of thine own nobler nature's strength and science,
Drawing two pinions, white as wings of swan,
From thy strong shoulders, to amaze the place
With holier light! that thou to woman's claim   10
And man's mightest join beside the angel's grace
Of a pure genius sanctified from blame,

Till child and maiden pressed to thine embrace
To kiss upon thy lips a stainless fame.

To George Sand

A Recognition

True genius, but true woman! dost deny
The woman's nature with a manly scorn,
And break away the gauds and armlets worn
By weaker women in captivity?
Ah, vain denial! that revolted cry   5
Is sobbed in by a woman's voice forlorn, –
Thy woman's hair, my sister, all unshorn
Floats back dishevelled strength in agony,
Disproving thy man's name: and while before
The world thou burnest in a poet-fire,   10
We see thy woman-heart beat evermore
Through the large flame. Beat purer, heart, and higher,
Till God unsex thee on the heavenly shore
Where unincarnate spirits purely aspire!

The Cry of the Children

Φεῦ, φεῦ, τί προσδέρκεσθέ μ' ὄμμασιν, τέκνα
Medea[1]

I

Do ye hear the children weeping, O my brothers,
 Ere the sorrow comes with years?
They are leaning their young heads against their mothers,
 And *that* cannot stop their tears.
The young lambs are bleating in the meadows,   5
 The young birds are chirping in the nest,
The young fawns are playing with the shadows,
 The young flowers are blowing toward the west –
But the young, young children, O my brothers,
 They are weeping bitterly!   10
They are weeping in the playtime of the others,
 In the country of the free.

---

[1] 'Alas, alas, why do you look at me with your eyes,
my children?'

II

Do you question the young children in the sorrow
        Why their tears are falling so?
The old man may weep for his to-morrow   15
        Which is lost in Long Ago;
The old tree is leafless in the forest,
    The old year is ending in the frost,
The old wound, if stricken, is the sorest,
    The old hope is hardest to be lost: 20
But the young, young children, O my brothers,
        Do you ask them why they stand
Weeping sore before the bosoms of their mothers,
        In our happy Fatherland?

III

They look up with their pale and sunken faces,   25
        And their looks are sad to see,
For the man's hoary anguish draws and presses
        Down the cheeks of infancy;
'Your old earth,' they say, 'is very dreary,
    Our young feet,' they say, 'are very weak;   30
Few paces have we taken, yet are weary –
    Our grave-rest is very far to seek:
Ask the aged why they weep, and not the children,
        For the outside earth is cold,
And we young ones stand without, in our bewildering,   35
        And the graves are for the old.

IV

'True,' say the children, 'it may happen
        That we die before our time:
Little Alice died last year, her grave is shapen
        Like a snowball, in the rime.   40
We looked into the pit prepared to take her:
    Was no room for any work in the close clay!
From the sleep wherein she lieth none will wake her,
    Crying, "Get up, little Alice! it is day."
If you listen by that grave, in sun and shower,   45
    With your ear down, little Alice never cries;
Could we see her face, be sure we should not know her,
    For the smile has time for growing in her eyes:
And merry go her moments, lulled and stilled in
        The shroud by the kirk-chime.   50

'It is good when it happens,' say the children,
    'That we die before our time.'

V

Alas, alas, the children! they are seeking
    Death in life, as best to have:
They are binding up their hearts away from breaking,   55
    With a cerement from the grave.
Go out, children, from the mine and from the city,
  Sing out, children, as the little thrushes do;
Pluck your handfuls of the meadow-cowslips pretty,
  Laugh aloud, to feel your fingers let them through!   60
But they answer, 'Are your cowslips of the meadows
    Like our weeds anear the mine?
Leave us quiet in the dark of the coal-shadows,
    From your pleasures fair and fine!

VI

'For oh,' say the children, 'we are weary,   65
    And we cannot run or leap;
If we cared for any meadows, it were merely
    To drop down in them and sleep.
Our knees tremble sorely in the stooping,
  We fall upon our faces, trying to go;   70
And, underneath our heavy eyelids drooping
  The reddest flower would look as pale as snow.
For, all day, we drag our burden tiring
    Through the coal-dark, underground;
Or, all day, we drive the wheels of iron   75
    In the factories, round and round.

VII

'For all day the wheels are droning, turning;
    Their wind comes in our faces,
Till our hearts turn, our heads with pulses burning,
    And the walls turn in their places: 80
Turns the sky in the high window, blank and reeling,
  Turns the long light that drops adown the wall,
Turn the black flies that crawl along the ceiling:
  All are turning, all the day, and we with all.
And all day the iron wheels are droning,   85
    And sometimes we could pray,

"O ye wheels" (breaking out in a mad moaning),
 "Stop! be silent for to-day!" '

VIII

Ay, be silent! Let them hear each other breathing
 For a moment, mouth to mouth!   90
Let them touch each other's hands, in a fresh wreathing
 Of their tender human youth!
Let them feel that this cold metallic motion
 Is not all the life God fashions or reveals:
Let them prove their living souls against the notion 95
 That they live in you, or under you, O wheels!
Still, all day, the iron wheels go onward,
 Grinding life down from its mark;
And the children's souls which God is calling sunward,
 Spin on blindly in the dark.   100

IX

Now tell the poor young children, O my brothers,
 To look up to Him and pray;
So the blessed One who blesseth all the others,
 Will bless them another day.
They answer, 'Who is God that He should hear us, 105
 While the rushing of the iron wheels is stirred?
When we sob aloud, the human creatures near us
 Pass by, hearing not, or answer not a word.
And *we* hear not (for the wheels in their resounding)
 Strangers speaking at the door: 110
Is it likely God, with angels singing round Him,
 Hears our weeping any more?

X

'Two words, indeed, of praying we remember,
 And at midnight's hour of harm,
"Our Father," looking upward in the chamber, 115
 We say softly for a charm.
We know no other words except "Our Father,"
 And we think that, in some pause of angels' song,
God may pluck them with the silence sweet to gather,
 And hold both within His right hand which is strong. 120
"Our Father!" If He heard us, He would surely
 (For they call Him good and mild)

Answer, smiling down the steep world very purely,
"Come and rest with me, my child."

XI

'But, no!' say the children, weeping faster,   125
        'He is speechless as a stone:
And they tell us, of His image is the master
        Who commands us to work on.
Go to!' say the children, – 'up in Heaven,
    Dark, wheel-like, turning clouds are all we find.   130
Do not mock us; grief has made us unbelieving:
    We look up for God, but tears have made us blind.'
Do you hear the children weeping and disproving,
        O my brothers, what ye preach?
For God's possible is taught by His world's loving,   135
        And the children doubt of each.

XII

And well may the children weep before you!
        They are weary ere they run;
They have never seen the sunshine, nor the glory
        Which is brighter than the sun.   140
They know the grief of man, without its wisdom;
    They sink in man's despair, without its calm;
Are slaves, without the liberty in Christdom,
    Are martyrs, by the pang without the palm:
Are worn as if with age, yet unretrievingly   145
        The harvest of its memories cannot reap, –
Are orphans of the earthly love and heavenly.
        Let them weep! let them weep!

XIII

They look up with their pale and sunken faces,
        And their look is dread to see,   150
For they mind you of their angels in high places,
        With eyes turned on Deity.
'How long,' they say, 'how long, O cruel nation,
    Will you stand, to move the world, on a child's heart, –
Stifle down with a mailed heel its palpitation,   155
    And tread onward to your throne amid the mart?
Our blood splashes upward, O gold-heaper,
        And your purple shows your path!

But the child's sob in the silence curses deeper
  Than the strong man in his wrath.'   160

The Runaway Slave at Pilgrim's Point

I

I stand on the mark beside the shore
  Of the first white pilgrim's bended knee,
Where exile turned to ancestor,
  And God was thanked for liberty.
I have run through the night, my skin is as dark,   5
I bend my knee down on this mark:
  I look on the sky and the sea.

II

O pilgrim-souls, I speak to you!
  I see you come proud and slow
From the land of the spirits pale as dew   10
  And round me and round me ye go.
O pilgrims, I have gasped and run
All night long from the whips of one
  Who in your names works sin and woe!

III

And thus I thought that I would come   15
  And kneel here where ye knelt before,
And feel your souls around me hum
  In undertone to the ocean's roar;
And lift my black face, my black hand,
Here, in your names, to curse this land   20
  Ye blessed in freedom's, evermore.

IV

I am black, I am black,
  And yet God made me, they say:
But if He did so, smiling back
  He must have cast His work away   25
Under the feet of His white creatures,
With a look of scorn, that the dusky features
  Might be trodden again to clay.

V

And yet He has made dark things
  To be glad and merry as light: 30
There's a little dark bird sits and sings,
  There's a dark stream ripples out of sight,
And the dark frogs chant in the safe morass,
And the sweetest stars are made to pass
  O'er the face of the darkest night. 35

VI

But *we* who are dark, we are dark!
  Ah God, we have no stars!
About our souls in care and cark
  Our blackness shuts like prison-bars:
The poor souls crouch so far behind 40
That never a comfort can they find
  By reaching through the prison-bars.

VII

Indeed we live beneath the sky,
  That great smooth Hand of God stretched out
On all His children fatherly, 45
  To save them from the dread and doubt
Which would be if, from this low place,
All opened straight up to His face
  Into the grand eternity.

VIII

And still God's sunshine and His frost,
  They make us hot, they make us cold, 50
As if we were not black and lost;
  And the beasts and birds, in wood and fold,
Do fear and take us for very men:
Could the whip-poor-will or the cat of the glen 55
  Look into my eyes and be bold?

IX

I am black, I am black!
  But, once, I laughed in girlish glee,

For one of my colour stood in the track
    Where the drivers drove, and looked at me,   60
And tender and full was the look he gave –
Could a slave look *so* at another slave? –
    I look at the sky and the sea.

X

And from that hour our spirits grew
    As free as if unsold, unbought: 65
Oh, strong enough, since we were two,
    To conquer the world, we thought.
The drivers drove us day by day;
We did not mind, we went one way,
    And no better a freedom sought.   70

XI

In the sunny ground between the canes,
    He said 'I love you' as he passed;
When the shingle-roof rang sharp with the rains,
    I heard how he vowed it fast:
While others shook he smiled in the hut,   75
As he carved me a bowl of the cocoa-nut
    Through the roar of the hurricanes.

XII

I sang his name instead of a song,
    Over and over I sang his name,
Upward and downward I drew it along   80
    My various notes, – the same, the same!
I sang it low, that the slave-girls near
Might never guess, from aught they could hear,
    It was only a name – a name.

XIII

I look on the sky and the sea.   85
    We were two to love, and two to pray:
Yes, two, O God, who cried to Thee,
    Though nothing didst Thou say!
Coldly Thou sat'st behind the sun:
And now I cry who am but one,   90
    Thou wilt not speak to-day.

XIV

We were black, we were black,
   We had no claim to love and bliss,
What marvel if each went to wrack?
   They wrung my cold hands out of his   95
They dragged him – where? I crawled to touch
His blood's mark in the dust . . . not much,
   Ye pilgrim-souls, though plain as *this!*

XV

Wrong, followed by a deeper wrong!
   Mere grief's too good for such as I: 100
So the white men brought the shame ere long
   To strangle the sob of my agony.
They would not leave me for my dull
Wet eyes! – it was too merciful
   To let me weep pure tears and die.   105

XVI

I am black, I am black!
   I wore a child upon my breast,
An amulet that hung too slack,
   And, in my unrest, could not rest:
Thus we went moaning, child and mother,   110
One to another, one to another,
   Until all ended for the best.

XVII

For hark! I will tell you low, low,
   I am black, you see, –
And the babe who lay on my bosom so,   115
   Was far too white, too white for me;
As white as the ladies who scorned to pray
Beside me at church but yesterday,
   Though my tears had washed a place for my knee.

XVIII

My own, own child! I could not bear   120
   To look in his face, it was so white;

I covered him up with a kerchief there,
   I covered his face in close and tight:
And he moaned and struggled, as well might be,
For the white child wanted his liberty –   125
   Ha, ha! he wanted the master-right.

XIX

He moaned and beat with his head and feet,
   His little feet that never grew;
He struck them out, as it was meet,
   Against my heart to break it through: 130
I might have sung and made him mild,
But I dared not sing to the white-faced child
   The only song I knew.

XX

I pulled the kerchief very close:
   He could not see the sun, I swear,   135
More, then, alive, than now he does
   From between the roots of the mango . . . where?
I know where. Close! A child and mother
Do wrong to look at one another
   When one is black and one is fair.   140

XXI

Why, in that single glance I had
   Of my child's face, . . . I tell you all,
I saw a look that made me mad!
   The *master's* look, that used to fall
On my soul like his lash . . . or worse!   145
And so, to save it from my curse,
   I twisted it round in my shawl.

XXII

And he moaned and trembled from foot to head,
   He shivered from head to foot;
Till after a time, he lay instead   150
   Too suddenly still and mute.
I felt, beside, a stiffening cold:
I dared to lift up just a fold,
   As in lifting a leaf of the mango-fruit.

XXIII

But *my* fruit . . . ha, ha! – there, had been   155
  (I laugh to think on't at this hour!)
Your fine white angels (who have seen
  Nearest the secret of God's power)
And plucked my fruit to make them wine,
And sucked the soul of that child of mine   160
  As the humming-bird sucks the soul of the flower.

XXIV

Ha, ha, the trick of the angels white!
  They freed the white child's spirit so.
I said not a word, but day and night
  I carried the body to and fro,   165
And it lay on my heart like a stone, as chill.
– The sun may shine out as much as he will:
  I am cold, though it happened a month ago.

XXV

From the white man's house, and the black man's hut,
  I carried the little body on;   170
The forest's arms did round us shut,
  And silence through the trees did run:
They asked no question as I went,
They stood too high for astonishment,
  They could see God sit on His throne.   175

XXVI

My little body, kerchiefed fast,
  I bore it on through the forest, on;
And when I felt it was tired at last,
  I scooped a hole beneath the moon:
Through the forest-tops the angels far,   180
With a white sharp finger from every star,
  Did point and mock at what was done.

XXVII

Yet when it was all done aright, –
  Earth, 'twixt me and my baby, strewed, –

All, changed to black earth, – nothing white, –   185
   A dark child in the dark! – ensued
Some comfort, and my heart grew young;
I sate down smiling there and sung
   The song I learnt in my maidenhood.

XXVIII

And thus we two were reconciled,   190
   The white child and black mother, thus;
For as I sang it soft and wild,
   The same song, more melodious,
Rose from the grave whereon I sate:
It was the dead child singing that,   195
   To join the souls of both of us.

XXIX

I look on the sea and the sky.
   Where the pilgrims' ships first anchored lay
The free sun rideth gloriously,
   But the pilgrim-ghosts have slid away   200
Through the earliest streaks of the morn:
My face is black, but it glares with a scorn
   Which they dare not meet by day.

XXX

Ha! – in their stead, their hunter sons!
   Ha, ha! they are on me – they hunt in a ring!   205
Keep off! I brave you all at once,
   I throw off your eyes like snakes that sting!
You have killed the black eagle at nest, I think:
Did you ever stand still in your triumph, and shrink
   From the stroke of her wounded wing?   210

XXXI

(Man, drop that stone you dared to lift! –)
   I wish you who stand there five abreast,
Each, for his own wife's joy and gift,
   A little corpse as safely at rest
As mine in the mangoes! Yes, but *she*   215
May keep live babies on her knee,
   And sing the song she likes the best.

XXXII

I am not mad: I am black.
    I see you staring in my face —
I know you staring, shrinking back,   220
    Ye are born of the Washington-race,
And this land is the free America,
And this mark on my wrist — (I prove what I say)
    Ropes tied me up here to the flogging-place.

XXXIII

You think I shrieked then? Not a sound!   225
    I hung, as a gourd hangs in the sun;
I only cursed them all around
    As softly as I might have done
My very own child: from these sands
Up to the mountains, lift your hands,   230
    O slaves, and end what I begun!

XXXIV

Whips, curses; these must answer those!
    For in this UNION you have set
Two kinds of men in adverse rows,
    Each loathing each; and all forget   235
The seven wounds in Christ's body fair,
While HE sees gaping everywhere
    Our countless wounds that pay no debt.

XXXV

Our wounds are different. Your white men
    Are, after all, not gods indeed,   240
Nor able to make Christs again
    Do good with bleeding. *We* who bleed
(Stand off!) we help not in our loss!
We are too heavy for our cross,
    And fall and crush you and your seed.   245

XXXVI

I fall, I swoon! I look at the sky.
    The clouds are breaking on my brain;

I am floated along, as if I should die
  Of liberty's exquisite pain.
In the name of the white child waiting for me   250
In the death-dark where we may kiss and agree,
White men, I leave you all curse-free
  In my broken heart's disdain!

Flush or Faunus

You see this dog; it was but yesterday
I mused forgetful of his presence here,
Till thought on thought drew downward tear on tear:
When from the pillow where wet-cheeked I lay,
A head as hairy as Faunus thrust its way   5
Right sudden against my face, two golden-clear
Great eyes astonished mine, a drooping ear
Did flap me on either cheek to dry the spray!
I started first as some Arcadian
Amazed by goatly god in twilight grove: 10
But as the bearded vision closelier ran
My tears off, I knew Flush, and rose above
Surprise and sadness, – thanking the true PAN
Who by low creatures leads to heights of love.

The Mask

I

I have a smiling face, she said,
  I have a jest for all I meet,
I have a garland for my head
  And all its flowers are sweet,
And so you call me gay, she said.   5

II

Grief taught to me this smile, she said,
  And Wrong did teach this jesting bold;
These flowers were plucked from garden-bed
  While a death-chime was tolled:
And what now will you say? – she said.   10

III

Behind no prison-grate, she said,
  Which slurs the sunshine half a mile,

Live captives so uncomforted
　　As souls behind a smile.
God's pity let us pray, she said.　　　　　　　　　　15

IV

I know my face is bright, she said, —
　　Such brightness dying suns diffuse:
I bear upon my forehead shed
　　The sign of what I lose,
The ending of my day, she said.　　　　　　　　　　20

V

If I dared leave this smile, she said,
　　And take a moan upon my mouth,
And tie a cypress round my head,
　　And let my tears run smooth,
It were the happier way, she said.　　　　　　　　　25

VI

And since that must not be, she said,
　　I fain your bitter world would leave.
How calmly, calmly smile the Dead,
　　Who do not, therefore, grieve!
The yea of Heaven is yea, she said.　　　　　　　　30

VII

But in your bitter world, she said,
　　Face-joy's a costly mask to wear;
'Tis bought with pangs long nourishèd,
　　And rounded to despair:
Grief's earnest makes life's play, she said.　　　　　35

VIII

Ye weep for those who weep? she said —
　　Ah fools! I bid you pass them by.
Go, weep for those whose hearts have bled
　　What time their eyes were dry.
Whom sadder can I say? she said.　　　　　　　　40

from *Sonnets from the Portuguese*

IV

Thou hast thy calling to some palace-floor,
Most gracious singer of high poems! where
The dancers will break footing, from the care
Of watching up thy pregnant lips for more.
And dost thou lift this house's latch too poor   5
For hand of thine? and canst thou think and bear
To let thy music drop here unaware
In folds of golden fulness at my door?
Look up and see the casement broken in,
The bats and owlets builders in the roof!   10
My cricket chirps against thy mandolin.
Hush, call no echo up in further proof
Of desolation! there's a voice within
That weeps ... as thou must sing ... alone, aloof.

V

I lift my heavy heart up solemnly,   15
As once Electra her sepulchral urn,
And, looking in thine eyes, I overturn
The ashes at thy feet. Behold and see
What a great heap of grief lay hid in me,
And how the red wild sparkles dimly burn   20
Through the ashen greyness. If thy foot in scorn
Could tread them out to darkness utterly,
It might be well perhaps. But if instead
Thou wait beside me for the wind to blow
The grey dust up, ... those laurels on thine head,   25
O my Belovèd, will not shield thee so,
That none of all the fires shall scorch and shred
The hair beneath. Stand farther off then! go.

XIII

And wilt thou have me fashion into speech
The love I bear thee, finding words enough,
And hold the torch out, while the winds are rough,   30
Between our faces, to cast light on each? —
I drop it at thy feet. I cannot teach
My hand to hold my spirit so far off
From myself — me — that I should bring thee proof   35
In words, of love hid in me out of reach.

Nay, let the silence of my womanhood
Commend my woman-love to thy belief, –
Seeing that I stand unwon, however wooed,
And rend the garment of my life, in brief,   40
By a most dauntless, voiceless fortitude,
Lest one touch of this heart convey its grief.

XLIII

How do I love thee? Let me count the ways.
I love thee to the depth and breadth and height
My soul can reach, when feeling out of sight   45
For the ends of Being and ideal Grace.
I love thee to the level of everyday's
Most quiet need, by sun and candle-light.
I love thee freely, as men strive for Right;
I love thee purely, as they turn from Praise.   50
I love thee with the passion put to use
In my old griefs, and with my childhood's faith.
I love thee with a love I seemed to lose
With my lost saints, – I love thee with the breath,
Smiles, tears, of all my life! – and, if God choose,   55
I shall but love thee better after death.

from *Casa Guidi Windows*

Part One

I heard last night a little child go singing
   'Neath Casa Guidi windows, by the church,
O bella libertà, O bella! stringing
   The same words still on notes he went in search
So high for, you concluded the upspringing   5
   Of such a nimble bird to sky from perch
Must leave the whole bush in a tremble green,
   And that the heart of Italy must beat,
While such a voice had leave to rise serene
   'Twixt church and palace of a Florence street!   10
A little child, too, who not long had been
   By mother's finger steadied on his feet,
And still *O bella libertà* he sang.

Then I thought, musing, of the innumerous
   Sweet songs which still for Italy outrang   15
From older singers' lips, who sang not thus
   Exultingly and purely, yet, with pang

Fast sheathed in music, touched the heart of us
   So finely, that the pity scarcely pained.
I thought how Filicaja led on others,   20
   Bewailers for their Italy enchained,
And how they called her childless among mothers,
   Widow of empires, ay, and scarce refrained
Cursing her beauty to her face, as brothers
   Might a shamed sister's, – 'Had she been less fair   25
She were less wretched,' – how, evoking so
   From congregated wrong and heaped despair
Of men and women writhing under blow,
   Harrowed and hideous in a filthy lair,
Some personating Image, wherein woe   30
   Was wrapt in beauty from offending much,
They called it Cybele, or Niobe,
   Or laid it corpse-like on a bier for such,
Where all the world might drop for Italy
   Those cadenced tears which burn not where they touch, –   35
'Juliet of nations, canst thou die as we?
   And was the violet crown that crowned thy head
So over-large, though new buds made it rough,
   It slipped down and across thine eyelids dead,
O sweet, fair Juliet?' Of such songs enough,   40
   Too many of such complaints! behold, instead,
Void at Verona, Juliet's marble trough.
   As void as that is, are all images
Men set between themselves and actual wrong,
   To catch the weight of pity, meet the stress   45
Of conscience, – since 'tis easier to gaze long
   On mournful masks, and sad effigies,
Than on real, live, weak creatures crushed by strong.

from *Aurora Leigh*

[Aurora, the daughter of an Italian mother and English father, both of whom are dead, has been reared from the age of thirteen by an English aunt. Her cousin Romney is the legitimate heir of the family estate, from which her father was disinherited when he married an Italian. In this section, Romney catches Aurora early one summer morning in the garden (Aurora means dawn), while she is crowning herself poet. He proceeds to make a proposal of marriage.]

Book II

Times followed one another. Came a morn
I stood upon the brink of twenty years,
And looked before and after, as I stood
Woman and artist, – either incomplete,
Both credulous of completion. There I held   5

The whole creation in my little cup,
And smiled with thirsty lips before I drank
'Good health to you and me, sweet neighbour mine,
And all these peoples.'
                I was glad, that day;
The June was in me, with its multitudes   10
Of nightingales all singing in the dark,
And rosebuds reddening where the calyx split.
I felt so young, so strong, so sure of God!
So glad, I could not choose be very wise!
And, old at twenty, was inclined to pull   15
My childhood backward in a childish jest
To see the face of't once more, and farewell!
In which fantastic mood I bounded forth
At early morning, – would not wait so long
As even to snatch my bonnet by the strings,   20
But, brushing a green trail across the lawn
With my gown in the dew, took will and way
Among the acacias of the shrubberies,
To fly my fancies in the open air
And keep my birthday, till my aunt awoke   25
To stop good dreams. Meanwhile I murmured on
As honeyed bees keep humming to themselves,
'The worthiest poets have remained uncrowned
Till death has bleached their foreheads to the bone;
And so with me it must be unless I prove   30
Unworthy of the grand adversity,
And certainly I would not fail so much.
What, therefore, if I crown myself to-day
In sport, not pride, to learn the feel of it,
Before my brows be numb as Dante's own   35
To all the tender pricking of such leaves?
Such leaves! what leaves?'
                  I pulled the branches down
To choose from.
            'Not the bay! I choose no bay,
(The fates deny us if we are overbold)
Nor myrtle – which means chiefly love; and love   40
Is something awful which one dares not touch
So early o' mornings. This verbena strains
The point of passionate fragrance; and hard by,
This guelder-rose, at far too slight a beck
Of the wind, will toss about her flower-apples.   45
Ah – there's my choice, – that ivy on the wall,
That headlong ivy! not a leaf will grow
But thinking of a wreath. Large leaves, smooth leaves,
Serrated like my vines, and half as green.
I like such ivy, bold to leap a height   50

'Twas strong to climb; as good to grow on graves
As twist about a thyrsus; pretty too,
(And that's not ill) when twisted round a comb.'
Thus speaking to myself, half singing it,
Because some thoughts are fashioned like a bell   55
To ring with once being touched, I drew a wreath
Drenched, blinding me with dew, across my brow,
And fastening it behind so, turning faced
. . My public! – cousin Romney – with a mouth
Twice graver than his eyes.
                                        I stood there fixed, –   60
My arms up, like the caryatid, sole
Of some abolished temple, helplessly
Persistent in a gesture which derides
A former purpose. Yet my blush was flame,
As if from flax, not stone.
                                        'Aurora Leigh,   65
The earliest of Auroras!'
                                Hand stretched out
I clasped, as shipwrecked men will clasp a hand,
Indifferent to the sort of palm. The tide
Had caught me at my pastime, writing down
My foolish name too near upon the sea   70
Which drowned me with a blush as foolish. 'You,
My cousin!'
                        The smile died out in his eyes
And dropped upon his lips, a cold dead weight,
For just a moment, 'Here's a book I found!
No name writ on it – poems, by the form;   75
Some Greek upon the margin, – lady's Greek
Without the accents. Read it? Not a word.
I saw at once the thing had witchcraft in't,
Whereof the reading calls up dangerous spirits:
I rather bring it to the witch.'
                                        'My book.   80
You found it'. .
                        'In the hollow by the stream
That beech leans down into – of which you said
The Oread in it has a Naiad's heart
And pines for waters.'
                                'Thank you.'
                                        'Thanks to *you*
My cousin! that I have seen you not too much   85
Witch, scholar, poet, dreamer, and the rest,
To be a woman also.'
                        With a glance
The smile rose in his eyes again and touched
The ivy on my forehead, light as air.

I answered gravely, 'Poets needs must be   90
Or men or women – more's the pity'
                                      'Ah,
But men, and still less women, happily,
Scarce need be poets. Keep to the green wreath,
Since even dreaming of the stone and bronze
Brings headaches, pretty cousin, and defiles   95
The clean white morning dresses.'
                          'So you judge!
Because I love the beautiful I must
Love pleasure chiefly, and be overcharged
For ease and whiteness! well, you know the world,
And only miss your cousin, 'tis not much.   100
But learn this; I would rather take my part
With God's Dead, who afford to walk in white
Yet spread His glory, than keep quiet here
And gather up my feet from even a step
For fear to soil my gown in so much dust.   105
I choose to walk at all risks. – Here, if heads
That hold a rhythmic thought, must ache perforce,
For my part I choose headaches – and to-day's
My birthday.'
                  'Dear Aurora, choose instead
To cure them. You have balsams.'
                                  'I perceive.   110
The headache is too noble for my sex.
You think the heartache would sound decenter,
Since that's the woman's special, proper ache,
And altogether tolerable, except
To a woman.'
                  Saying which, I loosed my wreath,   115
And swinging it beside me as I walked,
Half petulant, half playful, as we walked,
I sent a sidelong look to find his thought, –
As falcon set on falconer's finger may,
With sidelong head, and startled, braving eye,   120
Which means, 'You'll see – you'll see! I'll soon take flight,
You shall not hinder.' He, as shaking out
His hand and answering 'Fly then,' did not speak,
Except by such a gesture. Silently
We paced, until, just coming into sight   125
Of the house-windows, he abruptly caught
At one end of the swinging wreath, and said
'Aurora!' There I stopped short, breath and all.

'Aurora, let's be serious, and throw by
This game of head and heart. Life means, be sure,   130
Both heart and head, – both active, both complete,

And both in earnest. Men and women make
The world, as head and heart make human life.
Work man, work woman, since there's work to do
In this beleaguered earth, for head and heart,   135
And thought can never do the work of love:
But work for ends, I mean for uses, not
For such sleek fringes (do you call them ends,
Still less God's glory?) as we sew ourselves
Upon the velvet of those baldaquins   140
Held 'twixt us and the sun. That book of yours,
I have not read a page of; but I toss
A rose up – it falls calyx down, you see!
The chances are that, being a woman, young
And pure, with such a pair of large, calm eyes,   145
You write as well.. and ill.. upon the whole,
As other women. If as well, what then?
If even a little better,.. still, what then?
We want the Best in art now, or no art.
The time is done for facile settings up   150
Of minnow gods, nymphs here and tritons there;
The polytheists have gone out in God,
That unity of Bests. No best, no God!
And so with art, we say. Give art's divine,
Direct, indubitable, real as grief,   155
Or leave us to the grief we grow ourselves
Divine by overcoming with mere hope
And most prosaic patience. You, you are young
As Eve with nature's daybreak on her face,
But this same world you are come to, dearest coz,   160
Has done with keeping birthdays, saves her wreaths
To hang upon her ruins, – and forgets
To rhyme the cry with which she still beats back
Those savage, hungry dogs that hunt her down
To the empty grave of Christ. The world's hard pressed;   165
The sweat of labour in the early curse
Has (turning acrid in six thousand years)
Become the sweat of torture. Who has time,
An hour's time.. think! – to sit upon a bank
And hear the cymbal tinkle in white hands?   170
When Egypt's slain, I say, let Miriam sing! –
Before – where's Moses?'
                          'Ah, exactly that.
Where's Moses? – is a Moses to be found?
You'll seek him vainly in the bulrushes,
While I in vain touch cymbals. Yet concede,   175
Such sounding brass has done some actual good
(The application in a woman's hand,
If that were credible, being scarcely spoilt,)

In colonising beehives.'
            'There it is! —
You play beside a death-bed like a child,   180
Yet measure to yourself a prophet's place
To teach the living. None of all these things,
Can women understand. You generalise
Oh, nothing, — not even grief! Your quick-breathed hearts,
So sympathetic to the personal pang,   185
Close on each separate knife-stroke, yielding up
A whole life at each wound, incapable
Of deepening, widening a large lap of life
To hold the world-full woe. The human race
To you means, such a child, or such a man,   190
You saw one morning waiting in the cold,
Beside that gate, perhaps. You gather up
A few such cases, and when strong sometimes
Will write of factories and of slaves, as if
Your father were a negro, and your son   195
A spinner in the mills. All's yours and you,
All, coloured with your blood, or otherwise
Just nothing to you. Why, I call you hard
To general suffering. Here's the world half blind
With intellectual light, half brutalised   200
With civilisation, having caught the plague
In silks from Tarsus, shrieking east and west
Along a thousand railroads, mad with pain
And sin too .. does one woman of you all
(You who weep easily) grow pale to see   205
This tiger shake his cage? — does one of you
Stand still from dancing, stop from stringing pearls,
And pine and die because of the great sum
Of universal anguish? — Show me a tear
Wet as Cordelia's, in eyes bright as yours,   210
Because the world is mad. You cannot count,
That you should weep for this account, not you!
You weep for what you know. A red-haired child
Sick in a fever, if you touch him once,
Though but so little as with a finger-tip,   215
Will set you weeping; but a million sick ..
You could as soon weep for the rule of three
Or compound fractions. Therefore, this same world
Uncomprehended by you, must remain
Uninfluenced by you. — Women as you are,   220
Mere women, personal and passionate,
You give us doating mothers, and perfect wives,
Sublime Madonnas, and enduring saints
We get no Christ from you, — and verily
We shall not get a poet, in my mind.'   225

'With which conclusion you conclude' . .
                                    'But this:
That you, Aurora, with the large live brow
And steady eyelids, cannot condescend
To play at art, as children play at swords,
To show a pretty spirit, chiefly admired   230
Because true action is impossible.
You never can be satisfied with praise
Which men give women when they judge a book
Not as mere work but as mere woman's work,
Expressing the comparative respect   235
Which means the absolute scorn. 'Oh, excellent
'What grace, what facile turns, what fluent sweeps
'What delicate discernment . . almost thought!
'The book does honour to the sex, we hold.
'Among our female authors we make room   240
'For this fair writer, and congratulate
'The country that produces in these times
'Such women, competent to' . . spell.'
                                    'Stop there,'
I answered, burning through his thread of talk
With a quick flame of emotion, – 'You have read   245
My soul, if not my book, and argue well
I would not condescend . . we will not say
To such a kind of praise, (a worthless end
Is praise of all kinds) but to such a use
Of holy art and golden life. I am young,   250
And peradventure weak – you tell me so –
Through being a woman. And, for all the rest,
Take thanks for justice. I would rather dance
At fairs on tight-rope, till the babies dropped
Their gingerbread for joy, – than shift the types   255
For tolerable verse, intolerable
To men who act and suffer. Better far
Pursue a frivolous trade by serious means,
Than a sublime art frivolously.'
                                    'You,
Choose nobler work than either, O moist eyes   260
And hurrying lips and heaving heart! We are young
Aurora, you and I. The world, – look round, –
The world, we're come to late, is swollen hard
With perished generations and their sins:
The civiliser's spade grinds horribly   265
On dead men's bones, and cannot turn up soil
That's otherwise than fetid. All success
Proves partial failure; all advance implies
What's left behind; all triumph, something crushed
At the chariot-wheels; all government, some wrong: 270

And rich men make the poor, who curse the rich,
Who agonise together, rich and poor,
Under and over, in the social spasm
And crisis of the ages. Here's an age
That makes its own vocation! here we have stepped   275
Across the bounds of time! here's nought to see,
But just the rich man and just Lazarus,
And both in torments, with a mediate gulph,
Though not a hint of Abraham's bosom. Who
Being man, Aurora, can stand calmly by   280
And view these things, and never tease his soul
For some great cure? No physic for this grief,
In all the earth and heaven too?'
        'You believe
In God, for your part? – ay? that He who makes,
Can make good things from ill things, best from worst,   285
As men plant tulips upon dunghills when
They wish them finest?'
       'True. A death-heat is
The same as life-heat, to be accurate,
And in all nature is no death at all,
As men account of death, so long as God   290
Stands witnessing for life perpetually,
By being just God. That's abstract truth, I know,
Philosophy, or sympathy with God:
But I, I sympathise with man, not God,
(I think I was a man for chiefly this)   295
And when I stand beside a dying bed,
'Tis death to me. Observe, – it had not much
Consoled the race of mastodons to know,
Before they went to fossil, that anon
Their place would quicken with the elephant: 300
They were not elephants but mastodons;
And I, a man, as men are now and not
As men may be hereafter, feel with men
In the agonising present.'
       'Is it so,'
I said, 'my cousin? is the world so bad,   305
While I hear nothing of it through the trees?
The world was always evil, – but so bad?'

'So bad, Aurora. Dear, my soul is grey
With poring over the long sum of ill;
So much for vice, so much for discontent,   310
So much for the necessities of power,
So much for the connivances of fear,
Coherent in statistical despairs
With such a total of distracted life, . .

To see it down in figures on a page,   315
Plain, silent, clear, as God sees through the earth
The sense of all the graves, – that's terrible
For one who is not God, and cannot right
The wrong he looks on. May I choose indeed
But vow away my years, my means, my aims,   320
Among the helpers, if there's any help
In such a social strait? The common blood
That swings along my veins, is strong enough
To draw me to this duty.'
                    Then I spoke.
'I have not stood long on the strand of life,   325
And these salt waters have had scarcely time
To creep so high up as to wet my feet:
I cannot judge these tides – I shall, perhaps.
A woman's always younger than a man
At equal years, because she is disallowed   330
Maturing by the outdoor sun and air,
And kept in long-clothes past the age to walk.
Ah well, I know you men judge otherwise!
You think a woman ripens as a peach,
In the cheeks, chiefly. Pass it to me now;   335
I'm young in age, and younger still, I think,
As a woman. But a child may say amen
To a bishop's prayer and feel the way it goes,
And I, incapable to loose the knot
Of social questions, can approve, applaud   340
August compassion, christian thoughts that shoot
Beyond the vulgar white of personal aims.
Accept my reverence.'
                    There he glowed on me
With all his face and eyes. 'No other help?'
Said he – 'no more than so?'
                              'What help?' I asked.   345
'You'd scorn my help, – as Nature's self, you say,
Has scorned to put her music in my mouth
Because a woman's. Do you now turn round
And ask for what a woman cannot give?'

'For what she only can, I turn and ask,'   350
He answered, catching up my hands in his,
And dropping on me from his high-eaved brow
The full weight of his soul, – 'I ask for love,
And that, she can; for life in fellowship
Through bitter duties – that, I know she can;   355
For wifehood – will she?'
                         'Now,' I said, 'may God
Be witness 'twixt us two!' and with the word,

Meseemed I floated into a sudden light
Above his stature, – 'am I proved too weak
To stand alone, yet strong enough to bear   360
Such leaners on my shoulder? poor to think,
Yet rich enough to sympathise with thought?
Incompetent to sing, as blackbirds can,
Yet competent to love, like HIM?'
                        I paused;
Perhaps I darkened, as the light-house will   365
That turns upon the sea. 'It's always so.
Anything does for a wife.'
                 'Aurora, dear,
And dearly honoured,' – he pressed in at once
With eager utterance, – 'you translate me ill.
I do not contradict my thought of you   370
Which is most reverent, with another thought
Found less so. If your sex is weak for art,
(And I who said so, did but honour you
By using truth in courtship) it is strong
For life and duty. Place your fecund heart   375
In mine, and let us blossom for the world
That wants love's colour in the grey of time.
My talk, meanwhile, is arid to you, ay,
Since all my talk can only set you where
You look down coldly on the arena-heaps   380
Of headless bodies, shapeless, indistinct!
The Judgment-Angel scarce would find his way
Through such a heap of generalised distress
To the individual man with lips and eyes,
Much less Aurora. Ah my sweet, come down,   385
And hand in hand we'll go where yours shall touch
These victims, one by one! till, one by one,
The formless, nameless trunk of every man
Shall seem to wear a head with hair you know,
And every woman catch your mother's face   390
To melt you into passion.'
              'I am a girl,'
I answered slowly; 'you do well to name
My mother's face. Though far too early, alas,
God's hand did interpose 'twixt it and me,
I know so much of love as used to shine   395
In that face and another. Just so much;
No more indeed at all. I have not seen
So much love since, I pray you pardon me,
As answers even to make a marriage with
In this cold land of England. What you love,   400
Is not a woman, Romney, but a cause:
You want a helpmate, not a mistress, sir,

A wife to help your ends, – in her no end!
Your cause is noble, your ends excellent,
But I, being most unworthy of these and that,   405
Do otherwise conceive of love. Farewell.'

'Farewell, Aurora? you reject me thus?'
He said.
            'Sir, you were married long ago.
You have a wife already whom you love,
Your social theory. Bless you both, I say.   410
For my part, I am scarcely meek enough
To be the handmaid of a lawful spouse.
Do I look a Hagar think you?'
                              'So you jest.'

'Nay, so I speak in earnest,' I replied.
'You treat of marriage too much like, at least,   415
A chief apostle: you would bear with you
A wife .. a sister .. shall we speak it out?
A sister of charity.'
                      'Then, must it be
Indeed farewell? And was I so far wrong
In hope and in illusion, when I took   420
The woman to be nobler than the man,
Yourself the noblest woman, in the use
And comprehension of what love is, – love,
That generates the likeness of itself
Through all heroic duties? so far wrong,   425
In saying bluntly, venturing truth on love,
'Come, human creature, love and work with me,' –
Instead of, 'Lady, thou art wondrous fair,
'And, where the Graces walk before, the Muse
'Will follow at the lighting of their eyes,   430
'And where the Muse walks, lovers need to creep:
'Turn round and love me, or I die of love.'

With quiet indignation I broke in.
'You misconceive the question like a man,
Who sees a woman as the complement   435
Of his sex merely. You forget too much
That every creature, female as the male,
Stands single in responsible act and thought
As also in birth and death. Whoever says
To a loyal woman, 'Love and work with me,'   440
Will get fair answers if the work and love,
Being good themselves, are good for her – the best
She was born for. Women of a softer mood,
Surprised by men when scarcely awake to life,

Will sometimes only hear the first word, love, 445
And catch up with it any kind of work,
Indifferent, so that dear love go with it.
I do not blame such women, though, for love,
They pick much oakum; earth's fanatics make
Too frequently heaven's saints. But *me* your work 450
Is not the best for, – nor your love the best,
Nor able to commend the kind of work
For love's sake merely. Ah, you force me, sir,
To be over-bold in speaking of myself:
I too have my vocation, – work to do, 455
The heavens and earth have set me since I changed
My father's face for theirs, and, though your world
Were twice as wretched as you represent,
Most serious work, most necessary work
As any of the economists'. Reform; 460
Make trade a Christian possibility,
And individual right no general wrong;
Wipe out earth's furrows of the Thine and Mine,
And leave one green for men to play at bowls,
With innings for them all!.. what then, indeed, 465
If mortals are not greater by the head
Than any of their prosperities? what then,
Unless the artist keep up open roads
Betwixt the seen and unseen, – bursting through
The best of your conventions with his best. 470
The speakable, imaginable best
God bids him speak, to prove what lies beyond
Both speech and imagination? A starved man
Exceeds a fat beast: we'll not barter, sir,
The beautiful for barley. – And, even so, 475
I hold you will not compass your poor ends
Of barley-feeding and material ease,
Without a poet's individualism
To work your universal. It takes a soul,
To move a body: it takes a high-souled man, 480
To move the masses, even to a cleaner stye:
It takes the ideal, to blow a hair's-breadth off
The dust of the actual. – Ah, your Fouriers failed,
Because not poets enough to understand
That life develops from within. – For me, 485
Perhaps I am not worthy, as you say,
Of work like this: perhaps a woman's soul
Aspires, and not creates: yet we aspire,
And yet I'll try out your perhapses, sir,
And if I fail .. why, burn me up my straw 490
Like other false works – I'll not ask for grace;
Your scorn is better, cousin Romney. I

Who love my art, would never wish it lower
To suit my stature. I may love my art.
You'll grant that even a woman may love art,   495
Seeing that to waste true love on anything
Is womanly, past question.'
                I retain
The very last word which I said that day,
As you the creaking of the door, years past,
Which let upon you such disabling news   500
You ever after have been graver. He,
His eyes, the motions in his silent mouth,
Were fiery points on which my words were caught,
Transfixed for ever in my memory
For his sake, not their own. And yet I know   505
I did not love him .. nor he me .. that's sure ..
And what I said, is unrepented of,
As truth is always. Yet .. a princely man! –
If hard to me, heroic for himself!
He bears down on me through the slanting years,   510
The stronger for the distance. If he had loved,
Ah, loved me, with that retributive face, ..
I might have been a common woman now
And happier, less known and less left alone,
Perhaps a better woman after all,   515
With chubby children hanging on my neck
To keep me low and wise. Ah me, the vines
That bear such fruit, are proud to stoop with it.
The palm stands upright in a realm of sand.

And I, who spoke the truth then, stand upright,   520
Still worthy of having spoken out the truth,
By being content I spoke it though it set
Him there, me here. – O woman's vile remorse,
To hanker after a mere name, a show,
A supposition, a potential love!   525
Does every man who names love in our lives,
Become a power for that? is love's true thing
So much best to us, that what personates love
Is next best? A potential love, forsooth!
I'm not so vile. No, no – he cleaves, I think,   530
This man, this image, – chiefly for the wrong
And shock he gave my life, in finding me
Precisely where the devil of my youth
Had set me, on those mountain-peaks of hope
All glittering with the dawn-dew, all erect   535
And famished for the noon, – exclaiming, while
I looked for empire and much tribute, 'Come,
I have some worthy work for thee below.

Come, sweep my barns and keep my hospitals,
And I will pay thee with a current coin   540
Which men give women.'
                        As we spoke, the grass
Was trod in haste beside us, and my aunt,
With smile distorted by the sun, – face, voice
As much at issue with the summer-day
As if you brought a candle out of doors,   545
Broke in with, 'Romney, here! – My child, entreat
Your cousin to the house, and have your talk,
If girls must talk upon their birthdays. Come.'

He answered for me calmly, with pale lips
That seemed to motion for a smile in vain.   550
'The talk is ended – madam, where we stand.
Your brother's daughter has dismissed me here;
And all my answer can be better said
Beneath the trees, than wrong by such a word
Your house's hospitalities. Farewell.'   555

With that he vanished. I could hear his heel
Ring bluntly in the lane, as down he leapt
The short way from us. – Then a measured speech
Withdrew me. 'What means this, Aurora Leigh?
My brother's daughter has dismissed my guests?'   560
The lion in me felt the keeper's voice
Through all its quivering dewlaps; I was quelled
Before her, – meekened to the child she knew:
I prayed her pardon, said, 'I had little thought
To give dismissal to a guest of hers,   565
In letting go a friend of mine who came
To take me into service as a wife, –
No more than that, indeed.'
                        'No more, no more?
Pray Heaven,' she answered, 'that I was not mad.
I could not mean to tell her to her face   570
That Romney Leigh had asked me for a wife,
And I refused him?'
                    'Did he ask?' I said;
'I think he rather stooped to take me up
For certain uses which he found to do
For something called a wife. He never asked.'   575

'What stuff!' she answered; 'are they queens, these girls?
They must have mantles, stitched with twenty silks,
Spread out upon the ground, before they'll step
One footstep for the noblest lover born.'

'But I am born,' I said with firmness, 'I,   580
To walk another way than his, dear aunt.'

'You walk, you walk! A babe at thirteen months
Will walk as well as you,' she cried in haste,
'Without a steadying finger. Why, you child,
God help you, you are groping in the dark,   585
For all this sunlight. You suppose, perhaps,
That you, sole offspring of an opulent man,
Are rich and free to choose a way to walk?
You think, and it's a reasonable thought,
That I, beside, being well to do in life,   590
Will leave my handful in my niece's hand
When death shall paralyse these fingers? Pray,
Pray, child, albeit I know you love me not,
As if you loved me, that I may not die!
For when I die and leave you, out you go,   595
(Unless I make room for you in my grave)
Unhoused, unfed, my dear poor brother's lamb,
(Ah, heaven, – that pains!) – without a right to crop
A single blade of grass beneath these trees,
Or cast a lamb's small shadow on the lawn,   600
Unfed, unfolded! Ah, my brother, here's
The fruit you planted in your foreign loves! –
Ay, there's the fruit he planted! never look
Astonished at me with your mother's eyes,
For it was they who set you where you are,   605
An undowered orphan. Child, your father's choice
Of that said mother, disinherited
His daughter, his and hers. Men do not think
Of sons and daughters, when they fall in love,
So much more than of sisters; otherwise   610
He would have paused to ponder what he did,
And shrunk before that clause in the entail
Excluding offspring by a foreign wife,
(The clause set up a hundred years ago
By a Leigh who wedded a French dancing-girl   615
And had his heart danced over in return);
But this man shrank at nothing, never thought
Of you, Aurora, any more than me –
Your mother must have been a pretty thing,
For all the coarse Italian blacks and browns,   620
To make a good man, which my brother was,
Unchary of the duties to his house;
But so it fell indeed. Our cousin Vane,
Vane Leigh, the father of this Romney, wrote
Directly on your birth, to Italy,   625
'I ask your baby daughter for my son

'In whom the entail now merges by the law.
'Betroth her to us out of love, instead
'Of colder reasons, and she shall not lose
'By love or law from henceforth' – so he wrote;   630
A generous cousin, was my cousin Vane.
Remember how he drew you to his knee
The year you came here, just before he died,
And hollowed out his hands to hold your cheeks,
And wished them redder, – you remember Vane?   635
And now his son who represents our house
And holds the fiefs and manors in his place,
To whom reverts my pittance when I die,
(Except a few books and a pair of shawls)
The boy is generous like him, and prepared   640
To carry out his kindest word and thought
To you, Aurora. Yes, a fine young man
Is Romney Leigh; although the sun of youth
Has shone too straight upon his brain, I know,
And fevered him with dreams of doing good   645
To good-for-nothing people. But a wife
Will put all right, and stroke his temples cool
With healthy touches' . .
                          I broke in at that.
I could not lift my heavy heart to breathe
Till then, but then I raised it, and it fell   650
In broken words like these – 'No need to wait.
The dream of doing good to . . me, at least,
Is ended, without waiting for a wife
To cool the fever for him. We've escaped
That danger, – thank Heaven for it.'   655
                               'You,' she cried,
'Have got a fever. What, I talk and talk
An hour long to you, – I instruct you how
You cannot eat or drink or stand or sit
Or even die, like any decent wretch
In all this unroofed and unfurnished world,   660
Without your cousin, – and you still maintain
There's room 'twixt him and you, for flirting fans
And running knots in eyebrows? You must have
A pattern lover sighing on his knee?
You do not count enough, a noble heart   665
(Above book-patterns) which this very morn
Unclosed itself in two dear fathers' names
To embrace your orphaned life? fie, fie! But stay,
I write a word, and counteract this sin.'

She would have turned to leave me, but I clung.   670
'O sweet my father's sister, hear my word

Before you write yours. Cousin Vane did well,
And cousin Romney well, – and I well too,
In casting back with all my strength and will
The good they meant me. O my God, my God!   675
God meant me good, too, when he hindered me
From saying 'yes' this morning. If you write
A word, it shall be 'no.' I say no, no!
I tie up 'no' upon His altar-horns,
Quite out of reach of perjury! At least   680
My soul is not a pauper; I can live
At least my soul's life, without alms from men;
And if it must be in heaven instead of earth,
Let heaven look to it, – I am not afraid.'

She seized my hands with both hers, strained them fast,   685
And drew her probing and unscrupulous eyes
Right through me, body and heart. 'Yet, foolish Sweet,
You love this man. I've watched you when he came,
And when he went, and when we've talked of him:
I am not old for nothing; I can tell   690
The weather-signs of love: you love this man.'

Girls blush sometimes because they are alive,
Half wishing they were dead to save the shame.
The sudden blush devours them, neck and brow;
They have drawn too near the fire of life, like gnats,   695
And flare up bodily, wings and all. What then?
Who's sorry for a gnat .. or girl?
                              I blushed.
I feel the brand upon my forehead now
Strike hot, sear deep, as guiltless men may feel
The felon's iron, say, and scorn the mark   700
Of what they are not. Most illogical
Irrational nature of our womanhood,
That blushes one way, feels another way,
And prays, perhaps, another! After all,
We cannot be the equal of the male   705
Who rules his blood a little.
                              For although
I blushed indeed, as if I loved the man,
And her incisive smile, accrediting
That treason of false witness in my blush,
Did bow me downward like a swathe of grass   710
Below its level that struck me, – I attest
The conscious skies and all their daily suns,
I think I loved him not, – nor then, nor since,
Nor ever. Do we love the schoolmaster,
Being busy in the woods? much less, being poor,   715

The overseer of the parish? Do we keep
Our love to pay our debts with?
                White and cold
I grew next moment. As my blood recoiled
From that imputed ignominy, I made
My heart great with it. Then, at last, I spoke,   720
Spoke veritable words but passionate,
Too passionate perhaps . . ground up with sobs
To shapeless endings. She let fall my hands
And took her smile off, in sedate disgust,
As peradventure she had touched a snake, –   725
A dead snake, mind! – and turning round, replied,
'We'll leave Italian manners, if you please.
I think you had an English father, child,
And ought to find it possible to speak
A quiet 'yes' or 'no,' like English girls,   730
Without convulsions. In another month
We'll take another answer – no, or yes.'
With that, she left me in the garden-walk.

I had a father! yes, but long ago –
How long it seemed that moment. Oh, how far,   735
How far and safe, God, dost thou keep thy saints
When once gone from us! We may call against
The lighted windows of thy fair June-heaven
Where all the souls are happy, – and not one,
Not even my father, look from work or play   740
To ask, 'Who is it that cries after us,
Below there, in the dusk?' Yet formerly
He turned his face upon me quick enough,
If I said 'father.' Now I might cry loud;
The little lark reached higher with his song   745
Than I with crying. Oh, alone, alone, –
Not troubling any in heaven, nor any on earth,
I stood there in the garden, and looked up
The deaf blue sky that brings the roses out
On such June mornings.
                You who keep account   750
Of crisis and transition in this life,
Set down the first time Nature says plain 'no'
To some 'yes' in you, and walks over you
In gorgeous sweeps of scorn. We all begin
By singing with the birds, and running fast   755
With June-days, hand in hand: but once, for all,
The birds must sing against us, and the sun
Strike down upon us like a friend's sword caught
By an enemy to slay us, while we read
The dear name on the blade which bites at us! –   760

That's bitter and convincing: after that,
We seldom doubt that something in the large
Smooth order of creation, though no more
Than haply a man's footstep, has gone wrong.
Some tears fell down my cheeks, and then I smiled,   765
As those smile who have no face in the world
To smile back to them. I had lost a friend
In Romney Leigh; the thing was sure – a friend,
Who had looked at me most gently now and then,
And spoken of my favourite books, 'our books,'   770
With such a voice! Well, voice and look were now
More utterly shut out from me I felt,
Than even my father's. Romney now was turned
To a benefactor, to a generous man,
Who had tied himself to marry .. me, instead   775
Of such a woman, with low timorous lids
He lifted with a sudden word one day,
And left, perhaps, for my sake. – Ah, self-tied
By a contract, male Iphigenia bound
At a fatal Aulis for the winds to change,   780
(But loose him, they'll not change), he well might seem
A little cold and dominant in love!
He had a right to be dogmatical,
This poor, good Romney. Love, to him, was made
A simple law-clause. If I married him,   785
I should not dare to call my soul my own
Which so he had bought and paid for: every thought
And every heart-beat down there in the bill;
Not one found honestly deductible
From any use that pleased him! He might cut   790
My body into coins to give away
Among his other paupers; change my sons,
While I stood dumb as Griseld, for black babes
Or piteous foundlings; might unquestioned set
My right hand teaching in the Ragged Schools,   795
My left hand washing in the Public Baths,
What time my angel of the Ideal stretched
Both his to me in vain. I could not claim
The poor right of a mouse in a trap, to squeal,
And take so much as pity from myself.   800

Farewell, good Romney! if I loved you even,
I could but ill afford to let you be
So generous to me. Farewell, friend, since friend
Betwixt us two, forsooth, must be a word
So heavily overladen. And, since help   805
Must come to me from those who love me not,
Farewell, all helpers – I must help myself,

And am alone from henceforth. – Then I stooped
And lifted the soiled garland from the earth,
And set it on my head as bitterly   810
As when the Spanish monarch crowned the bones
Of his dead love. So be it. I preserve
That crown still, – in the drawer there! 'twas the first.
The rest are like it; – those Olympian crowns,
We run for, till we lose sight of the sun   815
In the dust of the racing chariots!

[Rejected by Aurora, Romney has made a proposal of marriage to a poor seamstress, Marian Erle, in conformity with his philanthropic ideals. Marian, however, failed to appear for the wedding. Instead, as a result of various machinations and mistakes, she was lured to France where, having been drugged and raped, she gave birth to a child. Aurora, now a published poet, is also in France on her way to Italy. In Paris, she catches sight of Marian's face in the crowd and determines to find her lost 'sister'.]

Book VI

                        ...A simple chance
Did all. I could not sleep last night, and, tired   420
Of turning on my pillow and harder thoughts,
Went out at early morning, when the air
Is delicate with some last starry touch,
To wander through the Market-place of Flowers
(The prettiest haunt in Paris), and make sure   425
At worst that there were roses in the world.
So wandering, musing, with the artist's eye,
That keeps the shade-side of the thing it loves,
Half-absent, whole-observing, while the crowd
Of young vivacious and black-braided heads   430
Dipped, quick as finches in a blossomed tree,
Among the nosegays, cheapening this and that
In such a cheerful twitter of rapid speech, –
My heart leapt in me, startled by a voice
That slowly, faintly, with long breaths that marked   435
The interval between the wish and word,
Inquired in stranger's French, 'Would *that* be much,
That branch of flowering mountain-gorse?' – 'So much?
Too much for me, then!' turning the face round
So close upon me that I felt the sigh   440
It turned with.
                'Marian, Marian!' – face to face –
'Marian! I find you. Shall I let you go?'
I held her two slight wrists with both my hands;
'Ah Marian, Marian, can I let you go?'
– She fluttered from me like a cyclamen,   445
As white, which taken in a sudden wind
Beats on against the palisade. – 'Let pass,'

She said at last. 'I will not,' I replied;
'I lost my sister Marian many days,
And sought her ever in my walks and prayers,   450
And, now I find her ... do we throw away
The bread we worked and prayed for, – crumble it
And drop it, .. to do even so by thee
Whom still I've hungered after more than bread,
My sister Marian? – can I hurt thee, dear?   455
Then why distrust me? Never tremble so.
Come with me rather where we'll talk and live
And none shall vex us. I've a home for you
And me and no one else' ...
                           She shook her head.
'A home for you and me and no one else   460
Ill-suits one of us: I prefer to such,
A roof of grass on which a flower might spring,
Less costly to me than the cheapest here;
And yet I could not, at this hour, afford
A like home even. That you offer yours,   465
I thank you. You are good as heaven itself –
As good as one I knew before .. Farewell.'

I loosed her hands, – 'In *his* name, no farewell!'
(She stood as if I held her.) 'For his sake,
For his sake, Romney's! by the good he meant,   470
Ay, always! by the love he pressed for once, –
And by the grief, reproach, abandonment,
He took in change' ..
                   'He Romney! who grieved *him?*
Who had the heart for't? what reproach touched *him?*
Be merciful, – speak quickly.'
                              'Therefore come,'   475
I answered with authority. – 'I think
We dare to speak such things and name such names
In the open squares of Paris!'
                           Not a word
She said, but in a gentle humbled way
(As one who had forgot herself in grief)   480
Turned round and followed closely where I went,
As if I led her by a narrow plank
Across devouring waters, step by step;
And so in silence we walked on a mile.

And then she stopped: her face was white as wax.   485
'We go much farther?'
                   'You are ill,' I asked,
'Or tired?'
           She looked the whiter for her smile.

'There's one at home,' she said, 'has need of me
By this time, – and I must not let him wait.'

'Not even,' I asked, 'to hear of Romney Leigh?'   490

'Not even,' she said, 'to hear of Mister Leigh.'

'In that case,' I resumed, 'I go with you,
And we can talk the same thing there as here.
None waits for me: I have my day to spend.'

Her lips moved in a spasm without a sound, –   495
But then she spoke. 'It shall be as you please;
And better so – 'tis shorter seen than told:
And though you will not find me worth your pains,
That, even, may be worth some pains to know
For one as good as you are.'
      Then she led   500
The way, and I, as by a narrow plank
Across devouring waters, followed her,
Stepping by her footsteps, breathing by her breath,
And holding her with eyes that would not slip;
And so, without a word, we walked a mile,   505
And so, another mile, without a word.
Until the peopled streets being all dismissed,
House-rows and groups all scattered like a flock,
The market-gardens thickened, and the long
White walls beyond, like spiders' outside threads,   510
Stretched, feeling blindly toward the country-fields
Through half-built habitations and half-dug
Foundations, – intervals of trenchant chalk
That bit betwixt the grassy uneven turfs
Where goats (vine-tendrils trailing from their mouths)   515
Stood perched on edges of the cellarage
Which should be, staring as about to leap
To find their coming Bacchus. All the place
Seemed less a cultivation than a waste.
Men work here, only, – scarce begin to live: 520
All's sad, the country struggling with the town,
Like an untamed hawk upon a strong man's fist,
That beats its wings and tries to get away,
And cannot choose be satisfied so soon
To hop through court-yards with his right foot tied,   525
The vintage plains and pastoral hills in sight.

We stopped beside a house too high and slim
To stand there by itself, but waiting till
Five others, two on this side, three on that,

Should grow up from the sullen second floor   530
They pause at now, to build it to a row.
The upper windows partly were unglazed
Meantime, – a meagre, unripe house: a line
Of rigid poplars elbowed it behind,
And, just in front, beyond the lime and bricks   535
That wronged the grass between it and the road,
A great acacia with its slender trunk
And overpoise of multitudinous leaves
(In which a hundred fields might spill their dew
And intense verdure, yet find room enough)   540
Stood reconciling all the place with green.

I followed up the stair upon her step.
She hurried upward, shot across a face,
A woman's, on the landing, – 'How now, now!
Is no one to have holidays but you?   545
You said an hour, and stay three hours, I think,
And Julie waiting for your betters here?
Why if he had waked he might have waked, for me.'
– Just murmuring an excusing word she passed
And shut the rest out with the chamber-door,   550
Myself shut in beside her.
                              'Twas a room
Scarce larger than a grave, and near as bare;
Two stools, a pallet-bed; I saw the room:
A mouse could find no sort of shelter in't,
Much less a greater secret; curtainless, –   555
The window fixed you with its torturing eye,
Defying you to take a step apart
If peradventure you would hide a thing.
I saw the whole room, I and Marian there
Alone.   560
          Alone? She threw her bonnet off,
Then, sighing as 'twere sighing the last time,
Approached the bed, and drew a shawl away:
You could not peel a fruit you fear to bruise
More calmly and more carefully than so, –
Nor would you find within, a rosier flushed   565
Pomegranate –
                    There he lay upon his back,
The yearling creature, warm and moist with life
To the bottom of his dimples, – to the ends
Of the lovely tumbled curls about his face;
For since he had been covered over-much   570
To keep him from the light-glare, both his cheeks
Were hot and scarlet as the first live rose
The shepherd's heart-blood ebbed away into

The faster for his love. And love was here
As instant; in the pretty baby-mouth,   575
Shut close as if for dreaming that it sucked,
The little naked feet, drawn up the way
Of nested birdlings; everything so soft
And tender, – to the tiny holdfast hands,
Which, closing on a finger into sleep,   580
Had kept the mould of't.
                    While we stood there dumb,
For oh, that it should take such innocence
To prove just guilt, I thought, and stood there dumb, –
The light upon his eyelids pricked them wide,
And, staring out at us with all their blue,   585
As half perplexed between the angelhood
He had been away to visit in his sleep,
And our most mortal presence, gradually
He saw his mother's face, accepting it
In change for heaven itself with such a smile   590
As might have well been learnt there, – never moved,
But smiled on, in a drowse of ecstasy,
So happy (half with her and half with heaven)
He could not have the trouble to be stirred,
But smiled and lay there. Like a rose, I said?   595
As red and still indeed as any rose,
That blows in all the silence of its leaves,
Content in blowing to fulfil its life.

She leaned above him (drinking him as wine)
In that extremity of love, 'twill pass   600
For agony or rapture, seeing that love
Includes the whole of nature, rounding it
To love .. no more, – since more can never be
Than just love. Self-forgot, cast out of self,
And drowning in the transport of the sight,   605
Her whole pale passionate face, mouth, forehead, eyes,
One gaze, she stood: then, slowly as he smiled
She smiled too, slowly, smiling unaware,
And drawing from his countenance to hers
A fainter red, as if she watched a flame   610
And stood in it a-glow. 'How beautiful,'
Said she.
          I answered, trying to be cold.
(Must sin have compensations, was my thought,
As if it were a holy thing like grief?
And is a woman to be fooled aside   615
From putting vice down, with that woman's toy
A baby?) – 'Ay! the child is well enough,'
I answered. 'If his mother's palms are clean

They need be glad of course in clasping such;
But if not, I would rather lay my hand,   620
Were I she, on God's brazen altar-bars
Red-hot with burning sacrificial lambs,
Than touch the sacred curls of such a child.'

She plunged her fingers in his clustering locks,
As one who would not be afraid of fire;   625
And then with indrawn steady utterance said,
'My lamb, my lamb! although, through such as thou,
The most unclean got courage and approach
To God, once, — now they cannot, even with men,
Find grace enough for pity and gentle words.'   630

'My Marian,' I made answer, grave and sad,
'The priest who stole a lamb to offer him,
Was still a thief. And if a woman steals
(Through God's own barrier-hedges of true love,
Which fence out licence in securing love)   635
A child like this, that smiles so in her face,
She is no mother but a kidnapper,
And he's a dismal orphan, not a son,
Whom all her kisses cannot feed so full
He will not miss hereafter a pure home   640
To live in, a pure heart to lean against,
A pure good mother's name and memory
To hope by, when the world grows thick and bad
And he feels out for virtue.'
                                    'Oh,' she smiled
With bitter patience, 'the child takes his chance;   645
Not much worse off in being fatherless
Than I was, fathered. He will say, belike,
His mother was the saddest creature born;
He'll say his mother lived so contrary
To joy, that even the kindest, seeing her,   650
Grew sometimes almost cruel: he'll not say
She flew contrarious in the face of God
With bat-wings of her vices. Stole my child, —
My flower of earth, my only flower on earth,
My sweet, my beauty!'.. Up she snatched the child,   655
And, breaking on him in a storm of tears,
Drew out her long sobs from their shivering roots,
Until he took it for a game, and stretched
His feet and flapped his eager arms like wings
And crowed and gurgled through his infant laugh: 660
'Mine, mine,' she said. 'I have as sure a right
As any glad proud mother in the world,
Who sets her darling down to cut his teeth

Upon her church-ring. If she talks of law,
I talk of law! I claim my mother-dues   665
By law, – the law which now is paramount, –
The common law, by which the poor and weak
Are trodden underfoot by vicious men,
And loathed for ever after by the good.
Let pass! I did not filch, – I found the child.'   670
'You found him, Marian?'
                          'Ay, I found him where
I found my curse, – in the gutter, with my shame!
What have you, any of you, to say to that,
Who all are happy, and sit safe and high,
And never spoke before to arraign my right   675
To grief itself? What, what,.. being beaten down
By hoofs of maddened oxen into a ditch,
Half-dead, whole mangled, when a girl at last
Breathes, sees.. and finds there, bedded in her flesh
Because of the extremity of the shock,   680
Some coin of price!.. and when a good man comes
(That's God! the best men are not quite as good)
And says, 'I dropped the coin there: take it you,
And keep it, – it shall pay you for the loss,' –
You all put up your finger – 'See the thief!   685
'Observe what precious thing she has come to filch.
'How bad those girls are!' Oh, my flower, my pet,
I dare forget I have you in my arms
And fly off to be angry with the world,
And fright you, hurt you with my tempers, till   690
You double up your lip? Why, that indeed
Is bad: a naughty mother!'
                          'You mistake,'
I interrupted; 'if I loved you not,
I should not, Marian, certainly be here.'

from *A Curse for a Nation*

Prologue

I heard an angel speak last night,
    And he said 'Write!
Write a Nation's curse for me,
And send it over the Western Sea.'

I faltered, taking up the word: 5
    'Not so, my lord!
If curses must be, choose another
To send thy curse against my brother.

'For I am bound by gratitude,
  By love and blood,   10
To brothers of mine across the sea,
Who stretch out kindly hands to me.'

'Therefore,' the voice said, 'shalt thou write
  My curse to-night.
From the summits of love a curse is driven,   15
As lightning is from the tops of heaven.'

'Not so,' I answered. 'Evermore
  My heart is sore
For my own land's sins: for little feet
Of children bleeding along the street: 20

'For parked-up honours that gainsay
  The right of way:
For almsgiving through a door that is
Not open enough for two friends to kiss:

'For love of freedom which abates   25
  Beyond the Straits:
For patriot virtue starved to vice on
Self-praise, self-interest, and suspicion:

'For an oligarchic parliament,
  And bribes well-meant.   30
What curse to another land assign,
When heavy-souled for the sins of mine?'

'Therefore,' the voice said, 'shalt thou write
  My curse to-night.
Because thou hast strength to see and hate   35
A foul thing done *within* thy gate.'

'Not so,' I answered once again.
  'To curse, choose men.
For I, a woman, have only known
How the heart melts and the tears run down.'   40

'Therefore,' the voice said, 'shalt thou write
  My curse to-night.
Some women weep and curse, I say
(And no one marvels), night and day

'And thou shalt take their part to-night,   45
  Weep and write.
A curse from the depths of womanhood
Is very salt, and bitter, and good.'

So thus I wrote, and mourned indeed,
  What all may read.   50
And thus, as was enjoined on me,
I send it over the Western Sea.

Lord Walter's Wife

I

'But why do you go?' said the lady, while both sat under the yew,
And her eyes were alive in their depth, as the kraken beneath the sea-blue.

II

'Because I fear you,' he answered; – 'because you are far too fair,
And able to strangle my soul in a mesh of your gold-coloured hair.'

III

'Oh, that,' she said, 'is no reason! Such knots are quickly undone,   5
And too much beauty, I reckon, is nothing but too much sun.'

IV

'Yet farewell so,' he answered; – 'the sunstroke's fatal at times.
I value your husband, Lord Walter, whose gallop rings still from the limes.'

V

'Oh, that,' she said, 'is no reason. You smell a rose through a fence:
If two should smell it, what matter? who grumbles, and where's the pretence?'   10

VI

'But I,' he replied, 'have promised another, when love was free,
To love her alone, alone, who alone and afar loves me.'

VII

'Why, that,' she said, 'is no reason. Love's always free, I am told.
Will you vow to be safe from the headache on Tuesday, and think it will hold?'

VIII

'But you,' he replied, 'have a daughter, a young little child, who was laid   15
In your lap to be pure; so I leave you: the angels would make me afraid.'

IX

'Oh, that,' she said, 'is no reason. The angels keep out of the way;
And Dora, the child, observes nothing, although you should please me and stay.'

X

At which he rose up in his anger, – 'Why, now, you no longer are fair!
Why, now, you no longer are fatal, but ugly and hateful, I swear.'   20

XI

At which she laughed out in her scorn: 'These men! Oh, these men overnice,
Who are shocked if a colour not virtuous is frankly put on by a vice.'

XII

Her eyes blazed upon him – 'And *you!* You bring us your vices so near
That we smell them! You think in our presence a thought 'twould defame
   us to hear!

XIII

'What reason had you, and what right, – I appeal to your soul from my life, –   25
To find me too fair as a woman? Why, sir, I am pure, and a wife.

XIV

'Is the day-star too fair up above you? It burns you not. Dare you imply
I brushed you more close than the star does, when Walter had set me as high?

XV

'If a man finds a woman too fair, he means simply adapted too much
To use unlawful and fatal. The praise! – shall I thank you for such?   30

XVI

'Too fair? – not unless you misuse us! and surely if, once in a while,
You attain to it, straightway you call us no longer too fair, but too vile.

XVII

'A moment, – I pray your attention! – I have a poor word in my head
I must utter, though womanly custom would set it down better unsaid.

XVIII

'You grew, sir, pale to impertinence, once when I showed you a ring.   35
You kissed my fan when I dropped it. No matter! – I've broken
    the thing.

XIX

'You did me the honour, perhaps, to be moved at my side now and then
In the senses – a vice, I have heard, which is common to beasts and
    some men.

XX

'Love's a virtue for heroes! – as white as the snow on high hills,
And immortal as every great soul is that struggles, endures, and fulfils.   40

XXI

'I love my Walter profoundly, – you, Maude, though you faltered a week,
For the sake of . . . what was it – an eyebrow? or, less still, a mole on a cheek?

XXII

'And since, when all's said, you're too noble to stoop to the frivolous cant
About crimes irresistible, virtues that swindle, betray and supplant,

XXIII

'I determined to prove to yourself that, whate'er you might dream or avow   45
By illusion, you wanted precisely no more of me than you have now.

XXIV

'There! Look me full in the face! – in the face. Understand, if you can,
That the eyes of such women as I am are clean as the palm of a man.

XXV

'Drop his hand, you insult him. Avoid us for fear we should cost you a scar –
You take us for harlots, I tell you, and not for the women we are.   50

XXVI

'You wronged me: but then I considered . . . there's Walter! And so at the end
I vowed that he should not be mulcted, by me, in the hand of a friend.

XXVII

'Have I hurt you indeed? We are quits then. Nay, friend of my Walter, be mine!
Come, Dora, my darling, my angel, and help me to ask him to dine.'

My Heart and I

I

Enough! we're tired, my heart and I.
  We sit beside the headstone thus,
  And wish that name were carved for us.
The moss reprints more tenderly
  The hard types of the mason's knife,   5
  As heaven's sweet life renews earth's life
With which we're tired, my heart and I.

II

You see we're tired, my heart and I.
  We dealt with books, we trusted men,
  And in our own blood drenched the pen,   10
As if such colours could not fly
  We walked too straight for fortune's end,
  We loved too true to keep a friend;
At last we're tired, my heart and I.

III

How tired we feel, my heart and I!   15
  We seem of no use in the world;
  Our fancies hang grey and uncurled
About men's eyes indifferently;
  Our voice which thrilled you so, will let
  You sleep; our tears are only wet: 20
What do we here, my heart and I?

IV

So tired, so tired, my heart and I!
  It was not thus in that old time
  When Ralph sat with me 'neath the lime
To watch the sunset from the sky.   25
  'Dear love, you're looking tired,' he said;
  I, smiling at him, shook my head:
'Tis now we're tired, my heart and I.

V

So tired, so tired, my heart and I!
  Though now none takes me on his arm   30
  To fold me close and kiss me warm
Till each quick breath end in a sigh
  Of happy languor. Now, alone,
  We lean upon this graveyard stone,
Uncheered, unkissed, my heart and I.   35

VI

Tired out we are, my heart and I.
  Suppose the world brought diadems
  To tempt us, crusted with loose gems
Of powers and pleasures? Let it try.
  We scarcely care to look at even   40
  A pretty child, or God's blue heaven,
We feel so tired, my heart and I.

VII

Yet who complains? My heart and I?
  In this abundant earth no doubt

Is little room for things worn out: 45
Disdain them, break them, throw them by!
  And if before the days grew rough
  We *once* were loved, used, — well enough,
I think, we've fared, my heart and I.

The Best Thing in the World

What's the best thing in the world?
June-rose, by May-dew impearled;
Sweet south-wind, that means no rain;
Truth, not cruel to a friend;
Pleasure, not in haste to end;   5
Beauty, not self-decked and curled
Till its pride is over-plain;
Light, that never makes you wink;
Memory, that gives no pain;
Love, when, *so*, you're loved again.   10
What's the best thing in the world?
— Something out of it, I think.

A Musical Instrument

I

What was he doing, the great god Pan,
  Down in the reeds by the river?
Spreading ruin and scattering ban,
Splashing and paddling with hoofs of a goat,
And breaking the golden lilies afloat   5
  With the dragon-fly on the river.

II

He tore out a reed, the great god Pan,
  From the deep cool bed of the river:
The limpid water turbidly ran,
And the broken lilies a-dying lay,   10
And the dragon-fly had fled away,
  Ere he brought it out of the river.

III

High on the shore sat the great god Pan
  While turbidly flowed the river;

And hacked and hewed as a great god can, 15
With his hard bleak steel at the patient reed,
Till there was not a sign of the leaf indeed
   To prove it fresh from the river.

IV

He cut it short, did the great god Pan,
   (How tall it stood in the river!) 20
Then drew the pith, like the heart of a man,
Steadily from the outside ring,
And notched the poor dry empty thing
   In holes, as he sat by the river.

V

'This is the way,' laughed the great god Pan 25
   (Laughed while he sat by the river),
'The only way, since gods began
To make sweet music, they could succeed.'
Then, dropping his mouth to a hole in the reed,
   He blew in power by the river. 30

VI

Sweet, sweet, sweet, O Pan!
   Piercing sweet by the river!
Blinding sweet, O great god Pan!
The sun on the hill forgot to die,
And the lilies revived, and the dragon-fly 35
   Came back to dream on the river.

VII

Yet half a beast is the great god Pan,
   To laugh as he sits by the river,
Making a poet out of a man:
The true gods sigh for the cost and pain, – 40
For the reed which grows nevermore again
   As a reed with the reeds in the river.

Mother and Poet[1]

Turin, after news from Gaeta, 1861

I

Dead! One of them shot by the sea in the east,
   And one of them shot in the west by the sea.
Dead! both my boys! When you sit at the feast
   And are wanting a great song for Italy free,
      Let none look at *me!*   5

II

Yet I was a poetess only last year,
   And good at my art, for a woman, men said;
But *this* woman, *this*, who is agonised here,
   – The east sea and west sea rhyme on in her head
      For ever instead.   10

III

What art can a woman be good at? Oh, vain!
   What art *is* she good at, but hurting her breast
With the milk-teeth of babes, and a smile at the pain?
   Ah boys, how you hurt! you were strong as you pressed,
      And I proud, by that test.   15

IV

What art's for a woman? To hold on her knees
   Both darlings! to feel all their arms round her throat,
Cling, strangle a little! to sew by degrees
   And 'broider the long-clothes and neat little coat;
      To dream and to doat.   20

V

To teach them ... It stings there! *I* made them indeed
   Speak plain the word *country. I* taught them, no doubt,
That a country's a thing men should die for at need.
   I prated of liberty, rights, and about
      The tyrant cast out.   25

[1 Laura Sauio, poet and patriot, lost two sons in the
struggle for unification.]

VI

And when their eyes flashed...O my beautiful eyes!...
  I exulted; nay, let them go forth at the wheels
Of the guns, and denied not. But then the surprise
  When one sits quite alone! Then one weeps, then one kneels!
    God, how the house feels!   30

VII

At first, happy news came, in gay letters moiled
  With my kisses, – of camp-life and glory, and how
They both loved me; and, soon coming home to be spoiled
  In return would fan off every fly from my brow
    With their green laurel-bough.   35

VIII

Then was triumph at Turin: 'Ancona was free!'
  And some one came out of the cheers in the street,
With a face pale as stone, to say something to me.
  My Guido was dead! I fell down at his feet,
    While they cheered in the street.   40

IX

I bore it; friends soothed me; my grief looked sublime
  As the ransom of Italy. One boy remained
To be leant on and walked with, recalling the time
  When the first grew immortal, while both of us strained
    To the height he had gained.   45

X

And letters still came, shorter, sadder, more strong,
  Writ now but in one hand, 'I was not to faint, –
One loved me for two – would be with me ere long:
  And *Viva l'Italia!* – *he* died for, our saint,
    Who forbids our complaint.'   50

XI

My Nanni would add, 'he was safe, and aware
  Of a presence that turned off the balls, – was imprest

It was Guido himself, who knew what I could bear,
  And how 'twas impossible, quite dispossessed
    To live on for the rest.'   55

XII

On which, without pause, up the telegraph line
  Swept smoothly the next news from Gaeta: – *Shot*.
Tell his mother. Ah, ah, 'his,' 'their' mother, – not 'mine,'
  No voice says '*My* mother' again to me. What!
    You think Guido forgot?   60

XIII

Are souls straight so happy that, dizzy with Heaven,
  They drop earth's affections, conceive not of woe?
I think not. Themselves were too lately forgiven
  Through THAT Love and Sorrow which reconciled so
    The Above and Below.   65

XIV

O Christ of the five wounds, who look'dst through the dark
  To the face of Thy mother! consider, I pray,
How we common mothers stand desolate, mark,
  Whose sons, not being Christs, die with eyes turned away,
    And no last word to say!   70

XV

Both boys dead? but that's out of nature. We all
  Have been patriots, yet each house must always keep one.
'Twere imbecile, hewing out roads to a wall;
  And, when Italy's made, for what end is it done
    If we have not a son?   75

XVI

Ah, ah, ah! when Gaeta's taken, what then?
  When the fair wicked queen sits no more at her sport
Of the fire-balls of death crashing souls out of men?
  When the guns of Cavalli with final retort
    Have cut the game short?   80

XVII

When Venice and Rome keep their new jubilee,
　　When your flag takes all heaven for its white, green, and red,
When *you* have your country from mountain to sea,
　　When King Victor has Italy's crown on his head,
　　　　(And *I* have my Dead) –　　　　　　　　　　　　　　　　85

XVIII

What then? Do not mock me. Ah, ring your bells low,
　　And burn your lights faintly! *My* country is *there*,
Above the star pricked by the last peak of snow:
　　My Italy's THERE, with my brave civic Pair,
　　　　To disfranchise despair!　　　　　　　　　　　　　　　　90

XIX

Forgive me. Some women bear children in strength,
　　And bite back the cry of their pain in self-scorn;
But the birth-pangs of nations will wring us at length
　　Into wail such as this – and we sit on forlorn
　　　　When the man-child is born.　　　　　　　　　　　　　　95

XX

Dead! One of them shot by the sea in the east,
　　And one of them shot in the west by the sea.
Both! both my boys! If in keeping the feast
　　You want a great song for your Italy free,
　　　　Let none look at *me!*　　　　　　　　　　　　　　　　100

Helen Dufferin (1807–1867)

Helen Selina Dufferin was one of the seven children, three daughters and four sons, of Henrietta Callander and Thomas Sheridan, whose father was the dramatist Richard Brinsley Sheridan. Her younger sister was Caroline Norton. When Henrietta and Thomas sailed to the Cape in hopes of improving her father's health, Helen was the only one of their children to travel with them. Thomas died of tuberculosis in 1817 so Helen and her mother returned to England to settle in grace and favour apartments at Hampton Court Palace. On their return journey their ship docked at St Helena and they saw Napoleon walking in his garden. Helen, like her sisters, was famous for her beauty and her accomplishments. It was said that her ear for music was so good that if she went to the opera you were sure to hear her singing the principal tunes the next day. She composed music for her own and for Caroline Norton's poems, and she was also an expert artist, embellishing her letters with sketches and caricatures, and illustrating her own satire on society in the story of 'The Honourable Impulsia Gushington'. Helen came out into London society at the age of seventeen and Price, heir to the Dufferin title, then a young Commander in the Navy, proposed. Mrs Sheridan, only too anxious to marry off her daughters, acquiesced, though the Blackwell family were less than enthusiastic. The couple married in 1825 and immediately set out for Italy in order to avoid the cold reception which they were promised by the husband's relatives. They lived in Siena and Florence where Helen's son was born. Her labour was a difficult one, and at one point, overhearing a discussion as to whose life should be saved, Helen cried out 'Never mind me! save my baby!'; an exclamation which her son declared to exemplify the governing passion of the rest of her days. Returning to England, the family settled in London where Helen made friends with Fanny Kemble among others and entertained all with her enthusiasm and merriment. Her lively wit could turn anything to a joke, a trait exhibited in both her poetry and her letters. Here, she is describing the events of a court case when her mother's silver and most of her own wardrobe were stolen in a burglary:

> I find that the idea of *personal property* is a fascinating illusion, for our goods belong, in fact, to our country and not to us: and that the petticoats and stockings which I have fondly imagined *mine* are really the petticoats of Great Britain and Ireland. I am now and then indulged with a distant glimpse of my most necessary garments in the hands of different policemen; but 'in this stage of the proceedings', may do not more than wistfully recognise them. Even on such occasions, the words of justice are: 'Policeman B 25, produce *your* gowns.' 'Letter A 36, identify *your* lace.' 'Letter C, tie up *your* stockings.' All that is harrowing to the feelings, but one cannot have *everything* in this life! We have obtained *justice*, and can easily wait for a change of linen . . . (Dufferin 1894: 63).

In 1839 Price came into the title of Lord Dufferin and inherited the family estate in Ireland. This eased the financial burden, but Helen was delicate and spent some time in Italy both before and after husband's early death in 1841 as the result of an accidental overdose of morphine. Helen devoted herself to making a home for her son who pursued a diplomatic career which meant that she accompanied him on trips to Egypt, the Holy Land, Greece and the Lebanon. During these years Helen received many proposals of marriage, the most insistent from the young Earl of Gifford, whom Helen liked, but refused on the grounds of the difference in age. In 1862 Gifford suffered an accident which meant that his life was threatened and so, after twenty years of friendship, Helen agreed to marry him, though he died only three months later. After this she again established her little salon and family home at Dufferin Lodge in Highgate, but this last period of happiness was short, for in 1866 Helen developed breast cancer. An operation, 'torture' as her son described it, gave but a short reprieve as the disease spread to her shoulder. Her last months were eased with morphine so that only two hours each day, morning and evening were conscious and free of pain. Her son built her a monument on the estate at Clandboye in Ireland, and this was the occasion for Alfred Tennyson's poem 'Helen's Tower', and Robert Browning's poem of the same name.

Dufferin's early poetry is essentially the light and entertaining verse designed to grace young ladies' albums. But her wit and aptitude make the poems memorable and amusing. her poem 'The Charming Woman' was written in her early twenties and it became a favourite piece for performance in drawing rooms. The idea of 'the charming woman' – vain, self-promoting, politically active and ambitious – became a shorthand phrase familiar in contemporary society. When Barrett Browning created the character of Lady Waldemar and called her a 'charming woman' (*Aurora Leigh*, V, 1041) she was referring to the terms of Dufferin's poem.

M.R.

Dufferin, Lady Helen (Countess of Gifford) (1894) *Songs, Poems and Verses: Edited with a memoir and some Account of the Sheridan family, by her son, The Marquess of Dufferin and Ava*, London.

Hickok, Kathleen (1984) *Representations of Women: Nineteenth-Century British Women's Poetry*, Westport, Conn. and London, Greenwood Press.
Nicolson, Harold (1937) *Helen's Tower*, London, Constable.

The Charming Woman

So Miss Myrtle is going to marry?
   What a number of hearts she will break!
There's Lord George, and Tom Brown, and Sir Harry,
   Who are dying of love for her sake!
'Tis a match that we all must approve, –   5
   Let gossips say all that they can!
For indeed she's a charming woman,
   And he's a most fortunate man!

Yes, indeed, she's a charming woman,
   And she reads both Latin and Greek, –   10
And I'm told that she solved a problem
   In Euclid before she could speak!
Had she been but a daughter of mine,
   I'd have taught her to hem and to sew, –
But her mother (a charming woman)   15
   Couldn't think of such trifles, you know!

Oh, she's really a charming woman!
   But, perhaps, a little too thin;
And no wonder such very late hours
   Should ruin her beautiful skin!   20
And her shoulders are rather too bare,
   And her gown's nearly up to her knees,
But I'm told that these charming women
   May dress themselves just as they please!

Yes, she's really a charming woman!   25
   But, I thought, I observed, by the bye,

A something – that's rather uncommon, –
   In the flash of that very bright eye?
It may be a mere fancy of mine,
   Tho' her voice has a very sharp tone, –   30
But I'm told that these charming women
   Are inclined to have wills of their own!

She sings like a bullfinch or linnet,
   And she talks like an Archbishop too;
Can play you a rubber and win it, –   35
   If she's got nothing better to do!
She can chatter of Poor-laws and Tithes,
   And the value of labour and land, –
'Tis a pity when charming women
   Talk of things which they don't understand!   40

I'm told that she hasn't a penny,
   Yet her gowns would make Maradan stare;
And I feel her bills must be many, –
   But that's only her husband's affair!
Such husbands are very uncommon,   45
   So regardless of prudence and pelf, –
But they say such a charming woman
   Is a fortune, you know, in herself!

She's brothers and sisters by dozens,
   And all charming people, they say!   50
And several tall Irish cousins,
   Whom she loves in a sisterly way.
O young men, if you'd take my advice,
   You would find it an excellent plan, –
Don't marry a charming woman,   55
   If you are a sensible man!

The Mother's Lament

Showing how a family resemblance is not always desirable

I

It is now nearly forty years, I guess,
   Since I was a girl coming out,
And Spriggins proposed – and I said, yes,
   At old Lady Mumble's rout
My match was reckon'd by no means bad,   5
   Take the marrying world as it goes –

But then I must own – Mr. Spriggins had
A remarkably ugly nose!

2

Now the length or shape of your husband's nose
Is a thing that don't signify –   10
As long as your mother and aunts suppose
There's enough to lead him by!
But I own it often has made me sigh,
At the time of our honeymoon's close –
To hear the folks who were passing by   15
Remark on my Spriggins's nose!

3

It wasn't round – nor was it square –
Nor three-corner'd as some noses be!
But upon my conscience I do declare
'Twas a mixture of all the three!   20
And oh! how painful it was to hear,
When our son was in swaddling clothes,
The nurses exclaim – "Oh, sweet little dear,
He has got his papa's own nose!"

4

Five daughters besides were born to me   25
To add to my woe and care –
Bell, Susan, Jemima, and Dorothee,
And Kate – who has sandy hair;
But it isn't the number that makes me grieve,
Tho' they cost me a mint in clothes,   30
– Five gawky girls! – but you'd hardly believe –
They have all got their father's nose!

5

They've been to Brighton for many years past,
And a season in London too,
And Bell nearly got a proposal at last –   35
But we found that it wouldn't do!
And oh! 'tis a grievous thing, I declare,
To be told, wherever one goes,
"I should know the Miss Sprigginses – anywhere –
They've all got the family nose!"   40

6

No beau will be seen in our company,
Do all that we possibly can,
Except Mr Green – who is fifty-three –
And Gubbins – the Doctor's young man!
There's Captain Hodson and Admiral Bluff,   45
I wonder they don't propose –
For really the girls are well enough –
If they hadn't their father's nose!

Caroline Norton (1808–1877)

On the evidence of some of her poems, it might be easy to mistake Caroline Norton as an apologist for the sentimental and decorative style of femininity '. . . let her eyes be grey/ The soft grey of the brooding dove, Full of the sweet and tender ray / Of modest love . . .', she wrote in 'A Visionary Portrait'. But the circumstances of Caroline's appalling married life turned her into an agitatrice such that her name became synonymous with suffering, wronged and angry womanhood. Caroline's grandfather was the dramatist Richard Brinsley Sheridan, and she and her two sisters (the eldest was Helen Selina Dufferin) were famous for their beauty and known in society as 'the three graces'. Her childhood was spent with relatives in Scotland while her parents removed to the Cape for the sake of her father's health. He died in 1817 and in that same year Caroline was sent to study with a governess in Surrey. This woman was the sister of the agent to Lord Grantley whose younger brother was the Hon. George Chapple Norton. The female members of the Norton family were friendly with Caroline's governess and used to invite her and a few favoured pupils to Lord Grantley's house. This is where Caroline's troubles began.

> A sister of Mr Norton's, an eccentric person who affected masculine habits and played a little on the violin, amused herself with my early verses and my love of music, and took more notice of me than of my companions. The occasions on which I saw this lady were not frequent; and still more rare were the occasions on which I had also seen her brother; it was therefore with a feeling of mere astonishment, that I received from my governess the intelligence that she thought it right to refuse me the indulgence of accompanying her again to Lord Grantley's till she had heard from my mother; as Mr Norton had professed his intention of asking me in marriage . . . (Norton 1855: 24).

In spite of the fact that Caroline had 'not exchanged six sentences' with George Norton, she was persuaded to the marriage apparently partly by her mother, partly by George's assurances of love, and partly by his pretence of financial independence where in fact, as a younger son, he had nothing. They married in 1827 and three sons were born in 1829, 1831 and 1833. These were exciting years for Caroline because she was writing and being published. But they were also miserable years as she learnt the truth of her domestic situation. Right from the beginning George insisted that, because she brought no dowry, Caroline and her family had a duty to support him and use their political connections to find him a lucrative place in the legal profession. Caroline and her mother complied, asking members of the royal family to intervene and besieging 'the great names linked with the career of my grandfather' (Norton 1855: 25). At the same time, Caroline settled down to write hoping to earn some money and in this she succeeded, publishing *The Sorrows of Rosalie* in 1829. 'It is not without a certain degree of romantic pride that I look back and know that the first expenses of my son's life were defrayed from that first creation of my brain' (Norton 1855: 25).

She also succeeded in her efforts for her husband, securing him an appointment as a magistrate for a thousand pounds a year. But George was indolent and lazy and soon lost both this appointment and his seat in the House of Commons, preferring instead to employ himself, much to Caroline's embarrassment, as her agent in suing for money owed to her for her writing and treating her publishers as his own bankers. Under the terms of the law at the time he was, of course, quite entitled to do this because a married woman could not own property which all passed to her husband. Her own sufferings on this account led Caroline to write *A Letter to the Queen on Lord Chancellor Cranworth's Marriage and Divorce Bill* (1855) in which she argued her own case but also made a forceful attack on the state of the law:

A married woman in England has *no legal existence*: her being is absorbed in that of her husband. Years of separation or desertion cannot alter this position. Unless divorced by special enactment in the House of Lords, the legal fiction holds her to be '*one*' with her husband, even though she may never see or hear of him . . .

An English wife cannot legally claim her own earnings. Whether wages for manual labour, or payment for intellectual exertion . . . her salary is *the husband's*; and he could compel a second payment, and treat the first as void, if paid to the wife without his sanction . . .

An English wife may not leave her husband's house. Not only can he sue her for 'restitution of conjugal rights', but he has a right to enter the house of any friend or relation with whom she may take refuge, and who may 'harbour her', – as it is termed, – and carry her away by force, with or without the aid of the police (Norton 1855: 8–10).

In 1835 Caroline did leave her husband. But under the law he had exclusive custody of their children and he refused to allow her to see them so that she was forced to return. Then in 1836 Norton accused Caroline of adultery and charged Lord Melbourne, then Prime Minister, with 'criminal conversation' suing for £10,000 compensation. The case went to court but the jury acquitted Melbourne without leaving the box. Caroline's relations with Melbourne would appear to have been political rather than sexual (she had been much interested in the passing of the parliamentary reform bill of 1832), but the case became a monument in legal history and entered popular legend. Famously, the frank and headstrong character of Diana Warwick in George Meredith's novel *Diana of the Crossways* (1885) was based upon Caroline Norton.

Caroline went to live with her mother and began her long campaigns to try and change the law over infant custody, marriage and divorce. Her agitation achieved both ends in the long term, but too late for Caroline herself. She lost her children who went to live with George's sister in Scotland, and, she lost her reputation especially while she insisted upon writing novels about outspoken women whose experiences were similar to her own; *The Wife* and *Woman's Reward* (1835) and *Lost and Saved* (1863). In 1877 when she was sixty-nine she married Sir William Stirling Maxwell, but she died a few months later, a 'bold Bradamante of the nineteenth century' according to John Mitchell Kemble.

Unlike her prose writings, Norton's poetry is graceful and pretty. Poems such as 'The Picture of Sappho' suggest a romantic longing for love and acceptance. Her Sappho is the idealized heterosexual Sappho typical of the early nineteenth century, whose literary fame cannot compensate for the loss of the man she loves. In this it very much resembles the conclusions of Hemans's 'Corinne at the Capitol' or Landon's *The Improvisatrice*. But there are also themes which suggest – with good reason – an anxiety about the likely errors entailed in the conventions of romantic love. 'A Visionary Portrait' offers such a sickly sweet image of man's ideal woman that it surely must be read ironically. And the sonnet 'Like an enfranchised bird' with its careful choice of the public and political word 'enfranchised' and its reference to the caged bird theme, derived from Mary Wollstone-craft's *Vindication of the Rights of Woman* (1792) and so familiar in nineteenth-century women's writing, is an effective extension of the metaphor to criticize the common terms of Victorian love and marriage. Like other 'mother' poems – Eliza Cook's 'The Old Arm-Chair' is an example – the poet speaker in 'Obscurity of Woman's Worth' acknow-ledges the disappearance of women from history and attempts to rectify that absence by re-inscribing her mother, and herself, for the edification of 'those who read/That trust in woman...' In some senses Norton's 'graveyard' poem marks a half way development in feminist consciousness between Grey's 'Elegy in a Country Churchyard' and George Eliot's conclusion to the Finale of *Middlemarch*.

M.R.

Norton, Caroline (1829) *The Sorrows of Rosalie. A Tale with Other Poems*, London.
—— (1830) *The Undying One and Other Poems*, London.
—— (1836) *A Voice from the Factories in serious verse*, London.
—— (1839) *A Plain Letter to the Lord Chancellor on the Infant Custody Bill*, London.
—— (1840) *The Dream, and Other Poems*, London.
—— (1854) *English Laws for Women in the Nineteenth Century*, London.
—— (1855) *A Letter to the Queen on Lord Chancellor Cranworth's Marriage and Divorce Bill*, London.

Acland, Alice (1948) *Caroline Norton*, London, Constable.
Hoge, James O. and Olney, Charles eds. (1974) *The Letters of Caroline Norton to Lord Melbourne*, Columbus, Ohio State University Press.
Huddleston, Joan ed. (1982) *Caroline Norton's Defense: English Laws for Women in the Nineteenth Century*, Chicago, Academy Chicago.

The Picture of Sappho

I

Thou! whose impassion'd face
The Painter loves to trace,

Theme of the Sculptor's art and Poet's story —
　　How many a wand'ring thought
　　Thy loveliness hath brought,　　　　　　　　　　5
Warming the heart with its imagined glory!

II

　　Yet, was it History's truth,
　　That tale of wasted youth,
Of endless grief, and Love forsaken pining?
　　What wert thou, thou whose woe　　　　　　10
　　The old traditions show
With Fame's cold light around thee vainly shining?

III

　　Didst thou indeed sit there
　　In languid lone despair —
Thy harp neglected by thee idly lying —　　　　15
　　Thy soft and earnest gaze
　　Watching the lingering rays
In the far west, where summer-day was dying —

IV

　　While with low rustling wings,
　　Among the quivering strings　　　　　　　　20
The murmuring breeze faint melody was making,
　　As though it wooed thy hand
　　To strike with new command,
Or mourn'd with thee because thy heart was breaking?

V

　　Didst thou, as day by day　　　　　　　　　25
　　Roll'd heavily away,
And left thee anxious, nerveless, and dejected,
　　Wandering thro' bowers beloved —
　　Roving where *he* had roved —
Yearn for his presence, as for one expected?　　　30

VI

Didst thou, with fond wild eyes
Fix'd on the starry skies,

Wait feverishly for each new day to waken –
   Trusting some glorious morn
   Might witness his return,   35
Unwilling to believe thyself forsaken?

VII

And when conviction came,
   Chilling that heart of flame,
Didst thou, O saddest of earth's grieving daughters!
   From the Leucadian steep   40
   Dash, with a desperate leap,
And hide thyself within the whelming waters?

VIII

Yea, in their hollow breast
   Thy heart at length found rest!
The ever-moving waves above thee closing –   45
   The winds, whose ruffling sigh
   Swept the blue waters by,
Disturb'd thee not! – thou wert in peace reposing!

IX

Such is the tale they tell!
   Vain was thy beauty's spell –   50
Vain all the praise thy song could still inspire –
   Though many a happy band
   Rung with less skilful hand
The borrowed love-notes of thy echoing lyre.

X

FAME, to thy breaking heart   55
   No comfort could impart,
In vain thy brow the laurel wreath was wearing;
   One grief and one alone
   Could bow thy bright head down –
Thou wert a WOMAN, and wert left despairing!   60

Obscurity of Woman's Worth

In many a village churchyard's simple grave,
Where all unmarked the cypress branches wave,
In many a vault where Death could only claim
The brief inscription of a woman's name;
Of different ranks, and different degrees,   5
From daily labour to a life of ease,
(From the rich wife who through the weary day
Wept in her jewels, grief's unceasing prey,
To the poor soul who trudged o'er marsh and moor,
And with her baby begged from door to door, –)   10
Lie hearts, which, ere they found that last release,
Had lost all memory of the blessing "Peace;"
Hearts, whose long struggle through unpitied years
None saw but Him who marks the mourner's tears;
The obscurely noble! who evaded not   15
The woe which He had willed should be their lot,
But nerved themselves to bear!
                              Of such art thou,
My Mother! With thy calm and holy brow,
And high devoted heart, which suffered still
Unmurmuring, through each degree of ill.   20
And, because Fate hath willed that mine should be
A Poet's soul (at least in my degree,) –
And that my verse would faintly shadow forth
What I have seen of pure unselfish worth, –
Therefore I speak of Thee; that those who read   25
That trust in woman, which is still my creed,
Thy early-widowed image may recall
And greet thy nature as the type of all!

Sonnet VII

Like an enfranchised bird, who wildly springs,
   With a keen sparkle in his glancing eye
And a strong effort in his quivering wings,
   Up to the blue vault of the happy sky, –
So my enamour'd heart, so long thine own,   5
   At length from Love's imprisonment set free,
Goes forth into the open world alone,
   Glad and exulting in its liberty:
But like that helpless bird, (confined so long,
   His weary wings have lost all power to soar,)   10
Who soon forgets to trill his joyous song,
   And, feebly fluttering, sinks to earth once more, –

So, from its former bonds released in vain,
My heart still feels the weight of that remember'd chain.

from *Marriage and Love*

The poorest peasant of the meanest soil,
The child of poverty, and heir to toil,
Early, from radiant love's impartial light,
Steals one small spark to cheer his world of night:
Dear spark! which oft, through winter's chilling woes.
Is all the warmth his little cottage knows!
                                        Sheridan

Laura was lightsome, gay, and free from guile;
Bright were her eyes, and beautiful her smile:
Women found fault, but men were heard to swear
That she *was* lovely, though she was not *fair*.
Her parents were not rich, nor very poor;   5
She had enough, nor breathed a wish for more;
Blithe were the mornings, gay the evenings spent,
And youthful eyes smiled back a calm content.
Yes, she was happy, and she was at rest,
Till the world filled with cares her little breast,   10
Taught her to fear all dowagers and mothers,
Smile on gay lords, and cut their younger brothers.
This last rule cost her now and then a sigh –
'Tis wrong to say so – but I know not why
Men, when they're handsome, are not liked the less,   15
And may be pleasant, though they're pennyless –
But Laura's mother never would agree
That needy men could pleasant partners be;
To gain *her* favour, vain was all exertion,
A younger brother was her great aversion.   20
The mother hoped and prayed – her prayer was granted,
A lordling came – the very thing she wanted –
'Oh! what a match, my dear!' – and Laura sighed
And hung her head, and timidly replied,
'She did not love,' – 'What put it in your head   25
That it was needful? – you are asked to *wed* –
Romantic love is all a childish folly,
So marry, dear! and don't look melancholy;
Besides, you cannot always live at home –
Another year your sister's turn will come –   30
And you will be *so* rich! – where *shall* we go?
Let us begin to think of your *trousseau!*'
And Laura laughed, and looked up at her mother:
She loved not *him* – but then, she loved no other!

Days passed away – she spent the last few hours 35
In pinning on lace veils and orange flowers;
With beating heart the maid to church was carried,
And Laura blushed, and trembled, and – was married!
Quickly the happy couple speed away,
And friends' congratulations end the day. 40
'Sweet girl! how well she look'd! dress'd with such care!
How the rich veil became her face and hair!
A lovely woman, certainly,' – and Laura
Left friends behind, with all the world before her!
Dwelt for a while (remembrance sad and strong!) 45
In Laura's mind her little brother's song –
The quick light step – the blue and sparkling eye,
The bright perfection of his infancy –
Her sister's gentle smile – all these arise,
Whilst damp'd her wedding veil her weeping eyes; 50
But soon consoled, again the maid grew gay,
Swift in amusement flew each busy day;
The country seat was exquisite; she found
New beauties every time she looked around;
The lawn so green, so smooth, so sunny too, 55
The flowers so bright, the heavens of *such* a blue! –
'Oh! this *was* happiness!' – It *might* have been,
Had there been no reverse of this fair scene.
But Laura's lord was not what lords should be; –
Cold, harsh, unfeeling, proud, alas! was he – 60
And yet a *very* fool – had he been stern,
She would have tried the tyrant's will to learn –
Had he been passionate, she still had loved –
Or jealous, time her virtue would have proved;
But, as he was, without a soul or mind 65
Too savage e'en to be in seeming kind –
The slave of petty feelings, every hour
He changed his will, to show he *had* the power;
And Laura wept, that she had linked her fate
With one too cold to love, too mean to hate. 70
A mother's hopes were left her, and she said,
'My child, at least, will love me!' days, months, sped –
She watched the grave, and wept the early dead!
The scene was changed: nought pleases Laura now,
Nor sunny sky, nor richly sweeping bough; 75
At the long window, opening to the ground,
She sits, while evening spreads its shadows round;
Or through the glowing noon, for weary hours,
Watches the bees that flutter o'er the flowers;
Or when the moon is up, and stars are out, 80
She leaves her lonely room to roam about;
And while the night breeze murmurs o'er her head,

Upbraids the living, or bewails the dead!
Both are alike insensible – her mate,
Weary of home, hath left her to her fate;   85
Nor recks he *now* that Laura weeps or sighs,
So he enjoy what Heaven to *her* denies.
But there was *one* who thought eyes blue and deep,
Like Laura's were too beautiful to weep;
Perchance he told her so – perchance she guessed   90
He deemed her lovelier than his words expressed –
A cousin he of Laura's moody lord,
But how unlike him! – every gentle word
And gentlier tone – the song, the walk, the book,
The graceful step, the bright expressive look,   95
Awoke in her a deep and sad regret
Of what he *might* have been – ah! might be yet!

from *A Voice from the Factories*

IX

Ever a toiling *child* doth make us sad:
'Tis an unnatural and mournful sight,
Because we feel their smiles should be so glad,
Because we know their eyes should be so bright.
What is it, then, when, tasked beyond their might,   5
They labour all day long for others' gain, –
Nay, trespass on the still and pleasant night,
While uncompleted hours of toil remain?
Poor little FACTORY SLAVES – for YOU these lines complain!

X

Beyond all sorrow which the wanderer knows,   10
Is that these little pent-up wretches feel;
Where the air thick and close and stagnant grows,
And the low whirring of the incessant wheel
Dizzies the head, and makes the senses reel:
There, shut for ever from the gladdening sky,   15
Vice premature and Care's corroding seal
Stamp on each sallow cheek their hateful die,
Line the smooth open brow, and sink the saddened eye.

XI

For them the fervid summer only brings
A double curse of stifling withering heat;   20

For them no flowers spring up, no wild bird sings,
No moss-grown walks refresh their weary feet; —
No river's murmuring sound; — no wood-walk, sweet
With many a flower the learned slight and pass; —
Nor meadow, with pale cowslips thickly set   25
Amid the soft leaves of its tufted grass, —
Lure *them* a childish stock of treasures to amass.

XII

Have we forgotten our own infancy,
That joys so simple are to them denied? —
Our boyhood's hopes — our wanderings far and free,   30
Where yellow gorse-bush left the common wide
And open to the breeze? — The active pride
Which made each obstacle a pleasure seem;
When, rashly glad, all danger we defied,
Dashed through the brook by twilight's fading gleam,   35
Or scorned the tottering plank, and leapt the narrow stream?

XIII

In lieu of this, — from short and bitter night,
Sullen and sad the infant labourer creeps;
He joys not in the glow of morning's light,
But with an idle yearning stands and weeps,   40
Envying the babe that in its cradle sleeps:
And ever as he slowly journeys on,
His listless tongue unbidden silence keeps;
His fellow-labourers (playmates hath he none)
Walk by, as sad as he, nor hail the morning sun.   45

XIV

Mark the result. Unnaturally debarred
All nature's fresh and innocent delights,
While yet each germing energy strives hard,
And pristine good with pristine evil fights;
When every passing dream the heart excites,   50
And makes even *guarded* virtue insecure;
Untaught, unchecked, they yield as vice invites:
With all around them cramped, confined, impure,
Fast spreads the moral plague which nothing new shall cure.

XV

Yes, this reproach is added; (infamous   55
In realms which own a Christian monarch's sway!)
Not suffering *only* is their portion, thus
Compelled to toil their youthful lives away:
Excessive labour works the SOUL'S decay –
Quenches the intellectual light within –   60
Crushes with iron weight the mind's free play –
Steals from us LEISURE purer thoughts to win –
And leaves us sunk and lost in dull and native sin.

XVI

Yet in the British Senate men rise up,
(The freeborn and the fathers of our land!)   65
And while these drink the dregs of Sorrow's cup,
Deny the sufferings of the pining band.
With nice-drawn calculations at command,
They prove – rebut – explain – and reason long;
Proud of each shallow argument they stand,   70
And prostitute their utmost powers of tongue
Feebly to justify this great and glaring wrong.

XVII

So rose, with such a plausible defence
Of the unalienable RIGHT OF GAIN,
Those who against Truth's brightest eloquence   75
Upheld the cause of torture and of pain:
And fear of Property's Decrease made vain,
For years, the hope of Christian Charity
To lift the curse from SLAVERY'S dark domain,
And send across the wide Atlantic sea   80
The watchword of brave men – the thrilling shout, 'BE FREE!'

XVIII

What is to be a slave? Is't not to spend
A life bowed down beneath a grinding ill? –
To labour on to serve another's end, –
To give up leisure, health, and strength, and skill –   85
And give up each of these *against your will?*
Hark to the angry answer: – 'Theirs is not
A life of slavery; if they labour, – still

We *pay* their toil. Free service is their lot;
And what their labour yields, by us is fairly got.'   90

XIX

Oh, Men! blaspheme not Freedom! Are they free
Who toil until the body's strength gives way?
Who may not set a term for Liberty,
Who have no time for food, or rest, or play,
But struggle through the long unwelcome day   95
Without the leisure to be good or glad?
Such is their service – call it what you may.
Poor little creatures, overtasked and sad,
Your Slavery hath no name, – yet is its Curse as bad!

XX

Again an answer. ' 'Tis their parents' choice.   100
By *some* employ the poor man's child must earn
Its daily bread; and infants have no voice
In what the allotted task shall be: they learn
What answers best, or suits the parents' turn.'
Mournful reply! Do not your hearts inquire   105
Who tempts the parents' penury? They yearn
Toward their offspring with a strong desire,
But those who starve *will* sell, even what they most require.

XXI

We grant their class must labour – young and old;
We grant the child the needy parents' tool: 110
But still our hearts a better plan behold;
No bright Utopia of some dreaming fool,
But rationally just, and good by rule.
Not against TOIL, but TOIL'S EXCESS we pray,
(Else were we nursed in Folly's simplest school);   115
That so our country's hardy children may
Learn not to loathe, but bless, the well apportioned day.

XXII

One more reply! The *last* reply – the great
Answer to all that sense or feeling shows,
To which all others are subordinate: –   120
'The Masters of the Factories must lose

By the abridgment of these infant woes.
Show us the remedy which shall combine
Our equal gain with their increased repose –
Which shall not make our trading class repine,   125
But to the proffered boon its strong effects confine.'

XXIII

Oh! shall it then be said that TYRANT acts
Are those which cause our country's looms to thrive?
That Merchant England's prosperous trade exacts
This bitter sacrifice, e'er she derive   130
That profit due, for which the feeble strive?
Is her commercial avarice so keen,
That in her busy multitudinous hive
Hundreds must die like insects, scarcely seen,
While the thick-thronged survivors work where they have been?   135

XXIV

Forbid it, Spirit of the glorious Past
Which gained our Isle the surname of 'The Free,'
And made our shores a refuge at the last
To all who would not bend the servile knee,
The vainly-vanquished sons of Liberty!   140
Here ever came the injured, the opprést,
Compelled from the Oppressor's face to flee –
And found a home of shelter and of rest
In the warm generous heart that beat in England's breast.

Frances Anne Kemble (1809–1893)

Fanny Kemble was the elder of two daughters born into a famous theatrical family.
Her mother, Maria Teresa, and her father, Charles, were both actors at the Drury Lane
and Covent Garden theatres. Her sister, Adelaide, became a famous opera singer and
her aunt was the great Sarah Siddons. A wilful child, Fanny describes how she was once
beaten, locked in a cellar and taken to a public execution in an attempt to subdue her.
She was educated mainly in France. At sixteen she returned to her parents' home in
Britain where she continued her education on her own and began to write poetry and
plays. By 1829 financial problems at Covent Garden were so acute that her father,
who was now its manager, persuaded his daughter to go on the stage. Her appearance
in the role of Juliet (her father playing Mercutio and her mother Lady Capulet) was a
great success, and her subsequent appearances for several consecutive seasons seem
temporarily to have saved the theatre. However, there is a hint of coercion and even
exploitation in this free use of a daughter. Fanny herself claimed that she always found

the theatre 'utterly distasteful' and only agreed to act out of 'duty and conformity to the will of my parents' (1878: II, 13). The rough publicity must also have been difficult to bear. It seems that some derogatory comments about her in *The Age* resulted in an actual physical assault by her father upon its editor.

In 1832, in the hope of solving further financial problems, he took his daughter on a two-year tour of America, where she met and then married Pierce Mease Butler, a Philadelphia plantation owner. The marriage was not a success. Fanny had once written to a friend that 'I do not think I am fit to marry, to make an obedient wife or affectionate mother' (1878: I, 220). Certainly her anti-slavery views, which were confirmed when she visited the plantations in the south, soon became a source of tension in the marriage. Eventually, in 1845, she was separated from her husband, and in 1849, divorced. Tragically, she was forced to leave her two daughters in his custody – a fact which gives added poignancy to the 'childless mother's' cry in the sonnet 'If there were any power...' and to the poem addressed to that campaigner for maternal child custody, Caroline Norton. In 1863, free of the prohibitions of her husband, she published her anti-slavery manifesto, *Journal of a Residence on a Georgian Plantation*.

After leaving America, Fanny spent some time with her sister in Rome (Italy being the beloved haven described, very much à la Barrett Browning, in 'Farewell to Italy'), and then returned to England where, for the next twenty years or so, she supported herself by acting, giving public readings and writing plays, poems and extensive memoirs. In 1854 she was in Rome again, where she became a close friend of the Brownings. Elizabeth, who had followed the story of Fanny's divorce with considerable interest, declared: 'I like her decidedly' (1983: III, 402), though she was amused by certain rigid eccentricities, such as Fanny's insistence on wearing her clothes in rotation, so that 'the white satin shoes' (III, 407) were always worn on fixed days, whatever the weather or occupation of the wearer. Fanny's reluctance to join the growing movement for women's emancipation (in America she was friendly with the feminist campaigner Margaret Fuller) was evidently the consequence both of her own 'individual superabundant sense of independence' (1891: I, 315), as she put it, and also of her own emotional mistakes. She once declared that the cause of women would be furthered much more by preventing them 'from becoming desperately in love with, and desperately afraid of, very contemptible men' than by 'all the speeches, pamphlets, and "platforms" in the world' (1891: I, 106). As she grew older, she became somewhat overbearing and dictatorial (see Mary Coleridge). After years of travelling and working to support herself, she eventually settled with her younger daughter in England, where she died at the age of eighty-four.

Kemble's poems are little more than asides in a life that was indefatigably active and independent, if also often unhappy. By comparison with that life, the poems can seem disappointingly impersonal and unpolitical, as if providing their author with a merely formulaic expression of poetical weariness. But here and there they are charged by the real sufferings, beliefs or resentments of this indomitable, and in her way, crusading woman.

A.L.

Kemble, Frances Anne (1883) *Poems*, London.
—— (1863) *Journal of a Residence on a Georgian Plantation in 1838–1839*, Philadelphia.
—— (1878) *Record of a Girlhood*, 3 vols, London.
—— (1891) *Further Records: 1848–1883*, 2 vols, London.

Barrett Browning, Elizabeth (1983) *The Letters of Elizabeth Barrett Browning to Mary Russell Mitford: 1836–1854,* 3 vols, eds Raymond and Meredith B. Mary Rose Sullivan, Winfield, Kan., Wedgestone Press.

Marshall, Dorothy (1977) *Fanny Kemble,* London, Weidenfeld & Nicolson.

To Mrs. Norton

I never shall forget thee – 'tis a word
  Thou oft must hear, for surely there be none
  On whom thy wondrous eyes have ever shone
But for a moment, or who e'er have heard
Thy voice's deep impassioned melody,   5
  Can lose the memory of that look or tone.
But, not as these, do I say unto thee,
  I never shall forget thee: – in thine eyes,
Whose light, like sunshine, makes the world rejoice,
  A stream of sad and solemn splendour lies;   10
And there is sorrow in thy gentle voice.
Thou art not like the scenes in which I found thee,
Thou art not like the beings that surround thee;
  To me thou art a dream of hope and fear;
Yet why of fear? – oh sure! the Power that lent   15
Such gifts, to make thee fair, and excellent;
Still watches one whom it has deigned to bless
With such a dower of grace and loveliness;
  Over the dangerous waves 'twill surely steer
The richly freighted bark, through storm and blast,   20
And guide it safely to the port at last.
Such is my prayer; 'tis warm as ever fell
From off my lips: accept it, and farewell!
And though in this strange world where first I met thee,
We meet no more – I never shall forget thee.   25

Lines

On Reading with Difficulty Some of Schiller's Early Love Poems

When of thy loves, and happy heavenly dreams
Of early life, O Bard! I strive to read,
Thy foreign utterance a riddle seems,
And hardly can I hold thy thought's bright thread.
When of the maiden's guilt, the mother's woe,   5
And the dark mystery of death and shame,
Thou speakest – then thy terrible numbers flow
As if the tongue we think in were the same.
Ah wherefore! but because all joy and love
Speak unfamiliar, unknown words to me,   10

A spirit of wishful wonder they may move,
Dreams of what might – but yet shall never be.
But the sharp cry of pain – the bitter moan
Of trust deceived – the horrible despair
Of hope and love for ever overthrown –   15
These strains of thine need no interpreter.
Ah! 'tis my native tongue! and howsoe'er
In foreign accents writ, that I did ne'er
Or speak, or hear, a woman's agony
Still utters a familiar voice to me.   20

Sonnet

If there were any power in human love,
    Or in th' intensest longing of the heart,
    Then should the oceans and the lands that part
Ye from my sight all unprevailing prove,
Then should the yearning of my bosom bring   5
    Ye here, through space and distance infinite;
And life 'gainst love should be a baffled thing,
    And circumstance 'gainst will lose all its might.
Shall not a childless mother's misery
    Conjure the earth with such a potent spell –   10
    A charm so desperate – as to compel
Nature to yield to her great agony?
    Can I not think of ye till ye arise,
    Alive, alive, before my very eyes?

Farewell to Italy

Farewell awhile, beautiful Italy!
My lonely bark is launched upon the sea
That clasps thy shore, and the soft evening gale
Breathes from thy coast, and fills my parting sail.
Ere morning dawn, a colder breeze will come,   5
And bear me onward to my northern home;
That home, where the pale sun is not so bright,
So glorious, at his noonday's fiercest height,
As when he throws his last glance o'er the sea,
And fires the heavens, that glow farewell on thee.   10
Fair Italy! perchance some future day
Upon thy coast again will see me stray;
Meantime, farewell! I sorrow, as I leave
Thy lovely shore behind me, as men grieve
When bending o'er a form, around whose charms,   15
Unconquered yet, death winds his icy arms:

While leaving the last kiss on some dear cheek,
Where beauty sheds her last autumnal streak,
Life's rosy flower just mantling into bloom,
Before it fades for ever in the tomb.   20
So I leave thee, oh! thou art lovely still!
Despite the clouds of infamy and ill
That gather thickly round thy fading form:
Still glow thy glorious skies, as bright and warm,
Still memory lingers fondly on thy strand,   25
And genius hails thee still her native land.
Land of my soul's adoption! o'er the sea,
Thy sunny shore is fading rapidly:
Fainter and fainter, from my gaze it dies,
Till like a line of distant light it lies,   30
A melting boundary 'twixt earth and sky,
And now 'tis gone; — farewell, fair Italy!

Charlotte Brontë (1816–1855)

Two years after Charlotte's death, Elizabeth Gaskell published her biography with
an epigraph taken from Barrett Browning's recently published *Aurora Leigh*: 'Oh my
God, / ... Thou hast knowledge, only Thou, / How dreary 'tis for women to sit
still / On Winter nights by solitary fires / And hear the nations praising them far off'
(Book v).

Charlotte had grown up reading the women poets who fretted over the female choice
between love and fame. She certainly knew Felicia Hemans's work, and gave a copy of
her poems to the sister of her close friend Ellen Nussey (Wise and Symington 1933: I,
284). But she didn't live to read *Aurora Leigh*, nor could she know that it would mark
a turning point in the self-conceptions of the nineteenth-century professional woman
writer. The irony in Barrett Browning's quotation is quite lost in the way Gaskell uses
it, and her mournful picture of the lonely Charlotte has had a powerful influence. From
Gaskell on, Charlotte's miserable lot has been offered to women as a dire warning
about the high cost of genius. The trouble is that, while this painful image tells a truth
about Charlotte, it wasn't the *writing* that made her life sad. Quite the contrary. Writing
was the only thing that made her life endurable.

Charlotte was the third daughter of Maria Branwell and the Revd Patrick Brontë. Her
mother married when she was twenty-nine and had been for some years 'perfectly my
own mistress, subject to no control whatever'. Yet she saw, or said she saw, this as a
disadvantage and told her new husband that 'I have deeply felt the want of a guide and
instructor' (Gaskell 1975 [1857]: 82). Whether she found this in the arrogant, short-
tempered and egotistical Patrick is doubtful. What she *did* find was occupation, first as
a mother – she bore six children in seven years – and then as an invalid, the consequence
of the first. She died in 1821 when Charlotte was five. Patrick retired to his study and
ignored the children. Their aunt Branwell came to run the household, and Maria, the
eldest at seven years, became mother to the babies. A local woman described these
early years to Gaskell: 'You would not have known that there was a child in the

house, they were such still, noiseless, good little creatures... I used to think them spiritless...' (Gaskell 1975[1857]: 87).

Oppressed they may have been, but their intellect, and especially Charlotte's, was a marvel, according to the servants Gaskell consulted. Mr Brontë himself described how the children invented plays for one another 'in which the Duke of Wellington, my daughter Charlotte's hero, was sure to come off conqueror' (Gaskell 1975 [1857]: 94). The other personae, adopted by the other children, were all heroes too, Napoleon, Hannibal and Caesar. Obviously, at this stage sexual difference mattered not a jot to the aspiring minds of the girls, but they were soon to learn that this would not do. When Patrick took notice of his 'timid' children he encouraged them to speak out boldly under cover of a mask:

> I asked Branwell what was the best way of knowing the difference between the intellects of men and women; he answered, 'By considering the difference between them as to their bodies.' I then asked Charlotte what was the best book in the world; she answered 'The Bible'. And what was the next best; she answered 'The Book of Nature'. I then asked the next [Elizabeth] what was the best mode of education for a woman; she answered, 'That which would make her rule her house well' (Gaskell 1975 [1857]: 94).

In July 1824 the two eldest girls, Maria and Elizabeth, were taken to the newly established school for daughters of the clergy at Cowan Bridge. In September Charlotte and Emily joined them. They were all delicate, having been suffering from childish diseases, and the school was run on economical lines which allowed neither tempting food nor adequate warmth. Maria was the especial target of harassment from one of the teachers and all this experience notoriously went into the imaginative stock of the young Charlotte to be transmuted into the school at Lowood which appears in *Jane Eyre*. Maria and later Elizabeth were both removed from the school, but they died of consumption aged eleven and ten. Charlotte and Emily were also removed for good in June 1845 (Gérin 1967: 16).

Back at Haworth the nine-year-old Charlotte became the leader in the children's education and pleasures. They read widely in the classics of literature (Scott, Wordsworth, Southey) and the newspapers of the day. At least one of the annuals, *Friendship's Offering* for 1829 found its way into the parsonage. When Branwell was given some wooden soldiers they began to invent their imaginary worlds in which Charlotte partnered Branwell as the chroniclers of Angria. Her hero then was the Byronic Duke of Zamorna and her childish writings were extravagant in tone, as Gaskell saw it, 'to the very borders of apparent delirium' (Gaskell 1975 [1857]: 119).

From 1831 to 1832 she studied at Miss Wooler's school at Roe Head where she met the great friend of her life, Ellen Nussey and others, such as Mary Taylor who valued her intellect. Mary said to Charlotte that the Brontës' fashion of 'making out' stories to compensate for their lack of society made her think they 'were like growing potatoes in a cellar'. Charlotte replied 'sadly, "Yes! I know we are"...' (Gaskell 1975 [1857]: 132). At home again, she instructed her sisters, took drawing lessons and corresponded with Ellen and Mary. In 1835 she returned to Miss Wooler's as a teacher where she worked without remitting. She seemed, wrote Mary Taylor, 'to have no interest or pleasure beyond the feeling of duty, and, when she could get, used to sit alone, and "make out"' (Gaskell 1975 [1857]: 160). The conflict between passion and reason, inclination and duty, which was to mark all of Charlotte's life and work was already shaping her character. To Ellen Nussey she wrote:

> My darling, if I were like you, I should have my face Zion-ward, though prejudice and error might occasionally fling a mist over the glorious vision before me – but *I am not like you.* If you knew my thoughts, the dreams that absorb me, and the fiery imagination that at times eats me up, and makes me feel society, as it is, wretchedly insipid, you would pity and I dare say despise me ... (Gaskell 1975 [1857]: 161).

At home at Christmas 1836, the family decided to see if their writings had any value in the opinion of the world. Charlotte wrote a letter to Robert Southey, the Poet Laureate, and Branwell addressed one to Wordsworth. Branwell's apparently received no reply, but Charlotte did:

> You evidently possess, and in no inconsiderable degree, what Wordsworth calls the 'faculty of verse'. I am not depreciating it when I say that in these times it is not rare ... But it is not with a view to distinction that you should cultivate this talent, if you consult your own happiness ... The day dreams in which you habitually indulge are likely to induce a distempered state of mind; and in proportion as all the ordinary uses of the world seem to you flat and unprofitable, you will be unfitted for them without becoming fitted for anything else. Literature cannot be the business of a woman's life, and it ought not to be. The more she is engaged in her proper duties, the less leisure will she have for it, even as an accomplishment and a recreation. To those duties you have not yet been called, and when you are you will be less eager for celebrity (Gaskell 1975 [1857]: 172–3).

Charlotte later told Gaskell that this letter was 'a little stringent, but it did me good' (Gaskell 1975 [1857]: 174). At the time she replied to the poet that she did indeed observe 'all the duties a woman ought to fulfil', and that she only wrote 'for its own sake' and that she would do so no more. Southey congratulated her on her good sense and, as Wordsworth had done in the case of Maria Jewsbury, invited her to visit. But there was no money and it never happened.

Forced to give up her position at Miss Wooler's because of ill health, she worked as a governess in 1839 and 1841, and then, with the idea of improving their education sufficiently to enable them to open a school, Charlotte and Emily went to Brussels to study with the Hegers. They came home when their aunt died, but Charlotte went back as a teacher in 1843, attracted, in part, by her deepening interest in Monsieur Heger. Madame, however, was not so keen. Ostensibly the rift was over Charlotte's Protestant disgust for the 'idolatry' of the Catholic church, but some sexual jealousy was also involved, and Charlotte came back to Haworth early in 1844. There she cared for her father, who was suffering from cataracts and, after Branwell's ignominious dismissal from his post as tutor, she coped, with her sisters, with his increasing violence and dissipation.

Then into this gloomy time came the old dream of publication. In Autumn 1845 Charlotte found Emily's manuscript poems and the three sisters agreed to put a book together. Probably remembering Southey, they decided not to attach their own names:

> Averse to personal publicity, we veiled our own names under those of Currer, Ellis, and Acton Bell; the ambiguous choice being dictated by a sort of

conscientious scruple at assuming christian names positively masculine, while we did not like to declare ourselves women, because – without at that time suspecting that our mode of writing and thinking was not what is called 'feminine' – we had a vague impression that authoresses are liable to be looked on with prejudice; we had noticed how critics sometimes use for chastisement the weapon of personality, and for their reward, a flattery which is not true praise' (Bronte 1850: viii–xi).

After being offered to many publishers, *Poems by Currer, Ellis and Acton Bell* was published by Aylott and Jones at the authors' expense of £31.10s. It may have been vanity publishing, but Charlotte was determined that their work should have the best and stipulated that she required quality of paper and size of type similar to 'Moxon's last edition of Wordsworth' (Gaskell 1975 [1857]: 287). The *Poems* only sold a few copies, it received only one review. But the idea of publication was in train and the three sisters started on a novel each. Charlotte's was *The Professor* and it was rejected everywhere, so, while in Manchester, nursing her father after an operation on his eyes, she began to write *Jane Eyre*. It was accepted by Smith and Elder in August 1847 and published in October.

The public reception accorded the book is well known. At home, Charlotte gave her father a copy, and when he came in to tea he said 'Girls, do you know that Charlotte has been writing a book, and it is much better than likely?' (Gaskell 1975 [1857]: 325). At last she had a real occupation, and Charlotte stuck to it. She stuck to it while Branwell drugged himself to oblivion, while Emily and Anne became ill and died, while her father demanded attention. In 1848–9, now the only one left, she wrote *Shirley* without the encouragement of her sisters, but with the consciousness of a place in the writing world. From the dreary home at Haworth she made occasional visits to London, the Lake District and Scotland and to see new friends Thackeray, G. H. Lewes, Harriet Martineau and Elizabeth Gaskell among them. To Gaskell she sent a copy of *Poems* saying of her own: 'Mine are chiefly juvenile productions, the restless effervescence of a mind that would not be still...' (Gaskell 1975 [1857]: 422). *Villette* was begun in 1853 while she was experiencing increasing weakness and depression. In December 1852 Arthur Bell Nicholls, her father's curate, proposed marriage. Patrick was adamantly against any change and Charlotte refused. But by April 1854 Patrick's continuing dependency, Charlotte's own illness, and Arthur's assurance that he would assist in her father's care, altered matters. They were married in June 1854 and Arthur moved into the parsonage as Charlotte's husband. In January 1855, pregnant, and suffering from extreme nausea, Charlotte stopped eating. She died in March of exhaustion and starvation.

Charlotte Brontë was a Romantic poet who learnt to distrust both Romanticism and poetry. Her early writings were clearly influenced by the work of Byron, Wordsworth and Shelley, but she put these away with other childish passions when she began, in the 1830s, to practise the self-control and discipline which dominated her life. Unlike either Emily or Anne, Charlotte mainly stopped writing poetry after her success with prose. Only the two poems written on the deaths of her sisters would seem to date from her later years. It is as though her governing set of dualities, passion versus reason, excitement versus duty, ambition versus home, also revealed themselves in her attitude to poetry. Prose, by contrast, was 'something cool and unromantic as Monday morning' (Brontë 1849: 3).

In terms of her technical faculty Brontë's poetry is not as innovative as Emily's, or as neatly achieved as Anne's. There is none of the rapid transfer from concrete to imaginary which characterizes Emily's work, nor is there the rational unfolding of argument which dignifies Anne's. Charlotte's poetry is quite ragged in comparison, but it is still powerful, mainly because it enacts the struggle between her early Romantic inclinations and her later Victorian suppressions. 'Unloved I love, unwept I weep' – typically called 'Reason' in the 1846 collection – sets out in classic Charlotte style the excesses of feeling in fervent excited language, only to pull that feeling sharply back into line with ordering discourses; 'Come Reason—Science—Learning—Thought— / To you my poor heart I dedicate'.

In 'Obscure and little seen my way' Brontë's poetic vocabulary is the same as that found in *Jane Eyre* and the situation observed here is close to the picture of Jane in the novel. But, as it is a poem about the speaker observing her own self, it resembles Anne's 'Self-Congratulation', and the 'mirror' poems of other writers who come both before and after Brontë such as Lindsay's 'To My Own Face', Webster's 'By the Looking-Glass' and Probyn's 'The Model'. All these recognize, as Brontë herself does, the dictates and constrictions in the socialization of women in the nineteenth century.

'My Dreams' ('Again I find myself alone') is also reminiscent of Brontë's novels but mainly in terms of the imaginative lives of Jane Eyre or Lucy Snowe. The weird and mysterious landscapes it presents appear vividly, for instance, in the pictures which Jane paints, or in the lurid fantasies of Lucy's dreams. In part, these are obviously Angrian landscapes, derived from Brontë's knowledge of the apocalyptic scenes painted by John Martin. But this is also a fantasized Italy and, as with other women poets (Hemans, who imagined it; Barrett Browning who knew it) this exotic, exaggerated, foreign place is a sensuous female world which offers an escape, an other world, where new freedoms might be explored. Difference and alienation are also the themes in 'Is this my tomb, this humble stone'. Like many of Rossetti's poems, but particularly the Song 'When I am dead, my dearest', the speaker in this poem is dead and yet alive, a ghost who haunts her self and judges her life. There is an eerie freedom in this situation and the bold alliance with nature scorns the meek fears of the merely living. Yet this is also a poem about the aspiration to write vivid poetry, and a poem of regret for all that the 'fettered tongue' might yet be able to utter in other, more mystic conditions. By the end of the poem the 'whole rich song divine' has at least been powerfully imagined, even if the speaker, constrained by context and time, ends up buried alive.

M.R.

Brontë, Charlotte (1846) *Poems by Currer, Ellis and Acton Bell*, London.
—— (1847) *Jane Eyre*, London.
—— (1849) *Shirley*, London.
—— (1855) *Villette*, London.
—— (1850) Biographical Notice of Ellis and Acton Bell, second edition of Emily Brontë's *Wuthering Heights*, London.
—— (1984) *The Poems of Charlotte Brontë: A New Annotated and Enlarged Edition of the Shakespeare Head Brontë*, ed. Tom Winnifrith, Oxford, The Shakespeare Head Press and Basil Blackwell.
Alexander, Christine (1983) *The Early Writings of Charlotte Brontë*, Oxford Blackwell.
Armstrong, Isabel (1993) *Victorian Poetry: Poetry, Poetics and Politics*, Routledge, London and New York.
Fraser, Rebecca (1988) *Charlotte Brontë*, London, Methuen.

Gaskell, Elizabeth (1975) [1857] *The Life of Charlotte Brontë*, Harmondsworth, Penguin.

Gérin, Winifred (1967) *Charlotte Brontë: The Evolution of Genius*, Oxford, Oxford University Press.

Gordon, Lyndall (1994) *Charlotte Brontë: A Passionate Life*, London, Chatto and Windus.

Kucich, John (1985) 'Passionate reserve and reserved passion in the works of Charlotte Brontë', *Journal of English Literary History*, vol. 52, pp. 913–37.

Tayler, Irene (1990) *Holy Ghosts: The Male Muses of Emily and Charlotte Brontë*, New York, Columbia University Press.

Wise, T. J. and Symington, J. A. (1933) *The Brontës: Their Lives, Friendships and Correspondence*, 4 vols, Oxford, Shakespeare Head.

Young Man Naughty's Adventure

Murk was the night: nor star, nor moon,
  Shone in the cloud-wrapped sky,
To break the dull, tenebrous gloom
  Of the arched vault on high,

When Naughty, with his dog and gun,   5
  Walked lonely o'er the moor;
True, the shooting-season had not begun, –
  But poachers commence before!

The howling winds blew fierce around,
  The rain drove in his face;   10
And, as Naughty heard the hollow sound,
  He quickened his creeping pace.

For as each hoarse sepulchral blast
  Drew slow and solemn near,
It seemed like spirits sailing past   15
  To his affrighted ear.

For he was on a dreadful errand bent
  To the ancient witch of the moor;
A delegate by his comrades sent
  To consult the beldam hoar.   20

Now yelled the wind with more terrible din,
  Now rattled the rain full fast;
And, noiselessly gliding, forms were seen,
  As around his eyes he cast;

When a rustling sound in the heather he heard: 25
  Starting, he turned about;
Was it a spirit? Was it a bird?
  No! a hare sprang trembling out.

The shot went 'Whizz!' and the gun went 'Bang!'
  A flash illumined the air;   30
Far and wide the moor with the echo rang
  As down dropped the luckless hare.

He ran to the spot, and, lo! there lay
  A woman on the hard heath-bed,
Whose soul had left its breathless clay,   35
  For the witch of the moor was dead!

The Lonely Lady

She was alone that evening – and alone
  She had been all that heavenly summer day.
She scarce had seen a face, or heard a tone
  And quietly the hours had slipped away,
Their passage through the silence hardly known   5
  Save when the clock with silver chime did say
The number of the hour, and all in peace
Listened to hear its own vibration cease.

Wearied with airy task, with tracing flowers
  Of snow on lace, with singing hymn or song   10
With trying all her harp's symphonious powers
  By striking full its quivering strings along,
And drawing out deep chords, and shaking showers
  Of brilliant sound, from shell and wires among,
Wearied with reading books, weary with weeping,   15
Heart-sick of Life, she sought for death in sleeping.

She lay down on her couch – but could she sleep?
  Could she forget existence in a dream
That blotting out reality might sweep
  Over her weariness, the healing stream   20
Of hope and hope's fruition? – Lo the deep
  And amber glow of that departing beam
Shot from that blood-red sun – points to her brow
Straight like a silent index, mark it now

Kindling her perfect features, bringing bloom   25
  Into the living marble, smooth and bright
As sculptured effigy on hallowed tomb
  Glimmering amid the dimmed and solemn light
  Native to Gothic pile – so wan, so white
In shadow gleamed that face, in rosy flush   30
Of setting sun, rich with a living blush.

Up rose the lonely lady, and her eyes
   Instinctive raised their fringe of raven shade
And fixed upon those vast and glorious skies
   Their lustre that in death alone might fade.   35
Skies fired with crimson clouds, burning with dyes
   Intense as blood – they arched above and rayed
The firmament with broad and vivid beams
That seemed to bend towards her all their gleams.

It was the arc of battle, leagues away   40
   In the direction of that setting sun
An army saw that livid summer day
   Closing their serried ranks and squared upon,
Saw it with awe, so deeply was the ray,
   The last ray tinged with blood – so wild it shone,   45
So strange the semblance gory, burning, given
To pool and stream and sea by that red heaven.

My Dreams

Again I find myself alone, and ever
   The same voice like an oracle begins
Its vague and mystic strain, forgetting never
   Reproaches for a hundred hidden sins,
And setting mournful penances in sight,   5
Terrors and tears for many a watchful night.

Fast change the scenes upon me all the same,
   In hue and drift the regions of a land
Peopled with phantoms, and how dark their aim
   As each dim guest lifts up its shadowy hand   10
And parts its veil to shew one withering look,
That mortal eye may scarce unblighted brook.

I try to find a pleasant path to guide
   To fairer scenes – but still they end in gloom;
The wilderness will open dark and wide   15
   As the sole vista to a vale of bloom,
Of rose and elm and verdure – as these fade
Their sere leaves fall on yonder sandy shade.

My dreams, the Gods of my religion, linger
   In foreign lands, each sundered from his own,   20
And there has passed a cold destroying finger
   O'er every image, and each sacred tone
Sounds low and at a distance, sometimes dying
Like an uncertain sob, or smothered sighing.

Sea-locked, a cliff surrounded, or afar   25
   Asleep upon a fountain's marble brim –
Asleep in heart, though yonder early star,
   The first that lit its taper soft and dim
By the great shrine of heaven, has fixed his eye
Unsmiling though unsealed on that blue sky.   30

Left by the sun, as he is left by hope:
   Bowed in dark, placid cloudlessness above,
As silent as the Island's palmy slope,
   All beach untrodden, all unpeopled grove,
A spot to catch each moonbeam as it smiled   35
Towards that thankless deep so wide and wild.

Thankless he too looks up, no grateful bliss
   Stirs him to feel the twilight-breeze diffuse
Its balm that bears in every spicy kiss
   The mingled breath of southern flowers and dews,   40
Cool and delicious as the fountain's spray
Showered on the shining pavement where he lay.

'Obscure and little seen my way'

Obscure and little seen my way
   Through life has ever been,
But winding from my earliest day
   Through many a wondrous scene.
None ever asked what feelings moved   5
   My heart, or flushed my cheek,
And if I hoped, or feared or loved
   No voice was heard to speak.

I watched, I thought, I studied long,
The crowds I moved unmarked among,   10
I nought to them and they to me
But shapes of strange variety.
The Great with all the elusive shine
Of power and wealth and lofty line
I long have marked and well I know.   15

'Is this my tomb, this humble stone'

Is this my tomb, this humble stone
   Above this narrow mound?
Is this my resting place, so lone,
   So green, so quiet round?

Not even a stately tree to shade 5
 The sunbeam from my bed,
Not even a flower in tribute laid
 As sacred to the dead.

I look along those evening hills,
 As mute as earth may be, 10
I hear not even the voice of rills —
 Not even a cloud I see.
How long is it since human tread
 Was heard on that dim track
Which, through the shadowy valleys led, 15
 Winds far, and farther back?

And was I not a lady once,
 My home a princely hall?
And did not hundreds make response
 Whene'er I deigned to call? 20
Methinks, as in a doubtful dream,
 That dwelling proud I see
Where I caught first the early beam
 Of being's day's spring face.

Methinks the flash is round me still 25
 Of mirrors broad and bright;
Methinks I see the torches fill
 My chambers with their light,
And o'er my limbs the draperies flow
 All gloss and silken shine, 30
On my cold brow the jewels glow
 As bright as festal wine.

Who then disrobed that worshipped form?
 Who wound this winding sheet?
Who turned the blood that ran so warm 35
 To Winter's frozen sleet?
O can it be that many a sun
 Has set, as that sets now,
Since last its fervid lustre shone
 Upon my living brow? 40

Have all the wild dark clouds of night
 Each eve for years drawn on
While I interred so far from light
 Have slumbered thus alone?
Has this green mound been wet with rain — 45
 Such rain as storms distil

When the wind's high and warning strain
  Swells loud on sunless hill?

And I have slept where roughest hind
  Had shuddered to pass by,   50
And no dread did my spirit find
  In all that snow-racked sky,
Though shook the iron-rails around
  As, swept by deepened breeze,
They gave a strange and hollow sound   55
  That living veins might freeze.

O was that music like my own? –
  Such as I used to play
When soft and clear and holy shone
  The summer moon's first ray,   60
And saw me lingering still to feel
  The influence of that sky?
O words may not the peace reveal
  That filled its concave high,

As rose and bower how far beneath   65
  Hung down o'ercharged with dew,
And sighed their sweet and fragrant breath
  To every gale that blew
The hour for music, but in vain,
  Each ancient stanza rose   70
To lips that could not with their strain
  Break Earth's and Heaven's repose.

Yet first a note and then a line
  The fettered tongue would say,
And then the whole rich song divine   75
  Found free a gushing way.
Past, lost, forgotten, I am here,
  They dug my chamber deep,
I know no hope, I feel no fear,
  I sleep – how calm I sleep!   80

The Orphan Child

My feet they are sore, and my limbs they are weary;
  Long is the way, and the mountains are wild;
Soon will the twilight close moonless and dreary
  Over the path of the poor orphan child.

Why did they send me so far and so lonely,   5
  Up where the moors spread and grey rocks are piled?

Men are hard-hearted, and kind angels only
   Watch o'er the steps of a poor orphan child.

Yet distant and soft the night-breeze is blowing,
   Clouds there are none, and clear stars beam mild;   10
God, in His mercy, protection is showing,
   Comfort and hope to the poor orphan child.

Even should I fall o'er the broken bridge passing,
   Or stray in the marshes, by false lights beguiled,
Still will my Father, with promise and blessing,   15
   Take to His bosom the poor orphan child.

There is a thought that for strength should avail me,
   Though both of shelter and kindred despoiled:
Heaven is a home, and a rest will not fail me;
   God is a friend to the poor orphan child.   20

'Like wolf – and black bull or goblin hound'

Like wolf – and black bull or goblin hound,
   Or come in guise of spirit
With wings and long wet waving hair
And at the fire its locks will dry,
   Which will be certain sign   5
That one beneath the roof must die
   Before the year's decline
Forget not now what I have said,
   Sit there till we return.
The hearth is hot – watch well the bread   10
   Lest haply it may burn.

Pilate's Wife's Dream

I've quenched my lamp, I struck it in that start
   Which every limb convulsed, I heard it fall –
The crash blent with my sleep, I saw depart
   Its light, even as I woke, on yonder wall;
Over against my bed, there shone a gleam   5
Strange, faint, and mingling also with my dream.

It sunk, and I am wrapt in utter gloom;
   How far is night advanced, and when will day
Re-tinge the dusk and livid air with bloom,
   And fill this void with warm, creative ray?   10
Would I could sleep again till, clear and red,
Morning shall on the mountain-tops be spread!

I'd call my women, but to break their sleep,
    Because my own is broken, were unjust;
They've wrought all day, and well-earned slumbers steep   15
    Their labours in forgetfulness, I trust;
Let me my feverish watch with patience bear,
Thankful that none with me its sufferings share.

Yet Oh! for light! one ray would tranquillize
    My nerves, my pulses, more than effort can;   20
I'll draw my curtain and consult the skies:
    These trembling stars at dead of night look wan,
Wild, restless, strange, yet cannot be more drear
Than this my couch, shared by a nameless fear.

All black — one great cloud, drawn from east to west,   25
    Conceals the heavens, but there are lights below;
Torches burn in Jerusalem, and cast
    On yonder stony mount a lurid glow.
I see men stationed there, and gleaming spears;
A sound, too, from afar, invades my ears.   30

Dull, measured strokes of axe and hammer ring
    From street to street, not loud, but through the night
Distinctly heard — and some strange spectral thing
    Is now upreared — and, fixed against the light
Of the pale lamps; defined upon that sky,   35
It stands up like a column, straight and high.

I see it all — I know the dusky sign —
    A cross on Calvary, which Jews uprear
While Romans watch; and when the dawn shall shine
    Pilate, to judge the victim, will appear,   40
Pass sentence — yield Him up to crucify;
And on that cross the spotless Christ must die.

Dreams, then, are true — for thus my vision ran;
    Surely some oracle has been with me,
The gods have chosen me to reveal their plan,   45
    To warn an unjust judge of destiny:
I, slumbering, heard and saw; awake I know,
Christ's coming death, and Pilate's life of woe.

I do not weep for Pilate — who could prove
    Regret for him whose cold and crushing sway   50
No prayer can soften, no appeal can move;
    Who tramples hearts as others trample clay,
Yet with a faltering, an uncertain tread,
That might stir up reprisal in the dead.

Forced to sit by his side and see his deeds;   55
  Forced to behold that visage, hour by hour,
In whose gaunt lines the abhorrent gazer reads
  A triple lust of gold, and blood, and power;
A soul whom motives fierce, yet abject, urge –
Rome's servile slave, and Judah's tyrant scourge.   60

How can I love, or mourn, or pity him?
  I, who so long my fettered hands have wrung;
I, who for grief have wept my eyesight dim;
  Because, while life for me was bright and young,
He robbed my youth – he quenched my life's fair ray –   65
He crushed my mind, and did my freedom slay.

And at this hour – although I be his wife –
  He has no more of tenderness from me
Than any other wretch of guilty life;
  Less, for I know his household privacy –   70
I see him as he is – without a screen;
And, by the gods, my soul abhors his mien!

Has he not sought my presence, dyed in blood –
  Innocent, righteous blood, shed shamelessly?
And have I not his red salute withstood?   75
  Ay, when, as erst, he plunged all Galilee
In dark bereavement – in affliction sore,
Mingling their very offerings with their gore.

Then came he – in his eyes a serpent-smile,
  Upon his lips some false, endearing word,   80
And, through the streets of Salem, clanged the while
  His slaughtering, hacking, sacrilegious sword –
And I, to see a man cause men such woe,
Trembled with ire I did not fear to show.

And now the envious Jewish priests have brought   85
  Jesus – whom they in mockery call their king –
To have, by this grim power, their vengeance wrought:
  By this mean reptile, innocence to sting.
Oh! could I but the purposed doom avert,
And shield the blameless head from cruel hurt!   90

Accessible is Pilate's heart to fear,
  Omens will shake his soul, like autumn leaf;
Could he this night's appalling vision hear,
  This just man's bonds were loosed, his life were safe,
Unless that bitter priesthood should prevail,   95
And make even terror to their malice quail.

Yet if I tell the dream – but let me pause.
  What dream? Erewhile the characters were clear,
Graved on my brain – at once some unknown cause
  Has dimmed and rased the thoughts, which now appear,   100
Like a vague remnant of some by-past scene; –
Not what will be, but what, long since, has been.

I suffered many things – I heard foretold
  A dreadful doom for Pilate, – lingering woes,
In far barbarian climes, where mountains cold   105
  Built up a solitude of trackless snows:
There he and grisly wolves prowled side by side,
There he lived famished – there, methought, he died;

But not of hunger, nor by malady;
  I saw the snow around him, stained with gore;   110
I said I had no tears for such as he,
  And lo! my cheek is wet – mine eyes run o'er.
I weep for mortal suffering, mortal guilt,
I weep the impious deed, the blood self-spilt.

More I recall not, yet the vision spread   115
  Into a world remote, an age to come –
And still the illumined name of Jesus shed
  A light, a clearness through the unfolding gloom –
And still I saw that sign which now I see,
That cross on yonder brow of Calvary.   120

What is this Hebrew Christ? – to me unknown
  His lineage – doctrine – mission; yet how clear
Is god-like goodness is his actions shewn,
  How straight and stainless in his life's career!
The ray of Deity that rests on him,   125
In my eyes makes Olympian glory dim.

The world advances; Greek or Roman rite
  Suffices not the inquiring mind to stay;
The searching soul demands a purer light
  To guide it on its upward, onward way;   130
Ashamed of sculptured gods, Religion turns
To where the unseen Jehovah's altar burns.

Our faith is rotten, all our rites defiled,
  Our temples sullied, and, methinks, this Man,
With His new ordinance, so wise and mild,   135
  Is come, even as He says, the chaff to fan
And sever from the wheat; but will His faith
Survive the terrors of to-morrow's death?

I feel a firmer trust – a higher hope
   Rise in my soul – it dawns with dawning day;   140
Lo! on the Temple's roof – on Moriah's slope
   Appears at length that clear and crimson ray
Which I so wished for when shut in by night;
Oh, opening skies, I hail, I bless your light!

Part, clouds and shadows! Glorious Sun, appear!   145
   Part, mental gloom! Come, insight from on high!
Dusk dawn in heaven still strives with daylight clear,
   The longing soul doth still uncertain sigh.
Oh! to behold the truth – that sun divine,
How doth my bosom pant, my spirit pine!   150

This day, Time travails with a mighty birth;
This day, Truth stoops from heaven and visits earth;
Ere night descends I shall more surely know
What guide to follow, in what path to go;
I wait in hope – I wait in solemn fear,   155
The oracle of God – the sole – true God – to hear.

Reason

Unloved I love, unwept I weep,
   Grief I restrain, hope I repress;
Vain is this anguish, fixed and deep,
   Vainer desires or means[1] of bliss.

My life is cold, love's fire being dead;   5
   That fire self-kindled, self-consumed;
What living warmth erewhile it shed,
   Now to how drear extinction doomed!

Devoid of charm how could I dream
   My unasked love would e'er return?   10
What fate, what influence lit the flame
   I still feel inly, deeply burn?

Alas! there are those who should not love;
   I to this dreary band belong;
This knowing let me henceforth prove   15
   Too wise to list delusion's song.

No, Syren! Beauty is not mine;
   Affection's joy I ne'er shall know;

---

[1] ?dreams

Lonely will be my life's decline,
  Even as my youth is lonely now.   20

Come Reason – Science – Learning – Thought –
  To you my heart I dedicate;
I have a faithful subject brought:
  Faithful because most desolate.

Fear not a wandering, feeble mind: 25
  Stern Sovereign, it is all your own
To crush, to cheer, to loose, to bind;
  Unclaimed, unshared, it seeks your throne.

Soft may the breeze of summer blow,
  Sweetly its sun in valleys shine;   30
All earth around with love may glow, –
  No warmth shall reach this heart of mine.

Vain boast and false! Even now the fire
  Though smothered, slacked, repelled, is burning
At my life's source; and stronger, higher,   35
  Waxes the spirit's trampled yearning.

It wakes but to be crushed again:
  Faint I will not, nor yield to sorrow;
Conflict and force will quell the brain;
  Doubt not I shall be strong to-morrow.   40

Have I not fled that I may conquer?
  Crost the dark sea in firmest faith
That I at last might plant my anchor
  Where love cannot prevail to death?

On the Death of Emily Jane Brontë

My darling, thou wilt never know
The grinding agony of woe
  That we have borne for thee.
Thus may we consolation tear
E'en from the depth of our despair   5
  And wasting misery.

The nightly anguish thou art spared
When all the crushing truth is bared
  To the awakening mind,
When the galled heart is pierced with grief,   10
Till wildly it implores relief,
  But small relief can find.

Nor know's thou what it is to lie
Looking forth with streaming eye
   On life's lone wilderness.   15
'Weary, weary, dark and drear,
How shall I the journey bear,
   The burden and distress?'

Then since thou art spared such pain
We will not wish thee here again;   20
   He that lives must mourn.
God help us through our misery
And give us rest and joy with thee
   When we reach our bourne!

On the Death of Anne Brontë

There's little joy in life for me,
   And little terror in the grave;
I've lived the parting hour to see
   Of one I would have died to save.

Calmly to watch the failing breath,   5
   Wishing each sigh might be the last;
Longing to see the shade of death
   O'er those belovèd features cast.

The cloud, the stillness that must part
   The darling of my life from me;   10
And then to thank God from my heart,
   To thank Him well and fervently;

Although I knew that we had lost
   The hope and glory of our life;
And now, benighted, tempest-tossed,   15
   Must bear alone the weary strife.

Isa Blagden (1816?–1873)

An important figure in the English community at Florence where she settled in 1849, very little is known about Isa Blagden before that date. The register of the Protestant cemetery in Florence gives her father's name as Thomas and her nationality as Swiss, but rumours in Florence gave her a more romantic heritage as the illegitimate daughter of an English father and Indian mother. Boase's *Dictionary of Literary Biography* gives her name as 'Isabella Jane' but there is no other source for this.

From 1850 onwards Isa was particularly close to the Brownings and it was to her that Robert turned after Elizabeth's death when she accompanied him and his son Pen to their new home in England. Her other friends included Theodosia Trollope and the American sculptor Harriet Hosmer. There seems to have been a brief romantic attachment to Robert Lytton who later became Viceroy of India, but nothing came of this. Otherwise, Isa Blagden lived in Florence, nursed her friends when need arose, travelled in Europe and wrote novels, mainly under the pseudonym of 'Ivory Beryl' to supplement her meagre income.

She was universally beloved and seemed to have a gift for making others happy and comfortable even though she described her own life as 'one long disappointment'. Her caring disposition extended to both human and animal strays, as Alfred Austin recalled.

I remember her writing to me in 1866, after a visit she had paid to Venice, and in the letter she described how she had rescued a poor poodle from the clutches of some boys, who, after shaving it till it resembled a white rat, were about to drown it in the Grand Canal. She took it back to Florence with her, and christened it after the Queen of the Adriatic: 'and thus', she added, 'I hear Venezia, Venezia, all day long.' Another member of the canine saved, a truly friendly fellow, was christened 'Keeley, or the low comedian', for his singularly unaristocratic, not to say comic appearance. A highly unpopular member of her dog community was 'Teddie' who scrapped at the whole world except its dear mistress . . .

One year when she spent the hot summer months at the Bagni di Lucca, she made the entire journey at considerable expense, by *vetturino* [coach and horses], because the 'Livorno–Empoli–Firenze' railway line would not allow her to have her dogs in the railway carriage with her . . .' (Blagden 1873: xxii–xxiii).

After Blagden's death in 1873 her manuscript poems were collected by Mme Linda (White) Mazini who asked the poet Alfred Austin to prepare an edition of them for the press. Robert Browning refused to subscribe to the volume because, much as he cared for Isa, he also hated Austin. In his memoir, Austin, who had met Isa in 1865, wrote of her work: 'Her real genius and strength lay, I am persuaded, in poetical composition. Such, too was her own conviction; and it is to be regretted that, what ever her other moral qualities, she lacked the solidity and continuity of purpose to devote herself wholly to the service of the Muses' (Blagden 1873: viii).

However convinced Austin may have been about her poetic faculty Blagden's poems do adopt conventional forms and prosaic sentiments, though they are not 'tiresome and unpalatable' as Edward McAleer described them (McAleer; 1951, xxix). Her one really interesting poem, 'To George Sand on her Interview with Elizabeth Barrett Browning', was inspired by Elizabeth's account of that meeting which took place in 1852: 'She received us very kindly, with hand stretched out, which I, with a natural emotion (I assure you my heart beat), stooped and kissed, when she said quickly, 'Mais non, je ne veux pas,' and kissed my lips . . .' (Kenyon 1897: II, 55).

Blagden's vision of the contrast between the two women, a saintly Elizabeth and a lurid George Sand, is forgivable given her partisan feelings, but it is also an amusing example of the high Victorian notion of the Virgin and Whore dichotomy.

M.R.

Blagden, Isa (1873) *Poems by Isa Blagden*, with a memoir by Alfred Austin, Edinburgh.

Kenyon, Frederic G. ed. (1897) *The Letters of Elizabeth Barrett Browning*, 2 vols, London.
McAleer, Edward C. ed. (1951) *Dearest Isa: Robert Browning's Letters to Isabella Blagden*, Austin, Tex. and Edinburgh, University of Texas Press.

To George Sand on her Interview with Elizabeth Barrett Browning

The late repentance, and the long despair,
The sin-bound soul's fierce struggle to be free,
A fettered maniac raging in her lair
    Are thine!

A life all musical with happy love,
An angel child who sings beside her knee,   5
Pulses which true to heavenly rhythms move,
    Are hers!

Dark hair strained backwards from a forehead broad,
Dark eyes, in whose chill light strange secrets live,
As in the deep grim monsters watch and ward,
    Are thine!

Soft curls which droop around an oval cheek,   10
Calm brows where holy thought has power to give
Transfigured glory to a woman meek,
    Are hers!

Her childhood smileth still around her mouth –
O'er thy white gleaming teeth, thy full lips part –
Eager for joys which may renew thy youth;   15
Some brief wild rapture which may cheat, yet warm,
Kindling the languor of a hopeless heart.
With thee life stagnates, or is flashing storm.

To shapeless horrors thou hast given name,
And woes, 'neath which poor tortured hearts had bowed   20
And borne till now in trembling patient shame,
Rose at thy call, and spoke their loud despair,
And women's wrongs, like opened graves, avowed
Their stark foul secrets to the startled air!

Thou wert Deliverer, but Victim too,   25
Th' avenger ever wears the martyr's palm;
It is the Orestes whom the fiends pursue –
Alone to foredoomed Hamlet's vengeful eyes

(While sleep the murtherous pair in guilty calm)
The spectre frowns, the boding shadows rise.   30

Stern as that voice which in the desert cried
Majestic prophecy and mystic woe,
And poured its warnings o'er the Jordan's tide –
Thou, 'mid the dreary wilderness of life,
With bleeding feet and burning soul didst go,   35
And flung thyself into th' arena's strife.

Naked and hungered, with what bitter scorn,
Banned from sweet charities of earth and sky,
By passions and impulsive senses torn,
At earthly banquets, poisonous yet sweet,   40
Didst thou thy Nature's ruthless wants supply,
Earth's locusts and its bitter honey eat!

Like forkèd tongues of fire round blackened wood
That leave charred ashes where was glowing flame,
Thy lurid idols made thy heart their food   45
And ruined and consumed it evermore,
And powerless now the best belovèd name
That cold dead heart to kindle or restore.

And therefore wears thy brow its sullen scorn,
And therefore glooms thy large prophetic eye,   50
And in thy song are cadences forlorn,
Which blend their sighs with lingering echoes fine
Of thrilling sweetness, yet of agony –
Grand revelations, utterances divine.

Not thus her song. The seraph chorus bowed   55
And leant entranced from jasper thrones to hear
A mortal's voice so nigh the throne of God.
Its rich Hellenic harmonies had power
Of wide reverberation far and near.
A woman's witness to her God they bore!   60

Amid the world's wild roar, that tender song,
Throughout its jarring discords heard between,
Rung out heroic protest against wrong.
Where coward souls had recklessly despaired,
That dove-like heart with fortitude serene   65
Through Sorrow's whelming flood victorious dared,

And won Faith's vernal promise; glowing words
Revealed eternal hopes, and music fraught
Ravished the silences with sweet accords.

Upon her lips the altar's living coal   70
With cherub glories circled mortal thought,
And birth consummate stirred within her soul.

Genius, God-born, full filled its worshipper,
And flowed God-voiced, as flows the sacred river,
Through holy places ever and for ever!   75
Mild guardian angels smiled above her head,
And round her hearth their shelt'ring pinions spread,
And o'er that face beloved a halo shed!

She came! – the tumult of thy soul subsided,
As erst beside the Gate called Beautiful,   80
A shining Angel o'er the waters glided.
Lo! the dark stream became a fountain blessed –
So did her presence all thy being lull,
As to thy lip that purest lip was pressed.

Thy genius to her stainless genius knelt,   85
And with pathetic reverential awe
The holiness of womanhood was felt
Deep in thy soul; to thee, she was a shrine
Of sanctuary – inexorable law –
The earthly human won to God's divine!   90

Ah! by that healing kiss, be thou assoiled!
The radiant Twins whose joys in Heaven are shown
(The Mortal and Immortal), thus uncoiled
The death-doom which was long the curse of One.
She, by that love which pressed to thine embrace,   95
By her own star-crowned soul has claimed thy place.

Frances Brown(e) (1816–1879)

Famous for a time as 'the Blind Poetess of Ulster', Frances's great-grandfather had
been a man of considerable property which he squandered so that her father was no
more than the village postmaster in Stranolar, County Donegal. She was the seventh
of twelve children and, suffering from smallpox at eighteen months, she was left
permanently blind. Frances received no formal schooling as a result, but listening
attentively while her brothers were learning their lessons suggested to her the idea of
persuading them to read aloud to her. In this way she became acquainted with the
whole of Hume's *History of England* and the twenty-one volumes of *Ancient Universal
History*, bribing her youthful assistants with promises of storytelling in return. Once
competent in knowledge, she assisted a younger sister in her schooling and trained her
to act as her guide and amanuensis. Frances began to write – or rather dictate – poems
in her seventh year. But when she was fifteen a friend lent her a copy of Homer and

a copy of Byron's *Childe Harold*. So disgusted was she at the comparative quality of her own meagre efforts that Frances destroyed all her manuscript writings and resolved to write no more. Then in about 1840 Frances heard some Irish poems which encouraged her to try again and to send contributions to the *Irish Penny Journal* and later to the *Athenaeum*. Through the interest of its editor Frances was awarded a literary pension of £20 per annum after the publication of *The Star of Attéghéi* in 1844. Frances began to write regularly for magazines and in 1847 she moved to Edinburgh and then, in 1852 to London in order to be in the thick of literary life. Like other 'working-class' or underprivileged poets such as Eliza Cook or Ellen Johnston, the chief charm for contemporary readers of Brown's poetry was not so much how well it was done, but that it was done at all. Under this flag she made a name for herself acquiring patrons, notably Lord Lansdown, and a wide admiring audience:

> Few episodes are to be met with in the range of metaphysical history more interesting than the life of this true poetess, who, debarred by an early visitation of Providence from participating in the active duties of the outer world, has worked out for herself a noble vocation in the inner sphere of thought. More eloquent, surely, of the power of mind than the deeds of the world's heroes, is the conquest of knowledge and wisdom by this lonely girl, under circumstances which would have doomed a less finely-constituted temperament to life-long darkness and inactivity...' (anon. *Men of the Time*, Appendix, Women of the Time, 1856).

Brown is a good storyteller and her early necessity clearly provided her with an excellent training. Her stories and novels for children were hugely popular, and her tales in *Granny's Wonderful Chair* (1857) have a curious subsequent history. When quite a young child this was the favourite book of the writer Frances Hodgson Burnett. But she lost her copy and could not discover the author. Years later when she was approached by a magazine for some children's stories, she decided to retell these lost tales of her youth and was charged with plagiarism until the error was revealed. Just as Brown's stories generally weave around some folk theme or tale, so her poetry from 1844 on tends to focus on some theme from, or reference to history, or legend whether the life of Napoleon, or the Irish tales of her youth. 'The Australian Emigrant' would appear to be based on real-life stories told to Brown by the Irish who left for a better life in the colony, but her curious picture of the woman singer who feels herself without a nationality, without a land, simply because of the disenfranchisement of her sex, is peculiar and original.

M.R.

Brown(e), Frances (1844) *The Star of Attéghéi; The Vision of Schwartz and Other Poems*, London.
—— (1848) *Lyrics and Miscellaneous Poems*, Edinburgh.
—— (1861) *My Share of the World: An Autobiography*, London.

Anon. (1856) *Men of the Time*, London.
Hay, Frances (1885) *Women of the Day*, London.

from *The Australian Emigrant*

A bark went forth, with the morning's smile,
That bore the maids of the western isle
Far, where the southern summers shine
On the glorious world beyond the line.
Theirs was a weary lot of toil,   5
And their hopes were turned to a better soil,
While their tears were shed for the island-shore –
They should look on its greenness never more!

But one was there – who shed no tears! –
A girl, in the blossom of her years; –   10
Yet bloom had she none from the roses caught,
For her cheek was withered with early thought, –
And her young brow bore the written doom
Of a lonely heart and a distant tomb; –
But still, in the light of her starry eye,   15
There shone a glory that could not die!

Silent she gazed on the shore and sea, –
And ever her glance was bright and free,
Like a spirit's, bound by no kindred ties, –
(For she had none beneath the skies!)   20
Till the mountains faded in misty blue, –
And louder the grief around her grew.
Then, turned the maid to that mourning throng, –
And poured the power of her soul in song!

How sadly mixed was that parting strain,   25
That told of the talent given in vain,
And the wisdom born of deep despair: –
With the tone of triumph blending there,
Through faintest fall and through wildest swell
Was heard the voice of the heart's farewell, –   30
As if the dream on her memory hung
Of a wasted love! – and thus she sung: –

'Whence flow these floods of sorrow? –
O, my gentle sisters, tell! –
Do the heart's deep fountains send their streams   35
To bid the land farewell?
Like a shadow passing from us
Is each mighty mountain's brow, –
But earth – the wide green earth – is ours, –
We have no country now!   40
But, oh! the old home track,

Where our first affections rest!
Alas! no time shall give them back –
Our earliest and our best!

'Oh! MAN may grieve to sever   45
From the hearth or from the soil, –
For still some hope, some right, was his,
Which lived through want and toil; –
The dwellers of the forest,
THEY may mourn their leafy lair; –   50
But why should WOMAN weep her land?
She has no portion there.
Woe – woe for deeds of worth,
That were only paid with ill! –
For to *her* the homes of earth   55
Are the house of bondage, still!'

Eliza Cook (1817–1889)

The success of Eliza Cook's working life was a peculiarly Victorian phenomonen. She was a working-class poet, self-educated and self-directed, and she made a virtue of this, presenting herself as a poet for the people whose credentials were an innocent wisdom and an honest sentiment. Eliza was the youngest of the eleven children of a respectable working man, a tinman and brazier from Southwark in London. When Eliza was about nine the family moved to a small farm in Sussex. Various stories about the difficulties of Eliza's early life appear in biographical dictionaries published from the middle of the century on. Sarah Hale in *Woman's Record* (1855) said that Eliza's father was of an 'eccentric' turn of mind and would not allow any of his children to take advantage of the educational opportunities offered them. Eliza, however, set about her own education and was encouraged in this by her mother, whom she adored, but who died when Eliza was about fifteen.

Eliza began to write verses at an early age, and her enthusiasm never waned:

My earliest rhymes, written from intuitive impulse, before hackneyed experience or politic judgement could dictate their tendency, were accepted and responded to by those whose good word is a 'tower of strength'. The first active breath of nature that swept over my heart strings, awoke wild but earnest melodies which I dotted down in simple notes; and when I found that others thought the tune worth learning... then I was made to think that my burning desire to pour out my soul's measure of music was given for a purpose. My young bosom throbbed with rapture... when I discovered that I held power over the affections of earth ...' (Cook 5 May 1849: 1).

Eliza's first book was, characteristically, *Lays of a Wild Harp* (1835), and from the 1830s when the family returned to London, Eliza sent numerous poems to literary magazines. These were signed only with initials and the reviewers, congratulating themselves upon the arrival of a new Burns, praised the poems' spontaneity, cheerfulness and wit. When the second edition of her next volume *Melaia, and Other Poems* appeared in 1840 it not only bore her name, but a sumptuous picture, to which Elizabeth Barrett Browning took exception: '. . . a full length of the lady in mourning à la mode & hair a la Brute & a determination of countenance "to be poetical" whatever nature may say to it' (EBB to Mary Russell Mitford, 13 December 1839: EBB 1983: I, 165), a facsimile signature, and a fulsome Preface by the author which showed that her youthful dedication to self-promotion was undimmed: '. . . the fierce malignity of the envious few, and the warm applause of the impartial many, assure me that there is some gold in the dross, which time and experience may refine into purer brilliancy' (ibid., 167).

Eliza and her poems became the rage of London. And William Jerdan, once the supporter, and possibly the lover of L.E.L., took up Eliza's cause in the *Literary Gazette*, and added her to his private collection of 'fair poetic saints' (EBB to MRM, 26 October 1841: EBB 1983: I, 297). Eliza continued to write for the journals with considerable success, but by 1845 she seems to have moved on to a new patron. It is Elizabeth Barrett, always good for a bit of gossip even if she did spend her days on a sofa, who relates the story:

> . . . for her position as governess in Alderman Harmer's family . . . I am *told* that her position in his family is of far tenderer, if of a less moral and didactic a character. *That* is the scandal . . . *a* scandal, perhaps! I will not answer for it or against it – & you have it as a piece of 'telling', just as it came to me. Her poetry, so called, I really cannot admire – though of course she has a *talent* in the way of putting verses together, of a respectable kind (EBB to MRM, 16 August 1845: EBB 1983: III, 136).

Once again, Eliza seems to have found herself a literary champion for in 1840 James Harmer had resigned as an alderman of London in order to become the proprietor of the *Weekly Dispatch* which published many of Eliza's poems.

In 1849 Eliza went into journalism on her own account and established *Eliza Cook's Journal*. It was published weekly at the price of $1\frac{1}{2}$d. and consisted mainly of work by Eliza herself; stories, poems, little morals, essays on contemporary issues and improving editorials with titles ranging from 'The Art of Being Happy' to 'The Health of the Skin' and 'Chemistry in the Kitchen'. The *Journal* achieved a wide circulation, but it ceased publication in 1854, mainly because Eliza was not a good businesswoman and she was then also suffering from ill health. In the 1860s Eliza published another volume of poems and seems to have taken up with yet another knight – in the person of John H. Ingram. He persuaded her to publish *Diamond Dust* (1865) a collection of 'wise saws and modern instances' such as: 'Gray hairs, like honest friends, are plucked out and cast aside for telling unpleasant truths', or 'Man and horse-radish are hottest when rubbed and grated', or 'Soldiers in peace are like chimneys in summer', or, 'Marrying for a home is a most tiresome way of getting a living' (Cook 1865: 47, 79, 154, 145).

Eliza herself was never married. She seems to have held strong views on the degraded position of women within marriage and published many articles on this subject in her *Journal*. She also published at least one defence of the status of 'old maid' which she described as 'one of the favourite subjects on which is exercised the courage

of the coward and the wit of the witless' (Cook 1865: 183). In later life Eliza was
dogged by ill health. She lived with relatives and wrote little, surviving on a Civil List
pension granted her in 1864. By the end of the century her poetry was thoroughly out
of fashion, but even so John H. Ingram attempted to rescue her reputation: 'Adverse
criticism notwithstanding, it may be confidently claimed for Eliza Cook that she was
and is a poet of the people: a poet whose works are filled with sympathy for the
downtrodden and helpless, the earth weary and oppressed. Her works are characterised
by purity of tone, a clearness of expression, and an entire absence of straining for effect
...' (Ingram 1907: 270). He probably thought he was doing her good, but this is really
just another way of saying that Cook's poems are simple. Certainly Barrett Browning
thought so – she wickedly agreed with Mitford that 'Cook' was a very apt name for
the writer of such verses (EBB 1983: I, 170) – and Rossetti thought so too –
challenging her brother to go ahead and just call her 'Eliza Cook' if he thought her
verses were quite that bad (W. M. Rossetti 1903: 88).

There are problems with Cook's verse: its predictable rhyming couplets; its relentless
sentimentality (an extraordinary percentage of her poems have 'old' in the title); its
embarrassing nationalist themes; and its condescending address to the 'little and poor'.
That said, her social poems are effective and add to the group of women writers who
felt it their duty to comment on injustice, whether in 'A Song for the Workers' which
was written in support of the movement to limit the hours of the working day, or
'"Our Father"' which, like Barrett Browning's 'The Cry of the Children' was based
upon R. H. Horne's report on the factory conditions for working children. Poems in
which Cook criticizes society also work well: 'The Song of the Imprisoned Bird'
because it lists the absurd prisons of convention; 'Song of the Modern Time' because
it is a funny mockery of middle-class pretension. There are occasions too when
Cook takes on subjects not generally found in verse: her 'The Surgeon's Knife' is
astonishingly gory and forthright given that she writes of an age without anaesthetics,
and her 'The Song of the Ugly Maiden' or 'The Idiot-Born' show how willing she was
to tackle difficult subjects, even if she does then make them a vehicle for pious
sermonizing. Like other women poets of her generation Cook finds a major theme in
writing about herself *writing* in 'To my Lyre' and 'Lines Suggested by the Song of a
Nightingale', but the latter is intriguing for its quick sketch of the working drudgery of
the writer's life. As far as more personal poems are concerned, Cook writes two poems
to the American actress Charlotte Cushman (only 'To Charlotte Cushman, Seeing her
Play "Bianca" is included here). Eliza obviously knew Charlotte Cushman well and the
actress's well-known lesbian associations with 'emancipated' women such as Matilda
Hays and Harriet Hosmer, has led to some recent speculation about Eliza's sexuality.
But Cook's love poems, if they can be so called, seem to be heterosexual and most of
them are addressed 'To—'. They also tend to a distinctive bitterness exemplified by
her short stanza 'On Seeing a Bird-Catcher', and poems such as ' 'Tis Well to Wake
the Theme of Love', where love is no pleasure but only torture, may reflect on her
disappointed attitudes to marriage and romance.

M.R.

Cook, Eliza (1849–1854) *Eliza Cook's Journal*, London.
—— (1874) *The Poetical Works of Eliza Cook*, Complete Edition, London.
—— (1865) *Diamond Dust*, London.

Barrett Browning, Elizabeth (1983) *The Letters of Elizabeth Barrett Browning to Mary Russell Mitford: 1836–1854*, 3 vols, eds Meredith B. Raymond and Mary Rose Sullivan, Winfield, Kan., Wedgestone Press.

Ingram, John H. (1907) *Poets of the Nineteenth Century*, London.

Rossetti, William Michael (1903) *Rossetti Papers: 1862 to 1870*, London, Sands.

The Old Arm-Chair

I love it, I love it; and who shall dare
To chide me for loving that old Arm-chair?
I've treasured it long as a sainted prize;
I've bedewed it with tears, and embalmed it with sighs.
'Tis bound by a thousand bands to my heart;   5
Not a tie will break, not a link will start.
Would ye learn the spell? – a mother sat there;
And a sacred thing is that old Arm-chair.

In Childhood's hour I lingered near
The hallowed seat with listening ear;   10
And gentle words that mother would give;
To fit me to die, and teach me to live.
She told me shame would never betide,
With truth for my creed and God for my guide;
She taught me to lisp my earliest prayer;   15
As I knelt beside that old Arm-chair.

I sat and watched her many a day,
When her eye grew dim, and her locks were grey:
And I almost worshipped her when she smiled,
And turned from her Bible, to bless her child.   20
Years rolled on; but the last one sped –
My idol was shattered; my earth-star fled:
I learnt how much the heart can bear,
When I saw her die in that old Arm-chair.

'Tis past, 'tis past, but I gaze on it now   25
With quivering breath and throbbing brow:
'Twas there she nursed me; 'twas there she died:
And Memory flows with lava tide.
Say it is folly, and deem me weak,
While the scalding drops start down my cheek;   30
But I love it, I love it; and cannot tear
My soul from a mother's old Arm-chair.

Song of the Rushlight

Oh! scorn me not as a fameless thing,
Nor turn with contempt from the song I sing
'Tis true, I am not suffered to be
On the ringing board of wassail glee:
My pallid gleam must never fall   5
In the gay saloon or lordly hall;
But many a tale does the Rushlight know
Of secret sorrow and lonely woe.

I am found in the closely-curtained room,
Where a stillness reigns that breathes of the tomb   10
Where the breaking heart, and heavy eye,
Are waiting to see a loved one die –
Where the doting child with noiseless tread
Steals warily to the mother's bed;
To mark if the faint and struggling breath   15
Is fluttering still in the grasp of Death.

The panting has ceased; the cheek is chill;
And the ear of the child bends closer still.
It rests on the lips, but listens in vain;
For those lips have done with life and pain.   20
I am wildly snatched, and held above
The precious wreck of hope and love:
The work is sealed, for my glimmering ray
Shows a glazing eye, and stiffening clay.

I am the light that quivering flits   25
In the joyless home where the fond wife sits;
Waiting the one that flies his hearth,
For the gambler's dice and drunkard's mirth.
Long hath she kept her wearying watch,
Now bitterly weeping, now breathless to catch   30
The welcome sound of a footstep near,
Till she weeps again, as it dies on her ear.

Her restless gaze, as the night wears late,
Is anxiously thrown on the dial-plate;
And a sob responds to the echoing sound   35
That tells the hand hath gone its round:
She mournfully trims my slender wick,
As she sees me fading and wasting quick;
And many a time has my spark expired,
And left her, still the weeping and tired.   40

I am the light that dimly shines
Where the friendless child of Genius pines –
Where the godlike mind is trampled down
By the callous sneer, and freezing frown.
Where Want is playing a demon part,   45
And sends its iron to the heart, –
Where the soul burns on in the bosom that mourns
Like the incense fire in funeral urns.

I see the hectic fingers fling
The thoughts intense, that flashingly spring;   50
And my flickering beam illumes the page
That may live in the fame of a future age.
I see the pale brow droop and mope,
Till the breast turns sick with blasted hope –
Till the harsh, cold world has done its worst,   55
And the goaded Spirit has groaned and burst.

I am the light that's doomed to share
The meanest lot that man can bear:
I see the scanty portion spread,
Where children struggle for scraps of bread –   60
Where squalid forms and faces seem
Like phantoms in a hideous dream –
Where the soul may look, with startled awe,
On the work of Poverty's vulture-claw.

Many a lesson the bosom learns   65
Of hapless grief while the Rushlight burns;
Many a scene unfolds to me
That the heart of Mercy would bleed to see.
Then scorn me not as a fameless thing,
Nor turn with contempt from the song I sing;   70
But smile as ye will, or scorn as ye may,
There's naught but truth to be found in my lay.

The Idiot-Born

'Out, thou silly moon-struck elf;
Back, poor fool, and hide thyself!'
This is what the wise ones say,
Should the Idiot cross their way:
But if we would closely mark,   5
We should see him not *all* dark;
We should find we must not scorn
The teaching of the Idiot-born.

He will screen the newt and frog;
He will cheer the famished dog;   10
He will seek to share his bread
With the orphan, parish fed:
He will offer up his seat
To the stranger's wearied feet:
Selfish tyrants, do not scorn   15
The teaching of the Idiot-born.

Use him fairly, he will prove
How the simple breast can love;
He will spring with infant glee
To the form he likes to see.   20
Gentle speech, or kindness done;
Truly binds the witless one.
Heartless traitors, do not scorn
The teaching of the Idiot-born.

He will point with vacant stare   25
At the robes proud churchmen wear;
But he'll pluck the rose, and tell,
God hath painted it right well.
He will kneel before his food,
Softly saying, 'God is good.'   30
Haughty prelates, do not scorn
The teaching of the Idiot-born.

Art thou great as man can be? –
The same hand moulded him and thee.
Hast thou talent? – Taunt and jeer   35
Must not fall upon his ear.
Spurn him not; the blemished part
Had better be the head than heart.
Thou wilt be the fool to scorn
The teaching of the Idiot-born.   40

' 'Tis Well to Wake the Theme of Love'

'Tis well to wake the theme of Love
    When chords of wild ecstatic fire
Fling from the harp, and amply prove
    The soul as joyous as the lyre.

Such theme is blissful when the heart   5
    Warms with the precious name we pour;
When our deep pulses glow and start
    Before the idol we adore.

Sing ye, whose doting eyes behold –
　　Whose ears can drink the dear one's tone;　　　　　　10
Whose hands may press, whose arms may fold –
　　The prized, the beautiful, thine own!

But should the ardent hopes of youth
　　Have cherished dreams that darkly fled;
Should passion, purity, and truth,　　　　　　　　　　15
　　Live on, despairing o'er the dead:

Should we have heard some sweet voice hushed,
　　Breathing our name in latest vow;
Should our fast heavy tears have gushed
　　Above a cold, yet worshipped brow:　　　　　　　　20

Oh! say, then, can the minstrel choose
　　The theme that gods and mortals praise?
No, no; the spirit will refuse,
　　And sadly shun such raptured lays.

For who can bear to touch the string　　　　　　　　　25
　　That yields but anguish in its strain;
Whose lightest notes have power to wring
　　The keenest pangs from breast and brain?

'Sing ye of Love in words that burn?'
　　Is what full many a lip will ask;　　　　　　　　　30
But love the dead, and ye will learn
　　Such bidding is no gentle task.

Oh! pause in mercy, ere ye blame
　　The one who lends not Love his lyre;
That which *ye* deem ethereal flame　　　　　　　　　35
　　May be to *him* a torture pyre.

On Seeing a Bird-Catcher

Health in his rags, Content upon his face,
He goes th' enslaver of a feathered race:
And cunning snares, warm hearts, like warblers, take;
The one to sing for sport, the other, break.

Song of the Imprisoned Bird

Ye may pass me by with pitying eye,
　　And cry 'Poor captive thing!'

But I'll prove ye are caged as safely as I,
　　If ye'll list to the notes I sing.

I flutter in thrall, and so do all; –　　　　　　　　　5
　　Ye have bonds ye cannot escape;
With only a little wider range,
　　And bars of another shape.

The noble ranks of fashion and birth
　　Are fettered by courtly rule;　　　　　　　　　10
They dare not rend the shackles that tend
　　To form the knave and fool.

The parasite, bound to kiss the hand
　　That, perchance, he may loathe to touch;
The maiden, high-born, wedding where she may scorn, –　　15
　　Oh! has earth worse chains than such?

The one who lives but to gather up wealth, –
　　Though great his treasures may be;
Yet, guarding with care and counting by stealth, –
　　What a captive wretch is he!　　　　　　　　　20

The vainly proud, who turn from the crowd,
　　And tremble lest they spoil
The feathers of the peacock plume
　　With a low, plebeian soil:

Oh! joy is mine to see them strut　　　　　　　　　25
　　In their chosen, narrow space;
They mount a perch, but ye need not search
　　For a closer prison-place.

The being of fitful, curbless wrath
　　May fiercely stamp and rave;　　　　　　　　　30
He will call himself free, but there cannot be
　　More mean and piteous slave; –

For the greatest victim, the fastest-bound,
　　Is the one who serves his rage;
The temper that governs will ever be found　　　　　　35
　　A fearful, torture-cage.

Each breathing spirit is chastened down
　　By the hated or the dear;
The gentle smile or tyrant frown
　　Will hold ye in love or fear.　　　　　　　　　40

How much there is self-will would do,
    Were it not for the dire dismay
That bids ye shrink, as ye suddenly think
    Of 'What will my neighbour say?'

Then pity me not; for mark mankind,   45
    Of every rank and age;
Look close to the heart, and ye'll ever find,
    That each is a bird in a cage.

The Surgeon's Knife

There are hearts — stout hearts — that own no fear
At the whirling sword or the darting spear, —
That are ready alike to bleed in the dust,
'Neath the sabre's cut or the bayonet's thrust;
They heed not the blows that Fate may deal,   5
From the murderer's dirk or the soldier's steel:
But lips that laugh at the dagger of strife
Turn silent and white from the surgeon's knife.

Though bright be the burnish and slender the blade,
Bring it nigh, and the bravest are strangely afraid;   10
And the rope on the beam or the axe on the block
Have less terror to daunt and less power to shock.
Science may wield it, and danger may ask
The hand to be quick in its gory task:
The hour with torture and death may be rife,   15
But death is less feared than the surgeon's knife.

It shines in the grasp — 'tis no weapon for play,
A shudder betrays it is speeding its way;
While the quivering muscle and severing joint
Are gashed by the keen edge and probed by the point. 20
It has reeked in the dark and welling flood,
Till purple and warm with the heart's quick blood;
Dripping it comes from the cells of life,
While glazing eyes turn from the surgeon's knife.

Braggarts in courage, and boasters of strength,   25
At the cannon's mouth or the lance's length;
Ye who have struggled sword to sword,
With your wide wounds drenching the battle-sward —
Oh! boast no more till your soul be found
Unmoved with a breathless silence around;   30
And a dread of the grave and a hope of life;
That rest on the work of the surgeon's knife.

To My Lyre

My LYRE! oh, let thy soothing power
Beguile once more the lonely hour;
Thy music ever serves to cheer,
To quell the sigh and chase the tear.
Thy notes can ever wile away   5
The sleepless night and weary day;
And howsoe'er the world may tire,
I care not while I've thee, my Lyre!

None were around to mark and praise
The breathings of thy first, rude lays;   10
But many a chiding taunt was thrown
To mock and crush thy earliest tone.
'Twas harshly done – yet, ah! how vain
The cruel hope to mar thy strain;
For the stern words that bade us part   15
But bound thee closer to my heart.

Let the bright laurel-wreath belong
To prouder harps of classic song;
I'll be content that thou shouldst bear
The wild flowers children love to wear.   20
If warmth be round thy chords, my Lyre,
'Tis Nature that shall yield the fire;
If one responsive tone be found,
'Tis Nature that shall yield the sound.

Gold may be scant – I ask it not;   25
There's peace with little – fairly got.
The hearts I prize may sadly prove
False to my hopes, my trust, my love.
Let all grow dark around, but still
I find a balm for every ill: 30
However cheqnered fate may be,
I find wealth, joy, and friends in thee.

What are the titles monarchs hold? –
Mere sounding nothings, bought and sold;
The highest rank that man can gain,   35
Fortune may bribe or fools attain.
But they who sweep the glowing strings,
Mock the supremacy of kings:
The Minstrel's skill is dearer far
Than Glory's crown or Triumph's car.   40

My Lyre! I feel thy chords are rife
With music ending but with life:
When the 'cold chain' shall round thee dwell,
'Twill bind this fervid breast as well.
My Lyre! my Lyre! I hang o'er thee   45
With lifted brow and bended knee,
And cry aloud, 'For every bliss
I thank thee, GOD! but most for this.'

Song of the Modern Time

Oh, how the world has altered since some fifty years ago!
When boots and shoes would *really* serve to keep out rain and snow
But double soles and broadcloth – oh, dear me, how very low,
To talk of such old-fashioned things! when every one must know
   That we are well-bred gentlefolks, all of the modern time.   5

We all meet now at midnight-hour, and form a 'glittering throng,'
Where lovely angels polk and waltz, and chant a German song:
Where 'nice young men,' with fierce moustache, trip mincingly along,
And the name of a good old country-dance would sound like a Chinese gong
   In the ears of well-bred gentlefolks, all of the modern time.   10

Your beardless boys, all brag and noise, must 'do the thing that's right;'
That is, they'll drink champagne and punch, and keep it up all night:
They'll smoke and swear till, sallying forth at peep of morning light,
They knock down some old woman, just to show how well they fight;
   Like brave young English gentlemen, all of the modern time.   15

At the good old hours of twelve and one our grandsires used to dine,
And quaff their horns of nut-brown ale and eat roast beef and chine;
But we must have our silver forks, ragouts, and foreign wine,
And not sit down till five or six, if we mean to 'cut a shine;'
   Like dashing, well-bred gentlefolks, all of the modern time.   20

Our daughters now at ten years old must learn to squall and strum,
And study shakes and quavers under Signor Fee-Foo-Fum;
They'll play concertos, sing bravuras, rattle, scream, and thrum,
Till you almost wish that you were deaf, or they, poor things, were dumb;
   But they must be like young gentlefolks, all of the modern time.   25

Our sons must jabber Latin verbs, and talk of a Greek root,
Before they've left off tunic skirts, cakes, lollypops, and fruit;
They all have 'splendid talents,' that the desk or bar would suit
Each darling boy would scorn to be 'a low mechanic brute;'
   They must be well-bred College 'men,' all of the modern time.   30

But bills will come at Christmas tide, alas! alack-a-day.
The creditors may call again, 'Papa's not in the way;
He's out of town, but certainly next week he'll call and pay;'
And then his name's in the 'Gazette;' and this I mean to say
    Oft winds up many gentlefolks, all of the modern time.   35

Song of the Ugly Maiden

Oh! the world gives little of love or light,
    Though my spirit pants for much;
For I have no beauty for the sight,
    No riches for the touch.
I hear men sing o'er the flowing cup   5
    Of woman's magic spell;
And vows of zeal they offer up,
    And eloquent tales they tell.
They bravely swear to guard the fair
    With strong, protecting arms;   10
But will they worship woman's worth
    Unblent with woman's charms?
No! ah, no! 'tis little they prize
Crookbacked forms and rayless eyes.

Oh! 'tis a saddening thing to be   15
    A poor and Ugly one:
In the sand Time puts in his glass for me,
    Few sparkling atoms run.
For my drawn lids bear no shadowing fringe,
    My locks are thin and dry;   20
My teeth wear not the rich pearl tinge,
    Nor my lips the henna dye.
I know full well I have nought of grace
    That maketh woman 'divine;'
The wooer's praise and doting gaze   25
    Have never yet been mine.
Where'er I go all eyes will shun
The loveless mien of the Ugly one.

I join the crowd where merry feet
    Keep pace with the merry strain;   30
I note the earnest words that greet
    The fair ones in the train,
The stripling youth has passed me by
    He leads another out!
She has a light and laughing eye,   35
    Like sunshine playing about.
The wise man scanneth calmly round,

But his gaze stops not with me;
It hath fixed on a head whose curls, unbound,
   Are bright as curls can be;   40
And he watches her through the winding dance
With smiling care and tender glance.

The gay cavalier has thrust me aside;
   Whom does he hurry to seek?
One with a curving lip of pride,   45
   And a forehead white and sleek.
The grey-haired veteran, young with wine,
   Would head the dance once more;
He looks for a hand, but passes mine,
   As all have passed before.   50
The pale, scarred face may sit alone,
   The unsightly brow may mope;
There cometh no tongue with winning tone
   To flatter Affection's hope.
Oh, Ugliness! thy desolate pain   55
Had served to set the stamp on Cain.

My quick brain hears the thoughtless jeers
   That are whispered with langhing grin;
As though I had fashioned my own dull orbs,
   And chosen my own seared skin.   60
Who shall dream of the withering pang,
   As I find myself forlorn –
Sitting apart, with lonely heart,
   'Mid cold neglect and scorn?
I could be glad as others are,   65
   For my soul is young and warm;
And kind it had been to darken and mar
   My feelings with my form;
For fondly and strong as my spirit may yearn
It gains no sweet love in return.   70

Man, just Man! I know thine eye
   Delighteth to dwell on those
Whose tresses shade, with curl or braid,
   Cheeks soft and round as the rose.
I know thou wilt ever gladly turn   75
   To the beautiful and bright;
But is it well that thou shouldst spurn
   The one GOD chose to blight?
Oh! why shouldst thou trace my shrinking face
   With coarse, deriding jest?   80
Oh! why forget that a charmless brow
   May abide with a gentle breast?

Oh! why forget that gold is found
Hidden beneath the roughest ground?

Would that I had passed away   85
   Ere I knew that I was born;
For I stand in the blessed light of day
   Like a weed among the corn, –
The black rock in the wide, blue sea –
   The snake in the jungle green,   90
Oh! who will stay in the fearful way
   Where such ugly things are seen?
Yet mine is the fate of lonelier state
   Than that of the snake or rock;
For those who behold me in their path   95
   Not only shun, but mock.
Oh, Ugliness! thy desolate pain
Had served to set the stamp on Cain.

To Charlotte Cushman

Seeing her play 'Bianca' in Milman's Tragedy of Fazio

I thought thee wondrous when thy soul portrayed
   The youth Verona bragged of; and the love
Of glowing, southern blood by thee was made
   Entrancing as the breath of orange-grove.

I felt the spirit of the great was thine: 5
   In the fond Boy's devotion and despair;
I knew thou wert a pilgrim at the shrine
   Where GOD's high ministers alone repair.

No rote-learned sighing filled thy doting moans;
   Thy grief was heavy as thy joy was light;   10
Passion and Poesy were in thy tones,
   And MIND flashed forth in its electric might.

I had seen many 'fret and strut their hour;'
   But my brain never had become such slave
To Fiction, as it did beneath thy power;   15
   Nor owned such homage as to thee it gave.

I did not think thou couldst arouse a throb
   Of deeper, stronger beating in my heart;
I did not deem thou couldst awake the sob
   Of choking fulness, and convulsive start.   20

But thy pale madness, and thy gasping woe,
    That breathed the torture of Bianca's pain;
Oh! never would my bosom ask to know
    Such sad and bitter sympathy again!

When the wife's anguish sears thy hopeless cheek,   25
    Let crowds behold and laud thee as they will;
But this poor breast, in shunning what *they* seek,
    May yield, perchance, a richer tribute still.

A Song for the Workers

Written for the Early Closing Movement

Let Man toil to win his living,
    Work is not a task to spurn;
Poor is gold of others' giving,
    To the silver that we earn.

Let Man proudly take his station   5
    At the smithy, loom, or plough;
The richest crown-pearls in a nation
    Hang from Labour's reeking brow.

Though her hand grows hard with duty,
    Filling up the common Fate;   10
Let fair Woman's cheek of beauty
    Never blush to own its state.

Let fond Woman's heart of feeling
    Never be ashamed to spread
Industry and honest dealing,   15
    As a barter for her bread.

Work on bravely, GOD's own daughters!
    Work on stanchly, GOD's own sons!
But when Life has too rough waters,
    Truth must fire her minute guns.   20

Shall ye be *unceasing* drudges?
    Shall the cry upon your lips
Never make your selfish judges
    Less severe with Despot-whips?

Shall the mercy that we cherish,   25
    As old England's primest boast,
See no slaves but those who perish
    On a far and foreign coast?

When we reckon hives of money,
  Owned by Luxury and Ease,   30
Is it just to grasp the honey
  While Oppression chokes the bees?

Is it just the poor and lowly
  Should be held as soulless things?
Have they not a claim as holy   35
  As rich men, to angels' wings?

Shall we burthen Boyhood's muscle?
  Shall the young Girl mope and lean,
Till we hear the dead leaves rustle
  On a tree that should be green?   40

Shall we bar the brain from thinking
  Of aught else than work and woe?
Shall we keep parched lips from drinking
  Where refreshing waters flow?

Shall we strive to shut out Reason,   45
  Knowledge, Liberty, and Health?
Shall all Spirit-light be treason
  To the mighty King of Wealth?

Shall we stint with niggard measure,
  Human joy, and human rest?   50
Leave no profit – give no pleasure,
  To the toiler's human breast?

Shall our Men, fatigued to loathing.
  Plod on sickly, worn, and bowed?
Shall our Maidens sew fine clothing,   55
  Dreaming of their own, white shroud?

No! for Right is up and asking
  Loudly for a juster lot;
And Commerce must not let her tasking
  Form a nation's canker spot.   60

Work on bravely, GOD's own daughters!
  Work on stanchly, GOD's own sons!
But till ye have smoother waters,
  Let Truth fire her minute guns!

'Our Father'

'Many of the children told me they always said their prayers at night, and the prayer they said was "Our Father". I naturally thought they meant that they repeated the Lord's Prayer, but I soon found that few of them knew it. They only repeated the first two words; they knew no more than "Our Father". These poor children, after their laborious day's work (nail-making, japanning, screw-making), lying down to sleep with this simple appeal, seemed to me inexpressibly affecting.'

Report of the Commissioners on the Employment of Children: Evidence of
R. H. Horne, Town of Wolverhampton

Pale, struggling blossoms of mankind,
   Born only to endure;
White, helpless slaves whom Christians bind;
   Sad children of the poor!
Ye walk in rags, ye breathe in dust,   5
   With souls too dead to ask
For aught beyond a scanty crust,
   And Labour's grinding task.
Ye ne'er have heard the code of love,
   Of Hope's eternal light;   10
Ye are not led to look above
   The clouds of earthly blight;
And yet 'mid Ignorance and Toil,
   Your lips, that ne'er have known
The 'milk and honey' of the soil,   15
   Sleep not before they own
          'Our Father!'

Unheeded workers in the marts
   Of England's boasted wealth,
Ye, who may carry ulcered hearts,
   If hands but keep their health;   20
Ye, whose young eyes have never watched
   June's roses come and go,
Whose hard-worn fingers ne'er have snatched
   The spring-flowers as they blow;
Who slave beneath the summer sun,   25
   With dull and torpid brain,
Ye, who lie down when work is done,
   To rise and work again:
Oh! even ye, poor, joyless things;
   Rest not, before you pray;   30
Striving to mount on fettered wings
   To Him who hears you say,
          'Our Father!'

Proud, easy tenants of the earth,
  Ye who have fairer lots;
Who live with Plenty, Love, and Mirth,   35
  On Fortune's golden spots;
Ye, who but eat, laugh, drink, and sleep,
  Who walk 'mid Eden's bloom,
Who know not what it is to weep
  In Poverty's cold gloom;   40
Oh! turn one moment from your way,
  And learn what these can teach,
Deign in your rosy path to stay,
  And hear the 'untaught' preach.
Then to your homes so bright and fair,   45
  And think it good to pray;
Since the sad children of Despair
  Can kneel in thanks and say,
                'Our Father!'

Lines

Suggested by the Song of a Nightingale

I am jealous! I am jealous! which I ne'er have been before;
And I trust by all I suffer, I shall never be so more;
For all the petty pangs of pain ne'er gave me half the smart
That this young, green-eyed viper does, now nibbling at my heart.

Full many trying moments have I passed through in my life,   5
While swallowing the bitter herbs that stir the blood of strife;
I've lost my place at spelling-class, to some still younger dunce,
And seen my cobbled fancy-work outrivalled more than once.

I've heard the dancing-master say the cruellest of things,
Declaring Miss Rosina was a fairy without wings;   10
While, as for me, he scarcely knew to what he could compare
My awkward steps in 'Lady's chain,' excepting to a bear.

I have been doomed to hear the praise of fairer skins than mine:
And listened while my neighbour's eyes were mentioned as divine –
While my poor cheeks and orbs were left unnoted in their hue, 15
And slighted, since they did not shine in brilliant pink and blue.

I've had a 'very, nice young man' keep flitting at my side,
And talking to me with a deal of eloquence and pride,
Till really, 'twixt the music and a little, iced champagne,
The nice, young man appeared to be my most devoted swain, 20

But some young lady-friend appeared, with sweet and gracious smile.
She wooed him with the softness of a tender flirting guile;
I stood alone, my beau had gone to join the *balancez*, –
My lady friend with wicked might, had carried him away.

And yet, amid these trials, I have stood with unmoved breast,   25
Not even having lovers pilfered, broke my spirit's rest;
And verily I have declared, with honest, upturned brow,
That never was my nature tinged with jealousy till now.

But only think, for some two hours have I been dreaming here,
Where summer trees are all full dressed, and summer skies are clear.   30
Without one line of carol song outpouring from my lyre,
Although I've asked, and begged, and prayed Apollo to inspire.

And all at once a Nightingale has perched above my head;
And burst into a strain that might almost arouse the dead.
So loud, so full, so exquisite, so gushing, and so long;   35
O! can I hear the lay, and not be jealous of the song?

So free, so pure, so spirit-filled, so tender, and so gay;
I do feel jealous; yes I do; and really, well I may,
When I have sought such weary while to breathe a few, choice notes
And find myself so mocked at by the tiniest of throats.   40

Now listen to that 'jug, jug, jug;' did ever jug pour out
Such liquid floods of ecstasy, in rapid streams about?
And now, that hissing, trembling tone, in one, long earnest shake;
Like quenching hosts of fiery stars in some ambrosial lake.

Again, that whistle did you hear? – that warble, now this trill?   45
See, it has made the ploughman and the gipsy-boy stand still!
Again, and louder, sweeter too; just hearken to its pipe;
And wonder not that I'm within the green-eyed monster's gripe.

I'm jealous! yes, indeed, I am! I'm pale with angry rage!
I almost wish the merry thing were trammelled in a cage!   50
But, stay, I'll have still more revenge, in evil thought, at least;
And wish him worse than ever fell to lot of bird or beast.

I'll wish he had to *write* his song beneath a midnight taper;
On pittance that would scarcely pay for goose-quill, ink, and paper;
And then, to crown his misery, and break his heart in splinters;   55
I'll wish he had to see his proofs, his publishers, and printers.

To the Late William Jerdan

If my poor Harp has ever poured
  A tone that Truth alone can give;
Thou wert the one who helped that tone
  To win the echo that shall live.

For thou didst bid me shun the theme   5
  Of morbid grief, or feigned delight;
Thou bad'st me *think* and *feel*, not dream
  And 'look into my heart and write.'

And looking in that heart just now;
  'Mid all the memories there concealed;   10
I find thy name still dearly claim
  The thanks in these few lines revealed.

The Mouse and the Cake

A mouse found a beautiful piece of plum-cake,
The richest and sweetest that mortal could make;
'Twas heavy with citron and fragrant with spice,
And covered with sugar all sparkling as ice.

'My stars!' cried the mouse, while his eye beamed with glee,   5
'Here's a treasure I've found; what a feast it will be:
But, hark! there's a noise, 'tis my brothers at play;
So I'll hide with the cake, lest they wander this way.

'Not a bit shall they have, for I know I can eat
Every morsel myself, and I'll have such a treat;'   10
So off went the mouse, as he held the cake fast;
While his hungry, young brothers went scampering past.

He nibbled, and nibbled, and panted, but still
He kept gulping it down till he made himself ill;
Yet he swallowed it all, and 'tis easy to guess,   15
He was soon so unwell that he groaned with distress.

His family heard him, and as he grew worse,
They sent for the doctor, who made him rehearse
How he'd eaten the cake to the very last crumb;
Without giving his playmates and relatives some.   20

'Ah me!' cried the doctor, 'advice is too late,
You must die before long, so prepare for your fate;

If you had but divided the cake with your brothers,
'Twould have done you no harm, and been good for the others.

'Had you shared it, the treat had been wholesome enough;   25
But eaten by *one*, it was dangerous stuff;
So prepare for the worst;' and the word had scarce fled,
When the doctor turned round, and the patient was dead.

Now all little people the lesson may take,
And *some* large ones may learn from the mouse and the cake; 30
Not to be over-selfish with what we may gain;
Or the best of our pleasures may turn into pain.

Emily Jane Brontë (1818–1848)

'Stronger than a man, simpler than a child, her nature stood alone' wrote Charlotte of her sister Emily (Brontë 1850: vi). Charlotte adored strong men and Emily was the best man she knew. In her life they didn't exist: her father was an irascible pedant, her teacher was a fussy coxcomb, her brother was a sulky failure. But in Emily, and in Emily's poetic persona, Charlotte found a man just to her taste: 'wild', 'terse', 'vigorous', 'unpretending', but possessed of 'a secret power and fire that might have kindled the veins of a hero'. Every word is taken from Charlotte's descriptions of Emily and her poetry, and every idea went into the making of Mr Rochester.

Emily was the fifth child in the Brontë family. She was two years old when they moved to Haworth and three when her mother died. Following Maria and Elizabeth, Charlotte and Emily went to Cowan Bridge in November 1824 and her brief sojourn there is recorded in the school register: 'Emily Brontë 5 $\frac{3}{4}$ 1824 Novbr 25th H Cough Reads very prettily & Works a little Left School June 1st 1825 Governess' (Chitham 1987: 35–7). For the next ten years Emily remained at home until she tried school again in July 1835 when she went to Miss Wooler's establishment at Roe Head where Charlotte was working as a teacher. After four months she was ill and desperately homesick so that Charlotte arranged for her release. 'Liberty was the breath of Emily's nostrils' Charlotte wrote, 'without it she perished. The change from her own home to a school and from her noiseless, very secluded but unrestrained and inartificial mode of life, to one of disciplined routine . . . was what she failed in enduring . . . I felt in my heart she would die if she did not go home . . .' (Gérin 1972: 55).

At Haworth Emily roamed the moors, 'Emily especially had a gleesome delight in these nooks of beauty, – her reserve for the time vanished' said Ellen Nussey (Wise and Symington 1933: I, 112), and she read widely. She worked at her Gondal writings, with and without Anne, living as much in that imagined world as in the real world where she made bread, ironed frills, cooked and sewed with efficiency and expertise. For Emily the real and the imaginary always intermeshed and the slide from one to the other was direct and uncomplicated:

This morning Branwell went down to Mr Driver's and brought news that Sir Robert Peel was going to be invited to stand for Leeds. Anne and I have been

peeling apples for Charlotte to make an apple pudding...Taby said just now
Come Anne pilloputate...Papa opened the door and gave Branwell a letter
saying Here Branwell read this and show it to your Aunt and Charlotte. The
Gondals are discovering the interior of Gaaldine. Sally Mosley is washing in the
back Kitchin.

It is past twelve o'clock Anne and I have not tided ourselves, done our
bedwork or done our lessons and we want to go out to play We are going to
have for dinner Boiled Beef, Turnips, potatoes and apple pudding. The kitchin
is in a very untidy state Anne and I have not done our music exercise which
consists of b major Taby said on my putting a pen in her face Ya pitter pottering
there instead of pilling a potate. I answered Dear, O Dear, O Dear I will derectly
With that I get up, take a knife and begin pilling. Finished pilling the potatoes
Papa going to walk Mr Sunderland expected.

Anne and I say I wonder what we shall be and where we shall be, if all goes
on well in the year 1874 (Wise and Symington 1933: I, 124–5).

In this diary paper for 1834 it looks very much as if Emily, like the other girls, was
expected to be employed in the feminine sphere of the kitchen while father and
Branwell went out into the world. But there are other stories which suggest how far
the family acknowledged what they perceived as Emily's masculine side. Patrick Brontë
had always made it his habit to carry a loaded firearm in his pocket and to sleep with
a pistol loaded and cocked by his bed, discharging it each morning from his bedroom
window. When his eyesight began to fail and Branwell was physically decrepit, it was
Emily whom he chose as deputy protector. John Greenwood, the Haworth stationer,
tells the story:

Mr Brontë...had such unbounded confidence in his daughter Emily, knowing as
he did, her unparalleled intrepidity and firmness, that he resolved to learn her to
shoot too. They used to practice with pistols. Let her be ever so busy in her
domestic duties, whether in the kitchen baking bread at which she had such a
dainty hand, or at her ironing, or at her studies, raped in a world of her own
creating – it mattered not; if he called her to take a lesson, she would put it all
down; his tender and affectionate 'Now my dear girl, let me see how well you can
shoot to-day' was irristable to her filial nature...she would...take the pistol,
which he had previously primed and loaded for her...with as firm a hand, and
as steady an eye as any veteran of the camp, and fire (Gérin 1972: 147–8).

Greenwood is also the source of another story of Emily's power and decision:

On one occasion a person went to tell them that Keeper and another great
powerful dog out of the village were fighting...She never spoke a word, nor
appeared in the least at a loss at what to do, but rushed at once into the kitchen,
took the pepper box, and away into the lane, where she found the two savage
brutes each holding the other by the throat...while several other animals, who
thought themselves men, were standing looking like cowards...watching this
fragile creature spring upon the beasts – seizing Keeper round the neck with one
arm, while with the other hand she dredges well their noses with pepper, and
separating them by force of her great will...(Gérin 1972: 146–7).

There are many other tales in this line and the bold heroine of Charlotte's *Shirley* (1849) was partly based on Emily. Elizabeth Gaskell first linked an incident in *Shirley* with the occasion when Emily seared her own wound with the kitchen tongs after being bitten by a rabid dog.

Emily had two more spells away from Haworth. In 1838 she tried to teach at a school in Law Hill near Halifax, but she only lasted six months there. In 1842 she went to Brussels with Charlotte and stuck it out from February to November until her aunt's death gave her the excuse to return home as well as a release from financial worries. 'Now' she wrote, 'I don't desire a school at all, and none of us have any great longing for it. We have cash enough for our present wants, with a prospect of accumulation... I am quite contented for myself: not as idle as formerly... and having learnt to make the most of the present... seldom or never troubled with nothing to do, and merely desiring that everybody could be as comfortable as myself and as undesponding... I must hurry off now to my turning and ironing...' (Wise and Symington 1933: II, 51).

While she studied with M. Heger in Brussels, his reports on Emily had described her as 'ignorant' and 'timid', but fifteen years later, probably influenced by Charlotte's own 1850 version of her sister, he offered Mrs Gaskell quite a different view of Emily's character. Now Emily had a genius which he valued above Charlotte's; she had 'a head for logic, and a capability of argument, unusual in a man, and rare indeed in a woman'. He went on: 'She should have been a man – a great navigator. Her powerful reason would have deduced new spheres of discovery from the knowledge of the old; and her strong, imperious will would never have been daunted by opposition or difficulty; never have given way but with life...' (Gaskell 1975 [1857]: 230). All the same, Emily was, according to Heger, 'egotistical and exacting'.

In the Autumn of 1845 all the girls were at home and Charlotte found Emily's volume of manuscript poems: 'Of course, I was not surprised, knowing that she could and did write verse: I looked it over, and something more than surprise seized me, – a deep conviction that these were not common effusions, nor at all like the poetry women generally write. I thought them condensed and terse, vigorous and genuine. To my ear, they also had a peculiar music – wild, melancholy, and elevating' (Brontë 1850: viii).

Emily was furious, and the quarrel which followed was long lasting. She seems never to have forgiven Charlotte's intrusion into her hidden life, though she did indeed settle down to promote her own literary ambitions and wrote *Wuthering Heights* which was published in 1847 with Anne's *Agnes Grey*. In the little time left to her, Emily continued to write poetry, selecting and copying it out into her careful notebooks. Towards the end of 1848 she was seriously ill with consumption and she declined fast, stubbornly refusing any medical aid. Charlotte had to reply when W. S. Williams offered advice, that 'It is best usually to leave her to form her own judgement, and *especially* not to advocate the side you wish her to favour; if you do, she is sure to lean in the opposite direction, and ten to one will argue herself into non-compliance' (Wise and Symington 1933: II, 286). Still not complying, Emily died in December 1848.

Charlotte's attitude to Emily and her writings fits with many contemporary notions of gender stereotypes and their awkward relation to intellect in women. In Charlotte's view Emily was a genius. Her poetry was so good exactly because it was *not* 'like the poetry women generally write'. Quite unlike the work of Felicia Hemans – who was almost certainly one of the poets Charlotte was thinking of – Emily's genius is masculine in character. Yet Charlotte's hagiographical intent in the Biographical Notice of her sister required that she toned down the unwomanly aspects of Emily's character.

And she did this by harping on her innocence. Emily, the world was told, possessed 'no worldly wisdom', she had no more knowledge of local life 'than a nun has of the country people who sometimes pass her convent gates'. Above all, Emily didn't know what she was doing when she allowed her imagination free rein, for 'the writer who possesses the creative gift owns something of which he is not always master' (Brontë 1850: ix).

Charlotte's invented Emily, part egotistical hero, part fierce and solitary witch, part holy fool, became a lively myth. And when, in the 1880s and 1890s public interest in the Brontës was renewed with the recovery of their letters and other documents, this mythological Emily became the very icon of what the woman poet should be. Mary Robinson wrote a eulogy masquerading as biography for the Eminent Women series, and Charlotte Mew recreated her in the stoic and wayward heroine of her unpublished story 'Elinor': 'He said you were like a queen and should have had an empire, but that your people would have killed and canonized you afterwards' (Mew 1982: 290).

Emily Brontë's poetry colludes in creating the image of her fierce independence. Her personae are very often 'alone' or 'lonely' – one of her favourite words, and probably responsible for her popularity with adolescents. Rejecting human company and the haunts of men, her poetry also distrusts conventional creeds. Her most famous claim to an independent mystical belief comes in 'No coward soul is mine' ('O God within my breast,/ Almighty ever-present deity') but there are indications of this same lawless self-sufficiency in other poems such as 'Riches I hold in light esteem', 'Aye there it is' and 'If grief for grief can touch thee'.

Turning in upon itself, Emily Brontë's poetry very often becomes a dialogue with her muse. Like Emily Dickinson, her muse is certainly male and she maintains an intense and erotic relation with him which is explicitly sexual and astonishingly direct in its insistence ('In summer's mellow midnight' and 'Ah! why, because the dazzling sun').

As in Rossetti's work, there is a charged and sensuous representation of the natural world. It is painful, cold, and decaying but there is also a tortured and pleasurable excitement in that distressing physicality. Images of the prison, death and the threshold express, as they do for Rossetti and Mew, the dualities of inside and outside. But one of Brontë's distinctive qualities is a dislocated emotion where the feeling is not in the speaker but in her apparent unexplained circumstances. This is what happens in 'The night is darkening round me' where the speaker is threatened by an unexplained 'tyrant spell' manifested in the malevolence of trees and wind and snow. The speaker consequently seems powerless until the last stanza where, typically for Emily, a clear choice is indicated ('I will not, cannot go') and the speaker remains alone in her masochistic ecstasy.

M.R.

Brontë, Emily (1992) *The Poems of Emily Brontë*, ed. Barbara Lloyd-Evans, London, Batsford.

Brontë, Charlotte (1850) Biographical Notice of Ellis and Acton Bell, second edition of *Wuthering Heights*, London.

Chitham, Edward (1987) *A Life of Emily Brontë*, Oxford, Basil Blackwell.

Davis, Stevie (1988) *Emily Brontë*, Hemel Hempstead, Harvester.

Gaskell, Elizabeth (1975) [1857] *The Life of Charlotte Brontë*, Harmondsworth, Penguin.

Gérin, Winifred (1972) *Emily Brontë: A Biography*, Oxford, Oxford University Press.

Grove, Robin (1976) ' "It Would Not Do": Emily Brontë as Poet', in *The Art of Emily Brontë*, ed. Anne Smith, London, Vision Press.

Hardy, Barbara (1976) 'The Lyricism of Emily Brontë', in *The Art of Emily Brontë* ed. Anne Smith, London, Vision Press.

Homans, Margaret (1980) *Women Writers and Poetic Identity: Dorothy Wordsworth, Emily Brontë and Emily Dickinson*, Princeton, Princeton University Press.

Mew, Charlotte (1982) *Collected Poems and Prose*, ed. Val Warner, London, Virago.

Miles, Rosalind (1976) 'A Baby God: The Creative Dynamism of Emily Brontë's Poetry' in *The Art of Emily Brontë*, ed. Anne Smith, London, Vision Press.

Pykett, Lyn (1989) *Emily Brontë*, Basingstoke, Macmillan.

Tayler, Irene (1990) *Holy Ghosts: The Male Muses of Emily and Charlotte Brontë*, New York, Columbia University Press.

Wise, T. J. and Symington, J. A., eds (1933) *The Brontës: Their Lives, Friendships and Correspondence*, 4 vols, Oxford, Shakespeare Head.

R. Alcona to J. Brenzaida

Cold in the earth and the deep snow piled above thee!
Far, far removed cold in the dreary grave!
Have I forgot, my Only Love to love thee,
Severed at last by Time's allwearing wave?

Now, when alone, do my thoughts no longer hover   5
Over the mountains on Angora's shore;
Resting their wings where heath and fern-leaves cover
That noble heart for ever, ever more?

Cold in the earth, and fifteen wild Decembers
From those brown hills have melted into spring –   10
Faithful indeed is the spirit that remembers
After such years of change and suffering!

Sweet Love of youth, forgive if I forget thee
While the world's tide is bearing me along
Sterner desires and darker Hopes beset me   15
Hopes which obscure but cannot do thee wrong –

No other sun has lightened up my heaven:
No other star has ever shone for me
All my life's bliss from thy dear life was given –
All my life's bliss is in the grave with thee!   20

But when the days of golden dreams had perished
And even Despair was powerless to destroy
Then did I learn how existence could be cherished
Strengthened and fed – without the aid of joy

Then did I check the tears of useless passion,   25
Weaned my young soul from yearning after thine;

Sternly denied its burning wish to hasten
Down to that tomb already more than mine!

And even yet, I dare not let it languish,
Dare not indulge in Memory's rapturous pain!   30
Once drinking deep of that divinest anguish
How could I seek the empty world again?

'The night is darkening round me'

The night is darkening round me,
The wild winds coldly blow,
But a tyrant spell has bound me
And I cannot, cannot go.

The giant trees are bending   5
Their bare boughs weighed with snow
And the storm is fast descending
And yet I cannot go.

Clouds beyond cloud above me,
Wastes beyond wastes below,   10
But nothing drear can move me,
I will not, cannot go.

'Why do I hate that lone green dell?'

Why do I hate that lone green dell?
Buried in moors and mountains wild
That is a spot I had loved too well
Had I but seen it when a child.

There are bones whitening there in the summer's heat   5
But it is not for that, and none can tell;
None but one can the secret repeat
Why I hate that lone green dell.

Noble foe, I pardon thee
All thy cold and scornful pride,   10
For thou wast a priceless friend to me
When my sad heart had none beside.

And leaning on thy generous arm
A breath of old times over me came;
The earth shone round with a long-lost charm;   15
Alas, I forgot I was not the same.

Before a day – an hour – passed by
My spirit knew itself once more;
I saw the gilded vapours fly
And leave me as I was before.   20

'The linnet in the rocky dells'

The linnet in the rocky dells,
The moorlark in the air,
The bee among the heather bells
That hide my lady fair –

The wild deer browse above her breast: 5
The wild birds raise their brood.
And they, her smiles of love caressed,
Have left her solitude!

I ween, that when the grave's dark wall
Did first her form retain   10
They thought their hearts could ne'er recall
The light of joy again –

They thought the tide of grief would flow
Unchecked through future years
But where is all their anguish now,   15
And where are all their tears?

Well, let them fight for Honour's breath
Or Pleasure's shade pursue –
The Dweller in the land of Death
Is changed and careless too –   20

And if their eyes should watch and weep
Till sorrows' source were dry
She would not, in her tranquil sleep,
Return a single sigh –

Blow, west wind, by the lonely mound   25
And murmur, summer streams,
There is no need of other sound
To soothe my Lady's dreams –

'Loud without the wind was roaring'

Loud without the wind was roaring
    Through the waned autumnal sky,

Drenching wet, the cold rain pouring
  Spoke of stormy winters nigh.

All too like that dreary eve,   5
Sighed, within repining grief –
Sighed at first – but sighed not long
Sweet. How softly sweet it came!
Wild words of an ancient song,
Undefined, without a name –   10

'It was spring, for the skylark was singing.'
Those words they awakened a spell –
They unlocked a deep fountain whose springing
Nor Absence nor Distance can quell.

In the gloom of a cloudy November   15
They uttered the music of May –
They kindled the perishing ember
Into fervour that could not decay

Awaken on all my dear moorlands
The wind in its glory and pride!   20
O call me from valleys and highlands
To walk by the hill river's side!

It swelled with the first snowy weather;
The rocks they are icy and hoar
And darker waves round the long heather   25
And the fern-leaves are sunny no more

There are no yellow-stars on the mountain
The blue-bells have long died away
From the brink of the moss bedded fountain,
From the side of the wintery brae –   30

But lovelier than corn-fields all waving
In emerald and scarlet and gold
Are the slopes where the north-wind is raving
And the glens where I wandered of old –

'It was morning, the bright sun was beaming.' 35
How sweetly that brought back to me
The time when nor labour nor dreaming
Broke the sleep of the happy and free.

But blithely we rose as the dusk heaven
Was melting to amber and blue   40
And swift were the wings to our feet given
While we traversed the meadows of dew.

For the moors, for the moors where the short grass
Like velvet beneath us should lie!
For the moors, for the moors where each high pass   45
Rose sunny against the clear sky!

For the moors, where the linnet was trilling
Its song on the old granite stone –
Where the lark – the wild sky-lark was filling
Every breast with delight like its own.   50

What language can utter the feeling
That rose when, in exile afar,
On the brow of a lonely hill kneeling
I saw the brown heath growing there.

It was scattered and stunted, and told me   55
That soon even that would be gone
It whispered; 'The grim walls enfold me;
'I have bloomed in my last summer's sun'

But not the loved music whose waking
Makes the soul of the Swiss die away   60
Has a spell more adored and heart-breaking
Than in its half-blighted-bells lay –

The Spirit that bent 'neath its power
How it longed, how it burned to be free!
If I could have wept in that hour   65
Those tears had been heaven to me –

Well, well the sad minutes are moving
Though loaded with trouble and pain –
And sometimes the loved and the loving
Shall meet on the mountains again –   70

'A little while, a little while'

A little while, a little while
The noisy crowd are barred away;
And I can sing and I can smile –
A little while I've holyday!

Where wilt thou go my harassed heart?   5
Full many a land invites thee now;
And places near, and far apart
Have rest for thee, my weary brow.

There is a spot mid barren hills
Where winter howls and driving rain 10
But if the dreary tempest chills
There is a light that warms again

The house is old, the trees are bare
And moonless bends the misty dome
But what on earth is half so dear – 15
So longed for as the hearth of home?

The mute bird sitting on the stone,
The dank moss dripping from the wall,
The garden-walk with weeds o'ergrown
I love them – how I love them all! 20

Shall I go there? or shall I seek
Another clime, another sky,
Where tongues familiar music speak
In accents dear to memory?

Yes, as I mused, the naked room, 25
The flickering firelight died away
And from the midst of cheerless gloom
I passed to bright, unclouded day.

A little and a lone green lane
That opened on a common wide 30
A distant, dreamy, dim blue chain
Of mountains circling every side –

A heaven so clear, an earth so calm,
So sweet, so soft, so hushed an air
And, deepening still the dreamlike charm 35
Wild moor-sheep feeding everywhere –

That was the scene – I knew it well
I knew the path-ways far and near
That winding o'er each billowy swell
Marked out the tracks of wandering deer 40

Could I have lingered but an hour
It well had paid a week of toil
But truth has banished fancy's power;
I hear thy dungeon bars recoil –

Even as I stood with raptured eye 45
Absorbed in bliss so deep and dear
My hour of rest had fleeted by
And given me back to weary care –

'Shall Earth no more inspire thee'

Shall Earth no more inspire thee,
Thou lonely dreamer now?
Since passion may not fire thee
Shall Nature cease to bow?

Thy mind is ever moving   5
In regions dark to thee;
Recall its useless roving –
Come back and dwell with me –

I know my mountain breezes
Enchant and soothe thee still.   10
I know my sunshine pleases
Despite thy wayward will –

When day with evening blending
Sinks from the summer sky,
I've seen thy spirit bending   15
In fond idolatry –

I've watched thee every hour.
I know my mighty sway –
I know my magic power
To drive thy griefs away –   20

Few hearts to mortals given
On earth so wildly pine
Yet none would ask a Heaven
More like the Earth than thine.

Then let my winds caress thee –   25
Thy comrade let me be.
Since nought beside can bless thee
Return and dwell with me –

'In summer's mellow midnight'

In summer's mellow midnight
A cloudless moon shone through
Our open parlour window
And rosetrees wet with dew –

I sat in silent musing –   5
The soft wind waved my hair

It told me Heaven was glorious
And sleeping Earth was fair

I needed not its breathing
To bring such thoughts to me   10
But still it whispered lowly
'How dark the woods will be! –

'The thick leaves in my murmur
Are rustling like a dream,
And all their myriad voices   15
Instinct with spirit seem.'

I said, 'Go gentle singer,
Thy wooing voice is kind
But do not think its music
Has power to reach my mind –   20

'Play with the scented flower,
The young tree's supple bough –
And leave my human feelings
In their own course to flow'

The Wanderer would not leave me   25
Its kiss grew warmer still –
'O come,' it sighed so sweetly
'I'll win thee 'gainst thy will –

'Have we not been from childhood friends?
Have I not loved thee long?   30
As long as thou hast loved the night
Whose silence wakes my song?

'And when thy heart is laid at rest
Beneath the church-yard stone
I shall have time enough to mourn   35
And thou to be alone' –

'Riches I hold in light esteem'

Riches I hold in light esteem
And Love I laugh to scorn
And lust of Fame was but a dream
That vanished with the morn –

And if I pray – the only prayer   5
That moves my lips for me

Is — 'Leave the heart that now I bear
'And give me liberty.'

Yes, as my swift days near their goal
'Tis all that I implore —   10
Through life and death, a chainless soul
With courage to endure! —

'Aye there it is! It wakes tonight'

Aye there it is! It wakes tonight
Sweet thoughts that will not die
And feeling's fires flash all as bright
As in the years gone by! —

And I can tell by thine altered cheek   5
And by thy kindled gaze
And by the words thou scarce dost speak,
How wildly fancy plays —

Yes I could swear that glorious wind
Has swept the world aside   10
Has dashed its memory from thy mind
Like foam-bells from the tide —

And thou art now a spirit pouring
Thy presence into all —
The essence of the Tempest's roaring   15
And of the Tempest's fall —

A universal influence
From Thine own influence free —
A principle of life intense
Lost to mortality —   20

Thus truly when that breast is cold
Thy prisoned soul shall rise
The dungeon mingle with the mould —
The captive with the skies —

'If grief for grief can touch thee'

If grief for grief can touch thee,
If answering woe for woe,
If any ruth can melt thee
Come to me now!

I cannot be more lonely, 5
More drear I cannot be!
My worn heart throbs as wildly
'Twill break for thee.

And when the world despises –
When Heaven repels my prayer 10
Will not mine angel comfort?
Mine idol hear?

Yes by the tears I've poured,
By all my hours of pain
O I shall surely win thee 15
Beloved, again!

' "Well, some may hate and some may scorn" '

'Well, some may hate and some may scorn
And some may quite forget thy name
But my sad heart must ever mourn
Thy ruined hopes, thy blighted fame' –

'Twas thus I thought an hour ago 5
Even weeping o'er that wretch's woe –
One word turned back my gushing tears
And lit my altered eye with sneers –

'Then bless the friendly dust' I said
'That hides thy unlamented head. 10
Vain as thou wert, and weak as vain
The slave of falsehood, pride and pain –
My heart has nought akin to thine
Thy soul is powerless over mine'

But these were thoughts that vanished too 15
Unwise, unholy, and untrue –
Do I despise the timid deer
Because his limbs are fleet with fear?
Or would I mock the wolf's death-howl
Because his form is gaunt and foul? 20
Or hear with joy the leveret's cry
Because it cannot bravely die?

No – then above his memory
Let pity's heart as tender be
Say, 'Earth, lie lightly on that breast, 25
And kind Heaven, grant that spirit rest!'

My Comforter

Well has thou spoken and yet not taught
A feeling strange or new –
Thou hast but roused a latent thought,
A cloud-closed beam of sunshine brought
To gleam in open view –   5

Deep down – concealed within my soul
That light lies hid from men
Yet glows unquenched though shadows roll,
Its gentle ray can not control,
– About the sullen den –   10

Was I not vexed, in these gloomy ways
To walk unlit so long?
Around me, wretches uttering praise
Or howling o'er their hopeless days –
And each with frenzy's tongue –   15

A Brotherhood of misery,
With smiles as sad as sighs –
Whose madness daily maddening me,
Turning into agony
The Bliss before my eyes –   20

So stood I – in Heaven's glorious sun
And, in the glare of Hell
My spirit drank a mingled tone
Of scraph's song and demon's groan.
– What thy soul bore thy soul alone   25
Within its self may tell –

Like a soft air above a sea
Tossed by the tempest's stir –
A thawwind melting quietly
The snowdrift on some wintery lea   30
– No – What sweet thing can match with thee,
My thoughtful Comforter?

And yet a little longer speak
Calm this resentful mood
And while the savage heart grows meek,   35
For other token do not seek,
But let the tear upon my cheek
Evince my gratitude –

To Imagination

When weary with the long day's care
And earthly change from pain to pain
And lost and ready to despair
Thy kind voice calls me back again –
O my true Friend, I am not lone   5
While thou canst speak with such a tone!

So hopeless is the world without
The world within I doubly prize
Thy world, where guile and hate and doubt
And cold suspicion never rise –   10
Where thou and I and Liberty
Have undisputed sovereignty.

What matters it that all around
Danger and grief and darkness lie
If but within our bosom's bound   15
We hold a bright unsullied sky
Warm with the thousand mingled rays
Of suns that know no winter days –

Reason indeed may oft complain
For Nature's sad reality   20
And tells the suffering heart how vain
Its cherished dreams must always be
And Truth may rudely trample down
The flowers of fancy newly blown

But thou art ever there to bring   25
The hovering visions back and breathe
New glories o'er the blighted spring
And call a lovelier life from death
And whisper with a voice divine
Of real worlds as bright as thine   30

I trust not to thy phantom bliss
Yet still in evening's quiet hour
With never failing thankfulness
I welcome thee benignant power
Sure Solacer of human cares   35
And brighter hope when hope despairs –

'O! thy bright eyes must answer now'

O! thy bright eyes must answer now,
When Reason, with a scornful brow,
Is mocking at my overthrow;
O, thy sweet tongue must plead for me
And tell why I have chosen thee!   5

Stern Reason is to judgement come
Arrayed in all her forms of gloom;
Wilt thou my advocate he dumb?
No radiant angel, speak and say
Why I did cast the world away: 10

Why I have persevered to shun
The common paths that others run
And on a strange road journeyed on,
Heedless alike of Wealth and Power –
Of Glory's wreath and Pleasure's flower –   15

These once indeed seemed Beings divine
And they perchance heard vows of mine
And saw my offerings on their shrine –
But, careless gifts are seldom prized
And mine were worthily despised;   20

So with a ready heart I swore
To seek their altar stone no more
And gave my spirit to adore
Thee, ever present, phantom thing.
My slave, my Comrade and my King!   25

A slave because I rule thee still
Incline thee to my changeful will
And make thy influence good or ill
A comrade, for by day and night
Thou art my intimate Delight –   30

My Darling Pain that wounds and sears
And wrings a blessing out from tears
By deadening me to real cares:
And yet a king – though prudence well
Have taught thy subject to rebel –   35

And am I wrong, to worship where
Faith cannot doubt, nor Hope despair,
Since my own soul can grant my prayer?
Speak God of visions, plead for me,
And tell why I have chosen thee!   40

'Ah! why, because the dazzling sun'

Ah! why, because the dazzling sun
Restored my earth to joy
Have you departed, everyone,
And left a desert sky?

All through the night, your glorious eyes   5
Were gazing down in mine
And with a full heart's thankful sighs
I blessed that watch divine!

I was at peace: and drank your beams
As they were life to me   10
And revelled in my changeful dreams
Like petrel on the sea –

Thought followed thought – star followed star
Through boundless regions on
While one sweet influence, near and far,   15
Thrilled through and proved us one.

Why did the morning rise to break
So great, so pure a spell,
And scorch with fire the tranquil cheek
Where your cool radiance fell?   20

Blood red he rose, and arrow-straight
His fierce beams struck my brow
The soul of Nature sprang elate,
But mine sank sad and low!

My lids closed down – yet through their veil   25
I saw him blazing still;
And bathe in gold the misty dale
And flash upon the hill –

I turned me to the pillow then
To call back Night, and see   30
Your worlds of solemn light again
Throb with my heart and me!

It would not do – the pillow glowed
And glowed both roof and floor
And birds sang loudly in the wood   35
And fresh winds shook the door.

The curtains waved, the wakened flies
Were murmuring round my room
Imprisoned there, till I should rise
And give them leave to roam –   40

O, Stars and Dreams and Gentle Night.
O, Night and Stars return!
And hide me from this hostile light
That does not warm, but burn –

That drains the blood of suffering men –   45
Drinks tears, instead of dew –
Let me sleep through his blinding reign
And only wake with you!

'No coward soul is mine'

No coward soul is mine
No trembler in the world's storm-troubled sphere.
I see Heaven's glories shine
And Faith shines equal arming me from Fear

O God within my breast   5
Almighty ever-present Deity
Life, that in me hast rest
As I Undying Life, have power in thee

Vain are the thousand creeds
That move men's hearts, unutterably vain,   10
Worthless as withered weeds
Or idlest froth amid the boundless main

To waken doubt in one
Holding so fast by thy infinity
So surely anchored on   15
The steadfast rock of Immortality

With wide-embracing love
Thy spirit animates eternal years
Pervades and broods above,
Changes, sustains, dissolves, creates and rears   20

Though Earth and moon were gone
And suns and universe ceased to be
And thou wert left alone
Every Existence would exist in thee

There is not room for Death   25
Nor atom that his might could render void
Since Thou art Being and Breath
And what thou art may never be destroyed

'Stanzas'

Often rebuked, yet always back returning
  To those first feelings that were born with me,
And leaving busy chase of wealth and learning
  For idle dreams of things which cannot be;

To-day, I will seek not the shadowy region;   5
  Its unsustaining vastness waxes drear;
And visions rising, legion after legion,
  Bring the unreal world too strangely near.

I'll walk, but not in old heroic traces,
  And not in paths of high morality,   10
And not among the half-distinguished faces,
  The clouded forms of long-past history.

I'll walk where my own nature would be leading:
  It vexes me to choose another guide:
Where the grey flocks in ferny glens are feeding;   15
  Where the wild wind blows on the mountain side.

What have those lonely mountains worth revealing?
  More glory and more grief than I can tell:
The earth that wakes *one* human heart to feeling
  Can centre both the worlds of Heaven and Hell.   20

Henrietta Tindal (1818–1879)

Henrietta Tindal (Mrs Acton Tindal) was the only child and 'heiress' of Elizabeth and
John Harrison. Her father was vicar of Binton, Buckinghamshire. Being a weakly child,
Henrietta was kept at home and given the usual, superficial girls' education. Later, she
became a close friend of Mary Russell Mitford, who helped her place poems in various
journals, including *Findens' Tableaux* where she appeared alongside Barrett Browning.
In 1846 she married Acton Tindal and subsequently bore five children, one of whom
died at the age of nine. Her poems about child mortality and death in childbirth are
particularly moving. So too are her verses about working-class hardship, like 'The Cry
of the Oppressed'. A copy of another poem, 'On the Hartley Colliery Accident, 16
January 1862' (not quoted here), was personally requested by the Queen. Tindal
published only two volumes of poems and one novel during her lifetime.

'The Birth Wail' is a good example of an unsentimental treatment of the subject of birth, and bears comparison, in particular, with the poems about motherhood by Clive, Ogilvy, Nesbit, Meynell and Sigerson.

A.L.

Tindal, Henrietta Mrs Acton [published under name of Tindal] (1850) *Lines and Leaves*, London.
—— (1879) *Rhymes and Legends*, London.

The Cry of the Oppressed

Bondmen, and helots, and serfs were we,
Slaves in plantation and stifling mill,
Pauper and 'prentice: from sea to sea,
Our bands are rising and gathering still.

We are the many who served the few;   5
We made their glory, and strength, and gain;
We passed as sand, when the west wind blew,
As the myriad drops of the autumn rain;

We sank at night off the surge-beat strand, –
The rotting bark and its living freight,   10
The o'erflowing swarm of a straitened land,
Who went forth bravely to seek their fate.

For a trader's gain our lives were sold –
The blooming mother, the maiden bright,
The vigorous father, the stripling bold,   15
With the rough and wrong of life to fight.

We are the souls who were pent within
The narrow street and the valley dim;
Bred in the darkness of want and sin,
We peopled the hulks and the prisons grim.   20

The blazing gas on the night was shed,
To lure our lips to the liquid flame;
And bitter upon our hard-earned bread
The poisonous fraud of the dealer came.

We breathed the heated and noisome air   25
In crowded chambers of daily toil;
And the green, slow, slimy drain was there,
Creeping below on the black wet soil.

Ha! we have blunted the hungry tooth
Of ev'ry plague that hath stalked the land;   30

It took our beauty, and strength, and youth,
Father, mother, and household band!

Yes! we have parched in the fever's fire,
Till madness throbbed in the whirling brain,
When fancy feasted the vain desire,   35
The suff'rer rose o'er his want and pain!

Mercy! for those we have left to die
Beyond your hearing, walled out from sight,
In the black close lane to the palace nigh –
For the body, food – for the spirit, light!   40

We ask no weary life of leisure,
That robs your joy of its bloom and zest –
Give us God's just and righteous measure,
The worth of labour, the hours of rest.

Ye lack emotions who live at ease   45
In bright warm chambers of prosp'rous life;
Ye tales of terror and sorrow please –
Look out around ye, they're rife, aye, – rife,

As berries in autumn, as leaves in May,
Seek! ye will find in the neighbouring street   50
Tragedies acted before the day,
That stir the heart to a quicker beat,
And draw the tear from its deepest seat.

The Birth Wail

Tum porro puer, ut sævis projectus ab undis
Navita, nudus humi jacet, infans, indigus omni
Vitali auxilio, cùm primùm in luminis oras
Nixibus ex alvo matris natura profudit;
Vagituque locum lugubri complet, ut æquum est
Cui tantum in vità restet transire malorum.
               Lucretius Book V, v. 223 et seq.

On parent knees, a naked new-born child,
Weeping thou sat'st when all around thee smiled.
               Sir Wm. Jones

That wail! 'tis prophecy. Oh, hush! be still:
Let the small voice the darken'd chamber thrill.
That little heart with life's first grief o'erflows,
And its first power is used to tell its woes.

Ye may rejoice, who meet the waking life 5
With busy thoughts and fond ambition rife,
With hopes that grasp this being's span of time,
And prayers the offspring of a faith sublime.
Let the babe weep! a pilgrim on the earth!
Tears are the dews that meetly grace his birth. 10
Well may his nascent soul in sad surprise
Review the tumult opening to his eyes,
And, startled by the sounds of coming strife,
Turn to yield back the doubtful boon of life.
Regret, methinks, as well as suffering, spoke 15
In the shrill wail that with the birth-pang broke.
What mystic memories fill that new-born mind
Of light forsaken, and love left behind,
Of time, not parcell'd into night or day,
Of powers seraphic, cumber'd not by clay! 20
When woke the spirit that within thy brain
Will sit enthroned till dust join dust again?
Hath it for ages dwelt amid the light
That saint and martyr view with shadow'd sight –
Sent a drear travail through our earth to make, 25
And learn the woe God bore for mortals' sake?
Or did thy soul to being spring this morn,
Clothed with the garment by thy Saviour worn?
We ne'er may know! A silence deep will seal
Those rosy lips that might so much reveal. 30
A blooming cherub reconciled to earth,
Words will be given to tell thy infant mirth,
Thy artless fancies, and thy glad surprise,
Not the dim secrets of the spirit's rise,
Young wanderer from the fount of mysteries! 35

Cecil Frances Alexander (1818–1895)

Cecil Frances Alexander led a privileged, blameless and exemplary life. Her father Major John Humphreys was a soldier and the family owned large estates in County Wicklow and Tyrone in Ireland. Their four daughters and two sons were well educated though the sons went to Oxford and the daughters stayed at home. Frances's early writing ventures included a weekly newspaper for her family with serious and comic verses, and a manuscript volume of poems 'My Poems for Mama, C.F.H.'. While she was a young woman she travelled to visit relatives and friends and met many notable people; Sir Walter Scott, Samuel Rogers and Agnes Strickland in Edinburgh, Charlotte Yonge and Edmund Keble at Winchester. At Ballykean she became very close to Harriet Howard, the daughter of Lord Wicklow and the two friends wrote a book of stories 'An Old Man's Rambles' together. They also shared a commitment to the philosophies of the Oxford Movement and wrote some pamphlets for Newman and

Keble, Harriet contributing the prose, and Frances the verse (1842–3, collected 1848). Harriet died young but Frances continued to write religious lyrics, dedicating her *Verses for the Holy Seasons* (1846) to Keble: 'To the author of the Christian Year, this attempt to adapt the great principle of his immortal work to the exigencies of the school room is inscribed with feelings of reverence and respect by one of the many thousands who have profited by his labours' (Alexander 1846: i). Frances also produced two books of prose and verse for children, and her popular *Hymns for Little Children* (1848) which included the most famous of her verses, 'There is a green hill far away' and the carol 'Once in Royal David's City'. Surprisingly, that old favourite of school assemblies began life as 'All Things Bright and Beauteous' which is the version included here.

In 1850 Frances married William Alexander, rector of Termonamongan in County Tyrone. His family objected to the marriage because Frances was six years older than William and, for this reason, he delicately refrained from giving her date of birth when he wrote a memoir of his wife. She bore four children and fulfilled her womanly rector's-wife duties, outdoors in all weathers and at home: '... she was consistently anxious for the spiritual welfare of her household, and carefully catechised her maids in her own simple, downright way' (Alexander 1913: 35). William worked his way up through serving increasingly prosperous parishes until in 1867 he was created Bishop of Derry and Raphoe where Frances founded a home for fallen women. In 1896, the year after Frances's death, William was created Archbishop of Armagh and Primate of All Ireland and he celebrated with an edition of his saintly wife's poems.

The simplicity of Alexander's vocabulary and the evocative images which she uses in depicting a pretty picture of the Holy Land means that her verses were not only suitable for children, but have been retained in the collective memory as harmless sentimental hymns. But times change and, more recently, Alexander's work has not been viewed as harmless. Her most famous work 'All Things Bright and Beauteous' has appeared in countless hymn books but, in the twentieth century, without the undemocratic verses about the proper order of society, 'The rich man in his castle/The poor man at his gate'. They are, however, restored here.

M.R.

Humphreys, later Alexander, Cecil Frances (1846) *Verses for the Holy Seasons*, London.
—— (1852) *Hymns for Little Children*, London.
—— (1896) *Poems*, edited with a Preface by William Alexander, London.
Alexander, Eleanor (1913) *Primate Alexander: Archbishop of Armagh*, London.

'All things bright and beauteous'

All things bright and beauteous,
All creatures great and small,
All things wise and wondrous,
The LORD GOD made them all.

Each little flower that opens,   5
Each little bird that sings,
He made their glowing colours,
He made their tiny wings.

The rich man in his castle,
The poor man at his gate,   10
GOD made them, high or lowly,
And ordered their estate.

The purple-headed mountain,
The river running by,
The sunset, and the morning,   15
That brightens up the sky,

The cold wind in the winter,
The pleasant summer sun,
The ripe fruits in the garden,
He made them every one.   20

The tall trees in the greenwood,
The meadows where we play,
The rushes by the water,
We gather every day; –

He gave us eyes to see them,   25
And lips that we might tell,
How great is GOD Almighty,
Who has made all things well.

George Eliot (Mary Ann Evans) (1819–1880)

Mary Ann Evans was the third child of Christiana and Robert Evans. Her father was a carpenter and Warwickshire land agent. The strongest influence on her childhood was the evangelical revivalism she encountered at her two schools. When she was sixteen her mother died, and some years later her father put the family business into the hands of his son, Isaac. In her early twenties Mary Ann became friendly with the freethinker Charles Bray, under whose influence her religious fervour started to wane. Her refusal to go to church at this time caused an angry rift between herself and her father, which was only mended when, after months of angry silence between them, she agreed to keep up appearances and attend services with him.

In 1843 she became acquainted with the scholar Dr Brabant, whose book challenging all theological dogmas never progressed beyond the first chapter. This early Casaubon in her life nicknamed her 'Deutera', which, she noted eagerly, '*sounds* a little like daughter' (1985: 28). The visits came to an abrupt end, however, when Mrs Brabant became suspicious of their intimacy. This was a situation which repeated itself in Mary Ann's life. Her ironic account, three years later, of the German professor who turned up at the door in search of 'a translator in the person of a wife', with, if possible, 'a very decided ugliness of person' (1985: 38), is knowingly self-mocking. Her 'worship' of Dr Brabant, and her willingness to serve as his secretary, was only, she admitted, for lack of any 'other deity' (1985: 39) in her life. By now she was translating Strauss's

Life of Jesus for the publisher Chapman, though the book's scientific critique of the gospel stories sometimes depressed her. In 1849 her father died after a long illness, during which she nursed him almost single-handed. The night of his death she wrote in anguish: 'What shall I be without my Father? It will seem as if a part of my moral nature were gone' (1985: 54). Father-figures, with their imagined moral authority, continued to exert a strong influence over her life.

Soon after the funeral Mary Ann went abroad, and spent the winter in a pension in Geneva. Returning to England, she took lodgings with Chapman, intending to earn her living by the pen. But the old problem of 'worship' returned. She quickly succeeded in rousing the jealousy both of Chapman's wife *and* his mistress, so that after ten weeks she was once again forced to leave. Two years later, however, he invited her to return and take on the editorship of the *Westminster Review*. By now her relations with the two other women of the household had relaxed. Under her anonymous editorship, from 1852 to 1854, the *Westminster* grew in intellectual stature. At this time she also formed a close friendship with the social scientist, Herbert Spencer, and in July 1852 wrote him an extraordinary letter of proposal, not dissimilar in its terms from the utilitarian request of the old professor. 'I could gather courage to work and make life valuable, if only I had you near me', she begged, promising to make no other demands. She admitted frankly, at the end, that 'no woman ever before wrote such a letter as this' (1985: 102). Spencer, who never married, turned her down. In the months which followed she became friendly with another regular contributor to the *Westminster*, who had recently founded the radical weekly, the *Leader*. The relationship with George Henry Lewes was to become, after all the eager false starts, the love which gave her 'courage to work'.

Lewes, however, was already married with three children. By 1852 his wife Agnes had borne another two by her lover. By registering them under his name, Lewes was seen to condone the adultery and thus forfeited the right to a divorce. By 1853 he was struggling to support Agnes and six children, and was often ill with overwork. Eventually, in July 1854, he and Mary Ann decided to face the opprobrium of society and left England for Germany. On returning, she took his name and they lived openly together, though shunned at first by 'respectable' members of society. On hearing the news, Isaac, in true brotherly fashion, cut off communication with his sister. His silence, which lasted for twenty-three years, is the hidden sounding-board for the loving childhood sections of *The Mill on the Floss* (1860) as well as the yearning reminiscences of the *Brother and Sister* sonnets (1874).

It was not till 1856 that Mary Ann, at the age of thirty-six, started writing fiction. Characteristically, it was Lewes who gave her the idea and the encouragement. 'He is', she once wrote, 'the prime blessing that has made all the rest possible to me' (1985: 211). Her first story, the first of *Scenes of Clerical Life*, was published anonymously in *Blackwood's* in 1857 and was an immediate success. In response to curiosity about its author, she informed her publisher that she wished to be known as 'George Eliot', a name which records her admiration both for her husband and, of course, for the daring French novelist, George Sand.

For the next twenty years of her life George Eliot travelled, wrote, and became immensely successful. Her early diagnosis of her emotional needs was evidently correct. She and Lewes enjoyed a long, supportive and, in her case, artistically productive relationship. While continuing to give financial support to Agnes, they themselves practised some form of birth control. With Barbara Bodichon and Emily Davies, George Eliot helped found Girton College, Cambridge, and later subscribed to Garrett

Anderson's hospital for women. In spite of her own unconventional union, however, she was usually reluctant to enter into debates on the 'Woman Question'. In some ways, her insistence on 'woman's peculiar constitution for a special moral influence' (1985: 351) is more reminiscent of Felicia Hemans, one of her early favourite poets, than of the liberal emancipationists, Harriet Taylor or John Stuart Mill. She once scolded a friend for agreeing 'to canvass on the Women's Suffrage question' on the grounds of its 'doubtful good' (1985: 335). No doubt the large, humanist commitments of her fiction made her indifferent to seemingly narrower causes. However her poetry is an exception. The heroine of her verse play, *Armgart* (1870), is ostentatiously torn between the conflicting demands of art and life, ambition and love, in the well-worn tradition of *Corinne*.

In 1878 Lewes died. Though desolate, Mary Ann's dauntingly clear-sighted perception of her needs came to her rescue. John Cross, the nephew who had managed their financial affairs, was one of her first visitors. By February 1879 she was writing to him: 'I do need your affection. Every sign of care for me from the beings I respect and love is a help to me' (1985: 504). In May 1880, at the age of sixty, she married the forty-year-old 'Johnnie', and they left for the continent together. The marriage also effected a long-desired reconciliation with Isaac. In Venice there was an odd incident, however, when John, suffering perhaps from fatigue at the strenuous round of reading and visiting, threw himself from the hotel window into the Grand Canal and had to be rescued. Apart from this lapse, whatever the reasons for it, the relationship seems to have been happy.

But it was short lived. On 19 December, soon after they had moved into a new home together, Mary Ann retired early to bed, complaining of a sore throat. She died that same night, probably of the kidney complaint which had troubled her for some years.

George Eliot's poetry is essentially the work of a novelist on leave. It does, however, reveal something of her attitudes to art and womanhood which the novels conceal. The delightful *Brother and Sister* sonnets which, like Webster's *Mother & Daughter* sequence, use the courtly love form for a new relationship, is loaded with autobiographical regret. It can be read, on the one hand, as a pleading letter from the cast-off sister to her beloved brother, or as an intriguing, mischievous rewriting of the story of Eden. Though Isaac is Adam to his sister's Eve, second only to the angels in her eyes, he is also the one who plucks 'The fruit that hung on high'. Meanwhile the 'little sister', against all the odds (the barge of fate, history and myth bearing hard upon her) triumphantly catches her 'silver perch'.

Armgart is obviously influenced by *Aurora Leigh*, which Eliot read at least three times and greatly admired. Its story of a famous opera singer who loses her voice offers an anxious, heavily moralistic revision of Barrett Browning's poem. Yet the split between the ruthless artistic dedication of scene ii, and the lesson of humiliation and human sympathy in scene v, is never psychologically resolved. Armgart's ferocious defence of her art against the emotional demands of men becomes an abject and unconvincing acceptance of her artistic ruin at the end. Yet the story of the maid Walpurga, whose ill-used faithfulness to her upper-class cousin is eventually acknowledged, offers another commentary on the love-or-fame story. According to Walpurga, Armgart's aristocratic vocation has ignored the 'million women' who drudge in poverty. Eliot's equivalent to the emotional sistering of Marian and Aurora, which Barrett Browning carelessly forgets at the end, is this absolute, political sistering of the great and poor. Armgart finally returns to Walpurga's birthplace, in a symbolic burying and rebirth of her own self. The 'moral nature' thus defeats the artist's careless selfishness, in a gesture which may be read as a rebuke to Barrett Browning, or as a piece of guilty self-castigation in an artist who never, herself, lost the voice of her powerful, all-demanding gift.

A.L.

Eliot., George (1874) *The Legend of Jubal and Other Poems*, London.

—— (1985) *Selections from George Eliot's Letters*, ed. Gordon S. Haight, New Haven and London.

Beer, Gillian (1986) *George Eliot*, Brighton, Harvester, pp. 200–28.

Blake, Kathleen (1980) '*Armgart* – George Eliot on the Woman Artist', *Victorian Poetry*, 18 (1980), 75–80.

Bodenheimer, Rosmarie (1990) 'Ambition and its Audiences: George Eliot's Performing Figures', *Victorian Studies*, 34 (1990), 7–31.

Brown, Susan (1995) 'Determined Heroines: George Eliot, Augusta Webster, and Closet Drama by Victorian Women', *Victorian Poetry*, 33 (1995).

Brother and Sister

I

I cannot choose but think upon the time
When our two lives grew like two buds that kiss
At lightest thrill from the bee's swinging chime,
Because the one so near the other is.

He was the elder and a little man   5
Of forty inches, bound to show no dread,
And I the girl that puppy-like now ran,
Now lagged behind my brother's larger tread.

I held him wise, and when he talked to me
Of snakes and birds, and which God loved the best,   10
I thought his knowledge marked the boundary
Where men grew blind, though angels knew the rest.

  If he said 'Hush!' I tried to hold my breath;
  Wherever he said 'Come!' I stepped in faith.

II

Long years have left their writing on my brow,   15
But yet the freshness and the dew-fed beam
Of those young mornings are about me now,
When we two wandered toward the far-off stream

With rod and line. Our basket held a store
Baked for us only, and I thought with joy   20
That I should have my share, though he had more,
Because he was the elder and a boy.

The firmaments of daisies since to me
Have had those mornings in their opening eyes,
The bunchèd cowslip's pale transparency   25
Carries that sunshine of sweet memories,

    And wild-rose branches take their finest scent
    From those blest hours of infantine content.

III

Our mother bade us keep the trodden ways,
Stroked down my tippet, set my brother's frill,   30
Then with the benediction of her gaze
Clung to us lessening, and pursued us still

Across the homestead to the rookery elms,
Whose tall old trunks had each a grassy mound,
So rich for us, we counted them as realms   35
With varied products: here were earth-nuts found,

And here the Lady-fingers in deep shade;
Here sloping toward the Moat the rushes grew,
The large to split for pith, the small to braid;
While over all the dark rooks cawing flew,   40

    And made a happy strange solemnity,
    A deep-toned chant from life unknown to me.

IV

Our meadow-path had memorable spots:
One where it bridged a tiny rivulet,
Deep hid by tangled blue Forget-me-nots;   45
And all along the waving grasses met

My little palm, or nodded to my cheek,
When flowers with upturned faces gazing drew
My wonder downward, seeming all to speak
With eyes of souls that dumbly heard and knew.   50

Then came the copse, where wild things rushed unseen,
And black-scathed grass betrayed the past abode

Of mystic gypsies, who still lurked between
Me and each hidden distance of the road.

   A gypsy once had startled me at play,   55
   Blotting with her dark smile my sunny day.

V

Thus rambling we were schooled in deepest lore,
And learned the meanings that give words a soul,
The fear, the love, the primal passionate store,
Whose shaping impulses make manhood whole.   60

Those hours were seed to all my after good;
My infant gladness, through eye, ear, and touch,
Took easily as warmth a various food
To nourish the sweet skill of loving much.

For who in age shall roam the earth and find   65
Reasons for loving that will strike out love
With sudden rod from the hard year-pressed mind?
Were reasons sown as thick as stars above,

   'Tis love must see them, as the eye sees light:
   Day is but Number to the darkened sight.   70

VI

Our brown canal was endless to my thought;
And on its banks I sat in dreamy peace,
Unknowing how the good I loved was wrought,
Untroubled by the fear that it would cease.

Slowly the barges floated into view   75
Rounding a grassy hill to me sublime
With some Unknown beyond it, whither flew
The parting cuckoo toward a fresh spring time.

The wide-arched bridge, the scented elder-flowers,
The wondrous watery rings that died too soon,   80
The echoes of the quarry, the still hours
With white robe sweeping-on the shadeless noon,

   Were but my growing self, are part of me,
   My present Past, my root of piety.

VII

Those long days measured by my little feet   85
Had chronicles which yield me many a text;
Where irony still finds an image meet
Of full-grown judgments in this world perplext.

One day my brother left me in high charge,
To mind the rod, while he went seeking bait,   90
And bade me, when I saw a nearing barge,
Snatch out the line, lest he should come too late.

Proud of the task, I watched with all my might
For one whole minute, till my eyes grew wide,
Till sky and earth took on a strange new light   95
And seemed a dream-world floating on some tide –

    A fair pavilioned boat for me alone
    Bearing me onward through the vast unknown.

VIII

But sudden came the barge's pitch-black prow,
Nearer and angrier came my brother's cry,   100
And all my soul was quivering fear, when lo!
Upon the imperilled line, suspended high,

A silver perch! My guilt that won the prey,
Now turned to merit, had a guerdon rich
Of hugs and praises, and made merry play,   105
Until my triumph reached its highest pitch

When all at home were told the wondrous feat,
And how the little sister had fished well.
In secret, though my fortune tasted sweet,
I wondered why this happiness befell.   110

    'The little lass had luck,' the gardener said:
    And so I learned, luck was with glory wed.

IX

We had the self-same world enlarged for each
By loving difference of girl and boy:
The fruit that hung on high beyond my reach   115
He plucked for me, and oft he must employ

A measuring glance to guide my tiny shoe
Where lay firm stepping-stones, or call to mind
'This thing I like my sister may not do,
For she is little, and I must be kind.'   120

Thus boyish Will the nobler mastery learned
Where inward vision over impulse reigns,
Widening its life with separate life discerned,
A Like unlike, a Self that self restrains.

　　His years with others must the sweeter be   125
　　For those brief days he spent in loving me.

                          X

His sorrow was my sorrow, and his joy
Sent little leaps and laughs through all my frame;
My doll seemed lifeless and no girlish toy
Had any reason when my brother came.   130

I knelt with him at marbles, marked his fling
Cut the ringed stem and make the apple drop,
Or watched him winding close the spiral string
That looped the orbits of the humming top.

Grasped by such fellowship my vagrant thought   135
Ceased with dream-fruit dream-wishes to fulfil;
My aëry-picturing fantasy was taught
Subjection to the harder, truer skill

　　That seeks with deeds to grave a thought-tracked line,
　　And by 'What is,' 'What will be' to define.   140

                         XI

School parted us; we never found again
That childish world where our two spirits mingled
Like scents from varying roses that remain
One sweetness, nor can evermore be singled.

Yet the twin habit of that early time   145
Lingered for long about the heart and tongue:
We had been natives of one happy clime
And its dear accent to our utterance clung.

Till the dire years whose awful name is Change
Had grasped our souls still yearning in divorce,   150

And pitiless shaped them in two forms that range
Two elements which sever their life's course.

But were another childhood-world my share,
I would be born a little sister there.

from *Armgart*

[Armgart, the opera singer, has had a brilliantly successful debut. The aristocratic
Graf Dornberg asks to marry her.]

Scene II

The same Salon, morning. ARMGART *seated, in her bonnet and walking dress. The* GRAF
standing near her against the piano.

GRAF

Armgart, to many minds the first success
Is reason for desisting. I have known
A man so versatile, he tried all arts,
But when in each by turns he had achieved
Just so much mastery as made men say,   5
'He could be king here if he would,' he threw
The lauded skill aside. He hates, said one,
The level of achieved pre-eminence,
He must be conquering still; but others said –

ARMGART

The truth, I hope: he had a meagre soul,   10
Holding no depth where love could root itself.
'Could if he would?' True greatness ever wills –
It lives in wholeness if it live at all,
And all its strength is knit with constancy.

GRAF

He used to say himself he was too sane   15
To give his life away for excellence
Which yet must stand, an ivory statuette
Wrought to perfection through long lonely years,
Huddled in the mart of mediocrities.
He said, the very finest doing wins   20
The admiring only; but to leave undone,
Promise and not fulfil, like buried youth,

Wins all the envious, makes them sigh your name
As that fair Absent, blameless Possible,
Which could alone impassion them; and thus,   25
Serene negation has free gift of all,
Panting achievement struggles, is denied,
Or wins to lose again. What say you, Armgart?
Truth has rough flavours if we bite it through;
I think this sarcasm came from out its core   30
Of bitter irony.

ARMGART

It is the truth
Mean souls select to feed upon. What then?
Their meanness is a truth, which I will spurn.
The praise I seek lives not in envious breath
Using my name to blight another's deed.   35
I sing for love of song and that renown
Which is the spreading act, the world-wide share,
Of good that I was born with. Had I failed –
Well, that had been a truth most pitiable.
I cannot bear to think what life would be   40
With high hope shrunk to endurance, stunted aims
Like broken lances ground to eating-knives,
A self sunk down to look with level eyes
At low achievement, doomed from day to day
To distaste of its consciousness. But I—   45

GRAF

Have won, not lost, in your decisive throw.
And I too glory in this issue; yet,
The public verdict has no potency
To sway my judgment of what Armgart is:
My pure delight in her would be but sullied,   50
If it o'erflowed with mixture of men's praise.
And had she failed, I should have said, 'The pearl
Remains a pearl for me, reflects the light
With the same fitness that first charmed my gaze –
Is worth as fine a setting now as then.'   55

ARMGART (rising)

O you are good! But why will you rehearse
The talk of cynics, who with insect eyes
Explore the secrets of the rubbish-heap?

I hate your epigrams and pointed saws
Whose narrow truth is but broad falsity.   60
Confess your friend was shallow.

GRAF

        I confess
Life is not rounded in an epigram,
And saying aught, we leave a world unsaid.
I quoted, merely to shape forth my thought
That high success has terrors when achieved –   65
Like preternatural spouses whose dire love
Hangs perilous on slight observances:
Whence it were possible that Armgart crowned
Might turn and listen to a pleading voice,
Though Armgart striving in the race was deaf.   70
You said you dared not think what life had been
Without the stamp of eminence; have you thought
How you will bear the poise of eminence
With dread of sliding? Paint the future out
As an unchecked and glorious career,   75
'Twill grow more strenuous by the very love
You bear to excellence, the very fate
Of human powers, which tread at every step
On possible verges.

ARMGART

            I accept the peril.
I choose to walk high with sublimer dread   80
Rather than crawl in safety. And, besides,
I am an artist as you are a noble:
I ought to bear the burthen of my rank.

GRAF

Such parallels, dear Armgart, are but snares
To catch the mind with seeming argument –   85
Small baits of likeness 'mid disparity.
Men rise the higher as their task is high,
The task being well achieved. A woman's rank
Lies in the fulness of her womanhood:
Therein alone she is royal.

ARMGART

Yes, I know 90
The oft-taught Gospel: 'Woman, thy desire
Shall be that all superlatives on earth
Belong to men, save the one highest kind –
To be a mother. Thou shalt not desire
To do aught best save pure subservience: 95
Nature has willed it so!' O blessed Nature!
Let her be arbitress; she gave me voice
Such as she only gives a woman child,
Best of its kind, gave me ambition too,
That sense transcendent which can taste the joy 100
Of swaying multitudes, of being adored
For such achievement, needed excellence,
As man's best art must wait for, or be dumb.
Men did not say, when I had sung last night,
' 'Twas good, nay, wonderful, considering 105
She is a woman' – and then turn to add,
'Tenor or baritone had sung her songs
Better, of course: she's but a woman spoiled.'
I beg your pardon, Graf, you said it.

GRAF

No!
How should I say it, Armgart? I who own 110
The magic of your nature-given art
As sweetest effluence of your womanhood
Which, being to my choice the best, must find
The best of utterance. But this I say:
Your fervid youth beguiles you; you mistake 115
A strain of lyric passion for a life
Which in the spending is a chronicle
With ugly pages. Trust me, Armgart, trust me;
Ambition exquisite as yours which soars
Toward something quintessential you call fame, 120
Is not robust enough for this gross world
Whose fame is dense with false and foolish breath.
Ardour, a-twin with nice refining thought,
Prepares a double pain. Pain had been saved,
Nay, purer glory reached, had you been throned 125
As woman only, holding all your art
As attribute to that dear sovereignty –
Concentering your power in home delights
Which penetrate and purify the world.

ARMGART

What, leave the opera with my part ill-sung   130
While I was warbling in a drawing-room?
Sing in the chimney-corner to inspire
My husband reading news? Let the world hear
My music only in his morning speech
Less stammering than most honourable men's?   135
No! tell me that my song is poor, my art
The piteous feat of weakness aping strength —
That were fit proem to your argument.
Till then, I am an artist by my birth —
By the same warrant that I am a woman: 140
Nay, in the added rarer gift I see
Supreme vocation: if a conflict comes,
Perish — no, not the woman, but the joys
Which men make narrow by their narrowness.
O I am happy! The great masters write   145
For women's voices, and great Music wants me!
I need not crush myself within a mould
Of theory called Nature: I have room
To breathe and grow unstunted.

GRAF

                    Armgart, hear me.
I meant not that our talk should hurry on   150
To such collision. Foresight of the ills
Thick shadowing your path, drew on my speech
Beyond intention. True, I came to ask
A great renunciation, but not this
Towards which my words at first perversely strayed,   155
As if in memory of their earlier suit,
Forgetful. . . . .
Armgart, do you remember too? the suit
Had but postponement, was not quite disdained —
Was told to wait and learn — what it has learned —   160
A more submissive speech.

ARMGART (*with some agitation*)

                    Then it forgot
Its lesson cruelly. As I remember,
'Twas not to speak save to the artist crowned,
Nor speak to her of casting off her crown.

GRAF

Nor will it, Armgart. I come not to seek   165
Any renunciation save the wife's,
Which turns away from other possible love
Future and worthier to take his love
Who asks the name of husband. He who sought
Armgart obscure, and heard her answer, 'Wait' –   170
May come without suspicion now to seek
Armgart applauded.

ARMGART (*turning towards him*)

      Yes, without suspicion
Of aught save what consists with faithfulness
In all expressed intent. Forgive me, Graf –
I am ungrateful to no soul that loves me –   175
To you most grateful. Yet the best intent
Grasps but a living present which may grow
Like any unfledged bird. You are a noble,
And have a high career; just now you said
'Twas higher far than aught a woman seeks   180
Beyond mere womanhood. You claim to be
More than a husband, but could not rejoice
That I were more than wife. What follows, then?
You choosing me with such persistency
As is but stretched-out rashness, soon must find   185
Our marriage asks concessions, asks resolve
To share renunciation or demand it.
Either we both renounce a mutual ease,
As in a nation's need both man and wife
Do public services, or one of us   190
Must yield that something else for which each lives
Besides the other. Men are reasoners:
That premiss of superior claims perforce
Urges conclusion – 'Armgart, it is you.'

GRAF

But if I say I have considered this   195
With strict prevision, counted all the cost
Which that great good of loving you demands –
Questioned my stores of patience, half-resolved
To live resigned without a bliss whose threat
Touched you as well as me – and finally,   200
With impetus of undivided will

Returned to say, 'You shall be free as now;
Only accept the refuge, shelter, guard,
My love will give your freedom' – then your words
Are hard accusal.

ARMGART

           Well, I accuse myself.   205
My love would be accomplice of your will.

GRAF

Again – my will?

ARMGART

           O your unspoken will.
Your silent tolerance would torture me,
And on that rack I should deny the good
I yet believed in.

GRAF

           Then I am the man   210
Whom you would love?

ARMGART

           Whom I refuse to love!
No, I will live alone and pour my pain
With passion into music, where it turns
To what is best within my better self.
I will not take for husband one who deems   215
The thing my soul acknowledges as good –
The thing I hold worth striving, suffering for,
To be a thing dispensed with easily,
Or else the idol of a mind infirm.

GRAF

Armgart, you are ungenerous; you strain   220
My thought beyond its mark. Our difference
Lies not so deep as love – as union
Through a mysterious fitness that transcends
Formal agreement.

ARMGART

                        It lies deep enough
To chafe the union. If many a man   225
Refrains, degraded, from the utmost right,
Because the pleadings of his wife's small fears
Are little serpents biting at his heel, –
How shall a woman keep her steadfastness
Beneath a frost within her husband's eyes   230
Where coldness scorches? Graf, it is your sorrow
That you love Armgart. Nay, it is her sorrow
That she may not love you.

GRAF

                              Woman, it seems,
Has enviable power to love or not
According to her will.

ARMGART

                              She has the will –   235
I have – who am one woman – not to take
Disloyal pledges that divide her will.
The man who marries me must wed my Art –
Honour and cherish it, not tolerate.

GRAF

The man is yet to come whose theory   240
Will weigh as nought with you against his love.

ARMGART

Whose theory will plead beside his love.

GRAF

Himself a singer, then? who knows no life
Out of the opera books, where tenor parts
Are found to suit him?

ARMGART

                  You are bitter, Graf.   245
Forgive me; seek the woman you deserve,
All grace, all goodness, who has not yet found
A meaning in her life, nor any end
Beyond fulfilling yours. The type abounds.

GRAF

And happily, for the world.

ARMGART

                  Yes, happily.   250
Let it excuse me that my kind is rare:
Commonness is its own security.

GRAF

Armgart, I would with all my soul I knew
The man so rare that he could make your life
As woman sweet to you, as artist safe.   255

ARMGART

O I can live unmated, but not live
Without the bliss of singing to the world,
And feeling all my world respond to me.

GRAF

May it be lasting. Then, we two must part?

ARMGART

I thank you from my heart for all. Farewell!   260

[A year later, Armgart has lost her voice. Her cousin and maid, Walpurga, reminds her of the lives of most women. Her teacher, the composer Leo, advises humility and endurance.]

Scene V

ARMGART, WALPURGA.

ARMGART

Walpurga, have you walked this morning?

WALPURGA

No.

ARMGART

Go, then, and walk; I wish to be alone.

WALPURGA

I will not leave you.

ARMGART

Will not, at my wish?

WALPURGA

Will not, because you wish it. Say no more,
But take this draught.

ARMGART

The Doctor gave it you?   5
It is an anodyne. Put it away.
He cured me of my voice, and now he wants
To cure me of my vision and resolve –
Drug me to sleep that I may wake again
Without a purpose, abject as the rest   10
To bear the yoke of life. He shall not cheat me
Of that fresh strength which anguish gives the soul,
The inspiration of revolt, ere rage
Slackens to faltering. Now I see the truth.

WALPURGA (*setting down the glass*)

Then you must see a future in your reach,   15
With happiness enough to make a dower
For two of modest claims.

ARMGART

                O you intone
That chant of consolation wherewith ease
Makes itself easier in the sight of pain.

WALPURGA

No; I would not console you, but rebuke.   20

ARMGART

That is more bearable. Forgive me, dear.
Say what you will. But now I want to write.
            (She rises and moves towards a table.)

WALPURGA

I say then, you are simply fevered, mad;
You cry aloud at horrors that would vanish
If you would change the light, throw into shade   25
The loss you aggrandise, and let day fall
On good remaining, nay on good refused
Which may be gain now. Did you not reject
A woman's lot more brilliant, as some held,
Than any singer's? It may still be yours.   30
Graf Dornberg loved you well.

ARMGART

                Not me, not me.
He loved one well who was like me in all
Save in a voice which made that All unlike
As diamond is to charcoal. O, a man's love!
Think you he loves a woman's inner self   35
Aching with loss of loveliness? — as mothers
Cleave to the palpitating pain that dwells
Within their misformed offspring?

WALPURGA

                But the Graf
Chose you as simple Armgart — had preferred
That you should never seek for any fame   40

But such as matrons have who rear great sons.
And therefore you rejected him; but now –

ARMGART

Ay, now – now he would see me as I am,
                    (*She takes up a hand-mirror.*)
Russet and songless as a missel-thrush.
An ordinary girl – a plain brown girl,   45
Who, if some meaning flash from out her words,
Shocks as a disproportioned thing – a Will
That, like an arm astretch and broken off,
Has nought to hurl – the torso of a soul.
I sang him into love of me: my song   50
Was consecration, lifted me apart
From the crowd chiselled like me, sister forms,
But empty of divineness. Nay, my charm
Was half that I could win fame yet renounce!
A wife with glory possible absorbed   55
Into her husband's actual.

WALPURGA

                    For shame!
Armgart, you slander him. What would you say
If now he came to you and asked again
That you would be his wife?

ARMGART

                    No, and thrice no!
It would be pitying constancy, not love,   60
That brought him to me now. I will not be
A pensioner in marriage. Sacraments
Are not to feed the paupers of the world.
If he were generous – I am generous too.

WALPURGA

Proud, Armgart, but not generous.

ARMGART

                    Say no more.   65
He will not know until –

WALPURGA

He knows already.

ARMGART (*quickly*)

Is he come back?

WALPURGA

Yes, and will soon be here.
The Doctor had twice seen him and would go
From hence again to see him.

ARMGART

Well, he knows.
It is all one.

WALPURGA

What if he were outside?   70
I hear a footstep in the ante-room.

ARMGART (*raising herself and assuming calmness*)

Why let him come, of course. I shall behave
Like what I am, a common personage
Who looks for nothing but civility.
I shall not play the fallen heroine,   75
Assume a tragic part and throw out cues
For a beseeching lover.

WALPURGA

Some one raps.
                    (*Goes to the door.*)
A letter — from the Graf.

ARMGART

Then open it.
                    (WALPURGA *still offers it.*)

Nay, my head swims. Read it. I cannot see.
(WALPURGA *opens it, reads and pauses*.)
Read it. Have done! No matter what it is.   80

WALPURGA (*reads in a low, hesitating voice*)

'I am deeply moved – my heart is rent, to hear of your illness and its cruel result,
just now communicated to me by Dr Grahn. But surely it is possible that this result
may not be permanent. For youth such as yours, Time may hold in store something
more than resignation: who shall say that it does not hold renewal? I have not dared
to ask admission to you in the hours of a recent shock, but I cannot depart on a long
mission without tendering my sympathy and my farewell. I start this evening for the
Caucasus, and thence I proceed to India, where I am intrusted by the Government with
business which may be of long duration.'

(WALPURGA *sits down dejectedly*.)

ARMGART (*after a slight shudder, bitterly*).

The Graf has much discretion. I am glad.
He spares us both a pain, not seeing me.
What I like least is that consoling hope –
That empty cup, so neatly ciphered 'Time,'
Handed me as a cordial for despair.   85
(*Slowly and dreamily*) Time – what a word to fling as charity!
Bland neutral word for slow, dull-beating pain –
Days, months, and years! – If I would wait for them!
            (*She takes up her hat and puts it on, then wraps her
                  mantle round her.* WALPURGA *leaves the room*.)
Why, this is but beginning. (WALP. *re-enters*.) Kiss me, dear.
I am going now – alone – out – for a walk.   90
Say you will never wound me any more
With such cajolery as nurses use
To patients amorous of a crippled life.
Flatter the blind: I see.

WALPURGA

            Well, I was wrong.
In haste to soothe, I snatched at flickers merely.   95
Believe me, I will flatter you no more.

ARMGART

Bear witness, I am calm. I read my lot
As soberly as if it were a tale

Writ by a creeping feuilletonist and called
'The Woman's Lot: a Tale of Everyday:'   100
A middling woman's, to impress the world
With high superfluousness; her thoughts a crop
Of chick-weed errors or of pot-herb facts,
Smiled at like some child's drawing on a slate.
'Genteel?' 'O yes, gives lessons; not so good   105
As any man's would be, but cheaper far.'
'Pretty?' 'No; yet she makes a figure fit
For good society. Poor thing, she sews
Both late and early, turns and alters all
To suit the changing mode. Some widower   110
Might do well, marrying her; but in these days! . . .
Well, she can somewhat eke her narrow gains
By writing, just to furnish her with gloves
And droschkies in the rain. They print her things
Often for charity.' – O a dog's life!   115
A harnessed dog's, that draws a little cart
Voted a nuisance! I am going now.

WALPURGA

Not now, the door is locked.

ARMGART

                              Give me the key!

WALPURGA

Locked on the outside. Gretchen has the key:
She is gone on errands.

ARMGART

                              What, you dare to keep me   120
Your prisoner?

WALPURGA

                              And have I not been yours?
Your wish has been a bolt to keep me in.
Perhaps that middling woman whom you paint
With far-off scorn . . . . .

ARMGART

                    I paint what I must be!
What is my soul to me without the voice   125
That gave it freedom? – gave it one grand touch
And made it nobly human? – Prisoned now,
Prisoned in all the petty mimicries
Called woman's knowledge, that will fit the world
As doll-clothes fit a man. I can do nought   130
Better than what a million women do –
Must drudge among the crowd and feel my life
Beating upon the world without response,
Beating with passion through an insect's horn
That moves a millet-seed laboriously.   135
If I *would* do it!

WALPURGA (*coldly*)

                    And why should you not?

ARMGART (*turning quickly*)

Because Heaven made me royal – wrought me out
With subtle finish towards pre-eminence,
Made every channel of my soul converge
To one high function, and then flung me down,   140
That breaking I might turn to subtlest pain.
An inborn passion gives a rebel's right:
I would rebel and die in twenty worlds
Sooner than bear the yoke of thwarted life,
Each keenest sense turned into keen distaste,   145
Hunger not satisfied but kept alive
Breathing in languor half a century.
All the world now is but a rack of threads
To twist and dwarf me into pettiness
And basely feigned content, the placid mask   150
Of women's misery.

WALPURGA (*indignantly*)

                    Ay, such a mask
As the few born like you to easy joy,
Cradled in privilege, take for natural
On all the lowly faces that must look
Upward to you! What revelation now   155
Shows you the mask or gives presentiment

Of sadness hidden? You who every day
These five years saw me limp to wait on you,
And thought the order perfect which gave *me*,
The girl without pretension to be aught,   160
A splendid cousin for my happiness:
To watch the night through when her brain was fired
With too much gladness – listen, always listen
To what *she* felt, who having power had right
To feel exorbitantly, and submerge   165
The souls around her with the poured-out flood
Of what must be ere she were satisfied!
That was feigned patience, was it? Why not love,
Love nurtured even with that strength of self
Which found no room save in another's life?   170
O such as I know joy by negatives,
And all their deepest passion is a pang
Till they accept their pauper's heritage,
And meekly live from out the general store
Of joy they were born stripped of. I accept –   175
Nay, now would sooner choose it than the wealth
Of natures you call royal, who can live
In mere mock knowledge of their fellows' woe,
Thinking their smiles may heal it.

ARMGART (*tremulously*)

      Nay, Walpurga,
I did not make a palace of my joy   180
To shut the world's truth from me. All my good
Was that I touched the world and made a part
In the world's dower of beauty, strength, and bliss;
It was the glimpse of consciousness divine
Which pours out day and sees the day is good.   185
Now I am fallen dark; I sit in gloom,
Remembering bitterly. Yet you speak truth;
I wearied you, it seems; took all your help
As cushioned nobles use a weary serf,
Not looking at his face.

WALPURGA

      O, I but stand   190
As a small symbol for a mighty sum –
The sum of claims unpaid for myriad lives;
I think you never set your loss beside
That mighty deficit. Is your work gone –
The prouder queenly work that paid itself   195

And yet was overpaid with men's applause?
Are you no longer chartered, privileged,
But sunk to simple woman's penury,
To ruthless Nature's chary average –
Where is the rebel's right for you alone?   200
Noble rebellion lifts a common load;
But what is he who flings his own load off
And leaves his fellows toiling? Rebel's right?
Say rather, the deserter's. O, you smiled
From your clear height on all the million lots   205
Which yet you brand as abject.

ARMGART

                    I was blind
With too much happiness: true vision comes
Only, it seems, with sorrow. Were there one
This moment near me, suffering what I feel,
And needing me for comfort in her pang –   210
Then it were worth the while to live; not else.

WALPURGA

One – near you – why, they throng! you hardly stir
But your act touches them. We touch afar.
For did not swarthy slaves of yesterday
Leap in their bondage at the Hebrews' flight,   215
Which touched them through the thrice millennial dark?
But you can find the sufferer you need
With touch less subtle.

ARMGART

                    Who has need of me?

WALPURGA

Love finds the need it fills. But you are hard.

ARMGART

Is it not you, Walpurga, who are hard?   220
You humoured all my wishes till to-day,
When fate has blighted me.

WALPURGA

You would not hear

The 'chant of consolation:' words of hope
Only embittered you. Then hear the truth –
A lame girl's truth, whom no one ever praised   225
For being cheerful. 'It is well,' they said:
'Were she cross-grained she could not be endured.'
A word of truth from her had startled you;
But you – you claimed the universe; nought less
Than all existence working in sure tracks   230
Towards your supremacy. The wheels might scathe
A myriad destinies – nay, must perforce;
But yours they must keep clear of; just for you
The seething atoms through the firmament
Must bear a human heart – which you had not!   235
For what is it to you that women, men,
Plod, faint, are weary, and espouse despair
Of aught but fellowship? Save that you spurn
To be among them? Now, then, you are lame –
Maimed, as you said, and levelled with the crowd: 240
Call it new birth – birth from that monstrous Self
Which, smiling down upon a race oppressed,
Says, 'All is good, for I am throned at ease.'
Dear Armgart – nay, you tremble – I am cruel.

ARMGART

O no! hark! Some one knocks. Come in! – come in!   245
(Enter LEO)

LEO

See, Gretchen let me in. I could not rest
Longer away from you.

ARMGART

Sit down, dear Leo.

Walpurga, I would speak with him alone.
(WALPURGA goes out)

LEO (<i>hesitatingly</i>)

You mean to walk?

ARMGART

No, I shall stay within.
(*She takes off her hat and mantle, and sits down
inmediately. After a pause, speaking in a subdued
tone to* LEO.)
How old are you?   250

LEO

Threescore and five.

ARMGART

That's old.
I never thought till now how you have lived.
They hardly ever play your music?

LEO (*raising his eyebrows and throwing out his lip*)

No!
Schubert too wrote for silence: half his work
Lay like a frozen Rhine till summers came   255
That warmed the grass above him. Even so!
His music lives now with a mighty youth.

ARMGART

Do you think yours will live when you are dead?

LEO

Pfui! The time was, I drank that home-brewed wine
And found it heady, while my blood was young: 260
Now it scarce warms me. Tipple it as I may,
I am sober still, and say: 'My old friend Leo,
Much grain is wasted in the world and rots;
Why not thy handful?'

ARMGART

Strange! since I have known you
Till now I never wondered how you lived.   265

When I sang well – that was your jubilee.
But you were old already.

LEO

                    Yes, child, yes:
Youth thinks itself the goal of each old life;
Age has but travelled from a far-off time
Just to be ready for youth's service. Well!   270
It was my chief delight to perfect you.

ARMGART

Good Leo! You have lived on little joys.
But your delight in me is crushed for ever.
Your pains, where are they now? They shaped intent
Which action frustrates; shaped an inward sense   275
Which is but keen despair, the agony
Of highest vision in the lowest pit.

LEO

Nay, nay, I have a thought: keep to the stage,
To drama without song; for you can act –
Who knows how well, when all the soul is poured   280
Into that sluice alone?

ARMGART

                    I know, and you:
The second or third best in tragedies
That cease to touch the fibre of the time.
No; song is gone, but nature's other gift,
Self-judgment, is not gone. Song was my speech,   285
And with its impulse only, action came:
Song was the battle's onset, when cool purpose
Glows into rage, becomes a warring god
And moves the limbs with miracle. But now –
O, I should stand hemmed in with thoughts and rules –   290
Say 'This way passion acts,' yet never feel
The might of passion. How should I declaim?
As monsters write with feet instead of hands.
I will not feed on doing great tasks ill,
Dull the world's sense with mediocrity,   285
And live by trash that smothers excellence.

One gift I had that ranked me with the best —
The secret of my frame — and that is gone.
For all life now I am a broken thing.
But silence there! Good Leo, advise me now.   300
I would take humble work and do it well —
Teach music, singing — what I can — not here,
But in some smaller town where I may bring
The method you have taught me, pass your gift
To others who can use it for delight.   305
You think I can do that?

(*She pauses with a sob in her voice*)

LEO

            Yes, yes, dear child!
And it were well, perhaps, to change the place —
Begin afresh as I did when I left
Vienna with a heart half broken.

ARMGART (*roused by surprise*)

            You?

LEO

Well, it is long ago. But I had lost —   310
No matter! We must bury our dead joys
And live above them with a living world.
But whither, think you, you would like to go?

ARMGART

To Freiburg.

LEO

            In the Breisgau? And why there?
It is too small.

ARMGART

            Walpurga was born there,
And loves the place. She quitted it for me
These five years past. Now I will take her there.
Dear Leo, I will bury my dead joy.

LEO

Mothers do so, bereaved; then learn to love
Another's living child.

ARMGART

O, it is hard
To take the little corpse, and lay it low,
And say, 'None misses it but me.'
She sings ...
I mean Paulina sings Fidelio,
And they will welcome her to-night.

LEO

Well, well,
'Tis better that our griefs should not spread far.

Anne Brontë (1820–1849)

Anne Brontë was the younger sister of Charlotte and Emily and the sixth child of Maria
Branwell and Patrick Brontë. Her mother died, worn out with childbearing, when Anne
was only twenty months old and some of Anne's 'modesty' – in the nineteenth-century
phrase, 'lack of self-esteem' in twentieth-century terminology – may be attributed to
this circumstance. Because few of Anne's letters and papers survive, posterity has had
to rely upon Charlotte's assessment of Anne in drawing a picture of her personality.
Although Charlotte was not as dismissive as their brother Branwell who described
Anne as 'nothing, absolutely nothing ... next door to an idiot' (Gérin 1961: 82), there
is no doubt that Charlotte had a low opinion of Anne's talents and her work. But
Charlotte was a poor reader of Anne's work, deeming her novel *The Tenant of Wildfell
Hall* 'a mistake' and keeping it out of print during her own lifetime. Anne's poetry she
read as straightforwardly autobiographical commenting that her verses had 'a sweet and
sincere pathos of their own' (Wise and Symington 1933: II, 79). But Charlotte also said
that Anne's poems were 'mournful' and the product of her sister's 'morbid' character
and her 'tinge of religious melancholy' (Charlotte Brontë 1850: vi–vii). So persuasive
has Charlotte's mythmaking been, as in the case of Emily also, that Anne's literary
reputation has only recently been rehabilitated.

The earliest story of Anne's life is now taken to reveal more about Charlotte's
attitude to Anne than about Anne herself. When Anne was a baby Charlotte rushed
into her father's study to announce that an angel was standing beside Anne's cradle
(Gérin 1959: 13). The next story we have about Anne is when she appears in the
account of the mask training which Mr Brontë used to encourage his children to speak
out under the guise of a persona not their own. Anne, who was four at the time, was

asked what she most lacked and her answer was 'age and experience' (Gaskell 1975 [1857]: 94). The tale is read by modern commentators as evidence of Anne's early strongminded determination to shape her own destiny. Certainly it strikes the keynote, for in her Birthday Note for 1841 Anne, at the age of twenty-one writes: 'What will the next four years bring? Providence only knows. But we ourselves have sustained very little alteration...I have the same faults that I had then, only I have more wisdom and experience, and a little more self-possession than I then enjoyed' (Wise and Symington 1933: I, 239). Self-possession seems to have meant a great deal to Anne and her poem 'A Fragment' bears that out.

Anne stayed at home when her four elder sisters went to Cowan Bridge School. She shared lessons with Branwell, acquiring a mastery of Latin much superior to Charlotte and Emily's. Anne also saw Branwell's early failures to get on at Haworth Grammar School and might then have developed a sceptical attitude to her brother's aptitude and character; a scepticism which was to prove all too sadly correct. When Charlotte and Emily returned to Haworth, Anne partnered Emily in composing the Gondal side of the Gondal and Angria fantasy, and the two girls were so close that Ellen Nussey described them as 'like twins'. Anne did later go to school when Charlotte was offered free schooling for a sister during her posting at Roe Head School. Emily, as the elder, had gone first, but her homesickness meant that she dropped out in October 1835. At Roe Head Anne was a model pupil and won a conduct prize. Unlike either of her sisters she was always willing to take the world and its systems on their own terms and she succeeded in adapting to the ways of convention without rebellion and heartbreak. In the past this has been seen as evidence of her weak-mindedness. Today it is interpreted as indicative of her wiliness and iron determination to win an independent place in the world beyond Haworth, beyond Gondal.

In 1837 Anne was ill and suffered a spiritual crisis. It was after this that she began to write much of her religious poetry. The year of 1838 was spent at home but in 1839, again when Emily failed to keep her job and came home, Anne left Haworth for a post as governess to the Ingham family of Blake Hall. She was dismissed at the end of the year because she couldn't manage her boisterous charges, and she spent four months at home, during which time she was once supposed to have developed an attachment to her father's curate, William Weightman. He died in September 1842. In May 1840 Anne took up another post with the Robinsons at Thorp Green. She remained with them for five years, becoming a valued friend of the girls she tutored, and only returning to Haworth twice each year for a month at Christmas and in June. This (meagrely) independent life was clearly valued by Anne who took none of the opportunities offered to return to home life at Haworth. But it all went badly wrong when Branwell arrived, on Anne's recommendation, to tutor the son of the family, and promptly began something, an affair? a flirtation? with Mrs Robinson. Suspecting his deception and misdemeanour, Anne, caught in the middle, became increasingly miserable: 'During my stay [at Thorp Green] I have had some unpleasant and undreamt-of experience of human nature' she wrote (Wise and Symington 1933: II, 52). In the back of her prayer book she scribbled 'Sick of mankind and their disgusting ways'.

Anne left her post in June 1845. Branwell was dismissed in July when all was discovered and he returned home to a life of alcohol and drug addiction which put great strain on all the sisters. That autumn Charlotte found Emily's manuscript poems and Anne offered her own contribution to the volume of *Poems* which resulted. Anne then set to work on her novel *Agnes Grey* which was published with Emily's *Wuthering*

Heights in 1847. *The Tenant of Wildfell Hall* followed with its picture of vicious dissolution in the portrait of Huntingdon, so clearly drawn from Anne's own experience of Branwell's decline. Anne's sense of morality and serious conviction that it was a woman's duty to speak things by their names is made clear in her Preface to the second edition of *The Tenant*, 'I wished to tell the truth' she wrote.

Branwell died in September 1848 and the swift breaking up of the family followed. Emily died in December and Anne by then was also ill, though she strove to recover and persuaded Charlotte and Ellen Nussey that a trip to Scarborough, which she loved, having spent much time there with the Robinsons, would do her good. The three visited York Minster and travelled on to Scarborough where Anne died, still anxious for Charlotte rather than herself; 'Take courage, Charlotte, *take courage*' (Wise and Symington 1933: II, 336). And at Scarborough Anne was buried, the only one of the family to lie away from Haworth, a small sign in death of her difference in life.

Anne Brontë's poems are of a high quality and, just as they often suffer in comparison with Emily's, so they benefit by being read in the wider context of the work of other women writers of the period. Anne Brontë's literary influences were drawn from the eighteenth century, whether the religious poetry of Moore, or the secular writings of Cowper. In this she is quite unlike Emily and Charlotte whose allegiences lie with the Romantics. Brontë's poetry is sparse and rigorously ordered rather than lush and imaginatively sensuous. But her logical drive and her delight in intellectual reasoning mean that the poems often develop into dialogue or narrative which gives them a pleasurable quality of argument or plot unfolded. This is the case with 'A Fragment'. It bears a Gondal signature so was apparently written for the saga, but tellingly, it was published in the 1846 collection under the title of 'Self-Congratulation'. The question and answer beginning of the poem means that the reader has to unravel the mystery of the speaker's behaviour. And it is typical of Anne Brontë that she is here interested in the story of a 'masquerade' which conceals, rather than reveals, emotion. The poem clearly recognizes, and in the most modern terms, the construction of the self as this speaker adjusts both dress, appearance and manner in order to make a false self for public presentation. Of course the poem also reveals, to the reader, the emotional turmoil of the speaker, but it is a most interesting account of the processes of repression and socialization demanded of Victorian woman. 'The Captive Dove', like other 'bird' poems of the period (Norton's 'Like an enfranchised bird', Blind's 'Entangled', Barrett Browning's *Aurora Leigh* Book 1), realizes a connection between the (woman) poet–speaker and the imprisoned bird. Here there is no joyous resolution in freedom, but rather the prison is made doubly restrictive by being a prison of isolation and solitary confinement. It is tempting to read the work as a 'governess' poem: not only is the speaker captive, exiled from 'thy native wood', and unable to develop her potential and fly with 'those useless wings', but it lives in a state which must be endured alone, without the companionship of a social equal. Finally, Anne Brontë's little lyric 'My soul is awakened, my spirit is soaring' is included because it is a nature poem, but it is very much an Anne poem, reflecting her love of the 'other place' where she wishes to be, at the seaside and not out on the moors with Emily and Charlotte. It is also endearing because of the immense sense of physicality in her enjoyment of the wind, a sensual and bodily-felt reaction which is only matched by the more untamed of Rossetti's rousing nursery poems such as 'Goblin Market' or 'Who has seen the wind?'.

M.R.

Brontë, Anne (1846) Poems by Currer, Ellis and Acton Bell [i.e. Charlotte, Emily and Anne Brontë], London.

—— (1979) *The Poems of Anne Brontë: A New Text and Commentary*, ed. Edward Chitham, London and Basingstoke, Macmillan.

Bell, Craig A. (1986) 'Anne Brontë: A Re-appraisal', *Quarterly Review*, cciv (1986), 315–21.

Brontë, Charlotte (1850) Biographical Notice of Ellis and Acton Bell, second edition of Emily Brontë's *Wuthering Heights*.

Gaskell, Elizabeth (1975) [1857] *The Life of Charlotte Brontë*, Harmondsworth, Penguin.

Gérin, Winifred (1959) *Anne Brontë*, London, Allen Lane.

—— (1961) *Branwell Brontë*, Toronto and New York, Thomas Nelson and Sons.

Gilligan, Carol (1982) *In a Different Voice*, Cambridge Mass., Harvard University Press.

Langland, Elizabeth (1989) *Anne Brontë: The Other One*, Basingstoke and London, Macmillan.

Scott, P. J. M. (1983) *Anne Brontë: A New Critical Assessment*, New York, Barnes and Nobel.

Wise, T. J. and Symington, J. A. eds (1933) *The Brontës: Their Lives, Friendships and Correspondence*, 4 vols, Oxford, Shakespeare Head.

A Fragment

'Maiden, thou wert thoughtless once
    Of beauty or of grace,
Simple and homely in attire
    Careless of form and face.
Then whence this change, and why so oft   5
    Dost smooth thy hazel hair?
And wherefore deck thy youthful form
    With such unwearied care?

'Tell us – and cease to tire our ears
    With yonder hackneyed strain –   10
Why wilt thou play those simple tunes
    So often o'er again?'
'Nay, gentle friends, I can but say
    That childhood's thoughts are gone.
Each year its own new feelings brings   15
    And years move swiftly on,

And for those little simple airs,
    I love to play them o'er –
So much I dare not promise now
    To play them never more.'   20
I answered and it was enough;
    They turned them to depart;

They could not read my secret thoughts
    Nor see my throbbing heart.

I've noticed many a youthful form   25
    Upon whose changeful face
The inmost workings of the soul
    The gazer's eye might trace.
The speaking eye, the changing lip,
    The ready blushing cheek,   30
The smiling or beclouded brow
    Their different feelings speak.

But, thank God! you might gaze on mine
    For hours and never know
The secret changes of my soul   35
    From joy to bitter woe.
Last night as we sat round the fire
    Conversing merrily,
We heard without approaching steps
    Of one well known to me.   40

There was no trembling in my voice,
    No blush upon my cheek,
No lustrous sparkle in my eyes
    Of hope or joy to speak.
But O my spirit burned within,   45
    My heart beat thick and fast.
He came not nigh – he went away
    And then my joy was past.

And yet my comrades marked it not,
    My voice was still the same;   50
They saw me smile, and o'er my face –
    No signs of sadness came;
They little knew my hidden thoughts
    And they will never know
The anguish of my drooping heart,   55
    The bitter aching woe!

'My soul is awakened, my spirit is soaring'

My soul is awakened, my spirit is soaring,
And carried aloft on the wings of the breeze;
For, above, and around me, the wild wind is roaring
Arousing to rapture the earth and the seas.

The long withered grass in the sunshine is glancing,   5
The bare trees are tossing their branches on high;

The dead leaves beneath them are merrily dancing,
The white clouds are scudding across the blue sky.

I wish I could see how the ocean is lashing
The foam of its billows to whirlwinds of spray,   10
I wish I could see how its proud waves are dashing
And hear the wild roar of their thunder today!

The Captive Dove

Poor restless Dove, I pity thee,
And when I hear thy plaintive moan
I'll mourn for thy captivity
And in thy woes forget mine own.

To see thee stand prepared to fly,   5
And flap those useless wings of thine,
And gaze into the distant sky
Would melt a harder heart than mine.

In vain! In vain! Thou canst not rise —
Thy prison roof confines thee there;   10
Its slender wires delude thine eyes,
And quench thy longing with despair.

O! thou wert made to wander free
In sunny mead and shady grove,
And far beyond the rolling sea   15
In distant climes at will to rove.

Yet hadst thou but one gentle mate
Thy little drooping heart to cheer
And share with thee thy captive state,
Thou couldst be happy even there.   20

Yes, even there, if listening by
One faithful dear companion stood,
While gazing on her full bright eye
Thou mightst forget thy native wood.

But thou, poor solitary dove,   25
Must make unheard thy joyless moan;
The heart that nature formed to love
Must pine neglected and alone.

Home

How brightly glistening in the sun
    The woodland ivy plays!
While yonder beeches from their barks
    Reflect his silver rays.

That sun surveys a lovely scene   5
    From softly smiling skies;
And wildly through unnumbered trees
    The wind of winter sighs:

Now loud, it thunders o'er my head,
    And now in distance dies.   10
But give me back my barren hills
    Where colder breezes rise:

Where scarce the scattered, stunted trees
    Can yield an answering swell,
But where a wilderness of heath   15
    Returns the sound as well.

For yonder garden, fair and wide,
    With groves of evergreen,
Long winding walks, and borders trim,
    And velvet lawns between;   20

Restore to me that little spot,
    With gray walls compassed round,
Where knotted grass neglected lies,
    And weeds usurp the ground.

Though all around this mansion high   25
    Invites the foot to roam,
And though its halls are fair within —
    Oh, give me back my home!

Night

I love the silent hour of night,
For blissful dreams may then arise,
Revealing to my charméd sight
What may not bless my waking eyes!

And then a voice may meet my ear   5
That death has silenced long ago;

> And hope and rapture may appear
> Instead of solitude and woe.
>
> Cold in the grave for years has lain
> The form it was my bliss to see,   10
> And only dreams can bring again
> The darling of my heart to me.

Menella Bute Smedley (1820–1877)

Like a pattern for many another Victorian woman poet, Menella Smedley had an inadequate father who gave her a sound classical education and little else, an intelligent mother who kept the household together, numerous brothers and sisters to support, and a melodramatic turn of imagination channelled effectively by indigence and lack of opportunity into good works.

Menella's father, Edward Smedley, married Mary Hume in 1815. He supplemented his income as a curate by preparing young men for university, and writing for the *British Critic* and the *Annual Register*, taking a post as editor of the *Encyclopaedia Metropolitana* in 1822. Increasing deafness meant that he could no longer teach or preach, and in 1827 the family of five children moved from London to Dulwich, where their father led an invalid's existence, apart from teaching the girls Latin and using their services as scribes. His one volume of poetry was published posthumously in 1837.

Menella was delicate as a child and for many years lived at Tenby on account of her health. Probably encouraged by her father's sister, one Mrs Hart who wrote stories and poems for children, she published under the pseudonym of 'S. M.', a number of stories from 1849, including *Twice Lost* (1866) which is a tale of deceit and abduction narrated by a 38-year-old governess who describes herself as a 'strong-minded woman'.

In the 1870s Menella worked as a district visitor to poor houses under the supervision of Mrs Nassau Senior who was then Inspector under the Local Government Board for the education of girls in Pauper Schools. She edited Mrs Senior's report published in the Blue Book for 1873–4 and this was issued as *Boarding Out and Pauper Schools for Girls* (1875).

For the most part Smedley's poetry consists of slight lyrics or extravagant and sensational narratives. Occasionally she rises above this, as in the haunting suggestiveness of 'A Face from the Past' and in the poems which were inspired by reports of the struggle for unification in Italy. As with other women poets, most notably Barrett Browning, she seems to have adopted a view of Italy as quintessentially female, and seen a personal reflection in that political endeavour. There is some stringent comment on the contemporary sexual double standard in 'A Contrast' where the bride is required to be saintly while the groom, though unexceptionable as far as the conventional world is concerned, is corrupt and licentious in comparison. Her poems for children, though published late in her life, are intriguing in their playfulness and are one of the places in her writings where the proprieties are thrown aside. A strong association with friends in Ireland led to her endearing poem 'The Irish Fairy' which was published along with 'The Sorrowful Seagull' in *Poems Written for a Child* by Two Friends (1895).

M.R.

Smedley, Menella Bute (1856) *Lays and Ballads from English History*, London.
—— (1863) *The Story of Queen Isabel and Other Verses*, London.
—— (1868) *Poems*, London.
—— (1868) *Poems Written for a Child* by Two Friends, London.

A Face from the Past

Out of the Past there has come a Face;
  Wherefore I do not know;
I did not call it from its place,
  I cannot make it go;
In the night it was very near,   5
  And it looks at me to-day,
With well-known eyes, so kind, so dear,
  And it will not go away.

I am the same that I was before,
  There is nothing new to say;   10
But *this* is with me evermore,
  As it was not yesterday;
It makes the Moment vague and vain,
  And (what a wondrous thing!)
I hear an old tale told again   15
  As if it was happening.

You talk, but scarce I understand;
  If you but pause for breath,
Straightway I am in that far land
  Beyond the seas of Death;   20
All living sights are dimly seen
  Across that mighty space –
How can I tell you what I mean?
  'Tis nothing but a Face.

O friends, who think me dull or cold,   25
  Why do you feel surprise?
Have *you* no memories that hold
  Your weary waking eyes?
I want to take all patiently,
  But I sometimes long to say,   30
A Face has come from the Past to me –
  Let me alone to-day!

The Irish Fairy

An Irish Fairy lost her way;
  Of course she could not find it.

She was so debonnair and gay,
　　She vow'd she did not mind it.
And far too vain to speak of pain,　　　　　　　　　5
　　Or own to fear's dominion,
She sang of you, Donnel Aboo,
　　As happy as a Fenian!

Sure all her ancestors were kings,
　　Who ruled and reign'd and thunder'd;　　　　10
And, if you talk'd of fifty things,
　　She'd gabble of a hundred!
She'd fun galore, and plenty more,
　　She was so bright and tricksy;
She liked a pig, an Irish pig,　　　　　　　　　15
　　And just a dhrop of whisky!

She was not fond of water, though,
　　And thought rags cool and pleasant;
She had no call to work, you know —
　　Would rather play at present.　　　　　　　　20
And heads she'd break at fair and wake,
　　And hearts too very gaily;
And if you spoke of John Bull's oak,
　　She'd flourish Pat's shillaly!

She snigger'd at the big Police,　　　　　　　　25
　　The craytures, they'll not hurt you!
And swans she made of all her geese,
　　Of all her faults a virtue.
In debt to run is only fun,
　　To drink is only jolly;　　　　　　　　　　　30
A little lie is 'cute and sly,
　　And telling truth a folly.

And *are* there other countries, then?
　　(Och! Ireland grand and great is!);
And *have* they women there, and men,　　　　35
　　And whisky, punch, and praties?
Of this she's sure, that rich or poor,
　　Or honest folks or rogues, oh!
Sorra a bit can *one* be fit
　　To tie ould Ireland's brogues, oh!　　　　　40

She wander'd on, she wander'd on.
　　And still she kept her eyes on
The place she'd set her heart upon —
　　And that was the horizon.
She murmur'd, 'Oh, if on I go,　　　　　　　　45

Unheeding gates and hedges,
  I'm sure that I must touch the sky,
    And stand upon the edges!'

And if you think the notion queer,
  Remember, she was Irish;   50
And on she went, poor little dear,
  Till she was rather tiredish!
Her shoes (a pair) she held with care –
  Her feet, you see, don't need 'em;
For Irish shoes are not for use,   55
  And Irish feet like freedom.

She went so far, that all the trees
  Were made of cherry-brandy,
And all the little pods of peas
  Held drops of sugar-candy,   60
And every well contain'd Moselle,
  And all the rivers sherry,
And eggs were made of marmalade –
  A charming country, very.

She reach'd the land where sea is earth,   65
  And earth is only water;
And people banquet on a dearth,
  And lives are saved by slaughter;
And dwarfs are tall, and giants small,
  And rascals bow demurely.   70
She said, 'Perhaps I know these chaps;
  I've seen this country, surely.'

She came to where the sky rains cats
  And dogs, to drown the miller;
And, in their mouths, the little brats   75
  Are born with spoons of siller.
And if you speak about next week,
  You'll find yourself pitch'd in it;
And no one knows how money goes,
  But still you do not win it.   80

Her shoes she carries in her hands
  (Not one of them she tries on);
And on she goes through lands and lands
  – She reaches the horizon!
She's there at last! Her heart beats fast –   85
  Oh, what will she discover?
She's on the ledge – the very edge;
  And then – she tumbles over!

The Sorrowful Sea-Gull

The Sea-gull *is* so sorry!
  She flings herself about,
And utters little wailing sounds,
  And flutters in and out.
The fishes do not sympathise: 5
  Fish are so very cool –
They make so many rules, you know,
  And who can *feel* by rule?

They have a rule for swimming,
  A rule for taking food;   10
They have a rule for pleasure-trips,
  A rule for doing good.
And people who make rules like that
  May dine, and work, and swim;
But never know how sweet a thing   15
  It is to take a whim!

I'd like to be a Sea-gull,
  With lovely beak and claws;
I would not like to be a fish,
  Subject to fishy laws.   20
And if they make more changes soon
  By Acts of Parliament
I won't consent to be a fish –
  I *never will* consent!

Rules are so very tiresome,   25
  And so is good advice;
I'd like to be a reckless bird –
  I think it would be nice!
Sea-gulls are sentimental, though;
  Fishes are dull and sly: 30
I don't object to sentiment,
  But dullness makes me cry.

I do distrust a herring,
  I quite despise a pike;
Of all the fish that ever lived,   35
  A cod I most dislike!
They're stupid and self-satisfied,
  And indolent and gruff.
I'm speaking of their characters –
  To eat, they're good enough.   40

Why is the Sea-gull sorry?
    I'm not allow'd to tell!
The fish, who will not sympathise,
    Know what's the matter well!
And you who'd feel with all your hearts,   45
    And give her love and tears,
Are not allow'd to hear a word —
    And such is life, my dears!

A Contrast

Trained tenderly by Heaven and Earth,
    Up grew she to her gentle height, —
    Grew to the level of the light
That shines by every placid hearth.

Her days so filled with joyful hopes,   5
    If any one should fade and fail,
    She hath no leisure to bewail;
As shuts the rose, the lily opes;

As blooms the lily, dies the rose;
    And she can hardly see to choose,   10
    Among the glitter of the dews,
'Twixt hope that comes and joy that goes.

For that she had was pure and sweet;
    It lies upon her breast, a balm;
    And that she seeks is sweet and calm;   15
It breathes a perfume at her feet.

And all around the world she looks,
    And wonders about grief and sin;
    She hath no evidence within;
She only knows of them in books.   20

Sometimes a little evil voice
    Speaks, and is silenced by a prayer;
    Sometimes she sees the face of Care,
That having wept, she may rejoice.

She touches sorrow with her hand,   25
    Taught softly not to shrink nor frown,
    But bring her pity bravely down
To depths she cannot understand.

The love which is her living fence
    (No barrier, but an atmosphere)   30

Makes all surrounding shapes of fear
Servants and shields for innocence.

Her daily food of joy endues
   Her aspect with such powers and signs,
   That for all sadder hearts she shines   35
A very angel of good news.

The glorying eyes that watch her growth
   Appeal to all the world around,
   'Was ever such a maiden found?'
And 'Who is worthy of her troth?'   40

Yet, under all, the feeling lurks,
   As ever since the world began,
   To make a helpmeet for a man
Is woman's perfectest of works.

So this fair pageant of her life,   45
   This gradual walk through upward ways,
   This melody of tuneful days,
Must finish in the name of wife.

But, slow of choice (no fairy now
   Brings the fit princess to her prince),   50
   Thought-shadows scarce have deepened since
Childhood lay smooth upon her brow.

And many a boldness fails before
   The bright composure of her glance,
   And stayed is many a swift advance,   55
And powerless much of worldly lore.

Checked hopes rebel; the mothers cry,
   'See to what end these dreamers come!
   She hath no heart except for home,
And man shall never hear her sigh!'   60

The sons among themselves aver
   Their taste is for a shallower strain;
   They have not cared to woo in vain;
They pass their blunders on to her.

But here and there a soul receives   65
   Unconscious vision of its queen,
   And fragrance as from flowers unseen
That have not yet come through the leaves.

You hear the soothing talk of some,
  'They would not, – if they would they might,'   70
  With vexed denials of the light,
And prophecies, 'Her day shall come.'

But she through all the tumult sings
  Delightsome melodies of dawn,
  And sees not any shadow drawn   75
Upon the whiteness of her wings.

How first her tardy trouble grew
  The watchers saw not; keen and wise
  To note a difference in her eyes,
Yet it was there before they knew.   80

A dream with no interpreter,
  The weaving of a happy spell
  With some mute pathos of farewell,
Not hers, but childhood leaving her.

As if pale opal depths should warm   85
  And kindle till the gem became
  A living miracle of flame
Without its first mysterious charm;

So that capacity which lay
  In the last petal of the flower   90
  Becomes a fire, a pang, a power,
To sweep the softer life away.

Reluctant and ashamed, she sees
  Her simple sovereignty depart;
  And loses patience with her heart,   95
And pleads for strength upon her knees,

And tells herself 'tis false, and shakes
  The trifle from her maiden fame;
  Yet blushes when she thinks his name,
And knows each movement that he makes;   100

And finds herself in sudden tears,
  Scorns her sweet nature as a crime,
  Looks to the coming calm of Time,
And longs to overleap the years.

O little garden in the wood,   105
  So full of safe and tender bloom!
  God guide the footsteps that presume
To break thy breezeless solitude.

God bless the deed! for it is done,
  The moment is proclaimed at last;   110
  A word divides her from her past;
Her song is sung, her life begun.

He came from unfamiliar ways
  To pluck this blossom for his breast,
  With this one merit, that he guessed   115
At treasures hidden from his gaze.

From unfamiliar ways he came;
  If you had set them side by side,
  His life and her unsullied tide,
You might have thought his love was shame.   120

So judge not men. His name stood well;
  He sneered his tedious modern sneer
  At everything above his sphere,
And was contented in his shell.

The cynic scorn, that should have mailed   125
  A finer thought, went through his soul;
  A mean ideal held the whole,
And kept his conscience unassailed.

He was not better than he seemed,
  Nor worse than he desired; he gazed   130
  With condescension and amazed
On good weak men who toiled and dreamed.

That old name-heritage, which grew
  In deeper days, is still the plan,
  Though our serener 'gentleman'   135
Shrink from the rigorous line it drew.

Not chivalrous, methinks, is he;
  Not very truthful, for he needs
  To hide at home his daily deeds,
On pretext 'women should not see.'   140

But brave at heart and blithe of cheer,
  A generous smile, a courtly glance,
  A foot unrivalled in the dance,
The bearing of a cavalier;

Smooth polished by his upper throng,   145
  And charitable as the light;
  For they who burn not for the right
Find free excuses for the wrong.

She, in her listening sweetness, tries
  The natural music of her part,   150
  And, looking upward, thinks his heart
As much above her as his eyes.

Too wise to share her childish heat,
  Too great to kindle when she moves,
  Yet lifting her, because he loves,   155
From her due station at his feet.

He puts each nobler utterance by,
  And scorns himself for what he is;
  She (how she trusts!) reveres in this
Some choice reserve of modesty.   160

'I talk, he does; 'tis English rule
  To do the deed and leave the talk;
  I too, when at his side I walk,
May learn in such a lofty school.'

She goes so gaily to her fate;   165
  They who might rescue stand afar:
  'He is a man as others are,
And fit for any woman's mate.'

He loves her; – what do women seek?
  Henceforth 'tis well; the two are one,   170
  And that unholy past is done
Of which she must not ask nor speak.

He drops into his purer place
  (These stronger beings must begin
  With their full privilege of sin).   175
If there be memories in his face

Which daze her, she need never know
  What comes between him and his bliss;
  She only asks for leave to kiss
Some sudden aching from his brow.   180

But how these daily lives can blend
  (I set a problem of the time),
  Whose thought shall sink and whose may climb,
And whence the light, and what the end,

'Tis hard to guess. The day may break   185
  When that slow painful pile of truth
  Is heaped at last, and all her youth
Has but to mount and die awake.

When, film by film, the colours fade,
   And she, where she believed, beholds,
   And has no further hope, and folds
Her life into a prayer for aid:

Or sometimes, with a weary smile,
   Remembers what she dreamed, and sighs,
   And shuts her unreproachful eyes,
And whispers, 'Yet a little while.'

Or her blind heart may stoop and lean
   To where he stands, until she move
   Under the burden of a love
Which will not let the sky be seen,

Till daily watch on ways of his
   Makes her degrade the type, because
   She will not see the broken laws; –
I think she will be saved from this.

Or – Let us lift the veil a space
   From the last chance! She takes his hand,
   While thoughts he does not understand
Have drawn the colour from her face.

'What is it, love?' He knows his power;
   He holds her gently. Then she speaks,
   And that pure paleness of her cheeks
Trembles and flushes like a flower.

'You must not frown. I have a shame,
   A something which you ought to know;
   I should have told it long ago, –
You will forgive, though you must blame:

'Before you wooed me I was sought, –
   I know not why. I told you true,
   I never cared for man but you,
Yet once I wavered in my thought.

'And I was vain, as girls are vain,
   But, O! it was a fault to play
   With one true spirit for a day!
I could not do the deed again.'

'So I, most confident of men,
   Was not the first!' She shook her head;
   For, 'O! it was a fault!' she said,
And 'I have wept for it since then.'

190

195

200

205

210

215

220

225

And 'O! it was a fault!' he says,
  And puts it from him as a jest;   230
  Yet takes the word into his breast,
To keep it there for many days.

The wonder of that fault! It grows,
  It speaks and thrills him in the night,
  Till his cleansed eyes perceive the light   235
Of something purer than he knows.

White soul, with such a fault! He thinks,
  Is, then, the darker soul more strong
  Because it does the deeper wrong?
Because it fails? because it sinks?   240

Lo, touch by touch, a hand unseen
  Paints a slow picture in his thought,
  He cannot choose but see it wrought;
He knows such beauty may have been;

He knows it is! He once was blind,   245
  But by this soft home-light discerns
  Things he believed not once, and learns
To think more truly of his kind.

So for a year he holds his peace,
  And meditates on noble things,   250
  And listens while a seraph sings,
And all the meaner voices cease.

Till, laughing once, she says with pride,
  'See, love, how sage your wife has grown!
  You never check her with that tone   255
Of fond contempt you gave your bride.'

He looks at her with reverent eyes,
  He clasps her with a generous shame;
  'There was a revelation came
From your angelic fault!' he cries.   260

Cavour

I met a woman, weeping by the sea,
Not patiently, as women sit and weep,
But running, white with passion, wild with fear,
And as she ran she cried, 'Cavour is dead!'
And cast the grey sea-sand upon her hair,   5

And cried, beating her breast, 'Cavour is dead!
Was any near him? Tell me how he look'd
When they came in and said that he must die?
Must shut the casket, open in his hand,
Whose wealth he had seen, not touch'd! Did not the gloom　　10
Of that immense regret, shared by the world,
Trouble his closing eyes; or were they void?
Void as the place he leaves among the powers!
In stifled murmurs from the watching crowd,
A sea of heads, still as that other sea　　15
When it awaits the tempest, he might hear
The first pathetic note of his own dirge,
Soon to swell out in thunder through the world
Vast sobs of grief, cleft by some clarion-tones
From foes who kept their silence while he lived;　　20
Ah, let them be content; they broke his heart, –
He died of Villafranca!'
　　　　　　　　　　　Here she paused,
And hid her face. But when I ask'd her name
She did not tell it, but she turn'd upon me,
And fronted me as stately and as pale　　25
As the moon stood on Ajalon, and waited
For the first shout of conquest; so she show'd
The fatal gift of beauty in her face,
And all the tearful traces of the Past;
And I beheld her while she answer'd me.　　30
'I am his Widow. Do not look at me
With that familiar pity, which was mine
Before he lived, but never while he lived:
I have forgotten how to suffer pity.
I am his Widow: bring me to his grave!　　35
I think I shall not die upon his grave,
But, when I take my place, and wear my crown,
And the world wonders, men shall stoop to read,
Upon the topmost step of my great throne,
An epitaph – "Here lies Cavour; a man　　40
Who built the throne of Italy, and died." '

Jean Ingelow (1820–1897)

Jean Ingelow was born in Boston, Lincolnshire. When her father's banking interests collapsed the family moved to various smaller homes in the south of England and then settled in London. Jean was friendly with Jane Taylor, the poet who wrote 'Twinkle, Twinkle, Little Star', while her cousin, Charlotte Barnard, later became famous as 'Claribel', author of sentimental drawing-room songs, some of them settings of Ingelow's own poems. Jean remained in the family home throughout her life,

occasionally undertaking good works, though she showed little sympathy for the poor
– 'almost all the misery, poverty, and sickness were caused by the faults of the people'
(Peters 1972: 97), she once declared. In 1860 she became a member of the Portfolio
Society, which was set up by Barbara Bodichon and Bessie Rayner Parkes as a forum
in which women might read their poems or show their paintings to each other. There
she met Adelaide Procter, Dora Greenwell and, briefly, Christina Rossetti. Her second
volume of verse, published in 1863, was immensely successful, going into thirty
editions, to the envy of Rossetti, and earning its author a considerable amount of money.
Ingelow was even more popular in the United States where 200,000 copies of her
Poems were sold and a ship was named after her. Her most popular work was the
pseudo-antique ballad 'High Tide on the Coast of Lincolnshire', which was much
quoted, but now sounds mawkishly high-pitched and melodramatic.

In 1870 she received an invitation from Tennyson, another Lincolnshire poet, to
visit him at home and, as she repeated, 'see what your study is like' (Peters 1972: 82).
Tennyson, it seems, genuinely admired her work. She later became friendly with Ruskin
as well as Robert Browning. Unfortunately, Ingelow's later volumes were never as
popular as the second, and by the end of the century her high-minded, impersonal
narrative mode was largely out of fashion. She died at home, having outlived many
younger members of her family.

Much of Ingelow's poetry now seems parochial and conventional. She belongs in
the genteel tradition of women's poetry – a tradition which offered moral and
emotional comforts in accessible verse forms. However, when fired by her love of
the Lincolnshire countryside or when writing fantasy tales for children, Ingelow
overcomes her inhibiting sense of propriety. 'Divided', for instance, is a stunning
evocation of her home landscape, the light-handed symbolism of the river only just
taking the poem over the edge into allegory. Written in the register of short diary
jottings, but flowing restlessly to its conclusion, this possibly personal poem may
be about lost love or inevitable death. But the ostentatiously female sex of the river,
which is almost a rival presence in the poem, hints that it might also be about poetry
and the muse – about the dancing, laughing but ultimately separating nature of poetic
creativity.

Ingelow's nonsense story for children, *Mopsa the Fairy*, like Sara Coleridge's *Phantasmion*, is a good example of that imaginative freedom which Victorian women found in
writing children's literature. This tale of a boy who crosses into fairyland and meets
curiously strange, sad or violent creatures there, is punctuated by songs which are
quirky and odd, and often disembodied from the storyline. 'Winding-Up Time' hints
at another time when the antique fighting of men and the decorous marrying of women
will both seem out of date, as the indifferent clock ticks on. 'A Story' portrays the
female storyteller as part-mother, part-lover and part-fate, while 'Little babe, . . .' sung
by one of the 'stone' people who long to return to mortality, might be read as a poem
about child mortality or about the mother's desire for a world of work and society
beyond her lot. In these, Ingelow overcomes the cramps of class respectability and
duty, and shows a poetic power which deserves re-appraisal.

A.L.

Ingelow, Jean (1863) *Poems*, London. (1869) *Mopsa the Fairy*, London.

Anon. (1901) *Recollections of Jean Ingelow*, London.
Black, H. C. (1893) *Notable Women Authors of the Day*, London.

Johnson, Heidi H. (1995) ' "Matters That a Woman Rules": Marginalized Maternity in Jean Ingelow's "A Story of Doom" ', *Victorian Poetry*, 33 (1995).

Peters, Maureen (1972) *Jean Ingelow: Victorian Poetess*, Ipswich, The Boydell Press.

Wagner, Jennifer (1993) 'In her "Proper Place": Ingelow's Fable of the Female Poet and Her Community in *Gladys and Her Island*', *Victorian Poetry*, 31 (1993), 227–40.

Divided

I

An empty sky, a world of heather,
  Purple of foxglove, yellow of broom;
We two among them wading together,
  Shaking out honey, treading perfume.

Crowds of bees are giddy with clover,   5
  Crowds of grasshoppers skip at our feet,
Crowds of larks at their matins hang over,
  Thanking the Lord for a life so sweet.

Flusheth the rise with her purple favour,
  Gloweth the cleft with her golden ring,   10
'Twixt the two brown butterflies waver,
  Lightly settle, and sleepily swing.

We two walk till the purple dieth
  And short dry grass under foot is brown,
But one little streak at a distance lieth   15
  Green like a ribbon to prank the down.

II

Over the grass we stepped unto it,
  And God He knoweth how blithe we were!
Never a voice to bid us eschew it:
  Hey the green ribbon that showed so fair!   20

Hey the green ribbon! we kneeled beside it,
  We parted the grasses dewy and sheen;
Drop over drop there filtered and slided,
  A tiny bright beck that trickled between.

Tinkle, tinkle, sweetly it sung to us,   25
  Light was our talk as of faëry bells;
Faëry wedding-bells faintly rung to us
  Down in their fortunate parallels.

Hand in hand, while the sun peered over,
  We lapped the grass on that youngling spring;   30
Swept back its rushes, smoothed its clover,
  And said, 'Let us follow it westering.'

III

A dappled sky, a world of meadows,
  Circling above us the black rooks fly
Forward, backward; lo their dark shadows   35
  Flit on the blossoming tapestry.

Flit on the beck, for her long grass parteth
  As hair from a maid's bright eyes blown back;
And, lo, the sun like a lover darteth
  His flattering smile on her wayward track.   40

Sing on! we sing in the glorious weather
  Till one steps over the tiny strand,
So narrow, in sooth, that still together
  On either brink we go hand in hand.

The beck grows wider, the hands must sever.   45
  On either margin, our songs all done,
We move apart, while she singeth ever,
  Taking the course of the stooping sun.

He prays, 'Come over' – I may not follow;
  I cry, 'Return' – but he cannot come: 50
We speak, we laugh, but with voices hollow;
  Our hands are hanging, our hearts are numb.

IV

A breathing sigh, a sigh for answer,
  A little talking of outward things;
The careless beck is a merry dancer,   55
  Keeping sweet time to the air she sings.

A little pain when the beck grows wider;
  'Cross to me now – for her wavelets swell:'
'I may not cross' – and the voice beside her
  Faintly reacheth, though heeded well.   60

No backward path; ah! no returning;
  No second crossing that ripple's flow:

'Come to me now, for the west is burning;
   Come ere it darkens;' – 'Ah, no! ah, no!'

Then cries of pain, and arms outreaching –   65
   The beck grows wider and swift and deep:
Passionate words as of one beseeching –
   The loud beck drowns them; we walk, and weep.

V

A yellow moon in splendour drooping,
   A tired queen with her state oppressed,   70
Low by rushes and swordgrass stooping,
   Lies she soft on the waves at rest.

The desert heavens have felt her sadness;
   Her earth will weep her some dewy tears;
The wild beck ends her tune of gladness,   75
   And goeth stilly as soul that fears.

We two walk on in our grassy places
   On either marge of the moonlit flood,
With the moon's own sadness in our faces,
   Where joy is withered, blossom and bud.   80

VI

A shady freshness, chafers whirring,
   A little piping of leaf-hid birds;
A flutter of wings, a fitful stirring,
   A cloud to the eastward snowy as curds.

Bare grassy slopes, where kids are tethered,   85
   Round valleys like nests all ferny-lined;
Round hills, with fluttering tree-tops feathered,
   Swell high in their freckled robes behind.

A rose-flush tender, a thrill, a quiver,
   When golden gleams to the tree-tops glide;   90
A flashing edge for the milk-white river,
   The beck, a river – with still sleek tide.

Broad and white, and polished as silver,
   On she goes under fruit-laden trees;
Sunk in leafage cooeth the culver,   95
   And 'plaineth of love's disloyalties.

Glitters the dew and shines the river,
  Up comes the lily and dries her bell;
But two are walking apart for ever,
  And wave their hands for a mute farewell.   100

VII

A braver swell, a swifter sliding;
  The river hasteth, her banks recede:
Wing-like sails on her bosom gliding
  Bear down the lily and drown the reed.

Stately prows are rising and bowing   105
  (Shouts of mariners winnow the air),
And level sands for banks endowing
  The tiny green ribbon that showed so fair.

While, O my heart! as white sails shiver,
  And crowds are passing, and banks stretch wide,   110
How hard to follow, with lips that quiver,
  That moving speck on the far-off side.

Farther, farther – I see it – know it –
  My eyes brim over, it melts away:
Only my heart to my heart shall show it   115
  As I walk desolate day by day.

VIII

And yet I know past all doubting, truly –
  A knowledge greater than grief can dim –
I know, as he loved, he will love me duly –
  Yea better – e'en better than I love him.   120

And as I walk by the vast calm river,
  The awful river so dread to see,
I say, 'Thy breadth and thy depth for ever
  Are bridged by his thoughts that cross to me.'

from *Mopsa the Fairy*

Winding-up Time

'Wake, baillie, wake! the crafts are out;
  Wake!' said the knight, 'be quick!
For high street, bye street, over the town
  They fight with poker and stick.'

Said the squire, 'A fight so fell was ne'er   5
   In all thy bailliewick.'
What said the old clock in the tower?
      'Tick, tick, tick!'

'Wake, daughter, wake! the hour draws on;
   Wake!' quoth the dame, 'be quick!   10
The meats are set, the guests are coming,
   The fiddler waxing his stick.'
She said, 'The bridegroom waiting and waiting
   To see thy face is sick.'
What said the new clock in her bower?   15
      'Tick, tick, tick!'

A Story

In the night she told a story,
   In the night and all night through,
While the moon was in her glory,
   And the branches dropped with dew.

'Twas my life she told, and round it   5
   Rose the years as from a deep;
In the world's great heart she found it,
   Cradled like a child asleep.

In the night I saw her weaving
   By the misty moonbeam cold,   10
All the weft her shuttle cleaving
   With a sacred thread of gold.

Ah! she wept me tears of sorrow,
   Lulling tears so mystic sweet;
Then she wove my last to-morrow,
   And her web lay at my feet.   15

Of my life she made the story:
   I must weep – so soon 'twas told!
But your name did lend it glory,
   And your love its thread of gold!   20

'Little babe, while burns the west,'

Little babe, while burns the west,
Warm thee, warm thee in my breast;
While the moon doth shine her best,
   And the dews distil not.

All the land so sad, so fair –   5
Sweet its toils are, blest its care.
Child, we may not enter there!
    Some there are that will not.

Fain would I thy margins know,
Land of work, and land of snow;   10
Land of life, whose rivers flow
    On, and on, and stay not.

Fain would I thy small limbs fold,
While the weary hours are told,
Little babe in cradle cold.   15
    Some there are that may not.

Dora Greenwell (1821–1882)

Dora Greenwell was one of five children born to Dorothy and William Thomas Greenwell. Her father was the owner of the Greenwell Ford estate in County Durham and a popular magistrate for the area. She was educated at home. In 1848, as a result of financial mismanagement, her father lost all his money and the estate was sold. This was also the year in which Dora published her first volume of poems. The family subsequently moved to Northumberland and then to Lancashire, where she became friends with Josephine Grey (later Butler), who would wage the long campaign against the Contagious Diseases Acts. It may have been this friendship which inspired Dora's own support for various social causes during her life.

After the death of her father she returned with her invalid mother to Durham in 1854. Although Jean Ingelow effusively commended Dora's ardent attachment to her mother (Dorling 1885: 162), a later commentator, Constance Maynard, hinted at the frustrations and tensions of these years, when Mrs Greenwell, it seems, made heavy demands on her dutiful daughter. 'They were certainly fond of each other,' she recalled, 'but under a perpetual sense of difficulty and the old lady could say very sarcastic things' (1926: 98). Possibly Dora's liberal opinions – she once lamented that she was 'almost the only *liberal* lady in Durham' (Dorling 1885: 55) – were not to the liking of her tetchy, conservative mother. The sometimes disappointing conventionality of Greenwell's poetry compared with her prose may have had something to do with this maternal influence and control. None the less, during these years Dora wrote a considerable amount, and busied herself in support of such causes as the education of 'idiots and imbeciles', about which she wrote an important essay in the *North British Review* in 1868, the anti-vivisection league (see 'Fidelity Rewarded'), the education of girls, the suffrage movement and women's right to work. Her essay, 'Our Single Women', refutes conservative arguments on the propriety of separate spheres, declaring unequivocally that the 'proper sphere of all human beings is the largest and highest which they are able to attain to' (*North British Review*, 36 (1862), 72). Her insights on poverty and child labour can also be surprisingly free of sentimental gloss. She writes, for instance, of child labour in the Fen country: 'It would be foolish to suppose there is anything *legally* compulsory in this, or to compare it, as the papers do, with negro slavery; but, as it is, it is sufficiently cruel and demoralizing; and the poor man, even when legally free, is oppressed because of his poverty, which can drive to as hard tasks as any overseer' (Dorling 1885: 100).

After the death of her mother in 1871 Dora was free to move, and in subsequent years settled in London, Torquay, and Clifton where her favourite brother lived. She had gained a name as a poet by this time, and was in contact with other poets with whom she was often compared, in particular Ingelow and Procter. She met Barrett Browning on one occasion – the two love sonnets to her suggesting the extent of her admiration – and she met and corresponded with Rossetti (see 'To Christina Rossetti'), though their letters have unfortunately not survived. Christina once wrote, in 1875, that she was visiting Dora, and was 'quite struck with her large-mindedness, really liking her', though adding: 'She is far more dilapidated than myself, poor thing' (Rossetti 1908: 51). Evidently Dora's health, which was always frail, was giving cause for concern. The fact that Rossetti goes on to ask her brother to sign an anti-vivisectionist petition suggests that conversations with Dora may have converted her to the cause. In 1881, after an accident which left her an invalid, Dora returned to Clifton where she died the following year. In 1897 an anonymous notice in the *Athenaeum* claimed that Ingelow, Greenwell and Rossetti had once entered a needlework contest with each other, but that Rossetti never completed her piece. Highly embroidered if not downright apocryphal, the story betrays a continuing uneasy fascination with the figure of the spinster woman poet.

Greenwell's work on the whole tends to reproduce familiar motifs and forms. She was modest in her own claims: 'I have never aimed or dreamed of anything more than the lyrical and subjective, knowing my own deficiency in objective force, formative power, and above all in imaginative strength' (Dorling 1885: 74). Her many religious poems, for which she was best known in her day, bear witness to a certain visionary streak in her sensibility, though these tend towards the orthodox and predictable, contrary to her own often repeated declaration that there should be 'an essential scepticism in the poet nature' (1875: 137).

Here and there, however, an imaginative or social cause gets the better of her caution. 'The Broken Chain' and 'The Sun-Flower' both play on the intriguing connections between desire and slavery; the double monologue 'Demeter and Cora' draws on the tensions and love Greenwell knew well in the relationship with her own mother, while 'Christina' (1851) (no reference to Rossetti), though ultimately less daring than other 'fallen woman' poems, must be credited, none the less, with being one of the first dramatic monologues on the subject. The fact that it is spoken in the first person, by the unnamed woman herself, is an act of literary and social transgression which will be repeated in women's poetry throughout the century. The 'chasm' between pure and impure, which cannot be crossed in the story, is eloquently crossed by the single, univocal, female voice of the poem. Interesting, too, is the underlying mother–daughter theme, with its suggestion that the fallen woman might take the place of the dead daughter, in a substitutive relationship which radically confuses holy and unholy families. This sistering, or mothering, event never happens, however, as the religious divide between good and evil reasserts its powerful hold at the end.

A.L.

Greenwell, Dora (1861) *Poems*, Edinburgh.
—— (1889) *Poems*, intro. William Dorling, London.

—— (1866) *Essays*, London.
—— (1875) *Liber Humanitatis*, London.

Dorling, William (1885) *Memoirs of Dora Greenwell*, London.
Kaplan, Cora (1986) 'Language and Gender' in *Sea Changes*, London, Verso.
Maynard, Constance (1926) *Dora Greenwell: A Prophet for Our Own Times on the Battleground of Our Faith*, London, H. R. Allenson.
Rossetti, Christina (1908) *Family Letters*, ed. W. M. Rossetti, London, Brown, Langham.

Christina

Father, when I am in my grave, kind Father,
Take thou this cross, – I had it from a girl, –
Take it to one that I will tell thee of, –
Unto Christina.

I may not part with it while I have life;   5
I kept it by me, treasured it through years
Of evil, when I dared not look upon it;
But of the love and reconciling mercy
Whereof it is a token, now it speaks.
Sore bitten by the fiery flying serpent,   10
Yet have I strength to raise my languid eyes,
And fix them on that sign, for sin uplift
Within the wilderness, and there my gaze –
My straining gaze – will fasten to the last,
Death-glazed, upon it. Oh! may then my soul   15
Be drawn up after it unperishing!

Thou knowest of my life, that I have been
Saved as by fire, – a brand plucked from the burning;
But not before the breath of flame had passed
On all my garments, not before my spirit   20
Shrunk up within it as a shrivelled scroll
Falls from the embers, black, – yet unconsumed,
For One in Heaven still loved me, one on earth.
O Father, I would speak to thee of Love;
We learn the price of goodliest things through losing.   25
They who have sat in darkness bless the light,
And sweetest songs have risen to Liberty
From souls once bound in misery and iron;
So, Father, I would speak to thee of Love.
Fain are my lips, and fain my heart to sing   30
The glad new song that both have learned so late.
Once, ere my soul had burst the fowler's snare,
I heard a wild stern man, that stood and cried
Within the market-place; a man by love
Of souls sent forth among the lanes and highways,   35

To seek, and haply save, some wandering one
Long strayed, like mine, from flock, and fold, and pastor.
His words were bold and vehement; as one
Set among flints, that strove to strike a spark
From out dull, hardened natures. Then he used   40
The terrors of the Lord in his persuading;
Death, Judgment, and their fearful after-looking,
Grew darker at his words: 'How long,' he said,
'O simple ones, will ye be fain to follow
Hard service and hard wages – Sin and Death?   45
Now, the world comes betwixt your souls and God;
Here, you can do without Him and be happy;
He speaks to you by love, ye put Him by;
But He will speak to you by wrath, and then
Vain will it be to shun Him, to forget –   50
In the next world ye may not do without Him:
Seek God, run after Him, for ye must *die!*'
Oh! then, I thought, if one like me might speak,
If I might find a voice, now would I raise
A yet more bitter and exceeding cry,   55
'Seek God, run after Him, for ye must LIVE!
I know not what it may be in that world,
The future world, the wide unknown hereafter,
That waits for us, to be afar from God;
Yet can I witness of a desolation   60
That I have known; can witness of a place
Where spirits wander up and down in torment,
And tell you what it is to want Him *here*.'

    I had no friends, no parents. I was poor
In all but beauty, and an innocence   65
That was not virtue – failing in the trial.
Mine is a common tale, and all the sadder
Because it is so common: I was sought
By one that wore me for a time, then flung
Me off; a rose with all its sweetness gone,   70
Yet with enough of bloom to flaunt awhile,
Although the worm was busy at its core.
So I lived on in splendour, lived through years
Of scorning, till my brow grew hard to meet it;
Though all the while, behind that brazen shield,   75
My spirit shrank before each hurtling arrow
That sang and whistled past me in the air.
On every wall methought I saw a Hand
Write evil things and bitter; yea, the stones
Took up a taunting parable against me.   80
I looked unto the right hand and the left,
But not for help, for there was none would know me,

I knew that no man carèd for my soul;
Yet One in heaven still loved me, one on earth!
But being then unto myself so hateful, 85
I deemed that all did hate me, hating all; –
Yet one there was I hated not, but envied,
A sad, despairing envy, having this
Of virtue, that it did not seek to soil
The whiteness that it gazed upon, and pined. 90
For I had loved Christina! we had been
Playmates in innocent childhood; girlish friends,
With hearts that, like the summer's half-oped buds,
Grew close, and hived their sweetness for each other.
She was not fair like me unto the eye, 95
But to the heart, that showed her by its light
Most lovely in the loveliness of love.
I parted from her on Life's cross-road, where
I parted from all good; yet even then,
Had prayers and tears prevailed, we had not parted. 100
Long after me I heard her kind voice calling,
'Return!' yet I went on; – our paths struck wide,
As were the issues that they led to, then
She lost me, but I never lost her: still
Across the world-wide gulf betwixt us set 105
My soul stretched out a bridge, a slender hair,
Whereon repassing swiftly to and fro,
It linked itself unseen with all her lot,
Oft seeking for a moment but to lose
The bitter consciousness of self, to be 110
Aught other e'en in thought than that I was.
I took a portion of her innocent life
Within myself; I watched her in her ways,
Unseen I looked upon her in her home,
Her humble home. Yes; I that once had scorned 115
At lowly poverty and honest love,
I know not if it were its joys or sorrows
I envied most! *Her* tears were like the dew
That lies all night upon the fruitful field
That Heaven hath blessed, and rises there again. 120
I was like blasted corn shrunk up and mildewed,
Like sere, dry grass upon the house-tops growing,
Whereof the mower filleth not his arms,
Nor he that bindeth up his sheaves his bosom.
Earth, earth methought and Heaven alike refused me; 125
None gave me the kind wish, the holy word.
I had no joys, no griefs; yet had I joyed,
Then none had said, 'God bless thee!' had I grieved,
Then none that passed had said, 'God pity thee!'

I said, Christina wept. Within her home   130
There was one only little one, a girl:
Oft had I marked her playing in the sunshine,
Oft by the hearth-light on her father's knee
I watched her (little did Christina think
Who stood without), but she was taken from her,   135
This child of many prayers and hopes: I saw
The little bier borne forth; this tender flower
That Love had nursed so warm, yet could not keep,
Did seem to leave a blank where it had been.
Christina wept; but still as one whose tears   140
Rained inward on her heart, whence rising oft
They filled her eyes, but did not overflow them:
For still she moved about the house, serene,
And when her husband sought his home at eve
She met him now, as ever, with a smile,   145
So sweet, I know not if he missed its joy.
But oft I tracked her thoughts unto a field,
Quiet, yet populous as the city round it –
Thick sown with graves; yet there the mother's heart
Had marked a place, and there her constant feet   150
Had worn a path. At early morn, I knew
Oft went she by the grave to weep unseen,
So oft at night-fall there I scattered flowers,
The fairest and the sweetest I could find.
I thought, she will not know whose hand hath strewed them,   155
So wonder and a loving guess may cheat
Her mind, a moment taking it from grief.
I stood beside that grave one summer night;
The skies were moonless, yet their dusk serene
Was grateful to my spirit, for it seemed   160
To wrap me from the world, myself, and heaven;
And all the air was soft and cool, methought
It kissed my cheek as if it were a child
That loved me, – sinless, shrinking not from sin.
Old legends say, that when the faithful join   165
On holy Sabbaths with one fervent voice,
Then doth prevailing prayer hold back awhile
The edge of torment, and the lost have rest.
So then, perchance, some gracious spirit wept,
And prayed for sinners, for the voices died,   170
The wailing ones, the mocking, at my heart;
And through the hush came up a wish, a yearning –
I know not where it took me – not to heaven, –
Yet, had I ever prayed, it had been then;
I sought not death, for that were but a change   175
Of being, and a passage to a world
Where thought would after me to hunt and vex,

But to cease utterly to be, to find
A place among the rocks, among the stones,
With things that lived not, that would never live, 180
To pass absorbed, and be at rest for ever.
So stood I, holding in that trance the flowers,
A wreath of white Immortelles, that as yet
I hung not on the gravestone, when I heard
A sudden step, and was aware that one 185
Had come upon me in the gloom; I felt
A grasp upon my arm, detaining kindly,
A hand that sought to fold itself in mine:
Before she spoke, I knew it was Christina.
'And who art thou, with charitable hand 190
Such kindness showing to the dead, the living?
Now let me look upon thy face, for long
My soul hath deemed of thee as of the angels
That come and go unseen, and only traced
By deeds that show some gracious Presence near; 195
Yet, surely thou art one whom earth hath taught
Through sorrow and through love this gentleness
With grieving hearts, with stricken ones; from mine
The blessing of the sorrowful be on Thee!'
But at her words a madness took my soul; 200
They seemed to mock me; falling one by one
Like gracious drops upon my heart, they smote
Its stagnant waters, stirring there no spring
Of life or wholesomeness; yet were they stirred.
Now would I speak with her, the fire was kindled; 205
Long had it smouldered, long enough consumed me.
Now by its flashes she shall read my soul
Methought, and look upon me as I am;
So, with a gesture of the hand, I led
Christina, following on my rapid steps 210
Like an unquestioning child, as if my will
Had power to draw her, till within the door
Of the great Minster passing, in the aisle's
Dim light we stood, together and alone.

Oft had I shunned Christina; now beneath 215
A steadfast lamp that burned before a shrine,
Confronting her, I said, 'Now look on me; –
Where is the blessing that thou speakest of?'
But to my words she answered not; methought
She did not catch their import – so her gaze 220
Was fastened on me – then her very soul
Gave way in tears; she took me in her arms, –
Me, wretched me, that never thought to feel,
In this world, or the after one, again

Such pure embrace around me; to her heart,   225
That heaved as if it could not hold a joy
Made out of such an anguish, close she pressed me,
And, sobbing, murm'ring to herself or heaven,
In language half articulate, the words
Came broken: 'I have found thee! I have found thee!'   230
'What hast thou found, Christina?' then I said,
And with the words unto my lips arose
A laugh of bitterness, whose mocking tones
Through all the dreary hollow of my heart
Woke up the echoes of its desolation;   235
'What hast thou found? Speak not to me of her
Whose name perchance thy lips are framing now, –
The Magdalene; my life hath been as hers
But not my heart, for she loved much – for this
The more forgiveness meeting; I love none!'   240
But then Christina pointed to the flowers
Still hanging on my arm; '*Thou* lovest none!'
And gently laid upon my mouth her hand,
A soft restraining curb that now my speech,
Like an ungovernable steed sore stung   245
And goaded into frenzy, spurned aside,
And sprang the wilder; 'None, not even thee!'
I cried; but then the whiteness of her face
Smote on my spirit, taming scorn to sadness.
'Why should I vex thee with my words; of love   250
I know but as I know of God, of good,
Of hope, of heaven, of all things counted holy –
Know only by their names, for nought in me
Gives witness to their natures; so, to speak
Of them is but to take their names in vain.   255
Oft hast thou told me how souls hang on God
Like leaves upon a gracious bough, that draw
Their juices from its fulness; long ago
Mine fell from off that Tree of Life, thereon
Retaining not its hold; – a withered leaf   260
It lies, and bears the lightning's brand upon it.'
'Yea, truly,' said Christina, 'it may bear
The spoiler's mark upon it, yet, like His[1]
Of whom the Scriptures tell us, may thy soul
(A watcher and an Holy One befriending)   265
Have yet a root within the earth; though bound
About with brass and iron, still the dews
Lie on it, and the tender grass around
Is wet with tears from heaven; so may it spring
Once more to greenness and to life, for all   270
The years it felt the pressure of the band

---

[1] Daniel iv.

So close and grievous round it.' But I cried,
'There is no root! a leaf, a withered leaf,
Long tossed upon the wind, and under foot
Of men long trodden in the streets and trampled, –   275
God will not gather it within His bosom!'
'And who art thou that answerest for God?
Now from this mouth of thine will I condemn thee;
For, saying that thou knowest nought of love,
How canst thou judge of Him whose name it is?'   280
But here she clasped her fervent hands, and all
The sternness melted from her: 'Look on me,
A sinner such as thou, – yet I have loved thee;
Remembering thee above my mirth, how oft
Beside the cheerful board that Heaven had blessed,   285
I ate my bread in heaviness; and then
Had I known where to seek thee, had risen up
And left my food untasted, till I brought
Thee in to share it; to my lips thy name
Rose never, *so* I feared some bitter word   290
Might chide it back within my wounded heart,
That shut it in from blame; but then my prayers
Grew dearer to me, for the thought that *here*,
In this pure Presence only, could I meet thee;
Here only to the Merciful could name thee,   295
Could love thee, plead for thee without rebuke.
Yes! even in my sleep my quest went on;
Through dreams I ever tracked thee, following hard
Upon thy steps, pursuing thee, and still
Before I reached thee (thus it is in dreams)   300
Came somewhat sundering us, and I awoke
With tearful eyes, and on my lips half-framed
Some loving word, – recalling so the past,
I thought thou couldst not turn from it away.
Yes! I have loved thee, I, a poor weak woman,   305
One like to thee, yet holding in my heart –
That else were dry and barren to all good –
One drop of love from out of God's great ocean.
And thinkest thou that we can love each other
As He loves us, – as He that made us loves us?   310
And sayest thou, "I am cast out from God?"
No! He hath lovèd thee from everlasting,
Therefore with loving-kindness will He draw thee
Oft doth He chide, yet earnestly remember,
Long waiting to be gracious: come, poor child, –   315
Thy brethren scorn thee, come unto thy Father!
Away from Him, in that far country dwelling,
Long hast thou fed upon the husks, too long
Hast hungered sore, while no man gave unto thee;

But there, within thy Father's house, is Bread 320
Enough and still to spare, and no upbraiding.
My little Child, my Innocent, that scarce
Had left His arms, nor angered Him, nor grieved,
Was not so welcome back to them as thou;
Even now, a great way off, even now He sees thee, 325
And comes to meet thee – rise and go to Him!
The home is distant, but the way is nigh.
Oh, Thou who, dying, madest us a way,
Who, living, for us keepest ever open
That access to the Father, look on us!' 330
So speaking solemn, looking up to Heaven,
She knelt down where we stood; upon my knees
Beside her drew me; holding both my hands
Firm folded 'twixt her own, she lifted them
Towards the Mercy-seat; within her arms 335
She held me still, supporting me; it seemed
As then the very fountains of her soul
Were broken up within her; so she wept,
So pleaded: 'Jesu, Lamb of God, O Thou
The Father's righteous Son, that takest all 340
The sin of earth away, have mercy on us!'
But I was passive in her arms, I knew
She wrestled sorely for me; yet as one
That feels in heavy dreams a strife go on,
And may not stir a finger, by the chain 345
Of slumber compassed; so my torpid soul
Slept numb, yet conscious, till within my heart,
That had no movement of its own, but rose
Upon Christina's heart that heaved beneath it,
At length this miracle of love was wrought: 350
Her spirit lay on mine, as once of old
The Prophet on the little clay-cold child
Outstretched, through warmth compelling warmth again,
And o'er the chaos of the void within
A breath moved lightly, and my soul stretched out 355
Its feelers darkly, as a broken vine
Puts forth its bruisèd tendrils to the sun:
A mighty yearning took me, and a sigh
Burst from my bosom, cleaving for my soul
A way to follow it, and in that hour 360
Methought I could have died, and known no pain
In parting from the body; then I cried,
'Oh, turn Thou me, and so shall I be turned!'

When we arose up from our knees, her face
Was calm and happy, then she kissed me, saying, 365
'I call thee not my Sister, as of old,
But come with me unto my home, and there

Be thou unto me even as a Daughter,
In place of her God gave and took again, –
So hath He given thee to me.' Thus she spoke,   370
And drew me on constraining; but my soul
Held other counsel, minded in itself
That I would look upon her face no more;
Though all my soul clave unto her, as he
From whom our Lord drave out the vexing demon,   375
Had followed fain upon his steps for ever,
So had I tarried by her well content;
And yet I answered her, 'Entreat me not,
This may not be, yet fear not thou for me;
I go upon my way, that crosses thine   380
Perchance no more; so give me counsel now
Upon my journey, for, as thou hast said,
The home I seek is far away, the road
Is strait and narrow, hard for erring feet
Like mine to walk in.' Then Christina said,   385
'I can but give thee counsel in the words
Of Him our Master, "Go and sin no more!"
Keep in the Way, and as thou goest, there
A Blessing will o'ertake thee; thou shalt meet
With One to pour within thy wounds the wine   390
And oil of consolation; He will set thee
On His own steed, and bring thee to an inn
Where thou may'st tarry till He comes again;
Yea! all thou spendest more He will account for,
For thou wert purchased and redeemed of old: 395
Now must I leave thee, for the night wears on.'
But still I held her closer, 'Not before
I too have blessed thee, even I, Christina;
May now the blessing of a soul wellnigh
To perishing be on thee! may thy love   400
Be poured, a thousandfold by God requited,
Within thy bosom.' Then Christina turned
Once more beneath the lamp, and smiled farewell; –
Smiled as if then the sweetness of her soul
Rose to her very lips and overflowed them,   405
But spoke not: passing swiftly through the porch,
The darkness took her from me.

   That same night
I left the guilty city far behind me;
Thou knowest, Father, of my life since then.   410
Here have I found the place Christina spoke of, –
A goodly inn, where they have cared for me,
These gracious souls, who loving so their Lord,
And covetous for Him, upon the coin

Long-lost, defaced, and soiled, could trace His image   415
And read His superscription, half out-worn, —
Soon must I leave it for a surer refuge.
I sent Christina long ago a token,
To tell her it was well with me, and now
Fain would I send this other one, a sign   420
From Him that loved me in the heavens, to her
That loved so true on earth. When I am gone,
Kind Father, to my rest, take thou this cross,
Take it to her that I have told thee of —
Unto Christina.   425

The Broken Chain

Captives, bound in iron bands,
    Half have learned to love their chain,
Slaves have held up ransomed hands,
    Praying to be slaves again:
So doth custom reconcile,   5
    Soothing even pain to smile;
So a sadness will remain
    In the breaking of the chain.

But if chain were wove of flower,
    Linked and looped to sister free,   10
With a Name and with an Hour,
    Running down its Rosary,
Light as gossamers on green,
    By their shining only seen;
Would not something sad remain   15
    In the breaking of the chain?

But if chain were woven shining,
    Firm as gold and fine as hair,
Twisting round the heart and twining,
    Binding all that centres there   20
In a knot, that like the olden
    May be cut, yet ne'er unfolden,
Would not something sharp remain
    In the breaking of the chain?

To Elizabeth Barrett Browning, in 1851

I lose myself within thy mind — from room
    To goodly room thou leadest me, and still
    Dost show me of thy glory more, until

My soul, like Sheba's Queen, faints, overcome,
And all my spirit dies within me, numb,   5
  Sucked in by thine, a larger star, at will;
  And hasting like thy bee, my hive to fill,
I 'swoon for very joy' amid thy bloom;
Till – not like that poor bird (as poets feign)
  That tried against the Lutanist's her skill,   10
  Crowding her thick precipitate notes, until
Her weak heart break above the contest vain –
  Did not thy strength a nobler thought instil,
I feel as if I ne'er could sing again!

To Elizabeth Barrett Browning, in 1861

I praised thee not while living; what to thee
  Was praise of mine? I mourned thee not when dead;
  I only loved thee, – love thee! oh thou fled
Fair spirit, free at last where all are free,
I only love thee, bless thee, that to me   5
  For ever thou hast made the rose more red,
  More sweet each word by olden singers said
In sadness, or by children in their glee;
  Once, only once in life I heard thee speak,
  Once, only once I kissed thee on the cheek,   10
And met thy kiss and blessing; scarce I knew
Thy smile, I only loved thee, only grew,
  Through wealth, through strength of thine, less poor, less weak;
  Oh, what hath death with souls like thine to do?

Demeter and Cora

'Speak, daughter, speak; art speaking now?'
'Seek, mother, seek; art seeking thou
Thy dear-loved Cora?' 'Daughter sweet,
I bend unto the earth my ear
To catch the sound of coming feet;   5
I listen long, but only hear
The deep, dark waters running clear.'
'Oh! my great mother, now the heat
Of thy strong heart in thickened beat
Hath reached thy Cora in her gloom,   10
Is't well with thee, my mother – tell?'
'Is't well with thee, my daughter?' 'Well
Or ill I know not; I through fate
Queen of a wide unmeasured tomb
Know not if it be love or hate   15

That holds me fast, but I am bound
For ever! What if I am found
Of thee, my mother, still the bars
Are round me, and the girdling night
Hath passed within my soul! the stars   20
Have risen[1] on me, but the light
Hath gone for ever.' 'Daughter, tell,
Doth thy dark lord, the King of Hell,
Still love thee?' 'Oh, too well, too well
He loves! he binds with unwrought chain.   25
I was not born to be thy mate,
Aïdes! nor the Queen of pain:
I was thy daughter Cora, vowed
To gladness in thy world above,
I loved the daffodil, I love   30
All lovely, free, and gentle things
Beloved of thee! a sound of wings
Is with me in captivity
Of birds, and bees, with her that sings
The shrill Cicula, ever gay   35
In noon's white heat.' 'But, daughter, say,
Dost love Aïdes?' 'Now, too bold
Thy question, mother; this be told,
I leave him not for love, for gold,
One lot we share, one life we know.   40
The Lord is he of wealth and rest,
As well as king of death and pain;
He folds me to a kingly breast,
He yields to me a rich domain.
I leave him not for aught above,   45
For any god's unsteadfast love
Or fairest mortal-form below;
Thou hast left heaven for earth; and thou
For thy poor Cora's sake, self-driven,
Hast fled its sunny heights in scorn   50
And hate, of Zeus unforgiven!
Do mortals love thee?' 'Daughter, yea.
They call me their great mother. Corn
And wine I give them when they pray;
Their love for me their little day   55
Of life lasts out; perchance they knew
It was not love for them that drew
Me down to wander where the wine
Is sweet to me, and breath of kine.
Art listening now, my Cora dear?   60

---

[1] When night has once passed into a human soul it
never leaves it, though the stars may rise. Victor Hugo

Art listening now, my child, – art near?
Oh, that thy kiss upon my cheek
Were warm! thy little hand in mine
Once more! Yet, let me hear thee speak,
And tell me of that garden rare, 65
And of thy flowers, dark, fiery, sweet,
That never breathe the upper air.'
'Oh, mother, they are fair, are fair;
Large-leaved are they, large-blossomed, frail,
And beautiful. No vexing gale 70
Comes ever nigh them; fed with fire
They kindle in a torch-light flame
Half ecstasy, half tender shame
Of bloom that must so soon expire.
But, mother, tell me of the wet, 75
Cool primrose! of the lilac-bough
And its warm gust of rapture, met
In summer days! – art listening yet?'
'Art near me, O my Cora, now?'

The Sun-Flower

Till the slow daylight pale,
    A willing slave, fast bound to one above,
I wait; he seems to speed, and change, and fail;
    I know he will not move.

I lift my golden orb 5
    To his, unsmitten when the roses die,
And in my broad and burning disk absorb
    The splendours of his eye.

His eye is like a clear
    Keen flame that searches through me: I must droop 10
Upon my stalk, I cannot reach his sphere;
    To mine he cannot stoop.

I win not my desire,
    And yet I fail not of my guerdon; lo!
A thousand flickering darts and tongues of fire 15
    Around me spread and glow.

All ray'd and crown'd, I miss
    No queenly state until the summer wane,
The hours flit by; none knoweth of my bliss,
    And none has guessed my pain. 20

I follow one above,
　　I track the shadow of his steps, I grow
Most like to him I love
　　Of all that shines below.

Fidelity Rewarded

We experimented on dogs — old, and otherwise useless.
　　　　　　　　　　Professor Rutherford

I was not useful? So
　　He says, nor young nor strong.
My master ought to know,
　　I've followed him so long.

For many and many a day   5
　　I followed well content,
Might I but go the way
　　That he, my master, went.

I listened for his foot,
　　I strove his thought to scan;   10
For I was but a brute,
　　And he I loved was man.

O'er all that he held dear,
　　A patient watch to keep,
With light, attentive ear   15
　　I listened in my sleep.

The stealthy foot withdrew,
　　The daring hand was stayed;
My growl the robber knew,
　　And fled the spot dismayed.   20

I knew my master's voice,
　　My nature's bounded plan
Had left my love no choice,
　　And he I loved was man.

And often would I watch   25
　　His inmost thought to prove,
His hidden will to catch:
　　A brute can only love.

I waited for a crumb,
　　From off his daily meal   30

To fall for me: a dumb
    Poor brute can only feel.

I thought he loved me well,
    But when my eye grew dim –
I leave the tale I tell   35
    As it is told by him –

Some secret hint to track
    Of life's poor trembling flame,
He nailed me to a rack,
    He pierced and tore my frame.   40

He saw me slowly die
    In agonies acute:
For he was man, and I
    Was nothing but a brute!

To Christina Rossetti

I have mingled my grapes and my wine.
The Song of Songs

Thou hast filled me a golden cup
With a drink divine that glows,
With the bloom that is flowing up
From the heart of the folded rose.
The grapes in their amber glow,   5
And the strength of the blood-red wine
All mingle and change and flow
In this golden cup of thine.
With the scent of the curling wine
With the balm of the rose's breath, –   10
For the voice of love is thine,
And thine is the Song of Death!

Jane Francesca Wilde (Speranza) (1821–1896)

Jane Frances Elgee's family were Irish and solidly middle-class, but she aspired to a more romantic and aristocratic inheritance. She changed her middle name to Francesca, never used Jane except in letters to tradesmen and others of no consequence, and devised an elaborate etymology for the name of Elgee via an Italian version of Algiati whereby she might claim kinship with Dante Alighieri. In appearance she was tall and stately, which in middle age she emphasized with flowing costumes, outsize jewellry and extravagant headresses. She attributed her aquiline features to the fact that she had been an eagle in a past life and told the young Yeats when she moved to London that she had to 'live in some high place, Primrose Hill or Highgate, because I was an eagle in my youth' (Ellmann 1987: 9). This formidable woman, known to nineteenth-century readers as the poet 'Speranza', is better known still to posterity as the mother of Oscar Wilde. 'All women become like their mothers. That is their tragedy. No man does. That is his' wrote Wilde in *The Importance of Being Earnest*. In his own case, however, Wilde's tragedy might have been that he did indeed become like his mother.

As a young woman, inspired by the significance of her own destiny and by an intense nationalistic fervour, Francesca submitted her early verses to the *Nation* under the pseudonym of Speranza, a name derived from her own motto 'Fidanza, Speranza, Constanza'. When the editor, Charles Gavan Duffy was arrested for sedition in 1848 she took over the writing of inflammatory editorials, succeeding so well in attracting the attention of the prosecutors that her articles were added to the charges against Duffy. At his trial, Francesca leapt up in the public gallery to denounce herself as the offending author. Duffy was eventually set free, and no charges were ever brought against Francesca – much to her own disappointment. 'I should like to rage through life', she wrote, '– this orthodox creeping is too tame for me – ah, this wild rebellious nature of mine. I wish I could satiate it with Empires, though a St Helena were the end' (Ellmann 1987: 8). In 1851 Francesca married William Robert Wilde, an eminent surgeon, and as she put it, 'at last my great soul is imprisoned within a woman's destiny' (Ellmann 1987: 9). Matters could only get worse as Francesca gave birth to two sons, Willie born in 1852, Oscar born in 1854 and daughter Isola, born in 1857. Francesca acknowledged her defeat with an epigram:

> Alas! the Fates are cruel
> Behold Speranza making gruel (Ellmann 1987: 46)

Not one to be downhearted for long Lady Wilde, as she became in 1864 when her husband was knighted, established a salon at her house in Merrion Square in Dublin and made herself the centre of an intellectual and political circle which encouraged the arts and supported the cause of Irish nationalism, though they both disassociated themselves from republican Fenianism in the 1860s for Lady Wilde, especially, was a lifelong anti-democrat. Otherwise, Francesca devoted herself to her children and to promoting her husband's career and his literary works on Irish themes. During the 1870s her light was again dimmed for a time while her husband was ill and she could not write poetry. After his death in 1876 Francesca suffered financial difficulties as she failed to extract payments from her recalcitrant tenants. In 1879 she sold the Dublin properties and moved to London, establishing again a brilliant artistic salon with herself at the centre and Oscar a willing, though teasing, acolyte for he laughed at her pretensions and parodied her conversation in *The Picture of Dorian Grey*: 'Sir Humpty Dumpty – you know – Afghan frontier. Russian intrigues: very successful man – wife killed by an elephant – quite inconsolable – wants to marry a beautiful American widow – everybody does nowadays – hates Mr Gladstone – but very much interested in beetles: ask him what he thinks of Schouvaloff.'

Francesca's financial situation was eased by pensions, obtained through Oscar's influence, from the Royal Literary Fund and the Civil List. She also continued to write and to publish and her name was such that during Oscar's tour of America in 1882 the *Irish Nation* described him in their headlines as 'Speranza's Son'. Very pleased with

Oscar's success in the world, Francesca spent much of her time keeping her two sons on good terms with one another and anxiously encouraging them both to marry advantageously. Oscar's brief triumph in the English literary scene was a cause for self-congratulation but his mother stood by him throughout his disgrace also. He stayed at her house in Chelsea between trials while she insisted that he defend himself or be disowned. After Oscar's sentence to hard labour the last year of Francesca's life was spent in illness and sorrow. She would not leave her room and saw no one. On her deathbed she asked to see Oscar, but he was not permitted leave from gaol. She left a private letter requesting that no one attend her funeral and was buried in Kensal Green cemetery. Oscar himself was not told of his beloved mother's death until fourteen days later because it took ten days to obtain leave for his wife to receive special permission to visit him with the news and another four days for her travel from Italy where she was convalescing.

In *De Profundis*, his long love letter to Alfred Douglas written from Reading Gaol, Oscar described his mother as ranking 'intellectually with Elizabeth Barrett Browning, and historically with Madame Roland'. The comparison with Barrett Browning was not a new one, for throughout her writing life Speranza glanced aside to measure herself by the older poet, and this extended even to a one-sided competition over offspring: '. . . what do you think of Mrs Browning's son who at six years old composes the most sublime poetry? Poor child, I should die of apprehension if Willie were like this' (Ellmann 1987: 17). In every way Speranza was jealous of her claim to literary fame, and scolded Oscar roundly, signing herself 'La Tua La Madre Dolorosa', when he reviewed Mrs Sharp's anthology *Women's Voices* in the November issue of the journal *The Woman's World* and there failed to mention the illustrious name of Speranza though he referred to other minnows: 'Why didn't you name *me* in the review of Mrs Sharp's book? Me, who hold such an historic place in Irish Literature? and you name Miss Tynan and Miss Mulholland!' (Ellmann 1987: 277).

Speranza's poetry has a character as bombastic as her own estimate of it. There can be no doubt that much of Oscar Wilde's capacity for memorable aphorisms or bathetic exaggeration was learned at his mother's knee: 'When you are as old as I, young man', she said when in her sixties, 'you will know that there is only one thing in the world worth living for, and that is sin' (Ellmann 1987: 13). The same large rhetorical tone is found in her poetry, and Speranza's early Irish nationalist poems are especially grand and vigorously orated productions. Exclamation marks figure prominently in these rousing addresses to 'pale victims' and 'ye children of sorrow', for Speranza took the role of the poet–prophet very seriously. That this made her self-conscious of her own calling is clear in the two poems 'The Poet's Destiny' and 'Désillusion'. These poems reveal the same reverence for the role of the artist which appears in so much of Oscar Wilde's work. They are also interesting for their use of lush images and a Romantic vocabulary which looks forward to the late Victorian aesthetic and decadent style of Walter Pater or Algernon Swinburne. Speranza's self-consciousness also extended to her sense of herself as a woman poet so that, like Hemans, like L.E.L. and Barrett Browning, she writes 'Corinne's Last Love-Song' out of the myth of the improvisatrice. But Speranza's version is very much a latter-day interpretation. Her Corinne may have lost her sense of self in the first stanza's 'dream' of love; and she may have lost herself again in the directionless second stanza, but the focus on herself as a poet, still singing and still proud of that role, is absolute and unconditional.

M.R.

Wilde, Jane Francesca (1864) *Poems by Speranza*, Dublin.

—— (1866) *Poems: Second Series: Translations*, Dublin.

—— (1871) *Poems*, Glasgow.

—— (1888) *Ancient Legends, Mystic Charms, and Superstitions of Ireland*, London.

—— (1907) *Poems by Speranza*, London, M. H. Gill & Son.

—— (1891) *Notes on Men, Women and Books*, London, chapters on George Eliot, Countess of Blessington, Harriet Martineau.

—— (1893) *Social Studies*, London.

Ellmann, Richard (1987) *Oscar Wilde*, London, Hamish Hamilton.

Who Will Show Us Any Good?

I

Beautiful IRELAND! Who will preach to thee?
   Souls are waiting for lips to vow;
And outstretched hands, that fain would reach to thee,
   Yearn to help, if they knew but how,
   To lift the thorn-wreath off thy brow.   5

II

Passionate dreamers have fought and died for thee,
   Poets poured forth their lava song;
But dreamer and poet have failed as a guide for thee —
   Still are unriven the chains of wrong.

III

Suffering Ireland! Martyr-Nation!   10
   Blind with tears thick as mountain mist;
Can none amidst all the new generation
   Change them to glory, as hills sun-kissed
   Flash lights of opal and amethyst?

IV

Welcome a Hero! A man to lead for us,   15
   Sifting true men from chaff and weeds;
Daring and doing as those who, indeed, for us
   Proved their zeal by their life and deeds.

V

Desolate Ireland! Saddest of mothers,
    Waits and weeps in her island home;   20
But the Western Land – has she help for others
Who feeds her eagles on blood of brothers?
    Not with cannon or roll of drum,
    Or foreign flag can our triumph come.

VI

Why seek aid from the arm of a stranger?   25
    Trust thy sons, O Mother! for good;
Braver can none be in hours of danger,
    Proudly claiming thy rights withstood.

VII

Then, Ireland! wake from thy vain despairing!
    Grand the uses of life may be;   30
Heights can be reached by heroic daring,
    Crowns are won by the brave and free,
    And Nations create their own destiny.

VIII

But, Time and the hour fleet fast unbidden,
    A turbid stream over golden sands;   35
And too often the gold is scattered or hidden,
    While we stand by with listless hands.

IX

Then seize the least grain as it glistens and passes,
    Swift and sure is that river's flight:
The glory of morning the bright wave glasses,   40
    But the gold and glory soon fade from sight,
    And noon-tide splendours will change to night.

X

Ah! life is too brief for languor or quarrel,
    Second by second the dead drop down;

And souls, all eager to strive for the laurel,   45
    Faint and fall ere they win the crown.

XI

Ireland rests mid the rush of progression,
    As a frozen ship in a frozen sea;
And the changeless stillness of life's stagnation,
    Is worse than the wildest waves could be,   50
    Rending the rocks eternally.

XII

Then, trumpet-tongued, to a people sleeping,
    Who will speak with magic command,
Bidding them rise – these dead men, keeping
    Watch by the dead in a silent land?   55

XIII

Grandly, solemnly, earnestly preaching,
    Man's great gospel of Truth and light;
With lips like saints' in their love beseeching,
    Hands as strong as a prophet's to smite
    The foes to Humanity's sacred right.   60

XIV

Earth is thrilling with new aspirations,
    Rending the fetters that bar and ban;
But we alone of the Christian nations
    Fall to the rear in the march of Man.

XV

Alas! can I help? but a nameless singer –   65
    Weak the words of a woman to save;
We wait the advent of some light-bringer,
    Strong to roll the stone from the grave,
    And summon to life the death-bound slave.

XVI

Down from heights of the Infinite drifting,   70
    Raising the prisoned soul from gloom;

Like the white angels of God uplifting
   Seal and stone from the Saviour's tomb.

XVII

Yet, hear me now, for a Nation pleading;
   Strike! but with swords yet keener than steel;   75
Flash on the path the new Age is treading,
   As sparks from grooves of the iron wheel,
   In star-flames its onward march reveal.

XVIII

Work by the shore where our broad ocean rages,
   Bridging it over by wraiths of steam;   80
Linking two worlds by a chain that sages
   Forged in the heat of a science dream.

XIX

For Nature has stamped us with brand immortal,
   Highway of nations our Land must be:
We hold the keys of the Old-world portal,   85
   We guard the pass of the Western Sea –
   Ireland, sole in her majesty!

XX

Work! there is work for the thinker and doer,
   And glory for all when the goal is won;
So we are true to our Country, or truer   90
   Than Planets are to the central Sun.

XXI

Call from the hills our own Irish Eagle,
   Spread its plumes on the 'The Green' of old;
With a sunrise blaze, as a mantle regal,
   Turning the dusk-brown wings to gold –   95
   Symbol and flag be it then unrolled!

XXII

Face Heaven's light with as proud a daring,
   Tread the heights with a step as grand,

Breast the wild storm with brave hearts unfearing
As kings might do for their rightful land.   100

XXIII

Irish daring by land and by river,
   Irish wealth from mountain and mine,
Irish courage so strong to deliver,
   Irish love as strong to combine
   Separate chords in one strain divine;   105

XXIV

These are the forces of conquering power,
   Chains to sever, if slaves we be;
Then strike in your might, O Men of the hour!
And Ireland springs on the path of the free!

Corinne's Last Love-Song

I

How beautiful, how beautiful you streamed upon my sight,
In glory and in grandeur, as a gorgeous sunset-light!
How softly, soul-subduing, fell your words upon mine ear,
Like low aerial music when some angel hovers near!
What tremulous, faint ecstacy to clasp your hand in mine,   5
Till the darkness fell upon me of a glory too divine!
The air around grew languid with our intermingled breath,
And in your beauty's shadow I sank motionless as death.
I saw you not, I heard not, for a mist was on my brain –
I only felt that life could give no joy like that again.   10

II

And this was Love – I knew it not, but blindly floated on,
And now I'm on the ocean waste, dark, desolate, alone;
The waves are raging round me – I'm reckless where they guide;
No hope is left to light me, no strength to stem the tide.
As a leaf along the torrent, a cloud across the sky,   15
As dust upon the whirlwind, so my life is drifting by.
The dream that drank the meteor's light – the form from Heav'n has flown –
The vision and the glory, they are passing – they are gone.
Oh! love is frantic agony, and life one throb of pain;
Yet I would bear its darkest woes to dream that dream again.   20

The Poet's Destiny

The Priest of Beauty, the Anointed One,
Through the wide world passes the Poet on.
All that is noble by his word is crown'd,
But on his brow th' Acanthus wreath is bound.
Eternal temples rise beneath his hand,   5
While his own griefs are written in the sand;
He plants the blooming gardens, trails the vine –
But others wear the flowers, drink the wine;
He plunges in the depths of life to seek
Rich joys for other hearts – his own may break.   10
Like the poor diver beneath Indian skies,
He flings the pearl upon the shore – and dies;

Désillusion

Too soon, alas! too soon I plunged into the world with tone and clang,
And they scarcely comprehended what the Poet wildly sang.
Not the spirit-glance deep gazing into nature's inmost soul,
Not the mystic aspirations that the Poet's words unroll.
Cold and spiritless and silent – yea, with scorn received they me,   5
Whilst on meaner brows around me wreath'd the laurel crown I see.
And I, who in my bosom felt the godlike nature glow,
I wore the mask of folly while I sang of deepest woe.
But, courage! years may pass – this mortal frame be laid in earth,
But my spirit reign triumphant in the country of my birth!   10

Eliza Ogilvy (1822–1912)

The daughter of Eliza Wintle and Abercrombie Dick, Eliza Anne Harris Dick was born at Perth in Scotland. She spent some time in India where her grandfather was a surgeon. In 1843 she married David Ogilvy and their first child, Rose, was born in March 1844. The delightful little poem 'A Natal Address to my Child' was written by Eliza on the day of the child's birth and later sent to David Ogilvy's aunt; '... they were begun in a serious mood, she says, but the Muse ran away with her. I doubt if such good verses were ever composed at so extraordinary a time' (Barrett Browning 1974: 178).

When Rose died the following year Ogilvy wrote *Rose Leaves* (1845), a small volume of privately published verses which are understandably more serious, but considerably less unconventional and moving than this first address. In 1846 she published *A Book of Highland Minstrelsy* which consists of anecdotes from Scottish history and legend which are developed into narrative poems accompanied by suitably fey story-book illustrations by R. R. McIan.

The family moved to Italy in 1848 and Eliza was given a letter of introduction to the Brownings. When the Ogilvys settled in Florence the two families became very close, especially after a shared holiday in Bagni di Lucca when the Ogilvys took the apartment below the Brownings in Casa Guidi in Florence. Inevitably Eliza and Elizabeth shared a baby-centred relationship for Eliza gave birth to her son Alexander in September 1848 and to her daughter Marcia in January 1850, while Elizabeth's only child, christened Robert Wiedemann though he was always called Penini or Pen, was born at Casa Guidi in March 1849. Eliza later recalled these days in a memoir of Elizabeth Barrett Browning.

My Eldest son was born in September and Mrs. Browning took a great interest in him. Her boy was born in March, six months later. She was often very low spirited about the event and afraid of not having a living child as she had already had several miscarriages . . .

In those days young infants wore lace caps with cockades of satin ribbon – a round cockade for a boy, an oval one for a girl. I used to make up these dainty caps, and decorate them with boys' cockades and take them to the despondent mother-expectant and holding them up before her I said 'There! does not that make you feel as if the little son were close at hand,' and she would smile and own it cheered her to see them . . . As Mrs. Browning could not suckle her baby, she had a balia or Italian wetnurse. The child throve very well while my boy six months older was cutting teeth and in alarmingly delicate health. Well do I recall the round full face of little Wiedeman enclosed in a red knitted hood with a full border of red knitted frilling – while my poor little man under a round straw hat showed one of those pallid sunken countenances with preternaturally large wistful eyes which are the anguish of mothers and nurses. Mrs. Browning did not expect my boy to live and often expressed her deep sympathy to friends, but never said anything to increase my own fears for him (Barrett Browning 1974: xxvi–xxvii and xxviii–xxix).

It was at the time of her confinement with Marcia that Ogilvy wrote 'Newly Dead and Newly Born'. The poem may end with a pious declaration of acquiescence to God's will, but it is still a touching account of a mother's anxiety for the life of her child. It is also one of those relatively rare poems which speaks directly of the particularities of a woman's life in the nineteenth century.

M.R.

Ogilvy, Eliza 1846 (1856) *Poems of Ten Years: 1846–1856*, London.

Barrett Browning, Elizabeth (1974) *Elizabeth Barrett Browning's Letters to Mrs. David Ogilvy 1849–1861*, ed. Peter N. Heydon and Philip Kelley, London, John Murray.

A Natal Address to My Child, March 19th 1844

Hail to thy puggy nose, my Darling,
Fair womankind's last added scrap,
That, callow as an unfledg'd starling,
Liest screaming in the Nurse's lap.

No locks thy tender cranium boasteth,   5
No lashes veil thy gummy eye
And, like some steak gridiron toasteth,
Thy skin is red and crisp and dry.

Thy mouth is swollen past describing
Its corners twisted as in scorn   10
Of all the Leech is now prescribing
To doctor thee, the newly born.

Sweet little lump of flannel binding,
Thou perfect cataract of clothes,
Thy many folds there's no unwinding   15
Small mummy without arms or toes!

And am I really then thy Mother?
My very child I cannot doubt thee,
Rememb'ring all the fuss and bother
And moans and groans I made about thee!   20

'Tis now thy turn to groan and grumble,
As if afraid to enter life,
To dare each whipping scar and tumble
And task and toil with which 'tis rife.

O Baby of the wise round forehead,   25
Be not too thoughtful ere thy time;
Life is not truly quite so horrid –
Oh! how she squalls! – she can't bear rhyme!

Newly Dead and Newly Born

The mother lies in travail bed,
  The babe beside her sleepeth,
When, hark! a chaunting for the dead
  Below her window creepeth.

It swelleth nearer, filling loud   5
  That vast Florentian palace,
Deaf is the corpse within its shroud
  To sympathy or malice.

Deaf as the little babe above
  To all its kindred's praises,
Both child and corpse are shut from love   10
  In mystery's awful mazes.

Hard by with round Etruscan arch
  Expands the church's portal,
'Mid smoking brands the funeral march
  Leads in those relics mortal.

As if 'twere round her infant's head
  The mother hears them singing,
While from the bier up to the bed
  Rise fumes of censers swinging.

Herself yet trembling on the verge
  Of scarce escaped danger,
A shudder takes her at this dirge
  From Death, the great all-changer.

And when the requiem's failing sighs
  Expire along the distance,
She turneth where her new-born lies
  To test its warm existence.

By touch, and sight, and fine-edged ear,
  To certify its thriving,
Then cry 'O Death, go with that bier,
  And leave this life surviving.'

Poor mother! look for higher things!
  To warnings rest beholden:
All human souls are born with wings
  Which but awhile are folden.

They sink or soar as God sees right
  When grown to full extension,
Pray, when arrives her hour of flight,
  The summons be ascension.

Grannie's Birthday

I

Happy Returns! the children say
Grannie is Sixty-three today
Her hair is white and her eyes are bleared
But she is'nt the sort that grows a beard!
You ca'nt expect to be 'Fair to see'
When you reach the age of *63*.

2

She lives by herself on her own small hoard
She asks no tendance, so no one's bored
The young are busy at work and play
Grannie might find herself in the way   10
So she trots down hill with a lonely glee
Thank Heaven, I'm hale at 63.

3

The day must come when her legs will fail
When a cough will lurk in the winter gale
When Grannie must sit in the ingle nook   15
With a bit of work, and a bit of book
But she hopes she never a fash may be
E'en if she lives to *73*!

Adelaide Anne Procter (1825–1864)

Adelaide Anne Procter was the first child and oldest daughter of Anne Benson Skepper and Bryan Waller Procter, the poet who wrote under the pseudonym of 'Barry Cornwall'. Her father, a lawyer, held a well-established place in literary London and was the friend and encourager of many younger writers, including Charles Dickens and Robert Browning. Her mother was described by friends as the centre of the household, witty, capable and clever, and Adelaide grew up in a literary and intellectual atmosphere where her education in literature, languages, mathematics, music and drawing was closely attended to by both parents. Her mother especially encouraged her, creating for the child a small handwritten album of favourite quotations which she used to carry about with her in preference to a doll. After Adelaide's early death this album clearly became a treasured family relic.

Her first poem in print was 'Ministering Angels' published in 1843 in *Heath's Book of Beauty* – one of the many fancy annuals produced for women and severely condemned by Lydgate in George Eliot's *Middlemarch* (1871–2). The title of Adelaide's poem is a sufficient guide to its subject matter and literary merit.

Some time between 1849 and 1851 Adelaide's piety took on a more public aspect when she and her two sisters became Roman Catholics. Bessie Rayner Parkes says that Adelaide never spoke of her conversion (Belloc 1895: 164), but it must have constituted something of a surprise in the Procter household, especially when Adelaide's sister Agnes joined the Irish Sisters of Mercy. In 1853 Adelaide visited her aunt Emily de Viry who lived at the Court of Turin and who was also a devout Roman Catholic. Passages from her letters home, however, reveal that Adelaide entered enthusiastically into Italian life, attending at least one peasant marriage and livening up proceedings by offering to dance with the bride and continuing to dance until she had to crawl home 'in an agony with the cramp' (Procter: 1866, xix).

Procter's career as a poet really began in the spring of 1853 when she sent a poem under the name of 'Miss Mary Berwick' to Charles Dickens as editor of *Household Words*. She had of course known Dickens since she was a child and practised this delicate subterfuge because she wished 'to take my chance fairly with the unknown volunteers' (Procter: 1866, xv). 'Miss Mary Berwick' became a regular contributor to *Household Words* and to *All the Year Round* after the deception was revealed in December 1854.

The great passion of Adelaide's life was causes, and according to Dickens, it was this dedication to 'her Christian duty to her neighbour' (Procter, 1866) which wore her out. Certainly she visited the sick, supported education for the poor, endeavoured to help the homeless, and gave all the money she earned from her writing to these enterprises. Bu the place where she was most active and most emotionally engaged, was in promoting the employment of women, and this was by no means the dry and automatic duty that Dickens makes out. Adelaide's *Legends and Lyrics* was dedicated to Matilda Hays with a quotation from Emerson: 'Our tokens of love are for the most part barbarous. Cold and lifeless, because they do not represent our life. The only gift is a portion of thyself. Therefore let the farmer give his corn; the miner, a gem; the sailor, coral and shells; the painter, his picture; and the poet, his poem.'

Matilda Hays was a remarkable woman whose varied career included intense friendships and long companionships with women, among them the actress Charlotte Cushman and the American sculptor Harriet Hosmer. Elizabeth Barrett Browning met her in Rome in the early 1850s and described her living in a house of 'emancipated women', dressing as a man from the waist up, and being a 'peculiar person altogether, decided, direct, truthful' (Huxley 1929: 196). At this time Hays lived in a 'female marriage' with Cushman where they 'have made vows of celibacy & of eternal attachment to each other – they live together, dress alike' (Elizabeth Barrett Browning to Isa Blagden, 13 February 1853, unpublished letter in the Berg Collection).

Through Hays, Procter met Bessie Rayner Parkes, Emily Faithfull, Anna Jameson and other stalwarts of the 1850s initiatives for women's rights. Together, and under the auspices of the 'Council of the National Association for the Promotion of a Social Science', they planned to find new channels for the employment of women. Bessie Parkes bought a small press and, with Emily Faithfull, learnt typesetting so that they could train women as compositors. The Victoria Press was opened in 1860 and took over the printing of the *English Woman's Journal* and the *Transactions of the Association for the Promotion of a Social Science*.

In 1861, Adelaide edited a volume called *Victoria Regia*, dedicated with special permission to the Queen. Its main aim was to provide a showcase for the technical skills of the Victoria Press and it included essays, stories and poems by Isa Blagden, Theodosia Trollope, Geraldine Jewsbury (Maria's younger sister, a novelist), Caroline Clive, Dinah Mulock, Anna Jameson, Matilda Hays, Caroline Norton, and Amelia B. Edwards among others. Procter herself contributed a poem 'Links with Heaven'. *A Chaplet of Verses*, published in 1861, was produced for the benefit of a Catholic refuge, the 'Providence Row Night Refuge for Homeless Women and Children'. By this time Adelaide was ill with tuberculosis and made a trip to Malvern hoping for recovery. But she died, in her mother's arms, after some fifteen months confined to bed.

When Charles Dickens was asked by Procter's parents to write a memoir for the 1866 edition of *Legends and Lyrics* he included the curious praise that she was not 'like a poet' in her person:

No claim can be set up for her, thank God, to the possession of any of the conventional poetical qualities. She never by any means held the opinion that she was among the greatest of human beings; she never suspected the existence of a conspiracy on the part of mankind against her; ... she never cultivated the luxury of being misunderstood and unappreciated; she would far rather have died without seeing a line of her composition in print, than that I should have maundered about her, as 'the Poet', or 'the Poetess' (Procter 1866: xxii).

This may say more about Dickens's own attitudes to the posing of characters such as Leigh Hunt, but it also reveals much about his opinions concerning the necessity for a proper humility in women poets. Certainly it says little about Procter's poetry which can sometimes be exactly what women's poetry of the nineteenth century was expected to be: pious, flowery, sentimental and sweet.

That Procter's work fulfilled these expectations is partly supported by the fact that her *Legends and Lyrics* remained surprisingly popular and was regularly reprinted up to 1913. Without doubt her most famous poem is 'A Lost Chord', which was set to music by Sir Arthur Sullivan. The poem's message that earthly sorrows will be calmed by heavenly rest, combined with the mystery of the origin of the 'lost chord' which cannot be recovered in life, easily explains its sentimental appeal. Her best and most interesting poem, however, is 'A Legend of Provence', which offers a moving version of the 'fallen woman' theme, as it tells of the nun who leaves the convent with a man, only to find, when she returns after years of dissipation, that her place has been kept for her by the Virgin Mary and her absence not noted. The idea of the double, the 'other self' encountered on the threshold, finds a powerful examplar here in a poem which is an original handling of a typical Victorian scene. Repetition and reinvention are techniques which Procter also uses skilfully in her other poems, whether narrative pieces such as 'Three Evenings in a Life', or in the suggestive progress of the three poems 'A Woman's Question', 'A Woman's Answer' and 'A Woman's Last Word' which appear separately, but cumulatively, in *Legends and Lyrics*. The rendering of the ironies of comparison and difference is also one of her poetic strengths and Procter frequently uses this for political ends, whether she is dealing with the injustice suffered by the homeless, whose plight is compared with the safe housing given to imprisoned criminals and chattels in 'Homeless', or with the sexual politics of the doctrine of the 'separate spheres' in 'Philip and Mildred'. Bitter and critical, Procter can appear saccharine where she is heavily ironic – witness her sanctimonious conclusion to 'Three Evenings in a Life' which cannot possibly be taken seriously.

For all this, it does have to be admitted that at least one contemporary reader was not much impressed, if only in private. In 1861 Elizabeth Barrett Browning wrote to Isa Blagden:

The new volume of Adelaide Procter's poems is not dedicated to Miss Hays, though the first was – The new volume we have sight of ... & I think there is progress. Only my surprise remains, that such writing, with so little form & originality, should have had so favorable a reception ... This is all between you & me – I admire her personally – & there's goodness & grace in what she writes – Moreover isn't there something kindly rhymed about Aurora Leigh in this volume. It would, in fact, be *horrible* for me to be heard nibbling at another woman's poems. I would as soon that people said I dyed my hair ... (Elizabeth

Barrett Browning to Isa Blagden, 3 February 1861, unpublished letter in the Berg Collection).

M.R.

Procter, Adelaide Anne (1858) *Legends and Lyrics. A Book of Verses*, London.
—— (1861) *A Chaplet of Verses*, London.
—— (1866) new edition of *Legends and Lyrics* with an introduction by Charles Dickens.

Barrett Browning, Elizabeth (1929) *Elizabeth Barrett Browning: Letters to Her Sister 1846–1859*, ed. Leonard Huxley, London, John Murray.
Belloc, Bessie Rayner Parkes (1895) *In a Walled Garden*, London.
Janku, Ferdinand (1912) 'Adelaide Anne Procter, ihr Leben und ihre Werke', in *Wiener Beiträge zur englischen Philogie*, vol. 38.
Maison, Margaret (29 April 1965) 'Queen Victoria's Favourite Poet', *The Listener*, pp. 636–7.

A Woman's Question

Before I trust my Fate to thee,
　Or place my hand in thine,
Before I let thy Future give
　Colour and form to mine,
Before I peril all for thee, question thy soul to-night for me.　　　5

I break all slighter bonds, nor feel
　A shadow of regret:
Is there one link within the Past,
　That holds thy spirit yet?
Or is thy Faith as clear and free as that which I can pledge to thee?　　10

Does there within thy dimmest dreams
　A possible future shine,
Wherein thy life could henceforth breathe,
　Untouched, unshared by mine?
If so, at any pain or cost, oh, tell me before all is lost.　　　15

Look deeper still. If thou canst feel
　Within thy inmost soul,
That thou hast kept a portion back,
　While I have staked the whole;
Let no false pity spare the blow, but in true mercy tell me so.　　20

Is there within thy heart a need
　That mine cannot fulfil?
One chord that any other hand
　Could better wake or still?
Speak now – lest at some future day my whole life wither and decay.　　25

Lives there within thy nature hid
  The demon-spirit Change,
Shedding a passing glory still
  On all things new and strange? –
It may not be thy fault alone – but shield my heart against thy own.   30

Couldst thou withdraw thy hand one day
  And answer to my claim,
That Fate, and that to-day's mistake,
  Not thou – had been to blame?
Some soothe their conscience thus: but thou, wilt surely warn and save me now.   35

Nay, answer *not* – I dare not hear,
  The words would come too late;
Yet I would spare thee all remorse,
  So, comfort thee, my Fate –
Whatever on my heart may fall – remember, I *would* risk it all!   40

My Journal

It is a dreary evening;
  The shadows rise and fall:
With strange and ghostly changes,
  They flicker on the wall.

Make the charred logs burn brighter;   5
  I will show you, by their blaze,
The half-forgotten record
  Of bygone things and days.

Bring here the ancient volume;
  The clasp is old and worn,   10
The gold is dim and tarnished,
  And the faded leaves are torn.

The dust has gathered on it –
  There are so few who care
To read what Time has written   15
  Of joy and sorrow there.

Look at the first fair pages;
  Yes – I remember all:
The joys now seem so trivial,
  The griefs so poor and small.   20

Let us read the dreams of glory
  That childish fancy made;

Turn to the next few pages,
  And see how soon they fade.

Here, where still waiting, dreaming,   25
  For some ideal Life,
The young heart all unconscious
  Had entered on the strife.

See how this page is blotted:
  What — could those tears be mine?   30
How coolly I can read you,
  Each blurred and trembling line.

Now I can reason calmly,
  And, looking back again,
Can see divinest meaning   35
  Threading each separate pain.

Here strong resolve — how broken;
  Rash hope, and foolish fear,
And prayers, which God in pity
  Refused to grant or hear.   40

Nay — I will turn the pages
  To where the tale is told
Of how a dawn diviner
  Flushed the dark clouds with gold.

And see, that light has gilded   45
  The story — nor shall set;
And, though in mist and shadow,
  You know I see it yet.

Here — well, it does not matter,
  I promised to read all;   50
I know not why I falter,
  Or why my tears should fall;

You see each grief is noted;
  Yet it was better so —
I can rejoice to-day — the pain   55
  Was over, long ago.

I read — my voice is failing,
  But you can understand
How the heart beat that guided
  This weak and trembling hand.   60

Pass over that long struggle,
  Read where the comfort came,
Where the first time is written
  Within the book your name.

Again it comes, and oftener,   65
  Linked, as it now must be,
With all the joy or sorrow
  That Life may bring to me.

So all the rest – you know it:
  Now shut the clasp again,   70
And put aside the record
  Of bygone hours of pain.

The dust shall gather on it,
  I will not read it more:
Give me your hand – what was it   75
  We were talking of before?

I know not why – but tell me
  Of something gay and bright.
It is strange – my heart is heavy,
  And my eyes are dim to-night.   80

A Legend of Provence

The lights extinguished, by the hearth I leant,
Half weary with a listless discontent.
The flickering giant-shadows, gathering near,
Closed round me with a dim and silent fear.
All dull, all dark; save when the leaping flame,   5
Glancing, lit up a Picture's ancient frame.
Above the hearth it hung. Perhaps the night,
My foolish tremors, or the gleaming light,
Lent power to that Portrait dark and quaint –
A Portrait such as Rembrandt loved to paint –   10
The likeness of a Nun. I seemed to trace
A world of sorrow in the patient face,
In the thin hands folded across her breast –
Its own and the room's shadow hid the rest.
I gazed and dreamed, and the dull embers stirred,   15
Till an old legend that I once had heard
Came back to me; linked to the mystic gloom
Of that dark Picture in the ghostly room.

In the far south, where clustering vines are hung;
Where first the old chivalric lays were sung,   20

Where earliest smiled that gracious child of France,
Angel and knight and fairy, called Romance,
I stood one day. The warm blue June was spread
Upon the earth; blue summer overhead,
Without a cloud to fleck its radiant glare,   25
Without a breath to stir its sultry air.
All still, all silent, save the sobbing rush
Of rippling waves, that lapsed in silver hush
Upon the beach; where, glittering towards the strand,
The purple Mediterranean kissed the land.   30

All still, all peaceful; when a convent chime
Broke on the mid-day silence for a time,
Then trembling into quiet, seemed to cease,
In deeper silence and more utter peace.
So as I turned to gaze, where gleaming white,   35
Half hid by shadowy trees from passers' sight,
The Convent lay, one who had dwelt for long
In that fair home of ancient tale and song,
Who knew the story of each cave and hill,
And every haunting fancy lingering still   40
Within the land, spake thus to me, and told
The Convent's treasured Legend, quaint and old:

  Long years ago, a dense and flowering wood,
Still more concealed where the white convent stood,
Borne on its perfumed wings the title came: 45
'Our Lady of the Hawthorns' is its name.
Then did that bell, which still rings out to-day,
Bid all the country rise, or eat, or pray.
Before that convent shrine, the haughty knight
Passed the long vigil of his perilous fight;   50
For humbler cottage strife or village brawl,
The Abbess listened, prayed, and settled all.
Young hearts that came, weighed down by love or wrong,
Left her kind presence comforted and strong.
Each passing pilgrim, and each beggar's right   55
Was food, and rest, and shelter for the night.
But, more than this, the Nuns could well impart
The deepest mysteries of the healing art;
Their store of herbs and simples was renowned,
And held in wondering faith for miles around.   60
Thus strife, love, sorrow, good and evil fate,
Found help and blessing at the convent gate.
Of all the nuns, no heart was half so light,
No eyelids veiling glances half as bright,
No step that glided with such noiseless feet,   65
No face that looked so tender or so sweet,

No voice that rose in choir so pure, so clear,
No heart to all the others half so dear,
So surely touched by others' pain or woe,
(Guessing the grief her young life could not know,)   70
No soul in childlike faith so undefiled,
As Sister Angela's, the 'Convent Child.'
For thus they loved to call her. She had known
No home, no love, no kindred, save their own.
An orphan, to their tender nursing given,   75
Child, plaything, pupil, now the Bride of Heaven.
And she it was who trimmed the lamp's red light
That swung before the altar, day and night;
Her hands it was whose patient skill could trace
The finest broidery, weave the costliest lace;   80
But most of all, her first and dearest care,
The office she would never miss or share,
Was every day to weave fresh garlands sweet,
To place before the shrine at Mary's feet.
Nature is bounteous in that region fair,   85
For even winter has her blossoms there.
Thus Angela loved to count each feast the best,
By telling with what flowers the shrine was dressed.
In pomp supreme the countless Roses passed,
Battalion on battalion thronging fast   90
Each with a different banner, flaming bright,
Damask, or striped, or crimson, pink, or white,
Until they bowed before a new born queen,
And the pure virgin Lily rose serene.
Though Angela always thought the Mother blest   95
Must love the time of her own hawthorn best,
Each evening through the year, with equal care,
She placed her flowers; then kneeling down in prayer,
As their faint perfume rose before the shrine,
So rose her thoughts, as pure and as divine.   100
She knelt until the shades grew dim without,
Till one by one the altar lights shone out,
Till one by one the Nuns, like shadows dim,
Gathered around to chant their vesper hymn;
Her voice then led the music's wingèd flight,   105
And 'Ave, Maris Stella' filled the night.

But wherefore linger on those days of peace?
When storms draw near, then quiet hours must cease.
War, cruel war, defaced the land, and came
So near the convent with its breath of flame,   110
That, seeking shelter, frightened peasants fled,
Sobbing out tales of coming fear and dread.
Till after a fierce skirmish, down the road,

One night came straggling soldiers, with their load
Of wounded, dying comrades; and the band,   115
Half pleading, yet as if they could command,
Summoned the trembling Sisters, craved their care,
Then rode away, and left the wounded there.
But soon compassion bade all fear depart,
And bidding every Sister do her part,   120
Some prepare simples, healing salves, or bands
The Abbess chose the more experienced hands,
To dress the wounds needing most skilful care;
Yet even the youngest Novice took her share
To Angela, who had but ready will   125
And tender pity, yet no special skill,
Was given the charge of a young foreign Knight,
Whose wounds were painful, but whose danger slight
Day after day she watched beside his bed,
And first in hushed repose the hours fled: 130
His feverish moans alone the silence stirred,
Or her soft voice, uttering some pious word.
At last the fever left him; day by day
The hours, no longer silent, passed away.
What could she speak of? First, to still his plaints,   135
She told him legends of the martyred Saints;
Described the pangs, which, through God's plenteous grace,
Had gained their souls so high and bright a place.
This pious artifice soon found success –
Or so she fancied – for he murmured less.   140
So she described the glorious pomp sublime,
In which the chapel shone at Easter time,
The Banners, Vestments, gold, and colours bright,
Counted how many tapers gave their light;
Then, in minute detail went on to say,   145
How the High Altar looked on Christmas-day:
The kings and shepherds, all in green and red,
And a bright star of jewels overhead.
Then told the sign by which they all had seen,
How even nature loved to greet her Queen   150
For, when Our Lady's last procession went
Down the long garden, every head was bent,
And, rosary in hand, each Sister prayed;
As the long floating banners were displayed,
They struck the hawthorn boughs, and showers and showers   155
Of buds and blossoms strewed her way with flowers.
The Knight unwearied listened; till at last,
He too described the glories of his past;
Tourney, and joust, and pageant bright and fair,
And all the lovely ladies who were there.   160
But half incredulous she heard. Could this –

This be the world? this place of love and bliss!
Where then was hid the strange and hideous charm,
That never failed to bring the gazer harm?
She crossed herself, yet asked, and listened still,   165
And still the Knight described with all his skill
The glorious world of joy, all joys above,
Transfigured in the golden mist of love.
Spread, spread your wings, ye angel guardians bright,
And shield these dazzling phantoms from her sight!   170
But no; days passed, matins and vespers rang,
And still the quiet Nuns toiled, prayed, and sang,
And never guessed the fatal, coiling net
Which every day drew near, and nearer yet,
Around their darling; for she went and came   175
About her duties, outwardly the same.
The same? ah, no! even when she knelt to pray,
Some charmèd dream kept all her heart away.
So days went on, until the convent gate
Opened one night. Who durst go forth so late?   180
Across the moonlit grass, with stealthy tread,
Two silent, shrouded figures passed and fled.
And all was silent, save the moaning seas,
That sobbed and pleaded, and a wailing breeze
That sighed among the perfumed hawthorn trees.   185

What need to tell that dream so bright and brief,
Of joy unchequered by a dread of grief?
What need to tell how all such dreams must fade,
Before the slow, foreboding, dreaded shade,
That floated nearer, until pomp and pride,   190
Pleasure and wealth, were summoned to her side,
To bid, at least, the noisy hours forget,
And clamour down the whispers of regret.
Still Angela strove to dream, and strove in vain;
Awakened once, she could not sleep again.   195
She saw, each day and hour, more worthless grown
The heart for which she cast away her own;
And her soul learnt, through bitterest inward strife,
The slight, frail love for which she wrecked her life,
The phantom for which all her hope was given,   200
The cold bleak earth for which she bartered heaven
But all in vain; would even the tenderest heart
Now stoop to take so poor an outcast's part?

Years fled, and she grew reckless more and more,
Until the humblest peasant closed his door,   205
And where she passed, fair dames, in scorn and pride,
Shuddered, and drew their rustling robes aside.

At last a yearning seemed to fill her soul,
A longing that was stronger than control:
Once more, just once again, to see the place   210
That knew her young and innocent; to retrace
The long and weary southern path; to gaze
Upon the haven of her childish days;
Once more beneath the convent roof to lie;
Once more to look upon her home – and die!   215

Weary and worn – her comrades, chill remorse
And black despair, yet a strange silent force
Within her heart, that drew her more and more –
Onward she crawled, and begged from door to door.
Weighed down with weary days, her failing strength   220
Grew less each hour, till one day's dawn at length,
As first its rays flooded the world with light,
Showed the broad waters, glittering blue and bright,
And where, amid the leafy hawthorn wood,
Just as of old the quiet cloister stood.   225
Would any know her? Nay, no fear. Her face
Had lost all trace of youth, of joy, of grace,
Of the pure happy soul they used to know –
The novice Angela – so long ago.
She rang the convent bell. The well-known sound   230
Smote on her heart, and bowed her to the ground,
And she, who had not wept for long dry years,
Felt the strange rush of unaccustomed tears;
Terror and anguish seemed to check her breath,
And stop her heart. Oh God! could this be death?   235
Crouching against the iron gate, she laid
Her weary head against the bars, and prayed:
But nearer footsteps drew, then seemed to wait;
And then she heard the opening of the grate,
And saw the withered face, on which awoke   240
Pity and sorrow, as the portress spoke,
And asked the stranger's bidding: 'Take me in,'
She faltered, 'Sister Monica, from sin,
And sorrow, and despair, that will not cease;
Oh, take me in, and let me die in peace!'   245
With soothing words the Sister bade her wait,
Until she brought the key to unbar the gate.
The beggar tried to thank her as she lay,
And heard the echoing footsteps die away.
But what soft voice was that which sounded near,   250
And stirred strange trouble in her heart to hear?
She raised her head; she saw – she seemed to know –
A face that came from long, long years ago:
Herself; yet not as when she fled away,

The young and blooming novice, fair and gay,   255
But a grave woman, gentle and serene:
The outcast knew it – *what she might have been*.
But, as she gazed and gazed, a radiance bright
Filled all the place with strange and sudden light;
The Nun was there no longer, but instead,   260
A figure with a circle round its head,
A ring of glory; and a face, so meek,
So soft, so tender. . . . Angela strove to speak,
And stretched her hands out, crying, 'Mary mild,
Mother of mercy, help me! – help your child!'   265
And Mary answered, 'From thy bitter past,
Welcome, my child! oh, welcome home at last!
I filled thy place. Thy flight is known to none,
For all thy daily duties I have done;
Gathered thy flowers, and prayed, and sung, and slept;   270
Didst thou not know, poor child, *thy place was kept?*
Kind hearts are here; yet would the tenderest one
Have limits to its mercy: God has none.
And man's forgiveness may be true and sweet,
But yet he stoops to give it. More complete   275
Is Love that lays forgiveness at thy feet,
And pleads with thee to raise it. Only Heaven
Means *crowned*, not *vanquished*, when it says "Forgiven!" '
Back hurried Sister Monica; but where
Was the poor beggar she left lying there?   280
Gone; and she searched in vain, and sought the place
For that wan woman, with the piteous face:
But only Angela at the gateway stood,
Laden with hawthorn blossoms from the wood.
And never did a day pass by again,   285
But the old portress, with a sigh of pain,
Would sorrow for her loitering: with a prayer
That the poor beggar, in her wild despair,
Might not have come to any ill; and when
She ended, 'God forgive her!' humbly then   290
Did Angela bow her head, and say 'Amen!'
How pitiful her heart was! all could trace
Something that dimmed the brightness of her face
After that day, which none had seen before;
Not trouble – but a shadow – nothing more.   295

Years passed away. Then, one dark day of dread
Saw all the sisters kneeling round a bed,
Where Angela lay dying; every breath
Struggling beneath the heavy hand of death.
But suddenly a flush lit up her cheek,   300
She raised her wan right hand, and strove to speak.

In sorrowing love they listened; not a sound
Or sigh disturbed the utter silence round.
The very tapers' flames were scarcely stirred,
In such hushed awe the sisters knelt and heard.   305
And through that silence Angela told her life:
Her sin, her flight; the sorrow and the strife,
And the return; and then clear, low and calm,
'Praise God for me, my sisters;' and the psalm
Rang up to heaven, far and clear and wide,   310
Again and yet again, then sank and died;
While her white face had such a smile of peace.
They saw she never heard the music cease;
And weeping sisters laid her in her tomb,
Crowned with a wreath of perfumed hawthorn bloom.
                                                                   315

  And thus the Legend ended. It may be
Something is hidden in the mystery,
Besides the lesson of God's pardon shown,
Never enough believed, or asked, or known.
Have we not all, amid life's petty strife,   320
Some pure ideal of a noble life
That once seemed possible? Did we not hear
The flutter of its wings, and feel it near,
And just within our reach? It was. And yet
We lost it in this daily jar and fret,   325
And now live idle in a vague regret.
But still *our place is kept*, and it will wait.
Ready for us to fill it, soon or late:
No star is ever lost we once have seen,
We always may be what we might have been.   330
Since Good, though only thought, has life and breath,
God's life – can always be redeemed from death;
And evil, in its nature, is decay,
And any hour can blot it all away;
The hopes that lost in some far distance seem,   335
May be the truer life, and this the dream.

A Lost Chord

Seated one day at the Organ,
  I was weary and ill at ease,
And my fingers wandered idly
  Over the noisy keys.

I do not know what I was playing,   5
  Or what I was dreaming then;
But I struck one chord of music,
  Like the sound of a great Amen.

It flooded the crimson twilight
    Like the close of an Angel's Psalm,   10
And it lay on my fevered spirit
    With a touch of infinite calm.

It quieted pain and sorrow,
    Like love overcoming strife;
It seemed the harmonious echo   15
    From our discordant life.

It linked all perplexèd meanings
    Into one perfect peace,
And trembled away into silence
    As if it were loth to cease.   20

I have sought, but I seek it vainly,
    That one lost chord divine,
Which came from the soul of the Organ,
    And entered into mine.

It may be that Death's bright angel   25
    Will speak in that chord again, –
It may be that only in Heaven
    I shall hear that grand Amen.

A Woman's Answer

I will not let you say a Woman's part
    Must be to give exclusive love alone;
Dearest, although I love you so, my heart
    Answers a thousand claims besides your own.

I love – what do I not love? earth and air   5
    Find space within my heart, and myriad things
You would not deign to heed, are cherished there,
    And vibrate on its very inmost strings.

I love the summer with her ebb and flow
    Of light, and warmth, and music that have nurst   10
Her tender buds to blossoms ... and you know
    It was in summer that I saw you first.

I love the winter dearly too, ... but then
    I owe it so much; on a winter's day,
Bleak, cold, and stormy, you returned again,   15
    When you had been those weary months away.

I love the Stars like friends; so many nights
    I gazed at them, when you were far from me,
Till I grew blind with tears.... those far off lights
    Could watch you, whom I longed in vain to see.   20

I love the Flowers; happy hours lie
    Shut up within their petals close and fast:
You have forgotten, dear: but they and I
    Keep every fragment of the golden Past.

I love, too, to be loved; all loving praise   25
    Seems like a crown upon my Life, – to make
It better worth the giving, and to raise
    Still nearer to your own the heart you take.

I love all good and noble souls; – I heard
    One speak of you but lately, and for days   30
Only to think of it, my soul was stirred
    In tender memory of such generous praise.

I love all those who love you; all who owe
    Comfort to you: and I can find regret
Even for those poorer hearts who once could know,   35
    And once could love you, and can now forget.

Well, is my heart so narrow – I, who spare
    Love for all these? Do I not even hold
My favourite books in special tender care,
    And prize them as a miser does his gold?   40

The Poets that you used to read to me
    While summer twilights faded in the sky;
But most of all I think Aurora Leigh,
    Because – because – do you remember why?

Will you be jealous? Did you guess before   45
    I loved so many things? – Still you the best: –
Dearest, remember that I love you more,
    Oh, more a thousand times than all the rest!

A Woman's Last Word

    Well – the links are broken,
        All is past;
    This farewell, when spoken,
        Is the last.
    I have tried and striven   5
        All in vain;

Such bonds must be riven,
　　Spite of pain,
And never, never, never
　　Knit again.　　　　　　　　　　　　　　　10

So I tell you plainly,
　　It must be:
I shall try, not vainly,
　　To be free;
Truer, happier chances　　　　　　　　　　15
　　Wait me yet,
While you, through fresh fancies,
　　Can forget; –
And life has nobler uses
　　Than Regret.　　　　　　　　　　　　　20

All past words retracing,
　　One by one,
Does not help effacing
　　What is done.
Let it be. Oh, stronger　　　　　　　　　　25
　　Links can break!
Had we dreamed still longer
　　We could wake, –
Yet let us part in kindness
　　For Love's sake.　　　　　　　　　　　30

Bitterness and sorrow
　　Will at last,
In some bright to-morrow,
　　Heal their past;
But future hearts will never　　　　　　　　35
　　Be as true
As mine was – is ever,
　　Dear, for you.....
Then must we part, when loving
　　As we do?　　　　　　　　　　　　　40

Three Evenings in a Life
I

I

Yes, it looked dark and dreary,
　　That long and narrow street:
Only the sound of the rain,
　　And the tramp of passing feet,
The duller glow of the fire,　　　　　　　　5

And gathering mists of night
To mark how slow and weary
The long day's cheerless flight!

II

Watching the sullen fire,
    Hearing the dismal rain,
Drop after drop, run down   10
    On the darkening window-pane:
Chill was the heart of Alice,
    Chill as that winter day, —
For the star of her life had risen   15
    Only to fade away.

III

The voice that had been so strong
    To bid the snare depart,
The true and earnest will,
    The calm and steadfast heart,   20
Were now weighed down by sorrow,
    Were quivering now with pain;
The clear path now seemed clouded,
    And all her grief in vain.

IV

Duty, Right, Truth, who promised   25
    To help and save their own,
Seemed spreading wide their pinions
    To leave her there alone.
So, turning from the Present
    To well-known days of yore,   30
She called on them to strengthen
    And guard her soul once more.

V

She thought how in her girlhood
    Her life was given away,
The solemn promise spoken   35
    She kept so well to-day;
How to her brother Herbert
    She had been help and guide,
And how his artist nature
    On her calm strength relied.   40

VI

How through life's fret and turmoil
   The passion and fire of art
In him was soothed and quickened
   By her true sister heart;
How future hopes had always   45
   Been for his sake alone;
And now, – what strange new feeling
   Possessed her as its own?

VII

Her home – each flower that breathed there,
   The wind's sigh, soft and low,   50
Each trembling spray of ivy,
   The river's murmuring flow,
The shadow of the forest,
   Sunset, or twilight dim –
Dear as they were, were dearer   55
   By leaving them for him.

VIII

And each year as it found her
   In the dull, feverish town,
Saw self still more forgotten,
   And selfish care kept down   60
By the calm joy of evening
   That brought him to her side,
To warn him with wise counsel,
   Or praise with tender pride.

IX

Her heart, her life, her future,   65
   Her genius, only meant
Another thing to give him,
   And be therewith content.
To-day, what words had stirred her,
   Her soul could not forget?   70
What dream had filled her spirit
   With strange and wild regret?

X

To leave him for another, —
  Could it indeed be so?
Could it have cost such anguish   75
  To bid this vision go?
Was this her faith? Was Herbert
  The second in her heart?
Did it need all this struggle
  To bid a dream depart?   80

XI

And yet, within her spirit
  A far-off land was seen,
A home, which might have held her,
  A love, which might have been.
And Life — not the mere being   85
  Of daily ebb and flow,
But Life itself had claimed her,
  And she had let it go!

XII

Within her heart there echoed
  Again the well-known tone   90
That promised this bright future,
  And asked her for her own:
Then words of sorrow, broken
  By half-reproachful pain;
And then a farewell, spoken   95
  In words of cold disdain.

XIII

Where now was the stern purpose
  That nerved her soul so long?
Whence came the words she uttered,
  So hard, so cold, so strong?   100
What right had she to banish
  A hope that God had given?
Why must she choose earth's portion,
  And turn aside from Heaven?

XIV

To-day! Was it this morning?   105
    If this long, fearful strife
Was but the work of hours,
    What would be years of life?
Why did a cruel Heaven
    For such great suffering call?   110
And why – Oh, still more cruel! –
    Must her own words do all?

XV

Did she repent? Oh Sorrow
    Why do we linger still
To take thy loving message,   115
    And do thy gentle will?
See, her tears fall more slowly,
    The passionate murmurs cease,
And back upon her spirit
    Flow strength, and love, and peace.   120

XVI

The fire burns more brightly,
    The rain has passed away,
Herbert will see no shadow
    Upon his home to-day;
Only that Alice greets him   125
    With doubly tender care,
Kissing a fonder blessing
    Down on his golden hair.

II

I

The Studio is deserted,
    Palette and brush laid by,   130
The sketch rests on the easel,
    The paint is scarcely dry;
And Silence – who seems always
    Within her depths to bear
The next sound that will utter –   135
    Now holds a dumb despair.

II

So Alice feels it: listening
  With breathless, stony fear,
Waiting the dreadful summons
  Each minute brings more near: 140
When the young life, now ebbing,
  Shall fail, and pass away
Into that mighty shadow
  Who shrouds the house to-day.

III

But why – when the sick chamber   145
  Is on the upper floor –
Why dares not Alice enter
  Within the close-shut door?
If he – her all – her Brother,
  Lies dying in that gloom,   150
What strange mysterious power
  Has sent her from the room?

IV

It is not one week's anguish
  That can have changed her so;
Joy has not died here lately,   155
  Struck down by one quick blow;
But cruel months have needed
  Their long relentless chain,
To teach that shrinking manner
  Of helpless, hopeless pain.   160

V

The struggle was scarce over
  Last Christmas Eve had brought:
The fibres still were quivering
  Of the one wounded thought,
When Herbert – who, unconscious,   165
  Had guessed no inward strife –
Bade her, in pride and pleasure,
  Welcome his fair young wife.

VI

Bade her rejoice, and smiling,
   Although his eyes were dim,   170
Thanked God he thus could pay her
   The care she gave to him.
This fresh bright life would bring her
   A new and joyous fate –
Oh, Alice, check the murmur   175
   That cries, 'Too late! too late!'

VII

Too late! Could she have known it
   A few short weeks before,
That his life was completed,
   And needing hers no more,   180
She might—Oh sad repining!
   What 'might have been,' forget;
'It was not,' should suffice us
   To stifle vain regret.

VIII

He needed her no longer,   185
   Each day it grew more plain;
First with a startled wonder,
   Then with a wondering pain.
Love: why, his wife best gave it;
   Comfort: durst Alice speak,   190
Or counsel, when resentment
   Flushed on the young wife's cheek?

IX

No more long talks by firelight
   Of childish times long past,
And dreams of future greatness   195
   Which he must reach at last;
Dreams, where her purer instinct
   With truth unerring told,
Where was the worthless gilding,
   And where refinèd gold.   200

X

Slowly, but surely ever,
    Dora's poor jealous pride,
Which she called love for Herbert,
    Drove Alice from his side;
And, spite of nervous effort   205
    To share their altered life,
She felt a check to Herbert,
    A burden to his wife.

XI

This was the least; for Alice
    Feared, dreaded, *knew* at length   210
How much his nature owed her
    Of truth, and power, and strength;
And watched the daily failing
    Of all his nobler part:
Low aims, weak purpose, telling   215
    In lower, weaker art.

XII

And now, when he is dying,
    The last words she could hear
Must not be hers, but given
    The bride of one short year   220
The last care is another's;
    The last prayer must not be
The one they learnt together
    Beside their mother's knee.

XIII

Summoned at last: she kisses   225
    The clay-cold stiffening hand;
And, reading pleading efforts
    To make her understand,
Answers, with solemn promise,
    In clear but trembling tone,   230
To Dora's life henceforward
    She will devote her own.

XIV

Now all is over. Alice
　　Dares not remain to weep,
But soothes the frightened Dora　　　　　　　　　235
　　Into a sobbing sleep.
The poor weak child will need her:
　　Oh, who can dare complain,
When God sends a new Duty
　　To comfort each new Pain!　　　　　　　　　240

III

I

The House is all deserted
　　In the dim evening gloom,
Only one figure passes
　　Slowly from room to room;
And, pausing at each doorway,　　　　　　　　　245
　　Seems gathering up again
Within her heart the relics
　　Of bygone joy and pain.

II

There is an earnest longing
　　In those who onward gaze,　　　　　　　　　250
Looking with weary patience
　　Towards the coming days.
There is a deeper longing,
　　More sad, more strong, more keen:
Those know it who look backward,　　　　　　　255
　　And yearn for what has been.

III

At every hearth she pauses,
　　Touches each well-known chair;
Gazes from every window,
　　Lingers on every stair.　　　　　　　　　　260
What have these months brought Alice
　　Now one more year is past?
This Christmas Eve shall tell us,
　　The third one and the last.

IV

The wilful, wayward Dora,   265
   In those first weeks of grief,
Could seek and find in Alice
   Strength, soothing, and relief;
And Alice – last sad comfort
   True woman-heart can take –   270
Had something still to suffer
   And bear for Herbert's sake.

V

Spring, with her western breezes,
   From Indian islands bore
To Alice news that Leonard   275
   Would seek his home once more.
What was it – joy, or sorrow?
   What were they – hopes, or féars?
That flushed her cheeks with crimson,
   And filled her eyes with tears?   280

VI

He came. And who so kindly
   Could ask and hear her tell
Herbert's last hours; for Leonard
   Had known and loved him well.
Daily he came; and Alice,   285
   Poor weary heart, at length,
Weighed down by others' weakness,
   Could lean upon his strength.

VII

Yet not the voice of Leonard
   Could her true care beguile,   290
That turned to watch, rejoicing,
   Dora's reviving smile.
So, from that little household
   The worst gloom passed away,
The one bright hour of evening   295
   Lit up the livelong day.

VIII

Days passed. The golden summer
  In sudden heat bore down
Its blue, bright, glowing sweetness
  Upon the scorching town.   300
And sights and sounds of country
  Came in the warm soft tune
Sung by the honeyed breezes
  Borne on the wings of June.

IX

One twilight hour, but earlier   305
  Than usual, Alice thought
She knew the fresh sweet fragrance
  Of flowers that Leonard brought;
Through opened doors and windows
  It stole up through the gloom,   310
And with appealing sweetness
  Drew Alice from her room.

X

Yes, he was there; and pausing
  Just near the opened door,
To check her heart's quick beating,   315
  She heard – and paused still more –
His low voice – Dora's answers –
  His pleading – Yes, she knew
The tone – the words – the accents:
  She once had heard them too.   320

XI

'Would Alice blame her?' Leonard's
  Low, tender answer came: –
'Alice was far too noble
  To think or dream of blame.'
'And was he sure he loved her?'   325
  'Yes, with the one love given
Once in a lifetime only,
  With one soul and one heaven!'

XII

Then came a plaintive murmur, –
   'Dora had once been told   330
That he and Alice' – 'Dearest,
   Alice is far too cold
To love; and I, my Dora,
   If once I fancied so,
It was a brief delusion,   335
   And over, – long ago.'

XIII

Between, the Past and Present,
   On that bleak moment's height,
She stood. As some lost traveller
   By a quick flash of light   340
Seeing a gulf before him,
   With dizzy, sick despair,
Reels backward, but to find it
   A deeper chasm there.

XIV

The twilight grew still darker,   345
   The fragrant flowers more sweet,
The stars shone out in heaven,
   The lamps gleamed down the street;
And hours passed in dreaming
   Over their new-found fate,   350
Ere they could think of wondering
   Why Alice was so late.

XV

She came, and calmly listened;
   In vain they strove to trace
If Herbert's memory shadowed   355
   In grief upon her face.
No blame, no wonder showed there,
   No feeling could be told;
Her voice was not less steady,
   Her manner not more cold.   360

XVI

They could not hear the anguish
  That broke in words of pain
Through the calm summer midnight, –
  'My Herbert – mine again!'
Yes, they have once been parted,   365
  But this day shall restore
The long lost one: she claims him:
  'My Herbert – mine once more!'

XVII

Now Christmas Eve returning,
  Saw Alice stand beside   370
The altar, greeting Dora,
  Again a smiling bride;
And now the gloomy evening
  Sees Alice pale and worn,
Leaving the house for ever,   375
  To wander out forlorn.

XVIII

Forlorn – nay, not so. Anguish
  Shall do its work at length;
Her soul, passed through the fire,
  Shall gain still purer strength.   380
Somewhere there waits for Alice
  An earnest noble part;
And, meanwhile God is with her, –
  God, and her own true heart!

Philip and Mildred

Lingering fade the rays of daylight, and the listening air is chilly;
  Voice of bird and forest murmur, insect hum and quivering spray,
Stir not in that quiet hour: through the valley, calm and stilly,
  All in hushed and loving silence watch the slow departing Day.

Till the last faint western cloudlet, faint and rosy, ceases blushing,   5
  And the blue grows deep and deeper where one trembling planet shines,
And the day has gone for ever – then, like some great ocean rushing,
  The sad night wind wails lamenting, sobbing through the moaning pines.

Such, of all day's changing hours, is the fittest and the meetest
 For a farewell hour – and parting looks less bitter and more blest; 10
Earth seems like a shrine for sorrow, Nature's mother-voice is sweetest,
 And her hand seems laid in chiding on the unquiet throbbing breast.

Words are lower, for the twilight seems rebuking sad repining,
 And wild murmur and rebellion, as all childish and in vain;
Breaking through dark future hours clustering starry hopes seem shining, 15
 Then the calm and tender midnight folds her shadow round the pain.

So they paced the shady lime-walk in that twilight dim and holy,
 Still the last farewell deferring, she could hear or he should say;
Every word, weighed down by sorrow, fell more tenderly and slowly –
 This, which now beheld their parting, should have been their wedding-day. 20

Should have been: her dreams of childhood, never straying, never faltering,
 Still had needed Philip's image to make future life complete;
Philip's young hopes of ambition, ever changing, ever altering,
 Needed Mildred's gentle presence even to make successes sweet.

This day should have seen their marriage; the calm crowning and assurance 25
 Of two hearts, fulfilling rather, and not changing, either life:
Now they must be rent asunder, and her heart must learn endurance,
 For he leaves their home, and enters on a world of work and strife.

But her gentle spirit long had learnt, unquestioning, submitting,
 To revere his youthful longings, and to marvel at the fate 30
That gave such a humble office, all unworthy and unfitting,
 To the genius of the village, who was born for something great.

When the learnèd Traveller came there who had gained renown at college,
 Whose abstruse research had won him even European fame,
Questioned Philip, praised his genius, marvelled at his self-taught knowledge, 35
 Could she murmur if he called him up to London and to fame?

Could she waver when he bade her take the burden of decision,
 Since his troth to her was plighted, and his life was now her own?
Could she doom him to inaction? could she, when a newborn vision
 Rose in glory for his future, check it for her sake alone? 40

So her little trembling fingers, that had toiled with such fond pleasure,
 Paused, and laid aside, and folded the unfinished wedding gown;
Faltering earnestly assurance, that she too could, in her measure,
 Prize for him the present honour, and the future's sure renown.

Now they pace the shady lime-walk, now the last words must be spoken, 45
 Words of trust, for neither dreaded more than waiting and delay;
Was not love still called eternal – could a plighted vow be broken? –
 See the crimson light of sunset fades in purple mist away.

'Yes, my Mildred,' Philip told her, 'one calm thought of joy and blessing,
 Like a guardian spirit by me, through the world's tumultuous stir,   50
Still will spread its wings above me, and now urging, now repressing,
 With my Mildred's voice will murmur thoughts of home, and love, and her.

'It will charm my peaceful leisure, sanctify my daily toiling,
 With a right none else possesses, touching my heart's inmost string;
And to keep its pure wings spotless I shall fly the world's touch, soiling   55
 Even in thought this Angel Guardian of my Mildred's Wedding Ring.

'Take it, dear; this little circlet is the first link, strong and holy,
 Of a life-long chain, and holds me from all other love apart;
Till the day when you may wear it as my wife – my own – mine wholly –
 Let me know it rests for ever near the beating of your heart.'   60

Dawn of day saw Philip speeding on his road to the Great City,
 Thinking how the stars gazed downward just with Mildred's patient eyes;
Dreams of work, and fame, and honour, struggling with a tender pity,
 Till the loving Past receding saw the conquering Future rise.

Daybreak still found Mildred watching, with the wonder of first sorrow,   65
 How the outward world unaltered shone the same this very day;
How unpitying and relentless busy life met this new morrow,
 Earth, and sky, and man unheeding that her joy had passed away.

Then the round of weary duties, cold and formal, came to meet her,
 With the life within departed that had given them each a soul;   70
And her sick heart even slighted gentle words that came to greet her;
 For Grief spread its shadowy pinions, like a blight upon the whole.

Jar one chord, the harp is silent; move one stone, the arch is shattered;
 One small clarion-cry of sorrow bids an armèd host awake;
One dark cloud can hide the sunlight; loose one string the pearls are scattered;   75
 Think one thought, a soul may perish; say one word, a heart may break!

Life went on, the two lives running side by side; the outward seeming,
 And the truer and diviner hidden in the heart and brain;
Dreams grow holy, put in action; work grows fair through starry dreaming;
 But where each flows on unmingling, both are fruitless and in vain.   80

Such was Mildred's life; her dreaming lay in some far-distant region,
 All the fairer, all the brighter, that its glories were but guessed;
And the daily round of duties seemed an unreal, airy legion –
 Nothing true save Philip's letters and the ring upon her breast.

Letters telling how he struggled, for some plan or vision aiming,   85
 And at last how he just grasped it as a fresh one spread its wings;
How the honour or the learning, once the climax, now were claiming,
 Only more and more, becoming merely steps to higher things.

Telling her of foreign countries: little store had she of learning,
   So her earnest, simple spirit answered as he touched the string;   90
Day by day, to these bright fancies all her silent thoughts were turning,
   Seeing every radiant picture framed within her golden Ring.

Oh, poor heart – love, if thou willest; but, thine own soul still possessing,
   Live thy life: not a reflection or a shadow of his own:
Lean as fondly, as completely, as thou willest but confessing   95
   That thy strength is God's, and therefore can at need be, stand alone.

Little means were there around her to make farther wider ranges,
   Where her loving gentle spirit could try any stronger flight;
And she turned aside, half fearing that fresh thoughts were fickle changes –
   That she *must* stay as he left her on that farewell summer night.   100

Love should still be guide and leader, like a herald should have risen,
   Lighting up the long dark vistas, conquering opposing fates;
But new claims, new thoughts, new duties found her heart a silent prison,
   And found Love, with folded pinions, like a jailer by the gates.

Yet why blame her? it had needed greater strength than she was given   105
   To have gone against the current that so calmly flowed along;
Nothing fresh came near the village save the rain and dew of heaven,
   And her nature was too passive, and her love perhaps too strong.

The great world of thought, that rushes down the years, and onward sweeping
   Bears upon its mighty billows in its progress each and all,   110
Flowed so far away, its murmur did not rouse them from their sleeping;
   Life and Time and Truth were speaking, but they did not hear their call.

Years flowed on; and every morning heard her prayer grow lower, deeper,
   As she called all blessings on him, and bade every ill depart,
And each night when the cold moonlight shone upon that quiet sleeper,   115
   It would show her ring that glittered with each throbbing of her heart.

Years passed on. Fame came for Philip in a full, o'erflowing measure;
   He was spoken of and honoured through the breadth of many lands,
And he wrote it all to Mildred, as if praise were only pleasure,
   As if fame were only honour, when he laid them in her hands.   120

Mildred heard it without wonder, as a sure result expected,
   For how could it fail, since merit and renown go side by side:
And the neighbours who first fancied genius ought to be suspected,
   Might at last give up their caution, and could own him now with pride.

Years flowed on. These empty honours led to others they called better,   125
   He had saved some slender fortune, and might claim his bride at last:
Mildred, grown so used to waiting, felt half startled by the letter
   That now made her future certain, and would consecrate her past.

And he came: grown sterner, older – changed indeed a grave reliance
    Had replaced his eager manner, and the quick short speech of old: 130
He had gone forth with a spirit half of hope and half defiance;
    He returned with proud assurance half disdainful and half cold.

Yet his old self seemed returning while he stood sometimes, and listened
    To her calm soft voice, relating all the thoughts of these long years;
And if Mildred's heart was heavy, and at times her blue eyes glistened,   135
    Still in thought she would not whisper aught of sorrow or of fears.

Autumn with its golden corn-fields, autumn with its storms and showers,
    Had been there to greet his coming with its forests gold and brown;
And the last leaves still were falling, fading still the year's last flowers,
    When he left the quiet village, and took back his bride to town.   140

Home – the home that she had pictured many a time in twilight, dwelling
    On that tender gentle fancy, folded round with loving care;
Here was home – the end, the haven; and what spirit voice seemed telling,
    That she only held the casket, with the gem no longer there?

Sad it may be to be longing, with a patience faint and weary,   145
    For a hope deferred – and sadder still to see it fade and fall;
Yet to grasp the thing we long for, and, with sorrow sick and dreary,
    Then to find how it can fail us, is the saddest pain of all.

What was wanting? He was gentle, kind, and generous still, deferring
    To her wishes always; nothing seemed to mar their tranquil life: 150
There are skies so calm and leaden that we long for storm-winds stirring,
    There is peace so cold and bitter, that we almost welcome strife.

Darker grew the clouds above her, and the slow conviction clearer,
    That he gave her home and pity, but that heart, and soul, and mind
Were beyond her now; he loved her, and in youth he had been near her,   155
    But he now had gone far onward, and had left her there behind.

Yes, beyond her: yes, quick-hearted, her Love helped her in revealing
    It was worthless, while so mighty; was too weak, although so strong;
There were courts she could not enter; depths she could not sound; yet feeling
    It was vain to strive or struggle, vainer still to mourn or long.   160

He would give her words of kindness, he would talk of home, but seeming
    With an absent look, forgetting if he held or dropped her hand;
And then turn with eager pleasure to his writing, reading, dreaming,
    Or to speak of things with others that she could not understand.

He had paid, and paid most nobly, all he owed; no need of blaming;   165
    It had cost him something, may be, that no future could restore:
In her heart of hearts she knew it; Love and Sorrow, not complaining,
    Only suffered all the deeper, only loved him all the more.

Sometimes then a stronger anguish, and more cruel, weighed upon her,
  That through all those years of waiting, he had slowly learnt the truth;   170
He had known himself mistaken, but that, bound to her in honour,
  He renounced his life, to pay her for the patience of her youth.

But a star was slowly rising from that mist of grief, and brighter
  Grew her eyes, for each slow hour surer comfort seemed to bring;
And she watched with strange sad smiling, how her trembling hands grew slighter,   175
  And how thin her slender finger, and how large her wedding-ring.

And the tears dropped slowly on it, as she kissed that golden token
  With a deeper love, it may be, than was in the far off past;
And remembering Philip's fancy, that so long ago was spoken,
  Thought her Ring's bright angel guardian had stayed near her to the last.   180

Grieving sorely, grieving truly, with a tender care and sorrow,
  Philip watched the slow, sure fading of his gentle patient wife;
Could he guess with what a yearning she was longing for the morrow,
  Could he guess the bitter knowledge that had wearied her of life?

Now with violets strewn upon her, Mildred lies in peaceful sleeping;   185
  All unbound her long, bright tresses, and her throbbing heart at rest,
And the cold, blue rays of moonlight, through the open casement creeping,
  Show the Ring upon her finger, and her hands crossed on her breast.

Peace at last. Of peace eternal is her calm sweet smile a token.
  Has some angel lingering near her let a radiant promise fall?   190
Has he told her Heaven unites again the links that Earth has broken?
  For on Earth so much is needed, but in Heaven Love is all!

Homeless

It is cold dark midnight, yet listen
  To that patter of tiny feet!
Is it one of your dogs, fair lady,
  Who whines in the bleak cold street? —
Is it one of your silken spaniels   5
  Shut out in the snow and the sleet?

My dogs sleep warm in their baskets,
  Safe from the darkness and snow;
All the beasts in our Christian England,
  Find pity wherever they go —   10
(Those are only the homeless children
  Who are wandering to and fro.)

Look out in the gusty darkness —
  I have seen it again and again,

That shadow, that flits so slowly 15
    Up and down past the window pane: –
It is surely some criminal lurking
    Out there in the frozen rain?

Nay, our Criminals all are sheltered,
    They are pitied and taught and fed; 20
That is only a sister-woman
    Who has got neither food nor bed –
And the Night cries 'sin to be living,'
    And the River cries 'sin to be dead.'

Look out at that farthest corner 25
    Where the wall stands blank and bare: –
Can that be a pack which a Pedlar
    Has left and forgotten there?
His goods lying out unsheltered
    Will be spoilt by the damp night air.

Nay; – goods in our thrifty England 30
    Are not left to lie and grow rotten,
For each man knows the market value
    Of silk or woollen or cotton...
But in counting the riches of England 35
    I think our Poor are forgotten.

Our Beasts and our Thieves and our Chattels
    Have weight for good or for ill;
But the Poor are only His image,
    His presence, His word, His will – 40
And so Lazarus lies at our doorstep
    And Dives neglects him still.

Envy

He was the first always: Fortune
    Shone bright in his face.
I fought for years; with no effort
    He conquered the place:
We ran; my feet were all bleeding, 5
    But he won the race.

Spite of his many successes
    Men loved him the same;
My one pale ray of good fortune
    Met scoffing and blame. 10
When we erred, they gave him pity,
    But me – only shame.

My home was still in the shadow,
  His lay in the sun:
I longed in vain: what he asked for   15
  It straightway was done.
Once I staked all my heart's treasure,
  We played – and he won.

Yes; and just now I have seen him
  Cold, smiling, and blest,   20
Laid in his coffin. God help me!
  While he is at rest,
I am cursed still to live: – even
  Death loved him the best.

Emily Pfeiffer (1827–1890)

Emily Jane Pfeiffer was the daughter of an army officer named Davis who married into the wealthy Tilsley family of Milford Hall in Montgomeryshire, Wales. When the bank in which Emily's father had invested failed, he lost his estate in Oxfordshire and the family was reduced to poverty. As a result of this Emily received no formal education, though she was encouraged in writing and painting by both her parents. In youth she was an anxious and depressive girl, always aware of her own shortcomings. When she published a small volume of verses in 1843, she prefaced it with an apology referring to her personal situation: 'The Authoress feels, even a greater portion of diffidence, than is normal to the young aspirant for fame, – as a severe family affliction has prevented her bestowing, on the revisal of her manuscript, the time and attention she could have wished to dedicate to her first literary production' (1843: ii).

After this Pfeiffer decided not to publish again until she had rectified the inadequacy of her education by settling to a rigorous course of study. These early experiences of her girlhood were not forgotten, and later in life Emily became an enthusiastic promoter of education for women, writing essays on the subject for the *Contemporary Review* and publishing *Women and Work* which argued the case for women's education, intellectual effort and profitable employment. Her anger over the failure to provide proper education for women continued throughout her life and included railing against Plato and 'the wisdom of Greece': 'How instructive is the whole of that fifth book of the "Republic" which treats of the "Education of Women"! – what a light it lets in on the history and tendency of Greek thought! It is the masculine spirit working alone that we trace in this portion of the wonderful Utopia . . .' (Pfeiffer 1885: 65). Her interests in women's issues also extended to the necessity of suffrage and the absurdity of female fashions which both figured in her contributions to magazines. Her poems reflect her political interests, the two sonnets 'Peace to the Odalisque', setting up a contrast between the decorative female who is little more than a harem slave, and the active working woman who will supersede her. Pfeiffer's poem to George Eliot 'The Lost Light' presents the older woman not so much as a poetic mentor as the leader and 'Pallas' of the band of 'insurgent womanhood'.

The rather melancholy tenor of Emily's existence was lightened in the 1850s when a friend took her on a tour of Europe. It was altogether changed in 1853 when she married Jurgen Edward Pfeiffer, a wealthy German-English merchant. Not only was he described as a generous and warm-hearted man, which mitigated the effects of the depression from which Emily still suffered, he also actively encouraged her writing and commitment to social reform. Although the marriage seems to have been very happy, and his death in 1889 was a blow, Pfeiffer maintained a sceptical attitude to the conduct of relations between the sexes. 'Any Husband to Many a Wife' is a version of the 'mirror' poem, though here the husband sees himself reflected positively in the eyes of his wife. The poem does not question the role of wife as moral standard because the speaker's husband is willing to live up to the challenge. But the very fact of Pfeiffer's noticing woman's role as the enlarging mirror to man suggests a foreshadowing of the arguments and images used by many later feminist critics, notably Virginia Woolf in *A Room of One's Own*.

Emily continued to travel, visiting Asia and America, and to write. Part of her considerable fortune went towards the founding of an orphanage (a project also favoured by her husband), but she also founded a school of dramatic art and promoted higher education for women. In 1895 some £2000 from this fund was allotted to assist in building Aberdare Hall at Cardiff for the accommodation of women students at university in Wales.

Pfeiffer's long lyrical poem 'From Out of the Night' is a variation on the 'fallen woman' theme which weaves the fate of her working-class speaker with the scenes along the riverbank which witness her story: the first meeting with her undergraduate lover at the boat race; his wooing in boats and woods by the river and her final decision, after his desertion, to throw herself into the river. The poem elevates the fallen woman to a saintly status, even going so far as to compare her with Christ given that she, in effect, gives her life, so that the life of her lover's father can be saved by his son's marrying a girl of a higher class. In giving her this sanctified role Pfeiffer follows the cleaning-up device used also by Procter in 'A Legend of Provence' and Barrett Browning in *Aurora Leigh*.

M.R.

Davis, Emily (1843) *The Holly-Branch: An Album for 1843*, London.
Pfeiffer, Emily (1876) *Poems*, London.
—— (1882) *Under the Aspens: Lyrical and Dramatic*, London.
—— (1885) *Flying Leaves from East and West*, London.
—— (1888) *Women and Work: An Essay Treating on the Relation to Health and Physical Development of the Higher Education of Girls . . .*, London.

from *From Out of the Night*

So the river – yes, the river; I have come to that at last;
   The river is my only friend, though changed with all the rest,
Dark and sullen, it has known me in the glory of my past
And has smiled upon me then; for very shame it could not cast
   Me forth if I should seek the barren haven of its breast.   5

Give me shelter, sullen river, hide me out of sight and ken,
   Keep your dreams, I have outdreamed them, all your golden visions keep;

Though with festering forms you hold me in some scooped-out, slimy den,
In your loathliest recesses, keep me safe from eyes of men,
  And for all the joy I had of you but give me quiet sleep.   10

No, that may not be awhile; I know that I must pass again
  By the ways that I have come, that when the waters enter in,
They will meet my lingering life and drive it backward through the brain;
I shall go to final peace as through a burning lake of pain; –
  Who can say but that the devils of that after-time may win?   15

Soft! the river did not hear them – has no knowledge of my foes,
  And it may be if it see no sign and hear no word of me,
It will pass and leave them sleeping, them and all their train of woes, –
And will only waken tenderly the pleasures that it knows,
  And so let me take farewell of love ere I have ceased to be!   20

But the pack of them that came again and found me in the church,
  And hunted me from place to place all day, yet never caught,
Till I heard the river call, and fled, and left them in the lurch,
And lay silent in the shadow, while they past me in their search –
  No, I think the river never knew that it was me they sought.   25

How they mocked me, how they scoffed at all, and most of all at him,
  As he knelt before the altar with that woman at his side,
Dressed in cobwebs spun in cellars where the spinners' eyes grow dim;
How the devils in their triumph yelled aloud and drowned the hymn,
  When they lifted up the cobwebs and his mother kissed the bride.   30

Hush, the river must not know that I had ever seen her face,
  Must not know she came and found me when my torturers had fled;
Hah! for me she had no kiss, but sat aloof in pride of race,
Though I yearned to her – his mother – till she offered me a place
  In the service of the living, never noting I was dead.   35

I had yearned to those cold eyes, because I saw his eyes look through,
  And, as out of frozen windows of a prison, gaze at me;
Had they softened with a tear, I think, my tears had fallen too,
And perhaps my heart in melting would have brought my life anew, –
  But to put to cruel uses – no! forbear my tears, let be!   40

It was she who kissed the bride, he dared not touch her in my sight,
  For he felt my ghostly presence and my shadow rise between;
But they past me by together, and she has him day and night,
With my shadow growing less and less until it dwindles quite,
  Or is swallowed of her substance, and abides with him unseen.   45

And she will be a growing power and potency, the years –
  The treacherous years will take her part and ravish him from me,

And she will make a title out of daily smiles and tears,
And will pass to fuller blessedness through weakness which endears,
   And I shall be as one forbid before I cease to be.   50

O thou blessed among women more than all of woman born!
   Be my sister, be my comforter; nay, wherefore cold and proud?
We are bound as in one web of Fate, the garland that was worn
Of thee to-day, but yestereen from off my brows was torn,
   And that costly bridal robe of thine must serve me for a shroud.   55

Be thou high of heart as happy, leave for me a little space
   In the silence of his thoughts, that while you pass from change to change,
I may, balmëd with the dead, lie still with dead unchanging face,
Making fragrant all his seasons – be this granted me for grace –
   With some magic of the morning that might else for him grow strange.   60

O my love that loved me truly in the days not long ago,
   I am young to perish wholly, let not all of me be lost;
Take me in, and never fear me – nay, I would not work you woe;
Keep for her the cheerful daylight, keep for her the firelight glow, –
   Let me wander in the twilight of your thoughts, a harmless ghost.   65

Let me steal upon your dreams, and make your broken life complete,
   Take me in, no mortal maiden, but the spirit of your youth;
I have done with earthly longings, and their memory, bitter sweet,
And would feed you with an essence you should only taste, not eat,
   And so keep your soul undying in its tenderness and truth.   70

I may rise from out the shadow, there is none upon my track;
   One might think the world was dead but for the city's ceaseless moan;
Not a foot of man or beast a-near; and for that demon pack,
They have lost and left me utterly – but, hist! they may come back –
   What is done between us, river, must be seen by us alone.   75

You are watching for me, waiting; let me be, my flesh recoils;
   What are you that you should sentence me – what evil have I done?
You have ever been my fate; you have and hold me in your toils; –
Yet, O life, I cannot live you, with your fevers and turmoils;
   Come and take me, lest it find me at the rising of the sun.   80

Let me look upon you, river – soh, how deep and still you are!
   You will hide me well, for you are dark and secret as the night;
I can see your bosom heave in the reflection of a star,
And it does not show so hard in you, and does not seem so far;
   As I drop into the darkness, I shall feel the kiss of light.   85

Yet the world is all blurred as with tears; I am looking my last;
   I can still hear its moan, though the worst of its sorrow is dumb; –

Farewell to the glimmer of lamps that grow pale in the blast,
And the clock that will measure the time, when my times shall be past! –
  See, he opens his arms – O my River-God, clasp me, I come!   90

Any Husband to Many a Wife

I scarcely know my worthless picture,
  As seen in those soft eyes and clear;
But oh, dear heart, I fear the stricture
  You pass on it when none are near.

Deep eyes that smiling give denial   5
  To tears that you have shed in vain;
Fond heart that summoned on my trial,
  Upbraids the witness of its pain.

Eyes, tender eyes, betray me never!
  Still hold the flattered image fast   10
Whereby I shape the fond endeavour
  To justify your faith at last.

'Peace to the odalisque, the facile slave'

Peace to the odalisque, the facile slave,
Whose uninvidious love rewards the brave,
Or cherishes the coward; she who yields
Her lord the fief of waste, uncultur'd fields
To perish in non-using; she whose hour   5
Is measur'd by her beauties' transient flower;
Who lives in him, as he in God, and dies
The death of parasites, no more to rise.
Graceful ephemera! Fair morning dream
  Of the young world! In vain would women's hearts   10
In love with sacrifice, withstand the stream
  Of human progress; other spheres, new parts
Await them. God be with them in their quest –
Our brave, sad working-women of the west!

Peace to the odalisque, whose morning glory   15
Is vanishing, to live alone in story.
Firm in her place, a dull-rob'd figure stands,
With wistful eyes, and earnest, grappling hands:
The working-woman, she whose soul and brain –
Her tardy right – is bought with honest pain.   20
Oh woman! sacrifice may still be thine –
More fruitful than the souls ye did resign

To sated masters; from your lives, so real,
Shall shape itself a pure and high ideal,
That ye shall seek with sad, wide-open eyes, 25
Till, finding nowhere, baffled love shall rise
To higher planes, where passion may look pale,
But charity's white light shall never fail.

The Lost Light

[George Eliot]

I

I never touched thy royal hand, dead queen,
  But from afar have looked upon thy face,
  Which, calm with conquest, carried still the trace
Of many a hard-fought battle that had been.
Since thou hast done with life, its toil and teen, 5
  Its pains and gains, and that no further grace
  Can come to us of thee, a poorer place
Shows the lorn world, – a dimlier lighted scene.

Lost queen and captain, Pallas of our band,
  Who late upon the height of glory stood, 10
Guarding from scorn – the ægis in thy hand –
  The banner of insurgent womanhood;
Who of our cause may take the high command?
  Who make with shining front our victory good?

II

Great student of the schools, who grew to be 15
  The greater teacher, having wandered wide
  In lonely strength of purity and pride
Through pathless sands, unfruitful as the sea.
Now warning words – and one clear act of thee,
  Bold pioneer who shouldst have been our guide – 20
  Affirm the track which Wisdom must abide; –
For man is bond, the beast alone is free.

So hast thou sought a larger good, so won
  Thy way to higher law, that by thy grave
We, thanking thee for lavish gifts, for none 25
  May owe thee more than that in quest so brave –
True to a light our onward feet must shun –
  Thou gavest nobler strength our strength to save.

Elizabeth Siddal (1829–1862)

Elizabeth, or Lizzie as she was usually known, was the third of eight children born to Elizabeth and Charles Siddal. Her Sheffield-born father ran a cutlery business in London. Little is known about her early life except that, in her teens, she nursed her much loved older brother Charles through a fatal illness. When she was about twenty, and working in a milliner's shop near Leicester Square, she met Walter Deverell, one of the young pre-Raphaelites, who was struck by her unusual beauty and invited her to model for one of his pictures. She went on to model for Holman Hunt, Dante Gabriel Rossetti and Millais – for whom she famously posed as the drowned Ophelia in a bath of cooling water, as a result of which she caught a bad cold, leading her father to threaten to sue the painter. From 1852 she became exclusively Rossetti's model and, under his tutelage, began to paint and write herself. Whether or not she also became his lover is not known. Evidently the Rossetti family was not too keen on the connection, as Lizzie seems never to have visited the family home. In 1854, however, Dante Gabriel persuaded Christina to call. At this time there was a plan that Lizzie should illustrate Christina's first volume of poems (*Goblin Market*), but like so many attempts to forge an artistic liaison between the 'sisters', it came to nothing. Perhaps Christina felt piqued at her brother's transferred enthusiasm, or perhaps her more clear-sighted assessment of Lizzie perceived the sad irony of his exploitative adulation. In any case, she seems to have offended him by failing to be 'adequately impressed' (W. M. Rossetti 1899: 45) by his protégée.

By contrast, many of the pre-Raphaelite circle regarded Lizzie as an artistic genius in her own right. In 1854 even Madox Brown had been converted, and was hailing her as 'a real artist, a woman without parallel' (W. M. Rossetti 1899: 19). Ruskin, already primed by Dante Gabriel – 'Ruskin...I know, will worship her' (D. G. Rossetti 1965–7: 186) – bought every one of her designs on first sight, proclaimed her a better painter than her tutor and settled £150 a year on her. 'Everyone adores and reveres Lizzy' (200), Dante Gabriel confidently proclaimed. Behind this barrage of adoration it is hard to find the real woman. Certainly, during these years Lizzie was often ill, and as Dante Gabriel's enthusiasm started to abate, a note of irritation creeps into his letters. Both Lizzie's and his own work was often interrupted by bouts of sickness. In 1855, Ruskin persuaded her to go south for the winter, but she spent most of the time in Paris, which she enjoyed, and then Nice, where she was bored. In May she returned to London to find Dante Gabriel flirting with other women and apparently no nearer fulfilling the promise of marriage which he continued to renew. Between 1857 and 1859 Lizzie's whereabouts are not known; it is possible that she returned to live with her family (Marsh 1991: 16). Bronfen suggests that her disappearances were themselves a ritual enactment of the death-like qualities idealized by Dante Gabriel (171–2).

Eventually, in May 1860, the long delayed marriage took place. 'Like all the important things I ever meant to do – to fulfil duty or secure happiness – this one has been deferred almost beyond possibility' (1965–7: 363), Dante Gabriel wrote, not very promisingly, to his mother. By this time Lizzie was quite weak, suffering bouts of faintness and vomiting. None the less, the couple went to Paris for their honeymoon and she recovered a little. Back in London, there were cheerful gatherings with the Burne-Jones's, the Morris's and Swinburne. Then, in May 1861, Lizzie gave birth to a stillborn child and fell into a deep depression. On 10 February 1862, returning home after dining with Swinburne (Dante Gabriel had gone out again to the Working Men's

College), she took an overdose of laudanum, whether intentionally or accidentally. In spite of the efforts to revive her, she died the next morning. Dante Gabriel, in his grief and guilt, buried a manuscript copy of his poems in her coffin which, seven years later, he decided to recover. The macabre story, put about by those at the exhumation, that Lizzie's hair had grown to fill the coffin, fuelled an already strong Victorian obsession with dead women and their hair (see Mew).

Siddal remains a sad and shadowy figure in the story of the pre-Raphaelites. The paintings and unpublished poems she left behind do not seem to be the works of a genius, and it may be that a major cause of her eventual breakdown was the overwhelming pressure on her to be an artist in spite of her strengths and abilities. None the less, her poems have a quiet, melancholy authority, which seems to touch a live nerve of emotional disappointment and regret. It is particularly interesting to compare her poem 'The Lust of the Eyes' with Rossetti's ' "Reflection" ' and 'In an Artist's Studio'. Both poets use the frame of the idealizing male gaze in order to release something which remains unseen and unknown in the woman: a secret self or soul. There is an intriguing, imaginative relationship between these two 'sister' women (see Rossetti) which emerges mainly in the mutual echoes of their poems. 'At Last' takes up the familiar Rossettian theme of woman's desire for death with a light-handed ease which, though lacking the playfulness and compressed sexual energy of 'When I am dead, my dearest', is nevertheless movingly purposeful and mysterious.

A.L.

Siddal, Elizabeth (1978) *Poems and Drawings*, eds Roger C. Lewis and Mark S. Lasner, Wolfville, Nova Scotia, The Wombat Press.

Bronfen, Elizabeth (1992) *Over Her Dead Body: Death, femininity and the aesthetic*, Manchester, Manchester University Press, pp. 168–78.

Marsh, Jan (1989) *The Legend of Elizabeth Siddal*, London, Quartet Books.

—— (1991) *Elizabeth Siddal 1829–1862*, The Ruskin Gallery.

Rossetti, D. G. (1965–7) *Letters*, 4 vols, eds O. Doughty and J. R. Wahl, Oxford, Clarendon Press.

Rossetti, W. M. (1899) *Ruskin: Rossetti: Preraphaelitism*, London.

—— (1906) *Some Reminiscences*, 2 vols, London.

The Lust of the Eyes

I care not for my Lady's soul
   Though I worship before her smile;
I care not where be my Lady's goal
   When her beauty shall lose its wile.

Low sit I down at my Lady's feet   5
   Gazing through her wild eyes
Smiling to think how my love will fleet
   When their starlike beauty dies.

I care not if my Lady pray
   To our Father which is in Heaven   10

But for joy my heart's quick pulses play
  For to me her love is given.

Then who shall close my Lady's eyes
  And who shall fold her hands?
Will any hearken if she cries   15
  Up to the unknown lands?

At Last

O mother, open the window wide
  And let the daylight in;
The hills grow darker to my sight
  And thoughts begin to swim.

And mother dear, take my young son,   5
  (Since I was born of thee)
And care for all his little ways
  And nurse him on thy knee.

And mother, wash my pale pale hands
  And then bind up my feet;   10
My body may no longer rest
  Out of its winding sheet.

And mother dear, take a sapling twig
  And green grass newly mown,
And lay them on my empty bed   15
  That my sorrow be not known.

And mother, find three berries red
  And pluck them from the stalk,
And burn them at the first cockcrow
  That my spirit may not walk.   20

And mother dear, break a willow wand,
  And if the sap be even,
Then save it for sweet Robert's sake
  And he'll know my soul's in heaven.

And mother, when the big tears fall,   25
  (And fall, God knows, they may)
Tell him I died of my great love
  And my dying heart was gay.

And mother dear, when the sun has set
  And the pale kirk grass waves,   30

Then carry me through the dim twilight
And hide me among the graves.

Bessie Rayner Parkes (1829–1925)

Born in Birmingham and educated in Warwickshire, even though her parents moved to London while Bessie was still a child, she described herself as having been 'born in the very bosom of Puritan England, and fed daily upon the strict letter of the Scripture from aged lips which I regarded with profound reverence' (Belloc 1895: 3). Bessie's father was a radical lawyer and a founder of the Reform Club. Her parents' involvement with a wide intellectual circle meant that Bessie made many lifelong friends with other girls from the same background. She was passionately attached to the feminist activist Barbara Leigh-Smith (later Bodichon) whom she knew from childhood and with whom she engaged in many personal and political ventures. Together, they travelled across Europe, unchaperoned in 1850. Together they drew up the petition over Married Women's Property which they persuaded many eminent women to sign in the 1850s. Bessie and Barbara also set up the *English Woman's Journal* in 1858. It was run by women for women with Bessie as editor and with a conscious brief of encouraging and exhorting its readers to personal endeavour and to celebrate women's achievements. One of her most valued contributors was Bessie's close friend Adelaide Procter. Bessie was at school with Adelaide's younger sister Agnes but did not come to know Adelaide well until after 1853. They collaborated over the Victoria Press, and when Bessie saw Adelaide on the evening of her death, Adelaide and Bessie worked on a poem of Bessie's ('Avignon') and talked about the poetry of Jean Ingelow (Belloc 1895: 171). Parkes had aspired to writing poetry since her early years and published three volumes of verse in the 1850s, but her poem 'For Adelaide' shows that she considered Procter the superior writer.

Other friends included George Eliot whom she met in Warwickshire in 1850, Elizabeth Gaskell, Anna Jameson the art critic, Mary Howitt, Matilda Hays and Elizabeth Barrett Browning. In 1856 when Barrett Browning was completing her verse-novel *Aurora Leigh* it was Bessie who shored her up as she faced male chauvinist criticism. 'Bessie Parkes', she wrote, 'is writing very vigorous articles on the woman question, in opposition to Mr Patmore, poet and husband, who expounds infamous doctrines on the same subject . . . if you heard Bessie Parkes and the rest of us militant foam with rage . . .' (EBB to Isa Blagden, 20 October 1856, unpublished letter in the Fitzwilliam Museum, Cambridge).

Having begun in a family of Unitarians, Bessie became agnostic during her most politically active years, but in 1864 she became a Catholic like so many other women of her generation. Mary Howitt remarked that it was not 'any surprise to us to learn that you had joined that great fellowship of saints and martyrs, for you and Adelaide Procter were kindred in so many ways' (Belloc 1895: 95). In 1867 Bessie married Louis Belloc and moved to France where she spent most of her married life. Two children were born, Hilaire Belloc and Marie Belloc-Lowndes. Louis, never very strong, died in 1872 and Bessie eventually returned to England 'absorbed in responsibilities which left me scant leisure for anything beyond the duties of every hour' (Belloc 1895: 94).

Parkes's poetry is pleasing and accomplished, but most effective when she uses it to argue on her special theme of women's rights, for, as she says in 'For Adelaide' her own sphere is not the imagination's realm but the public forums of debate: 'with bent brow and all too anxious heart,/ I walk with hurrying step the crowded mart,/ And look abroad on men with faithless eyes ...'. In this vein her 'To An Author who Loved Truth More than Fame' is especially interesting because it is addressed to a female writer and sets out the difficulties of obtaining an audience and the restrictions on the woman poet. On the one hand they must work to escape 'the ban which men/ Would set upon thee', while at the same time they must forego the easy security of the fashionable pet of 'drawing-room renown'. The extract from Parkes's narrative poem *Summer Sketches* is, along with Barrett Browning's *Aurora Leigh*, one of the few bold attempts to tackle the 'woman question' in verse and it is clearly influenced by the voice of the older writer. Her argument, that men are considered to be still striving to reach an ideal of development while women are conventionally believed to have achieved perfection in theirs and therefore should evolve no further, is persuasively set out and interesting for the Darwinian context it implies.

M.R.

Parkes, Bessie Rayner (1852) *Poems*, London.
—— (1854) *Summer Sketches and Other Poems*, London.
—— (1854) *Remarks on the Education of Girls*, London.
—— (1865) *Essays on Woman's Work*, London.
Belloc, Bessie Rayner Parkes (1895) *In a Walled Garden*, [Miscellaneous Essays], London.
—— (1904) *In Fifty Years*, London.

For Adelaide

Who is the Poet? He who sings
 Of high, abstruse, and hidden things,
Or rather he who with a liberal voice
Does with the glad hearts of all earth rejoice?
O sweetest Singer! rather would I be 5
Gifted with thy kind human melody
Than weave mysterious rhymes and such as seem
Born in the dim depths of some sage's dream:
But I have no such art; they will not choose
The utterance of my harsh ungenial muse 10
For any cradle chant; I shall not aid
The mournful mother or the loving maid
To find relief in song. I shall not be
Placed side by side, O Poet dear, with thee
In any grateful thoughts, yet be it known 15
By all who read how much thou hast mine own!
When, with bent brow and all too anxious heart,
I walk with hurrying step the crowded mart,
And look abroad on men with faithless eyes,
Then do sweet snatches of thy song arise, 20

And float into my heart like melodies
Down dropping from the far blue deeps of heaven,
Or sweet bells wafted over fields at even.
Therefore, if thanks for any gifts be due,
If any service be esteemèd true, 25
If any virtues do to verse belong,
Take thou the Poet's name, by right of song!
Suffer that I, who never yet did give
False words to that dear art by which I live,
Pluck down bright bay-leaves from the eternal tree, 30
And place them where they have true right to be!

To an Author who Loved Truth More than Fame

Not the sharp torture of the critic's pen,
The curse of genius in our days, tho' scorn'd,
Nor full fore-knowledge of the ban which men
Would set upon thee, Lady, have suborn'd
Thee from the simple truth; nor that gay crown 5
Of dry gilt leaves and roses overblown,
Which intellectual cliques delight to give
To wits and scribes of drawing-room renown,
And they, debased, on bended knees receive,
Weighs 'gainst the awful claims of that which you believe. 10

What you assert the critics will deny,
What you deplore pronounce eternal law,
Sneer at the echo of your bitterest sigh,
At home lock up your book, abroad decry,
Quashing your doctrine with some dusty saw. 15
Sincerely vow'd to every high command,
And bent on duty with a stedfast soul,
Truth for your only monarch, hand in hand
With all who own the same august control,
No word of pity, if the storm should beat, 20
Need any voice bestow which calls you dear;
You will not quail beneath the foolish heat,
Nor mourn anathemas you do not fear.
Truth is, your strong and loyal heart will say,
Of all her martyrs the sufficing friend, 25
And, when the lamp of love has paled away,
Will without fail her own great glory lend.
Oh voices raised in passionate protest once,
Brave spirits from whose pains our freedoms spring,
Who dared your birthright of delights renounce, 30
And, finding God, feel rich in everything, –
How long shall we your noble names revere,

And write your actions where our sons may see,
Your ancient utterance in our hearts ensphere,
And, when your steps are follow'd, turn and flee?   35

To Elizabeth Barrett Browning

I was a child when first I read your books,
And loved you dearly, so far as I could see
Your obvious meanings, your more subtle depths
Being then (as still, perhaps,) a mystery.
I had no awe of you, so much does love,   5
In simple daring, all shy fears transcend;
And when they told me, 'You shall travel south,'
I chiefly thought, 'In Florence dwells my friend!'
In those first days I seldom heard your name,
You seem'd in my strange fancy all my own,   10
Or else as if you were some saint in Heaven
Whose image took my bookcase for a throne.
As time went on, your words flew far and wide,
I heard them quoted, critically scann'd
With grave intentness, learnt, half mournfully,   15
That you were *a great Poet in the land*,
So far, so far from me, who loved you so,
And never might one human blessing claim;
Yet oh! how I rejoiced that you were great,
And all my heart exulted in your fame;   20
A woman's fame, and *yours!* I use no words
Of any careful beauty, being plain
As earnestness, and quiet as that Truth
Which shrinks from any flattering speech with pain.
Indeed, I should not dare – but that this love,   25
Long nursed, demands expression, and alone
Speaks by love's dear strength – to approach near you
In words so weak and poor beside your own.

from *Summer Sketches*

Lilian's Second Letter

Ah! with no careless pen would I report
Our words on such a topic, 't is a text
For divine sermons, did the angels preach,
Its bearings wide as half the human race.
Let no untimely deed, no crude desire   5
Profane our aspiration, it should rise
And swell and broaden like the blessed light

Which momently, yet with so soft a sound
We cannot hear its coming, opens out
Its silver wings and mounts the slopes of dawn.   10
It should, like an accumulating flood,
Gather its forces from a thousand rills,
Until by its unquestionable might
It sweep the rocks away, yet scarcely show
A foam-flake on its bosom, steadfastly   15
Careering to the sea. A spirit moves
Amidst the silk of gilded drawing-rooms
And in laborious homes, with equal voice
It summons us to labour and to prayer, –
To labour which *is* prayer, and which alone   20
Can solve the question which the age demands,
'What is a woman's right, and fitting sphere?'
How best she may, with free and willing mind,
Develope every special genius,
Retaining and perfecting every charm   25
And sweetness sung of old, so, evenpaced,
Walk in a joint obedience with man,
And equal freedom of the law of God,
Up to the height of an immortal hope.
Vainly would any poet, tho' he own'd   30
The 'double-nature' of the poet breed,
Paint the completed circle of her powers,
Whose germs await the future, undisclosed.
What she will be, she can alone define,
Nor knows she yet, but, dimly feeling, strives   35
To gain the fair ideal; what she will do
Is folded in her nature, as the flower
Is folded in the bud, or masterpiece
Of statuary in marble. She is not
Like some dead animal whose nerves and veins,   40
Bones, muscles, functions, powers and highest use
Can be defined by an anatomist
Brooding above her with a sharpen'd knife.

Suppose some small philosopher declared
'Man is a creature framed to such an end,   45
And this is his ideal, which attain'd
He will not top; this is the possible
Of his capacity, perhaps a fact
At which ambitious strugglers will rebel,
But none less true for that, let him sit down   50
And swallow it in silence.' – Witness all,
That this is said of women every day.
Diverse in nature, with unsparing creed
They limit hers, unseeing where it tends. –

Girdle with iron bands the sapling tree,   55
It shoots into deformity, but He
Who first its feeble breath of life inspired,
Ordain'd its growth by an interior law
To full development of loveliness,
Whereof the planter wots not till he leaves   60
It to the kindly care of elements
And the free seasons' change of storm and shine.
Not for a moment would I underrate
That sweet ideal which has charm'd the world
For ages, and will never cease to charm.   65
Fair as the creatures of an upper sphere,
Women among the charities of home
Walk noiseless, undefiled; ah! who would wish
To turn from this green fertilizing course
Such rills of promise! let each amplify   70
In its own proper measure far and wide,
According to its bounty; sacred be
The radiant tresses of such ministers,
And beautiful their feet; but with my voice,
And with my pen, and with mine uttermost,   75
I say this is not all, and even this,
This loveliest life to hidden music set,
Must be a blossom of spontaneous growth,
Must spring from aptitude and natural use
Of gracious deeds, not hardly forced on all   80
As the sole good and fit, lest it decay
Under the pressure to a loathsome thing,
A thing of idleness and sensuous mind,
At which the angels weep. If this be all,
Speak, thou true heart, out from the hungry sea   85
Which suck'd thee down just in thy fruit of life,
Speak, wife and mother, from that unmark'd grave
Which those so vainly seek who loved thee well,
Speak, rather, Margaret, from thy seat in heaven,
Where thou, in knowledge larger, but in love   90
Scarce more perfected, dost those days recall
Spent in strong aspiration and pursuit
Of dim ideals, now reveal'd in full,
With shape sustain'd and meanings more divine.
Ah, could I give thy dear and honour'd name   95
Some little tribute, who wert brave and bold,
And faithful, as are few! 'T is a small thing,
An easy thing, to write such witty words
As Lowell wrote of thee; 't is a hard thing,
A royal thing, to live so kind a life, –   100
Dying, to leave so dear a memory,
And such a want where thou wast wont to be.

Now let these earnest martyrs, and this hope
Which ferments round, one special prayer suggest;
That, as the founders of a colony   105
Create a nation's heart, so we, who strive
For the foundation of a principle,
May work with pure hands and a clean heart,
Regarding nought as trivial; be it said, –
As of those noble hearts who left their land   110
And planted a new empire with the seeds
Of piety and strength, – 'they very much
Did labour for the world, and the mere rights
Of man amidst his fellows, but, with zeal
Far more inclusive, gave their lives to God.'   115

Christina G. Rossetti (1830–1894)

Christina Rossetti was the youngest of four children born to Gabriele and Frances
Mary Rossetti. Her father, a poet and revolutionary exile from Bourbon Italy, was tutor
of Italian at King's College, London. Her mother, a second generation Italian and sister
of John Polidori, Byron's physician and author of *The Vampyre*, was a pious Anglican,
whose moral influence over Christina was lifelong. In temperament, Christina
resembled her eldest brother, Dante Gabriel, the pre-Raphaelite painter and poet.
Passionate, unruly and given to tantrums, she once ripped up her arm with a pair of
scissors to vent her anger against her mother. By contrast, Maria, who became a nun,
and William Michael, an editor and critic, were the pacific members of the family.

   In her mid teens, Christina suffered an emotional and religious crisis which she later
fictionalized in her short story, *Maude*. Outwardly, it took the form of a mania for
self-abnegation: she gave up playing chess and going to the theatre because she felt
their pleasures too keenly. Inwardly, it shaped itself into a death-wish, a form of
imaginative self-mortification, which then became the driving impulse of her verse.
At about this time, too, she rejected a proposal of marriage from the pre-Raphaelite
painter James Collinson, ostensibly because of his religious indecisiveness. It is hard to
judge how seriously this affected her. It did, however, give her a lifelong topos for her
poetry: that of lost love and impending death, epitomized by the lyric 'When I am dead,
my dearest' which was written at about this time. Whether life gave her the theme or
the theme dictated her life is difficult to say. At any rate, for the next forty years or
more Christina lived at home with the mother whom she adored. She twice considered
the possibility of setting up a school, but thankfully changed her mind when financial
problems eased; she applied to join Florence Nightingale in the Crimea, but was turned
down as too young; for some years she was a lay helper at a home for fallen women,
but this was short-lived. Like Barrett Browning and Emily Dickinson, Rossetti seems
to have turned her state of indefinable invalidism into a convenient pretext for
dedicating herself to art.

   She was not, however, contrary to later legends, a neurotic recluse. Although shy,
she was often found at pre-Raphaelite gatherings in the 1850s. Madox Brown recalled
a four-day visit in 1855 when Christina seemed peculiarly uncommunicative: 'She works

at worsted ever, and talks sparingly' (W. M. Rossetti 1899: 46). He also observed that there was some jealousy at this time between Christina and Dante Gabriel's much vaunted new model, Lizzie Siddal. 'In an Artist's Studio', written a year later, is a touching tribute by the ousted sister (Christina had posed for a number of Dante Gabriel's early works, including 'Girlhood of Mary Virgin') to the new star, whose beauty ambiguously feeds the artist's ravaging addiction. The 'sister' poems of these years (*Goblin Market*, 'Cousin Kate', 'Noble Sisters') all play out a drama of rivalry and sisterhood which is suggestively familial. After Lizzie's death in 1862 Christina tried to make amends for past coldness by suggesting to her brother that she publish some of Lizzie's verses jointly with her own. But on reading them she thought they were 'almost too hopelessly sad for publication', and, with an irresistible last taunt of superiority, demanded of Dante Gabriel: 'talk of my bogieism, is it not by comparison jovial?' (W. M. Rossetti 1903: 78). Certainly, the transparently obvious melancholy of Siddal's verses throws into relief the idiosyncratically whimsical and jokey nature of Rossetti's.

Christina was also in communication with other women poets of the day: Dora Greenwell, Jean Ingelow and Adelaide Procter. It is with women that she invariably compares herself as a poet. However, she was not above feeling a certain 'green tinge' of envy at a prospective eighth reprint from Ingelow, whose poetry she found some-what 'dismal' and 'oppressive' (Troxell 1937: 144), or a certain confident superiority when, confronted with Dante Gabriel's suggested emendations to her own verse, she answered roundly: 'call me "Eliza Cook" at once and be happy' (W. M. Rossetti 1903: 88). As a rule, she was polite and evasive when asked for opinions of contemporary women poets. But there were three exceptions. The first was Barrett Browning. Although Christina never met her, she remained throughout her life an ardent admirer of the older poet, staunchly defending her political 'many-sidedness' (1908: 31) against Dante Gabriel's criticisms. Rossetti's own ballads and sonnets are considerably indebted to Barrett Browning's. The second was Augusta Webster, with whom, as she put it, she once 'had a courteous tilt in the strong-minded woman lists' (1908: 97). Webster's pamphlet on 'Parliamentary Franchise for Women Ratepayers' (1878) provoked a passionate and muddled answer from Christina, who deplored women's suffrage on biblical grounds, but also argued that married women should not be excluded from the vote and that in principle women might be MPs like men. Meanwhile, the two poets exchanged volumes of their verse and maintained an admiring, if distant, friendship. The third poet was Emily Dickinson, whom Rossetti read in 1890, commenting on her 'wonderfully Blakean gift' in spite of 'a startling recklessness of poetic ways and means' (1908: 176).

In 1861 and 1865 Christina took two trips to the continent, the first to France and the second to her beloved Italy. The myth of the south, of warmth and fruit, is never a glibly untested ideal in her work, though the pull of it is strong. Later, in the 1860s, she received another proposal of marriage, from the timid scholar, Charles Cayley, whose religious half-heartedness (and perhaps emotional dithering – see 'A Sketch' and 'The heart knoweth...') gave her the old excuse to turn him down, though William Michael believed she retained a profound love for him. In her later years, suffering from Graves' disease which discoloured her face, Christina did withdraw from social life and became increasingly morbid and fanatical. In 1882 she nursed Dante Gabriel through his last illness, and in 1886, her mother. After this, she lived with some aunts. In 1892 she underwent an operation for cancer of the breast, but it recurred the following year and by 1894 she was in considerable pain – her screams, perhaps caused by the opiates she was taking, causing one of the neighbours to write a letter of complaint. To the surprise of her agnostic brother William, this most scrupulous of believers was plagued by guilt and fears of hell on her deathbed. This is not an inconsistency, however, as Rossetti's imagination was always vividly at odds with the requirements of her faith (see 'The Convent Threshold'). She died, in December 1894, at the age of sixty-four.

Rossetti is undoubtedly one of the greatest poets of the nineteenth century. As a lyricist she is unsurpassed. Like many Victorian women poets her reputation suffered as a result of the modernist cult of difficulty and experimentation in the twentieth century. However, the limpid musicality of her lyrics, though simple sounding, is never trite or superficial. Her great gift as a poet is the ability to sound the depths of the transparent – to open up, beneath the perfect, fluent metres of her verse, a perspective of troubled coldness and strangeness. These are haunted poems, in which the chilly, futuristic landscapes of the grave suggest a state of mind removed from the grip of immediate experience. Rossetti's obsession with being dead, with a state of posthumous exclusion from the world (see 'Sappho', 'At Home', 'Remember', 'When I am dead, my dearest', 'Autumn', 'A Pause', 'Cobwebs', 'A Chilly Night') may be interpreted in several ways: as a form of worldly renunciation, the imaginative equivalent to religious mortification; as a morbid and macabre scepticism, which fails ultimately to accept the idea of salvation; as a form of indirect social protest (women's lives are effectively a life-in-death); as a whimsical bid for imaginative liberty, without moral or emotional purpose. Certainly, comparing Rossetti's poems with L.E.L.'s, and there are many similarities between them (see her poem 'L.E.L.'), it is evident that Rossetti's poetic melancholy is much more casual and capricious. The speaker in 'Sappho' or the Sphinx-like woman in ' "Reflection" ' have an enigmatic coolness and self-sufficiency which is missing in L.E.L.'s noisier, unhappier heroines. Although Rossetti also exploits the tradition of the woman poet as a suffering singer, a Sappho full of grief and woe, she does so in an oddly light-hearted, careless, even mischievous manner. Her many nonsense poems for children ('The peacock has a score of eyes', 'Who has seen the wind?' 'A pin has a head...') hint at this streak of the absurd running through much of her poetry.

Goblin Market is the work which epitomizes this transgressive playfulness. Treading a thin line between fairytale and sexual fantasy, nonsense poem and cautionary tale, religious parable and socio-economic allegory, it evades resolution into any one interpretation. Like the wayward, perverse metres in which it is written, it constantly slips its own moral framework. The goblins' fruit may, after all, represent original sin, Eucharistic redemption, sexual desire, prostitution, the nurturing south, economic power, imperial capitalism, masculinity, or even, as Gilbert and Gubar suggest, language and poetry. All of these are 'marketed' in the poem's extraordinary changes and exchanges of meaning. The fruit may even just be fruit, literally, and the poem about 'shopping' – that new popular pastime for women in the early 1860s. The brilliance of the work, however, lies not in one meaning, but in its heady mix of secular and spiritual, sociological and mythical, contemporary and folkloric, as if Rossetti were probing the very nature and constitution of contemporary ideology, particularly sexual ideology.

Like the sister ballads which were written at about this time, *Goblin Market* is also a 'fallen woman' poem. Influenced by *Aurora Leigh*, which Rossetti had read recently, it too asserts a strong, suggestively erotic relationship between sister women, who defy the myth of sexual contamination by undergoing the same 'fall' (though 'paying' differently for it), by curing each other of the fruit-induced disease, and by returning to respectability and family life at the end – though it is a family which excludes both goblins and men.

Rossetti's reputation as a minor lyricist and unfashionably religious poet has only been challenged in the last decade or so. Hers is a genius which has, in a sense, worked under cover of the simple, the spontaneous and the sincere – attributes all too readily ascribed to Victorian women's verse – to produce poems which open up, below their own surface, unsettlingly dark and curious perspectives.

A.L.

Rossetti, Christina (1904) *Poetical Works*, with Memoir and Notes by W. M. Rossetti, London, Macmillan.
—— (1908) *Family Letters*, ed. W. M. Rossetti, London, Brown, Langham.
—— (1979–90) *Complete Poems: A Variorum Edition*, 3 vols, ed. R. W. Crump, Baton Rouge and London, Louisiana State University Press.

Armstrong, Isobel (1987) 'Christina Rossetti: Diary of a Feminist Reading', in *Women Reading Women's Writing*, ed. Sue Roe, Brighton, Harvester Press, pp. 117–37.
Belsey, Andrew, and Belsey, Catherine (1988) 'Christina Rossetti: Sister to the Brotherhood', *Textual Practice*, 2 (1988), 30–50.
Campbell, Elizabeth (1990) 'Of Mothers and Merchants: Female Economics in Christina Rossetti's "Goblin Market"', *Victorian Studies*, 33 (1990), 393–410.
Carpenter, Mary Wilson (1991) '"Eat me, drink me, love me": The Consumable Female Body in Christina Rossetti's *Goblin Market*', *Victorian Poetry*, 29 (1991), 415–34.
Connor, Steven (1984) '"Speaking Likenesses": Language and Repetition in Christina Rossetti's *Goblin Market*', *Victorian Poetry*, 22 (1984), 439–48.
Garlick, Barbara (1991) 'Christina Rossetti and the Gender Politics of Fantasy', in *The Victorian Fantasists*, ed. Kath Filmer, Basingstoke, Macmillan, pp. 133–52.
Gilbert, Sandra M. and Gubar, Susan (1979) *The Madwoman in the Attic*, New Haven and London, Yale University Press.
Harrison, Antony H. (1988) *Christina Rossetti in Context*, Brighton, Harvester Press.
Helsinger, Elizabeth K. (1991) 'Consumer Power and the Utopia of Desire: Christina Rossetti's "Goblin Market"', *English Literary History*, 58 (1991), 903–33.
Holt, Terrence (1990) '"Men sell not such in any town": Exchange in *Goblin Market*', *Victorian Poetry*, 28 (1990), 51–67.
Jones, Kathleen (1991) *Learning Not To Be First: The Life of Christina Rossetti*, Gloucestershire, Windrush Press.
Kent, David A. ed. (1987) *The Achievement of Christina Rossetti*, Ithaca and London, Cornell University Press.
Leighton, Angela (1992) *Victorian Women Poets*, Hemel Hempstead, Harvester, pp. 118–63.
McGann, Jerome J. (1980) 'Christina Rossetti's Poems: A New Edition and a Revaluation', *Victorian Studies*, 23 (1980), 237–54.
—— (1983) 'The Religious Poetry of Christina Rossetti', *Critical Inquiry*, 10 (1983), 127–44.
Marshall, Linda E. (1994) '"Transfigured to His Likeness": Sensible Transcendentalism in Christina Rossetti's "Goblin Market"', *University of Toronto Quarterly*, 63 (1994), 429–50.

Mermin, Dorothy (1983) 'Heroic Sisterhood in *Goblin Market*', *Victorian Poetry*, 21 (1983), 107–18.

Michie, Helena (1989) 'There is no Friend Like a Sister: Sisterhood as Sexual Difference', *English Literary History*, 56 (1989), 401–22.

Packer, Lona Mosk (1963) *Christina Rossetti*, Cambridge, Cambridge University Press.

Rosenblum, Dolores (1983) *Christina Rossetti: The Poetry of Endurance*, Carbondale, Southern Illinois University Press.

Rossetti, W. M. (1899) *Ruskin: Rossetti: Preraphaelitism: Papers 1854 to 1862*, London.

—— (1903) *Rossetti Papers: 1862 to 1870*, London, Sands.

Thomas, Eleanor Walter (1931) *Christina Georgina Rossetti*, New York, Columbia University Press.

Thomas, Frances (1994) *Christina Rossettri: A Biography*, London, Virago.

Thompson, Deborah Ann (1992) 'Anorexia as Lived Trope: Christina Rossetti's "Goblin Market" ', *Mosaic*, 24 (1992), 89–106.

Troxell, J. C. ed. (1937) *Three Rossettis: Unpublished Letters to and from Dante Gabriel, Christina, William*, Cambridge, Mass., Harvard University Press.

Sappho

I sigh at day-dawn, and I sigh
When the dull day is passing by.
I sigh at evening, and again
I sigh when night brings sleep to men.
Oh! it were better far to die   5
Than thus for ever mourn and sigh,
And in death's dreamless sleep to be
Unconscious that none weep for me;
Eased from my weight of heaviness,
Forgetful of forgetfulness,   10
Resting from pain and care and sorrow
Thro' the long night that knows no morrow;
Living unloved, to die unknown,
Unwept, untended and alone.

Song

When I am dead, my dearest,
  Sing no sad songs for me;
Plant thou no roses at my head,
  Nor shady cypress tree:
Be the green grass above me   5
  With showers and dewdrops wet;
And if thou wilt, remember,
  And if thou wilt, forget.

I shall not see the shadows,
  I shall not feel the rain;   10

I shall not hear the nightingale
    Sing on, as if in pain:
And dreaming through the twilight
    That doth not rise nor set,
Haply I may remember,   15
    And haply may forget.

Three Stages

I

I looked for that which is not, nor can be,
    And hope deferred made my heart sick in truth;
But years must pass before a hope of youth
    Is resigned utterly.

I watched and waited with a steadfast will: 5
    And though the object seemed to flee away
That I so longed for; ever, day by day,
    I watched and waited still.

Sometimes I said: This thing shall be no more:
    My expectation wearies and shall cease;   10
I will resign it now and be at peace: –
    Yet never gave it o'er.

Sometimes I said: It is an empty name
    I long for; to a name why should I give
The peace of all the days I have to live? –   15
    Yet gave it all the same.

Alas, thou foolish one! alike unfit
    For healthy joy and salutary pain;
Thou knowest the chase useless, and again
    Turnest to follow it.   20

2

My happy happy dream is finished with,
    My dream in which alone I lived so long.
My heart slept – woe is me, it wakeneth;
    Was weak – I thought it strong.

Oh weary wakening from a life-true dream: 25
    Oh pleasant dream from which I wake in pain:
I rested all my trust on things that seem,
    And all my trust is vain.

I must pull down my palace that I built,
   Dig up the pleasure-gardens of my soul;   30
Must change my laughter to sad tears for guilt,
    My freedom to control.

Now all the cherished secrets of my heart,
   Now all my hidden hopes are turned to sin:
Part of my life is dead, part sick, and part   35
    Is all on fire within.

The fruitless thought of what I might have been
   Haunting me ever will not let me rest:
A cold north wind has withered all my green,
    My sun is in the west.   40

But where my palace stood, with the same stone,
   I will uprear a shady hermitage;
And there my spirit shall keep house alone,
    Accomplishing its age:

There other garden beds shall lie around   45
   Full of sweet-briar and incense-bearing thyme;
There I will sit, and listen for the sound
    Of the last lingering chime.

3

I thought to deal the death-stroke at a blow,
   To give all, once for all, but nevermore; –   50
Then sit to hear the low waves fret the shore,
    Or watch the silent snow.

'Oh rest,' I thought, 'in silence and the dark;
   Oh rest, if nothing else, from head to feet:
Though I may see no more the poppied wheat,   55
    Or sunny soaring lark.

'These chimes are slow, but surely strike at last;
   This sand is slow, but surely droppeth thro';
And much there is to suffer, much to do,
    Before the time be past.   60

'So will I labour, but will not rejoice:
   Will do and bear, but will not hope again;
Gone dead alike to pulses of quick pain,
    And pleasure's counterpoise:'

I said so in my heart, and so I thought 65
   My life would lapse, a tedious monotone:
   I thought to shut myself, and dwell alone
     Unseeking and unsought.

But first I tired, and then my care grew slack;
   Till my heart slumbered, may-be wandered too: – 70
   I felt the sunshine glow again, and knew
     The swallow on its track;

All birds awoke to building in the leaves,
   All buds awoke to fulness and sweet scent,
   Ah, too, my heart woke unawares, intent 75
     On fruitful harvest sheaves.

Full pulse of life, that I had deemed was dead,
   Full throb of youth, that I had deemed at rest, –
   Alas, I cannot build myself a nest,
     I cannot crown my head 80

With royal purple blossoms for the feast,
   Nor flush with laughter, nor exult in song; –
   These joys may drift, as time now drifts along;
     And cease, as once they ceased.

I may pursue, and yet may not attain, 85
   Athirst and panting all the days I live:
   Or seem to hold, yet nerve myself to give
     What once I gave, again.

Remember

Remember me when I am gone away,
   Gone far away into the silent land;
   When you can no more hold me by the hand,
Nor I half turn to go yet turning stay.
Remember me when no more day by day 5
   You tell me of our future that you planned:
   Only remember me; you understand
It will be late to counsel then or pray.
Yet if you should forget me for a while
   And afterwards remember, do not grieve: 10
   For if the darkness and corruption leave
   A vestige of the thoughts that once I had,
Better by far you should forget and smile
   Than that you should remember and be sad.

A Pause

They made the chamber sweet with flowers and leaves,
    And the bed sweet with flowers on which I lay;
    While my soul, love-bound, loitered on its way.
I did not hear the birds about the eaves,
Nor hear the reapers talk among the sheaves: 5
    Only my soul kept watch from day to day,
    My thirsty soul kept watch for one away: —
Perhaps he loves, I thought, remembers, grieves.
At length there came the step upon the stair,
    Upon the lock the old familiar hand: 10
Then first my spirit seemed to scent the air
    Of Paradise; then first the tardy sand
Of time ran golden; and I felt my hair
    Put on a glory, and my soul expand.

A Study (A Soul)

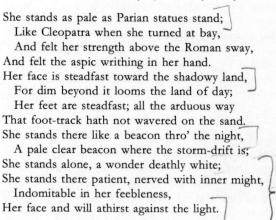

She stands as pale as Parian statues stand;
    Like Cleopatra when she turned at bay,
    And felt her strength above the Roman sway,
And felt the aspic writhing in her hand.
Her face is steadfast toward the shadowy land,   5
    For dim beyond it looms the land of day;
    Her feet are steadfast; all the arduous way
That foot-track hath not wavered on the sand.
She stands there like a beacon thro' the night,
    A pale clear beacon where the storm-drift is;   10
She stands alone, a wonder deathly white;
She stands there patient, nerved with inner might,
    Indomitable in her feebleness,
Her face and will athirst against the light.

Echo

Come to me in the silence of the night;
    Come in the speaking silence of a dream;
Come with soft rounded cheeks and eyes as bright
    As sunlight on a stream;
        Come back in tears,   5
O memory, hope, love of finished years.

Oh dream how sweet, too sweet, too bitter sweet,
    Whose wakening should have been in Paradise,
Where souls brimfull of love abide and meet;

Where thirsting longing eyes 10
　Watch the slow door
That opening, letting in, lets out no more.

Yet come to me in dreams, that I may live
　My very life again tho' cold in death:
Come back to me in dreams, that I may give 15
　Pulse for pulse, breath for breath:
　　Speak low, lean low,
As long ago, my love, how long ago.

My Dream

Hear now a curious dream I dreamed last night,
Each word whereof is weighed and sifted truth.

I stood beside Euphrates while it swelled
Like overflowing Jordan in its youth:
It waxed and coloured sensibly to sight, 5
Till out of myriad pregnant waves there welled
Young crocodiles, a gaunt blunt-featured crew,
Fresh-hatched perhaps and daubed with birthday dew.
The rest if I should tell, I fear my friend,
My closest friend would deem the facts untrue; 10
And therefore it were wisely left untold;·
Yet if you will, why, hear it to the end.

Each crocodile was girt with massive gold
And polished stones that with their wearers grew:
But one there was who waxed beyond the rest, 15
Wore kinglier girdle and a kingly crown,
Whilst crowns and orbs and sceptres starred his breast.
All gleamed compact and green with scale on scale,
But special burnishment adorned his mail
And special terror weighed upon his frown; 20
His punier brethren quaked before his tail,
Broad as a rafter, potent as a flail.
So he grew lord and master of his kin:
But who shall tell the tale of all their woes?
An execrable appetite arose, 25
He battened on them, crunched, and sucked them in.
He knew no law, he feared no binding law,
But ground them with inexorable jaw:
The luscious fat distilled upon his chin,
Exuded from his nostrils and his eyes, 30
While still like hungry death he fed his maw;
Till every minor crocodile being dead

And buried too, himself gorged to the full,
He slept with breath oppressed and unstrung claw.
Oh marvel passing strange which next I saw: 35
In sleep he dwindled to the common size,
And all the empire faded from his coat.
Then from far off a wingèd vessel came,
Swift as a swallow, subtle as a flame:
I know not what it bore of freight or host,   40
But white it was as an avenging ghost.
It levelled strong Euphrates in its course;
Supreme yet weightless as an idle mote
It seemed to tame the waters without force
Till not a murmur swelled or billow beat: 45
Lo, as the purple shadow swept the sands,
The prudent crocodile rose on his feet
And shed appropriate tears and wrung his hands.

What can it mean? you ask. I answer not
For meaning, but myself must echo, What?   50
And tell it as I saw it on the spot.

Cobwebs

It is a land with neither night nor day,
    Nor heat nor cold, nor any wind, nor rain,
    Nor hills nor valleys; but one even plain
Stretches thro' long unbroken miles away:
While thro' the sluggish air a twilight grey   5
    Broodeth; no moons or seasons wax and wane,
    No ebb and flow are there along the main,
No bud-time no leaf-falling there for aye,
No ripple on the sea, no shifting sand,
    No beat of wings to stir the stagnant space,   10
No pulse of life thro' all the loveless land:
And loveless sea; no trace of days before,
    No guarded home, no toil-won restingplace
No future hope no fear for evermore.

A Chilly Night

I rose at the dead of night
    And went to the lattice alone
To look for my Mother's ghost
    Where the ghostly moonlight shone.

My friends had failed one by one,   5
    Middleaged, young, and old,

Till the ghosts were warmer to me
  Than my friends that had grown cold.

I looked and I saw the ghosts
  Dotting plain and mound: 10
They stood in the blank moonlight
  But no shadow lay on the ground;
They spoke without a voice
  And they leapt without a sound.

I called: 'O my Mother dear,' –   15
  I sobbed: 'O my Mother kind,
Make a lonely bed for me
  And shelter it from the wind:

'Tell the others not to come
  To see me night or day;   20
But I need not tell my friends
  To be sure to keep away.'

My Mother raised her eyes,
  They were blank and could not see;
Yet they held me with their stare   25
  While they seemed to look at me.

She opened her mouth and spoke,
  I could not hear a word
While my flesh crept on my bones
  And every hair was stirred.   30

She knew that I could not hear
  The message that she told
Whether I had long to wait
  Or soon should sleep in the mould:
I saw her toss her shadowless hair   35
  And wring her hands in the cold.

I strained to catch her words
  And she strained to make me hear,
But never a sound of words
  Fell on my straining ear.   40

From midnight to the cockcrow
  I kept my watch in pain
While the subtle ghosts grew subtler
  In the sad night on the wane.

From midnight to the cockcrow   45
  I watched till all were gone,

Some to sleep in the shifting sea
  And some under turf and stone:
Living had failed and dead had failed
  And I was indeed alone.   50

A Bed of Forget-me-nots

Is love so prone to change and rot
We are fain to rear forget-me-not
By measure in a garden plot? –

I love its growth at large and free
By untrod path and unlopped tree,   5
Or nodding by the unpruned hedge,
Or on the water's dangerous edge
Where flags and meadowsweet blow rank
With rushes on the quaking bank.

Love is not taught in learning's school,   10
Love is not parcelled out by rule;
Hath curb or call an answer got? –
So free must be forget-me-not.
Give me the flame no dampness dulls,
The passion of the instinctive pulse,   15
Love steadfast as a fixèd star,
Tender as doves with nestlings are,
More large than time, more strong than death:
This all creation travails of –
She groans not for a passing breath –   20
This is forget-me-not and love.

In an Artist's Studio

One face looks out from all his canvasses,
  One selfsame figure sits or walks or leans;
  We found her hidden just behind those screens,
That mirror gave back all her loveliness.
A queen in opal or in ruby dress,   5
  A nameless girl in freshest summer greens,
  A saint, an angel; – every canvass means
The same one meaning, neither more nor less.
He feeds upon her face by day and night,
  And she with true kind eyes looks back on him   10
Fair as the moon and joyful as the light:
  Not wan with waiting, not with sorrow dim;
Not as she is, but was when hope shone bright;
  Not as she is, but as she fills his dream.

Introspective

I wish it were over the terrible pain,
Pang after pang again and again;
First the shattering ruining blow,
Then the probing steady and slow.

Did I wince? I did not faint: 5
My soul broke but was not bent;
Up I stand like a blasted tree
By the shore of the shivering sea.

On my boughs neither leaf nor fruit,
No sap in my uttermost root,   10
Brooding in an anguish dumb
On the short past and the long to come.

Dumb I was when the ruin fell,
Dumb I remain and will never tell:
O my soul I talk with thee   15
But not another the sight must see.

I did not start when the torture stung,
I did not faint when the torture wrung;
Let it come tenfold if come it must
But I will not groan when I bite the dust.   20

'Reflection'

Gazing thro' her chamber window
   Sits my soul's dear soul;
Looking northward, looking southward,
   Looking to the goal,
   Looking back without control. –   5

I have strewn thy path, beloved,
   With plumed meadowsweet,
Iris and pale perfumed lilies,
   Roses most complete:
   Wherefore pause on listless feet? –   10

But she sits and never answers;
   Gazing gazing still
On swift fountain, shadowed valley,
   Cedared sunlit hill:
   Who can guess or read her will?   15

Who can guess or read the spirit
   Shrined within her eyes,
Part a longing, part a languor,
   Part a mere surprize,
     While slow mists do rise and rise? —   20

Is it love she looks and longs for;
   Is it rest or peace;
Is it slumber self-forgetful
   In its utter ease;
     Is it one or all of these?   25

So she sits and doth not answer
   With her dreaming eyes,
With her languid look delicious
   Almost Paradise,
     Less than happy, over wise.   30

Answer me, O self-forgetful —
   Or of what beside? —
Is it day dream of a maiden,
   Vision of a bride,
     Is it knowledge, love, or pride?   35

Cold she sits thro' all my kindling,
   Deaf to all I pray:
I have wasted might and wisdom,
   Wasted night and day:
     Deaf she dreams to all I say.   40

Now if I could guess her secret
   Were it worth the guess? —
Time is lessening, hope is lessening,
   Love grows less and less:
     What care I for *no* or *yes?* —   45

I will give her stately burial,
   Tho', when she lies dead:
For dear memory of the past time,
   Of her royal head,
     Of the much I strove and said.   50

I will give her stately burial,
   Willow branches bent;
Have her carved in alabaster,
   As she dreamed and leant
     While I wondered what she meant.   55

A Birthday

My heart is like a singing bird
  Whose nest is in a watered shoot;
My heart is like an apple tree
  Whose boughs are bent with thickset fruit;
My heart is like a rainbow shell   5
  That paddles in a halcyon sea;
My heart is gladder than all these
  Because my love is come to me.

Raise me a dais of silk and down;
  Hang it with vair and purple dyes;   10
Carve it in doves and pomegranates,
  And peacocks with a hundred eyes;
Work it in gold and silver grapes,
  In leaves and silver fleurs-de-lys;
Because the birthday of my life   15
  Is come, my love is come to me.

Winter: My Secret

I tell my secret? No indeed, not I:
Perhaps some day, who knows?
But not today; it froze, and blows, and snows,
And you're too curious: fie!
You want to hear it? well: 5
Only, my secret's mine, and I won't tell.

Or, after all, perhaps there's none:
Suppose there is no secret after all,
But only just my fun.
Today's a nipping day, a biting day;   10
In which one wants a shawl,
A veil, a cloak, and other wraps:
I cannot ope to every one who taps,
And let the draughts come whistling thro' my hall;
Come bounding and surrounding me,   15
Come buffeting, astounding me,
Nipping and clipping thro' my wraps and all.
I wear my mask for warmth: who ever shows
His nose to Russian snows
To be pecked at by every wind that blows?   20
You would not peck? I thank you for good will,
Believe, but leave that truth untested still.

Spring's an expansive time: yet I don't trust
March with its peck of dust,
Nor April with its rainbow-crowned brief showers,   25
Nor even May, whose flowers
One frost may wither thro' the sunless hours.

Perhaps some languid summer day,
When drowsy birds sing less and less,
And golden fruit is ripening to excess,   30
If there's not too much sun nor too much cloud,
And the warm wind is neither still nor loud,
Perhaps my secret I may say,
Or you may guess.

A Better Resurrection

I have no wit, no words, no tears;
　My heart within me like a stone
Is numbed too much for hopes or fears;
　Look right, look left, I dwell alone;
I lift mine eyes, but dimmed with grief   5
　No everlasting hills I see;
My life is in the falling leaf:
　O Jesus, quicken me.

My life is like a faded leaf,
　My harvest dwindled to a husk;   10
Truly my life is void and brief
　And tedious in the barren dusk;
My life is like a frozen thing,
　No bud nor greenness can I see:
Yet rise it shall — the sap of Spring;   15
　O Jesus, rise in me.

My life is like a broken bowl,
　A broken bowl that cannot hold
One drop of water for my soul
　Or cordial in the searching cold;   20
Cast in the fire the perished thing,
　Melt and remould it, till it be
A royal cup for Him my King:
　O Jesus, drink of me.

'The heart knoweth its own bitterness'

When all the over-work of life
　Is finished once, and fast asleep

We swerve no more beneath the knife
　But taste that silence cool and deep;
Forgetful of the highways rough,　　　　　　　　　　　5
　Forgetful of the thorny scourge,
　Forgetful of the tossing surge,
Then shall we find it is enough? —

How can we say 'enough' on earth;
　'Enough' with such a craving heart:　　　　　　　10
I have not found it since my birth
　But still have bartered part for part.
I have not held and hugged the whole,
　But paid the old to gain the new;
　Much have I paid, yet much is due,　　　　　　　15
Till I am beggared sense and soul.

I used to labour, used to strive
　For pleasure with a restless will:
Now if I save my soul alive
　All else what matters, good or ill?　　　　　　　20
I used to dream alone, to plan
　Unspoken hopes and days to come: —
　Of all my past this is the sum:
I will not lean on child of man.

To give, to give, not to receive,　　　　　　　　　25
　I long to pour myself, my soul,
Not to keep back or count or leave
　But king with king to give the whole:
I long for one to stir my deep —
　I have had enough of help and gift —　　　　　　30
　I long for one to search and sift
Myself, to take myself and keep.

You scratch my surface with your pin;
　You stroke me smooth with hushing breath; —
Nay pierce, nay probe, nay dig within,　　　　　　35
　Probe my quick core and sound my depth.
You call me with a puny call,
　You talk, you smile, you nothing do;
　How should I spend my heart on you,
My heart that so outweighs you all?　　　　　　　40

Your vessels are by much too strait;
　Were I to pour you could not hold,
Bear with me: I must bear to wait
　A fountain sealed thro' heat and cold.
Bear with me days or months or years;　　　　　　45

Deep must call deep until the end
  When friend shall no more envy friend
Nor vex his friend at unawares.

Not in this world of hope deferred,
  This world of perishable stuff; — 50
Eye hath not seen, nor ear hath heard,
  Nor heart conceived that full 'enough':
Here moans the separating sea,
  Here harvests fail, here breaks the heart;
  There God shall join and no man part, 55
I full of Christ and Christ of me.

Autumn

I dwell alone — I dwell alone, alone,
  Whilst full my river flows down to the sea,
    Gilded with flashing boats
      That bring no friend to me:
O love-songs, gurgling from a hundred throats, 5
      O love-pangs, let me be.

Fair fall the freighted boats which gold and stone
        And spices bear to sea:
Slim, gleaming maidens swell their mellow notes,
      Love-promising, entreating — 10
        Ah! sweet, but fleeting —
  Beneath the shivering, snow-white sails.
  Hush! the wind flags and fails —
Hush! they will lie becalmed in sight of strand —
  Sight of my strand, where I do dwell alone; 15
Their songs wake singing echoes in my land —
  They cannot hear me moan.

One latest, solitary swallow flies
  Across the sea, rough autumn-tempest tost,
    Poor bird, shall it be lost? 20
Dropped down into this uncongenial sea,
      With no kind eyes
      To watch it while it dies,
    Unguessed, uncared for, free:
      Set free at last, 25
      The short pang past,
In sleep, in death, in dreamless sleep locked fast.

Mine avenue is all a growth of oaks,
      Some rent by thunder strokes,

Some rustling leaves and acorns in the breeze;   30
    Fair fall my fertile trees,
That rear their goodly heads, and live at ease.

A spider's web blocks all mine avenue;
  He catches down and foolish painted flies,
    That spider wary and wise.   35
Each morn it hangs a rainbow strung with dew
  Betwixt boughs green with sap,
    So fair, few creatures guess it is a trap:
    I will not mar the web,
Tho' sad I am to see the small lives ebb.   40

It shakes – my trees shake – for a wind is roused
    In cavern where it housed:
    Each white and quivering sail,
    Of boats among the water leaves
Hollows and strains in the full-throated gale: 45
    Each maiden sings again –
Each languid maiden, whom the calm
Had lulled to sleep with rest and spice and balm.
    Miles down my river to the sea
    They float and wane,   50
    Long miles away from me.

Perhaps they say: 'She grieves,
    Uplifted, like a beacon, on her tower.'
    Perhaps they say: 'One hour
More, and we dance among the golden sheaves.'   55
    Perhaps they say: 'One hour
      More, and we stand,
      Face to face, hand in hand;
Make haste, O slack gale, to the looked-for land!'

    My trees are not in flower,   60
    I have no bower,
    And gusty creaks my tower,
And lonesome, very lonesome, is my strand.

At Home

When I was dead, my spirit turned
  To seek the much frequented house:
I passed the door, and saw my friends
  Feasting beneath green orange boughs;
From hand to hand they pushed the wine,   5
  They sucked the pulp of plum and peach;

They sang, they jested, and they laughed,
  For each was loved of each.

I listened to their honest chat:
  Said one: 'Tomorrow we shall be   10
Plod plod along the featureless sands
  And coasting miles and miles of sea.'
Said one: 'Before the turn of tide
  We will achieve the eyrie-seat.'
Said one: 'Tomorrow shall be like   15
  Today, but much more sweet.'

'Tomorrow,' said they, strong with hope,
  And dwelt upon the pleasant way:
'Tomorrow,' cried they one and all,
  While no one spoke of yesterday.   20
Their life stood full at blessed noon;
  I, only I, had passed away:
'Tomorrow and today,' they cried;
  I was of yesterday.

I shivered comfortless, but cast   25
  No chill across the tablecloth;
I all-forgotten shivered, sad
  To stay and yet to part how loth:
I passed from the familiar room,
  I who from love had passed away,   30
Like the remembrance of a guest
  That tarrieth but a day.

The Convent Threshold

There's blood between us, love, my love,
There's father's blood, there's brother's blood;
And blood's a bar I cannot pass:
I choose the stairs that mount above,
Stair after golden skyward stair,   5
To city and to sea of glass.
My lily feet are soiled with mud,
With scarlet mud which tells a tale
Of hope that was, of guilt that was,
Of love that shall not yet avail;   10
Alas, my heart, if I could bare
My heart, this selfsame stain is there:
I seek the sea of glass and fire
To wash the spot, to burn the snare;
Lo, stairs are meant to lift us higher: 15
Mount with me, mount the kindled stair.

Your eyes look earthward, mine look up.
I see the far-off city grand,
Beyond the hills a watered land,
Beyond the gulf a gleaming strand   20
Of mansions where the righteous sup;
Who sleep at ease among their trees,
Or wake to sing a cadenced hymn
With Cherubim and Seraphim;
They bore the Cross, they drained the cup,   25
Racked, roasted, crushed, wrenched limb from limb,
They the offscouring of the world:
The heaven of starry heavens unfurled,
The sun before their face is dim.

You looking earthward, what see you?   30
Milk-white, wine-flushed among the vines,
Up and down leaping, to and fro,
Most glad, most full, made strong with wines,
Blooming as peaches pearled with dew,
Their golden windy hair afloat,   35
Love-music warbling in their throat,
Young men and women come and go.

You linger, yet the time is short:
Flee for your life, gird up your strength
To flee; the shadows stretched at length   40
Show that day wanes, that night draws nigh;
Flee to the mountain, tarry not.
Is this a time for smile and sigh,
For songs among the secret trees
Where sudden blue birds nest and sport?   45
The time is short and yet you stay:
Today while it is called today
Kneel, wrestle, knock, do violence, pray;
Today is short, tomorrow nigh:
Why will you die? why will you die?   50

You sinned with me a pleasant sin:
Repent with me, for I repent.
Woe's me the lore I must unlearn!
Woe's me that easy way we went,
So rugged when I would return!   55
How long until my sleep begin,
How long shall stretch these nights and days?
Surely, clean Angels cry, she prays;
She laves her soul with tedious tears:
How long must stretch these years and years?   60

I turn from you my cheeks and eyes,
My hair which you shall see no more –
Alas for joy that went before,
For joy that dies, for love that dies.
Only my lips still turn to you,   65
My livid lips that cry, Repent.
Oh weary life, Oh weary Lent,
Oh weary time whose stars are few.

How should I rest in Paradise,
Or sit on steps of heaven alone?   70
If Saints and Angels spoke of love
Should I not answer from my throne:
Have pity upon me, ye my friends,
For I have heard the sound thereof:
Should I not turn with yearning eyes,   75
Turn earthwards with a pitiful pang?
Oh save me from a pang in heaven.
By all the gifts we took and gave,
Repent, repent, and be forgiven:
This life is long, but yet it ends;   80
Repent and purge your soul and save:
No gladder song the morning stars
Upon their birthday morning sang
Than Angels sing when one repents.

I tell you what I dreamed last night: 85
A spirit with transfigured face
Fire-footed clomb an infinite space.
I heard his hundred pinions clang,
Heaven-bells rejoicing rang and rang,
Heaven-air was thrilled with subtle scents,   90
Worlds spun upon their rushing cars:
He mounted shrieking: 'Give me light.'
Still light was poured on him, more light;
Angels, Archangels he outstripped
Exultant in exceeding might,   95
And trod the skirts of Cherubim.
Still 'Give me light,' he shrieked; and dipped
His thirsty face, and drank a sea,
Athirst with thirst it could not slake.
I saw him, drunk with knowledge, take   100
From aching brows the aureole crown –
His locks writhed like a cloven snake –
He left his throne to grovel down
And lick the dust of Seraphs' feet:
For what is knowledge duly weighed?   105
Knowledge is strong, but love is sweet;

Yea all the progress he had made
Was but to learn that all is small
Save love, for love is all in all.

I tell you what I dreamed last night: 110
It was not dark, it was not light,
Cold dews had drenched my plenteous hair
Thro' clay; you came to seek me there.
And 'Do you dream of me?' you said.
My heart was dust that used to leap   115
To you; I answered half asleep:
'My pillow is damp, my sheets are red,
There's a leaden tester to my bed:
Find you a warmer playfellow,
A warmer pillow for your head,   120
A kinder love to love than mine.'
You wrung your hands; while I like lead
Crushed downwards thro' the sodden earth:
You smote your hands but not in mirth,
And reeled but were not drunk with wine.   125

For all night long I dreamed of you:
I woke and prayed against my will,
Then slept to dream of you again.
At length I rose and knelt and prayed:
I cannot write the words I said,   130
My words were slow, my tears were few;
But thro' the dark my silence spoke
Like thunder. When this morning broke,
My face was pinched, my hair was grey,
And frozen blood was on the sill   135
Where stifling in my struggle I lay.

If now you saw me you would say:
Where is the face I used to love?
And I would answer: Gone before;
It tarries veiled in paradise.   140
When once the morning star shall rise,
When earth with shadow flees away
And we stand safe within the door,
Then you shall lift the veil thereof.
Look up, rise up: for far above   145
Our palms are grown, our place is set;
There we shall meet as once we met
And love with old familiar love.

L.E.L.

Whose heart was breaking for a little love.[1]

Downstairs I laugh, I sport and jest with all:
  But in my solitary room above
I turn my face in silence to the wall;
  My heart is breaking for a little love.
    Tho' winter frosts are done,   5
    And birds pair every one,
And leaves peep out, for springtide is begun.

I feel no spring, while spring is wellnigh blown,
  I find no nest, while nests are in the grove:
Woe's me for mine own heart that dwells alone,   10
  My heart that breaketh for a little love.
    While golden in the sun
    Rivulets rise and run,
While lilies bud, for springtide is begun.

All love, are loved, save only I; their hearts   15
  Beat warm with love and joy, beat full thereof:
They cannot guess, who play the pleasant parts,
  My heart is breaking for a little love.
    While beehives wake and whirr,
    And rabbit thins his fur,   20
In living spring that sets the world astir.

I deck myself with silks and jewelry,
  I plume myself like any mated dove:
They praise my rustling show, and never see
  My heart is breaking for a little love.   25
    While sprouts green lavender
    With rosemary and myrrh,
For in quick spring the sap is all astir.

Perhaps some saints in glory guess the truth,
  Perhaps some angels read it as they move,   30
And cry one to another full of ruth,
  'Her heart is breaking for a little love.'
    Tho' other things have birth,
    And leap and sing for mirth,
When springtime wakes and clothes and feeds the earth.   35

---

[1] Elizabeth Barrett Browning, 'L. E. L.'s Last Question', l. 39.

Yet saith a saint: 'Take patience for thy scathe;'
   Yet saith an angel: 'Wait, for thou shalt prove
True best is last, true life is born of death,
    O thou, heart-broken for a little love.
      Then love shall fill thy girth,   40
      And love make fat thy dearth,
When new spring builds new heaven and clean new earth.'

Goblin Market

Morning and evening
Maids heard the goblins cry:
'Come buy our orchard fruits,
Come buy, come buy:
Apples and quinces,   5
Lemons and oranges,
Plump unpecked cherries,
Melons and raspberries,
Bloom-down-cheeked peaches,
Swart-headed mulberries,   10
Wild free-born cranberries,
Crab-apples, dewberries,
Pine-apples, blackberries,
Apricots, strawberries; –
All ripe together   15
In summer weather, –
Morns that pass by,
Fair eves that fly;
Come buy, come buy:
Our grapes fresh from the vine,   20
Pomegranates full and fine,
Dates and sharp bullaces,
Rare pears and greengages,
Damsons and bilberries,
Taste them and try: 25
Currants and gooseberries,
Bright-fire-like barberries,
Figs to fill your mouth,
Citrons from the South,
Sweet to tongue and sound to eye;   30
Come buy, come buy.'

Evening by evening
Among the brookside rushes,
Laura bowed her head to hear,
Lizzie veiled her blushes: 35
Crouching close together

In the cooling weather,
With clasping arms and cautioning lips,
With tingling cheeks and finger tips.
'Lie close,' Laura said,   40
Pricking up her golden head:
'We must not look at goblin men,
We must not buy their fruits:
Who knows upon what soil they fed
Their hungry thirsty roots?'   45
'Come buy,' call the goblins
Hobbling down the glen.
'Oh,' cried Lizzie, 'Laura, Laura,
You should not peep at goblin men.'
Lizzie covered up her eyes,   50
Covered close lest they should look;
Laura reared her glossy head,
And whispered like the restless brook:
'Look, Lizzie, look, Lizzie,
Down the glen tramp little men.   55
One hauls a basket,
One bears a plate,
One lugs a golden dish
Of many pounds weight.
How fair the vine must grow   60
Whose grapes are so luscious;
How warm the wind must blow
Thro' those fruit bushes.'
'No,' said Lizzie: 'No, no, no;
Their offers should not charm us,   65
Their evil gifts would harm us.'
She thrust a dimpled finger
In each ear, shut eyes and ran:
Curious Laura chose to linger
Wondering at each merchant man.   70
One had a cat's face,
One whisked a tail,
One tramped at a rat's pace,
One crawled like a snail,
One like a wombat prowled obtuse and furry,   75
One like a ratel tumbled hurry skurry.
She heard a voice like voice of doves
Cooing all together:
They sounded kind and full of loves
In the pleasant weather.   80

Laura stretched her gleaming neck
Like a rush-imbedded swan,
Like a lily from the beck,

Like a moonlit poplar branch,
Like a vessel at the launch   85
When its last restraint is gone.

Backwards up the mossy glen
Turned and trooped the goblin men,
With their shrill repeated cry,
'Come buy, come buy.'   90
When they reached where Laura was
They stood stock still upon the moss,
Leering at each other,
Brother with queer brother;
Signalling each other,   95
Brother with sly brother.
One set his basket down,
One reared his plate;
One began to weave a crown
Of tendrils, leaves and rough nuts brown   100
(Men sell not such in any town);
One heaved the golden weight
Of dish and fruit to offer her:
'Come buy, come buy,' was still their cry.

Laura stared but did not stir,   105
Longed but had no money:
The whisk-tailed merchant bade her taste
In tones as smooth as honey,
The cat-faced purr'd,
The rat-paced spoke a word   110
Of welcome, and the snail-paced even was heard;
One parrot-voiced and jolly
Cried 'Pretty Goblin' still for 'Pretty Polly;' –
One whistled like a bird.

But sweet-tooth Laura spoke in haste: 115
'Good folk, I have no coin;
To take were to purloin:
I have no copper in my purse,
I have no silver either,
And all my gold is on the furze   120
That shakes in windy weather
Above the rusty heather.'
'You have much gold upon your head,'
They answered all together:
'Buy from us with a golden curl.'   125
She clipped a precious golden lock,
She dropped a tear more rare than pearl,
Then sucked their fruit globes fair or red:

Sweeter than honey from the rock,
Stronger than man-rejoicing wine,   130
Clearer than water flowed that juice;
She never tasted such before,
How should it cloy with length of use?
She sucked and sucked and sucked the more
Fruits which that unknown orchard bore;   135
She sucked until her lips were sore;
Then flung the emptied rinds away
But gathered up one kernel-stone,
And knew not was it night or day
As she turned home alone.   140

Lizzie met her at the gate
Full of wise upbraidings:
'Dear, you should not stay so late,
Twilight is not good for maidens;
Should not loiter in the glen   145
In the haunts of goblin men.
Do you not remember Jeanie,
How she met them in the moonlight,
Took their gifts both choice and many,
Ate their fruits and wore their flowers   150
Plucked from bowers
Where summer ripens at all hours?
But ever in the noonlight
She pined and pined away;
Sought them by night and day,   155
Found them no more but dwindled and grew grey;
Then fell with the first snow,
While to this day no grass will grow
Where she lies low:
I planted daisies there a year ago   160
That never blow.
You should not loiter so.'
'Nay, hush,' said Laura:
'Nay, hush, my sister:
I ate and ate my fill,   165
Yet my mouth waters still;
Tomorrow night I will
Buy more:' and kissed her:
'Have done with sorrow;
I'll bring you plums tomorrow   170
Fresh on their mother twigs,
Cherries worth getting;
You cannot think what figs
My teeth have met in,
What melons icy-cold   175

Piled on a dish of gold
Too huge for me to hold,
What peaches with a velvet nap,
Pellucid grapes without one seed:
Odorous indeed must be the mead   180
Whereon they grow, and pure the wave they drink
With lilies at the brink,
And sugar-sweet their sap.'

Golden head by golden head,
Like two pigeons in one nest   185
Folded in each other's wings,
They lay down in their curtained bed:
Like two blossoms on one stem,
Like two flakes of new-fall'n snow,
Like two wands of ivory   190
Tipped with gold for awful kings.
Moon and stars gazed in at them,
Wind sang to them lullaby,
Lumbering owls forbore to fly,
Not a bat flapped to and fro   195
Round their rest:
Cheek to cheek and breast to breast
Locked together in one nest.

Early in the morning
When the first cock crowed his warning,   200
Neat like bees, as sweet and busy,
Laura rose with Lizzie:
Fetched in honey, milked the cows,
Aired and set to rights the house,
Kneaded cakes of whitest wheat,   205
Cakes for dainty mouths to eat,
Next churned butter, whipped up cream,
Fed their poultry, sat and sewed;
Talked as modest maidens should:
Lizzie with an open heart,   210
Laura in an absent dream,
One content, one sick in part;
One warbling for the mere bright day's delight,
One longing for the night.

At length slow evening came: 215
They went with pitchers to the reedy brook;
Lizzie most placid in her look,
Laura most like a leaping flame.
They drew the gurgling water from its deep;
Lizzie plucked purple and rich golden flags,   220

Then turning homewards said: 'The sunset flushes
Those furthest loftiest crags;
Come, Laura, not another maiden lags,
No wilful squirrel wags,
The beasts and birds are fast asleep.'   225
But Laura loitered still among the rushes
And said the bank was steep.

And said the hour was early still,
The dew not fall'n, the wind not chill:
Listening ever, but not catching   230
The customary cry,
'Come buy, come buy,'
With its iterated jingle
Of sugar-baited words:
Not for all her watching   235
Once discerning even one goblin
Racing, whisking, tumbling, hobbling;
Let alone the herds
That used to tramp along the glen,
In groups or single,   240
Of brisk fruit-merchant men.
Till Lizzie urged, 'O Laura, come;
I hear the fruit-call but I dare not look:
You should not loiter longer at this brook:
Come with me home.   245
The stars rise, the moon bends her arc,
Each glowworm winks her spark,
Let us get home before the night grows dark:
For clouds may gather
Tho' this is summer weather,   250
Put out the lights and drench us thro';
Then if we lost our way what should we do?'

Laura turned cold as stone
To find her sister heard that cry alone,
That goblin cry,   255
'Come buy our fruits, come buy.'
Must she then buy no more such dainty fruit?
Must she no more such succous pasture find,
Gone deaf and blind?
Her tree of life drooped from the root: 260
She said not one word in her heart's sore ache;
But peering thro' the dimness, nought discerning,
Trudged home, her pitcher dripping all the way;
So crept to bed, and lay
Silent till Lizzie slept;   265
Then sat up in a passionate yearning,

And gnashed her teeth for baulked desire, and wept
As if her heart would break.

Day after day, night after night,
Laura kept watch in vain   270
In sullen silence of exceeding pain.
She never caught again the goblin cry:
'Come buy, come buy;' –
She never spied the goblin men
Hawking their fruits along the glen: 275
But when the noon waxed bright
Her hair grew thin and gray;
She dwindled, as the fair full moon doth turn
To swift decay and burn
Her fire away.   280

One day remembering her kernel-stone
She set it by a wall that faced the south;
Dewed it with tears, hoped for a root,
Watched for a waxing shoot,
But there came none;   285
It never saw the sun,
It never felt the trickling moisture run:
While with sunk eyes and faded mouth
She dreamed of melons, as a traveller sees
False waves in desert drouth   290
With shade of leaf-crowned trees,
And burns the thirstier in the sandful breeze.

She no more swept the house,
Tended the fowls or cows,
Fetched honey, kneaded cakes of wheat,   295
Brought water from the brook:
But sat down listless in the chimney-nook
And would not eat.

Tender Lizzie could not bear
To watch her sister's cankerous care   300
Yet not to share.
She night and morning
Caught the goblins' cry:
'Come buy our orchard fruits,
Come buy, come buy:' –   305
Beside the brook, along the glen,
She heard the tramp of goblin men,
The voice and stir
Poor Laura could not hear;
Longed to buy fruit to comfort her,   310

But feared to pay too dear.
She thought of Jeanie in her grave,
Who should have been a bride;
But who for joys brides hope to have
Fell sick and died   315
In her gay prime,
In earliest Winter time,
With the first glazing rime,
With the first snow-fall of crisp Winter time.

Till Laura dwindling   320
Seemed knocking at Death's door:
Then Lizzie weighed no more
Better and worse;
But put a silver penny in her purse,
Kissed Laura, crossed the heath with clumps of furze   325
At twilight, halted by the brook:
And for the first time in her life
Began to listen and look.

Laughed every goblin
When they spied her peeping: 330
Came towards her hobbling,
Flying, running, leaping,
Puffing and blowing,
Chuckling, clapping, crowing,
Clucking and gobbling,   335
Mopping and mowing,
Full of airs and graces,
Pulling wry faces,
Demure grimaces,
Cat-like and rat-like,   340
Ratel- and wombat-like,
Snail-paced in a hurry,
Parrot-voiced and whistler,
Helter skelter, hurry skurry,
Chattering like magpies,   345
Fluttering like pigeons,
Gliding like fishes, –
Hugged her and kissed her,
Squeezed and caressed her:
Stretched up their dishes,   350
Panniers, and plates:
'Look at our apples
Russet and dun,
Bob at our cherries,
Bite at our peaches,   355
Citrons and dates,

Grapes for the asking,
Pears red with basking
Out in the sun,
Plums on their twigs;   360
Pluck them and suck them,
Pomegranates, figs.' –

'Good folk,' said Lizzie,
Mindful of Jeanie:
'Give me much and many:' –   365
Held out her apron,
Tossed them her penny.
'Nay, take a seat with us,
Honour and eat with us,'
They answered grinning: 370
'Our feast is but beginning.
Night yet is early,
Warm and dew-pearly,
Wakeful and starry:
Such fruits as these   375
No man can carry;
Half their bloom would fly,
Half their dew would dry,
Half their flavour would pass by.
Sit down and feast with us,   380
Be welcome guest with us,
Cheer you and rest with us.' –
'Thank you,' said Lizzie: 'But one waits
At home alone for me:
So without further parleying,   385
If you will not sell me any
Of your fruits tho' much and many,
Give me back my silver penny
I tossed you for a fee.' –
They began to scratch their pates,   390
No longer wagging, purring,
But visibly demurring,
Grunting and snarling.
One called her proud,
Cross-grained, uncivil;   395
Their tones waxed loud,
Their looks were evil.
Lashing their tails
They trod and hustled her,
Elbowed and jostled her,   400
Clawed with their nails,
Barking, mewing, hissing, mocking,
Tore her gown and soiled her stocking,

Twitched her hair out by the roots,
Stamped upon her tender feet,   405
Held her hands and squeezed their fruits
Against her mouth to make her eat.
White and golden Lizzie stood,
Like a lily in a flood, –
Like a rock of blue-veined stone   410
Lashed by tides obstreperously, –
Like a beacon left alone
In a hoary roaring sea,
Sending up a golden fire, –
Like a fruit-crowned orange-tree   415
White with blossoms honey-sweet
Sore beset by wasp and bee, –
Like a royal virgin town
Topped with gilded dome and spire
Close beleaguered by a fleet   420
Mad to tug her standard down.

One may lead a horse to water,
Twenty cannot make him drink.
Tho' the goblins cuffed and caught her,
Coaxed and fought her,   425
Bullied and besought her,
Scratched her, pinched her black as ink,
Kicked and knocked her,
Mauled and mocked her,
Lizzie uttered not a word;   430
Would not open lip from lip
Lest they should cram a mouthful in:
But laughed in heart to feel the drip
Of juice that syrupped all her face,
And lodged in dimples of her chin,   435
And streaked her neck which quaked like curd.
At last the evil people
Worn out by her resistance
Flung back her penny, kicked their fruit
Along whichever road they took,   440
Not leaving root or stone or shoot;
Some writhed into the ground,
Some dived into the brook
With ring and ripple,
Some scudded on the gale without a sound,   445
Some vanished in the distance.

In a smart, ache, tingle,
Lizzie went her way;
Knew not was it night or day;

Sprang up the bank, tore thro' the furze,   450
Threaded copse and dingle,
And heard her penny jingle
Bouncing in her purse,
Its bounce was music to her ear.
She ran and ran   455
As if she feared some goblin man
Dogged her with gibe or curse
Or something worse:
But not one goblin skurried after,
Nor was she pricked by fear;   460
The kind heart made her windy-paced
That urged her home quite out of breath with haste
And inward laughter.

She cried 'Laura,' up the garden,
'Did you miss me?   465
Come and kiss me.
Never mind my bruises,
Hug me, kiss me, suck my juices
Squeezed from goblin fruits for you,
Goblin pulp and goblin dew.   470
Eat me, drink me, love me;
Laura, make much of me:
For your sake I have braved the glen
And had to do with goblin merchant men.'

Laura started from her chair,   475
Flung her arms up in the air,
Clutched her hair:
'Lizzie, Lizzie, have you tasted
For my sake the fruit forbidden?
Must your light like mine be hidden,   480
Your young life like mine be wasted,
Undone in mine undoing
And ruined in my ruin,
Thirsty, cankered, goblin-ridden?' –
She clung about her sister,   485
Kissed and kissed and kissed her:
Tears once again
Refreshed her shrunken eyes,
Dropping like rain
After long sultry drouth;   490
Shaking with aguish fear, and pain,
She kissed and kissed her with a hungry mouth.

Her lips began to scorch,
That juice was wormwood to her tongue,

She loathed the feast: 495
Writhing as one possessed she leaped and sung,
Rent all her robe, and wrung
Her hands in lamentable haste,
And beat her breast.
Her locks streamed like the torch   500
Borne by a racer at full speed,
Or like the mane of horses in their flight,
Or like an eagle when she stems the light
Straight toward the sun,
Or like a caged thing freed,   505
Or like a flying flag when armies run.

Swift fire spread thro' her veins, knocked at her heart,
Met the fire smouldering there
And overbore its lesser flame;
She gorged on bitterness without a name: 510
Ah! fool, to choose such part
Of soul-consuming care!
Sense failed in the mortal strife:
Like the watch-tower of a town
Which an earthquake shatters down,   515
Like a lightning-stricken mast,
Like a wind-uprooted tree
Spun about,
Like a foam-topped waterspout
Cast down headlong in the sea,   520
She fell at last;
Pleasure past and anguish past,
Is it death or is it life?

Life out of death.
That night long Lizzie watched by her,   525
Counted her pulse's flagging stir,
Felt for her breath,
Held water to her lips, and cooled her face
With tears and fanning leaves:
But when the first birds chirped about their eaves,   530
And early reapers plodded to the place
Of golden sheaves,
And dew-wet grass
Bowed in the morning winds so brisk to pass,
And new buds with new day   535
Opened of cup-like lilies on the stream,
Laura awoke as from a dream,
Laughed in the innocent old way,
Hugged Lizzie but not twice or thrice;
Her gleaming locks showed not one thread of grey,   540

Her breath was sweet as May
And light danced in her eyes.

Days, weeks, months, years
Afterwards, when both were wives
With children of their own;   545
Their mother-hearts beset with fears,
Their lives bound up in tender lives;
Laura would call the little ones
And tell them of her early prime,
Those pleasant days long gone   550
Of not-returning time:
Would talk about the haunted glen,
The wicked, quaint fruit-merchant men,
Their fruits like honey to the throat
But poison in the blood;   555
(Men sell not such in any town:)
Would tell them how her sister stood
In deadly peril to do her good,
And win the fiery antidote:
Then joining hands to little hands   560
Would bid them cling together,
'For there is no friend like a sister
In calm or stormy weather;
To cheer one on the tedious way,
To fetch one if one goes astray,   565
To lift one if one totters down,
To strengthen whilst one stands.'

Cousin Kate

I was a cottage maiden
    Hardened by sun and air,
Contented with my cottage mates,
    Not mindful I was fair.
Why did a great lord find me out,   5
    And praise my flaxen hair?
Why did a great lord find me out
    To fill my heart with care?

He lured me to his palace home –
    Woe's me for joy thereof –   10
To lead a shameless shameful life,
    His plaything and his love.
He wore me like a silken knot,
    He changed me like a glove;
So now I moan, an unclean thing,   15
    Who might have been a dove.

O Lady Kate, my cousin Kate,
  You grew more fair than I:
He saw you at your father's gate,
  Chose you, and cast me by.   20
He watched your steps along the lane,
  Your work among the rye;
He lifted you from mean estate
  To sit with him on high.

Because you were so good and pure   25
  He bound you with his ring:
The neighbours call you good and pure,
  Call me an outcast thing.
Even so I sit and howl in dust,
  You sit in gold and sing: 30
Now which of us has tenderer heart?
  You had the stronger wing.

O cousin Kate, my love was true,
  Your love was writ in sand:
If he had fooled not me but you,   35
  If you stood where I stand,
He'd not have won me with his love
  Nor bought me with his land;
I would have spit into his face
  And not have taken his hand.   40

Yet I've a gift you have not got,
  And seem not like to get:
For all your clothes and wedding-ring
  I've little doubt you fret.
My fair-haired son, my shame, my pride,   45
  Cling closer, closer yet:
Your father would give lands for one
  To wear his coronet.

Noble Sisters

'Now did you mark a falcon,
  Sister dear, sister dear,
Flying toward my window
  In the morning cool and clear?
With jingling bells about her neck,   5
  But what beneath her wing?
It may have been a ribbon,
  Or it may have been a ring.' –
    'I marked a falcon swooping
      At the break of day: 10

And for your love, my sister dove,
 I 'frayed the thief away.' –

'Or did you spy a ruddy hound,
 Sister fair and tall,
Went snuffing round my garden bound,   15
 Or crouched by my bower wall?
With a silken leash about his neck;
 But in his mouth may be
A chain of gold and silver links,
 Or a letter writ to me.' –   20
  'I heard a hound, highborn sister,
   Stood baying at the moon:
  I rose and drove him from your wall
   Lest you should wake too soon.' –

'Or did you meet a pretty page   25
 Sat swinging on the gate;
Sat whistling whistling like a bird,
 Or may be slept too late:
With eaglets broidered on his cap,
 And eaglets on his glove?   30
If you had turned his pockets out,
 You had found some pledge of love.' –
  'I met him at this daybreak,
   Scarce the east was red:
  Lest the creaking gate should anger you,   35
   I packed him home to bed.' –

'Oh patience, sister. Did you see
 A young man tall and strong,
Swift-footed to uphold the right
 And to uproot the wrong,   40
Come home across the desolate sea
 To woo me for his wife?
And in his heart my heart is locked,
 And in his life my life.' –
  'I met a nameless man, sister,   45
   Who loitered round our door:
  I said: Her husband loves her much,
   And yet she loves him more.' –

'Fie, sister, fie, a wicked lie,
 A lie, a wicked lie,   50
I have none other love but him,
 Nor will have till I die.
And you have turned him from our door,
 And stabbed him with a lie:

I will go seek him thro' the world   55
  In sorrow till I die.' –
    'Go seek in sorrow, sister,
      And find in sorrow too:
    If thus you shame our father's name
      My curse go forth with you.'   60

On the Wing

Once in a dream (for once I dreamed of you)
  We stood together in an open field;
  Above our heads two swift-winged pigeons wheeled,
Sporting at ease and courting full in view.
When loftier still a broadening darkness flew,   5
  Down-swooping, and a ravenous hawk revealed;
  Too weak to fight, too fond to fly, they yield;
So farewell life and love and pleasures new.
Then as their plumes fell fluttering to the ground,
  Their snow-white plumage flecked with crimson drops, 10
    I wept, and thought I turned towards you to weep:
  But you were gone; while rustling hedgerow tops
Bent in a wind which bore to me a sound
    Of far-off piteous bleat of lambs and sheep.

Twice

I took my heart in my hand
  (O my love, O my love),
I said: Let me fall or stand,
  Let me live or die,
But this once hear me speak –   5
  (O my love, O my love) –
Yet a woman's words are weak;
  You should speak, not I.

You took my heart in your hand
  With a friendly smile,   10
With a critical eye you scanned,
  Then set it down,
And said: It is still unripe,
  Better wait awhile;
Wait while the skylarks pipe,   15
  Till the corn grows brown.

As you set it down it broke –
  Broke, but I did not wince;

I smiled at the speech you spoke,
　　At your judgment that I heard: 20
But I have not often smiled
　　Since then, nor questioned since,
Nor cared for corn-flowers wild,
　　Nor sung with the singing bird.

I take my heart in my hand,   25
　　O my God, O my God,
My broken heart in my hand:
　　Thou hast seen, judge Thou.
My hope was written on sand,
　　O my God, O my God;   30
Now let Thy judgment stand –
　　Yea, judge me now.

This contemned of a man,
　　This marred one heedless day,
This heart take Thou to scan   35
　　Both within and without:
Refine with fire its gold,
　　Purge Thou its dross away –
Yea hold it in Thy hold,
　　Whence none can pluck it out.   40

I take my heart in my hand –
　　I shall not die, but live –
Before Thy face I stand;
　　I, for Thou callest such:
All that I have I bring,   45
　　All that I am I give,
Smile Thou and I shall sing,
　　But shall not question much.

Under Willows

Under willows among the graves
　　One was walking, ah welladay!
Where each willow her green boughs waves
　　Come April prime, come May.
Under willows among the graves   5
　　She met her lost love, ah welladay!
Where in Autumn each wild wind raves
　　And whirls sere leaves away.

He looked at her with a smile,
　　She looked at him with a sigh,   10

Both paused to look awhile;
  Then he passed by,
Passed by and whistled a tune;
  She stood silent and still:
It was the sunniest day in June,   15
  Yet one felt a chill.

Under willows among the graves
  I know a certain black black pool
Scarce wrinkled when Autumn raves;
  Under the turf is cool;   20
Under the water it must be cold;
  Winter comes cold when Summer's past;
Though she live to be old, so old,
  She shall die at last.

A Sketch

The blindest buzzard that I know
  Does not wear wings to spread and stir,
  Nor does my special mole wear fur
And grub among the roots below;
  He sports a tail indeed, but then   5
  It's to a coat; he's man with men;
    His quill is cut to a pen.

In other points our friend's a mole,
  A buzzard, beyond scope of speech:
  He sees not what's within his reach, 10
Misreads the part, ignores the whole.
  Misreads the part so reads in vain,
  Ignores the whole tho' patent plain,
    Misreads both parts again.

My blindest buzzard that I know,   15
  My special mole, when will you see?
  Oh no, you must not look at me,
There's nothing hid for me to show.
  I might show facts as plain as day;
  But since your eyes are blind, you'd say: 20
    Where? What? and turn away.

From Sunset to Star Rise

Go from me, summer friends, and tarry not:
  I am no summer friend, but wintry cold,

A silly sheep benighted from the fold,
A sluggard with a thorn-choked garden plot.
Take counsel, sever from my lot your lot,   5
    Dwell in your pleasant places, hoard your gold;
    Lest you with me should shiver on the wold,
Athirst and hungering on a barren spot.
For I have hedged me with a thorny hedge,
    I live alone, I look to die alone: 10
Yet sometimes when a wind sighs through the sedge
    Ghosts of my buried years and friends come back,
My heart goes sighing after swallows flown
    On sometime summer's unreturning track.

'Italia, Io Ti Saluto!'

To come back from the sweet South, to the North
    Where I was born, bred, look to die;
Come back to do my day's work in its day,
        Play out my play –
    Amen, amen, say I.   5

To see no more the country half my own,
    Nor hear the half familiar speech,
Amen, I say; I turn to that bleak North
        Whence I came forth –
    The South lies out of reach.   10

But when our swallows fly back to the South,
    To the sweet South, to the sweet South,
The tears may come again into my eyes
        On the old wise,
    And the sweet name to my mouth.   15

A Christmas Carol

In the bleak mid-winter
    Frosty wind made moan,
Earth stood hard as iron,
    Water like a stone;
Snow had fallen, snow on snow,   5
    Snow on snow,
In the bleak mid-winter
    Long ago.

Our God, Heaven cannot hold Him
    Nor earth sustain;   10

Heaven and earth shall flee away
　　When He comes to reign:
In the bleak mid-winter
　　A stable-place sufficed
The Lord God Almighty　　　　　　　　　15
　　Jesus Christ.

Enough for Him whom cherubim
　　Worship night and day,
A breastful of milk
　　And a mangerful of hay;　　　　　　20
Enough for Him whom angels
　　Fall down before,
The ox and ass and camel
　　Which adore.

Angels and archangels　　　　　　　　25
　　May have gathered there,
Cherubim and seraphim
　　Throng'd the air,
But only His mother
　　In her maiden bliss　　　　　　　　30
Worshipped the Beloved
　　With a kiss.

What can I give Him,
　　Poor as I am?
If I were a shepherd　　　　　　　　　35
　　I would bring a lamb,
If I were a wise man
　　I would do my part, –
Yet what I can I give Him,
　　Give my heart.　　　　　　　　　　40

from *Sing-Song: A Nursery Rhyme Book*

'Why did baby die'

Why did baby die,
Making Father sigh,
Mother cry?

Flowers, that bloom to die,
Make no reply　　　　　　　　　　　5
Of 'why?'
But bow and die.

'If a pig wore a wig'

If a pig wore a wig,
    What could we say?
Treat him as a gentleman,
    And say 'Good day.'

If his tail chanced to fail,   5
    What could we do? —
Send him to the tailoress
    To get one new.

'A pin has a head, but has no hair'

A pin has a head, but has no hair;
A clock has a face, but no mouth there;
Needles have eyes, but they cannot see;
A fly has a trunk without lock or key;
A timepiece may lose, but cannot win;   5
A corn-field dimples without a chin;
A hill has no leg, but has a foot;
A wine-glass a stem, but not a root;
A watch has hands, but no thumb or finger;
A boot has a tongue, but is no singer;   10
Rivers run, though they have no feet;
A saw has teeth, but it does not eat;
Ash-trees have keys, yet never a lock;
And baby crows, without being a cock.

'Hopping frog, hop here and be seen'

Hopping frog, hop here and be seen,
    I'll not pelt you with stick or stone:
Your cap is laced and your coat is green;
    Good bye, we'll let each other alone.

Plodding toad, plod here and be looked at,   5
You the finger of scorn is crooked at:
But though you're lumpish, you're harmless too;
You won't hurt me, and I won't hurt you.

'When fishes set umbrellas up'

When fishes set umbrellas up
    If the rain-drops run,
Lizards will want their parasols
    To shade them from the sun.

'The peacock has a score of eyes'

The peacock has a score of eyes,
　With which he cannot see;
The cod-fish has a silent sound,
　However that may be;

No dandelions tell the time,　　　　　　　　　　　5
　Although they turn to clocks;
Cat's-cradle does not hold the cat,
　Nor foxglove fit the fox.

'Who has seen the wind?'

Who has seen the wind?
　Neither I nor you:
But when the leaves hang trembling
　The wind is passing thro'.

Who has seen the wind?　　　　　　　　　　　　5
　Neither you nor I:
But when the trees bow down their heads
　The wind is passing by.

'Baby lies so fast asleep'

Baby lies so fast asleep
　That we cannot wake her:
Will the Angels clad in white
　Fly from heaven to take her?

Baby lies so fast asleep　　　　　　　　　　　　5
　That no pain can grieve her;
Put a snowdrop in her hand,
　Kiss her once and leave her.

'A handy Mole who plied no shovel'

A handy Mole who plied no shovel
To excavate his vaulted hovel,
While hard at work met in mid-furrow
An Earthworm boring out his burrow.
Our Mole had dined and must grow thinner　　　5
Before he gulped a second dinner,
And on no other terms cared he
To meet a worm of low degree.
The Mole turned on his blindest eye
Passing that base mechanic by;　　　　　　　　10
The Worm entrenched in actual blindness
Ignored or kindness or unkindness;

Each wrought his own exclusive tunnel
To reach his own exclusive funnel.

A plough its flawless track pursuing   15
Involved them in one common ruin.
Where now the mine and countermine,
The dined-on and the one to dine?
The impartial ploughshare of extinction
Annulled them all without distinction.   20

from *Later Life*

Sonnet 26

This Life is full of numbness and of balk,
    Of haltingness and baffled short-coming,
    Of promise unfulfilled, of everything
That is puffed vanity and empty talk:
Its very bud hangs cankered on the stalk,   5
    Its very song-bird trails a broken wing,
    Its very Spring is not indeed like Spring,
But sighs like Autumn round an aimless walk.
This Life we live is dead for all its breath;
    Death's self it is, set off on pilgrimage,   10
    Travelling with tottering steps the first short stage:
        The second stage is one mere desert dust
        Where Death sits veiled amid creation's rust: –
Unveil thy face, O Death who art not Death.

Soeur Louise de la Miséricorde (1674)[1]

I have desired, and I have been desired;
    But now the days are over of desire,
    Now dust and dying embers mock my fire;
Where is the hire for which my life was hired?
    Oh vanity of vanities, desire!   5

Longing and love, pangs of a perished pleasure,
    Longing and love, a disenkindled fire,
    And memory a bottomless gulf of mire,
And love a fount of tears outrunning measure;
    Oh vanity of vanities, desire!   10

---

[1] Louise de la Vallière, mistress of Louis XIV, who
retired to a convent.

Now from my heart, love's deathbed, trickles, trickles,
  Drop by drop slowly, drop by drop of fire,
  The dross of life, of love, of spent desire;
Alas, my rose of life gone all to prickles, –
  Oh vanity of vanities, desire!   15

Oh vanity of vanities, desire;
  Stunting my hope which might have strained up higher,
  Turning my garden plot to barren mire;
Oh death-struck love, oh disenkindled fire,
  Oh vanity of vanities, desire!   20

An Old-World Thicket

Una selva oscura.[1]
[Dante]

Awake or sleeping (for I know not which)
  I was or was not mazed within a wood
  Where every mother-bird brought up her brood
    Safe in some leafy niche
  Of oak or ash, of cypress or of beech,   5

Of silvery aspen trembling delicately,
  Of plane or warmer-tinted sycomore,
  Of elm that dies in secret from the core,
    Of ivy weak and free,
  Of pines, of all green lofty things that be.   10

Such birds they seemed as challenged each desire;
  Like spots of azure heaven upon the wing,
  Like downy emeralds that alight and sing,
    Like actual coals on fire,
  Like anything they seemed, and everything.   15

Such mirth they made, such warblings and such chat
  With tongue of music in a well-tuned beak,
  They seemed to speak more wisdom than we speak,
    To make our music flat
  And all our subtlest reasonings wild or weak.   20

Their meat was nought but flowers like butterflies,
  With berries coral-coloured or like gold;
  Their drink was only dew, which blossoms hold
    Deep where the honey lies;
Their wings and tails were lit by sparkling eyes.   25

---

[1] A dark wood

The shade wherein they revelled was a shade
   That danced and twinkled to the unseen sun;
   Branches and leaves cast shadows one by one,
     And all their shadows swayed
In breaths of air that rustled and that played.   30

A sound of waters neither rose nor sank,
   And spread a sense of freshness through the air;
   It seemed not here or there, but everywhere,
     As if the whole earth drank,
Root fathom deep and strawberry on its bank.   35

But I who saw such things as I have said,
   Was overdone with utter weariness;
   And walked in care, as one whom fears oppress
     Because above his head
Death hangs, or damage, or the dearth of bread.   40

Each sore defeat of my defeated life
   Faced and outfaced me in that bitter hour;
   And turned to yearning palsy all my power,
     And all my peace to strife,
Self stabbing self with keen lack-pity knife.   45

Sweetness of beauty moved me to despair,
   Stung me to anger by its mere content,
   Made me all lonely on that way I went,
     Piled care upon my care,
Brimmed full my cup, and stripped me empty and bare: 50

For all that was but showed what all was not,
   But gave clear proof of what might never be;
   Making more destitute my poverty,
     And yet more blank my lot,
And me much sadder by its jubilee.   55

Therefore I sat me down: for wherefore walk?
   And closed mine eyes: for wherefore see or hear?
   Alas, I had no shutter to mine ear,
     And could not shun the talk
Of all rejoicing creatures far or near.   60

Without my will I hearkened and I heard
   (Asleep or waking, for I know not which),
   Till note by note the music changed its pitch;
     Bird ceased to answer bird,
And every wind sighed softly if it stirred.   65

The drip of widening waters seemed to weep,
  All fountains sobbed and gurgled as they sprang,
Somewhere a cataract cried out in its leap
    Sheer down a headlong steep;
    High over all cloud-thunders gave a clang.   70

Such universal sound of lamentation
  I heard and felt, fain not to feel or hear;
  Nought else there seemed but anguish far and near;
    Nought else but all creation
  Moaning and groaning wrung by pain or fear,   75

Shuddering in the misery of its doom:
  My heart then rose a rebel against light,
  Scouring all earth and heaven and depth and height,
    Ingathering wrath and gloom,
  Ingathering wrath to wrath and night to night.   80

Ah me, the bitterness of such revolt,
  All impotent, all hateful, and all hate,
That kicks and breaks itself against the bolt
    Of an imprisoning fate,
  And vainly shakes, and cannot shake the gate.   85

Agony to agony, deep called to deep,
  Out of the deep I called of my desire;
  My strength was weakness and my heart was fire;
    Mine eyes that would not weep
Or sleep, scaled height and depth, and could not sleep;   90

The eyes, I mean, of my rebellious soul,
  For still my bodily eyes were closed and dark:
  A random thing I seemed without a mark,
    Racing without a goal,
  Adrift upon life's sea without an ark.   95

More leaden than the actual self of lead
  Outer and inner darkness weighed on me.
  The tide of anger ebbed. Then fierce and free
    Surged full above my head
  The moaning tide of helpless misery.   100

Why should I breathe, whose breath was but a sigh?
  Why should I live, who drew such painful breath?
Oh weary work, the unanswerable why! —
    Yet I, why should I die,
  Who had no hope in life, no hope in death?   105

Grasses and mosses and the fallen leaf
  Make peaceful bed for an indefinite term;
But underneath the grass there gnaws a worm –
  Haply, there gnaws a grief –
Both, haply always; not, as now, so brief.   110

The pleasure I remember, it is past;
  The pain I feel, is passing passing by;
  Thus all the world is passing, and thus I:
    All things that cannot last
  Have grown familiar, and are born to die.   115

And being familiar, have so long been borne
  That habit trains us not to break but bend:
Mourning grows natural to us who mourn
    In foresight of an end,
  But that which ends not who shall brave or mend?   120

Surely the ripe fruits tremble on their bough,
  They cling and linger trembling till they drop:
I, trembling, cling to dying life; for how
    Face the perpetual Now?
  Birthless and deathless, void of start or stop,   125

Void of repentance, void of hope and fear,
  Of possibility, alternative,
  Of all that ever made us bear to live
    From night to morning here,
  Of promise even which has no gift to give.   130

The wood, and every creature of the wood,
  Seemed mourning with me in an undertone;
  Soft scattered chirpings and a windy moan,
    Trees rustling where they stood
And shivered, showed compassion for my mood.   135

Rage to despair; and now despair had turned
  Back to self-pity and mere weariness,
With yearnings like a smouldering fire that burned,
    And might grow more or less,
  And might die out or wax to white excess.   140

Without, within me, music seemed to be;
  Something not music, yet most musical,
Silence and sound in heavenly harmony;
    At length a pattering fall
  Of feet, a bell, and bleatings, broke through all.   145

Then I looked up. The wood lay in a glow
  From golden sunset and from ruddy sky;
    The sun had stooped to earth though once so high;
    Had stooped to earth, in slow
Warm dying loveliness brought near and low.   150

Each water drop made answer to the light,
  Lit up a spark and showed the sun his face;
    Soft purple shadows paved the grassy space
    And crept from height to height,
  From height to loftier height crept up apace.   155

While opposite the sun a gazing moon
  Put on his glory for her coronet,
Kindling her luminous coldness to its noon,
    As his great splendour set;
  One only star made up her train as yet.   160

Each twig was tipped with gold, each leaf was edged
  And veined with gold from the gold-flooded west;
Each mother-bird, and mate-bird, and unfledged
    Nestling, and curious nest,
  Displayed a gilded moss or beak or breast.   165

And filing peacefully between the trees,
  Having the moon behind them, and the sun
Full in their meek mild faces, walked at ease
    A homeward flock, at peace
  With one another and with every one.   170

A patriarchal ram with tinkling bell
  Led all his kin; sometimes one browsing sheep
  Hung back a moment, or one lamb would leap
    And frolic in a dell;
Yet still they kept together, journeying well,   175

And bleating, one or other, many or few,
  Journeying together toward the sunlit west;
  Mild face by face, and woolly breast by breast,
    Patient, sun-brightened too,
  Still journeying toward the sunset and their rest.   180

Ellen Johnston (1835–1873)

Little is known about the working-class poet who wrote under the name of 'Ellen Johnston, the "Factory Girl" ', except what can be gleaned from the 'Autobiography' which prefixes her two volumes of poems. She was the only child of a Glaswegian stone-mason, James Johnston, who was himself a poet, and his wife Mary, whom he married when she was eighteen. When Ellen was only a few months old her father decided to emigrate to America. At the last minute, however, when about to board ship, her 'strong-minded' (1869: xii) mother decided not to go. Returning to her father's house in Bridgeton, she supported herself as a seamstress and milliner. Some eight years later, having heard that her first husband was dead, she married a power-loom worker. This, it seems, marked the end of a happy childhood for Ellen. When the girl was ten, her stepfather took exception to her bookish ways and sent her to work in the weaving factory. Subsequent events are obscure, but it seems that he sexually assaulted her. She writes that 'no language can paint the suffering which I afterwards endured from my tormentor' (1867: 7), and that 'to preserve [her] virtue and end [her] sufferings' (1869: xv) she ran away from home, and even contemplated killing herself. However, she was discovered by a member of the family, returned to her mother and severely beaten. Nevertheless, she remained silent about 'the cause which first disturbed [her] peace', though enduring further torments and running away from home on five subsequent occasions. At this time, only her 'heart's first love' (1867: 9), who remains unnamed, and the stirrings of her poetic ability, kept her from suicide.

It is probable that this 'first love' then became the father of Ellen's child. She writes that 'I was falsely accused by those who knew me as a fallen woman, while I was as innocent of the charge as the unborn babe.' The father absconded, but another man then stepped into his place, and, as she put it, 'offered . . . his heart – without the form of legal protection' (1867: 10). In September 1852, at the age of seventeen, Ellen gave birth to a daughter, Mary Achenvole, thus becoming a single mother. All the details of this event were excised from the second version of the *Autobiography*. Too frail to return to factory work, Ellen started contributing poems to the weekly newspapers. In 1854 her poem 'Lord Raglan's Address to the Allied Armies' was printed in the *Glasgow Examiner*, gaining her a gift of £10 from Lord Raglan himself. Another poem, strategically sent to the owner of a dockyard, gained her another £10 to start a 'small business' (1867: 12). However, these sporadic earnings were not sufficient to keep the whole family. Ellen, by now, was supporting her mother and stepfather as well as her daughter, the second anonymous protector having also disappeared (if he ever existed). So she returned to factory work. In 1857 she went to Belfast and worked in James Kennedy's Mill – a happy time, judging by the number of poems praising its philanthropic owner and recalling, a little too prettily, cheerful workers' outings. However the passionate poem, 'A Mother's Love', also tells how Ellen missed the daughter she had left at home. In 1859 she worked in Manchester for a few months, but then returned to Glasgow. She found her mother an invalid, as well as grief-stricken by the discovery that her first husband was not dead, that he had found out about her marriage and had subsequently killed himself. This information perhaps encouraged Ellen finally to disclose the 'dark history' of her own life, which, she declared, always 'haunted [her] like a vampire' (1867: 6). Her beloved mother died in 1861.

Ellen then moved with her child to Dundee where she worked in a weaving factory. Her poetic ambitions seem to have been the cause of some envy and distrust here. After two years she was dismissed without notice by the foreman, but, alert to her rights, she successfully sued him for a week's wages. Sadly, however, her fellow workers did not support her. 'But if I was envied by my sister sex... for my talent before this affair happened,' she recalled, 'they hated me with a perfect hatred after I had struggled for and gained my rights' (1867: 14). Persecuted and hounded, sometimes physically attacked in the streets by other women, she went hungry and without work for some months.

However, by now Johnston was finding recognition as a poet. Having contributed for some years to the *People's Journal*, which regularly published verses by working men and women, she then discovered the *Penny Post*. Her publications in this cheap and accessible magazine drew letters of 'sympathy, friendship, and love' (1867: 15) from many quarters, but especially from women. Under the encouragement of its editor and with the help of a body of subscribers, she put together a long awaited volume of poems in 1867. This carries the moving dedication: 'To all men and women, of every class, sect, and party, who by their skill, labour, science, art, literature, and poetry, promote the moral and social elevation of humanity...' The second edition of 1869 contains a few more poems and a significantly censored version of the *Autobiography*. Evidently, a decade after *Aurora Leigh*, the story of the unmarried working mother was still a cause of disrepute and scandal. Nothing more is known about Ellen Johnston, except that she died in the Barony Poorhouse in Glasgow in 1873 (see Boos, 1995). She was thirty-eight years old.

Johnston's poetry is striking for the extent to which it answers to a public even more than a private need. Although her own life was tragically hard, much of her poetry is concerned with the general hardships and sufferings of her class. She never put her own experience of sexual abuse into verse. With the exception of Bevington's 'One More Bruised Heart!' that subject remains one of the great silences of Victorian poetry, the roundabout phrases of Johnston's *Autobiography* suggesting just how unapproachable it was. She also offered her volumes of poems as a sort of public rather than private property. Her two editions contain, not only the prominent and representative 'witness' of the *Autobiography* – the story, no doubt, of innumerable working-class girls – but also poems by other women, to which she herself wrote versified responses. 'Lines to Ellen, the Factory Girl', for instance, suggests how far her poems were read as true-life stories which encouraged others to write back. The publication of these responses then turns the collection into a communal opportunity for being read and noticed. Other poems by Johnston are subtitled 'Written by Request', as if she saw her role as supplying professional poetic services to friends and acquaintances. Certainly, the heroic but short career of 'the Factory Girl' begins to shape a powerful, much needed model of the worker poet, speaking to and for others of her class.

Johnston's best poems are probably those written in Scots dialect. These avoid the archaic poeticisms of some of her English verses and have a colloquial, gritty lilt which is authentically her own. 'The Working Man' is a lively exhortation to independence and self-respect, in the tradition of Chartist freedom songs. 'Nelly's Lament for the Pirnhouse Cat', on the other hand, is a delightful, none too squeamish elegy, which mock-heroically laments the death of the 'we cheetie' with a rich mixture of realism and pathos. Especially interesting is the autobiographical 'Address to Nature on its Cruelty', which berates the aristocratic assumptions of the critics. Their disappointment and disbelief at the Factory Girl's smallness and plainness stand, in the end, as just another tribute to her poetry's energy, independence and generous populist spirit. Johnston's life, however, is a reminder that being a single working mother in the nineteenth century, for all the popular poetic mythology, could still be crushingly difficult.

A.L.

Johnston, Ellen (1867) *Autobiography, Poems and Songs*, Glasgow.
—— (1869) *Autobiography, Poems, and Songs*, Glasgow. (Second edition with shortened *Autobiography* and additional poems.)

Boos, Florence (1995) 'Cauld Engle-Cheek: Working-Class Women Poets in Victorian Scotland', *Victorian Poetry*, 33 (1995).

Swindells, Julia (1985) *Victorian Writing and Working Women: The Other Side of Silence*, Cambridge, Polity Press.

Vicinus, Martha (1974) *The Industrial Muse: A Study of Nineteenth-Century British Working-Class Literature*, London, Croom Helm.

A Mother's Love[1]

I love thee, I love thee, and life will depart
Ere thy mother forgets thee, sweet child of her heart;
Yea, death's shadows only my memory can dim,
For thou'rt dearer than life to me – Mary Achin.

I love thee, I love thee, and six years hath now fled   5
Since first on my bosom I pillow'd thy head;
Since I first did behold thee in sorrow and sin,
Thou sweet offspring of false love – my Mary Achin.

I love thee, I love thee, and twelve months hath now past,
My sweet child, since I gazed on thy fairy form last;   10
And our parting brought sorrow, known only to Him
Who can see through the heart's depths – my Mary Achin.

I love thee, I love thee, oh! when shalt thou rest
Thy sweet angel face on this heart-burning breast;
Thy last parting kiss lingers still on my chin,   15
Embalmed with a blessing from Mary Achin.

I love thee, I love thee, thy beauty and youth
Are spotless and pure as the fountain of truth;
Thou'rt my star in the night, till daybreak begin,
And my sunshine by noontide – my Mary Achin.   20

---

[1] Written for Miss Mary Achenvole. Born, 14th September, 1852. Written in Belfast, 1858.

I love thee, I love thee, wherever I go
Thou'rt shrined in my bosom in joy or in woe;
A murmuring music my fancy doth win,
'Tis the voice of my darling – Mary Achin.

I love thee, I love thee, is ever my lay,   25
I sigh it by night and I sing it by day,
Its chorus swells forth like the stern patriot's hymn,
Thrice hallowed with visions of Mary Achin.

I love thee, I love thee, though now far away
Thou'rt nearer and dearer to me every day;   30
Would they give me my choice – a nation to win –
I would not exchange with my Mary Achin.

Lines: To a Young Gentleman of Surpassing Beauty

Hail! gentle youth, and do not deem me rude
    Because I dare to sing thy beauty's fame;
But I have heard that thou art kind and good,
    And freely hope you will forgive the same.
Thou canst not turn with cold contempt on me,   5
I am a stranger quite unknown to thee.

Pause not to ask why thou to me are known,
    While I as yet remain unknown to thee;
'Midst thy conjectures do not spurn me from
    The heaven-lit chamber of thy mem'ry;   10
Through thy mind's eye still gaze upon my form,
And deem me fairer than the Queen of Morn.

Ah! what am I? – A hapless child of song,
    Musing upon thy matchless beauty bright,
Tracing thy footsteps through the mazy throng,   15
    And gazing on thee with love-born delight.
It cheers me onward through my hopeless doom
To dream upon thy beauty's sweetest bloom.

And what art thou? – An honour'd son of wealth,
    Gay fortune's diadem sits on thy brow;   20
Bless'd with a generous heart, with youth and health,
    And beauty's self before thy shadow bow;
Yet thou may'st never know whose humble lays
In sadness sung thy dazzling beauty's praise.

The Working Man

The spring is come at last, my freens, cheer up, you sons of toil,
Let the seeds of independence be sown in labour's soil,
And tho' the nipping blast of care should blight your wee bit crop,
Oh dinna let your spirits sink, cling closer aye to hope.

If youth and health be on your side, you ha'e a richer boon   5
Than him that's dressed in royal robes and wears a diamond crown;
Nae widow's curse lies in your cup, you bear nae orphan's blame;
Nae guilty conscience haunts your dreams wi' visions of the slain.

Tho' light your purse, and worn your coat the darkest hour of night,
Is whiles the very ane[1] that is before it dawns daylight;   10
And tho' your lot looks unco[2] hard, your future prospects drear,
Hope's sun may burst through sorrow's cloud, your sinking soul to cheer.

The summer's drawing near, my freens, cheer up ye sons of toil,
Let the sun of independence aye greet ye wi' a smile;
His genial beams will light your hearth when it is mirk[3] wi' care,   15
When ye ha'e little for to spend, and far less for to spare.

Let him that ne'er kent[4] labour's yoke but come to Glasgow toon,
And let him take a cannie[5] walk her bonny buildings roon,
And let him wi' his lady hands, his cheeks sae pale and wan,
Stand face to face, without a blush, before the Working Man.   20

But the man who wins fair fortune wi' labour's anxious pain,
He is the man who's justly earned her favour and her fame;
And may he aye keep flourishing wherever he may gang,[6]
And ne'er forget the days now gane when but a Working Man.

The harvest soon will be, my freens, cheer up, you sons of toil,   25
And the fu'some hand of plenty will store your domicile;
Ye are the sons of nature's art, aye forming some new plan,
Oh what would bonny Scotland do without the Working Man?

Nelly's Lament for the Pirnhouse[1] Cat

Killed by the Elevator,[2] C—e Factory, Dundee

Oh! fare-ye-weel my bonnie cat,
Nae mair I'll smooth yer skin sae black.

---

1   one
2   very
3   dark
4   know
5   attentive

6   go

1   Weaving shed
2   lift or ascending chamber

Mony a time I stroked yer back,
    Puir wee craiter;[3]
Ye've gane yer last lang sleep tae tak'.
    The Elevator   5

Has sent ye aff tae your lang hame,
Whaur hunger ne'er will jag[4] yer wame,[5]
Whaur ye shall ne'er put in a claim
    For meal or milk;   10
Yer in the 'pond,' free frae a' blame,
    Boiled like a whelk.

Puir hapless beast, what was't that took
Ye hunting into yon dark nook?
Whaur 'Death' sat cooring[6] wi' his hook   15
    Tae nip yer neck.
I'll think upon yer deein' look
    Wi' sad respect.

My very brain ran roon about
When I saw Archie tak' ye oot,   20
Wi' scalped pow[7] and bluidy snoot.
    Heigh, when I think,
A stane tied roon yer neck, nae doot
    Tae gar[8] ye sink.

Jist yesterday, my bonnie beast,   25
I held ye close unto my breast;
When, ye as proud as ony priest,
    Did cock yer lug;[9]
Syne aff ye ran tae get a feast
    Frae yer milk mug.   30

But noo nae mair in oor pirnhouse
Ye'll hunt the rats, nor catch a moose,
Nor on the counter sit fu' douse,[10]
    And mew and yell,
And shoot yer humph[11] sae prude and spruce   35
    At rhyming Nell.

Your race upon the earth was ran,
Puir puss, ere it was weel began;

---

[3] creature
[4] torment
[5] belly
[6] cowering
[7] head

[8] to make
[9] prick up your ears
[10] so content
[11] arch your back

Ye've gane whaur beastie, boy, and man
  Are doomed tae go.   40
Omnipotence in His vast plan
  Ordained it so.

There's nane has deign'd tae mourn ye here,
Unless mysel' wi' grief sincere;
Though but a cat I'll still revere   45
  Thy worth wi' pity,
And ower yer memory drap a tear,
  Puir we cheetie.[12]

Lines to Ellen, the Factory Girl

Dear Ellen, when you read these lines, O, throw them not aside!
O, do not laugh at them in scorn, or turn away in pride!
I know 'tis a presumptuous thought for me to thee to write,
For, Ellen, feeble are the words that my pen can indite.

Had fortune smiled upon thy birth and favoured thee with wealth, 5
Then, Ellen, I would be content with praying for your health;
But since I know that you, like me, are forced your bread to win,
Exposed to many dangers 'mid the factory's smoke and din,

I know you have a feeling heart – that you will not be stern,
Nor deem it curiosity your history to learn;   10
Although I never saw thy face, yet I have read thy lays,
And 'tis my earnest prayer for thee that thou'lt see many days

A year ago this very month I read your touching song –
Your last farewell to your betrothed, just after he had gone;
My thoughts were with you ever since – I thought of writing then, 15
But courage I could not call forth, and fear held back my pen.

Hast thou no mother, Ellen dear, to know thy griefs and fears,
No sister who hath shared thy joys through all thy childish years,
No brother's merry coaxing ways to welcome thee at home,
No father dear, in his arm-chair – are all those loved ones gone? 20

I know your heart is sensitive, and that you ill can brook
The sneer from those you work beside, the cold contemptuous look;
Tho' I have met with some of those, the number is but few –
The most of those I work beside are friends sincere and true.

I rise each morn at six o'clock, and pray that God will guide 25
Me through the duties of the day, whatever ill betide;

---

12 puss

And when at night I lay me down, in calm and quiet repose,
I sleep the dreamless sleep of health contentment only knows.

For, dearest, in this world, you know, the sun's not always shining,
But underneath each heavy cloud there lies a silver lining;   30
Although thou art companionless, with no friend save thy cat,
I trust 'twill not be so with thee when thy betrothed comes back.

Thine eyes with love shall sparkling beam when he comes back again
To claim the hand thou promised him before he crossed the main;
Then I will wake my feeble muse, and let my song be heard,   35
A marriage sonnet unto him – St Ninian's noble bard.

ISABEL
Glasgow, Nov. 21, 1866

An Address to Nature on its Cruelty

O Nature, thou to me was cruel,
That made me up so small a jewel;
I am so small I cannot shine
Amidst the great that read my rhyme.
When men of genius pass me by,   5
I am so small they can't descry
One little mark or single trace
Of Burns' science in my face.
Those publications that I sold,
Some typed in blue and some on gold,   10
Learned critics who have seen them
Says origin dwells within them;
But when myself perchance they see.
They laugh and say, 'O is it she?
Well, I think the little boaster   15
Is nothing but a fair impostor;
She looks so poor-like and so small,
She's next unto a nought-at-all;
Such wit and words quite out-furl
The learning of "A Factory Girl." '   20
At first they do my name exalt,
And with my works find little fault;
But when upon myself they gaze,
They say some other claims the praise.
O Nature, had'st thou taken time   25
And made me up somewhat sublime,
With handsome form and pretty face,
And eyes of language – smiles of grace;
With snowy brow and ringlets fair,
A beauty quite beyond compare;   30

Winning the charms of fortune's smile.
Still dressed in grandeur all the while;
Then those who see me would believe
I never tried for to deceive
By bringing out a publication   35
Of borrowed lines or yet quotation.
But those who see me in this dress,
So small and thin I must confess,
Well may they dare the words to use.
Can such a vase distil Love's muse;   40
Well may they ask dare I profess
The talent of an authoress?
Oh who could deem to gaze on me,
That e'er I mused on land or sea,
That I have sat in shady bower   45
Musing on thy fairest flower;
That I have sought the silvery stream
At midnight hour, calm and serene,
When skies of diamond sparkling flame
Shed pearly tears of heartsick shame;   50
To see me bound in hardship's blight,
Whilst man did rob me of my right.
And critics read my simple rhyme
And dared to say it was not mine?
Imperfect though my lays may be,   55
Still they belong to none but me.
My blighted breast is their abode,
They were placed there by nature's God;
And though my years are spent in pain,
Still seeking fortune's smiles in vain,   60
Still sighing youth's sweet years away,
Changing life's light into clay;
Hard toiling for my daily bread
With burning heart and aching head.
A vision of delusion's dream,   65
Hastening downward death's dark stream;
Yet nature between you and I,
Beneath the universal sky,
Who dares to say I have bereft
Another genius of their gift.   70

Frances Ridley Havergal (1836–1879)

Frances Havergal was the youngest of six children born to Jane and William Havergal. Her father was Rector of various parishes in Worcestershire as well as a composer of church music. In an 'Autobiography' written when she was twenty-three, Frances remembered her childhood as a time of rebellion, unsubdued even by the death of her mother in 1848. Two years later, to her 'great delight' (1880: 30), she was sent to school. Her intellectual ambition was checked, however, when she developed erysipelas (a nervous inflammation of the face) and was forced to give up studying and return home. By this time she had begun to be troubled by religious scruples. A brief period at school in Germany in 1853 led her to worry that 'I grew more eager for my lessons, and less earnest in seeking Jesus' (1880: 46). The conflict between religious and intellectual dedication, reminiscent of Christina Rossetti's at about the same age, increasingly resolved itself into a passion for self-denial. She thanked God when, as a result of ill health, she was no longer able to enjoy 'the pleasure of public applause when singing in the Philharmonic concerts' (73). Her gift for composition was also rigorously restricted to the writing of hymns. While Rossetti never succeeded in subduing her imagination, Havergal triumphed over hers, and her life became a studied, sometimes pernickety quest for saintliness: 'Every one calls me sweet tempered; but oh, I have been so ruffled two or three times' (92).

Apart from energetic walking holidays in Switzerland, Wales and Scotland, which also involved some missionary activity – giving out bibles or surprising other travellers with impromptu hymns ('Tell it out among the heathen' is one of Havergal's own hymns) – Frances's life was outwardly uneventful. She refused a number of suitors on the grounds of their spiritual half-heartedness, and lived at home with her father, and then, after his death, with her sister, writing verses which, she claimed, came to her 'Minerva fashion, full grown' (1880: 93). She generally sent the proceeds for these to the Church Missionary Society or the Young Women's Christian Association. When, in 1876, the entire stereotype of a new book of music by her was destroyed in a fire at the publishers, she welcomed it as another lesson in self-mortification. Evidently some lingering desire for fame still needed to be killed off.

For most of her life, Havergal regarded her poetry as a direct gift or dictation from the 'Master', as she called her God, curiously echoing Emily Dickinson's similar appellation for her muse. But in Havergal's case there is no confusion of poetic and religious inspiration. 'I have felt so very strongly and sweetly hitherto that my pen was to be used *only* for the Master' (1885: 334), she wrote in the last year of her life. However, she often suffered from her Master's capricious silences: 'I have been feeling very down, and I hope really humbled; it seemed rather marked, His not letting me write at all this year' (1880: 114). Her hymns invoking the Master characteristically resolve conflict into submission. 'Men may feel differently, but a true woman's submission is inseparable from deep love' (1880: 138), she once declared.

In 1874 Frances caught typhoid fever from which she never fully recovered. Then, in 1879, she suffered an attack of peritonitis and died a few days later, surrounded by her family and, according to her sister, rejoicing and singing hymns to the last.

The immense popularity of Havergal's verses and hymns, and the semi-canonization of her in memoirs after her death (memoirs which were almost more popular than her works), bear witness to that strong Victorian need for female Anglican saints. Like Rossetti, Greenwell and Meynell, Havergal felt the pressure of this confusion in the public mind between women poets and saints. Unlike them, however, her verse gener-ally lacks the contrary tension of the secular, the ambiguous and the pleasure-loving. One exception is to be found in her *Enigmas and Charades*, poems written as social pastimes and showing a certain witty ability (see 'Enigma No. 6') to turn poems into verbal games, like crosswords.

A.L.

Havergal, Frances Ridley (1880) *Memorials*, by M. V. G. Havergal, London.
—— (1884) *Poetical Works*, 2 vols, London.
—— (1885) *Letters*, ed. by her Sister, London.

Just When Thou Wilt[1]

I

Just when Thou wilt, O Master, call!
Or at the noon, or evening fall,
Or in the dark, or in the light, –
Just when Thou wilt, it must be right.

II

Just when Thou wilt, O Saviour, come,   5
Take me to dwell in Thy bright home!
Or when the snows have crowned my head,
Or ere it hath one silver thread.

III

Just when Thou wilt, O Bridegroom, say,
'Rise up, my love, and come away!'   10
Open to me Thy golden gate
Just when Thou wilt, or soon, or late.

IV

Just when Thou wilt – Thy time is best –
Thou shalt appoint my hour of rest,
Marked by the Sun of perfect love,   15
Shining unchangeably above.

V

Just when Thou wilt! – no choice for me!
Life is a gift to use for Thee;
Death is a hushed and glorious tryst,
With Thee, my King, my Saviour, Christ!   20

---

[1] Dictated in illness

Enigma No. 6

Seventeen hundred and sixty yards,
A maiden's name and a term at cards,
A halting leg, something stronger than beer,
A river to many a student dear,
A fragrant tree, and a foreign fruit,   5
A government coach on a postal route,
Honiton, Brussels, or Valenciennes,
A spice preceding bishops and deans,
A sin of the tongue, and the stronger sex,
The state of the sea when no tempests vex,   10
What you look for three or four times a day,
What the Prince of Wales to the crown will lay,
Three Scripture names, and a region wide,
What an archer takes his shaft to guide:
With six little letters all these are framed;   15
When each you have duly and rightly named,
They form what I hope you will never dare
Against friend or foe in your heart to bear.

Augusta Webster (1837–1894)

Not much is known about Augusta Webster. She was born in Dorset, but spent her early years on board ship, her father, George Davies, being a Vice-Admiral. He later became Chief Constable of Cambridgeshire. Augusta received a good classical education and then attended the Cambridge School of Art. In 1863 she married Thomas Webster, a law lecturer at Trinity College, Cambridge, and subsequently bore one child, a daughter – a fact celebrated in the touching and unusual sonnet sequence, *Mother & Daughter* (1895). Webster's first two volumes of verse and one novel were published under the pseudonym 'Cecil Home'. She subsequently published both poetry and plays under her own name.

At some point in the 1860s the family moved to London, where Augusta became increasingly active, alongside Frances Power Cobbe and John Stuart Mill, in the women's suffrage movement. She also served on the London School Board where she was a keen promoter of education for women. Her regular articles for *The Examiner* were collected in 1879 under the title *A Housewife's Opinions*. In them, she inveighs with wit and humour against the expense and unhealthiness of women's clothes, against the waste of their time in social entertaining, against 'Matrimony as a Means of Livelihood' for unprovided girls, and against society's attitudes to single women. She also issues a strong condemnation of the protectionist attempts to curtail women's work on the false and hypocritical ground of sexual propriety.

But her strongest statements concern education and the vote. At a time when the House of Commons was debating the issue of university degrees for women, she ridiculed the system at Cambridge which allowed women to attend courses and sit exams, but awarded them no degree at the end. It was, she argued, 'like the Wonderland "caucus-race", which all the runners began when and where they happened to be, and everybody had won' (1879: 99). Only the dignity of a publicly recognized reward, gained in equal and unfavoured competition, would remedy this academic nonsense. The availability of higher education for women would, she reasoned, finally give value to a woman's time, which was too often treated as 'open property of no value to anyone' (1879: 159), least of all, the owner.

In 1878 Webster wrote an article on 'Parliamentary Franchise for Women Ratepayers', which was subsequently issued as a pamphlet. She sent a copy to Christina Rossetti, whose poetry she greatly admired. In it, she points to the obvious injustice of denying the vote to those women who possess 'the same legal qualifications as their male neighbours' (1878: 1): namely, that they pay taxes to the state. Furthermore she derides, as arguments against the vote, the various mystifications offered in Parliament: from 'the theory of marriage, Adam and Eve, ministering angels, Tennyson's Princess, physiology, psychology, and things in general' (1878: 4). As a poet, too, Webster distrusts the myths and fairytales which give enchanted views of women's lives. In her own poems there are few courtly heroines and princesses, but there are many real, old, plain, unhappy or bored women. Poets, she argues in one place, 'may deal with high themes and poetic visions, or with the humblest details of existence and the vicissitudes of the money market, but the faculty at work is the same' (1879: 214). Her own imaginative interest in the substructures of money and economic survival is one of the great innovative strengths of her work.

After her death in 1894, an obituary in the *Athenaeum* placed Webster, George Eliot and Frances Power Cobbe together, as the major humanitarian, liberal thinkers of the age. Meanwhile, however, critics were already anxiously calling her plain-speaking register of secular commonsense 'masculine' or 'virile'. Moreover, by the 1880s and 90s her social realism and political commitment were largely out of fashion, as aestheticism turned poetry inwards once again towards the private vision. Thereafter, for much of the twentieth century, the name of Augusta Webster was almost entirely forgotten.

Webster's best poetry consists of the dramatic monologues in her two major volumes of 1866 and 1870. Made popular by Robert Browning in the 1850s, the dramatic monologue is used by her to turn the spotlight on women. Unlike him, she is not intrigued by the criminal, alienated or artistic consciousness, which he presents as male, but by ordinary, humble, downtrodden women, who have no great resources of inner strength or vision. Even Circe is, ultimately, not a dangerous seductress but a lonely, frustrated woman, with none too high an opinion of men. 'Faded' exploits a genre often used by women poets to explore the way inner subjectivity is determined by the frame of social assumptions and sexual prejudices. The old woman finds in the reflections of the mirror an inescapable, stereotypical distortion of herself, but one which none the less dictates who she is, both to herself and the world outside.

The most powerful of these monologues is 'A Castaway'. Here Webster enters the by now well-established tradition of the 'fallen woman' poem – but with a difference. Unlike most of her predecessors, she offers neither a metaphorical nor a religious solution to the problem of prostitution. The Castaway speaks in a familiarly colloquial language, which is never heightened or distanced by poetic play, as in Rossetti's *Goblin Market*, and never punished or forgiven in a moral conversion at the end, as in Greenwell's 'Christina', Procter's 'Legend of Provence' and even, to some extent, Barrett Browning's *Aurora Leigh*. Instead, Webster investigates the various social inequalities which force women into prostitution: their lack of education and training for work, their poor knowledge of the world, the vicissitudes of the labour market, the difficulty of re-entering society after a 'fall'. Meanwhile, she challengingly questions whether, as a trade, prostitution is any more immoral than others: journalism, the law, even, perhaps, marriage. The argument remains always on the level of the secular realities of money and the market, thus refusing the temptation either to sentimentalize or sermonize on the subject.

Although sometimes long-drawn-out, 'A Castaway' is none the less a fitting culmination to a poetic career which deserves much more notice than it has received, either today or in its own time. Webster remains, as Rossetti always maintained, one of the 'most formidable' (1908: 175) of voices among nineteenth-century women poets, and the socio-political sharpness of her poetry is unique. Even more than Barrett Browning, she reduces every shining myth or idealism of her time to the social facts of class, money and power. She is, probably, the most ruthlessly materialist of all Victorian women poets.

A.L.

Webster, Augusta (1866) *Dramatic Studies*, London and Cambridge.
—— (1870; 1893) *Portraits*, London.
—— (1878) *Parliamentary Franchise for Women Ratepayers*, London.
—— (1879) *A Housewife's Opinions*, London.
—— (1895) *Mother & Daughter: An Uncompleted Sonnet-Sequence*, intro. W. M. Rossetti, London.

Brown, Susan (1991) 'Economical Representations: Dante Gabriel Rossetti's "Jenny", Augusta Webster's "A Castaway", and the Campaign against the Contagious Diseases Acts', *Victorian Review*, 17 (1991), 78–95.
—— (1995) 'Determined Heroines: George Eliot, Augusta Webster, and Closet Drama by Victorian Women', *Victorian Poetry*, 33 (1995).
Leighton, Angela (1992) *Victorian Women Poets*, Hemel Hempstead, Harvester, pp. 164–201.
Rossetti, Christina (1908) *Family Letters*, ed. W. M. Rossetti, London, Brown, Langham.
Sackville-West, V. (1929) *The Eighteen-Seventies*, Cambridge, Cambridge University Press, pp. 122–4.

By the Looking-Glass

Alone at last in my room –
How sick I grow of the glitter and din,
Of the lips that smile and the voices that prate
To a ballroom tune for the fashion's sake:
Light and laughters without, but what within?   5
Are these like me? Do the pleasure and state
Weary them under the seeming they make? –
But I see all through my gloom.

For why should a light young heart
Not leap to a merry moving air,   10

Not laugh with the joy of the flying hour
And feed upon pleasure just for a while?
But the right of a woman is being fair,
And her heart must starve if she miss that dower,
For how should she purchase the look and the smile?   15
And I have not had my part.

A girl, and so plain a face!
Once more, as I learn by heart every line
In the pitiless mirror, night by night,
Let me try to think it is not my own.   20
Come, stranger with features something like mine,
Let me place close by you the tell-tale light;
Can I find in you now some charm unknown,
Only one softening grace?

Alas! it is I, I, I,   25
Ungainly, common. The other night
I heard one say 'Why, she is not so plain.
See, the mouth is shapely, the nose not ill.'
If I could but believe his judgement right!
But I try to dupe my eyesight in vain,   30
For I, who have partly a painter's skill,
I cannot put knowledge by.

He had not fed, as I feed
On beauty, till beauty itself must seem
Me, my own, a part and essence of me,   35
My right and my being – Why! how am I plain?
I feel as if this were almost a dream
From which I should waken, as it might be,
And open my eyes on beauty again
And know it myself indeed.   40

Oh idle! oh folly! look,
There, looking back from the glass, is my fate,
A clumsy creature smelling of earth,
What fancy could lend her the angel's wings?
She looks like a boorish peasant's fit mate.   45
Why! what a mock at the pride of birth,
Fashioned by nature for menial things,
With her name in the red-bound book.

Oh! to forget me a while,
Feeling myself but as one in the throng,   50
Losing myself in the joy of my youth!
Then surely some pleasure might lie in my reach.
But the sense of myself is ever strong,

And I read in all eyes the bitter truth,
And I fancy scorning in every speech   55
And mocking in every smile.

Ah! yes, it was so to-night,
And I moved so heavily through the dance,
And answered uncouthly like one ill taught,
And knew that ungentleness seemed on my brow,   60
While it was but pain at each meeting glance,
For I knew that all who looked at me thought
'How ugly she is! one sees it more now
With the other young faces so bright.'

I might be more like the rest,   65
Like those that laugh with a girlish grace
And make bright nothings an eloquence;
I might seem gentler and softer souled;
But I needs must shape myself to my place,
Softness in me would seem clumsy pretence,   70
Would they not deem my laughters bold?
I hide in myself as is best.

Do I grow bitter sometimes?
They say it, ah me! and I fear it is true,
And I shrink from that curse of bitterness,   75
And I pray on my knees that it may not come;
But how should I envy – they say that I do –
All the love which others' young lives may bless?
Because *my* age will be lone in its home
Do I weep at the wedding chimes?   80

Ah no, for they judge me ill,
Judging me doubtless by that which I look,
Do I not joy for another's delight?
Do I not grieve for another's regret?
And I have been true where others forsook   85
And kind where others bore hatred and spite,
For there I could think myself welcome – and yet
My care is unpitied still.

Yes, who can think it such pain
Not to be fair 'Such a trifling thing.'   90
And 'Goodness may be where beauty is not'
And 'How weak to sorrow for outward show!'
Ah! if they knew what a poisonful sting
Has this sense of shame, how a woman's lot
Is darkened throughout! – Oh yes I know   95
How weak – but I know in vain.

I hoped in vain, for I thought,
When first I grew to a woman's days,
Woman enough to feel what it means
To be a woman and not be fair,   100
That I need not sigh for the voice of praise
And the beauty's triumph in courtly scenes
Where she queens with her maiden-royal air,
Ah! and so worshipped and sought.

But I, oh my dreaming! deemed   105
With a woman's yearning and faith in love,
With a woman's faith in her lovingness,
That that joy might brighten on me, even me,
For which all the force of my nature strove,
Joy of daily smiles and voices that bless,   110
And one deeper other love it might be –
Hush, *that* was wrong to have dreamed.

I thank God, I have not loved,
Loved as one says it whose life has gone out
Into another's for evermore,   115
Loved as I know what love might be
Writhing but living through poison of doubt,
Drinking the gall of the sweetness before,
Drinking strange deep strength from the bitter lee –
Love, love in a falsehood proved!   120

Loving him on to the end,
Through the weary weeping hours of the night,
Through the wearier laughing hours of the day;
Knowing him less than the love I gave,
But this one fond dream left my life for its light   125
To do him some service and pass away;
Not daring, for sin, to think of the grave
Lest it seemed the only friend.

Thank God that it was not so,
And I have my scatheless maidenly pride,   130
But it might have been – for did he not speak
With that slow sweet cadence that seemed made deep
By a meaning – Hush! he has chosen his bride.
Oh! happy smile on her lips and her cheek,
My darling! And I have no cause to weep,   135
I have not bowed me so low.

But would he have wooed in vain?
Would not my heart have leaped to his will,
If he had not changed? – How, *changed* do I say?

Was I not mocked with an idle thought,   140
Dreaming and dreaming so foolishly still?
By the sweet glad smile and the winning way
And the grace of beauty alone is love bought.
He woo me! Am I not plain?

But yet I was not alone   145
To fancy I might be something to him.
They thought it, I know, though it seems so wild
Now, in this bitterer Now's hard light.
Vain that I was! could his sight grow dim?
How could he love me? But she, when she smiled   150
Once, the first once, by her beauty's right
Had made all his soul her own.

It is well that no busy tongue
Has vexed her heart with those bygone tales.
But I think he fears he did me some wrong,   155
I see him watch me at times, and his cheek
Crimsons a little, a little pales,
If his eye meets mine for a moment long.
But he need not fear, I am not so weak
Though I *am* a woman and young.   160

I had not grown to my love,
Though it might have been. And I give no blame:
Nothing was spoken to bind him to me,
Nothing had been that could make him think
My heart beat stronger and fast when he came,   165
And if he *had* loved me, was he not free,
When the fancy passed, to loose that vague link
That only such fancy wove?

No he has done no such ill
But that I can bear it, nor shame in my heart   170
To call him my brother and see her his,
The one little pearl that gleams through our gloom:
He has no dishonour to bar them apart.
I loving her so, am rested in this;
Else I would speak though I spoke her doom,   175
Though grief had the power to kill.

When she came a while ago,
My young fair sister bright with her bloom,
Back to a home which is little glad,
I thought 'Here is one who should know no care,   180
A little wild bird flown into a room
From its far free woods; will she droop and grow sad?

But, here even, love smiles upon one so fair.
And I too might feel that glow.'

But now she will fly away!   185
Ah me! and I love her so deep in my heart
And worship her beauty as he might do.
If I could but have kept her a little time!
Ah she will go! So the sunbeams depart
That brightened the winter's sky into blue,   190
And the dews of the chill dusk freeze into rime,
And cold cold mists hang grey.

I think she loved me till now –
Nay doubtless she loves me quietly yet,
But his lightest fancy is more, far more,   195
To her than all the love that I live.
But I cannot blame (as if love were a debt)
That, though I love, he is held far before;
And is it not well that a bride should give
All, all her heart with her vow?   200

But ah, if I smiled more sweet
And spoke more soft as one fairer could,
Had not love indeed been more surely mine?
Folly to say that a woman's grace
Is only strong o'er a man's light mood!   205
Even the hearts of the nearest incline
With a gentler thought to the lovely face,
And the winning eyes that entreat.

But I – yes flicker pale light,
Fade into darkness and hide it away,   210
The poor dull face that looks out from the glass,
Oh wearily wearily back to me!
Yes, I will sleep, for my wild thoughts stray
Weakly, selfishly – yes let them pass,
Let self and this sadness of self leave me free,   215
Lost in the peace of the night.

Faded

Ah face, young face, sweet with unpassionate joy,
Possessful joy of having all to hope –
Rich, measureless, nameless, formless, *all* to hope –
Fair, happy, face with the girl's questioning smile
Expectant of an answer from the days,   5
Fair, happy, morning, face who wast myself,

Talk with me, with this later drearier self.
Oftenest I dare not see thee: but alone,
Thou and I in the quiet, while, without,
Dim eve goes dwindling her hushed, hueless, light   10
And makes the leaden dusk before the stars –
While, if my duller eyes through envious tears
Reply to thine, there's none at hand to note,
Nor yet thyself, in the sad and pensive calm,
Wilt flout me for my faded look of thee,   15
As when thou mock'st me in the untender noon –
While now we two a little time are one,
Elder and girl, the blossoming and the sere,
One blended, dateless, woman for an hour –
Thou and I thus alone, I read from thee   20
My lesson what I was; which (ah, poor heart!)
Means trulier my lesson, bitter to learn,
Of what I cease to be.

            Fie, cruel face!
Too comely, thou. Thy round curves shame my cheeks;
Thy gloss of almond-bloom in the March sun   25
Affronts my hardened reds; thy satiny brow,
Like smooth magnolia petals warmly white,
Enforces all my tale of fretted lines;
The quivering woof of sunshine through thy hairs
Shows mine's spent russets deader. All in thee   30
That's likest me to-day is proof the more
Of my to-day's unlikeness. Ah! I have waned,
As every summer wanes, that, all the while,
Seems to grow still more summer, till, one day,
The first dead leaves are falling and all's past.   35
Myself has faded from me; I am old.

    Well, well, what's that to fret for? Yet, indeed,
'Tis pity for a woman to be old.
Youth going lessens us of more than youth:
We lose the very instinct of our lives –   40
Song-birds left voiceless, diswinged flies of the air.
And the loss comes so soon; and ere we know:
We have so many many after years,
To use away (the unmarried ones at least)
In only withering leisurely. Ah me!   45
Men jeer us clinging, clinging pitiably,
To that themselves account whole all for us:
Aye, but what man of them could bear, as we must,
To live life's worth a stinted dozen years.
And the long sequel all for learning age.   50
Why, if we try to cheat the merciless world

That bids us grow old meekly and to the hour,
(Like babes that must not cry when bed-time comes)
And, being old, be nothing – try, maybe,
To cheat our lingering selves as if Time lingered –   55
Is our fault other than the toil in vain
Of any shipwrecked swimmer who, miles from land,
No sail in sight, breasts the resistless sea,
And perishing will not perish? Oh, 'tis known
How bankrupt men will hopelessly, impotent,   60
Battle each inch with unforgiving ruin,
Waste their tired brains on schemes a child should laugh at,
Befool their hearts with more unbodied hopes
Than shadows flung by momentary spray,
Tease their unwilling faces into smiles   65
And loathingly look contentment – but, at best,
To gain some futile hour from certainty:
But we in our utter loss, outlawed from life,
Irretrievable bankrupts of our very selves,
We must give ruin welcome, blaze our fact   70
Of nothingness – 'good friends, perceive I am old;
Pray laugh and leave me.' We are fools, we sin,
Abjectly, past all pardon, past all pity,
We women, if we linger, if, maybe,
We use our petty melancholy arts   75
And are still women some filched year or two –
Still women and not ghosts, not lifeless husks,
Spent memories that slink through the world and breathe,
As if they lived, and yet they know they are dead.

    Once, long ago, I dreamed I had truly died: 80
My numb void body, in its winding-sheet,
Lay ignorant, but I, grown viewlessness,
Met my home's dear ones still; I spoke, methought,
Words which they marked not, smiled unanswered smiles,
And then I wept, and clung about their necks,   85
Closer, with vain embracing; and one said
(Another ghost, a voice, I searched not what)
'Thou art all dead for them; they cannot know,'
And still replied 'They felt not,' or 'They heard not,'
'They cannot, thou being dead,' until ere long   90
The anguish of it waked me – to be thus,
With them yet so forlorn of sense of theirs!
'Twas in my happiest days, when, like new fronds
Uncurling coil by coil on ferns in May
And widening to the light and dews and air,   95
The girl grows woman gladly, but, untold,
That dream clung like a sorrow, and, for pity,
I hoped the poor lone dead should bide apart,

Never among their living. Like that dream,
Lost and alone, I haunt our world to-day.   100

   How strange life is! – a woman's – if, I mean,
One miss a woman's destiny and sole hope,
The wife's dear service with its round of tasks
And sweet humilities and glad fatigues,
And anxious joy of mothers – strange indeed!   105
To wait and wait, like the flower upon its stalk,
For nothing save to wither! And the while
Knows she that she is waiting? Maybe, yes:
And maybe, no. That new-made shallow lake,
Asleep there in the park, knows not, asleep,   110
It waits the brook next rain-fall shall let loose
To brim it with full waters, bear it on
Filling its further channel: girls so wait,
Careless and calm, not judging what shall be;
Only they know life has not reached them yet,   115
And till life come they'll dream and laugh in the sun.
And the sun shines, and the dumb days flit by
And make no sign for working... till, at time,
To her whom life and love need the voice comes
Which names her wife among the happier many: 120
And till to her, maybe, who not again
Shall know rest and sweet dreams, nor in the world
Call anywhere her home, nor laugh at ease,
Nor spend her toils on those who'll love her for them,
Dawns change and the hour of wonder while she wakes   125
Alone in the eastwinds of a barren world:
And till to her to whom life never comes,
Whether by joy or sorrows or by toil,
The sunshine has grown drought, the calm, decay;
And there's the woman old.   130
                Poor imaged mock,
Thou art more than I to-day; thou hast my right,
My womanhood's lost right to meet pleased eyes
And please by being happy. Many a time
I note, forgotten, how thy youth, that lasts,
Earns thee companionship of lingering looks,   135
Thy smile a tenderness whereof nought's mine.
Thou hast a being still; but what am I?
A shadow and an echo – one that was.

   Well, Time's thy tyrant too: there waits for thee
In the sure end the day thou wilt have faded.   140
Carelessly thou'lt be lifted from thy place,
Too long usurped, where there'll, room being given,
Bloom some such other face, nor thine be missed –

As a newer rose, alike as roses are,
Makes us the self-same sweet as yesterday's –   145
As in the river's stream an on-come wave,
That is to pass, fills all the other filled
That took the drift before it and has passed –
As we have our succession, woman to woman,
And so no smiles are missed, there being enough.   150
I shall not know it: winters of many years
Before then long may have annulled my grave,
My date may be so back past household talk
'Tis out of guess whose the vague counterfeit
That on the canvas has past memory   155
Smiled peering through the dirt-crust and the cracks.
Yes; after me thou'lt years and years be thus,
Be young, be fair, be, dumb unconscious toy,
Beloved for youth and fairness; but at the end
Age and decay for thee too. Face of mine,   160
Forgotten self, thou art woman after all:
Sooner or later we are one again:
Both shall have had our fate ... decay, neglect,
Loneliness, and then die and never a one
In the busy world the poorer for our loss.   165

How dusk it is! Have I sat indeed so long?
I had not marked. Time to have been long since
In the merry drawing-room with its lights and talk
And my young sisters' music. Hark! that's sweet.
Maudie's clear voice sends me my favourite song,   170
Filling my stillness here. She sings it well.

Circe[1]

The sun drops luridly into the west;
Darkness has raised her arms to draw him down
Before the time, not waiting as of wont
Till he has come to her behind the sea;
And the smooth waves grow sullen in the gloom   5
And wear their threatening purple; more and more
The plain of waters sways and seems to rise
Convexly from its level of the shores;
And low dull thunder rolls along the beach:
There will be storm at last, storm, glorious storm!   10

---

[1]   In the *Odyssey* Circe is an enchantress who turns
men to swine. Odysseus is protected from her powers
by the herb moly.

Oh welcome, welcome, though it rend my bowers,
Scattering my blossomed roses like the dust,
Splitting the shrieking branches, tossing down
My riotous vines with their young half-tinged grapes
Like small round amethysts or beryls strung   15
Tumultuously in clusters; though it sate
Its ravenous spite among my goodliest pines
Standing there round and still against the sky
That makes blue lakes between their sombre tufts,
Or harry from my silvery olive slopes   20
Some hoary king whose gnarled fantastic limbs
Wear rugged armour of a thousand years;
Though it will hurl high on my flowery shores
The hostile wave that rives at the poor sward
And drags it down the slants, that swirls its foam   25
Over my terraces, shakes their firm blocks
Of great bright marbles into tumbled heaps,
And makes my pleached and mossy labyrinths,
Where the small odorous blossoms grow like stars
Strewn in the milky way, a briny marsh.   30
What matter? let it come and bring me change,
Breaking the sickly sweet monotony.

I am too weary of this long bright calm;
Always the same blue sky, always the sea
The same blue perfect likeness of the sky,   35
One rose to match the other that has waned,
To-morrow's dawn the twin of yesterday's;
And every night the ceaseless crickets chirp
The same long joy and the late strain of birds
Repeats their strain of all the even month;   40
And changelessly the petty plashing surfs
Bubble their chiming burden round the stones;
Dusk after dusk brings the same languid trance
Upon the shadowy hills, and in the fields
The waves of fireflies come and go the same,   45
Making the very flash of light and stir
Vex one like dronings of the shuttles at task.

Give me some change. Must life be only sweet,
All honey-pap as babes would have their food?
And, if my heart must always be adrowse   50
In a hush of stagnant sunshine, give me, then,
Something outside me stirring; let the storm
Break up the sluggish beauty, let it fall
Beaten below the feet of passionate winds,
And then to-morrow waken jubilant   55
In a new birth; let me see subtle joy
Of anguish and of hopes, of change and growth.

What fate is mine, who, far apart from pains
And fears and turmoils of the cross-grained world,
Dwell like a lonely god in a charmed isle   60
Where I am first and only, and, like one
Who should love poisonous savours more than mead,
Long for a tempest on me and grow sick
Of rest and of divine free carelessness!
Oh me, I am a woman, not a god;   65
Yea, those who tend me, even, are more than I,
My nymphs who have the souls of flowers and birds
Singing and blossoming immortally.

Ah me! these love a day and laugh again,
And loving, laughing, find a full content;   70
But I know nought of peace, and have not loved.

Where is my love? Does someone cry for me
Not knowing whom he calls? Does his soul cry
For mine to grow beside it, grow in it?
Does he beseech the gods to give him me,   75
The one unknown rare woman by whose side
No other woman thrice as beautiful
Could once seem fair to him; to whose voice heard
In any common tones no sweetest sound
Of love made melody on silver lutes,   80
Or singing like Apollo's when the gods
Grow pale with happy listening, might be peered
For making music to him; whom once found
There will be no more seeking anything?

Oh love, oh love, oh love, art not yet come   85
Out of the waiting shadows into life?
Art not yet come after so many years
That I have longed for thee? Come! I am here.

Not yet. For surely I should feel a sound
Of his far answer if now in the world   90
He sought me who will seek me – Oh, ye gods,
Will he not seek me? Is it all a dream?
Will there be only these, these bestial things
Who wallow in their styes, or mop and mow
Among the trees, or munch in pens and byres,   95
Or snarl and filch behind their wattled coops;
These things who had believed that they were men?

Nay, but he *will* come. Why am I so fair,
And marvellously minded, and with sight
Which flashes suddenly on hidden things,   100

As the gods see, who do not need to look?
Why wear I in my eyes that stronger power
Than basilisks, whose gaze can only kill,
To draw men's souls to me to live or die
As I would have them? Why am I given pride   105
Which yet longs to be broken, and this scorn,
Cruel and vengeful, for the lesser men
Who meet the smiles I waste for lack of him,
And grow too glad? Why am I who I am?
But for the sake of him whom fate will send   110
One day to be my master utterly,
That he should take me, the desire of all,
Whom only he in the world could bow to him.

    Oh, sunlike glory of pale glittering hairs,
Bright as the filmy wires my weavers take   115
To make me golden gauzes – Oh, deep eyes,
Darker and softer than the bluest dusk
Of August violets, darker and deep
Like crystal fathomless lakes in summer noons –
Oh, sad sweet longing smile – Oh, lips that tempt   120
My very self to kisses – oh, round cheeks
Tenderly radiant with the even flush
Of pale smoothed coral – perfect lovely face
Answering my gaze from out this fleckless pool –
Wonder of glossy shoulders, chiselled limbs –   125
Should I be so your lover as I am,
Drinking an exquisite joy to watch you thus
In all a hundred changes through the day,
But that I love you for him till he comes,
But that my beauty means his loving it?   130

    Oh, look! a speck on this side of the sun,
Coming – yes, coming with the rising wind
That frays the darkening cloud-wrack on the verge
And in a little while will leap abroad,
Spattering the sky with rushing blacknesses,   135
Dashing the hissing mountainous waves at the stars.
'Twill drive me that black speck a shuddering hulk
Caught in the buffeting waves, dashed impotent
From ridge to ridge, will drive it in the night
With that dull jarring crash upon the beach,   140
And the cries for help and the cries of fear and hope.

    And then to-morrow they will thoughtfully,
With grave low voices, count their perils up,
And thank the gods for having let them live
And tell of wives and mothers in their homes,   145

And children, who would have such loss in them
That they must weep (and maybe I weep too)
With fancy of the weepings had they died.
And the next morrow they will feel their ease
And sigh with sleek content, or laugh elate,   150
Tasting delight of rest and revelling,
Music and perfumes, joyaunce for the eyes
Of rosy faces and luxurious pomps,
The savour of the banquet and the glow
And fragrance of the wine-cup; and they'll talk   155
How good it is to house in palaces
Out of the storms and struggles, and what luck
Strewed their good ship on our accessless coast.
Then the next day the beast in them will wake,
And one will strike and bicker, and one swell   160
With puffed-up greatness, and one gibe and strut
In apish pranks, and one will line his sleeve
With pilfered booties, and one snatch the gems
Out of the carven goblets as they pass,
One will grow mad with fever of the wine,   165
And one will sluggishly besot himself,
And one be lewd, and one be gluttonous;
And I shall sickly look and loathe them all.

Oh my rare cup! my pure and crystal cup,
With not one speck of colour to make false   170
The entering lights, or flaw to make them swerve!
My cup of Truth! How the lost fools will laugh
And thank me for my boon, as if I gave
Some momentary flash of the gods' joy,
To drink where *I* have drunk and touch the touch   175
Of *my* lips with their own! Aye, let them touch.

Too cruel, am I? And the silly beasts,
Crowding around me when I pass their way,
Glower on me and, although they love me still,
(With their poor sorts of love such as they could)   180
Call wrath and vengeance to their humid eyes
To scare me into mercy, or creep near
With piteous fawnings, supplicating bleats.
Too cruel? Did I choose them what they are?
Or change them from themselves by poisonous charms?   185
But any draught, pure water, natural wine,
Out of my cup, revealed them to themselves
And to each other. Change? there was no change;
Only disguise gone from them unawares:
And had there been one true right man of them   190
He would have drunk the draught as I had drunk,

And stood unharmed and looked me in the eyes,
Abashing me before him. But these things –
Why, which of them has even shown the kind
Of some one nobler beast? Pah! yapping wolves,   195
And pitiless stealthy wild-cats, curs, and apes,
And gorging swine, and slinking venomous snakes –
All false and ravenous and sensual brutes
That shame the Earth that bore them, these they are.

Lo, lo! the shivering blueness darting forth   200
On half the heavens, and the forked thin fire
Strikes to the sea: and hark, the sudden voice
That rushes through the trees before the storm,
And shuddering of the branches. Yet the sky
Is blue against them still, and early stars   205
Sparkle above the pine-tops; and the air
Clings faint and motionless around me here.

Another burst of flame – and the black speck
Shows in the glare, lashed onwards. It were well
I bade make ready for our guests to-night.   210

A Castaway

Poor little diary, with its simple thoughts,
Its good resolves, its 'Studied French an hour,'
'Read Modern History,' 'Trimmed up my grey hat,'
'Darned stockings,' 'Tatted,' 'Practised my new song,'
'Went to the daily service,' 'Took Bess soup,'   5
'Went out to tea.' Poor simple diary!
And did *I* write it? Was I this good girl,
This budding colourless young rose of home?
Did I so live content in such a life,
Seeing no larger scope, nor asking it,   10
Than this small constant round – old clothes to mend,
New clothes to make, then go and say my prayers,
Or carry soup, or take a little walk
And pick the ragged-robins in the hedge?
Then, for ambition, (was there ever life   15
That could forego that?) to improve my mind
And know French better and sing harder songs;
For gaiety, to go, in my best white
Well washed and starched and freshened with new bows,
And take tea out to meet the clergyman.   20
No wishes and no cares, almost no hopes,
Only the young girl's hazed and golden dreams
That veil the Future from her.

            So long since:
And now it seems a jest to talk of me
As if I could be one with her, of me   25
Who am . . . me.

         And what is that? My looking-glass
Answers it passably; a woman sure,
No fiend, no slimy thing out of the pools,
A woman with a ripe and smiling lip
That has no venom in its touch I think,   30
With a white brow on which there is no brand;
A woman none dare call not beautiful,
Not womanly in every woman's grace.

  Aye, let me feed upon my beauty thus,
Be glad in it like painters when they see   35
At last the face they dreamed but could not find
Look from their canvas on them, triumph in it,
The dearest thing I have. Why, 'tis my all,
Let me make much of it: is it not this,
This beauty, my own curse at once and tool   40
To snare men's souls, (I know what the good say
Of beauty in such creatures) is it not this
That makes me feel myself a woman still,
With still some little pride, some little –

          . Stop!
'Some little pride, some little' – Here's a jest!   45
What word will fit the sense but modesty?
A wanton I, but modest!

         Modest, true;
I'm not drunk in the streets, ply not for hire
At infamous corners with my likenesses
Of the humbler kind; yes, modesty's my word –   50
'Twould shape my mouth well too, I think I'll try:
'Sir, Mr. What-you-will, Lord Who-knows-what,
My present lover or my next to come,
Value me at my worth, fill your purse full,
For I am modest; yes, and honour me   55
As though your schoolgirl sister or your wife
Could let her skirts brush mine or talk of me;
For I am modest.'

        Well, I flout myself:
But yet, but yet —

        Fie, poor fantastic fool,
Why do I play the hypocrite alone,   60

Who am no hypocrite with others by?
Where should be my 'But yet'? I am that thing
Called half a dozen dainty names, and none
Dainty enough to serve the turn and hide
The one coarse English word that lurks beneath: 65
Just that, no worse, no better.

                    And, for me,
I say let no one be above her trade;
I own my kindredship with any drab
Who sells herself as I, although she crouch
In fetid garrets and I have a home 70
All velvet and marqueterie and pastilles,
Although she hide her skeleton in rags
And I set fashions and wear cobweb lace:
The difference lies but in my choicer ware,
That I sell beauty and she ugliness; 75
Our traffic's one – I'm no sweet slaver-tongue
To gloze upon it and explain myself
A sort of fractious angel misconceived –
Our traffic's one: I own it. And what then?
I know of worse that are called honourable. 80
Our lawyers, who with noble eloquence
And virtuous outbursts lie to hang a man,
Or lie to save him, which way goes the fee:
Our preachers, gloating on your future hell
For not believing what they doubt themselves: 85
Our doctors, who sort poisons out by chance
And wonder how they'll answer, and grow rich:
Our journalists, whose business is to fib
And juggle truths and falsehoods to and fro:
Our tradesmen, who must keep unspotted names 90
And cheat the least like stealing that they can:
Our—all of them, the virtuous worthy men
Who feed on the world's follies, vices, wants,
And do their businesses of lies and shams
Honestly, reputably, while the world 95
Claps hands and cries 'good luck,' which of their trades,
Their honourable trades, barefaced like mine,
All secrets brazened out, would shew more white?

    And whom do I hurt more than they? as much?
The wives? Poor fools, what do I take from them 100
Worth crying for or keeping? If they knew
What their fine husbands look like seen by eyes
That may perceive there are more men than one!
But, if they can, let them just take the pains
To keep them: 'tis not such a mighty task 105

To pin an idiot to your apron-string;
And wives have an advantage over us,
(The good and blind ones have) the smile or pout
Leaves them no secret nausea at odd times.
Oh, they could keep their husbands if they cared,   110
But 'tis an easier life to let them go,
And whimper at it for morality.

   Oh! those shrill carping virtues, safely housed
From reach of even a smile that should put red
On a decorous cheek, who rail at us   115
With such a spiteful scorn and rancorousness,
(Which maybe is half envy at the heart)
And boast themselves so measurelessly good
And us so measurelessly unlike them,
What is their wondrous merit that they stay   120
In comfortable homes whence not a soul
Has ever thought of tempting them, and wear
No kisses but a husband's upon lips
There is no other man desires to kiss —
Refrain in fact from sin impossible?   125
How dare they hate us so? what have they done,
What borne, to prove them other than we are?
What right have they to scorn us — glass-case saints,
Dianas under lock and key — what right
More than the well-fed helpless barn-door fowl   130
To scorn the larcenous wild-birds?

                       Pshaw, let be!
Scorn or no scorn, what matter for their scorn?
I have outfaced my own — that's harder work.
Aye, let their virtuous malice dribble on —
Mock snowstorms on the stage — I'm proof long since: 135
I have looked coolly on my what and why,
And I accept myself.

           Oh, I'll endorse
The shamefullest revilings mouthed at me,
Cry 'True! Oh perfect picture! Yes, that's I!'
And add a telling blackness here and there,   140
And then dare swear you, every nine of ten,
My judges and accusers, I'd not change
My conscience against yours, you who tread out
Your devil's pilgrimage along the roads
That take in church and chapel, and arrange   145
A roundabout and decent way to hell.

   Well, mine's a short way and a merry one:
So says my pious hash of ohs and ahs,

Choice texts and choicer threats, appropriate names,
(Rahabs and Jezebels) some fierce Tartuffe   150
Hurled at me through the post. We had rare fun
Over that tract digested with champagne.
Where is it? where's my rich repertory
Of insults Biblical? *'I prey on souls'* –
Only my men have oftenest none I think: 155
'I snare the simple ones' – but in these days
There seem to be none simple and none snared
And most men have their favourite sinnings planned
To do them civilly and sensibly:
'I braid my hair' – but braids are out of date: 160
'I paint my cheeks' – I always wear them pale:
'I –'

      Pshaw! the trash is savourless to-day:
One cannot laugh alone. There, let it burn.
What, does the windy dullard think one needs
His wisdom dove-tailed on to Solomon's,   165
His threats out-threatening God's, to teach the news
That those who need not sin have safer souls?
We know it, but we've bodies to save too;
And so we earn our living.

          Well lit, tract!
At least you've made me a good leaping blaze.   170
Up, up, how the flame shoots! and now 'tis dead.
Oh proper finish, preaching to the last –
No such bad omen either; sudden end,
And no sad withering horrible old age.
How one would clutch at youth to hold it tight!   175
And then to know it gone, to see it gone,
Be taught its absence by harsh careless looks,
To live forgotten, solitary, old –
The cruellest word that ever woman learns.
Old – that's to be nothing, or to be at best   180
A blurred memorial that in better days
There was a woman once with such a name.
No, no, I could not bear it: death itself
Shows kinder promise ... even death itself,
Since it must come one day –

          Oh this grey gloom!   185
This rain, rain, rain, what wretched thoughts it brings!
Death: I'll not think of it.

          Will no one come?
'Tis dreary work alone.

                    Why did I read
That silly diary? Now, sing-song, ding-dong,
Come the old vexing echoes back again,   190
Church bells and nursery good-books, back again
Upon my shrinking ears that had forgotten –
I hate the useless memories: 'tis fools' work
Singing the hacknied dirge of 'better days':
Best take Now kindly, give the past good-bye,   195
Whether it were a better or a worse.

    Yes, yes, I listened to the echoes once,
The echoes and the thoughts from the old days.
The worse for me: I lost my richest friend,
And that was all the difference. For the world,   200
I would not have that flight known. How they'd roar:
'What! Eulalie, when she refused us all,
"Ill" and "away," was doing Magdalene,
Tears, ashes, and her Bible, and then off
To hide her in a Refuge . . . for a week!'   205

    A wild whim that, to fancy I could change
My new self for my old because I wished!
Since then, when in my languid days there comes
That craving, like homesickness, to go back
To the good days, the dear old stupid days,   210
To the quiet and the innocence, I know
'Tis a sick fancy and try palliatives.

    What is it? You go back to the old home,
And 'tis not *your* home, has no place for you,
And, if it had, you could not fit you in it.   215
And could I fit me to my former self?
If I had had the wit, like some of us,
To sow my wild-oats into three per cents,
Could I not find me shelter in the peace
Of some far nook where none of them would come,   220
Nor whisper travel from this scurrilous world
(That gloats, and moralizes through its leers)
To blast me with my fashionable shame?
There I might – oh my castle in the clouds!
And where's its rent? – but there, were there a there,   225
I might again live the grave blameless life
Among such simple pleasures, simple cares:
But could they be my pleasures, be my cares?
The blameless life, but never the content –
Never. How could I henceforth be content   230
With any life but one that sets the brain
In a hot merry fever with its stir?

What would there be in quiet rustic days,
Each like the other, full of time to think,
To keep one bold enough to live at all?   235
Quiet is hell, I say — as if a woman
Could bear to sit alone, quiet all day,
And loathe herself and sicken on her thoughts.

    They tried it at the Refuge, and I failed:
I could not bear it. Dreary hideous room,   240
Coarse pittance, prison rules, one might bear these
And keep one's purpose; but so much alone,
And then made faint and weak and fanciful
By change from pampering to half-famishing —
Good God, what thoughts come! Only one week more   245
And 'twould have ended: but in one day more
I must have killed myself. And I loathe death,
The dreadful foul corruption with who knows
What future after it.

                        Well, I came back,
Back to my slough. Who says I had my choice?   250
Could I stay there to die of some mad death?
And if I rambled out into the world
Sinless but penniless, what else were that
But slower death, slow pining shivering death
By misery and hunger? Choice! what choice   255
Of living well or ill? could I have that?
And who would give it me? I think indeed
If some kind hand, a woman's — I hate men —
Had stretched itself to help me to firm ground,
Taken a chance and risked my falling back,   260
I could have gone my way not falling back:
But, let her be all brave, all charitable,
How could she do it? Such a trifling boon —
A little work to live by, 'tis not much —
And I might have found will enough to last: 265
But where's the work? More sempstresses than shirts;
And defter hands at white work than are mine
Drop starved at last: dressmakers, milliners,
Too many too they say; and then their trades
Need skill, apprenticeship. And who so bold   270
As hire me for their humblest drudgery?
Not even for scullery slut; not even, I think,
For governess although they'd get me cheap.
And after all it would be something hard,
With the marts for decent women overfull,   275
If I could elbow in and snatch a chance
And oust some good girl so, who then perforce
Must come and snatch her chance among our crowd.

Why, if the worthy men who think all's done
If we'll but come where we can hear them preach,   280
Could bring us all, or any half of us,
Into their fold, teach all us wandering sheep,
Or only half of us, to stand in rows
And baa them hymns and moral songs, good lack,
What would they do with us? what could they do?   285
Just think! with were't but half of us on hand
To find work for ... or husbands. Would they try
To ship us to the colonies for wives?

Well, well, I know the wise ones talk and talk:
'Here's cause, here's cure:' 'No, here it is, and here:'   290
And find society to blame, or law,
The Church, the men, the women, too few schools,
Too many schools, too much, too little taught:
Somewhere or somehow someone is to blame:
But I say all the fault's with God himself   295
Who puts too many women in the world.
We ought to die off reasonably and leave
As many as the men want, none to waste.
Here's cause; the woman's superfluity:
And for the cure, why, if it were the law,   300
Say, every year, in due percentages,
Balancing them with males as the times need,
To kill off female infants, 'twould make room;
And some of us would not have lost too much,
Losing life ere we know what it *can* mean.   305

The other day I saw a woman weep
Beside her dead child's bed: the little thing
Lay smiling, and the mother wailed half mad,
Shrieking to God to give it back again.
I could have laughed aloud: the little girl   310
Living had but her mother's life to live;
There she lay smiling, and her mother wept
To know her gone!

                    My mother would have wept.

Oh, mother, mother, did you ever dream,
You good grave simple mother, you pure soul   315
No evil could come nigh, did you once dream
In all your dying cares for your lone girl
Left to fight out her fortune helplessly
That there would be *this* danger? – for *your* girl,
Taught by you, lapped in a sweet ignorance,   320
Scarcely more wise of what things sin could be

Than some young child a summer six months old,
Where in the north the summer makes a day,
Of what is darkness . . . darkness that will come
To-morrow suddenly. Thank God at least   325
For this much of my life, that when you died,
That when you kissed me dying, not a thought
Of this made sorrow for you, that I too
Was pure of even fear.

           Oh yes, I thought,
Still new in my insipid treadmill life,   330
(My father so late dead), and hopeful still,
There might be something pleasant somewhere in it,
Some sudden fairy come, no doubt, to turn
My pumpkin to a chariot, I thought then
That I might plod and plod and drum the sounds   335
Of useless facts into unwilling ears,
Tease children with dull questions half the day
Then con dull answers in my room at night
Ready for next day's questions, mend quill pens
And cut my fingers, add up sums done wrong   340
And never get them right; teach, teach, and teach –
What I half knew, or not at all – teach, teach
For years, a lifetime – *I!*

          And yet, who knows?
It might have been, for I was patient once,
And willing, and meant well; it might have been   345
Had I but still clung on in my first place –
A safe dull place, where mostly there were smiles
But never merry-makings; where all days
Jogged on sedately busy, with no haste;
Where all seemed measured out, but margins broad: 350
A dull home but a peaceful, where I felt
My pupils would be dear young sisters soon,
And felt their mother take me to her heart,
Motherly to all lonely harmless things.
But I must have a conscience, must blurt out   355
My great discovery of my ignorance!
And who required it of me? And who gained?
What did it matter for a more or less
The girls learnt in their schoolbooks, to forget
In their first season? We did well together: 360
They loved me and I them: but I went off
To housemaid's pay, six crossgrained brats to teach,
Wrangles and jangles, doubts, disgrace . . . then this;
And they had a perfection found for them,
Who has all ladies' learning in her head   365

Abridged and scheduled, speaks five languages,
Knows botany and conchology and globes,
Draws, paints, plays, sings, embroiders, teaches all
On a patent method never known to fail:
And now they're finished and, I hear, poor things,   370
Are the worst dancers and worst dressers out.
And where's their profit of those prison years
All gone to make them wise in lesson-books?
Who wants his wife to know weeds' Latin names?
Who ever chose a girl for saying dates?   375
Or asked if she had learned to trace a map?

   Well, well, the silly rules this silly world
Makes about women! This is one of them.
Why must there be pretence of teaching them
What no one ever cares that they should know,   380
What, grown out of the schoolroom, they cast off
Like the schoolroom pinafore, no better fit
For any use of real grown-up life,
For any use to her who seeks or waits
The husband and the home, for any use,   385
For any shallowest pretence of use,
To her who has them? Do I not know this,
I, like my betters, that a woman's life,
Her natural life, her good life, her one life,
Is in her husband, God on earth to her,   390
And what she knows and what she can and is
Is only good as it brings good to him?

   Oh God, do I not know it? I the thing
Of shame and rottenness, the animal
That feed men's lusts and prey on them, I, I,   395
Who should not dare to take the name of wife
On my polluted lips, who in the word
Hear but my own reviling, I know that.
I could have lived by that rule, how content:
My pleasure to make him some pleasure, pride   400
To be as he would have me, duty, care,
To fit all to his taste, rule my small sphere
To his intention; then to lean on him,
Be guided, tutored, loved – no not that word,
That *loved* which between men and women means   405
All selfishness, all cloying talk, all lust,
All vanity, all idiocy – not loved,
But cared for. I've been loved myself, I think,
Some once or twice since my poor mother died,
But *cared for*, never: – that's a word for homes,   410
Kind homes, good homes, where simple children come

And ask their mother is this right or wrong,
Because they know she's perfect, cannot err;
Their father told them so, and he knows all,
Being so wise and good and wonderful,   415
Even enough to scold even her at times
And tell her everything she does not know.
Ah the sweet nursery logic!

                    Fool! thrice fool!
Do I hanker after that too? Fancy me
Infallible nursery saint, live code of law!   420
Me preaching! teaching innocence to be good! –
A mother!

          Yet the baby thing that woke
And wailed an hour or two, and then was dead,
Was mine, and had he lived . . . why then my name
Would have been mother. But 'twas well he died: 425
I could have been no mother, I, lost then
Beyond his saving. Had he come before
And lived, come to me in the doubtful days
When shame and boldness had not grown one sense,
For his sake, with the courage come of him,   430
I might have struggled back.

               But how? But how?
His father would not then have let me go:
His time had not yet come to make an end
Of my 'for ever' with a hireling's fee
And civil light dismissal. None but him   435
To claim a bit of bread of if I went,
Child or no child: would he have given it me?
He! no; he had not done with me. No help,
No help, no help. Some ways can be trodden back,
But never our way, we who one wild day   440
Have given goodbye to what in our deep hearts
The lowest woman still holds best in life,
Good name – good name though given by the world
That mouths and garbles with its decent prate,
And wraps it in respectable grave shams,   445
And patches conscience partly by the rule
Of what one's neighbour thinks, but something more
By what his eyes are sharp enough to see.
How I could scorn it with its Pharisees,
If it could not scorn me: but yet, but yet –   450
Oh God, if I could look it in the face!

   Oh I am wild, am ill, I think, to-night:
Will no one come and laugh with me? No feast,

No merriment to-night. So long alone!
Will no one come?

   At least there's a new dress   455
To try, and grumble at – they never fit
To one's ideal. Yes, a new rich dress,
With lace like this too, that's a soothing balm
For any fretting woman, cannot fail;
I've heard men say it . . . and they know so well   460
What's in all women's hearts, especially
Women like me.

   No help! no help! no help!
How could it be? It was too late long since –
Even at the first too late. Whose blame is that?
There are some kindly people in the world,   465
But what can *they* do? If one hurls oneself
Into a quicksand, what can be the end,
But that one sinks and sinks? Cry out for help?
Ah yes, and, if it came, who is so strong
To strain from the firm ground and lift one out? 470
And how, so firmly clutching the stretched hand
As death's pursuing terror bids, even so,
How can one reach firm land, having to foot
The treacherous crumbling soil that slides and gives
And sucks one in again? Impossible path!   475
No, why waste struggles, I or any one?
What is must be. What then? I where I am,
Sinking and sinking; let the wise pass by
And keep their wisdom for an apter use,
Let me sink merrily as I best may.   480

 Only, I think my brother – I forgot;
He stopped his brotherhood some years ago –
But if he had been just so much less good
As to remember mercy. Did he think
How once I was his sister, prizing him   485
As sisters do, content to learn for him
The lesson girls with brothers all must learn,
To do without?

   I have heard girls lament
That doing so without all things one would,
But I saw never aught to murmur at,   490
For men must be made ready for their work
And women all have more or less their chance
Of husbands to work for them, keep them safe
Like summer roses in soft greenhouse air
That never guess 'tis winter out of doors: 495

No, I saw never aught to murmur at,
Content with stinted fare and shabby clothes
And cloistered silent life to save expense,
Teaching myself out of my borrowed books,
While he for some one pastime, (needful, true,   500
To keep him of his rank; 'twas not his fault)
Spent in a month what could have given me
My teachers for a year.

         'Twas no one's fault:
For could he be launched forth on the rude sea
Of this contentious world and left to find   505
Oars and the boatman's skill by some good chance?
'Twas no one's fault: yet still he might have thought
Of our so different youths and owned at least
'Tis pitiful when a mere nerveless girl
Untutored must put forth upon that sea,   510
Not in the woman's true place, the wife's place,
To trust a husband and be borne along,
But impotent blind pilot to herself.

    Merciless, merciless — like the prudent world
That will not have the flawed soul prank itself   515
With a hoped second virtue, will not have
The woman fallen once lift up herself . . .
Lest she should fall again. Oh how his taunts,
His loathing fierce reproaches, scarred and seared
Like branding iron hissing in a wound!   520
And it was true — *that* killed me: and I felt
A hideous hopeless shame burn out my heart,
And knew myself for ever that he said,
That which I was — Oh it was true, true, true.

    No, not true then. I was not all that then.   525
Oh, I have drifted on before mad winds
And made ignoble shipwreck; not to-day
Could any breeze of heaven prosper me
Into the track again, nor any hand
Snatch me out of the whirlpool I have reached;   530
But then?

        Nay, he judged very well: he knew
Repentance was too dear a luxury
For a beggar's buying, knew it earns no bread —
And knew me a too base and nerveless thing
To bear my first fault's sequel and just die.   535
And how could he have helped me? Held my hand,
Owned me for his, fronted the angry world

Clothed with my ignominy? Or maybe
Taken me to his home to damn him worse?
What did I look for? for what less would serve   540
That he could do, a man without a purse?
He meant me well, he sent me that five pounds,
Much to him then; and, if he bade me work
And never vex him more with news of me,
We both knew him too poor for pensioners.   545
I see he did his best; I could wish now
Sending it back I had professed some thanks.

   But there! I was too wretched to be meek:
It seemed to me as if he, every one,
The whole great world, were guilty of my guilt,   550
Abettors and avengers: in my heart
I gibed them back their gibings; I was wild.

   I see clear now and know one has one's life
In hand at first to spend or spare or give
Like any other coin; spend it, or give,   555
Or drop it in the mire, can the world see
You get your value for it, or bar off
The hurrying of its marts to grope it up
And give it back to you for better use?
And if you spend or give, that is your choice;   560
And if you let it slip, that's your choice too,
You should have held it firmer. Yours the blame,
And not another's, not the indifferent world's
Which goes on steadily, statistically,
And count by censuses not separate souls –   565
And if it somehow needs to its worst use
So many lives of women, useless else,
It buys us of ourselves; we could hold back,
Free all of us to starve, and some of us,
(Those who have done no ill, and are in luck)   570
To slave their lives out and have food and clothes
Until they grow unserviceably old.

   Oh, I blame no one – scarcely even myself.
It was to be: the very good in me
Has always turned to hurt; all I thought right   575
At the hot moment, judged of afterwards,
Shows reckless.

                    Why, look at it, had I taken
The pay my dead child's father offered me
For having been its mother, I could then
Have kept life in me – many have to do it,   580

That swarm in the back alleys, on no more,
Cold sometimes, mostly hungry, but they live —
I could have gained a respite trying it,
And maybe found at last some humble work
To eke the pittance out. Not I, forsooth,   585
I must have spirit, must have womanly pride,
Must dash back his contemptuous wages, I
Who had not scorned to earn them, dash them back
The fiercer that he dared to count our boy
In my appraising: and yet now I think   590
I might have taken it for my dead boy's sake;
It would have been *his* gift.

                But I went forth
With my fine scorn, and whither did it lead?
Money's the root of evil do they say?
Money is virtue, strength: money to me   595
Would then have been repentance: could I live
Upon my idiot's pride?

                Well, it fell soon.
I had prayed Clement might believe me dead,
And yet I begged of him — That's like me too,
Beg of him and then send him back his alms!   600
What if he gave as to a whining wretch
That holds her hand and lies? I am less to him
Than such a one; her rags do him no wrong,
But I, I wrong him merely that I live,
Being his sister. Could I not at least   605
Have still let him forget me? But 'tis past:
And naturally he may hope I am long dead.

   Good God! to think that we were what we were
One to the other ... and now!

                He has done well;
Married a sort of heiress, I have heard,   610
A dapper little madam dimple cheeked
And dimple brained, who makes him a good wife —
No doubt she'd never own but just to him,
And in a whisper, she can even suspect
That we exist, we other women things: 615
What would she say if she could learn one day
She has a sister-in-law? So he and I
Must stand apart till doomsday.

                But the jest,
To think how she would look! — Her fright, poor thing!

The notion! – I could laugh outright . . . or else,   620
For I feel near it, roll on the ground and sob.

   Well, after all, there's not much difference
Between the two sometimes.

                 Was that the bell?
Someone at last, thank goodness. There's a voice,
And that's a pleasure. Whose though? Ah, I know.   625
Why did she come alone, the cackling goose?
Why not have brought her sister? – she tells more
And titters less. No matter; half a loaf
Is better than no bread.

              Oh, is it you?
Most welcome, dear: one gets so moped alone.   630

Sonnets from *Mother and Daughter*

VIII

A little child she, half defiant came
  Reasoning her case – 'twas not so long ago –
  'I cannot mind your scolding, for I know
However bad I were you'd love the same.'
And I, what countering answer could I frame?   5
  'Twas true, and true, and God's self told her so.
  One does but ask one's child to smile and grow,
And each rebuke has love for its right name.

And yet, methinks, sad mothers who for years,
  Watching the child pass forth that was their boast,   10
Have counted all the footsteps by new fears
Till even lost fears seem hopes whereof they're reft
And of all mother's good love sole is left –
  Is their Love, Love, or some remembered ghost?

XI

Love's Mourner

'Tis men who say that through all hurt and pain   15
  The woman's love, wife's, mother's, still will hold,
  And breathes the sweeter and will more unfold
For winds that tear it, and the sorrowful rain.
So in a thousand voices has the strain

Of this dear patient madness been retold,   10
   That men call woman's love. Ah! they are bold,
Naming for love that grief which *does* remain.

Love faints that looks on baseness face to face:
   Love pardons all; but by the pardonings dies,
     With a fresh wound of each pierced through the breast.   15
And there stand pityingly in Love's void place
   Kindness of household wont familiar-wise,
   And faith to Love – faith to our dead at rest.

XV

That some day Death who has us all for jest
   Shall hide me in the dark and voiceless mould,   20
   And him whose living hand has mine in hold,
Where loving comes not nor the looks that rest,
Shall make us nought where we are known the best,
   Forgotten things that leave their track untold
   As in the August night the sky's dropped gold –   25
This seems no strangeness, but Death's natural hest.

But looking on the dawn that is her face
   To know she too is Death's seems misbelief;
She should not find decay, but, as the sun
Moves mightier from the veil that hides his place,   30
Keep ceaseless radiance. Life is Death begun:
   But Death and her! That's strangeness passing grief.

XX

There's one I miss. A little questioning maid
   That held my finger, trotting by my side,
   And smiled out of her pleased eyes open wide,   35
Wondering and wiser at each word I said.
And I must help her frolics if she played,
   And I must feel her trouble if she cried;
   My lap was hers past right to be denied;
She did my bidding, but I more obeyed.   40

Dearer she is to-day, dearer and more;
   Closer to me, since sister womanhoods meet;
Yet, like poor mothers some long while bereft,
I dwell on toward ways, quaint memories left,
   I miss the approaching sound of pit-pat feet,   45
The eager baby voice outside my door.

XXVII

Since first my little one lay on my breast
   I never needed such a second good,
   Nor felt a void left in my motherhood
She filled not always to the utterest.
The summer linnet, by glad yearnings pressed,   5
   Builds room enough to house a callow brood:
   I prayed not for another child – nor could;
My solitary bird had my heart's nest.

But she is cause that any baby thing
   If it but smile, is one of mine in truth,   10
   And every child becomes my natural joy:
And, if my heart gives all youth fostering,
   Her sister, brother, seems the girl or boy:
My darling makes me mother to their youth.

Harriet Hamilton King (1840–1920)

Harriet Eleanor Baillie Hamilton was the daughter of Lady Harriet and Admiral William Alexander Baillie Hamilton. The early passion of her life, as for so many other women poets at this time, was the cause of Italian unification, and she corresponded with the Italian patriot Giuseppe Mazzini from 1862. Late in life these letters became the core of her *Letters and Recollections of Mazzini* (1912) though she herself did not complete the editing which was undertaken by G. M. Trevelyan.

    Otherwise, Harriet's life took a conventional course. She married a banker, Henry Samuel King in 1863 and bore him seven children, whose care devolved entirely upon her on his death in 1878. Her poetry seems to have been encouraged by her husband rather then otherwise, for he financed the private publication of her first work, an apologia for Felice Orsini, the Italian patriot who attempted to assassinate Napoleon III. More poems on the Italian theme appeared in her *Aspromonte and Other Poems* (1869), while *The Disciples* (1873) tells the story of Mazzini's followers and their trials after his death. This poem may have been her most popular – it was a great favourite with Cardinal Manning – but it is conventional in comparison with the eerie poems which appeared in her collection *A Book of Dreams* (1883). The three poems included here are taken from this book and each one powerfully suggests the suppressed imaginative life of an otherwise dutiful wife and mother. 'A Dream Maiden' in particular, with its strange landscape and wandering spirit brought back, at the end, to the realization of the imperatives of family duty and relations, is curiously unsettling. The wild moonlight landscapes and the insistent journeying spirits who haunt these poems produce the impression of a restless and questioning mind.

    In later life, Harriet became a Catholic and most of her work from that time consists of religious verse published in *The Prophecy of Westminster* (1895) and two books of ballads and lyrics published in 1889 and 1902.

M.R.

King, Harriet Hamilton (1883) *A Book of Dreams*, London.

A Dream Maiden

My baby is sleeping overhead,
  My husband is in the town;
In my large white bed uncurtained,
  All alone I lay me down.

And dreamily I have said my prayers,   5
  And dreamily closed my eyes,
And the youth in my blood moves sweetly
  As my pulses fall and rise.

I lie so peaceful and lonely,
  A maiden in spirit-land,   10
With the moonbeams in at the window.
  And hand laid close to hand.

I wander forth in the moonbeams,
  All free of heart alone,
Neither awake nor dreaming,   15
  To-night it is all one.

Light of step across the carpet
  Of the flower-entangled spring,
Light of spirit through the haunted
  Wood pathways murmuring.   20

The earth is telling her secrets,
  Never shy or strange to me;
My heart beating only silence,
  One with her mystery.

All over the beautiful distance   25
  The air is so fresh and pure,
The night is so cool and silvery,
  The calm is so secure.

And afar, down into the sunrise,
  The glittering dream-worlds shine;   30
And by this free heart triumphant
  I pass on to make them mine.

O elfin maiden, turn homeward,
  And dream not so cold and wild! −
Have I not turned a woman?   35
  Have I not husband and child?

A Moonlight Ride

Through the lands low-lying, fast and free
  I ride alone and under the moon;
An empty road that is strange to me,
  Yet at every turn remembered soon:
A road like a racecourse, even and wide,   5
With grassy margins on either side;
In a rapture of blowing air I ride,
  With a heart that is beating tune.

Light as on turf the hoof-beats fall,
  As on spongy sod as fast and fleet,   10
For the road is smooth and moist withal,
  And the water springs under the horse's feet:
And to every stride sounds a soft plash yet.
For all the length of the way is wet
With many a runnel and rivulet   15
  That under the moonlight meet.

O surely the water lilies should be
  Sunk away and safe folded to rest!
But, no; they are shining open and free,
  White and awake on the water's breast: 20
On the long and shimmering waterway,
All silver-spread to the full moon's ray,
The shallow dykes that straggle and stray
  With their floating fringes drest.

The road will flow winding and winding away   25
  Through the sleeping country to-night;
All one long level of dusky grey,
  The border hedges slip past in flight;
Turning and twisting in many a lane,
Mile after mile of a labyrinth chain   30
I have seen before, I shall see again,
  Yet remember not aright.

And somewhere all out of sight there stands
  A sleeping house that is white and low,
Hid in the heart of the level lands,   35
  The lands where the waters wander slow,
Embowered all round by the thickset ways,
Set in a silent and stately maze
Of high-grown ilex, arbutus, bays, –
  If I ever saw it, I do not know.   40

Shall I ever reach it? or ere the day
Breaks, will it all have passed away?
   If only the night might last!
While the mists of moonlight the warm air fill,
Out of boskage and bower so deep and still   45
There reaches afar the glimmer, the thrill, –
   O the night is flying too fast!

Summer Lost

What is the summer
   Of which they speak?
How shall we find it?
   Where shall we seek?

The spring has passed over,   5
   It would not stay;
It was too bright,
   So it vanished away.

I saw the white stars
   Over the grass,   10
And the daffodils golden
   Arise and pass.

The merles were singing
   As evening fell
Of something coming   15
   Too sweet to tell.

A whisper flushed
   Through the twilight pale;
The lily, the rose,
   And the nightingale.   20

I listen for them; –
   And what has come?
The leaves are falling,
   The birds are dumb.

The scentless sunflowers   25
   Are open brown;
Through empty branches
   The rain pours down.

Is this the summer
   I waited for?
Is it come? or coming   30
   Nevermore?

Mathilde Blind (1841–1896)

Writing to the American poet Walt Whitman, William Michael Rossetti described Mathilde Blind as 'a woman of singular ability and independence of mind and a most earnest believer in the author of *Leaves of Grass*' (Peattie 1990: 332). In his *Reminiscences* William Michael wrote of Mathilde's 'fine, animated speaking countenance, and . . . ample stock of interesting conversation' (Rossetti 1906: II, 388).

This remarkable woman came from a remarkable family. She was the daughter of a German Jewish banker who died soon after her birth. Her mother then married Karl Blind who was one of leaders in the Baden insurrection of 1848–9 and the family fled to England after its suppression. Her brother, Ferdinand Cohen, followed his step-father's example and attempted to assassinate Bismarck just before the Austro-Prussian war of 1866.

Mathilde's own revolutionary fervour went rather into a personal and political effort to live the independent life of a 'New Woman'. While studying in Zurich she tried to get into university lectures forbidden to women. She failed, but her determination to behave like any young male student led to her making a walking tour of the Swiss Alps alone at the age of nineteen. 'For once I felt truly free' she wrote. All the same, the adventure was not without its amusing moments:

Suddenly as I was walking along I saw the evil-looking Frenchman whom I had noticed and instinctively avoided for several evenings at the table d'hôte. It had begun to thunder, lighten and rain. The guide had dropped behind. In turning an angle of the road, I completely lost sight of him. Before I knew how, the Frenchman had come up to me and suddenly addressed me with 'Pardon Mademoiselle; mais nous allons avoir un orage terrible; you have nothing to protect yourself from the storm. Allow me to offer you my cloak.' I thanked him very shortly and remarked that I had all I needed and walked on very fast to make him understand I had no wish for his company; but he hurried after me, panting a little, for he was stout and heavily built and kept uttering notes of admiration about my courage and Amazonian [blank] which I thought rude and impertinent, & which made me feel most uncomfortable. 'Ah Mademoiselle', he sighed when he had again come up with me 'I wish we had young ladies like you in France – there would be some temptation for men to get married then.' I walked in a stony silence and tried to hide the nervousness that I began to feel. He still urged me to accept his cloak and protested hotly that I would catch my death of cold. I walked on in silence when suddenly to my unspeakable amazement he flopped down on his fat short legs on the wet miry ground and seizing hold of my skirt said that I must at least allow him to pin it up for me. The suddeness of the action rendered me motionless with surprise for an instant. A shudder of horror and repulsion rooted me to the ground. Suddenly a flash of lightening seemed to rend the heavens asunder, lighting up the [blank] and away in wild cloudlands snow-laden peaks and glaciers of the Matterhorn. The flash seemed to go right through me and as if the spirit of the lightening had entered my frail human body I lifted my arm and hit the cowardly Frenchman such a blow right in the face that he fell back, the blood streaming from somewhere, probably his nose – but I did not stop. I simply raced clouds and running rills – on and on as if I had become a part and parcel of this Sabbath of the Elements which I loved more than aught human (Blind, BL Add. Ms. 61930, fol. 48r–49r).

Back in England Mathilde was a popular member of the pre-Raphaelite circle. She lived for long periods with the Madox Browns in Manchester in spite of occasional quarrels with Ford Madox Brown's daughters. These may have had some basis in the rumour which began after Emma Brown's death that Ford Madox Brown wished to marry Mathilde. If he ever asked her, Mathilde's turning him down is really no surprise because all her strong friendships and loyalties were with women, among them Eleanor Marx (whom she knew through her German connections) and the novelist Mona Caird. The exceptions to this rule were her admiration for Mazzini whom she knew well and to whom she dedicated her first volume of poems (1867), and her passion for the poet Shelley. In 1872, the year in which she published a collection of his poems with a memoir, William Michael showed Mathilde a piece of Shelley's skull: 'It was curious to observe the different feelings with which the sight of the fragment of Shelley's skull was received by different people. Mathilde Blind changed countenance in a moment: her eyes suffused, and she put the fragment reverently to her lips' (Bornand 1977: 171).

A staunch adherent of the woman's suffrage campaign, Mathilde was also energetic in promoting women's education, and bequeathed her estate to Newnham College, Cambridge to found a Scholarship for Language and Literature. Her political commitments overlapped with her literary interests in her biographies for the 'Eminent Women' series of *George Eliot* (1883) and *Madame Roland* (1886), and in her translation of the *Journal of Marie Bashkirtseff* (1890) where Mathilde wrote in the introduction:

Now here is a girl, the story of whose life as told by herself may be called the drama of woman's soul at odds with destiny, as such a soul must needs be, when endowed with great powers and possibilities, under the present social conditions; where the wish to live, of letting whatever energies you possess have their full play in action, is continually thwarted by the impediments and restrictions of sex ... Did we but know it the same revolts, the same struggles, the same helpless rage, have gone on in many another woman's life for want of scope for her latent powers and faculties (Blind 1890: vii–viii).

A feminist, a revolutionary, a socialist, Mathilde also seems to have been a sceptic in religious matters. Certainly she fell out with the novelist Rosa Carey, with whom she had been at school, because Rosa was high church and disapproved of Mathilde's views. And in 1881 the publishers of her long poem *The Prophecy of St Oran* withdrew the book shortly after publication because of its 'atheistic character' (Peattie 1990: 400). Never very strong, Mathilde suffered especially from headaches, though she did, for a while, find a way of combating this problem by taking up dancing (Bornand 1977: 219).

The chief interest of Blind's poetry lies with its political affiliations and her collection *Dramas in Miniature* (1891), from which 'The Russian Student's Tale' is taken, addresses the inequity of the sexes. Her epic poem *The Ascent of Man* (1889) was inspired by a reading of Charles Darwin and, like other women poets she used the concept of evolution to criticize the state of civilization in the late nineteenth century. The work is not as well-informed as the evolutionary poems of Constance Naden, nor as witty as May Kendall's, but it does convey a conviction that women's sphere should include both the worlds of poetry and that of science in an argument that is typical of the 1880s and 1890s. Less portenteously, Blind was an 'intense admirer' (Bornand 1977: 170) of Christina Rossetti's nursery poems in *Sing-Song* and her lighthearted poem 'A Fantasy' may have been influenced by Rossetti's work.

M.R.

Blind, Mathilde (1867) *Poems*, [published under the pseudonym of Claude Lake], London.
—— (1872) *Percy Bysshe Shelley: A Biography*, London.
—— (1881) *The Prophecy of St Oran and other Poems*, London.
—— (1883) *George Eliot*, in the Eminent Women series, London.
—— (1886) *The Heather on Fire*, London.
—— (1886) *Madame Roland*, in the Eminent Women series, London.
—— (1889) *The Ascent of Man*, London.
—— (1890), ed. *The Journal of Marie Bashkirtseff*, 2 vols, London.
—— (1891) *Dramas in Miniature*, London.
—— (1895) *Birds of Passage: Songs of the Orient and Occident*, London.
—— (1900) *The Poetical Works of Mathilde Blind*, ed. Arthur Symons, with a Memoir by Richard Garnett, London, T. F. Unwin.
—— (n.d.) Fragments of unpublished and incomplete autobiography in the British Library, Add. Ms. 61930, fol. 1r–55r.

Bornand, Odette ed. (1977) *The Diary of William Michael Rossetti*, Oxford, Clarendon Press.
Peattie, Roger W. ed. (1990) *Selected Letters of William Michael Rossetti*, University Park and London, Pennsylvannia University Press.
Rossetti, William Michael (1906) *Some Reminiscences of William Michael Rossetti*, 2 vols, London, Brown, Langham.

The Russian Student's Tale

The midnight sun with phantom glare
Shone on the soundless thoroughfare
Whose shuttered houses, closed and still,
Seemed bodies without heart or will;
Yea, all the stony city lay   5
Impassive in that phantom day,
As amid livid wastes of sand
The sphinxes of the desert stand.

And we, we two, turned night to day,
As, whistling many a student's lay.   10
We sped along each ghostly street,
With girls whose lightly tripping feet
Well matched our longer, stronger stride.
In hurrying to the water-side.
We took a boat; each seized an oar.   15
And put his will into each stroke,

Until on either hand the shore
Slipped backwards, as our voices woke
Far echoes, mingling like a dream
With swirl and tumult of the stream.   20
On – on – away, beneath the ray
Of midnight in the mask of day;
By great wharves where the masts at peace
Look like the ocean's barren trees;
Past palaces and glimmering towers,   25
And gardens fairy-like with flowers.
And parks of twilight green and closes,
The very Paradise of roses.
The waters flow; on, on we row,
Now laughing loud, now whispering low;   30
And through the splendour of the white
Electrically glowing night,
Wind-wafted from some perfumed dell,
Tumultuously there loudly rose
Above the Neva's surge and swell,   35
With amorous ecstasies and throes,
And lyric spasms of wildest wail,
The love song of a nightingale.

I see her still beside me. Yea,
As if it were but yesterday,
I see her – see her as she smiled;   40
Her face that of a little child
For innocent sweetness undefiled;
And that pathetie flower-like blue
Of eyes which, as they looked at you.   45
Seemed yet to stab your bosom through.
I rowed, she steered; oars dipped and flashed,
The broadening river roared and splashed,
So that we hardly seemed to hear
Our comrades' voices, though so near;   50
Their faces seeming far away.
As still beneath that phantom day
I looked at her, she smiled at me!
And then we landed – I and she.

There's an old Café in the wood;   55
A student's haunt on summer eves,
Round which responsive poplar leaves
Quiver to each æolian mood
Like some wild harp a poet smites
On visionary summer nights.   60
I ordered supper, took a room
Green-curtained by the tremulous gloom

Of those fraternal poplar trees
Shaking together in the breeze;
My pulse, too, like a poplar tree,   65
Shook wildly as she smiled at me.
Eye in eye, and hand in hand.
Awake amid the slumberous land.
I told her all my love that night –
How I had loved her at first sight;   70
How I was hers, and seemed to be
Her own to all eternity.
And through the splendour of the white
Electrically glowing night,
Wind-wafted from some perfumed dell.   75
Tumultuously there loudly rose
Above the Neva's surge and swell,
With amorous ecstasies and throes,
And lyric spasms of wildest wail,
The love-song of a nightingale.   80

I see her still beside me. Yea.
As if it were but yesterday.
I hear her tell with cheek aflame
Her ineradicable shame –
So sweet a flower in such vile hands!   85
Oh, loved and lost beyond recall!
Like one who hardly understands,
I heard the story of her fall,
The odious barter of her youth,
Of beauty, innocence, and truth,   90
Of all that honest women hold
Most sacred – for the sake of gold.
A weary seamstress, half a child,
Left unprotected in the street,
Where, when so hungry, you would meet   95
All sorts of tempters that beguiled.
Oh, infamous and senseless clods.
Basely to taint so pure a heart,
And make a maid fit for the gods
A creature of the common mart!   100
She spoke quite simply of things vile
Of devils with an angel's face;
It seemed the sunshine of her smile
Must purify the foulest place.
She told me all – she would be true –   105
Told me of things too sad, too bad;
And, looking in her eyes' clear blue
My passion nearly drove me mad!
I tried to speak, but tried in vain;

A sob rose to my throat as dry 110
As ashes – for between us twain
A murdered virgin seemed to lie.
And through the splendour of the white
Electrically glowing night,
Wind wafted from some perfumed dell, 115
Tumultuously there loudly rose,
Above the Neva's surge and swell,
With amorous ecstasies and throes,
And lyric spasms of wildest wail,
The love-song of a nightingale. 120

Poor craven creature! What was I,
To sit in judgment on her life,
Who dared not make this child my wife,
And lift her up to love's own sky?
This poor lost child we all – yes, all – 125
Had helped to hurry to her fall,
Making a social leper of
God's creature consecrate to love.
I looked at her – she smiled no more;
She understood it all before 130
A syllable had passed my lips;
And like a horrible eclipse,
Which blots the sunlight from the skies.
A blankness overspread her eyes –
The blankness as of one who dies. 135
I knew how much she loved me – knew
How pure and passionately true
Her love for me, which made her tell
What scorched her like the flames of hell.
And I, I loved her too, so much, 140
So dearly, that I dared not touch
Her lips that had been kissed in sin;
But with a reverential thrill
I took her work-worn hand and thin,
And kissed her fingers, showing still 145
Where needle-pricks had marred the skin.
And, ere I knew, a hot tear fell,
Scalding the place which I had kissed,
As between clenching teeth I hissed
Our irretrievable farewell. 150
And through the smouldering glow of night,
Mixed with the shining morning light
Wind-wafted from some perfumed dell,
Above the Neva's surge and swell,
With lyric spasms, as from a throat 155
Which dying breathes a faltering note,

There faded o'er the silent vale
The last sob of a nightingale.

A Fantasy

I was an Arab,
  I loved my horse;
Swift as an arrow
  He swept the course.

Sweet as a lamb   5
  He came to hand;
He was the flower
  Of all the land.

Through lonely nights
  I rode afar;   10
God lit His lights –
  Star upon star.

God's in the desert;
  His breath the air:
Beautiful desert,   15
  Boundless and bare!

Free as the wild wind,
  Light as a foal;
Ah, there is room there
  To stretch one's soul.   20

Far reached my thought.
  Scant were my needs:
A few bananas
  And lotus seeds.

Sparkling as water   25
  Cool in the shade,
Ibrahim's daughter,
  Beautiful maid.

Out of thy Kulleh,
  Fairest and first,   30
Give me to drink,
  Quencher of thirst.

I am athirst, girl;
  Parched with desire.
Love in my bosom   35
  Burns as a fire.

Green thy oasis,
  Waving with Palms;
Oh, be no niggard,
  Maid, with thy alms.   40

Kiss me with kisses,
  Buds of thy mouth,
Sweeter than Cassia
  Fresh from the South.

Bind me with tresses,   45
  Clasp with a curl;
And in caresses
  Stifle me, girl.

I was an Arab
  Ages ago!   50
Hence this home-sickness
  And all my woe.

Entangled

I stood as one enchanted,
  All in the forest deep:
As one that wond'ring wanders,
  Dream-bound within his sleep.

A thousand rustling footsteps   5
  Pattered upon the ground;
A thousand whisp'ring voices
  Made the wide silence, sound.

Some murmured deep and deeper,
  Like waves in solemn seas;   10
Some breathèd sweet and sweeter,
  Like elves on moon-lit leas.

Tall ferns, washed down in sunlight,
  Beckoned with fingers green;
Tall flowers nodded strangely,   15
  With white and glimm'ring sheen;

They sighed, they sang so softly,
  They stretched their arms to me;
My heart, it throbbed so wildly,
  In weird tumultuous glee.   20

I staggered in the mosses,
  It seemed to drag me down

Into the gleaming bushes;
  To fall, to sink, to drown.

When lo! thro' scared foliage,   25
  A lovely bird did fly;
And looked at me so knowing,
  With bright and curious eye;

It broke out into warbles,
  And singing sped away;   30
But I, like one awakened,
  Fled down the mossy way.

The Beautiful Beeshareen Boy

Beautiful, black-eyed boy,
  O lithe-limbed Beeshareen!
Face that finds no maid coy,
  Page for some peerless queen:
Some Orient queen of old,   5
Sumptuous in woven gold,
Close-clinging fold on fold,
  Lightning, with gems between.

Bred in the desert, where
  Only to breathe and be   10
Alive in living air
  Is finest ecstasy;
Where just to ride or rove,
With sun or stars above,
Intoxicates like love,   15
  When love shall come to thee.

Thy lovely limbs are bare;
  Only a rag, in haste,
Draped with a princely air,
  Girdles thy slender waist.   20
And gaudy beads and charms,
Dangling from neck and arms,
Ward off dread spells and harms
  Of Efreets of the waste.

Caressed of wind and sun,   25
  Across the white-walled town
Fawnlike we saw thee run,
  Light Love in Mocha brown!
Wild Cupid, without wings,

Twanging thy viol strings!   30
With crocodiles and rings
    Bartered for half a crown.

Spoilt darling of our bark,
    Smiling with teeth as white
As when across the dark   35
    There breaks a flash of light.
And what a careless grace
Showed in thy gait and pace
Eyes starlike in a face
    Sweet as a Nubian night!   40

Better than Felt or Fez,
    High on thy forehead set,
Countless in lock and tress,
    Waved a wild mane of jet.
Kings well might envy thee   45
What courts but rarely see,
Curls of rich ebony
    Coiled in a coronet.

Lo – in dim days long since –
    The strolling Almehs tell,   50
Thou shouldst have been a prince,
    Boy of the ebon fell!
If truth the poet sings,
Thy tribe, oh Beduin, springs
From those lost tribes of Kings,   55
    Once Kings in Israel.

Ah me! the camp-fires gleam
    Out yonder, where the sands
Fade like a lotos dream
    In hollow twilight lands.   60
Our sail swells to the blast,
Our boat speeds far and fast,
Farewell! And to the last
    Smile, waving friendly hands.

From England' storm-girt isle,   65
    O'er seas where seagulls wail,
Rocked on the rippling Nile,
    We drift with drooping sail.
On waters hushed at night,
Where stars of Egypt write   70
In hieroglyphs of light
    Their undeciphered tale.

Forlorn sits Assouan;
　Where is her boy, her pride? –
Now in the lamplit Khan,			75
　Now by the riverside,
Or where the Soudanese,
Under mimosa trees,
Chaunt mournful melodies,
　We've sought him far and wide.			80

Oh, desert-nurtured Child,
　How dared they carry thee,
Far from thy native Wild,
　Across the Western Sea?
Packed off, poor boy, at last,			85
With many a plaster cast
Of plinth and pillar vast,
　And waxen mummies piled!

Ah! just like other ware,
　For a lump sum or so			90
Shipped to the World's great Fair –
　The big Chicago Show!
With mythic beasts and thin
Beetles and bulls with wings,
And imitation Sphinx,			95
　Ranged row on curious row!

Beautiful, black-eyed boy;
　Ah me! how strange it is
That thou, the desert's joy,
　Whom heavenly winds would kiss,			100
With Ching and Chan-hwa ware,
Blue pots and bronzes rare,
Shouldst now be over there
　Shown at Porkopolis.

Gone like a lovely dream,			105
　Child of the starry smile;
Gone from the glowing stream
　Glassing its greenest isle!
We've sought, but sought in vain;
Thou wilt not come again,			110
Never for bliss or pain,
　Home to thy orphaned Nile.

On a Forsaken Lark's Nest

Lo, where left 'mid the sheaves, cut down by the iron-fanged reaper,
Eating its way as it clangs fast through the wavering wheat,
Lies the nest of a lark, whose little brown eggs could not keep her
As she, affrighted and scared, fled from the harvester's feet.

Ah, what a heartful of song that now will never awaken, 5
Closely packed in the shell, awaited love's fostering,
That should have quickened to life what, now a-cold and forsaken,
Never, enamoured of light, will meet the dawn on the wing.

Ah, what pæans of joy, what raptures no mortal can measure,
Sweet as honey that's sealed in the cells of the honeycomb, 10
Would have ascended on high in jets of mellifluous pleasure,
Would have dropped from the clouds to nest in its gold-curtained home.

Poor, pathetic brown eggs! Oh, pulses that never will quicken
Music mute in the shell that hath been turned to a tomb!
Many a sweet human singer, chilled and adversity-stricken, 15
Withers benumbed in a world his joy might have helped to illume.

from *The Ascent of Man*

As compressed within the bounded shell
Boundless Ocean seems to surge and swell,
Haunting echoes of an infinite whole
Moan and murmur through Man's finite soul.

Chaunts of Life

I

Struck out of dim fluctuant forces and shock of electrical vapour,
Repelled and attracted the atoms flashed mingling in union primeval,
And over the face of the waters far heaving in limitless twilight
Auroral pulsations thrilled faintly, and, striking the blank heaving surface,
The measureless speed of their motion now leaped into light on the waters. 5
And lo, from the womb of the waters, upheaved in volcanic convulsion,
Ribbed and ravaged and rent there rose bald peaks and the rocky
Heights of confederate mountains compelling the fugitive vapours
To take a form as they passed them and float as clouds through the azure.
Mountains, the broad-bosomed mothers of torrents and rivers perennial, 10
Feeding the rivers and plains with patient persistence, till slowly,
In the swift passage of æons recorded in stone by Time's graver,
There germ grey films of the lichen and mosses and palm-ferns gigantic,

And jungle of tropical forest fantastical branches entwining,
And limitless deserts of sand and wildernesses primeval.　　　　　15

II

Lo, moving o'er chaotic waters,
　　Love dawned upon the seething waste,
Transformed in ever new avatars
　　It moved without or pause or haste:
Like sap that moulds the leaves of May　　　　　20
It wrought within the ductile clay.

And vaguely in the pregnant deep,
　　Clasped by the glowing arms of light
From an eternity of sleep
　　Within unfathomed gulfs of night　　　　　25
A pulse stirred in the plastic slime
Responsive to the rhythm of Time.

Enkindled in the mystic dark
　　Life built herself a myriad forms,
And, flashing its electric spark　　　　　30
　　Through films and cells and pulps and worms,
Flew shuttlewise above, beneath,
Weaving the web of life and death.

And multiplying in the ocean,
　　Amorphous, rude, colossal things　　　　　35
Lolled on the ooze in lazy motion,
　　Armed with grim jaws or uncouth wings;
Helpless to lift their cumbering bulk
They lurch like some dismasted hulk.

And virgin forest, verdant plain,　　　　　40
　　The briny sea, the balmy air,
Each blade of grass and globe of rain,
　　And glimmering cave and gloomy lair
Began to swarm with beasts and birds,
With floating fish and fleet-foot herds.　　　　　45

The lust of life's delirious fires
　　Burned like a fever in their blood,
Now pricked them on with fierce desires,
　　Now drove them famishing for food,
To seize coy females in the fray,　　　　　50
Or hotly hunted hunt for prey.

And amorously urged them on
  In wood or wild to court their mate,
Proudly displaying in the sun
  With antics strange and looks elate,   55
The vigour of their mighty thews
Or charm of million-coloured hues.

There crouching 'mid the scarlet bloom,
  Voluptuously the leopard lies,
And through the tropic forest gloom   60
  The flaming of his feline eyes
Stirs with intoxicating stress
The pulses of the leopardess.

Or two swart bulls of self-same age
  Meet furiously with thunderous roar,   65
And lash together, blind with rage,
  And clanging horns that fain would gore
Their rival, and so win the prize
Of those impassive female eyes.

Or in the nuptial days of spring,   70
  When April kindles bush and brier,
Like rainbows that have taken wing,
  Or palpitating gems of fire,
Bright butterflies in one brief day
Live but to love and pass away.   75

And herds of horses scour the plains,
  The thickets scream with bird and beast
The love of life burns in their veins,
  And from the mightiest to the least
Each preys upon the other's life   80
In inextinguishable strife.

War rages on the teeming earth;
  The hot and sanguinary fight
Begins with each new creature's birth:
  A dreadful war where might is right;   85
Where still the strongest slay and win,
Where weakness is the only sin.

There is no truce to this drawn battle,
  Which ends but to begin again;
The drip of blood, the hoarse death-rattle,   90
  The roar of rage, the shriek of pain,
Are rife in fairest grove and dell,
Turning earth's flowery haunts to hell.

A hell of hunger, hatred, lust,
 Which goads all creatures here below,   95
Or blindworm wriggling in the dust,
 Or penguin in the Polar snow:
A hell where there is none to save,
Where life is life's insatiate grave.

And in the long portentous strife,   100
 Where types are tried even as by fire,
Where life is whetted upon life
 And step by panting step mounts higher,
Apes lifting hairy arms now stand
And free the wonder-working hand.   105

They raise a light, aërial house
 On shafts of widely branching trees,
Where, harboured warily, each spouse
 May feed her little ape in peace,
Green cradled in his heaven-roofed bed,   110
Leaves rustling lullabies o'erhead.

And lo, 'mid reeking swarms of earth
 Grim struggling in the primal wood,
A new strange creature hath its birth:
 Wild – stammering – nameless – shameless – nude; 115
Spurred on by want, held in by fear,
He hides his head in caverns drear.

Most unprotected of earth's kin,
 His fight for life that seems so vain
Sharpens his senses, till within   120
 The twilight mazes of his brain,
Like embryos within the womb,
Thought pushes feelers through the gloom.

And slowly in the fateful race
 It grows unconscious, till at length   125
The helpless savage dares to face
 The cave-bear in his grisly strength;
For stronger than its bulky thews
He feels a force that grows with use.

From age to dumb unnumbered age,   130
 By dim gradations long and slow,
He reaches on from stage to stage,
 Through fear and famine, weal and woe
And, compassed round with danger, still
Prolongs his life by craft and skill.   135

With cunning hand he shapes the flint,
　　He carves the horn with strange device,
He splits the rebel block by dint
　　Of effort – till one day there flies
A spark of fire from out the stone:　　　　　　　　　　　　140
Fire which shall make the world his own . . .

The Leading of Sorrow

. . . Peace ye call this? Call this justice, meted
　　Equally to rich and poor alike?
Better than this peace the battle's heated
　　Cannon-balls that ask not whom they strike!
Better than this masquerade of culture　　　　　　　　　　5
　　Hiding strange hyæna appetites,
The frank ravening of the raw-necked vulture
　　As its beak the senseless carrion smites.

What of men in bondage, toiling blunted
　　In the roaring factory's lurid gloom?　　　　　　　　　10
What of cradled infants starved and stunted?
　　What of woman's nameless martyrdom?
The all-seeing sun shines on unheeding,
　　Shines by night the calm, unruffled moon,
Though the human myriads, preying, bleeding,　　　　　　　15
　　Put creation harshly out of tune.

'Hence, ah, hence' – I sobbed in quivering passion –
　　'From these fearful haunts of fiendish men!
Better far the plain, carnivorous fashion
　　Which is practised in the lion's den.'　　　　　　　　　20
And I fled – yet staggering still did follow
　　In the footprints of my shrouded guide –
To the sea-caves echoing with the hollow
　　Immemorial moaning of the tide.

Sinking, swelling roared the wintry ocean,　　　　　　　　25
　　Pitch-black chasms struck with flying blaze,
As the cloud-winged storm-sky's sheer commotion
　　Showed the blank Moon's mute Medusa face
White o'er wastes of water – surges crashing
　　Over surges in the formless gloom,　　　　　　　　　　30
And a mastless hulk, with great seas washing
　　Her scourged flanks, pitched toppling to her doom.

Through the crash of wave on wave gigantic,
　　Through the thunder of the hurricane,
My wild heart in breaking shrilled with frantic　　　　　　35
　　Exultation – 'Chaos come again!

Yea, let earth be split and cloven asunder
   With man's still accumulating curse –
Life is but a momentary blunder
   In the cycle of the Universe.   40

'Yea, let earth with forest-belted mountains,
   Hills and valleys, cataracts and plains,
With her clouds and storms and fires and fountains,
   Pass with all her rolling sphere contains,
Melt, dissolve again into the ocean,   45
   Ocean fade into a nebulous haze!'
And I sank back without sense or motion
   'Neath the blank Moon's mute Medusa face.

Moments, years, or ages passed, when, lifting
   Freezing lids, I felt the heavens on high,   50
And, innumerable as the sea-sands drifting,
   Stars unnumbered drifted through the sky.
Rhythmical in luminous rotation,
   In dædalian maze they reel and fly,
And their rushing light is Time's pulsation   55
   In his passage through Eternity.

Constellated suns, fresh lit, declining,
   Were ignited now, now quenched in space,
Rolling round each other, or inclining
   Orb to orb in multi-coloured rays.   60
Ever showering from their flaming fountains
   Light more light on each far-circling earth,
Till life stirred crepuscular seas, and mountains
   Heaved convulsive with the throes of birth.

And the noble brotherhood of planets,   65
   Knitted each to each by links of light,
Circled round their suns, nor knew a minute's
   Lapse or languor in their ceaseless flight.
And pale moons and rings and burning splinters
   Of wrecked worlds swept round their parent spheres,   70
Clothed with spring or sunk in polar winters
   As their sun draws nigh or disappears.

Still new vistas of new stars – far dwindling –
   Through the firmament like dewdrops roll,
Torches of the Cosmos which enkindling   75
   Flash their revelation on the soul.
Yea, One spake there – though nor form nor feature
   Shown – a Voice came from the peaks of time: –
'Wilt thou judge me, wilt thou curse me, Creature
   Whom I raised up from the Ocean slime?   80

'Long I waited – ages rolled o'er ages –
  As I crystallized in granite rocks,
Struggling dumb through immemorial stages,
  Glacial æons, fiery earthquake shocks.
In fierce throbs of flame or slow upheaval,   85
  Speck by tiny speck, I topped the seas,
Leaped from earth's dark womb, and in primeval
  Forests shot up shafts of mammoth trees.

'Through a myriad forms I yearned and panted,
  Putting forth quick shoots in endless swarms –   90
Giant-hoofed, sharp-tusked, or finned or planted
  Writhing on the reef with pinioned arms.
I have climbed from reek of sanguine revels
  In Cimmerian wood and thorny wild,
Slowly upwards to the dawnlit levels   95
  Where I bore thee, oh my youngest Child!

'Oh, my heir and hope of my to-morrow,
  I – I draw thee on through fume and fret,
Croon to thee in pain and call through sorrow,
  Flowers and stars take for thy alphabet.   100
Through the eyes of animals appealing,
  Feel my fettered spirit yearn to thine,
Who in storm of will and clash of feeling,
  Shape the life that shall be – the divine.

'Oh, redeem me from my tiger rages,   105
  Reptile greed, and foul hyæna lust;
With the hero's deeds, the thoughts of sages,
  Sow and fructify this passive dust;
Drop in dew and healing love of woman
  On the bloodstained hands of hungry strife,   110
Till there break from passion of the Human
  Morning-glory of transfigured life.

'I have cast my burden on thy shoulder;
  Unimagined potencies have given
That from formless Chaos thou shalt mould her   115
  And translate gross earth to luminous heaven.
Bear, oh, bear the terrible compulsion,
  Flinch not from the path thy fathers trod,
From Man's martyrdom in slow convulsion
  Will be born the infinite goodness – God.'   120

Ceased the Voice: and as it ceased it drifted
  Like the seashell's inarticulate moan;
From the Deep, on wings of flame uplifted,
  Rose the sun rejoicing and alone.

Laughed in light upon the living ocean, 125
    Danced and rocked itself upon the spray,
And its shivered beams in twinkling motion
    Gleamed like star-motes of the Milky Way.

And beside me in the golden morning
    I beheld my shrouded phantom-guide; 130
But no longer sorrow-veiled and mourning –
    It became transfigured by my side.
And I knew – as one escaped from prison
    Sees old things again with fresh surprise –
It was Love himself, Love re-arisen 135
    With the Eternal shining through his eyes.

'Violet Fane' (1843–1905)

Mary Montgomerie Lamb was the daughter of a gentleman whose estate was in Beauport, Sussex. She began to write when she was quite young adopting the pseudonym of 'Violet Fane' because she feared parental disapproval. She married an Irish landowner Henry Singleton in 1864 and bore four children. From 1872 onwards she also started to publish, producing volumes of poetry, a verse-novel, several novels and collection of essays. After her husband's death in 1893 she married Sir Philip Henry Wodehouse Currie (later Baron Currie of Hawley) who was an ambassador which meant that she lived in Constantinople and later in Rome.

Violet Fane's attitude to the purpose of poetry is probably summed up in 'The Poet': 'The poet was not born to teach/ A moral lesson to mankind;/ He hath no solemn creed to preach,/ But, fancy-free and unconfined,/ By sunlit glade or gray sea-beach/ His lyre wakes to the shifting wind.// And if he be a minstrel true,/ Its ev'ry sound should charm your ears ...' (Fane 1880: 53). 'Charming' though many of her verses are, she also writes on some social issues, most notably little ballads on the 'fallen woman' theme where, typically, the lord betrays the peasant girl and she dies with her baby. Her removal to foreign parts late in life does seem to have given her a new strand and tone in *Under Cross and Crescent* (1896) and *Betwixt Two Seas* (1900). Cynical and brittle though these poems are, 'The Siren' offers a pleasing irony in the defamiliarization of the Siren's point of view, and an effective antidote to the numerous 'dead adored women' poems written by Victorian men.

M.R.

Fane, Violet (1880) *Collected Verses*, London.
—— (1896) *Under Cross and Crescent, Poems*, London.

In an Irish Churchyard

Amongst these graves where good men lie,
    Mute, ozier-bound, in dreamless sleep,

Above whose heads the browsing sheep
And careless painted butterfly
   Pasture and sport in summer grass,   5

Brown as the blasted Dead-Sea fruit,
  As banned to barrenness and dearth,
  Behold yon patch of rusty earth,
Whereon no turf has taken root,
   No summer shadows flit and pass,   10

Whilst here, a garden neat and trim,
  All fuchsia-fringed and pansy-starred,
  With gilded gateways locked and barred,
And double-daisies for a rim
   Surrounds a tomb, with foot and head   15

Guarded by angel-forms that weep,
  In marble from Carrara's mines,
  Whilst Fame a laurel chaplet twines,
And golden letters, graven deep,
   Blazon the honours of the dead.   20

He died as clarions smote the air
  To tell of vict'ry and renown;
  They brought him to his native town,
Near which the lands and lordships were
   That owed him fealty in the west   25

She died in those despairing days,
  Bowed down by all the griefs she had,
  And only that they deemed her mad,
They buried her by no cross-ways,
   And drove no stake into her breast.   30

She sleeps beneath yon rusty peat,
  Withered as by avenging fires;
  Amongst the noblest of his sires
He lies with angels at his feet,
   And golden gates to keep secure.   35

And 'twixt the two, all ozier-bound,
  Half melted into mother earth,
  Scarce two feet long, by one in girth,
A little nameless baby-mound
   Pleads for the sins of rich and poor.   40

The Siren

'My voice is sweeter than the lute,
  My form is passing fair,
My lips are like the scarlet fruit
  The coral branches bear.

'My teeth are whiter than the pearls   5
  Men seek beneath the brine,
And when I shake my dripping curls
  Far brighter jewels shine;

'My russet curls, whose golden tips
  Half hide a breast that swells   10
As pink and pearly as the lips
  That laugh on spike-back'd shells;

'My eyes reflect the glimmer cast
  When seas lie calm and deep,
Where, under rotting spar and mast,   15
  The silent sailors sleep.

'Oft have I dragged them from the sands, –
  They cannot make demur, –
And pull'd the gold rings from their hands:
  They neither speak nor stir,   20

'So stark they lie! Yet one, alone,
  Awoke to find me fair, –
(This harp is made of his breast-bone,
  Its strings were once his hair!)

'A merry moon we pass'd, and more,   25
  And then upon him came
Some wanton mem'ry of the shore,
  He breathed a woman's name;

'Wherefore I made him sleep again,
  So sound, he could not stir;   30
But first I suck'd his heart and brain,
  Lest he should dream of her,

'Before he slept he spake strange words;
  These were the words he said:
"Your song is blither than the birds',   35
  Your lips are ripe and red,

' "Your breast is white, your eyes are blue,
　　Yet you cannot understand,
Or love your love as the maidens do
　　That live upon the land."　　　　　　　　　　　　　　40

'So, since, whene'er the sun is low,
　　And length'ning shadows fall,
And straying lovers come and go
　　Along the grey sea-wall,

'Amongst the rocks I crouch me down　　　　　　　　45
　　To hear what they may say,
And learn this thing I have not known –
　　To love the land-girls' way!

'But oft I hear them moan and sigh,
　　And often weep for woe;　　　　　　　　　　　　　50
The summer nights are going by,
　　Yet this is all I know!

'So, mine must be the wiser way,
　　For all my sweetheart said!
I made far merrier than they　　　　　　　　　　　　55
　　The moon that I was wed!

'And he was mine, – my very own!
　　I clasp'd him firm and fair! . . .
(This harp is made of his breast-bone,
　　Its strings were once his hair!)'　　　　　　　　　60

Caroline Lindsay (1844–1912)

The daughter of Hannah Mayer Rothschild and Henry Fitzroy MP, Caroline Lady Lindsay grew up in a privileged circle and spent her life among artistic people who encouraged her talents for painting, music and writing. All the same she had her trials. Caroline married Sir Henry Coutts Lindsay in 1864 but separated from him in the early 1880s. It was after this that she began her writing career with a curious novel called *Caroline* (1889) where the heroine is heir to a large estate and suffers many trials as the result of the attentions of fortune hunters. The fictional Caroline gets the right man in the end, but the real one apparently didn't. A long and debilitating illness followed, commemorated in a slight but touching little volume called *About Robins* (1889) where Caroline contemplates the cheeriness of the robin and takes it as a totem for human life.

It clearly worked, – for throughout the 1890s and right up until her death Caroline published three more novels, numerous volumes of poetry, four plays, verses for children, a patriotic poem on the Boer War (*For England*, 1900) which was dedicated by permission to the Princess of Wales, a volume of bracing verses for hospital patients, and a fourteen-page pamphlet published by Hatchards the booksellers on *The Art of Poetry with Regard to Women Writers* (1899). Caroline also spend some time in Venice and corresponded with artistic and literary friends especially John Everett Millais, the Burne-Joneses and Robert Browning.

Lady Lindsay's best work is in the lyric vein and her style is most effective when controlled by an exact form – the two sonnets included here are good examples. 'Love or Fame' sets up the common Victorian dilemma for the woman writer, and it's interesting to note that the passage of time and the rallying cries of the 'women's-righters' during the nineteenth century make no difference at all to the conclusions of this poem which can be directly compared with Felicia Hemans's 'Woman and Fame' where the same sentiments are expressed. 'To My Own Face', on the other hand, is a significant development in women's poetry because it makes the poet herself the subject of the poem by using the mirror or portrait which reflects back another self. This figure, where the woman poet makes herself into her own Muse, does appear in Victorian women's poetry – see the opening passages of Barrett Browning's *Aurora Leigh* – but it is much more common in the work of twentieth-century writers.

M.R.

Lindsay, Caroline (1889) *Caroline*, [A Novel], London.
—— (1889) *Lyrics and Other Poems*, London.
—— (1889) *About Robins. Songs, facts, and legends collected and illustrated by Caroline Lindsay*, London.
—— (1894) *The King's Last Vigil*, London.
—— (1899) *The Art of Poetry with Regard to Women Writers*, London.

Love or Fame

A maiden to the Delphic temple came,
And hid her brows, and at the shrine bent low.
'What wilt thou?' 'Fain would I the future know.'
'Of two gifts then have one. Choose: Love or Fame?'
'O Sun-God! Laurels grant, a deathless name!   5
So at my song far nations' tears may flow,
And men remember though from hence I go;
For in my breast I feel the sacred flame.'

Years pass. A weeping woman kneels again,
For mercy to the oracle she sues: 10
'O give me Love! Take back the bay-crown'd lyre!
Life dawns for me; till now I've lived in vain.
Content am I all earthly fame to lose
If one true heart me for its guest desire.'

To My Own Face

A greeting to thee, O most trusty friend!
That hast so steadfastly companioned me.
What other, say, in this can equal thee,

Who cam'st to life with me, with me shalt end?
Poor face of mine! Right often dost thou lend   5
A smile to hide some smileless thoughts that be
Bound deep in heart, and oft thy kind eyes see
My soul's great grief and bid their ears attend.

Ah, childish fairness, seeming near, yet far,
Prized tenderly by dear ones pass'd away,   10
Fain I'd recall it! Next, an oval grace
Of girlhood; for thy woman's sorrows are
Stamped now on lips and forehead day by day,
Yet God's own image thou – O human face!

L. S. Bevington (1845–1895)

Louisa Sarah Bevington was the eldest of eight children (seven of them girls) born to Quaker parents, Louisa and Alexander Bevington. She was brought up in London, and published her first volume of poems in 1876 under the Barrett Browningesque pseudonym of 'Arbor Leigh'. These already show signs of the evolutionary meliorism and religious questioning which mark her later work. Her article on 'Atheism and Morality', published in the *Nineteenth Century* in 1879, elicited a strong reply from a cleric defending the Christian basis of morality. Like George Eliot and Constance Naden, Bevington was influenced by the work of Herbert Spencer. In 1881, at his request, she wrote a reply to another attack on the ethics of evolutionary theory. In it, she forcefully defends the larger moral scope of rationalism, on the grounds that religious conservatism has traditionally supported the worst British atrocities in the Colonies, including the recent suppression by Governor Eyre of the Morant Bay uprising in Jamaica. 'Orthodox Conservatism', she declares, 'is inclined to keep its theory of world-wide humanity for its wife and children to listen to, duly couched in Jewish phraseology, on Sunday' (*Fortnightly Review*, 36 (August 1881), 191). As a result, she concludes, 'one may long for the time when religion shall no longer have the power to paralyse the morality it professes to patronise' (194). In 1883 she married a German artist, Ignatz Guggenberger, but it seems the marriage only lasted a few years.

By the early 1890s Louisa had joined the increasingly vocal and internationally organized anarchist movement, of which the mild-mannered exile, Prince Kropotkin, was the main figurehead in Britain. For much of the 1880s and 90s the anarchists jostled for public notice against the growing socialist and trade union movements, eventually to be absorbed by them. Charlotte Wilson, who founded and supported the anarchist journal *Freedom*, was also a key member of the Fabians and friend of E. Nesbit, whom Bevington may have met. Anarchism, however, was always more eccentric and utopian than socialism, and perhaps for that reason was especially attractive to women. None the less, its espousal of violence finally alienated the general public. In the early 1890s Louisa was writing regularly for the anarchist journals, *Freedom, Commonweal* and *Liberty*, as well as lecturing at the Autonomie club on atheism and religion. In 1894 her article 'Why I Am an Expropriationist' was issued as a pamphlet, in a series which included William Morris's 'Why I Am a Communist'. Here

Bevington takes a straightforwardly Proudhonian line that 'property-holding is an abuse in itself' (1894: 10), and argues for a society in which government has been banished and all goods are held in common. Characteristically, the romantic and primitivist ideals of anarchism overwhelm the practical realities of social organization. The self-evident injustices and evils of late Victorian England, regularly exposed in all the anarchist journals, provided sufficient justification for an extremist, utopian goal.

When, in 1894, a suspected anarchist blew himself up while carrying a bomb towards the Greenwich Observatory (the incident which inspired Conrad's *The Secret Agent*), one of Bevington's letters was quoted to prove, though far from definitively, that the culprit had been set up by the police (Oliver 1983: 105–6). Evidently she was familiar with many of the London anarchist set by this time. In an article on 'Anarchism and Violence', published by the Liberty Press after her death, Bevington condones the use of violence as a final resort against institutionalized injustice: 'For the blind and their leaders all violence is held to be vile, except legalised and privileged violence on an enormous scale' (1896: 9). There is, she declares, 'such a thing as warring against the causes of war' (10).

When she died in 1895 Bevington was a recognized anarchist poet. The journal *The Torch*, which was founded and printed by the children of William Michael Rossetti (nieces and nephews of Christina), carried as epigraph to each edition four lines from a poem by Bevington:

> 'Tis our generation must fight the last fight against Warfare,
> Must hurl the God Mammon in depths of oblivion's sea,
> Unmask and drive from us all tyrannous powers of Darkness,
> And make the sweet planet a home of humanity – FREE.

The announcement of Bevington's death in the December issue of 1895, only a year after the death of Christina Rossetti, carried the pointed (and typically misprinted) comment that her funeral was 'withont any religious ceremony whatever' (*The Torch of Anarchy*, 2 (18 December 1895), 104). The differences as well as the connection between the two poets is a reminder of the sheer diversity of beliefs and attitudes in late Victorian society. Rossetti's tormented faith finds in Bevington's crusading atheism both a powerful opposite and, perhaps, a hidden explanation.

Paradoxically, however, Bevington's poetry lacks the darker, imaginative recesses of Rossetti's, and often sounds, in spite of its secularist goals, more religious and high-minded than hers. No doubt something of her early Quakerism was displaced into her equally fervent anarchism, as the poem ' "Dreamers?" ' with its fond memory of a 'comrade' Christ, suggests. Elsewhere, her verse draws on evolutionary theory to decentre, as do Field, Naden and Blind, the egocentric power of human passion ("Egoisme à Deux" ' and 'Measurements'), as well as to propose a progressivist political vision of the future ('In Memoriam'). Darwinism, with its large-scale, natural, geological imagery, provided a useful model for the idea of inevitable social change. Probably her most moving poem, however, is 'One More Bruised Heart!' which, like many of the news items in *The Torch* (though more decorously than they), touches on the issue of child sexual abuse. As in the case of many of these women poets, Bevington uses the traditionally courtly sonnet form for an ironically different and, in this case, brutal subject matter.

A.L.

Bevington, L. S. (1882) *Poems, Lyrics, and Sonnets*, London.
—— (1894) 'Why I Am an Expropriationist' [pamphlet].
—— (1895) *Liberty Lyrics*, London, James Tochatti's Liberty Press.
—— (1896) 'Anarchism and Violence' [article], London, Liberty Press.

Horowitz, Irving Louis ed. (1964) *The Anarchists*, New York, Dell.
Oliver, Hermia (1983) *The International Anarchist Movement in Late Victorian London*, London and Canberra, Croom Helm.

'Egoisme à Deux'

When the great universe hung nebulous
  Betwixt the unprevented and the need,
Was it foreseen that you and I should be? –
    Was it decreed?

While time leaned onward through eternities,   5
  Unrippled by a breath and undistraught,
Lay there at leisure Will that we should breathe? –
    Waited a Thought?

When the warm swirl of chaos-elements
  Fashioned the chance that woke to sentient strife,   10
Did there a Longing seek, and hasten on
    Our mutual life?

That flux of many accidents but now
  That brought you near and linked your hand in mine, –
That fused our souls in love's most final faith, –   15
    Was it divine?

Measurements

Our world is very little in the sky,
  Far off she must be just a mote to see;
  And on the tiny ball creep tinier we,
To live a very little while, and die.

My love is very great within my heart;   5
  It sees in two dear eyes, infinity,
  It finds in one sweet hour, eternity,
It has one measure: – nearness, or apart.

Ah, well! both things are true as truth can be!
  The world is little and my love is great;   10
  Yet who would rise triumphant over fate
Earth's breadth, love's narrowness, must learn to see.

One More Bruised Heart!

One more bruised heart laid bare! one victim more!
  One more wail heard! Oh, is there never end
  Of all these passionate agonies, that rend
Young hopes to tatters through enslavements sore?
So long, pale child, your patient spirit bore   5
  Its wrong in secret, ere you sought a friend;
  And yet, what love of mine can ever mend
Again for you the veil your tyrant tore?

Oh, there are woes too bitter to be shown!
  Oh, there are tears too burning to be seen!   10
  Yet purest sympathy, select and clean,
May feel the agony its very own.
Sweet slave-child, whom your voiceless griefs oppress,
I cannot cure; I may in part express.

'Dreamers?'

'Dreamers?' Ah, no! else he was a dreamer,
  Our crucified brother of long, long ago;
Arrested, and jeered at; 'seditious;' 'blasphemer;'
  And legally slain, lest the people should *know*

Offence against privileged, orthodox 'order,'   5
  That stirring of crowds by the straight word and true;
No wonder respectable Dives condemned him,
  And politic Roman, and clerical Jew.

Remember the agonised cry of desertion
  Lest haply the whole had been suffered in vain;   10
Ah! would he could know of this tardy awakening
  Of Peoples at last, as the message grows plain.

That 'Kingdom' *is coming*, on earth as 'within you,'
  The reign of sweet peace, and goodwill amongst men;
'Tis suffering violence? Yes, in the taking;   15
  Yet, taken, there shall not be fighting again.

Dear comrades, hold on, 'mid reproach and derision,
  To rid the old world of its thraldom and woe;
And still in the pauses of conflict remember
  That lone one, our comrade of long, long ago.   20

In Memoriam

Mad, as the world calls mad,
  See Anarchy's few;
Fighting the False and the Bad
  In all that they do;
Foreing a way for the Glad,   5
  The Pure, and the True.

Bolder and clearer it grows –
  The Anarchist task;
Liberty's plausible foes
  To assail and unmask;   10
Handing the torch as it glows
  To all who may ask.

Great! oh, exceedingly great,
  The Anarchists' claim!
Fusing the falsehood of State   15
  In unquenchable flame;
Breaking the fetters of fate
  In Humanity's name.

Breathing with fiery breath
  On the mammonite crew;   20
Fearless, in splendor of faith,
  Of the worst they can do;
Blessed, in life and in death,
  O beneficent few!

Emily Hickey (1845–1924)

Emily Hickey was born in Macmine Castle, Co. Wexford, where her father was Rector. At her strictly Protestant school such 'frivolous' authors as Shakespeare were banned, but later in her teens she discovered the poetry of Barrett Browning and started to write verse herself. In her early twenties she moved to London, where she lived for a time with the publishers Macmillans, who introduced her into various literary circles. She later took lodgings of her own and worked as a secretary, a private tutor and a governess. She attended lectures at University College and became a keen supporter of higher education for women. For eighteen years she was lecturer in English Literature at the famous North London Collegiate School for Girls, founded in 1850 by Miss Buss. She was friendly with Robert Browning and frequently gave readings of his work. In 1881 she became co-founder and honorary secretary of the Browning Society.

    In that same year she published a collection of poems, *A Sculptor and Other Poems*, which was followed by *Verse-Tales, Lyrics, and Translations* (1889). Her most interesting volume, however, was *Michael Villiers, Idealist, and Other Poems* (1891). Clearly influenced by *Aurora Leigh*, this verse-tale tells the story of the philanthropist and radical, Michael Villiers (based on the aristocratic, socialist poet Roden Noel), who opts for the simple life with a fellow philanthropist, Lucy Vere, and gives his land and property to the poor. The most interesting sections of this discursive poem are the discussions about Irish poverty and Home Rule, which challengingly point out the connections between political and psychological domination in a colonial context. However, as Emily became increasingly drawn to High Church Anglicanism, she decided to withdraw the volume from circulation, largely on account of a single offending line: 'the Galilean with the eagle eye'. With a scrupulosity comparable to Rossetti's, she inked out the Swinburnean line in her own copy. As with so many poets of the time, an early freethinking or agnostic spirit was liable to give way to a reaction of profound self-censure. In the end, like many of her generation, Emily became a Roman Catholic, and thus returned, as she put it, to 'the servants' church' (Dennis 1927: 38) of her childhood.

In spite of her friendships with other women, most notably the poet Emily Pfeiffer, Hickey became increasingly isolated and lonely in her later years. She seems to have suffered some kind of mental breakdown at one point, and then, two years before her death, became blind. However, she was able to continue writing on that new instrument, the typewriter, almost to the end of her long life.

Hickey's poetry is strongly influenced by Barrett Browning's. In particular, *Michael Villiers, Idealist*, takes up the issue of the use of philanthropic-political activism, but unlike *Aurora Leigh*, this activism is not set against the alternative, aesthetic (and feminized) purposes of poetry. Instead, poetry becomes the forum for an extended debate on the relationship between rich and poor, men and women, England and Ireland. Book V is particularly interesting for its hard-headed analysis of the links between colonial domination and poverty, both material and psychological. This poem is a reminder that, even in the decadent, escapist Nineties, women's verse was often firmly rooted in the real world of power, class and race. ' "For Richer, For Poorer" ', on the other hand, touches on the old topic of 'the fallen', but, as the title suggests, with an added irony arising from the economic implications of the words of the marriage service. This is essentially a love poem spoken by one of the wise to one of the foolish virgins, who thus offers her fallen sister an alternative 'marriage' to that offered by the Bridegroom (Christ) in the New Testament parable.

A.L.

Hickey, Emily (1881) *A Sculptor and Other Poems*, London.
—— (1889) *Verse-Tales, Lyrics, and Translations*, Liverpool.
—— (1891) *Michael Villiers, Idealist, and Other Poems*, London.

Dennis, Enid (1927) *Emily Hickey: Poet, Essayist – Pilgrim*, London, Harding and More.

'For Richer, For Poorer'

'Oh, give us of your oil, our lamps go out;
   Your well-fed lamps are clear and bright to see;
   And, if we go to buy us oil, maybe,
Far off our ears shall hear the jubilant shout,
"Behold the Bridegroom cometh, zoned about

5

With utter light and utter harmony."
Then leave us not to weep continually
In darkness, for our souls' hunger and drought.'

Then turned one virgin of the virgins wise
   To one among the foolish, with a low   10
Sweet cry, and looked her, lovelike, in the eyes,
   Saying, 'My oil is thine; for weal, for woe,
     We two are one, and where thou goest I go,
One lot being ours for aye, where'er it lies.'

from *Michael Villiers, Idealist*

[Michael Villiers, the son of a wealthy English landowner and his Irish wife, is an idealistic socialist and supporter of Home Rule. He eventually marries Lucy Vere, a fellow philanthropist, and relinquishes his inheritance for a simple life amongst the poor. In Book V he discusses the Irish question with an old college friend.]

Book V

He spoke with one, a friend of college days,
Of Ireland and the Irish; land and folk
That Gordon Moore, albeit, like Michael's self,
His earliest breath was drawn on Irish soil,
Loved not, but almost hated; once he talked   5
After this fashion:
              'Villiers, it's absurd
Of you to say you're half an Irishman –
At least that you have anything to do
With what they call the Irish people. Now,
I'll tell you what this Irish people is. –   10
A set of dirty, lazy priest-rid loons,
Who would not stir a foot to mend a fence
That any spancilled[1] cow could overleap:
Who grub on half-boiled roots and buttermilk,
And swill the fiery stuff that makes 'em mad   15
To fight and break each other's empty heads.
They laugh, and lie, and bask i' the sun half nude,
Or cower up close upon their stinking peat,
And breed like rabbits. – Nay, 'twas thus they were,
Until those cursed demagogues came round   20
And pricked the vermin till they used their stings
To sting the harmless passers-by to death –
Nay, hang the metaphor, they shot them down,
The brutal cowards; shot the innocent

---

[1] Hobbled

Good wives and children of the luckless men   25
Who owned the soil by immemorial right,
And those who dared to pay their lawful dues,
Or maimed them, body and mind; they fired the crops,
And burned the poor brute cattle in the byres,
Or houghed them; faugh! 'tis a disgusting theme!   30
And these you call a people! ay, maybe,
Of elemental times; a savage brood
The Vikings should have slaughtered long ago;
The English yet must tame; we'll tame them yet,
If we die for it.'
     Suddenly he stopped,   35
For Michael's eyes had flashed a look on him,
That dazed him into silence. Michael spoke,
The passion of his soul alive beneath
The calmness of his voice.
       'I'll tell you, Moore,
If you will listen, what the Irish are.   40

'A folk that has not had a chance to be
A nation; overcome by a strong race,
Good cross-breed meetly fused of strong and strong,
Ere its own day had come for clan and clan
To be one people. What is for a land   45
Gripped ere it gain a nation's unity?
Gripped, but not held; they knew not how to hold!
A folk with all its own laws flung to ground,
Trampled beneath a strange law's heavy heel,
A better law, you say, but not its own: 50
Forbidden in vain by edicts writ in blood,
The fusion of race with race; for English veins
'Neath Irish skies ran only Irish blood,
And English there thought only Irish thought;
While English here hounded the Irishry   55
Down to the earth, savages unreclaimed,
Keltic or Norman, Irish all alike.
And all the land was watered with their blood, –
Their stript dead bodies lay upon the hills,
Which looked i' the distance, like a pasture-land   60
Whereon there swarmed a flock of night-lulled sheep.
They were but – savages – and when they slew
And burned in vengeance, they were savages
And we were always men and Englishmen!
Their mother-tongue was dumb for want of use;   65
Their priests, like very vermin, hunted down;
Their faith doomed to the pangs of martyrdom,
Without its glory; a cross without a crown;
Their tribelands seized and parcelled out amiss

To the unkind, unkinned, of other kith;   70
Each effort made to right their land against
The bitter winds of evil chance annulled;
Her industries made one mere ruin-heap;
Her acres gript by men who only cared
To wring their rent, unwitting what it cost,   75
And only saw the houses and the lands
He owned across Saint George's Channel, when
The time of year to beat the coverts came.

   '"Dirty and thriftless!" Ay, it is the use
To call their peasants so! You know full well   80
When any among them seemed to thrive, the eyes
Of the good agent took a greedy glare,
As who should say, "Why if these cunning hinds
Have wherewithal to thatch their roofs anew,
And dress their womenfolk in comely gear,   85
And deck their window-frames with mignonette,
They must have some fair hoard i' the Savingsbank,
Were better in the pocket of my lord."
It was not well to seem as if one throve;
So John and Pat and Mick abode in dirt,   90
And let the rotten fences be, and saw
The prashogue[1] eat the earth, the poppies choke
The corn; and learned their lesson well – to sit
In apathy; that is a vice which wears
The look of that sweet virtue, patience' self!   95
But patience feeds the heart, and apathy
Drains the good lifeblood dry.
              'They lie, you say:
I think that all men lie who are not free.
Serfs lie, and slaves, and men who are bound with those
Thrice deadly bonds which bind the coward in   100
Upon the heart, the man being left outside.
You like to have them lie when lying means
You shall not have to face some ugly truth:
You scorn to hear them lie, when lies of theirs
Muffle away some truth you'd care to see: 105
You laugh to hear them lie, when 'tis your mood
To be amused.
           'You hate your native land,
Except for tickling your æsthetic sense
With her brave mountains, and her quick sea's breath,
And gentle undulating fields of green,   110
And steep magnificence of crags that meet

---

[1] Charlock, *Sinapis arvensis*

The wild winds' strength, and wrestle a fall, and win;
And here and there a maiden lovely-eyed,
With delicate blooming cheek, and raven hair;
Or barefoot urchin with the laughing face   115
You could not trust, and would not, if you could.
That's all you like in Ireland, save the sport
These farmers whom you curse have barred you from.
You are a scion of the dominant race,
And England is a good homeland to you;   120
And never a touch of Irish accent fouls
The limpid pureness of your faultless speech:
And when the famine comes, as come it does,
You stroll in languidly to some bazaar,
Where pretty women sell you buttonholes   125
For guineas, "to relieve the sore distress
Of the poor Irish: don't you know they live
In huts with walls of peat and roofs of sod,
Chimneyless, windowless; and the children go
The equals of the pigs! Alas, poor things,   130
They scarce have heard at all of God or Christ;
They are mere heathens; when their need is o'er
Of common food, it might be charity
To have them christianized." You laugh, and take
Your guinea's worth, and pay, and chatter on   135
At leisure of the pretty stallkeeper.
You have heard me long enough, and I have done.
Ye gete no more of me but ye wol rede
The original that telleth al the cas!'

'And what's the original?'
                          'Ireland's history.'   140

  'But, Villiers, you're unjust; in the old time,
Some wrong was done to Ireland, there's no doubt,
But England long ago had seen that wrong,
And striven to make amends; and still she strives,
With all her might and main.'
                          'I know it well,'   145
Said Michael, 'and I would not be unjust;
But it may be that vision came too late,
And that amendment cannot now be done!
The bitterest punishment of punishments
To nations or to men is impotence   150
To mend a wrong they knew not when they did.'

Michael Field Katherine Bradley (1846–1914) and Edith Cooper (1862–1913)

The two women who wrote under the name of Michael Field were an aunt and her niece. Katherine Bradley, the daughter of a tobacco manufacturer who died when she was two, was educated at home, briefly in Paris, and then at Newnham College, Cambridge. She published her first volume of poems in 1875 under the pseudonym 'Arran Leigh' – a name, like Bevington's 'Arbor Leigh', obviously recalling Barrett Browning's poet heroine. At about this time she became a member of Ruskin's Guild of St George, but was expelled for atheism when she informed its founder that she had 'lost God and found a Skye Terrier' (1933: 155). In 1878 she attended classes at Bristol University with her niece, Edith Cooper, whom she had reared from childhood. It seems that at about this time the two women also became lovers. The poem, 'Prologue', records their vow to be, in the face of the world's disapproval, 'Poets and lovers evermore'. This rare love poem from one woman to another sets its implicitly collaborative authorship against the traditional subject–object, poet–muse dichotomies of the romantic tradition. At this time Katherine and Edith were supporters of the suffrage movement and, even more importantly to them, of the anti-vivisection league.

Subsequently, they embarked on a life of writing and travelling together. Their many plays and poems were composed collaboratively – 'like mosaic work – the mingled, various product of our two brains' (1933: 3) – and were published in ornamental, limited editions in the fashion of the day. Robert Browning, receiving one of them, enthusiastically acclaimed the '*genius*' (1933: 2) of its authors, and subsequently took to calling them his 'two dear Greek women' (20). Though Katherine and Edith speak openly of being lovers (their unpublished journals proving that the relationship was sexual), the precise nature of that love was not probed or named by most of their contemporaries. In 1889 they brought out their first joint volume of poems, *Long Ago*. This acknowledges the inspiration of Henry Wharton's edition of Sappho (1885), which, for the first time in English history, restored the female pronoun for the object of address. Michael Field's poems are translations and elaborations of the Sapphic fragments, some of them, like 'Maids, not to you my mind doth change' and 'Come, Gorgo, put the rug in place', being overtly sensual expressions of love between women. These mark the culmination of a long tradition of 'Sappho' poems among nineteenth-century women poets, but it is not until Michael Field that the lesbian connotations are made apparent.

In the years that followed Katherine and Edith travelled abroad: to Germany once, where Edith caught scarlet fever and almost died, to France, where they visited the Paris morgue, and most often to Italy, where they stayed with Pen Browning in Asolo and Vernon Lee in Florence. These trips stopped, however, when they acquired a Chow dog whom they could not bear to leave behind. In London, they met most of the literary figures of the day. They attended Pater's almost inaudible lectures, dined at the 'Vegetarian' with Havelock Ellis, frequently encountered Oscar Wilde, whose snobbery amused and annoyed them, attended the famous poetry reading given by Verlaine in 1893 and, in the early 1900s, invited the nervous young Yeats to dinner. They may also have met Olive Schreiner and E. Nesbit in the late 1880s at the 'Fellowship of the New Life', the group which later gave birth to the breakaway

Fabians, though Katherine and Edith, who cultivated a sort of haughty aestheticism, were never drawn to socialism. In their later years they became increasingly touchy and eccentric, imagining, perhaps justifiably, a conspiracy of silence against their work, and retreating ever more into their private life together. They also vehemently rejected fin-de-siècle decadence, condemning the work of Zola, Huysmans and Beardsley, for instance, for its depravity: 'one must go to one's Wordsworth & Shelley to be fumigated', they once expostulated. In their disapproval at its increasing outrageousness and stridency, they withdrew one of their poems from the *Yellow Book*. This streak of *hauteur*, in both their private and public lives, probably contributed to their growing isolation from the main literary movements of the day.

A crucial turning point in their lives came in 1906 when their beloved dog died. This not only inspired an extraordinary collection of love poems, *Whym Chow: Flame of Love*, but also, so Edith claimed, brought about their conversion to Roman Catholicism. This time, by a neat reversal, the dog was exchanged for God. By the same token, sexual love was exchanged for chastity, and the headily sensual poetry of the early volumes for the baroque religiosity of the later. Like many of their contemporaries, they abandoned 'sin' for an equally potent and lavish rite of repentance.

Then, in 1911, Edith was diagnosed as having cancer. She faced her last months with unflinching courage, refusing to take opium so that she could keep writing to the end. Katherine, in fact, survived her lover by only eight months. She too was suffering from cancer (see 'Lo, my loved is dying'), but kept it a secret from Edith. Two days after the funeral she suffered a severe haemorrhage. In the months which remained she compiled several more volumes of verse, and died in September 1914.

The poetry of Michael Field is prolific and uneven, and benefits from selection. The best of it was inspired by the hedonistic paganism of their early years together rather than by the repentant Catholicism of the last, as the quiet retrospective of 'A Palimpsest' suggests. The early work invokes as its muse the classical Bacchus, the god of wine, frenzy and, of course, feminist revenge (the maenads, his followers, abandoned their homes and turned on their husbands and sons). In some sense the fiery Whym Chow (who once, on a visit, killed Kipling's pet rabbit) personifies the amoral energy of the Dionysiac impulse. The poem 'Trinity', for instance, presents the god–dog as a conduit of love between the two women, thus establishing a new threesome, not of Father, Son and Holy Ghost, but of two women – mother and daughter even – and their animal 'spirit'.

This streak of baroque unorthodoxy runs through their work. In the earlier poetry, the pagan and aestheticist ideal of pleasure for its own sake becomes attached to the notion of an impersonal, Darwinian life-force which cannot be repressed. 'Eros', for instance, specifically invokes, not Aphrodite, but the other god of love, whom A. J. Symonds, in his privately printed *A Problem in Greek Ethics* (1883), identified as the tutelary god of homosexual desire. Yet Michael Field's 'Eros' is also associated with the natural forces of life and death, where love is recognized as a 'hunger' at the very heart of things. Like 'Nests in Elms', this is a nature poem which carries no heartwarming, Wordsworthian consolations, but, instead, a quite exhilarating bleakness and agnosticism. Like so many women poets of the time, Michael Field invokes the classical gods less for their literary resonances than for their challenge to Christian orthodoxy. The evolutionary perspective also offers, as it does Constance Naden (whose poetry they may have known), a drastic revision of the terms of romantic love – a revision which implicitly widens the sphere of reference to include other forms of love. The legendary romance of the Brownings once provoked Katherine to overt emotional competition: *'we are closer married'* (1933: 16), she declared.

Other poems, like ' "A Girl" ' and ' "It was deep April..." ' have an almost modernist ease and informality about them, their free forms pointing forward to the work of Amy Lowell and H. D. At a time when most of their contemporaries were still tied to the metrical stanza form, Michael Field experiments with open-ended, improvised metres, which delight in the surprise of an unexpected rhyme. ' "A Girl" ', which was singled out for special praise in a review in the *Athenaeum* (9 September (1893), 346), beautifully suspends the moment of its own writing in a final, punning invitation to the girl to 'come to it'. Shorter poems, like 'Cyclamens' and 'A Flaw', have the miniature clarity of Imagist verse, while 'Embalmment' and 'The Mummy Invokes his Soul', though drawing on the fashionable Egyptianism of the Nineties (see Mary Coleridge 'A Day-dream'), do so with a light-handed, far-fetched wit which deflates their exotic orientalism.

The last poems, written in the face of death for both women, bear witness to a continuing struggle between the old pagan energy and Christian submission. Edith's last verse, 'They Shall Look on Him' is less a hymn of faith than a 'swan-song' to the dawn's natural light, while 'Fellowship', one of Katherine's last poems, which was written after Edith's death, movingly reclaims the pagan spirit of the past, and returns to the laughing, combative energy first invoked in ' "It was deep April..." ' Instinctively, both poets seem to have known that the inspiration for their best work lay in a fellowship, both emotional and professional, which belonged outside the heritage of Christianity as well as, ultimately, outside the male erotic ventures of the aesthetes. The poetry of Michael Field, charged as it is with the eroticism of a love which crosses so many ideological and moral boundaries, brings a whole new perspective and voice to the tradition of Victorian women's poetry.

A.L.

Field, Michael (1889) *Long Ago*, London.
—— (1892) *Sight and Song*, London.
—— (1893) *Underneath the Bough, A Book of Verses*, London.
—— (1908) *Wild Honey from Various Thyme*, London, Fisher Unwin.
—— (1913) *Mystic Trees*, London. Eveleigh Nash.
—— (1914) *Dedicated: An Early Work of Michael Field*, London, G. Bell.
—— (1914) *Whym Chow: Flame of Love*, London, privately printed at the Eragny Press.
—— (1928) *An Anthology of 'Nineties' Verse*, ed A. J. A. Symons, London, Elkin Matthews and Marrot.
—— (1930) *The Wattlefold: Unpublished Poems*, collected by Emily C. Fortey, Oxford, Blackwell.
—— (1933) *Works and Days: From the Journal of Michael Field*, eds T. and D. C. Sturge Moore, London, John Murray.
[Note: the poem 'To Christina Rossetti' was published only in *The Academy* 1248 (1896), 248.]

Faderman, Lillian (1981) *Surpassing the Love of Men*, London, Women's Press.
Laird, Holly (1995) 'Contradictory Legacies: Michael Field and Feminist Restoration', *Victorian Poetry*, 33 (1995).
Leighton, Angela (1992) *Victorian Women Poets*, Hemel Hempstead, Harvester, pp. 202–43.

Moriarty, David J. (1986) ' "Michael Field" (Edith Cooper and Katherine Bradley) and Their Male Critics', in *Nineteenth-Century Women Writers of the English-Speaking World*, New York, Greenwood Press, pp. 121–42.

Prins, Yopie (1995) 'A Metaphorical Field: Katherine Bradley and Edith Cooper,' *Victorian Poetry*, 33 (1995).

—— (1995) 'Sappho Doubled: Michael Field', *Yale Journal of Criticism*.

Symonds, J. A. (1883) *A Problem in Greek Ethics*, London.

White, Christine (1990) ' "Poets and lovers evermore": Interpreting Female Love in the Poetry and Journals of Michael Field', *Textual Practice*, 4 (1990), 197–212.

'Maids, not to you my mind doth change'

Ταῖς κάλαις ὔμμιν [τὸ] νόημα τὦμον
οὐ διάμειπτον[1]

Maids, not to you my mind doth change;
Men I defy, allure, estrange,
Prostrate, make bond or free:
Soft as the stream beneath the plane
To you I sing my love's refrain;   5
Between us is no thought of pain, Peril, satiety.

Soon doth a lover's patience tire,
But ye to manifold desire
Can yield response, ye know
When for long, museful days I pine,   10
The presage at my heart divine;
To you I never breathe a sign
Of inward want or woe.

When injuries my spirit bruise,
Allaying virtue ye infuse   15
With unobtrusive skill:
And if care frets ye come to me
As fresh as nymph from stream or tree,
And with your soft vitality
My weary bosom fill.   20

'Come, Gorgo, put the rug in place'

'Αλλά, μὴ μεγαλύνεο δακτυλίῳ πέρι[2]

Come, Gorgo, put the rug in place,
And passionate recline;
I love to see thee in thy grace,
Dark, virulent, divine.

---

[1] To you, fair maids, my mind changes not   [2] Foolish woman, pride not thyself on a ring

But wherefore thus thy proud eyes fix 5
  Upon a jewelled band?
Art thou so glad the sardonyx
  Becomes thy shapely hand?

Bethink thee! 'Tis for such as thou
  Zeus leaves his lofty seat; 10
'Tis at thy beauty's bidding how
  Man's mortal life shall fleet;
Those fairest hands – dost thou forget
  Their power to thrill and cling?
O foolish woman, dost thou set 15
  Thy pride upon a ring?

A Portrait

Bartolommeo Veneto

The Städel'sche Institut at Frankfurt

A crystal, flawless beauty on the brows
Where neither love nor time has conquered space
On which to live; her leftward smile endows
The gazer with no tidings from the face;
About the clear mounds of the lip it winds with silvery pace 5
  And in the umber eyes it is a light
Chill as a glowworm's when the moon embrowns an August night.

She saw her beauty often in the glass,
Sharp on the dazzling surface, and she knew
The haughty custom of her grace must pass: 10
  Though more persistent in all charm it grew
As with a desperate joy her hair across her throat she drew
  In crinkled locks stiff as dead, yellow snakes . . .
Until at last within her soul the resolution wakes

She will be painted, she who is so strong 15
In loveliness, so fugitive in years:
Forth to the field she goes and questions long
Which flowers to choose of those the summer bears;
She plucks a violet larkspur, – then a columbine appears
  Of perfect yellow, – daisies choicely wide; 20
These simple things with finest touch she gathers in her pride.

Next on her head, veiled with well-bleachen white
And bound across the brow with azure-blue,
She sets the box-tree leaf and coils it tight
In spiky wreath of green, immortal hue; 25

Then, to the prompting of her strange, emphatic insight true,
    She bares one breast, half-freeing it of robe,
And hangs green-water gem and cord beside the naked globe.

    So was she painted and for centuries
    Has held the fading field-flowers in her hand   30
    Austerely as a sign. O fearful eyes
    And soft lips of the courtesan who planned
To give her fragile shapeliness to art, whose reason spanned
    Her doom, who bade her beauty in its cold
And vacant eminence persist for all men to behold!   35

    She had no memories save of herself
    And her slow-fostered graces, naught to say
    Of love in gift or boon; her cruel pelf
    Had left her with no hopes that grow and stay;
She found default in everything that happened night or day,   40
    Yet stooped in calm to passion's dizziest strife
And gave to art a fair, blank form, unverified by life.

    Thus has she conquered death: her eyes are fresh,
    Clear as her frontlet jewel, firm in shade
    And definite as on the linen mesh   45
    Of her white hood the box-tree's sombre braid,
That glitters leaf by leaf and with the year's waste will not fade.
    The small, close mouth, leaving no room for breath,
In perfect, still pollution smiles – Lo, she has conquered death!

'O Wind, thou hast thy kingdom in the trees'

O Wind, thou hast thy kingdom in the trees,
    And all thy royalties
Sweep through the land to-day.
    It is mid June,
And thou, with all thine instruments in tune,   5
    Thine orchestra
Of heaving fields, and heavy, swinging fir,
    Strikest a lay
    That doth rehearse
Her ancient freedom to the universe.   10
    All other sound in awe
      Repeals its law;
    The bird is mute, the sea
    Sucks up its waves, from rain
    The burthened clouds refrain,   15
    To listen to thee in thy leafery,
      Thou unconfined,
Lavish, large, soothing, refluent summer-wind!

'Ah, Eros doth not always smite'

Ah, Eros doth not always smite
   With cruel, shining dart,
Whose bitter point with sudden might
   Rends the unhappy heart –
Not thus forever purple-stained,   5
   And sore with steely touch,
Else were its living fountain drained
   Too oft and overmuch.
O'er it sometimes the boy will deign
   Sweep the shaft's feathered end;   10
And friendship rises without pain
   Where the white plumes descend.

'Sometimes I do despatch my heart'

Sometimes I do despatch my heart
    Among the graves to dwell apart:
On some the tablets are erased,
Some earthquake-tumbled, some defaced,
And some that have forgotten lain   5
A fall of tears makes green again;
And my brave heart can overtread
Her brood of hopes, her infant dead,
And pass with quickened footsteps by
The headstone of hoar memory,   10
    Till she hath found
    One swelling mound
With just her name writ and *beloved*;
From that she cannot be removed.

'So jealous of your beauty'

So jealous of your beauty,
   You will not wed
    For dread
That hymeneal duty
   Should touch and mar   5
The lovely thing you are?
Come to your garden-bed!

Learn there another lesson:
   This poppy-head,
    Instead   10

Of having crimson dress on,
  Is now a fruit,
Whose marvellous pale suit
Transcends the glossy red.

What, count the colour   15
  Of apricot,
    Ungot,
Warming in August, duller
  Than those most shy,
Frail flowers that spread and die   20
Before the sun is hot!

Lady, the hues unsightly,
  And best forgot,
    Are not
Berries and seeds set brightly,   25
  But withered blooms:
  Alack, vainglory dooms
You to their ragged lot!

'Love rises up some days'

Love rises up some days
From a blue couch of light
  Upon the summer sky;
He wakes, and waking plays
With beams and dewdrops white;   5
His laugh is like the sunniest rain,
  And patters through his voice;
He is so lovely, tolerant, and sane,
  That the heart questions why
It doth not, every hour it beats, rejoice.   10

Yet sometimes Love awakes
On a black, hellish bed,
  And rises up as hate:
He drinks the hurtful lakes,
He joys to toss and spread   15
Sparkles of pitchy, rankling flame,
  He joys to play with death;
But when we look on him he is the same
  Quaint child we blest of late,
And every word that once he said he saith.   20

'Already to mine eyelids' shore'

Already to mine eyelids' shore
　　The gathering waters swell,
For thinking of the grief in store
　　When thou wilt say 'Farewell.'
I dare not let thee leave me, sweet,　　　　　　5
　　Lest it should be for ever;
Tears dew my kisses ere we meet,
　　Foreboding we must sever:
Since we can neither meet nor part,
Methinks the moral is, sweetheart,　　　　　　10
　　That we must dwell together.

'A Girl'

A Girl,
　　Her soul a deep-wave pearl
Dim, lucent of all lovely mysteries;
　　A face flowered for heart's ease,
　　A brow's grace soft as seas　　　　　　5
　　Seen through faint forest-trees:
　　A mouth, the lips apart,
Like aspen-leaflets trembling in the breeze
From her tempestuous heart.
Such: and our souls so knit,　　　　　　10
I leave a page half-writ –
　　The work begun
Will be to heaven's conception done,
　　If she come to it.

'I sing thee with the stock-dove's throat'

I sing thee with the stock-dove's throat,
　　Warm, crooning, superstitious note,
That on its dearie so doth dote
　　It falls to sorrow,
And from the fair, white swans afloat　　　　　　5
　　A dirge must borrow.

In thee I have such deep content,
I can but murmur a lament;
It is as though my heart were rent
　　By thy perfection,　　　　　　10
And all my passion's torrent spent
　　In recollection.

Unbosoming

The love that breeds
  In my heart for thee!
As the iris is full, brimful of seeds,
And all that it flowered for among the reeds
Is packed in a thousand vermilion-beads   5
That push, and riot, and squeeze, and clip,
Till they burst the sides of the silver scrip,
And at last we see
What the bloom, with its tremulous, bowery fold
Of zephyr-petal at heart did hold: 10
So my breast is rent
With the burthen and strain of its great content;
For the summer of fragrance and sighs is dead,
The harvest-secret is burning red,
And I would give thee, after my kind,   15
The final issues of heart and mind.

'It was deep April'

It was deep April, and the morn
    Shakespere was born;
The world was on us, pressing sore;
My Love and I took hands and swore,
  Against the world, to be   5
Poets and lovers evermore,
To laugh and dream on Lethe's shore,
To sing to Charon in his boat,
Heartening the timid souls afloat;
Of judgment never to take heed,   10
But to those fast-locked souls to speed,
Who never from Apollo fled,
Who spent no hour among the dead;
    Continually
      With them to dwell,   15
Indifferent to heaven and hell.

'As two fair vessels side by side'

As two fair vessels side by side,
    No bond had tied
   Our floating peace;
We thought that it would never cease,
But like swan-creatures we should always glide: 5

And this is love
  We sighed.

As two grim vessels side by side,
    Through wind and tide
    War grappled us,   10
With bond as strong as death, and thus
We drove on mortally allied:
    And this is hate
      We cried.

Cyclamens

They are terribly white:
    There is snow on the ground,
And a moon on the snow at night;
    The sky is cut by the winter light;
Yet I, who have all these things in ken,   5
Am struck to the heart by the chiselled white
    Of this handful of cyclamen.

A Flaw

To give me its bright plumes, they shot a jay:
On the fresh jewels, blood! Oh, sharp remorse!
The glittering symbols of the little corse
I buried where the wood was noisome, blind,
Praying that I might nevermore betray   5
The universe, so whole within my mind.

Penetration[1]

I love thee; never dream that I am dumb:
By day, by night, my tongue besiegeth thee,
As a bat's voice, set in too fine a key,
Too tender in its circumstance to come
To ears beset by havoc and harsh hum   5
Of the arraigning world; yet secretly
I may attain: lo, even a dead bee
Dropt sudden from thy open hand by some
Too careless wind is laid among thy flowers,
Dear to thee as the bees that sing and roam: 10
Thou watchest when the angry moon drops foam;

---

[1] Perhaps spoken by Syrinx to Pan

Thou answerest the faun's soft-footed stare;
No influence, but thou feelest it is there,
And drawest it, profound, into thy hours.

To the Winter Aphrodite

O Winter Aphrodite! (O acute,
Ice-eating pains, thine arrows!) shivering
By thy cold altar-stones, to thee I bring
Thy myrtle with its Erebus-black fruit,
Locked up, provocative, profoundly mute,   5
Muter than snow or any melting thing,
Muter than fall'n winds, or bird's dead wing,
Secret as music of a fresh-struck lute
Laid by a little while and yet for aye –
By all that jealously thou dost enwomb,   10
By Sappho's words hid of thee in a tomb,
Pondered of thee where no man passeth by,
Use thou my heart awhile for Love's own room,
O Winter Aphrodite, ere I die!

Embalmment

Let not a star suspect the mystery!
A cave that haunts thee in the dreams of night
Keep me as treasure hidden from thy sight,
And only thine while thou dost covet me!
As the Asmonæan queen perpetually   5
Embalmed in honey, cold to thy delight,
Cold to thy touch, a sleeping eremite,
Beside thee never sleeping I would be.

Or thou might'st lay me in a sepulchre,
And every line of life will keep its bloom,   10
Long as thou seal'st me from the common air.
Speak not, reveal not... There will be
In the unchallenged dark a mystery,
And golden hair sprung rapid in a tomb.

After Soufrière

It is not grief or pain;
But like the even dropping of the rain
That thou are gone.
It is not like a grave
To weep upon;   5

But like the rise and falling of a wave
    When the vessel's gone.

It is like the sudden void
When the city is destroyed,
Where the sun shone: 10
There is neither grief or pain,
But the wide waste come again.

Fifty Quatrains

'Twas fifty quatrains: and from unknown strands
The Woman came who sang them on the floor.
I saw her, I was leaning by the door,
– Saw her strange raiment and her lovely hands;
And saw ... but that I think she sang – the bands   5
Of low-voiced women on a happy shore:
Incomparable was the haze, and bore
The many blossoms of soft orchard lands.
'Twas fifty quatrains, for I caught the measure;
And all the royal house was full of kings,   10
Who listened and beheld her and were dumb;
Nor dared to seize the marvellous rich pleasure,
Too fearful even to ask in whisperings,
The ramparts being closed, whence she had come.

Nests in Elms

The rooks are cawing up and down the trees!
Among their nests they caw. O sound I treasure,
Ripe as old music is, the summer's measure,
Sleep at her gossip, sylvan mysteries,
With prate and clamour to give zest of these –   5
In rune I trace the ancient law of pleasure,
Of love, of all the busy-ness of leisure,
With dream on dream of never-thwarted ease.
O homely birds, whose cry is harbinger
Of nothing sad, who know not anything   10
Of sea-birds' loneliness, of Procne's strife,
Rock round me when I die! So sweet it were
To die by open doors, with you on wing
Humming the deep security of life.

'I love you with my life'

I love you with my life – 'tis so I love you;
    I give you as a ring

The cycle of my days till death:
    I worship with the breath
That keeps me in the world with you and spring: 5
And God may dwell behind, but not above you.

Mine, in the dark, before the world's beginning:
    The claim of every sense,
    Secret and source of every need;
      The goal to which I speed,   10
And at my heart a vigour more immense
Than will itself to urge me to its winning.

The Mummy Invokes his Soul

Down to me quickly, down! I am such dust,
Baked, pressed together; let my flesh be fanned
With thy fresh breath; come from thy reedy land
Voiceful with birds; divert me, for I lust
To break, to crumble – prick with pores this crust! –   5
And fall apart, delicious, loosening sand.
Oh, joy, I feel thy breath, I feel thy hand
That searches for my heart, and trembles just
Where once it beat. How light thy touch, thy frame!
Surely thou perchest on the summer trees ...   10
And the garden that we loved? Soul, take thine ease,
I am content, so thou enjoy the same
Sweet terraces and founts, content, for thee,
To burn in this immense torpidity.

Sullenness

The year is sullen, sullen is the day;
Nor is the heaviness for summer gone:
It issues from a garden wrapt in clay,
And shooting boughs of pale mezereon.
The wind heaves slow, and yet no dirge is rung;   5
There is no burthen from a distant shore;
A strain, a cry is there for things so long,
So very far away, so long before.
Nor is there any pain regret can bring
Of so sharp pang as virgin appetite   10
That can but brood upon its famishing,
Till unwarmed suns shall furnish its delight.
So long the winter dures, breath is so brief!
– If one should fail before the flower has leaf?

Leaves

Where are they? I have never missed before
The whole wide kingdom of the cherishing leaves,
Or waft, or drifted into golden heaves
With all their scents, or dead upon the floor!
We left at sundown; but shall see no more   5
The air a film of multitudinous leaves;
For, lo, a sudden ravishing bereaves
The air that threaded them, the earth that bore!
And now of all their gorgeous, solemn realms
No sign: of unseen arrows came their fall;   10
They are not. Clematis and ivy curl
Their wavering tissues on the river wall –
Nothing afloat: the river a dark pearl;
The jagged acacia and the misted elms.

Ebbtide at Sundown

How larger is remembrance than desire!
How deeper than all longing is regret!
The tide is gone, the sands are rippled yet;
The sun is gone; the hills are lifted higher,
Crested with rose. Ah, why should we require   5
Sight of the sea, the sun? The sands are wet,
And in their glassy flaws huge record set
Of the ebbed stream, the little ball of fire.
Gone, they are gone! But, oh, so freshly gone,
So rich in vanishing we ask not where –   10
So close upon us is the bliss that shone,
And, oh, so thickly it impregns the air!
Closer in beating heart we could not be
To the sunk sun, the far, surrendered sea.

Life Plastic

O Life, who art thou that with scarcely scanned
Mysterious aspect breakest on my way,
And vanishest, leaving a lump of clay
As gift, as symbol, shapeless in my hand?
Kindling and mute, thou gavest no command;   5
Yet am I left as prompted to obey,
With a great peril at my heart. Oh, say,
Am I a creature from achievement banned?
In my despair, my idle hands are cast,
Are plunged into the clay: they grip, they hold,   10

I feel them chafing on a moistened line;
Unconsciously my warmth is in the cold.
O Life, I am the Potter, and at last
The secret of my loneliness is mine.

Eros

O Eros of the mountains, of the earth,
One thing I know of thee that thou art old,
Far, sovereign, lonesome tyrant of the dearth
Of chaos, ruler of the primal cold!
None gave thee nurture: chaos' icy rings   5
Pressed on thy plenitude. O fostering power,
Thine the first voice, first warmth, first golden wings,
First blowing zephyr, earliest opened flower,
Thine the first smile of Time: thou hast no mate,
Thou art alone forever, giving all: 10
After thine image, Love, thou did'st create
Man to be poor, man to be prodigal;
And thus, O awful god, he is endued
With the raw hungers of thy solitude.

Elsewhere

Beauteous thou art, the spirit knows not how;
'Tis not the serpent-way thine iris slips,
Nor confluence of the temples and the brow,
Nor marge nor parting of the trembled lips:

Beauteous thou art; but never with thy face   5
Dwelleth thy beauty: all its riches are
Freighting for thee in distant argosies,
While thou art poor, save for a tranquil grace.

Beauty forever with the god doth keep
Backward, a few steps off, beside the shrine: 10
It is thy dreaming when thou art asleep;

Waking thou dost not wear it as a sign;
Yet wheresoe'er thou goest it limns thee, sweet,
As finest air a-quiver with the heat.

Nightfall

She sits beside: through four low panes of glass
The sun, a misty meadow, and the stream;

Falling through rounded elms the last sunbeam.
Through night's thick fibre sudden barges pass
With great forelights of gold, with trailing mass   5
Of timber: rearward of their transient gleam
The shadows settle, and profounder dream
Enters, fulfils the shadows. Vale and grass
Are now no more; a last leaf strays about,
Then every wandering ceases; we remain.   10
Clear dusk, the face of wind is on the sky:
The eyes I love lift to the upper pane –
Their voice gives note of welcome quietly
'I love the air in which the stars come out.'

Constancy

I love her with the seasons, with the winds,
As the stars worship, as anemones
Shudder in secret for the sun, as bees
Buzz round an open flower: in all kinds
My love is perfect, and in each she finds   5
Herself the goal: then why, intent to teaze
And rob her delicate spirit of its ease,
Hastes she to range me with inconstant minds?
If she should die, if I were left at large
On earth without her – I, on earth, the same   10
Quick mortal with a thousand cries, her spell
She fears would break. And I confront the charge
As sorrowing, and as careless of my fame
As Christ intact before the infidel.

Sweet-Briar in Rose

So sweet, all sweet – the body as the shyer
Sweet senses, and the Spirit sweet as those:
For me the fragrance of a whole sweet-briar
            Beside the rose!

Your Rose is Dead

   Your *rose* is *dead*,
   They said,
The Grand Mogul – for so her splendour
Exceeded, masterful, it seemed her due
By dominant male titles to commend her: 5
   But I, her lover, knew

That myriad-coloured blackness, wrought with fire,
Was woman to the rage of my desire.
My rose was dead? She lay
Against the sulphur, lemon and blush-gray   10
Of younger blooms, transformed, morose,
Her shrivelling petals gathered round her close,
   And where before,
Coils twisted thickest at her core
A round, black hollow: it had come to pass   15
Hints of tobacco, leather, brass,
Confounded, gave her texture and her colour.
I watched her, as I watched her, growing duller,
   Majestic in recession
   From flesh to mould.   20
My rose is dead — I echo the confession,
And they pass to pluck another;
While I, drawn on to vague, prodigious pleasure,
   Fondle my treasure.
O sweet, let death prevail   25
Upon you, as your nervous outlines thicken
And totter, as your crimsons stale,
I feel fresh rhythms quicken,
Fresh music follows you. Corrupt, grow old,
Drop inwardly to ashes, smother   30
Your burning spices, and entoil
My senses till you sink a clod of fragrant soil!

A Palimpsest

. . . The rest
Of our life must be a palimpsest —
The old writing written there the best.

In the parchment hoary
Lies a golden story,   5
As 'mid secret feather of a dove,
As 'mid moonbeams shifted through a cloud:

Let us write it over,
O my lover,
For the far Time to discover,   10
As 'mid secret feathers of a dove,
As 'mid moonbeams shifted through a cloud!

Trinity

I did not love him for myself alone:
I loved him that he loved my dearest love.
O God, no blasphemy
It is to feel we loved in trinity,
To tell Thee that I loved him as Thy Dove   5
Is loved, and is Thy own,
That comforted the moan
Of Thy Beloved, when earth could give no balm
And in Thy Presence makes His tenderest calm.

So I possess this creature of Love's flame,   10
So loving what I love he lives from me;
Not white, a thing of fire,
Of seraph plumèd limbs and one desire,
That is my heart's own, and shall ever be:
An animal — with aim   15
Thy Dove avers the same....
O symbol of our perfect union, strange
Unconscious Bearer of Love's interchange.

The Goad

Eros, why should one or two small notes
     Of thrilled birds in Spring —
Why should one or two gay motes
Tangled round the beams on wing —
Why should delicate, first flowers,   5
          Have such powers
That all music sweeps me wild,
That all light of June is piled
In my eyes, and gardens flow
All the colour to me they shall grow?   10

By thy eloquence, O God of Love,
     We are made alive ...
Thou with art all arts above
Dost against our slumber drive
Little shudderings of voice,   15
          Clear and choice;
Stroke of slender rays to wake
Our desire that summer break
On us in meridian heat,
Primroses by roses made effete.   20

To Christina Rossetti

Lady, we would behold thee moving bright
As Beatrice or Matilda 'mid the trees,
Alas! thy moan was as a moan for ease
And passage through cool shadows to the night:
Fleeing from love, hadst thou not poet's right   5
To slip into the universe? The seas
Are fathomless to rivers drowned in these,
And sorrow is secure in leafy light.
Ah, had this secret touched thee, in a tomb
Thou hadst not buried thy enchanting self,   10
As happy Syrinx murmuring with the wind,
Or Daphne thrilled through all her mystic bloom,
From safe recess as genius or as elf,
Thou hadst breathed joy in earth and in thy kind.

'Beloved, my glory in thee is not ceased'

Beloved, my glory in thee is not ceased,
Whereas, as thou art waning, forests wane:
Unmoved, as by the victim is the priest,
I pass the world's great altitudes of pain.
But when the stars are gathered for a feast,   5
Or shadows threaten on a radiant plain,
Or many golden cornfields wave amain,
Oh then, as one from a filled shuttle weaves,
    My spirit grieves.

'She is singing to thee, *Domine!*'

She is singing to Thee, *Domine!*
    Dost hear her now?
She is singing to Thee from a burning throat,
And melancholy as the owl's love-note;
She is singing to Thee from the utmost bough   5
    Of the tree of Golgotha, where it is bare,
And the fruit torn from it that fruited there;
She is singing . . . Canst Thou stop the strain,
    The homage of such pain?
Domine, stoop down to her again!   10

'Loved, on a sudden thou didst come to me'

Loved, on a sudden thou didst come to me
On our own doorstep, still I see thee stand

In thy bleared welcome, with the grim command
From Heaven that we must sever presently;
And no farewell was in the misery ...   5
So you condemned me; did not understand
O lovely and gay-coloured tulip-land,
I would not break on thee my wrathful sea;
   Back to the flood-gates, firm to my defence –
So hard, as thou complainest, so apart;   10
But had I not held tight from thee my sense,
My memory, my will against my heart,
But one defeat, the rupture of one sigh
How little of the world had been left dry!

An Almoner

Who is this? An almoner
By the lovely stoop of her,
By her smiling, by her quick
Footstep as she sought the sick.
'Tis a lovely almoner.   5
But I ask not speech with her;
I am going to my grave-bed,
Something from my heart there smote –
'Coins for Charon's ferry-boat,
Coins, give me coins for my dead.'   10

Fiercely did I press my tolls,
And the figure changed its pace,
Drew a veil across the face,
Left me with my pagan-tongue:
And a whispering came along –   15
'I am Mary of the Holy Souls.'

A Picture

Love, you were dying and one came and drew
The story of your sickness and your pain –
Forlorn you stooped; lover nor loved you knew,
Sucking the salt of sorrow, grain on grain.
You saw my grief for you, thus quite undone   5
How as at day of judgment you appealed
And sent for an old picture by the sun
As he saw you years ago in a green field –
A vision of your beauty very clear
Of open lip, yet something flashed between   10
That held and awed and made the face appear

As a shell under water, secret, keen.
O Catholic, sweet face, O gift, O truth
And revelation of thy Spirit's youth.

'Lo, my loved is dying'

Lo, my loved is dying, and the call
Is come that I must die,
All the leaves are dying, all
Dying, drifting by.
Every leaf is lonely in its fall,   5
Every flower has its speck and stain;
The birds from hedge and tree
Lisp mournfully,
And the great reconciliation of this pain
Lies in the full, soft rain.   10

They Shall Look on Him[1]

Jesus, my Light,
How, when it comes through darkness I love light,
Mysterious air's adornment, white
Chrysolite of the water, striking free,
    And beamingly   5
Through the dull currents of the stream at dawn
      Beam after beam
From the suspended jewel drawn;
      While swans go by,
Swans through the jewel pass, go by,   10
    Ponder and go along
Through gem-strokes strong,
        O perfect sight
        Of entire chrysolite!

Fellowship

I

In the old accents I will sing, my Glory, my Delight,
In the old accents, tipped with flame, before we knew the right,
True way of singing with reserve. O Love, with pagan might,

---

[1]   Edith Cooper's last poem

II

White in our steeds, and white too in our armour let us ride,
Immortal, white, triumphing, flashing downward side by side   5
To where our friends, the Argonauts, are fighting with the tide.

III

Let us draw calm to them, Beloved, the souls on heavenly voyage bound,
Saluting as one presence. Great disaster were it found,
If one with half-fed lambency should halt and flicker round.

IV

O friends so fondly loving, so beloved, look up to us,   10
In constellation breaking on your errand, prosperous,
O Argonauts!

          Now, faded from their sight,
We cling and joy. It was thy intercession gave me right
My Fellow, to this fellowship. My Glory, my Delight!

Alice Meynell (1847–1922)

Alice Meynell was the second of two daughters born to Christiana and Thomas Thompson.
Her mother was a concert pianist whose career was cut short by marriage; her father
inherited a modest private income. With her elder sister Elizabeth (later Butler), who
became the well-known painter of battle scenes, Alice was brought up mainly in Italy – a
country to which she returned throughout her life. The girls were educated by their father,
a liberal but reticent man, whose silence exercised a strong influence over Alice's
imagination. In an essay on him, 'A Remembrance', she once wrote: 'Where shall I find a
pen fastidious enough to define and limit and enforce so many significant negatives?' (1947:
226). Yet if the fastidious and the negative were the virtues of her own poetry (see 'To the
Beloved', 'To Silence'), they could also easily turn into vices.

The family returned to England in 1864. Some years later, Alice, like many of her
contemporaries (and her mother before her), became a Roman Catholic. Her love for
the young priest who received her into the church is recorded in the much antho-
logized sonnet 'Renouncement', which expresses the 'negative' passion of much of her
writing. Significantly, only her own father and this Father in the church seem to have
inspired her to write love poems. In 1877 she married Wilfrid Meynell, a Catholic
journalist, and embarked on a life of demanding domestic duties (she bore eight
children, one of whom died), unremitting journalistic work (editing, with Wilfrid *The
Weekly Register*, *Merry England* and, for a time, *The Pen*) and, later, of political action (she
became a staunch supporter of the non-militant suffragists).

During this time she also produced several volumes of poetry. The first of these, *Preludes* (1875), was much praised by Tennyson and Ruskin ('To a Daisy' found special favour with Ruskin), while later works gained her the friendship of the poets Francis Thompson, Coventry Patmore and George Meredith. Each of these seems to have been to some extent in love with her. Thompson was rescued by the Meynells from a life of destitution and drug addiction, and subsequently regarded Alice as his saving Madonna. Patmore was adoring but neurotically jealous of her friendships with other men, while the elderly Meredith remained probably the most supportive friend and mentor, though he too was inclined to cavil over minute improprieties in her work. The strain of this erotic idealization no doubt took its toll of Alice's life as well as her poetry. She became a prey to incapacitating headaches and suffered from long creative blocks, when the silence she claimed to admire became a painful and hampering reality. The requirement to be at once a mother, madonna and muse to these demanding and vulnerable men must have been difficult to accommodate to her own needs as a poet.

Probably the happiest years of her life were the last twenty or so, when, freed from the pressures of a young family, she was able to travel. She went to France, Germany and, most often, Italy — 'Nothing but Italy could have drawn me away from all I love' (V. Meynell 1929: 280), she once wrote. Her poem 'The Watershed' suggests how deep and 'altering' an experience Italy was for her. In 1901 she undertook a six-month lecturing tour in the United States, where she travelled tirelessly along the length and breadth of the country, delaying her return home when her friend, the poet Agnes Tobin, became ill. Women friends seem to have become increasingly important to her in these later years. One of the closest of them was Katharine Tynan, another Catholic poet, with whom Alice corresponded for many years and with whom she seems to have enjoyed a confiding and relatively untroubled friendship. 'I love you much. I have always loved you' (John Rylands Library, MS *Letters*: 115), she once affirmed, and in a curiously roundabout gesture of affection informed her friend: 'You know you are the only other woman he [Wilfrid] would have wanted to marry' (104). These years also saw Alice becoming active in the suffrage movement. She marched alongside Ethel Smyth, Cicely Hamilton and May Sinclair in the big demonstrations of 1910–12, and was a prominent member of the Society of Women Journalists. The title poem of her 1917 volume, 'A Father of Women', powerfully turns a private cry to her own dead father into an anguished call to the fathers of the land to grant their daughters the vote.

In spite of her political and journalistic activity, Meynell's poetry remains largely personal and lyrical. She can sometimes be over-scrupulous in her sentiments, the reticence she admired becoming a mere daintiness in places. However, her best poetry conceals, behind its deceptive simplicity of form, a complexity of attitude which resists resolution into easy messages. In particular her poems about motherhood ('Cradle-Song at Twilight', 'The Modern Mother', 'Maternity', 'The Girl on the Land') draw on her own ambiguous feelings about being a mother (she herself was notoriously absent-minded about her children, addressing them all, at times of stress, as 'child'). There is a long tradition of verse about motherhood amongst Victorian women poets, much of it uneasy, questioning and sceptical as well as rapturous and satisfied. But Meynell is probably the first poet overtly to acknowledge the 'unmaternal' instincts as well as the wider social and political pressures of parenthood. Far from being a source of joy and consolation, her own motherhood seems to have filled her with a sense of oppression and misgiving. Most of her 'mother' poems movingly exploit the failure of passion, the feeling of anxious, guilty detachment, which is the key motif of much of her verse.

When she writes about parents and children, Meynell's unsentimental abstemiousness and resonant silences bring to the topic a notably modern sense of uncertainty and foreboding.

Interestingly, her one poem on the old sexual theme of the fallen woman, 'A Study', which was omitted from her *Collected Poems* of 1913, is in fact about a mother and her son. In this strange dramatic monologue, the fact of having borne an illegitimate child is curiously confused with being a child oneself, whether literally or metaphorically. As in 'A Letter from a Girl to her own Old Age' and even 'Cradle-Song at Twilight', mothering, for Meynell, suggests as much a changed relationship to the self as a sexual relationship of guilt or redemption to another. The father is nowhere evident in this poem. Instead, it is the subjectivity of the mother, her loss of 'childhood in [her] heart', which is poignantly and regretfully explored.

A.L.

Meynell, Alice (1913) *Collected Poems*, London, Burnes & Oates.
—— (1940) *Poems*, London, Oxford University Press.
—— (1947) *Prose and Poetry*, introduction by V. Sackville-West, London, Jonathan Cape.

Badeni, June (1981) *The Slender Tree: A Life of Alice Meynell*, Padstow, Tabb House.
Leighton, Angela (1992) *Victorian Women Poets*, Hemel Hempstead, Harvester, pp. 244–65.
Meynell, Viola (1929) *Alice Meynell: A Memoir*, London, Jonathan Cape:
Schlack, Beverly Ann 'The poetess of poets: Alice Meynell rediscovered', *Women's Studies*, 7 (1980), 111–26.

To the Beloved

Oh, not more subtly silence strays
    Amongst the winds, between the voices,
Mingling alike with pensive lays,
    And with the music that rejoices,
Than thou art present in my days.   5

My silence, life returns to thee
    In all the pauses of her breath.
Hush back to rest the melody
    That out of thee awakeneth;
And thou, wake ever, wake for me!   10

Thou art like silence all unvexed,
    Though wild words part my soul from thee.
Thou art like silence unperplexed,
    A secret and a mystery
Between one footfall and the next.   15

Most dear pause in a mellow lay!
    Thou art inwoven with every air.
With thee the wildest tempests play,

And snatches of thee everywhere
Make little heavens throughout a day.   20

Darkness and solitude shine, for me.
    For life's fair outward part are rife
The silver noises; let them be.
    It is the very soul of life
Listens for thee, listens for thee.   25

O pause between the sobs of cares;
    O thought within all thought that is;
Trance between laughters unawares:
    Thou art the shape of melodies,
And thou the ecstasy of prayers!   30

A Letter from a Girl to her own Old Age

Listen, and when thy hand this paper presses,
O time-worn woman, think of her who blesses
What thy thin fingers touch, with her caresses.

O mother, for the weight of years that break thee!
O daughter, for slow time must yet awake thee,   5
And from the changes of my heart must make thee!

O fainting traveller, morn is grey in heaven.
Dost thou remember how the clouds were driven?
And are they calm about the fall of even?

Pause near the ending of thy long migration,   10
For this one sudden hour of desolation
Appeals to one hour of thy meditation.

Suffer, O silent one, that I remind thee
Of the great hills that stormed the sky behind thee,
Of the wild winds of power that have resigned thee.   15

Know that the mournful plain where thou must wander
Is but a grey and silent world, but ponder
The misty mountains of the morning yonder.

Listen: – the mountain winds with rain were fretting,
And sudden gleams the mountain-tops besetting.   20
I cannot let thee fade to death, forgetting.

What part of this wild heart of mine I know not
Will follow with thee where the great winds blow not,
And where the young flowers of the mountain grow not.

Yet let my letter with my lost thoughts in it   25
Tell what the way was when thou didst begin it,
And win with thee the goal when thou shalt win it.

Oh, in some hour of thine my thoughts shall guide thee.
Suddenly, though time, darkness, silence, hide thee,
This wind from thy lost country flits beside thee, —   30

Telling thee: all thy memories moved the maiden,
With thy regrets was morning over-shaden,
With sorrow, thou hast left, her life was laden.

But whither shall my thoughts turn to pursue thee?
Life changes, and the years and days renew thee.   35
Oh, Nature brings my straying heart unto thee.

Her winds will join us, with their constant kisses
Upon the evening as the morning tresses,
Her summers breathe the same unchanging blisses.

And we, so altered in our shifting phases,   40
Track one another 'mid the many mazes
By the eternal child-breath of the daisies.

I have not writ this letter of divining
To make a glory of thy silent pining,
A triumph of thy mute and strange declining.   45

Only one youth, and the bright life was shrouded.
Only one morning, and the day was clouded.
And one old age with all regrets is crowded.

O hush, O hush! Thy tears my words are steeping.
O hush, hush, hush! So full, the fount of weeping?   50
Poor eyes, so quickly moved, so near to sleeping?

Pardon the girl; such strange desires beset her.
Poor woman, lay aside the mournful letter
That breaks thy heart; the one who wrote, forget her:

The one who now thy faded features guesses,   55
With filial fingers thy grey hair caresses,
With morning tears thy mournful twilight blesses.

To a Daisy

Slight as thou art, thou art enough to hide
  Like all created things, secrets from me,

And stand a barrier to eternity.
And I, how can I praise thee well and wide
From where I dwell – upon the hither side?   5
 Thou little veil for so great mystery,
 When shall I penetrate all things and thee,
And then look back? For this I must abide,

Till thou shalt grow and fold and be unfurled
Literally between me and the world.   10
 Then I shall drink from in beneath a spring,
And from a poet's side shall read his book.
O daisy mine, what will it be to look
 From God's side even of such a simple thing?

A Study

In three monologues, with interruptions

I

Before Light

Among the first to wake. What wakes with me?
A blind wind and a few birds and a star.
With tremor of darkened flowers and whisper of birds,
Oh, with a tremor, with a tremor of heart –
Begins the day i' the dark. I, newly waked,   5
Grope backwards for my dreams, thinking to slide
Back unawares to dreams, in vain, in vain.
There is a sorrow for me in this day.
It watched me from afar the livelong night,
And now draws near, but has not touched me yet.   10
In from my garden flits the secret wind, –
My garden. – This great day with all its hours
(Its hours, my soul!) will be like other days
Among my flowers. The morning will awake,
Like to the lonely waking of a child   15
Who grows uneasily to a sense of tears,
Because his mother had come and wept and gone;
The morning grass and lilies will be wet,
In all their happiness, with mysterious dews.
And I shall leave the high noon in my garden,   20
The sun enthroned and all his court my flowers,
And go my journey as I live, – alone.
Then in the ripe rays of the later day
All the small blades of thin grass one by one,
Looked through with sun, will make each a long shade,   25
And daisies' heads will bend with butterflies.

And one will come with secrets at her heart,
Evening, whose darkening eyes hide all her heart,
And poppy-crowned move 'mid my lonely flowers.
And shall another, I wonder, come with her, –   30
I, with a heavy secret at my heart,
Uncrowned of all crowns to my garden and flowers?
Thou little home of mine, fair be thy day.
These things will be, but oh, across the hills,
Behind me in the dark, what things will be?   35
– Well, even if sorrow fills me through and through
Until my life be pain and pain my life,
Shall I not bear myself and my own life?
– A little life, O Lord, a little sorrow.
And I remember once when I was ill   40
That the whole world seemed breaking through with me,
Who lay so light and still; stillness availed not,
My weakness being a thing of power, I thought.

'Come to the Port to-morrow', says the letter,
And little more, except a few calm words,   45
Intended to prepare me (and I guess,
I guess for what). He never was too kind,
This man, the one i' the world, kin to my son,
Who knew my crime, who watched me with cold eyes,
And stayed me with calm hands, and hid the thing,   50
For horror more than pity; and took my son;
And mercifully let me ebb away
In this grey town of undesigned grey lives,
Five years already. To-day he sends for me.
And now I will prevent the dawn with prayers.   55

2

About Noon

She shut her five years up within the house.
And towards the noon she lifted up her eyes,
Looked to the gentle hills with a stirred heart,
Moved with the mystery of unknown places
Near to a long-known home; smiled, as she could,   60
A difficult smile that hurt half of her mouth,
Until she passed the streets and all sharp looks.

'Sharp looks, and since I was a child, sharp looks!
These know not, certainly, who scan me so,
That not a girl of all their brightest girls   65
Has such an eager heart for smiles as I.
It is no doubt the fault of my cold face

And reticent eyes that never make appeal,
Or plead for the small pale bewildered soul.
If they but knew what a poor child I am!   70
– Oh, born of all the past, what a poor child!
I could waste golden days and showers of words,
And laugh for nothing, and read my poets again,
And tend a voice I had, songless for ever; –
I would not if I might. I would not cease,   75
Not if I might, the penance and the pain
For that lost soul down somewhere in the past,
That soul of mine that did and knew such things,
If I could choose; and yet I wish, I wish,
Such little wishes, and so longingly.   80
Who would believe me, knowing what I am?

'Now from these noontide hills my home, my time,
My life for years lies underneath mine eyes,
And all the years that led up to these years.
I can judge now, and not the world for me.   85
And I, being what I am, and having done
What I have done, look back upon my youth
– Before my crime, I mean, – and testify:
It was not happy, no, it was not white,
It was not innocent, no, the young fair time.   90
The people and the years passed in my glass;
And all the insincerity of my thoughts
I laid upon the pure and simple Nature
(Now all the hills and fields are free of me),
Smiling at my elaborate sigh the smile   95
Of any Greek composing sunny gods.
And now begins my one true white child-time,
This time of desolate altars and all ruins.
For Pan is dead and the altars are in ruins.

'The world is full of endings for me, I find,   100
Emotions lost, and words and thoughts forgotten.
Yet amid all these *last* things, there is one,
But one Beginning, a seed within my soul.
Come quickly! and go by quickly, O my years!
Strip me of things and thoughts; as I have seen   105
The ilex changing leaves; for day by day
A little innocent life grows in my life,
A little ignorant life i' the world-worn life;
And I become a child with a world to learn,
Timorous, with another world to learn,   110
Timorous, younger, whiter towards my death.'

She turned to the strange sea that five long years
Had sent her letters of his misty winds,

Bearing a cry of storms in other lands,
And songs of mariners singing over seas;   115
And having long conjectured of his face,
Seeing his face, paused, thinking of the past.
Down the hills came she to the town and sea,
And met her child's friend where he waited her.
She swayed to his words unsaid, as the green canes   120
Murmur i' the quiet unto a wind that comes:

'I sent for you, mind, for your sake alone.
– No, my dear ward is well. But it has chanced
(I know it's a hard thing for you to bear,
But you are strong, I know) that he has learnt   125
What I had faithfully kept, – your life, your past,
Your secret. Well, we hope that you repent,
At least, your son and I.'

             'God bless my son,
My little son hopes I repent at least.'

'When he had read the papers – by mischance –   130
I would have kept them from him, broken down,
Beside himself at first, though the young heart
Recovered and is calm now, he resolved
On the completest parting, for he thinks
He could not live under one sky with you.   135
But being unwilling to disturb you now
And vex you in your harmless life, gives up
His hopes in England, his career, and sails
To-night to make a new life in the States.
As to the question of your seeing him   140
(He is in the town here), I persuaded him
To let you choose, this being probably
The last time in this world. It rests with you.'

'I pray you, as we pray morning and night,
Save me from the sick eyes of my one child;   145
But let me see my one child once. Amen.

'I never came across the hills before
In all these years; now all these years are done.
Who would have said it, yesterday at this hour?
Now my son knows, and I have crossed the hills,   150
And sure my poor face faces other things.
Not back! not home! anything, anything,
Anything – no, don't turn, I am very calm.
Not back the way I came to-day, not home.
Oh, anything but home and a long life.'   155

'Am I the arbiter? Besides, what fate
Can you desire more merciful than home
And hidden life? And then remember him.
You have borne the separation as it seems
With the most perfect patience. And your life   160
Ending (as to the world), owes this at least –
It is not much – to his bright beginning life,
Absence and perfect silence till you die.
I've done my duty, as I think, to both.
If you seemed in the least to ask for pity   165
I well could pity you. I hope that time
Will bring you a softer heart. Good-bye.'

    'Good-bye.'

3

At Twilight

Gone, O my child forsaking me, my flower.
Yet I forsaken pity you with tears,
Gone while I learn a world to learn a world.   170
I am to have no part with you again,
And you have many things to share; it's keen, –
I love you, I love you; but more keen is this, –
That you will have no part with me again;
And what have I to share? Pain, happy child.   175
Gone, gone into the west, for ever gone,
O little one, my flower; not you alone,
My son who are leaving me, but he, the child
Of five years back. That is the worst farewell.
I had not thought him lost until to-day.   180
But he had kept with me until to-day; –
Never seen, never heard; but he was there,
Behind the door on which I laid my hand,
Out in the garden when I sat within,
A turn of road before me in my walks.   185
As others greet a presence I did greet
An absence, O my sweet, my sweet surprise!
How will it be now? for he is so changed
I hardly knew the face I saw pass by.
And yet it is the one that must of needs   190
Grow from that long ago face innocent,
Grave with the presage of a human life.
So, child, giving again in thought my kiss,
My last, long since, I kiss you tall and changed
In that one kiss, and kiss you a man and old,   195
And so I kiss you dead. And yet, O child,

O child, a certain soul goes from my days;
They fall together like a rosary told,
Not aves now, but beads, – you being gone.

I was not worthy to be comfortless,   200
I find, and feasts broke in upon my fasts;
And innocent distractions and desires
Surprised me in my penitential tears.
For my absent child God gives me a child in Spring;
New seasons and the fresh and innocent earth,   205
Ever new years and children of the years,
Kin to the young thoughts of my weary heart,
Chime with the young thoughts of my weary heart,
My kin in all the world. And He Himself
Is young i' the quiet time of cold and snows.   210
(Mary! who fledst to Egypt with Him; Joseph!
And thou whose tomb I kissed in Padua,
Protect this perilous childhood in my heart!)
But oh, to-night, I know not why, to-night
Out of the earth and sky, out of the sea   215
My consolations fade. These empty arms
I stretch no more unto the beautiful world,
But clasp them close about the lonely heart
No other arms will clasp. What is thy pain,
What is thy pain, inexplicable heart?   220
Sorrow for ruined and for desolate days.
Failing in penitence, I, who fail in all,
Leave all my thoughts alone, and lift mine eyes
Quietly to One who makes amends for me.
Peace, O my soul, for thou hast failed in all: 225
(One thought, at last, that I might take to Heaven!)
It's well I never guessed this thing before,
I mean the weakness and the littleness
Of that which by God's grace begins in me.
Oh, earthly hopes and wishes, stay with me   230
(He will be patient); linger, O my loves
And phases of myself, and play with this
New life of grace (as He whose gift it is
Played with the children, a child). How could I bear
To see how little is perfect yet – a speck   235
If all things else should suddenly wither away?
(And yet they wither away, they wither away.)
Less than I knew, less than I know am I,
Returning childless, but, O Father, a child.

She therefore turned unto the Eastern hills,   240
Thrilled with a west wind sowing stars. She saw
Her lonely upward way climb to the verge

And ending of the day-time; and she knew
The downward way in presence of the night.
She heard the fitful sheep-bells in the glen   245
Move like a child's thoughts. There she felt the earth
Lonely in space. And all things suddenly   80
Shook with her tears. She went with shadowless feet,
Moving along the shadow of the world,
Faring alone to home and a long life,   250
Setting a twilight face to meet the stars.

Renouncement

I must not think of thee; and, tired yet strong,
  I shun the thought that lurks in all delight –
    The thought of thee – and in the blue Heaven's height,
And in the sweetest passage of a song.
O just beyond the fairest thoughts that throng   5
  This breast, the thought of thee waits hidden yet bright;
    But it must never, never come in sight;
I must stop short of thee the whole day long.

But when sleep comes to close each difficult day,
  When night gives pause to the long watch I keep,   10
    And all my bonds I needs must loose apart,
Must doff my will as raiment laid away, –
  With the first dream that comes with the first sleep
    I run, I run, I am gathered to thy heart.

Parentage

*When Augustus Cæsar legislated against the unmarried citizens of Rome, he declared them to
be, in some sort, slayers of the people.*

    Ah! no, not these!
These, who were childless, are not they who gave
So many dead unto the journeying wave,
The helpless nurslings of the cradling seas;
Not they who doomed by infallible decrees   5
Unnumbered man to the innumerable grave.

    But those who slay
Are fathers. Theirs are armies. Death is theirs –
The death of innocences and despairs;
The dying of the golden and the grey.   10
The sentence, when these speak it, has no Nay.
And she who slays is she who bears, who bears.

Cradle-Song at Twilight

The child not yet is lulled to rest.
    Too young a nurse, the slender Night
So laxly holds him to her breast
    That throbs with flight.

He plays with her, and will not sleep.   5
    For other playfellows she sighs;
An unmaternal fondness keep
    Her alien eyes.

The Modern Mother

        Oh, what a kiss
With filial passion overcharged is this!
        To this misgiving breast
This child runs, as a child ne'er ran to rest
Upon the light heart and the unoppressed.   5

        Unhoped, unsought!
A little tenderness, this mother thought
        The utmost of her meed.
She looked for gratitude; content indeed
With thus much that her nine years' love had bought.   10

        Nay, even with less.
This mother, giver of life, death, peace, distress,
        Desired ah! not so much
Thanks as forgiveness; and the passing touch
Expected, and the slight, the brief caress.   15

        O filial light
Strong in these childish eyes, these new, these bright
        Intelligible stars! Their rays
Are near the constant earth, guides in the maze,
Natural, true, keen in this dusk of days.   20

The Watershed

Lines written between Munich and Verona

Black mountains pricked with pointed pine
    A melancholy sky.
Out-distanced was the German vine,
    The sterile fields lay high.

From swarthy Alps I travelled forth
Aloft; it was the north, the north;
   Bound for the Noon was I.   5

I seemed to breast the streams that day;
   I met, opposed, withstood
The northward rivers on their way,   10
   My heart against the flood –
My heart that pressed to rise and reach,
And felt the love of altering speech,
   Of frontiers, in its blood.

But O the unfolding South! the burst   15
   Of summer! O to see
Of all the southward brooks the first!
   The travelling heart went free
With endless streams; that strife was stopped;
And down a thousand vales I dropped,   20
   I flowed to Italy.

Maternity

One wept whose only child was dead,
   New-born, ten years ago.
'Weep not; he is in bliss,' they said.
   She answered, 'Even so,

'Ten years ago was born in pain   5
   A child, not now forlorn.
But oh, ten years ago, in vain,
   A mother, a mother was born.'

Christ in the Universe

   With this ambiguous earth
His dealings have been told us. These abide:
The signal to a maid, the human birth,
The lesson, and the young Man crucified.

   But not a star of all   5
The innumerable host of stars has heard
How He administered this terrestrial ball.
Our race have kept their Lord's entrusted Word.

   Of His earth-visiting feet
None knows the secret, cherished, perilous,   10

The terrible, shamefast, frightened, whispered, sweet,
Heart-shattering secret of His way with us.

No planet knows that this
Our wayside planet, carrying land and wave,
Love and life multiplied, and pain and bliss,
Bears, as chief treasure, one forsaken grave.

Nor, in our little day,
May His devices with the heavens be guessed,
His pilgrimage to thread the Milky Way,
Or His bestowals there be manifest.

But in the eternities,
Doubtless we shall compare together, hear
A million alien Gospels, in what guise
He trod the Pleiades, the Lyre, the Bear.

O be prepared, my soul!
To read the inconceivable, to scan
The million forms of God those stars unroll
When, in our turn, we show to them a Man.

A Father of Women

Ad Sororem E. B.[1]
'Thy father was transfused into thy blood.
Dryden *Ode to Mrs. Anne Killigrew*

Our father works in us,
The daughters of his manhood. Not undone
Is he, not wasted, though transmuted thus,
And though he left no son.

Therefore on him I cry
To arm me: 'For my delicate mind a casque,
A breastplate for my heart, courage to die,
Of thee, captain, I ask.

'Nor strengthen only; press
A finger on this violent blood and pale,
Over this rash will let thy tenderness
A while pause, and prevail.

'And shepherd-father, thou
Whose staff folded my thoughts before my birth,

15

20

25

5

10

[1 To my sister]

Control them now I am of earth, and now   15
    Thou art no more of earth.

'O liberal, constant, dear,
Crush in my nature the ungenerous art
Of the inferior; set me high, and here,
    Here garner up thy heart!'   20

Like to him now are they,
The million living fathers of the War –
Mourning the crippled world, the bitter day –
    Whose striplings are no more.

The crippled world! Come then,   25
Fathers of women with your honour in trust,
Approve, accept, know them daughters of men,
    Now that your sons are dust.

To Silence

'Space, the bound of a solid': Silence, then, the form of a melody

Not, Silence, for thine idleness I raise
My silence-bounded singing in thy praise,
But for thy moulding of my Mozart's tune,
Thy hold upon the bird that sings the moon,
    Thy magisterial ways.   5

Man's lovely definite melody-shapes are thine,
Outlined, controlled, compressed, complete, divine.
Also thy fine intrusions do I trace,
Thy afterthoughts, thy wandering, thy grace,
    Within the poet's line.   10

Thy secret is the song that is to be.
Music had never stature but for thee,
Sculptor! strong as the sculptor Space whose hand
Urged the Discobolus and bade him stand.

Man, on his way to Silence, stops to hear and see.   15

The Girl on the Land

'When have I known a boy
Kinder than this my daughter, or his kiss
More filial, or the clasping of his joy
    Closer than this?'

> Thus did a mother think; 5
> And yet her daughter had been long away,
> Estranged, on other business; but the link
> Was fast to-day.
>
> This mother, who was she?
> I know she was the earth, she was the land. 10
> Her daughter, a gay girl, toiled happily,
> Sheaves in her hand.

May Probyn (dates unknown)

The facts of May Probyn's life are obscure and nothing can be discovered beyond a few indications in her published works. May lived in Weybridge and would seem to have had a happy childhood shared with a sister and a brother if the dedication to 'my mother and a thousand happy memories' (Probyn 1878: 1) is to be believed. Her first book (1878) was an adventure novel about heiresses and elopements, but her second, *Who Killed Cock Robin?* was published by the Literary Production Committee after May won second prize in a competition for amateur authors. Her book of *Poems* (1881) was dedicated to Thomas Westwood, an aspiring poet in the 1840s who had once sought out Barrett Browning because he admired her poetry and corresponded with her in the 1840s and 50s. He moved to Belgium where he became director of a railroad and he would have been in his sixties by the time May knew him. The wistful little lyric about lost opportunity 'A Song Out of Season' may be addressed to him.

By the time she published *A Ballad of the Road and Other Poems* (1883), May seems to have gone up in the poetical world because it is dedicated to Alfred Tennyson. For the next ten years her work was published in magazines and anthologies, among them Miles's *The Poets and the Poetry of the Century* (1891). Then in 1895 a final collection called *Pansies* appeared with a note from the publisher saying that her other work was long out of print, and that she had been silent for ten years: 'Miss Probyn is a convert to Catholicism and her new book will contain some fervent religious poetry often tinged with medieval mannerism. Her carols might have been written by some very devout and simple monk of the middle ages' (Probyn [1895]: 15).

We may know as little of Probyn's life as of a monk in the middle ages, but the voice in her poetry is distinctive. Explicitly feminist in tone, some of her poems re-work the themes of other women poets. 'The Model' is a poem about the male gaze where the artist constructs the woman without ever seeing her real self. In this it resembles Rossetti's 'In an Artist's Studio' and Siddal's 'The Lust of the Eyes'. But Probyn takes the argument a stage further and makes the connection between this male failure of vision and sexual betrayal. In this way the serious political implications of what appears to be a simple case of sexual stereotyping are made absolutely clear. 'The Model' is also a mirror poem like Lindsay's 'To My Own Face' because the model looks at her own face in the mirror to read her self through the images stamped there. And it is a picture poem, like the scene in Book II of Barrett Browning's *Aurora Leigh*. Like Aurora, Probyn's model self-consciously tries out poses and the possibilities of various representations of woman. Interestingly, both the picture she imagines that the artist will paint, and the picture which he had already painted, are without doubt pre-Raphaelite paintings given their trappings and props: the 'great gold serpents coiled about the throat' for Herodias and 'a spinning wheel' and 'groups of lilies' for the Virgin. It would seem highly likely that Probyn knew Dante Gabriel Rossetti's paintings and one wonders how much she knew of Lizzie Siddal's story.

Like other poems of the 1880s, notably Augusta Webster's 'A Castaway', Probyn's 'The Model' uses the dramatic monologue to give a voice to those who are silenced. In 'The End of the Journey' she takes up the cause of the native woman betrayed by the white man. In its sympathy for the woman who is colonized along with her land, the poem resembles Barrett Browning's 'The Runaway Slave', but the brief reference in the last stanza which compares her tenacious adoration with a 'dog's dumb patient look' aligns the poem with others about animals (Greenwell's 'Fidelity Rewarded') and children (Barrett Browning's 'The Cry of the Children', Cook's ' "Our Father" ') which plead for all dispossessed and exploited classes, women, slaves, natives, children and animals alike.

Probyn's poetic vocabulary is disarmingly simple when she writes lyrics. As in Rossetti's work, this is deceptive. In 'Changes' the scenes are prettily drawn to the extent of seeming babyish, but the placing of the repeated word 'only' means that the syntax of the poem forces the reader to imagine what is not said, – a technique very much in the manner of Rossetti's eloquent repeated negatives in 'Song' (When I am dead, my dearest'). The method adapts effectively to her 'Triolets' which are witty and sharp and economical, and, yet which, in all their nerviness and oddity, provide a vivid sketch of Victorian scenes that reveals more than any history book.

M. R.

Probyn, May (1880) *Who Killed Cock Robin?*, London.
—— (1883) *A Ballad of the Road and Other Poems*, London.
—— (n.d. 1895) Proof copy of *Pansies* with manuscript corrections in the author's hand, in the Bodleian Library.
—— (1895) *Pansies*, London.

The Model

Not three years since – and now he asks my name!
Not know me? – God! am I so changed, so changed?

Now that I stay to seek it, how it stares
Out of this scrap of wretched looking-glass,
Just big enough to hold my face, no more.   5
'Twas in this same, small, ragged bit of glass
I looked, when first I wore the little pearls
He gave me for my ears, three Easters back –
Poor little paltry things enough they are!
But then, they seemed almost too beautiful   10
To wear in such a weekday world as mine.

Still looking for it – yes, I understand,
I see the reason why he sent to-day,

And fetched me, having passed me in the street.
Herodias is his picture, and my face   15
Will make her all he wants. Strange luck he has!
(I've heard him say it fifty times before)
Unfailingly just finds the face he needs.
Tis hard to see in this unlighted place,
With but one guttering wick – yet, even here,   20
It only wants the shoulder-slipping garb,
The great gold serpents coiled about the throat,
And writhing up the large, round, naked arm –
It only wants the hair, cloud-falling – so!
And, lo, Herodias gleams there in the glass!   25
'Tis but to drop the chin into the palm,
Thrust both a little forward – thus! as though
Inviting hatred from a world contemned,
And there she sits, the beautiful, bad thing,
With superciliously defiant eyes,   30
And stealthy smile beneath the half-dropped lids,
Cruel as panther crouching for the spring.
Add but the whiteness of a bosom bared,
Large jewelled hoops for earrings – cast away
These clumsy shoes, and bind about with gold   35
The sleek, ripe-rounded ankles – and enough!
'Tis she, just as he paints her – nothing lacks –
Half animal, half fiend – not old, not young –
Steeped to the brows in splendid shamelessness.

Curse on this draught that takes the candle flame!   40
'Twill flicker out for end of all its flare –
And if I hold it up, for better view,
The roof will be on fire, it slopes so low.
Who'd choose the garret for their dwelling place?
Oven in the summer, ice-hole in the frost,   45
Rain dripping through, and rats for company,
Half a day's climb to reach it – Once, indeed,
To be so high seemed but the nearer heaven!
And there was one that mounted – was it I? –
The steep, uneven stair, three steps at once,   50
Sweet singing like some soul in Paradise.
And violet scents would linger in the air –
A little jar, set here upon the shelf,
Weighting the place with breath as fine and faint
As when the incense cloud goes floating up   55
Among the fretted aisles, and in the hush
The Host is lifted, and the organ dies.
Perhaps he gave the violets – I forget!
He gave me many things, in idleness,
As one might give a child. Here, too, at nights,   60

If you were pleasure-loving, you could lean
Both arms upon the sill, and see beneath
The lamps all twinkling, twinkling through the town,
And hear the half articulate music sound
From off the boulevard and the gaslit trees,   65
While out of heaven the great white stars looked down,
And trembled where they hung – the whole night through
One felt them shine athwart the uncurtained pane,
Like friends of old, and turned, and dreamed anew;
And in the morning, long before the light,   70
How loud the swallows cheeped beneath the eaves,
Until their twitter drove the dreams apart,
And waking seemed mere joy of being alive!
But that was long ago! three years ago!
I was young, then, and he was painting me   75
As Mary Maiden, grave and innocent,
Sitting untroubled at a spinning-wheel,
With sunset flaming through a pane behind,
And groups of lilies, and a garden plot,
Before the angel came.

                And now, to-day,   80
He looked, looked twice and thrice – and asked my name!

He stirred as though the dead had come to life –
He thought of his Maid-Mother first, I know,
And would not credit, and 'Thank God,' he said,
– Thick muttered in his throat, but I could hear –   85
'Thank God I never loved her!' And I laughed –
Herodias must have laughed that very laugh!
Full-eyed I faced him, as he turned about,
And cried between his teeth, 'You think I loved?
Not I! not I! Never so near I came,   90
But at the last, a look was in your eyes
That said no man could love you and be blest,
And on the brink I stayed – for that, thank God!'
Then up I sprang – 'Pity, in sooth,' I said –
More hiss than speech it sounded to myself,   95
As though a snake had spat into his face –
'Pity, in sooth, to have squandered, all in vain,
Such love as yours, most perfect man of love!'
The mesh of silk, wherein his subtle hand
Had wound me, half across the room I flung,   100
And snatched my old, dim, faded cloak again,
And dragged its hood above my storm of hair –
'One thing alone Herodias lacked,' I said,
'She should have smitten, herself, with her own palm,
The scorner, the rebuker' – and stepped close,   105

And lifted up my slim, unfolded hand,
And struck him, slightly, swiftly, in the face,
And nodded him farewell, and went, or ere
The outraged red could spring into his cheek.

So now, belike, he will not brook again   110
That I should sit to him; or if he do,
Belike I shall not go. To me all's one,
His loathing or his loving – yet, sometimes,
I think that had he loved me in those days,
Never so little, only for one hour,   115
To-day, perhaps, I were not all I am –
Perhaps Herodias had not worn my face.

'As the Flower of the Grass'

    Crack! crack!
A rocket that soared, with a shower of fire, through the black —

How they trembled and murmured, the gaslit, mysterious trees,
And the swell of the music went swooning away on the breeze,
And she, with a face like a flower, and a flower at her throat,   5
And a slim, scented glove just touching the sleeve of my coat,
Whispered and walked; and I knew, while I stared in her face,
Half the men in the crowd were thirsting to stand in my place,
And, like mirrors, the women that watched her, next day would repeat
The rose at her ear and the pearl-buckled shoes on her feet.   10
The mad, merry chime of the valses, half passion, half game,
That shivered and sobbed through its laughter, was called by her name,
Her name, that we shouted whenever the winecups were filled,
Till swords would leap out of the scabbard, and blood would be spilled –
The fountains shot higher, the people pressed round in a lane,   15
As she passed to her carriage, with lordling and prince in her train –

    Crack! crack!
The rocket soared upward, and rushed out of sight through the black . . .

The rose leaves have faded, and fallen, and mixed with the dust,
The roses that kissed the small ear, where the diamond was thrust.   20
'Mid twanging of fiddles, and lamps like a rainbow that shine,
Not hers are the fingers that plunge the camellias in wine,
Not hers the white bosom we crush, as the valse eddies by –
When the goblet foams over, 'tis no more her name that we cry –
And she –? Nay, I know not! I fancied, indeed, that to-day   25
One passed me, with face like to hers, when she turned it my way,
With lavish carnations and lilies, washed streak upon streak,
The mask of despair, on her throat and her haggard young cheek –

What of that? Vogue la galère! The rose, that is queen of to-day,
Lurks under the brim of a shepherdess hat, as at play;   30
The hand, that half-clings to my coat-sleeve, is naked and white,
The hair is gold-dusted, that brushes my shoulder tonight –

> Crack! crack!
Another red rocket, that soars out of sight through the black.

Barcarolle

Last night we sailed, my love and I,
  Last night and years ago –
Was it moon or sea, we drifted through?
  I think I shall never know!
    We had no oar –   5
    We neared no shore –
  We floated with the tide;
    The moon was white,
    And the sea alight,
And none in the world beside.   10

I and my love, we said farewell –
  It is years and years away.
We kissed our last in a life gone by –
  I think it was yesterday!
    Oh! for heaven, give me   15
    A moon and a sea
  To sail, when we both have died,
    With never an oar –
    With never a shore –
Drifting on with the tide!   20

Ballade of Lovers

Double Refrain.

For the man was she made by the Eden tree,
  To be decked in soft raiment, and worn on his sleeve,
To be fondled so long as they both agree,
  A thing to take, or a thing to leave.
  But for her, let her live through one long summer eve,   5
Just the stars, and the moon, and the man, and she –
  And her soul will escape her beyond reprieve,
And, alas! the whole of her world is he.

To-morrow brings plenty as lovesome, maybe –
  If she break when he handles her, why should he grieve?   10
She is only one pearl in a pearl-crowded sea,

A thing to take, or a thing to leave.
But she, though she knows he has kissed to deceive
And forsakes her, still only clings on at his knee –
When life has gone, what further loss can bereave? 15
And, alas! the whole of her world is he.

For the man was she made upon Eden lea,
To be helpmeet what time there is burden to heave,
White-footed, to follow where he walks free,
A thing to take, or a thing to leave, – 20
White-fingered, to weave and to interweave
Her woof with his warp and a tear two or three,
Till clear his way out through her web he cleave,
And, alas! the whole of her world is he.

Envoi

Did he own her no more, when he named her Eve, 25
Than a thing to take, or a thing to leave?
A flower-filled plot, that unlocks to his key –
But, alas! the whole of her world is he.

Blossom

In the orchard grass, through the daisies and clover,
She wandered along by the side of her lover.

She pulled the bloom from the bough above her;
And the lover watched, and stood still to reprove her.

'Appleflower for a farewell token – 5
To-morrow,' she said, 'my heart will have broken.

'You may come back when the rose is in bower,
But no summer can bring back the appleflower.

'Rains may water, and suns may dapple,
But these will never grow to the apple. 10

'Bloom and germ will have perished to-morrow –
Take it,' she said, ' 'tis the token of sorrow!'

Appleflower, and the look of a lover –
Then the orchard gate – and all of it over.

Anniversaries

Near, and more near, without sight or sound,
　　The suns and the seasons shape it;
And the day comes round, the day comes round,
　　And none of us can escape it.

We have baffled the thoughts, we have held them at bay;　　　　5
　　We have hidden their rags and tatters;
We have turned our faces the other way;
　　We have talked of other matters.

But we could not stay the leaves on the tree
　　From yellowing and falling;　　　　　　　　　　　　　　10
We could not wither the buds on the lea,
　　Nor hush the cuckoo's calling.

We cannot banish the bird that cried
　　As the well-beloved departed,
Nor the flowers that bloomed when the dear one died,　　　15
　　And we sat broken hearted.

Year upon year, without sight or sound,
　　The moons and the midnights shape it –
And the day comes round – the day comes round –
　　Would God we could escape it!　　　　　　　　　　　20

The End of the Journey

She had travelled through nights and days,
　　Barely staying to rest,
By lonely, perilous ways,
　　Farther and farther west,
Till a beach and a long blue race　　　　　　　　　　　5
　　And a sail came into sight,
And she knew she should look on his face
　　Before she lay down that night.

In the dust, a track of red
　　Followed her naked feet;　　　　　　　　　　　　　10
On her small, uncovered head
　　The blaze of the sunset beat;
No sense remained of cold,
　　Or heat, or hope of rest,
Only the strength to hold　　　　　　　　　　　　　15
　　His baby to her breast;

And ever, with sound the same,
  She hailed and questioned each,
Knowing no word but his name
  In all the white man's speech.   20

Where scarlet passion flowers
  Hung in the cedar trees,
She crouched through the twilight hours,
  With the babe across her knees –
'Mid the snakes and the evening damps   25
  A shadow, unreproved –
And beyond, in a glimmer of lamps,
  The fair white woman moved.

His hand unlatched the gate;
  His footstep crushed the grass;   30
A shadow desolate,
  She rose, where he should pass.
No trick she knew, nor spell
  Of wayward witcheries –
Before his feet she fell,   35
  And held him by the knees.
'Where the salt marsh currents drift,
  And the wrack is seaward swung,
I have journeyed,' she said, in her swift
  Soft-flowing Indian tongue,   40
'Across the rushing creek,
  Through the windy prairie place,
Only to hear thee speak!
  Only to look in thy face!'

He tore her hands in twain,   45
  And spurned her out of his path;
But her fingers locked again,
  And held him yet in his wrath;
With a dog's dumb, patient look,
  Undriven by blows apart,   50
She clung at his knee, and took
  His knife into her heart.

A Song Out of Season

To T. W.

What you will have it named, even that it is,
And so it shall be so.

Taming of the Shrew.

In summer-time, when all the sky was blue,
  And all the garden walks with flowers arrayed,

I sent, dear love, a little song to you.
I heard, you read it where the roses grew,
   And then you said, such songs were only made   5
In summer-time, when all the sky is blue.
So, since you nothing care to prove me true,
   I'll fret you not with any homage paid,
Save, love, that little song I sent to you –
I do but ask you, with no thought of rue,   10
   While I shall stand afar off in the shade,
Remember once, when all your sky is blue,
That little summer song I sent to you!

Changes

Only a cottage border,
   And a scent of mignonette,
And beans and peas in order,
   And a row of beehives set.
A pipkin and a platter   5
   Laid out for an evening meal;
A cage, and a magpie's chatter,
   And the whirr of a spinning wheel.
Only a woman hearkening
   For a step along the lane –   10
A shadow the doorway darkening –
   A kiss and a kiss again.

Only a church bell tolling,
   And a funeral winding slow,
And a sound of earth-sods rolling   15
   On a coffin-lid below.
Only the grass grown wavy
   On a grave, where the swallows flit –
And a cradle, and a baby,
   And no mother rocking it.   20

'More than They that Watch for the Morning'

Dear, in the terrible hour
   When the dark and the daylight meet,
When dread clangs the chime from the tower,
   And like death is the hush in the street,
While the noise of the wind-beaten rain   5
Stayed me from sleeping again,
Dear, I looked into my lot,
And I knew that I loved thee not.

Old thoughts gathered pale round the bed –
    And I knew I had never loved,   10
For the thing that seemed Love, lay dead,
    And I looked on its corpse unmoved.
In the dim and desolate dawn,
While I felt that all life was forlorn,
God did I thank through my moan   15
That Love is not this we have known.

Dear, thou shalt thank Him, too,
    Some day, when the pain is past;
Thou shalt find there is better to do,
    When thou readest thine heart at last.   20
When thou shalt have gone to the right,
And I to the left out of sight,
Dear, all the dark will be done,
And life will have just begun.

Rondelet

    'Which way he went?'
I know not – how should I go spy
    Which way he went?
I only know him gone. 'Relent?'
He never will – unless I die!   5
And then, what will it signify
    Which way he went?

Rondelet

    Say what you please,
But know, I shall not change my mind!
    Say what you please,
Even, if you wish it, on your knees –
And, when you hear me next defined   5
As something lighter than the wind,
    Say what you please!

Triolets

Tête-à-Tête

Behind her big fan,
    With its storks and pagoda,
What a nook for a man!
Behind her big fan

My enchantment began,
　Till my whole heart I showed her
Behind her big fan,
　With its storks and pagoda.

China Maniacs

'I've cracked the blue bowl!' –
'You adorable creature!' –
'Are you mad, my sweet soul?
I've *cracked* the blue bowl –'
'Why, its air new and whole
　Was its faultiest feature.'
'I've cracked the blue bowl,
　You adorable creature!'

I

Before

'Did I step on your train?' –
　'Nay, dearest, no matter!'
'My pet brown again –
Did I step on the train?'
'You wanted, 'tis plain,
　An excuse, sir, to flatter!'
'*Did* I step on your train?'
　'Nay, my dearest! what matter?'

II

After

'Your foot's on my gown' –
　'Well, it doesn't much matter!'
'You Vandal! you clown!
Your foot's on my gown' –
'Such an ugly dull brown –
　'Tisn't worth all this chatter!'
'*Your foot's on my gown!*'
　'Well, what does it matter!'

Love in Mayfair

I must tell you, my dear,
　I'm in love with him, vastly!
Twenty thousand a year,
I must tell you, my dear!
He will soon be a peer –

And such diamonds! – and, lastly,
I must tell you, my dear,
    I'm in love with him, vastly!

Masquerading

At dawn she unmasked –
    And – oh, heaven! 'twas her sister!
All her love I had asked
Ere at dawn she unmasked;
In her smile I had basked,
    I had coyed her, had kissed her –
At dawn she unmasked –
    And – oh, heaven! 'twas her sister!

Frustrated

Not a thing could I see
    But her coalscuttle bonnet!
Fair enough she may be –
Not a thing could I see!
'Twould give shelter to three –
    What induced her to don it?
Not a thing could I see
    But her coalscuttle bonnet!

Lai

Hark! the wood doves' moan,
Fondest tender tone –
    Coo, coo.

What brings life fresh-blown?
What means heaven full-grown?
    Two, two.

Here's the one alone
I will make my own –
    You, you!

Kyrielle

A rose in her hand, a rose in her breast,
A rose for the pillow her cheek has pressed.
The sun must shine though the rose is shed,
And I must live though she is dead.
The nightingale sings on as loud
Although they wind her in her shroud;

The garden stays when the flowers have fled.
And I must live though she is dead.

Each month had seemed as summer weather
Could we have braved each month together;   10
But Winter's come while the rose is red,
And I must live though she is dead.

We vowed that none should part us ever –
Ah God, the foolish, poor endeavour!
She could not stay though we were wed,   15
And I must live though she is dead.

A. Mary F. Robinson (1857–1944)

Agnes Mary Frances Robinson was the elder daughter of the archidiaconal architect for
Coventry and she was born in Leamington. Her younger sister, Mabel, was born a year
later. Mary was a delicate child and spent much of her time in her father's library reading
and educating herself until she went to school in Brussels in 1870. Later she studied in
Italy and at University College London where she worked for seven years concentrating
upon Greek literature. Mary's parents were the friends of many literary people from
Robert Browning to Oscar Wilde and when Mary came of age in 1878 her parents
offered her a choice: she could either have a grand coming-out ball or she could have a
volume of her verses published. Scholarly and ambitious, Mary chose the latter and so
her *A Handful of Honeysuckle* was privately printed in 1878 with a dedication to her
parents and some poems addressed to her close friend Vernon Lee. The poems in this
volume are pretty, fey, delicate and melancholy, and literary London soon became
interested in this young attractive woman poet. So much so that Eric Robertson said
later that there was a time when Mary Robinson was the universal topic of conversation
and speculation just as L.E.L. had once been (Robertson 1883: 376). Mary continued to
live in London and to write, publishing many volumes of verse, a novel, and a biography
of Emily Brontë (1883) for the 'Eminent Women' series. In 1888 she married James
Darmesteter, a French scholar and Professor of Persian in Paris. They were deeply
attached to one another and sought both to promote their writings by translating each
other's work, and to bring about a closer alliance between British and European cultures.
Mary's Paris salon became a fashionable intellectual and cultural centre. After Darmesteter's death in 1894 Mary remained in France and married Emile Duclaux, a French
scientist, in 1901, and moved to Olmet in the Cantal region. He died in 1904 but Mary
continued to live, and to write, well into the twentieth century. Her *Images and Meditations*
(1923) was dedicated 'to Mabel, Only Sister, Dearest Friend'.

Robinson claimed that 'I have never been able to write about what was not known
to me and near' (Robinson 1902: ii), but her poems often have a wistful otherworldly
tone which is oblique and distinctive. She also claimed that the ballad was a special
women's form and valuable for its authenticity of experience:

'Some persons of culture have refused me the right to express myself in those
simple forms of popular song which I have loved since childhood and as

sincerely as any peasant. If the critics would only believe it, they have come as naturally to me, if less happily, than they came of old to a Lady Wardlaw, a Lady Lindsay, or a Lady Nairn. We women have a privilege in these matters ... We have always been the prime makers of ballads and love songs, of anonymous snatches and screeds of popular song. We meet together no longer on Mayday, as of old in Provençe, to set the fashion in tensos and sonnets. But some old wife or other, crooning over her fire of sticks, in Scotland or the Val d'Aosta, in Roumania or Gascony, is probably at the beginning of most romantic ballads ...' (Robinson 1902: iii).

Robinson does indeed offer her versions of peasant songs and ballads in the Rispetti 'Tuscan Olives' or in her 'Stornelli and Strambotti', but her skills are so much more than that, and there is always an impressive variety in form and tone in all of her collections of verse. 'Venetian Nocturne', for instance, is strange and mysterious in its conjuring up of a treacherous and secretive beauty typical of Venice, but it is achieved with hardly any representational description. On the other hand, poems such as 'Darwinism', 'The Valley' and *'Unum est Necessarium'* have a mastery of argument which is powerful and authoritative. 'The Idea' is a short poem, but an accomplished one in its capacity to evoke a world beyond the physical which is none the less as secure as concepts of 'Number' or 'Sound'. Other little poems such as 'Pallor' or 'Posies' are clever and pleasing because of the oppositions they set up and their quirky, gentle indication of a joke being shared with the reader, while 'Celia's Homecoming' written for her sister Mabel, wittily parodies the style of Pope yet still retains a convincing emotion. 'An Oasis' is not so much a 'mirror' poem as it might appear at first glance, but rather one of those nineteenth-century artist-and-model poems which so sceptically and intelligently analyse the process of the 'male gaze' which wipes out the woman's individuality to make her only into a vehicle for reflecting his own image. 'Art and Life', 'A Search for Apollo' 'Love, Death and Art' and 'To My Muse' are all self-reflexive poems about Robinson's writing of poetry and all suggest the subtlety and slipperiness which poetry's form meant to her, even while she determinedly carries on in her own resilient path: 'Take heart, therefore, and sing the thing that seems, / And watch the world's disaster with smile'.

M. R.

Robinson, A. Mary F. (1883) *Emily Brontë* in the Eminent Women series, London.
—— (1902) *The Collected Poems, Lyrical and Narrative of Mary Robinson (Madame Duclaux)*, London, T. Fisher Unwin.

Robertson, Eric (1883) *English Poetesses*, London.

Venetian Nocturne

Down the narrow Calle where the moonlight cannot enter,
    The houses are so high;
Silent and alone we pierced the night's dim core and centre –
    Only you and I.

Clear and sad our footsteps rang along the hollow pavement,   5
    Sounding like a bell;

Sounding like a voice that cries to souls in Life's enslavement,
　　'There is Death as well!'

Down the narrow dark we went, until a sudden whiteness
　　Made us hold our breath;　　　　　　　　　　　　　10
All the white Salute towers and domes in moonlit brightness, —
　　Ah! could this be Death?

Stornelli and Strambotti

I

　　Flower of the vine!
I scarcely knew or saw how love began;
So mean a flower brings forth the sweetest wine!

O mandolines that thrill the moonlit street,
　　O lemon flowers so faint and freshly blown,　　　　5
O seas that lap a solemn music sweet
　　Through all the pallid night against the stone,
O lovers tramping past with happy feet,
　　O heart that hast a memory of thine own —
For Mercy's sake no more, no more repeat　　　　　10
　　The word it is so hard to hear alone!

　　Flowers in the hay!
My heart and all the fields are full of flowers;
So tall they grow before the mowing-day.

II

　　Rose in the rain!　　　　　　　　　　　　　15
We part; I dare not look upon your tears:
So frail, so white, they shatter and they stain.

Love is a bird that breaks its voice with singing,
　　Love is a rose blown open till it fall,
Love is a bee that dies of its own stinging,　　　　20
　　And Love the tinsel cross upon a pall.
Love is the Siren, towards a quicksand bringing
　　Enchanted fishermen that hear her call.
Love is a broken heart, — Farewell, — the wringing
　　Of dying hands. Ah, do not love at all!　　　　25

　　Rosemary leaves!
She who remembers cannot love again.
She who remembers sits at home and grieves.

An Oasis

You wandered in the desert waste, athirst;
  My soul I gave you as a well to drink;
  A little while you lingered at the brink,
And then you went, nor either blessed or cursed.

The image of your face, which sank that day   5
  Into the magic waters of the well,
  Still haunts their clearness, still remains to tell
Of one who looked and drank and could not stay.

The sun shines down, the moon slants over it,
  The stars look in and are reflected not;   10
  Only your face, unchanged and unforgot,
Shines through the deep, till all the waves are lit.

My soul I gave you as a well to drink,
  And in its depths your face is clearer far
  Than any shine of sun or moon or star –   15
Since then you pause by many a greener brink.

A Search for Apollo

Indeed I have sought thee too long, O Apollo,
  Nights and days, by brakes and bowers,
By wind-haunted waters, by wolf-haunted hollow,
  And where the city smoke-cloud lowers;
And I have listened hours on hours   5
  Where the holy Omphé of violins
The organ oracle overpowers,
  While the musical tumult thickens and thins,
Till the singing women begin to sing,
Invoking as I do their Master and King;   10
  But thou tarriest long, O Apollo!

Could I find but thy footprints, oh, there would I follow.
  Thou God of wanderers show the way!
But never I found thee as yet, my Apollo,
  Save indeed in a dream one day.   15
(If that or this be the dream, who shall say?)
  A man passed playing a quaint sweet lyre,
His face was young though his hair was grey,
  And his blue eyes gleamed with a wasting fire
As he sang the songs of an ancient land –   20
A singing no hearer could half understand....
  Can this have been Thou, my Apollo?

Tuscan Olives

Seven Rispetti

I

The colour of the olives who shall say?
  In winter on the yellow earth they're blue,
A wind can change the green to white or grey,
  But they are olives still in every hue;

But they are olives always, green or white,   5
As love is love in torment or delight;
But they are olives, ruffled or at rest,
As love is always love in tears or jest.

II

We walked along the terraced olive-yard,
  And talked together till we lost the way;   10
We met a peasant, bent with age and hard,
  Bruising the grape-skins in a vase of clay;

Bruising the grape-skins for the second wine,
We did not drink, and left him, Love of mine;
Bruising the grapes already bruised enough: 15
He had his meagre wine, and we our love.

III

We climbed one morning to the sunny height
  Where chestnuts grow no more and olives grow;
Far-off the circling mountains cinder-white,
  The yellow river and the gorge below.   20

'Turn round,' you said, O flower of Paradise;
I did not turn, I looked upon your eyes.
'Turn round,' you said, 'turn round and see the view!'
I did not turn, my Love, I looked at you.

IV

How hot it was! Across the white-hot wall   25
  Pale olives stretch towards the blazing street;
You broke a branch, you never spoke at all,
  But gave it me to fan with in the heat;

You gave it me without a sign or word,
And yet, my dear, I think you knew I heard.   30
You gave it me without a word or sign:
Under the olives first I called you mine.

                              V

At Lucca, for the autumn festival,
    The streets are tulip-gay; but you and I
Forgot them, seeing over church and wall   35
    Guinigi's tower soar i' the black-blue sky;

A stem of delicate rose against the blue;
And on the top two lonely olives grew,
Crowning the tower, far from the hills, alone;
As on our risen love our lives are grown.   40

                             VI

Who would have thought we should stand again together,
    Here, with the convent a frown of towers above us;
Here, mid the sere-wooded hills and wintry weather;
    Here, where the olives bend down and seem to love us;

Here, where the fruit-laden olives half remember   45
All that began in their shadow last November;
Here, where we knew we must part, must part and sever;
Here, where we know we shall love for aye and ever.

                             VII

Reach up and pluck a branch, and give it me,
    That I may hang it in my Northern room,   50
That I may find it there, and wake and see
    – Not you! not you! – dead leaves and wintry gloom.

O senseless olives, wherefore should I take
Your leaves to balm a heart that can but ache?
Why should I take you hence, that can but show   55
How much is left behind? I do not know.

Love, Death, and Art

Lord, give me Love! give me the silent bliss
Of meeting souls, of answering eyes and hands;

The comfort of one heart that understands;
The thrill and rapture of Love's sealing kiss.

Or grant me – lest I weary of all this –   5
The quiet of Death's unimagined lands,
Wherein the longed-for Tree of Knowledge stands,
Where Thou art, Lord – and the great mysteries.

Nay, let me sing, my God, and I'll forego,
Love's smiling mouth, Death's sweetlier smiling eyes.   10
Better my life long mourn in glorious woe,
Than love unheard in a mute Paradise –

For no grief, no despair, can quail me long,
While I can make these sweet to me in song.

Song

Oh for the wings of a dove,
    To fly far away from my own soul,
    Reach and be merged in the vast whole
Heaven of infinite Love!

Oh that I were as the rain,   5
    To fall and be lost in the great sea,
    One with the waves, till the drowned Me
Might not be severed again!

Infinite arms of the air,
    Surrounding the stars and without strife   10
    Blending our life with their large life,
Lift me and carry me there!

The Dead Friend

I

When you were alive, at least,
    There were days I never met you.
In the study, at the feast
    By the hearth, I could forget you.

Moods there were of many days   5
    When, methinks, I did not mind you.
Now, oh now, in any place
    Whereso'ever I go, I find you!

You ... but how profoundly changed,
  O you dear-belov'd dead woman!   10
Made mysterious and estranged,
  All-pervading, superhuman.

Ah! to meet you as of yore,
  Kind, alert, and quick to laughter:
You, the friend I loved Before;   15
  Not this tragic friend of After.

II

The house was empty where you came no more;
  I sat in awe and dread;
When, lo! I heard a hand that shook the door,
  And knew it was the Dead.   20

One moment – ah! – the anguish took my side,
  The fainting of the will.
'God of the living, leave me not!' I cried,
  And all my flesh grew chill.

One moment; then I opened wide my heart   25
  And open flung the door:
'What matter whence thou comest, what thou art? –
  Come to me!' ... Nevermore.

III

They lie at peace, the darkness fills
  The hollow of their empty gaze.   30
The dust falls in their ears and stills
  The echo of our fruitless days;

The earth takes back their baser part;
  The brain no longer bounds the dream;
The broken vial of the heart   35
  Lets out its passion in a stream.

And in this silence that they have
  One inner vision grows more bright:
The Dead remember in the grave
  As I remember here to-night.   40

Celia's Home-Coming

To F. M. R.

Maidens, kilt your skirts and go
  Down the stormy garden-ways,
Pluck the last sweet pinks that blow,
  Gather roses, gather bays,
Since our Celia comes to-day   5
That has been too long away.

Crowd her chamber with your sweets –
  Not a flower but grows for her!
Make her bed with linen sheets
  That have lain in lavender;   10
Light a fire before she come
Lest she find us chill at home.

Ah, what joy when Celia stands
  By the leaping blaze at last
Stooping down to warm her hands   15
  All benumbèd with the blast,
While we hide her cloak away
To assure us of her stay.

Cyder bring and cowslip wine,
  Fruits and flavours from the East,   20
Pears and pippins too, and fine
  Saffron loaves to make a feast:
China dishes, silver cups,
For the board where Celia sups!

Then, when all the feasting's done,   25
  She shall draw us round the blaze,
Laugh, and tell us every one
  Of her far triumphant days –
Celia, out of doors a star,
By the hearth a holier Lar!   30

To My Muse

The vast Parnassus never knew thy face,
  O Muse of mine, O frail and tender elf
  That dancest in a moonbeam to thyself
Where olives rustle in a lonely place!

And yet... thou hast a sort of Tuscan grace;   5
  Thou may'st outlive me! Some unborn Filelf

One day may range thee on his studious shelf
With Lenau, Leopardi, and their race.

And so, some time, the sole sad scholar's friend,
The melancholy comrade of his dreams,   10
Thou may'st, O Muse, escape a little while
The none the less inevitable end:
Take heart, therefore, and sing the thing that seems,
And watch the world's disaster with a smile.

Darwinism

When first the unflowering Fern-forest
Shadowed the dim lagoons of old,
A vague, unconscious, long unrest
Swayed the great fronds of green and gold.

Until the flexible stem grew rude,   5
The fronds began to branch and bower,
And lo! upon the unblossoming wood
There breaks a dawn of apple-flower.

Then on the fruitful forest-boughs
For ages long the unquiet ape   10
Swung happy in his airy house
And plucked the apple, and sucked the grape.

Until at length in him there stirred
The old, unchanged, remote distress,
That pierced his world of wind and bird   15
With some divine unhappiness.

Not love, nor the wild fruits he sought,
Nor the fierce battles of his clan
Could still the unborn and aching thought,
Until the brute became the man.   20

Long since; and now the same unrest
Goads to the same invisible goal,
Till some new gift, undream'd, unguess'd,
End the new travail of the soul.

The Valley

When August and the sultry summer's drouth
Parch all the plains and pale the mountain-tops
Where thick the pasture springs,

Unchanged, our valley sloping to the south
 Is greener than the Irish isle, and drops   5
  With waterfalls and springs.

The meadows by the river, tall with flowers,
 The fountain leaping from the rocks above,
  The simple ways of man,
The farms and forests of this vale of ours,   10
 Are such, methinks, as gods and shepherds love,
  And wait the flute of Pan.

The vale has seen unchanged a thousand years
 Or more, and Mercury might wander back
  And find, the same Auverne,   15
And greet the hollows of the mountain meres
 Where round the crater's brim the rocks are black
  Amid the beds of fern.

For neither he nor I have ever seen
 The lava rushing from the crater's edge,   20
  The rocks cast up like foam;
Though somewhile, as I dreamed amid the green,
 I thought I saw, beyond the cypress-hedge,
  Those torrents blast my home.

Fire, flood, fierce earthquakes of an elder world,   25
 Red flames and smoke of swirling lava streams,
  Tempests of ash and snow,
Whereby the rock I stand upon was hurl'd
 Down hither, oft ye haunt, ye haunt my dreams,
  O storms of long ago!   30

That FORCE unchain'd, volcanic, belching fire,
 Which shook the mountains then, and filled the combs
  With groaning tongues of flame,
Where is it? Still, they say, as dread, as dire,
 Sprung undiminished from a world of tombs,   35
  It dwells in us the same.

And yet how tranquil sleeps the mountain now!
 The water runnels trace their crystal rings
  And, thro' the grasses, gleam;
The tawny oxen pull the trident plough   40
 And turn the soil, while soft the farmer sings
  To cheer the straining team.

How tranquil smiles the valley, broad and calm!
 Those elemental energies of old
  Swoon they indeed beneath?   45

Whisper, O wind, made sweet with musk and balm;
   On sunset, rain an influence in thy gold;
      Answer, O cirrus-wreath!

Nay, thou shalt be mine answer, vale of rest
   That wast so wild and art so beautiful: 50
      Behold, I understand . . .
As waterfalls, that clear the mountain crest
   In torrents, fill the runnels clear and full
      That nourish all our land;

So, through a myriad channels, bound in peace   55
   And fruitful, runs the Force of primitive fire,
      Divided and divine:
The unnumbered travail of our earth's increase,
   The lives of men who toil, foresee, aspire,
      The growth of grain and vine;   60

The patient oxen ploughing through the clod,
   The very dragonflies about the stream,
      The larks that sing and soar,
Employ the force of that tremendous God
   Who lurks behind our thought, beyond our dream,   65
      And whom the worlds adore.

Unum est Necessarium

I thought that I was ravished to a height
   Whence earth was lost with all I once had known;
I saw the stars flash dwindling thro' the night,
   Like sparklets from a blackening yule-log thrown;
And nothing else remained of all that is   5
   Save the essential life of souls alone.

Behold! Like flowers of light against the abyss
   I watched them move and shine – how soft and clear!
With trailing rays of light, with streams of bliss,
   With haloes of a heavenly atmosphere: 10
Like flowers at dusk, when first the froth and bloom
   Of blond immense chrysanthemums appear
To shake a loose, fresh aureole o'er the gloom
   (If human sense and common vision might
   Divine the splendours of that Upper Room   15
Where motion, joy, and life are one with light) –
   Like flowers made meteors, then, or meteors flowers,
   The radiant spirits circled holy-bright.

And lo! I heard a voice from Heaven, not ours,
  'This is the Race,' it cried, 'this is the Race   20
  Of Radiating Souls, the large in heart,
And where they circle is a holy place!
  Yet not of them, O Gazer, know thou art:
  Look further!'
                Then with anxious sight astrain
I pierced the depth of space from part to part,   25
  And lo! adrift as leaves that eddy in vain,
  I watched the vacant, vagrant, aimless dance
Of Souls concentred in their bliss or pain:
  Unneighboured souls, the drift of time and chance.

  O bright, unthrifty stars that glow and spend   30
Your radiance unregarding, when my glance
  Fell from the fulgence where your orbits trend,
  So far, I felt as men who smile in dreams
And wake, at rainy dawn, without a friend!
  So bare they looked, bereft of all their beams;   35
  Poor spheres that trail their cloudy mantles dim
Where throb and fret a few faint feverish gleams.
  'Look,' said the Voice, 'for thou art such an one
  Many are ye; the uncentred Souls are few!'

  I gazed; and as we used to fix the sun   40
In London thro' the fogs our valleys knew,
  Beneath their shrouds I saw these too were bright.
'Be thankful!' then acclaimed the Voice anew,
  'Adore, and learn that all men love the Light!'
And, as the motion of their muffled fires   45
  Grew more distinct to mine undazzled sight,
  I half-forgot those glad and gracious quires,
  In pity of their dearth who dream and yearn,
Pent up and shrouded in their lone desires.

  Aye, even as plants that grow in chambers turn   50
  Their twisted branches towards the window space,
And languish for the daylight they discern,
  So longed these spirits for the Light of Grace!
  And aye their passionate yearning would attract
Some beam within their cloudy dwelling-place,   55
  Some dewy star-beam to their parch'd contàct;
  But, even as dew or raindrop, when they fall
Upon the insatiate earth, are changed in the act,
  Cease to be water, and no more at all
  Are either dew or rain – but only mire! –   60
So the benignant rays of Heaven would pall
  And faint into a maze of misty fire

At touch of these concentred spirits aye
Locked in their long ungenerous desire.
   Thus, shrouded each alone, nor far nor nigh   65
   Their shine was shed, nor shared by any mate;
Secret and still each burned, a separate I,
   Lost in no general glory, penetrate
   With no sweet mutual marvels of the sky,
And bitter isolation was their state.   70

   'Unjust Eternity!' I mourned aghast.
   'O dread, unchanging, predetermined Fate,
Shall evermore the Future ape the Past?'

   'Thou seest nor Past nor Future,' cried the Voice.
   'Such is the life thou leadest, such thou wast,   75
Art, shalt be; such thy bent is and thy choice,
   O centre-seeking Soul that cannot love,
   Nor radiate, nor relinquish, nor rejoice!
Know, they are wise who squander: Look above!'

   And lo! a beam of their transcendent bliss   80
   Who, ever giving, ever losing, move
In self-abandoned bounty through the abyss,
   Pierced to my soul with so divine a dart,
   I swooned with pain, I wakened to a kiss:
'Blessèd,' I sang, 'are ye the large in heart   85
   Irradiate with the light in alien eyes;
For ye have chosen indeed the brighter part,
   And where ye circle is our Paradise.'

Art and Life

A Sonnet

When autumn comes, my orchard trees alone,
Shall bear no fruit to deck the reddening year –
   When apple gatherers climb the branches sere
Only on mine no harvest shall be grown.
For when the pearly blossom first was blown,   5
   I filled my hands with delicate buds and dear,
   I dipped them in thine icy waters clear,
O well of Art! and turned them all to stone.

Therefore, when winter comes, I shall not eat
Of mellow apples such as others prize: 10
   I shall go hungry in a magic spring! –
All round my head and bright before mine eyes

The barren, strange, eternal blossoms meet,
  While I, not less an-hungered, gaze and sing.

The Sibyl

Behold, the old earth is young again!
The blackthorn whitens in the rain,
The flowers come baffling wind and hail,
The gay, wild nightingale
Cries out his heart in wood and vale.   5
(*And in my heart there rises too*
    A dim free longing
For some delight I never knew!)

O Spring, thou art a subtle thing,
Wiser than we, thou Sibyl, Spring!   10
Thy tresses blown across our face
In Life's mid-race
Remind us of some holier place –
(*And unawares the dullest find*
    A new religion   15
That all their doubts have left behind!)

The Idea

Beneath this world of stars and flowers
  That rolls in visible deity,
I dream another world is ours
  And is the soul of all we see.

It hath no form, it hath no spirit;   5
  It is perchance the Eternal Mind;
Beyond the sense that we inherit
  I feel it dim and undefined.

How far below the depth of being,
  How wide beyond the starry bound   10
It rolls unconscious and unseeing,
  And is as Number or as Sound.

And through the vast fantastic visions
  Of all this actual universe,
It moves unswerved by our decisions,   15
  And is the play that we rehearse.

Personality

A Sestina

As one who goes between high garden walls,
Along a road that never has an end,
With still the empty way behind, in front,
Which he must pace for evermore alone –
So, even so, is Life to every soul,   5
Walled in with barriers which no Love can break.

And yet, ah me! how often would we break
Through fence and fold, and overleap the walls,
To link ourselves to some belovèd soul;
Hearing her answering voice until the end,   10
Going her chosen way, no more alone,
But happy comrades, seeing Heaven in front.

But, ah, the barrier's high! and still my front
I dash against the stones in vain, nor break
A passage through, but still remain alone.   15
Sometimes I hear across high garden walls
A voice the wind brings over, or an end
Of song that sinks like dew into my soul.

Since others sing, let me forget, my Soul,
How dreary-long the road goes on in front,   20
And tow'rds how flat, inevitable an end.
Come, let me look for daisies, let me break
The gillyflowers that shelter in the walls –
But, ah! it is so sad to be alone!

For ever, irremediably alone,   25
Not only I or thou, but every soul,
Each cased and fastened with invisible walls.
Shall we go mad with it? or bear a front
Of desperate courage doomed to fail and break?
Or trudge in sullen patience till the end?   30

Ah, hope of every heart, there *is* an end!
An end when each shall be no more alone,
But strong enough and bold enough to break
This prisoning self and find that larger Soul
(Neither of thee nor me) enthroned in front   35
Of Time, beyond the world's remotest walls!

I trust the end; I sing within my walls,
Sing all alone, to bid some listening soul
Wait till the day break, watch for me in front!

The Scape-Goat

She lived in the hovel alone, the beautiful child.
    Alas, that it should have been so!
But her father died of the drink, and the sons were wild,
    And where was the girl to go?

Her brothers left her alone in the lonely hut.   5
    Ah, it was dreary at night
When the wind whistled right thro' the door that never would shut,
    And sent her sobbing with fright.

She never had slept alone; when the stifling room
    Held her, brothers, father – all.   10
Ah, better their violence, better their threats, than the gloom
    That now hung close as a pall!

When the hard day's washing was done, it was sweeter to stand
    Hearkening praises and vows,
To feel her cold fingers kept warm in a sheltering hand,   15
    Than crouch in the desolate house.

Ah, me! she was only a child; and yet so aware
    Of the shame which follows on sin.
A poor, lost, terrified child! she stept in the snare,
    Knowing the toils she was in.   20

Yet, now, when I watch her pass with a heavy reel,
    Shouting her villainous song,
It is only pity or shame, do you think, that I feel
    For the infinite sorrow and wrong?

With a sick, strange wonder I ask, Who shall answer the sin,   25
    Thou, lover, brothers of thine?
Or he who left standing thy hovel to perish in?
    Or I, who gave no sign?

The Wise-Woman

In the last low cottage in Blackthorn Lane
    The Wise-woman lives alone;
The broken thatch lets in the rain,
The glass is shattered in every pane
    With stones the boys have thrown.   5

For who would not throw stones at a witch?
    Take any safe revenge

For the father's lameness, the mother's stitch,
The sheep that died on its back in a ditch,
   And the mildewed corn in the grange?   10

Only be sure to be out of sight
   Of the witch's baleful eye!
So the stones, for the most, are thrown at night,
Then a scuffle of feet, a hurry of fright —
   How fast those urchins fly!   15

The witch's garden is run to weeds,
   Never a phlox or a rose,
But infamous growths her brewing needs,
Or slimy mosses the rank soil breeds,
   Or tares such as no man sows.   20

This is the house. Lift up the latch —
   Faugh, the smoke and the smell!
A broken bench, some rags that catch
The drip of the rain from the broken thatch —
   Are these the wages of Hell?   25

The witch — who wonders? — is bent with cramp.
   Satan himself cannot cure her,
For the beaten floor is oozing damp,
And the moon, through the roof, might serve for a lamp,
   Only a rushlight's surer.   30

And here some night she will die alone,
   When the cramp clutches tight at her heart,
Let her cry in her anguish, and sob, and moan,
The tenderest woman the village has known
   Would shudder — but keep apart.   35

May she die in her bed! A likelier chance
   Were the dog's death, drowned in the pond.
The witch when she passes it looks askance:
They ducked her once, when the horse bit Nance;
   She remembers, and looks beyond.   40

For then she had perished in very truth,
   But the Squire's son, home from college,
Rushed to the rescue, himself forsooth
Plunged after the witch. — Yes, I like the youth
   For all his new-fangled knowledge. —   45

How he stormed at the cowards! What a rage
   Heroic flashed in his eyes!

But many a struggle and many an age
Must pass ere the same broad heritage
  Be given the fools and the wise.   50

'Cowards!' he cried. He was lord of the land
  He was mighty to them, and rich.
They let him rant; but on either hand
They shrank from the devil's unseen brand
  On the sallow face of the witch.   55

They let him rant; but, deep in his heart,
  Each thought of some thing of his own
Wounded or hurt by the Wise-woman's art;
Some friend estranged, or some lover apart.
  Their hearts grew cold as stone.   60

And the Heir spoke on, in his eager youth,
  His blue eyes full of flame;
And he claspt the witch, as he spoke of the Truth;
And the dead, cold Past; and of Love and of Ruth –
  But their hearts were still the same,   65

Till at last – 'For the sake of Christ who died,
  Mother, forgive them,' he said.
'Come, let us kneel, let us pray!' he cried . . .
But horror-stricken, aghast, from his side
  The witch broke loose and fled!   70

Fled right fast from the brave amends
  He would make her then and there;
From the chance that Heaven so seldom sends
To turn our bitterest foes to friends, –
  Fled, at the name of a prayer!   75

Poor lad, he stared so, amazed and grieved.
  He had argued half an hour;
And yet the beldam herself believed,
No less than the villagers she deceived,
  In her own unholy power!   80

Though surely a witch should know very well
  'Tis the lie for which she will burn.
She must have learned that the deepest spell
Her art includes could ne'er compel
  A quart of cream to turn.   85

And why, knowing this, should one sell one's soul
  To gain such a life as hers –

The life of the bat and the burrowing mole –
To gain no vision and no control,
   Not even the power to curse?   90

'Tis strange, and a riddle still in my mind
   To-day as well as then.
There's never an answer I could find
Unless – O folly of humankind!
   O vanity born with men!   95

Rather it may be than merely remain
   A woman poor and old,
No longer like to be courted again
For the sallow face deep lined with pain,
   Or the heart grown sad and cold.   100

Such bitter souls may there be, I think,
   So craving the power that slips,
Rather than lose it, they would drink
The waters of Hell, and lie at the brink
   Of the grave, with eager lips.   105

They sooner would, than slip from sight,
   Meet every eye askance;
Sooner be counted an imp of the night,
Sooner live on as a curse and a blight
   Than just be forgotten?
                Perchance.   110

Posies

I made a posy for my love
   As fair as she is soft and fine:
The lilac thrift I made it of,
   And lemon-yellow columbine.

But woe is me for my despair,   5
   For my pale flowers, woe is me
A bolder man has given her
   A branch of crimson peony!

Pallor

The great white lilies in the grass
   Are pallid as the smile of death;
For they remember still – alas! –
   The graves they sprang from underneath.

> The angels up in heaven are pale –   5
> For all have died, when all is said;
> Nor shall the lutes of Eden avail
> To let them dream they are not dead.

Constance Naden (1858–1889)

Constance Caroline Woodhill Naden was the only child of Thomas and Caroline Naden. Her mother died within a fortnight of giving birth to her and Constance was brought up by her maternal grandparents near Birmingham. She attended a Unitarian day school and, in 1879, enrolled in botany classes at the Birmingham Midland Institute. She subsequently became a student at the Mason Science College where 'she distinguished herself particularly in Logic and Philosophy' (1894: 10). Here, she became a devotee of the work of Herbert Spencer (see also Eliot and Bevington), whose scientific philosophy, emphasizing the physical basis of all ethics, influenced her own humanist beliefs. She published articles in the *Journal of Science* and the *Agnostic Annual*, lectured on scientific and evolutionary theories and, in accordance with Spencer's dictum that 'science opens up realms of poetry' (1894: 7), started writing verse which humorously propagates a Darwinian perspective in human affairs. She was also a painter, one of her pictures being accepted by the Birmingham Society of Artists.

For a time she taught at a Home for Friendless Girls in Birmingham. Then, in, 1887, on the death of her grandmother, she inherited a large sum of money and set out on a nine-month tour of Palestine, Egypt and India. Her friendship with Elizabeth Garrett Anderson led her to take a special interest in the medical needs of Indian women, a cause which she supported on her return, along with the new Garrett Anderson hospital for women. In 1888, she was elected a member of the Aristotelian Society. It seems that Naden was also friendly with Michael Field. In a manuscript letter dated July 1889 she warmly invites Edith Cooper to stay with her, and hints at an earlier family connection. 'I should so enjoy a long talk with you' (Bod. MS Eng. Lett. e. 33, fol. 59v.), she declares, and expresses her admiration for one of Michael Field's plays. Five months later, however, after a serious operation, she died of an infection probably contracted in India. She was thirty-one.

Many letters of praise and condolence attest to the esteem in which Naden was held by both the scientific and literary communities. She was, as one contemporary pointed out, 'not only a poet, but a chemist, a psychologist, and – may I say, alas! – a Freethinker' (1894: 8). Gladstone praised her highly in an article on women poets in the *Spectator*. It seems that Naden's disappearance from literary history was only hastened by her unusual scientific background as well as by her less unusual early death.

The implicitly atheist or anti-theist bent of her poetry is unequivocally expounded by her friend and mentor, Robert Lewins. In his Foreword to her *Complete Poetical Works*, he explains that her verse is based on the theory of 'Hylo-Idealism', in which 'physical conditions' are regarded as the matrix of spiritual and moral ideals (1894: ix). According to this humanist-scientific creed, self is the only 'law, standard, criterion, and *final* court of appeal' (xii). Religious faith is to be regarded as no more than 'a childish illusion' (xi), soon to be superseded by 'reason' (viii). Lewins leaves the reader in no doubt as to the atheistic implications of this theory: 'All religious ideals and systems – none more than the Christian – are based on hideous immorality' (xi). Naden's own pamphlet, *What Is Religion? A Vindication of Freethought*, similarly proposes that scientific values will inevitably outgrow religious ones, so that 'we shall no longer be able to distinguish between matter and spirit, and shall be forced to find in Hylo-Idealism the reconciliation of poetry, philosophy and science' (1883: 26). Nature and the world of physical matter, now no longer cut off from the 'higher' forms of life in the Darwinian scheme of things, provide a new source of moral as well as poetic truth. Like Michael Field, Bevington, Blind and Kendall, Naden advocates an attitude to nature which is freed of all spiritual or emotional accretions.

Many of her verses cheerfully appropriate a scientific vocabulary to the subject of romance. The four poems headed 'Evolutional Erotics': 'Scientific Wooing', 'The New Orthodoxy,' 'Natural Selection' and 'Solomon Redivivus', three of which are included here, all call on a Darwinian model of selection in affairs of the heart, thus robustly exploding the romance value of 'true love'. Although not overtly feminist in her themes (in fact Naden often adopts the male voice or point of view), the difficult choice of love or work, marriage or vocation, is still presented as primarily a female one ('The Sister of Mercy' and 'Love Versus Learning'). High Romantic notions of genius are briskly mocked in 'Moonlight and Gas' and 'The Two Artists', while poem after poem implicitly challenges the assumption of religious truth. 'The Pantheist's Song of Immortality' uncannily echoes, and perhaps helps reinterpret, Rossetti's 'Song' 'When I am dead, my dearest'. Using the familiar 'Remember me' motif (see Hemans, L. E. L., Barrett Browning and Rossetti), but, like Rossetti, rejecting its egotistical emotionalism, she advocates a stoical and unrewarded acceptance of life and death in the face of nature's vast processes of change. In her pamphlet on religion, Naden interestingly asserts that 'Pantheism is but the mystical converse of Materialism' (1883: 19).

All in all, her imagination finds in the new Darwinian spirit of the age not only a challenge to traditional, emotional and religious faiths, but also an enlivening new creed of materialistic honesty and humility, as well as a poetic language which has largely shed the archaic mannerisms of much contemporary verse. Catchy and contemporary, these are poems which come at the old themes of love and death from a cheerfully new angle. As a scientist herself, Naden has no time for aestheticized mysteries, and she very often opposes to the language of faith and love that of intellectual enlightenment and truth. In 'Poet and Botanist', she wittily dissects the self-indulgent egotism of the former in favour of the useful cruelty of the latter. Her resonantly unorthodox poetic voice suggests the extent to which Victorian women's poetry cannot easily be fixed in any one lyrical mould.

A.L.

Naden, Constance (1883) *What Is Religion? A Vindication of Freethought*, London.
—— (1893) *Selections from the Philosophical and Poetical Works*, compiled by Emily and Edith Hughes, London.
—— (1894) *Complete Poetical Works*, with a Foreword by Robert Lewins, London.

Hughes, William R. (1890) *Constance Naden: A Memoir*, London.
Smith, Philip E. and Smith, Susan Harris (1977) 'Constance Naden: Late Victorian Feminist, Poet and Philosopher', *Victorian Poetry*, 15 (1977), 367–70

The Sister of Mercy

Speak not of passion, for my heart is tired,
I should but grieve thee with unheeding ears;
Speak not of hope, nor flash thy soul inspired
In haggard eyes, that do but shine with tears.
Think not I weep because my task is o'er;   5
This is but weakness – I must rest to-day:
Nay, let me bid farewell and go my way,
Then shall I soon be patient as before.
Yes, thou art grateful, that I nursed thee well;
This is not love, for love comes swift and free: 10
Yet might I long with one so kind to dwell,
Cared for as in thy need I cared for thee:
And sometimes when at night beside thy bed
I sat and held thy hand, or bathed thy head,
And heard the wild delirious words, and knew   15
Even by these, how brave thou wert, and true,
Almost I loved – but many valiant men
These hands have tended, and shall tend again;
And now thou art not fevered or distressed
I hold thee nothing dearer than the rest.   20
Nay, tell me not thy strong young heart will break
If to thy prayer such cold response I make;
It will not break – hearts cannot break, I know,
Or this weak heart had broken long ago.
Ah no! I would not love thee, if I could;   25
And when I cry, in some rebellious mood,
'To live for others is to live alone;
Oh, for a love that is not gratitude,
Oh, for a little joy that is my own!'
Then shall I think of thee, and shall be strong,   30
Knowing thee noblest, best, yet undesired:
Ah, for what other, by what passion fired,
Could I desert my life-work, loved so long?
I marvel grief like thine can move me still,
Who have seen death, and worse than death, ere now –   35
Nay, look not glad, rise up; thou shalt not bow
Thy knee, as if these tears thy hope fulfil:
Farewell! I am not bound by any vow;
This is the voice of mine own steadfast will.

The Pantheist's Song of Immortality

Bring snow-white lilies, pallid heart-flushed roses,
  Enwreathe her brow with heavy-scented flowers;

In soft undreaming sleep her head reposes,
    While, unregretted, pass the sunlit hours.

Few sorrows did she know – and all are over;   5
    A thousand joys – but they are all forgot:
Her life was one fair dream of friend and lover;
    And were they false – ah, well, she knows it not.

Look in her face, and lose thy dread of dying;
    Weep not, that rest will come, that toil will cease: 10
Is it not well, to lie as she is lying,
    In utter silence, and in perfect peace?

Canst thou repine that sentient days are numbered?
    Death is unconscious Life, that waits for birth:
So didst thou live, while yet thy embryo slumbered,   15
    Senseless, unbreathing, e'en as heaven and earth.

Then shrink no more from Death, though Life be gladness,
    Nor seek him, restless in thy lonely pain:
The law of joy ordains each hour of sadness,
    And firm or frail, thou canst not live in vain.   20

What though thy name by no sad lips be spoken,
    And no fond heart shall keep thy memory green?
Thou yet shalt leave thine own enduring token,
    For earth is not as though thou ne'er hadst been.

See yon broad current, hasting to the ocean,   25
    Its ripples glorious in the western red:
Each wavelet passes, trackless; yet its motion
    Has changed for evermore the river bed.

Ah, wherefore weep, although the form and fashion
    Of what thou seemest, fades like sunset flame?   30
The uncreated Source of toil and passion,
    Through everlasting change abides the same.

Yes, thou shalt die: but these almighty forces,
    That meet to form thee, live for evermore:
They hold the suns in their eternal courses,   35
    And shape the tiny sand-grains on the shore.

Be calmly glad, thine own true kindred seeing
    In fire and storm, in flowers with dew impearled;
Rejoice in thine imperishable being,
    One with the Essence of the boundless world.   40

Love Versus Learning

Alas, for the blight of my fancies!
　Alas, for the fall of my pride!
I planned, in my girlish romances,
　To be a philosopher's bride.

I pictured him learned and witty,　　　　　　　　　　　5
　The sage and the lover combined,
Not scorning to say I was pretty,
　Nor only adoring my *mind*.

No elderly, spectacled Mentor,
　But one who would worship and woo;　　　　　　　　10
Perhaps I might take an inventor,
　Or even a poet would do.

And tender and gay and well-favoured,
　My fate overtook me at last:
I saw, and I heard, and I wavered,　　　　　　　　　　15
　I smiled, and my freedom was past.

He promised to love me for ever,
　He pleaded, and what could I say?
I thought he must surely be clever,
　For he is an Oxford M.A.　　　　　　　　　　　　　20

But now, I begin to discover
　My visions are fatally marred;
Perfection itself as a lover,
　He's neither a sage nor a bard.

He's mastered the usual knowledge,　　　　　　　　　25
　And says it's a terrible bore;
He formed his opinions at college,
　Then why should he think any more?

My logic he sets at defiance,
　Declares that my Latin's no use,　　　　　　　　　　30
And when I begin to talk Science
　He calls me a dear little goose.

He says that my lips are too rosy
　To speak in a language that's dead,
And all that is dismal and prosy　　　　　　　　　　　35
　Should fly from so sunny a head.

He scoffs at each grave occupation,
  Turns everything off with a pun;
And says that his sole calculation
  Is how to make two into one.   40

He says Mathematics may vary,
  Geometry cease to be true,
But scorning the slightest vagary
  He still will continue to woo.

He says that the sun may stop action,   45
  But he will not swerve from his course;
For love is his law of attraction,
  A smile his centripetal force.

His levity's truly terrific,
  And often I think we must part,   50
But compliments so scientific
  Recapture my fluttering heart.

Yet sometimes 'tis very confusing,
  This conflict of love and of lore –
But hark! I must cease from my musing,   55
  For that is his knock at the door!

Moonlight and Gas

The poet in theory worships the moon,
  But how can he linger, to gaze on her light?
With proof-sheets and copy the table is strewn,
  A poem lies there, to be finished to-night.
He silently watches the queen of the sky,   5
  But orbs more prosaic must dawn for him soon –
The gas must be lighted; he turns with a sigh,
  Lets down his venetians and shuts out the moon.

'This is but a symbol,' he sadly exclaims,
  'Heaven's glory must yield to the lustre of earth; 10
More golden, less distant, less pure are the flames
  That shine for the world over sorrow and mirth.
When Wisdom sublime sheds her beams o'er the night,
  I turn with a sigh from the coveted boon,
And choosing instead a more practical light   15
  Let down my venetians and shut out the moon.'

He sits to his desk and he mutters 'Alas,
  My muse will not waken, and yet I must write!'

But great is Diana: venetians and gas
    Have not been sufficient to banish her quite.   20
She peeps through the blinds and is bright as before,
    He smiles and he blesses the hint opportune,
And feels he can still, when his labour is o'er,
    Draw up his venetians and welcome the moon.

The Two Artists

'Edith is fair,' the painter said,
    'Her cheek so richly glows,
My palette ne'er could match the red
    Of that pure damask rose.

'Perchance, the evening rain-drops light,   5
    Soft sprinkling from above,
Have caught the sunset's colour bright,
    And borne it to my love.

'In distant regions I must seek
    For tints before unknown,   10
Ere I can paint the brilliant cheek
    That blooms for me alone.'

All this his little sister heard,
    Who frolicked by his side;
To check such theories absurd,   15
    That gay young sprite replied:

'Oh, I can tell you where to get
    That pretty crimson bloom,
For in a bottle it is set
    In Cousin Edith's room.   20

'I'm sure that I could find the place,
    If you want some to keep;
I watched her put it on her face –
    She didn't see me peep!

'So nicely she laid on the pink,   25
    As well as *you* could do,
And really, I almost think
    She is an artist, too.'

The maddened painter tore his hair,
    And vowed he ne'er would wed,   30
And never since, to maiden fair,

A tender word has said.
Bright ruby cheeks, and skin of pearl,
  He knows a shower may spoil,
And when he wants a blooming girl   35
  Paints one himself in oil.

Love's Mirror

I live with love encompassed round,
  And glowing light that is not mine,
    And yet am sad; for, truth to tell,
    It is not I you love so well;
Some fair Immortal, robed and crowned,   5
  You hold within your heart's dear shrine.

Cast out the Goddess! let me in;
  Faulty I am, yet all your own,
  But this bright phantom you enthrone
Is such as mortal may not win.   10

And yet this beauty that you see
  Is like to mine, though nobler far;
  Your radiant guest resembles me
E'en as the sun is like a star.

Then keep her in your heart of hearts,   15
  And let me look upon her face,
  And learn of that transcendent grace,
Till all my meaner self departs,

And, while I love you more and more,
  My spirit, gazing on the light,   20
  Becomes, in loveliness and might,
The glorious Vision you adore.

Scientific Wooing

I was a youth of studious mind,
Fair Science was my mistress kind,
  And held me with attraction chemic;
No germs of Love attacked my heart,
Secured as by Pasteurian art   5
  Against that fatal epidemic.

For when my daily task was o'er
I dreamed of H_2SO_4,

While stealing through my slumbers placid
Came Iodine, with violet fumes,   10
And Sulphur, with its yellow blooms,
   And whiffs of Hydrochloric Acid.

My daily visions, thoughts, and schemes
With wildest hope illumed my dreams,
   The daring dreams of trustful twenty: 15
I might accomplish my desire,
And set the river Thames on fire
   If but Potassium were in plenty!

Alas! that yearnings so sublime
Should all be blasted in their prime   20
   By hazel eyes and lips vermilion!
Ye gods! restore the halcyon days
While yet I walked in Wisdom's ways,
   And knew not Mary Maud Trevylyan!

Yet nay! the sacrilegious prayer   25
Was not mine own, oh fairest fair!
   Thee, dear one, will I ever cherish;
Thy worshipped image shall remain
In the grey thought-cells of my brain
   Until their form and function perish.   30

Away with books, away with cram
For Intermediate Exam.!
   Away with every college duty!
Though once Agnostic to the core,
A virgin Saint I now adore,   35
   And swear belief in Love and Beauty.
Yet when I meet her tranquil gaze,
I dare not plead, I dare not praise,
   Like other men with other lasses;
She's never kind, she's never coy,   40
She treats me simply as a boy,
   And asks me how I like my classes!

I covet not her golden dower –
Yet surely Love's attractive power
   Directly as the mass must vary –   45
But ah! inversely as the square
Of distance! shall I ever dare
   To cross the gulf, and gain my Mary?

So chill she seems – and yet she might
Welcome with radiant heat and light   50

My courtship, if I once began it;
For is not e'en the palest star
That gleams so coldly from afar
    A sun to some revolving planet?

My Mary! be a solar sphere!   55
Envy no comet's mad career,
    No arid, airless lunar crescent!
Oh for a spectroscope to show
That in thy gentle eyes doth glow
    Love's vapour, pure and incandescent!   60

Bright fancy! can I fail to please
If with similitudes like these
    I lure the maid to sweet communion?
My suit, with Optics well begun,
By Magnetism shall be won,   65
    And closed at last in Chemic union!

At this I'll aim, for this I'll toil,
And this I'll reach—I will, by Boyle,
    By Avogadro, and by Davy!
When every science lends a trope   70
To feed my love, to fire my hope,
    Her maiden pride must cry 'Peccavi!'

I'll sing a deep Darwinian lay
Of little birds with plumage gay,
    Who solved by courtship Life's enigma;   75
I'll teach her how the wild-flowers love,
Any why the trembling stamens move,
    And how the anthers kiss the stigma.

Or Mathematically true
With rigorous Logic will I woo,   80
    And not a word I'll say at random;
Till urged by Syllogistic stress,
She falter forth a tearful 'Yes,'
    A sweet 'Quod erat demonstrandum!'

Natural Selection

I had found out a gift for my fair,
    I had found where the cave-men were laid;
Skull, femur, and pelvis were there,
    And spears, that of silex they made.
But he ne'er could be true, she averred,   5
    Who would dig up an ancestor's grave –

And I loved her the more when I heard
  Such filial regard for the Cave.

My shelves, they are furnished with stones
  All sorted and labelled with care,   10
And a splendid collection of bones,
  Each one of them ancient and rare;

One would think she might like to retire
  To my study – she calls it a 'hole!'
Not a fossil I heard her admire,   15
  But I begged it, or borrowed, or stole.

But there comes an idealess lad,
  With a strut, and a stare, and a smirk;
And I watch, scientific though sad,
  The Law of Selection at work.   20

Of Science he hasn't a trace,
  He seeks not the How and the Why,
But he sings with an amateur's grace,
  And he dances much better than I.

And we know the more dandified males   25
  By dance and by song win their wives –
'Tis a law that with *Aves* prevails,
  And even in *Homo* survives.

Shall I rage as they whirl in the valse?
  Shall I sneer as they carol and coo?   30
Ah no! for since Chloe is false,
  I'm certain that Darwin is true!

Solomon Redivivus, 1886

What am I? Ah, you know it,
  I am the modern Sage,
Seer, savant, merchant, poet –
  I am, in brief, the Age.

Look not upon my glory   5
  Of gold and sandal-wood,
But sit and hear a story
  From Darwin and from Buddh.

Count not my Indian treasures,
  All wrought in curious shapes,   10

My labours and my pleasures,
  My peacocks and my apes;

For when you ask me riddles,
  And when I answer each,
Until my fifes and fiddles   15
  Burst in and drown our speech,

Oh then your soul astonished
  Must surely faint and fail,
Unless, by me admonished,
  You hear our wondrous tale.   20

We were a soft Amœba
  In ages past and gone,
Ere you were Queen of Sheba,
  And I King Solomon.

Unorganed, undivided,   25
  We lived in happy sloth,
And all that you did I did,
  One dinner nourished both:

Till you incurred the odium
  Of fission and divorce –   30
A severed pseudopodium
  You strayed your lonely course.

When next we met together
  Our cycles to fulfil,
Each was a bag of leather,   35
  With stomach and with gill.

But our Ascidian morals
  Recalled that old mischance,
And we avoided quarrels
  By separate maintenance.   40

Long ages passed – our wishes
  Were fetterless and free,
For we were jolly fishes,
  A-swimming in the sea.

We roamed by groves of coral,   45
  We watched the youngsters play –

The memory and the moral
  Had vanished quite away.

Next, each became a reptile,
  With fangs to sting and slay;   50
No wiser ever crept, I'll
  Assert, deny who may.

But now, disdaining trammels
  Of scale and limbless coil,
Through every grade of mammals   55
  We passed with upward toil.

Till, anthropoid and wary
  Appeared the parent ape,
And soon we grew less hairy,
  And soon began to drape.   60

So, from that soft Amœba,
  In ages past and gone,
You've grown the Queen of Sheba,
  And I King Solomon.

The Pessimist's Vision

I dreamed, and saw a modern Hell, more dread
  Than Dante's pageant; not with gloom and glare,
  But all new forms of madness and despair
Filled it with complex tortures, some Earth-bred,
Some born in Hell: eternally full-fed   5
  Ghosts of all foul disease-germs thronged the air:
  And as with trembling feet I entered there,
A Demon barred the way, and mocking said –

'Through our dim vales and gulfs thou need'st not rove;
  From thine own Earth and from its happiest lot   10
    Thy lust for pain may draw full nourishment,
  With poignant spice of passion; knowest thou not
Fiends wed for hate as mortals wed for love,
  Yet find not much more anguish? Be content.'

Poet and Botanist

Fair are the bells of this bright-flowering weed;
  Nectar and pollen treasuries, where grope
  Innocent thieves; the Poet lets them ope
And bloom, and wither, leaving fruit and seed
To ripen; but the Botanist will speed   5
  To win the secret of the blossom's hope,

And with his cruel knife and microscope
Reveal the embryo life, too early freed.

Yet the mild Poet can be ruthless too,
    Crushing the tender leaves to work a spell   10
      Of love or fame; the record of the bud
    He will not seek, but only bids it tell
His thoughts, and render up its deepest hue
    To tinge his verse as with his own heart's blood.

E. Nesbit (1858–1924)

Edith was the youngest of five children born to Sarah and John Nesbit. Her father ran an agricultural college in South London, but much of Edith's childhood was spent travelling on the continent with her mother and older sister Mary, who was consumptive. (Mary died in the first year of her marriage to the blind poet Philip Marston.) In 1877 Edith met Hubert Bland, later one of the founder members of the Fabians and a well-known journalist. To the dismay of her family she fell in love, moved into a flat of her own and, after some prevarication on Hubert's part, was married in 1880, by which time she was seven months pregnant. Unknown to Edith, Maggie Doran, the paid companion of her mother-in-law, was also pregnant by Hubert at this time. For the next ten years he spent three nights a week at his mother's house, to be with Maggie. In time, the Blands' marriage accommodated itself both to Hubert's chronic philandering and to Edith's later affairs with younger men. Bernard Shaw once suggested that Edith was even grateful to have some 'assistance' (Briggs 1989: 104) in answering Hubert's voracious needs.

In 1882 Edith met Alice Hoatson at the offices of *Sylvia's Home Journal* where she worked. The two became close friends – Alice nursed Edith through the birth of her third (stillborn) child – and a year later Edith persuaded Alice to give up her job and move in with the family. She did so in 1886, and later that year herself gave birth to a daughter – by Hubert. Edith formally adopted the child, as she did a later son of Alice's. It is hard to know whether this action was prompted by fear of losing her husband, real affection for Alice, or perhaps fondness for the baby (she had, after all, recently lost her own – a pattern which repeated itself some years later). In any case, Alice remained in the family home and became the main nurse and rearer of all the children, Edith's as well as her own. It is perhaps not surprising, given this unconventional reproduction of mothering in the household, that E. Nesbit should have written such memorable and intense 'baby' poems as 'O baby, baby, baby dear', 'Haunted' and 'The Dead to the Living'.

With the founding of the Fabian society in 1884, Edith was introduced to a new circle of friends which included such emancipated women as Eleanor Marx, Charlotte Wilson and Annie Besant, though she was never much in sympathy with the suffrage movement. She also became friendly with Shaw, who rejected her several overtures, and later with H. G. Wells. Through Charlotte Wilson (see Bevington) she was also drawn into the anarchist group surrounding the Russian exiles Kropotkin and Stepniak – the latter providing the model for the Russian gentleman in *The Railway*

Children. By this time she was writing stories for various magazines, often jointly with Hubert, and in 1886 her first volume of poems, *Lays and Legends*, was published. This was well received, and encouraged Edith to believe (wrongly in fact) that her real gift was for poetry. A later edition was dedicated to Alice Hoatson and Charlotte Wilson.

It was not until the 1890s that Edith started to write the children's stories for which she became famous. This work was often done 'on the nights Hubert went to his mother' (Briggs: 122), and in the company of Alice, who herself wrote under the pseudonym of 'Uncle Harry'. At first, stories were written to illustrate a picture. Later, as Edith gained in confidence, she developed her own plots. Her early training in journalistic hackwork stood her in good stead, and her output of stories, verses and novels was prodigious.

As the five children grew up, domestic pressures eased, and Edith became intimate with a succession of younger admirers and lovers, who were accepted into the household and often accompanied her on family holidays. In 1893 Maggie Doran also joined the family, to be nursed in her final illness before she entered a hospital. Neighbours noticed with disapproval the bohemian atmosphere of the house which was usually full of visitors, the women in bloomers or smoking cigarettes, after the fashion of the day. There were many tensions, however, as Hubert's sexual philandering, undiminished by his conversion to Catholicism, continued to find objects of seduction, even amongst his own daughters and their school-friends. When Edith's youngest son Fabian died, as a result of an incompetently managed operation at home, for which his parents' carelessness was partly to blame, underlying divisions surfaced and there were harsh recriminations. However, it was not until after Hubert's death in 1914, and Edith's subsequent second marriage, in 1917, to Thomas Tucker, a sea captain, that Alice moved out into lodgings of her own. Edith finally cut the ties of a lifetime when, in her will, she disinherited Alice's two children.

E. Nesbit once claimed that 'Only my socialist poems are *real me*, and not drama' (Briggs: 71). While verses like 'A Great Industrial Centre' show an energetic awareness of the plight of the poor, Nesbit's best poems, contrary to her own beliefs, are those which catch the flavour of her ambiguous emotional life. The companion pieces, 'The Husband of To-day' and 'The Wife of All Ages', hint at the modern contradictions of her own 'free' marriage, whilst preserving the well-worn ideal of woman's essential faithfulness. '*Vies Manquées*', on the other hand, is a wittily ironic comment on the distorting obsessions of love. Instead of providing the goal and motive of the lyrical impulse, romantic love in these verses is the object of wry and ambivalent scrutiny. Like her near contemporary, Alice Meynell, Nesbit's imaginative and emotional allegiance is primarily to children. The very popular and much quoted song, 'O baby, baby, baby dear', is in fact part of a longer poem in which the young mother is abandoned by the man with whom she had formed an idealistic free union. The icon of mother and child is thus shadowed, for all its ecstatic self-containment, by the darker connotations of the father's absence – an absence which runs through Victorian women's poetry from Hemans onwards. In 'The Dead to the Living', Nesbit intriguingly turns an elegy on the death of a child into a poem of political hope for future generations, thus, in a rare combination, making a political statement out of a private, domestic and quintessentially female experience of loss.

A.L.

Nesbit, E. (1886) *Lays and Legends*, London.
—— (1898) *Songs of Love and Empire*, London.
—— (1905) *The Rainbow and the Rose*, London, Longmans.
—— (1908) *Ballads and Lyrics of Socialism*, London, Fabian Society.

Briggs, Julia (1987; 1989) *A Woman of Passion: The Life of E. Nesbit*, London, Penguin.

Song

Oh, baby, baby, baby dear,
We lie alone together here;
The snowy gown and cap and sheet
With lavender are fresh and sweet;
Through half-closed blinds the roses peer   5
To see and love you, baby dear.

We are so tired, we like to lie
Just doing nothing, you and I,
Within the darkened quiet room.
The sun sends dusk rays through the gloom,   10
Which is no gloom since you are here,
My little life, my baby dear.

Soft sleepy mouth so vaguely pressed
Against your new-made mother's breast.
Soft little hands in mine I fold,   15
Soft little feet I kiss and hold,
Round soft smooth head and tiny ear,
All mine, my own, my baby dear.

And he we love is far away!
But he will come some happy day,   20
You need but me, and I can rest
At peace with you beside me pressed.
There are no questions, longings vain,
No murmuring, nor doubt, nor pain,
Only content and we are here,   25
        My baby dear.

The Husband of To-Day

Eyes caught by beauty, fancy by eyes caught;
   Sweet possibilities, question, and wonder –
What did her smile say? What has her brain thought?
     Her standard, what? Am I o'er it or under?
       Flutter in meeting – in absence dreaming;   5
       Tremor in greeting – for meeting scheming;

Caught by the senses, and yet all through
True with the heart of me, sweetheart, to you.

Only the brute in me yields to the pressure
    Of longings inherent – of vices acquired;   10
All this, my darling, is folly – not pleasure,
    Only my fancy – not soul – has been fired.
      Sense thrills exalted, thrills to love-madness;
      Fancy grown sad becomes almost love-sadness;
And yet love has with it nothing to do,   15
Love is fast fettered, sweetheart, to you.

Lacking fresh fancies, time flags – grows wingless;
    Life without folly would fail – fall flat;
But the love that lights life, and makes death's self stingless –
    You, and you only, have wakened that.   20
      Sweet are all women, you are the best of them;
      You are so dear because dear are the rest of them;
      After each fancy has sprung, grown, and died,
      Back I come ever, dear, to your side.
The strongest of passions – in joy – seeks the new,   25
But in grief I turn ever, sweetheart, to you.

The Wife of All Ages

I do not catch these subtle shades of feeling,
    Your fine distinctions are too fine for me;
This meeting, scheming, longing, trembling, dreaming,
    To me mean love, and only love, you see;
In me at least 'tis love, you will admit,   5
And you the only man who wakens it.

Suppose *I* yearned, and longed, and dreamed, and fluttered,
    What would you say or think, or further, do?
Why should one rule be fit for me to follow,
    While there exists a different law for you?   10
If all these fires and fancies came my way,
Would you believe love was so far away?

On all these other women – never doubt it –
    'Tis love you lavish, love you promised me!
What do I care to be the first, or fiftieth?   15
    It is the *only one* I care to be.
Dear, I would be your sun, as mine you are,
Not the most radiant wonder of a star.

And so, good-bye! Among such sheaves of roses
    You will not miss the flower I take from you;   20

Amid the music of so many voices
   You will forget the little songs I knew –
The foolish tender words I used to say,
The little common sweets of every day.

The world, no doubt, has fairest fruits and blossoms   25
   To give to you; but what, ah! what for me?
Nay, after all I am your slave and bondmaid,
   And all my world is in my slavery.
So, as before, I welcome any part
Which you may choose to give me of your heart.   30

Vies Manquées

A year ago we walked the wood –
   A year ago to-day;
A blackbird fluttered round her brood
   Deep in the white-flowered may.

We trod the happy woodland ways,   5
   Where sunset streamed between
The hazel stems in long dusk rays,
   And turned to gold the green.

A thrush sang where the ferns uncurled,
   And clouds of wind-flowers grew: 10
I missed the meaning of the world
   From lack of love for you.

You missed the beauty of the year,
   And failed its self to see,
Through too much doubt and too much fear,   15
   And too much love of me.

This year we hear the birds' glad strain,
   Again the sunset glows,
We walk the wild wet woods again,
   Again the wind-flower blows.   20

In cloudy white the falling may
   Drifts down the scented wind,
And so the secret drifts away
   Which we shall never find.

Our drifted spirits are not free   25
   Spring's secret springs to touch,
For now you do not care for me,
   And I love you too much.

The Goose-Girl

I wandered lonely by the sea,
  As is my daily use,
I saw her drive across the lea
  The gander and the goose.
The gander and the gray, gray goose,   5
  She drove them all together;
Her cheeks were rose, her gold hair loose,
  All in the wild gray weather.

'O dainty maid who drive the geese
  Across the common wide,   10
Turn, turn your pretty back on these
  And come and be my bride.
I am a poet from the town,
  And, 'mid the ladies there,
There is not one would wear a crown   15
  With half your charming air!'

She laughed, she shook her pretty head.
  'I want no poet's hand;
Go read your fairy-books,' she said,
  'For this is fairy-land.   20
My Prince comes riding o'er the leas;
  He fitly comes to woo,
For I'm a Princess, and my geese
  Were poets, once, like you!'

Haunted

The house is haunted; when the little feet
  Go pattering about it in their play,
I tremble lest the little one should meet
  The ghosts that haunt the happy night and day.

And yet I think they only come to me;   5
  They come through night of ease and pleasant day
To whisper of the torment that must be
  If I some day should be, alas! as they.

And when the child is lying warm asleep,
  The ghosts draw back the curtain of my bed,   10
And past them through the dreadful dark I creep,
  Clasp close the child, and so am comforted.

Cling close, cling close, my darling, my delight,
   Sad voices on the wind come thin and wild,
Ghosts of poor mothers crying in the night –   15
   'Father, have pity – once I had a child!'

The Things That Matter

Now that I've nearly done my days,
   And grown too stiff to sweep or sew,
I sit and think, till I'm amaze,
   About what lots of things I know:
Things as I've found out one by one –   5
   And when I'm fast down in the clay,
My knowing things and how they're done
   Will all be lost and thrown away.

There's things, I know, as won't be lost,
   Things as folks write and talk about: 10
The way to keep your roots from frost,
   And how to get your ink spots out.
What medicine's good for sores and sprains,
   What way to salt your butter down,
What charms will cure your different pains,   15
   And what will bright your faded gown.

But more important things than these,
   They can't be written in a book:
How fast to boil your greens and peas,
   And how good bacon ought to look;   20
The feel of real good wearing stuff,
   The kind of apple as will keep,
The look of bread that's rose enough,
   And how to get a child asleep.

Whether the jam is fit to pot,   25
   Whether the milk is going to turn,
Whether a hen will lay or not,
   Is things as some folks never learn.
I know the weather by the sky,
   I know what herbs grow in what lane;   30
And if sick men are going to die,
   Or if they'll get about again.

Young wives come in, a-smiling, grave,
   With secrets that they itch to tell:
I know what sort of times they'll have,   35
   And if they'll have a boy or gell.

And if a lad is ill to bind,
 Or some young maid is hard to lead,
I know when you should speak 'em kind,
 And when it's scolding as they need.   40

I used to know where birds ud set,
 And likely spots for trout or hare,
And God may want me to forget
 The way to set a line or snare;
But not the way to truss a chick,   45
 To fry a fish, or baste a roast,
Nor how to tell, when folks are sick,
 What kind of herb will ease them most!

Forgetting seems such silly waste!
 I know so many little things,   50
And now the Angels will make haste
 To dust it all away with wings!
O God, you made me like to know,
 You kept the things straight in my head,
Please God, if you can make it so,   55
 Let me know *something* when I'm dead.

The Dead to the Living

Work while it is day: the night cometh, when no man can work

In the childhood of April, while purple woods
 With the young year's blood in them smiled,
I passed through the lanes and the wakened fields,
 And stood by the grave of the child.
And the pain awoke that is never dead   5
 Though it sometimes sleeps, and again
It set its teeth in this heart of mine,
 And fastened its claws in my brain:
For it seemed so hard that the little hands
 And the little well-loved head   10
Should be out of reach of my living lips,
 And be side by side with the dead —
Not side by side with us who had loved,
 But with these who had never seen
The grace of the smile, the gold of the hair,   15
 And the eyes of my baby-queen.
Yet with trees about where the brown birds build,
 And with long green grass above,
She lies in the cold, sweet breast of earth
 Beyond the reach of our love;   20
Whatever befalls in the coarse, loud world,

We know she will never wake.
When I thought of the sorrow she might have known,
   I was almost glad for her sake....
Tears might have tired those kiss-closed eyes,   25
   Grief hardened the mouth I kissed;
I was almost glad that my dear was dead
   Because of the pain she had missed.
Oh, if I could but have died a child
   With a white child-soul like hers,   30
As pure as the wind-flowers down in the copse,
   Where the soul of the spring's self stirs;
Or, if I had only done with it all,
   And might lie by her side unmoved!
I envied the very clods of earth   35
   Their place near the child I loved!

And my soul rose up in revolt at life,
   As I stood dry-eyed by her grave,
When sudden the grass of the churchyard sod
   Rolled back like a green, smooth wave;   40
The brown earth looked like the brown sea rocks,
   The tombstones were white like spray,
And white like surf were the curling folds
   Of the shrouds where the dead men lay;
For each in his place with his quiet face   45
   I saw the dead lie low,
Who had worked and suffered and found life sad,
   So many sad years ago.
Unchanged by time I saw them lie
   As when first they were laid to rest,   50
The tired eyes closed, the sad lips still,
   And the work-worn hands on the breast.
There were some who had found the green world so grey
   They had left it before their time,
And some were little ones like my dear,   55
   And some had died in their prime;
And some were old, they had had their fill
   Of bitter, unfruitful hours,
And knew that none of them, none, had known
   A flower of a hope like ours!   60

Through their shut eyelids the dead looked up,
   And without a voice they said:
'We lived without hope, without hope we died,
   And hopeless we lie here dead;
And death *is* better than life that draws   65
   Pain in, as it draws in breath,
If life never dreams of a coming day

When life shall not envy death.
Through the dark of our hours and our times we lived,
  Uncheered by a single ray   70
Of such hope as lightens the lives of you
  Who are finding life hard to-day;
With our little lanterns of human love
  We lighted our dark, warm night –
But you in the chill of the dawn are set   75
  With your face to the eastern light.
Freedom is waiting with hands held out
  Till you tear the veil from her face –
And when once men have seen the light of her eyes,
  And felt her divine embrace,   80
The light of the world will be risen indeed,
  And will shine in the eyes of men,
And those who come after will find life fair,
  And their lives worth living then!
Will you strive to the light in your loud, rough world,   85
  That these things may come to pass,
Or lie in the shadow beside the child,
  And strive to the sun through the grass?'
'My world while I may,' I cried; 'but you
  Whose lives were as dark as your grave?'   90
'We too are a part of the coming night,'
  They called through the smooth, green wave.
Their white shrouds gleamed as the flood of green
  Rolled over and hid them from me –
Hid all but the little hands and the hair,   95
  And the face that I always see.

A Great Industrial Centre

Squalid street after squalid street,
  Endless rows of them, each the same,
Black dust under your weary feet,
Dust upon every face you meet,
Dust in their hearts, too – or so it seems –   5
  Dust in the place of dreams.

Spring in her beauty thrills and thrives,
  Here men hardly have heard her name.
Work is the end and aim of their lives –
Work, work, work! for children and wives;   10
Work for a life which, when it is won,
  Is the saddest under the sun!

Work – one dark and unending round
  In black dull workshops, out of the light;

Work that others' ease may abound,   15
Work that delight for them may be found,
Work without hope, without pause, without peace,
    That only in death can cease.

Brothers, who live glad lives in the sun,
    What of these men, at work in the night?   20
God will ask you what you have done;
Their lives be required of you – every one –
Ye, who were glad and who liked life well,
    While they did your work – in hell!

Rosamund Marriott Watson
('Graham R. Tomson') (1860–1911)

Rosamund Marriott Watson lived a pretty free and unconventional life. Born Rosamund Ball, she married George Francis Armytage at the age of eighteen and, five years later, published her first volume of poems anonymously. Soon afterwards, in January 1885, she was legally separated from her husband, who, it seems, disapproved of her literary ambitions and social success. When, in October 1886, Rosamund went to live in Cornwall with the painter, Arthur Graham Tomson, George divorced her and she lost custody of her two daughters. She married Arthur in September 1887 and, a month later, gave birth to a son. At this time she subsumed her name into her husband's and published under the pseudonym of 'Graham R. Tomson'.

These were years of considerable social and literary renown. The publication of 'Tomson's' second volume, *The Bird- Bride* (1889), led to a friendship and flirtation with Thomas Hardy, in which, it seems, he was the disappointed partner. He may have used her as the model for the character of Mrs Pine-Avon in *The Pursuit of the Well-Beloved*, while she published two indiscreet articles about him in 1894, which probably ended their already cooled friendship (Millgate 1973: 254). During these years Rosamund was also friendly with the feminist novelist and journalist, Mona Caird, whose polemical essays against marriage in the *Westminster Review* were famous, as well as with E. Nesbit, Alice Meynell (to whom she dedicated her fourth volume of poems) and, briefly, Amy Levy. She edited *Sylvia's Journal* from 1893 to 1894 and was herself a regular contributor to many journals, including *The Yellow Book*.

In 1895 she met H. B. Marriott Watson, a young journalist, essayist and aspiring novelist from New Zealand. She became pregnant by him and, once again, left her husband, was served with divorce papers, lost custody of yet another child and adopted another name under which to publish – though this one at least retains something of her own. Although she did not marry again, this second divorce divided Rosamund's friends and was probably the cause of her social and literary downfall. Even in the 1890s it was rare to encounter such tolerance as that of the critic E. C. Stedman, who wrote to Robert Bridges: 'The Armytage – Tomson – Watson sequence is interesting. Well, a woman who can write such ballads has a right to be her own mistress' (in Mix 1960: 130). Between 1904 and 1911 she was poetry editor of the *Athenaeum*, though by now her own reputation as a poet had waned. She died at the age of fifty-one, having published seven volumes of verse.

Marriott Watson was best known in her day for her ballads, and these retain their ghostly, unnerving power. 'Ballad of the Bird-Bride' and 'A Ballad of the Were-Wolf' use the devious register of fairytale to tell stories of domestic violence, betrayal and terror. Marriage, in them, is under threat from unknown destructive forces in the woman – forces which, in both poems, are associated with animal freedom and ferocity. The sympathetic kinship between women and animals, which runs through nineteenth-century women's poetry, here becomes a ruthless and destructive identification. In both ballads, the woman's freedom implicates children, possibly even to the death (Hughes 1994: 103). In 'Children of the Mist' and 'The White Lady', too, there is a covert drama of the broken relationship between parents and children. A haunting guilt about the real children Rosamund left behind perhaps toughens the lyrical smoothness of these poems. The 'cages' of marriage, ideology, custom or even love are only escaped at a cost.

Altogether, the quality of moral irresolution, of whiteness, in Marriott Watson's work suggests comparison with her two contemporaries, Coleridge and Mew. Like them, she disguises the personal or ideological charge of her work in a folkloric or lyrical register, which results in verses which are apparently enigmatic, but also uneasily tense and questioning.

A.L.

Marriott Watson, Rosamund (1912) *Poems*, London, John Lane The Bodley Head.

Hughes, Linda K. (1992) 'Fair Rosamund: Sexual Politics and the Poetry of Graham R. Tomson / Rosamund Marriott Watson', *Journal of the Eighteen Nineties Society*, 19/20 (1992), 3–17.

—— (1994) ' "Fair Hymen holdeth hid a world of woes": Myth and Marriage in Poems by "Graham R. Tomson" (Rosamund Marriott Watson)', *Victorian Poetry*, 32 (1994), 97–120.

Millgate, Michael (1973) 'Thomas Hardy and Rosamund Tomson,' *Notes and Queries*, NS 20 (1973), 253–5.

Mix, Katherine Lyon (1960) *A Study in Yellow: The 'Yellow Book' and Its Contributors*, London, Constable and Company Ltd.

Nirvana

Sleep will He give His beloved?
   Not dreams, but the precious guerdon of deepest rest?
Aye, surely! Look on the grave-closed eyes,
   And cold hands folded on tranquil breast.
Will *not* the All-Great be just, and forgive?   5
   For He knows (though we make no prayer nor cry)
How our lone souls ached when our pale star waned,
   How we watch the promiseless sky.
Life hereafter? Ah no! we have lived enough.
   Life eternal? Pray God it may *not* be so.   10
Have we not suffered and striven, loved and endured,
   Run through the whole wide gamut of passion and woe?

Strangest illusion! sprung from a fevered habit of hope,
  Wild enthusiast's dream of blatant perfection at best.
Give us darkness for anguished eyes, stillness for weary feet,   15
  Silence, and sleep; but no heaven of glittering, loud unrest.
No more the lifelong labour of smoothing the stone-strewn way;
  No more the shuddering outlook athwart the sterile plain,
Where every step we take, every word we say,
  Each warm, living hand that we cling to, is but a fence against pain.   20

And nothing may perish, but lives again? Where? Out of thought, out of sight?
And where is your cresset's flame that the rough wind slew last night?

Ballad of the Bird-Bride

(Eskimo)

They never come back, though I loved them well;
  I watch the South in vain;
The snow-bound skies are blear and grey,
Waste and wide is the wild gull's way,
  And she comes never again.   5

Years agone, on the flat white strand,
  I won my sweet sea-girl:
Wrapped in my coat of the snow-white fur,
I watched the wild birds settle and stir,
  The grey gulls gather and whirl.   10

One, the greatest of all the flock,
  Perched on an ice-floe bare,
Called and cried as her heart were broke,
And straight they were changed, that fleet bird-folk,
  To women young and fair.   15

Swift I sprang from my hiding-place
  And held the fairest fast;
I held her fast, the sweet, strange thing:
Her comrades skirled, but they all took wing,
  And smote me as they passed.   20

I bore her safe to my warm snow house;
  Full sweetly there she smiled;
And yet, whenever the shrill winds blew,
She would beat her long white arms anew,
  And her eyes glanced quick and wild.   25

But I took her to wife, and clothed her warm
  With skins of the gleaming seal;

Her wandering glances sank to rest
When she held a babe to her fair, warm breast,
  And she loved me dear and leal.   30

Together we tracked the fox and the seal,
  And at her behest I swore
That bird and beast my bow might slay
For meat and for raiment, day by day,
  But never a grey gull more.   35

A weariful watch I keep for aye
  'Mid the snow and the changeless frost:
Woe is me for my broken word!
Woe, woe's me for my bonny bird,
  My bird and the love-time lost!   40

Have ye forgotten the old keen life?
  The hut with the skin-strewn floor?
O winged white wife, and children three,
Is there no room left in your hearts for me,
  Or our home on the low sea-shore?   45

Once the quarry was scarce and shy,
  Sharp hunger gnawed us sore,
My spoken oath was clean forgot,
My bow twanged thrice with a swift, straight shot,
  And slew me sea-gulls four.   50

The sun hung red on the sky's dull breast,
  The snow was wet and red;
Her voice shrilled out in a woeful cry,
She beat her long white arms on high,
  'The hour is here,' she said.   55

She beat her arms, and she cried full fain
  As she swayed and wavered there.
'Fetch me the feathers, my children three,
Feathers and plumes for you and me,
  Bonny grey wings to wear!'   60

They ran to her side, our children three,
  With the plumage black and grey;
Then she bent her down and drew them near,
She laid the plumes on our children dear,
  'Mid the snow and the salt sea-spray.   65

'Babes of mine, of the wild wind's kin,
  Feather ye quick, nor stay.

Oh, oho! but the wild winds blow!
Babes of mine, it is time to go:
   Up, dear hearts, and away!'   70

And lo! the grey plumes covered them all,
   Shoulder and breast and brow.
I felt the wind of their whirling flight:
Was it sea or sky? was it day or night?
   It is always night-time now.   75

Dear, will you never relent, come back?
   I loved you long and true.
O winged white wife, and our children three,
Of the wild wind's kin though ye surely be,
   Are ye not of my kin too?   80

Ay, ye once were mine, and, till I forget,
   Ye are mine forever and aye,
Mine, wherever your wild wings go,
While shrill winds whistle across the snow
   And the skies are blear and grey.   85

A Ballad of the Were-Wolf

The gudewife sits i' the chimney-neuk,
   An' looks on the louping[1] flame;
The rain fa's chill, and the win' ca's shrill,
   Ere the auld gudeman comes hame.

'Oh, why is your cheek sae wan, gudewife?   5
   An' why do ye glower on me?
Sae dour ye luik i' the chimney-neuk,
   Wi' the red licht in your e'e!

'Yet this nicht should ye welcome me,
   This ae nicht mair than a',   10
For I hae scotched[2] yon great grey wolf
   That took our bairnies[3] twa.

' 'Twas a sair, sair strife for my very life,
   As I warstled[4] there my lane;[5]
But I'll hae her heart or e'er we part,   15
   Gin ever we meet again.

---

[1] leaping
[2] maim, cripple
[3] children
[4] wrestled
[5] alone

'An' 'twas ae sharp stroke o' my bonny knife
    That gar'd[6] her haud[7] awa';
Fu' fast she went out-owre the bent[8]
    Wi'outen her right fore-paw.   20

'Gae tak' the foot o' the drumlie[9] brute,
    And hang it upo' the wa';
An' the next time that we meet, gudewife,
    The tane[10] of us shall fa'.'

He's flung his pouch on the gudewife's lap,   25
    I' the firelicht shinin' fair,
Yet naught they saw o' the grey wolf's paw,
    For a bluidy hand lay there.

O hooly, hooly[11] rose she up,
    Wi' the red licht in her e'e,   30
Till she stude but a span frae the auld gudeman
    Whiles never a word spak' she.

But she stripped the claiths frae her lang richt arm,
    That were wrappit roun' and roun',
The first was white, an' the last was red;   35
    And the fresh bluid dreeped adown.

She stretchit him out her lang right arm,
    An' cauld as the deid stude he.
The flames louped bricht i' the gloamin' licht –
    There was nae hand there to see!   40

The White Bird

Zigeunerkind hat keiner Ruh.[1]

The wild bird 'bode in the tame bird's tether,
    The stray white bird with the broken wing,
    And the quick, bright eyes like a hunted thing –
'Twas here, where the roofs crowd close together,
    He came one day in a stormy Spring.   5

Flung by a freak of the west wind hither,
    'Tis well, said we, with our vagrant guest,

---

6 forced
7 hold
8 heath
9 gloomy

10 one
11 softly

1 The gipsy child has no rest.

The white wild bird in the tame bird's nest,
No more the sport of the whence and whither,
   But calm kind fortunes of ease and rest.   10

Here in the fine town fenced and tended,
   Sheltered and safe from day to day,
   Went never a wandering thought astray?
Did he dream, perchance, of the old life ended,
   The wide world's joy and the wide world's way?   15

The low sun's fire and the long low shadows
   On outland valleys; and oh, once more
   Thunder of surf on the sounding shore,
The grey sea-marshes, the wide sea-meadows,
   Wind-bent boughs of the sycamore?   20

The wild bird came and the wild bird tarried,
   In a green courtyard guarded well –
   The first buds broke and the last leaves fell –
What was the summons the storm-wind carried,
   And what the sign of the broken spell?   25

Oh, the word of the wind and the winged white weather!
   The swift shrill call of the whirling blast,
   And the bond is snapped and the sojourn past –
At the sight, at the touch of a white snow-feather
   The wanderer's child goes free at last.   30

Children of the Mist

The cold airs from the river creep
   About the murky town,
The spectral willows, half asleep,
   Trail their thin tresses down
Where the dim tide goes wandering slow,   5
Sad with perpetual ebb and flow.

The great blind river, cold and wide,
   Goes groping by the shore,
And still where water and land divide
   He murmurs evermore   10
The overword of an old song,
The echo of an ancient wrong.

There is no sound 'twixt stream and sky,
   But white mists walk the strand,
Waifs of the night that wander by,   15

Wraiths from the river-land –
While here, beneath the dripping trees,
Stray other souls more lost than these.

Voiceless and visionless they fare,
    Known all too well to me –   20
Ghosts of the years that never were,
    The years that could not be –
And still, beneath the eternal skies
The old blind river gropes and sighs.

The White Lady

The white stone lady on the grass
    Beneath the walnut tree,
She never smiles to see me pass,
    Or blows a kiss to me.

She holds a cup in both her hands   5
    With doves upon its brink,
And ho, so very still she stands
    The thrushes come to drink.

She will not listen when I speak,
    She never seemed to know,   10
When once I climbed to kiss her cheek
    And brush away the snow.

She never took the daisy ring
    I gave her yesterday;
She never cares to hear me sing,   15
    Or watch me at my play.

But, still she looks through sun or rain,
    Towards the garden door,
As though some child should come again
    Who often came before.   20

Some little child who went away,
    Before they knew of me,
Another child who used to play
    Beneath the walnut tree.

The Cage

Amid the medley of ironic things
    We break our hearts upon from age to age

Glimmers a question, – Had the bird no wings
Who would have taken thought to build a cage?

Amy Levy (1861–1889)

Amy Levy was the second daughter of Jewish parents, Isabelle and Lewis Levy, of whom little is known except that the latter was an editor. She was educated in Brighton and in 1879 went to Newnham College, Cambridge, where she was the first Jewish student. She had already published a poem in the feminist journal *The Pelican* at the age of thirteen, and she continued to publish poems and stories while at university. Her first volume, *Xantippe and Other Poems*, appeared in 1881. The title work is a dramatic monologue spoken by the humiliated wife of Socrates who expresses her resentment at being excluded from the intellectual company of her husband and his friends. Its overt feminist protest, perhaps implicitly a protest against the ambiguous status of women at Cambridge, is a sign of a lifelong imaginative commitment.

Whatever the reason, after only four terms Amy returned to her parents' home in London. She started contributing stories and poems to various journals, including the *Victoria Magazine*, *Woman's World* and the *Jewish Chronicle*. In 1884 she brought out a second volume of poems, *A Minor Poet and other Verse*. Then, in the winter of 1885 she went to Italy with her close friend, Clementina Black, the socialist and suffragist, who would later become a prominent campaigner for equal pay for women and a founder of the Women's Trade Union Association. In Florence she stayed with the controversial novelist and philosopher, Vernon Lee (Violet Paget), whose passionate and traumatic friendships with women were well known. Ethel Smyth would later surmise that Violet's repressed lesbianism was the source of much of her unhappiness. It is difficult to know how Amy responded to this charged atmosphere of female friendship and artistic activity. Her poem 'To Vernon Lee' recalls idyllic days spent wandering in the hills round Bellosguardo, but ends with the characteristic assertion that the gods had bequeathed opposite gifts to the two women: 'Hope unto you, and unto me Despair'. (See also 'A Reminiscence'.)

Back in London, she continued to publish articles and poems, two of her verses appearing in Elizabeth Sharp's pioneering anthology, *Women's Voices* (1887). During these years she was also active as secretary of the Beaumont Trust, run by her father to solicit funds for educational facilities for the East End. As Levy became increasingly 'noted for her stories of Jewish life' (Beckson 1987: 47), she also became friendly with a number of writers, including Eleanor Marx, who was so impressed by her novel, *Reuben Sachs* (1888), that she translated it into German a year after its publication. She was also to be found at London literary gatherings where she met, for example, Mathilde Blind, Oscar Wilde and William Michael Rossetti. However, her increasing deafness at this time may have made participation difficult. In their diary of 1891 Michael Field reports that the Radfords 'knew Amy Levy + a delightful, silent smoking-companion she could be. She was deaf & often quiet' (BL Add. Ms. 46779, fol. 33b). Whether she suffered from constitutional melancholy, from despair at her disabling ailment or from some more general sense of thwarting in her life must be a matter for speculation. Clementina Black recalled that she suffered from recurrent 'fits of extreme depression' (*Athenaeum* (5 October 1889): 457). In 1889, a week after completing the proofs of her third volume, Amy killed herself by inhaling fumes of charcoal from a stove in her father's house. She was twenty-seven years old.

A few years after her death a curious rumour appeared in the *Pall Mall Gazette*:

> ...two literary ladies...one of whom is widely famous – were spending a holiday at the seaside together, and both were indulging in very gloomy views of life. After discussing the question they both decided to commit suicide, and the younger hurried home and but too effectually carried out her purpose. The other happily thought better of the matter, and refused to fulfil her terms of the contract (*Pall Mall Gazette* (1 April 1892) 2).

Although this smacks of a tasteless joke, it is certainly true that, a month before her death, Amy had gone to the seaside with Olive Schreiner, with whom she had formed an intimate friendship. Olive wrote to Havelock Ellis roundly refuting the rumour of a suicide pact, asserting that she 'was always trying to cheer up Amy Levy'. According to her, a last note from Amy gave a different reason for her death: 'You care for science and art and helping your fellow-men, therefore life is worth living to you: to me it is worth nothing'. The night before her suicide, Amy returned Olive's copy of a work by Edward Carpenter with the explanation: 'It might have helped me once; it is too late now; philosophy cannot help me' (Schreiner 1924: 207). A few weeks later, Olive left for South Africa. When Arthur Symons heard the news of Levy's death, he immediately surmised that 'It will be a great blow to O.S., who thought her the most fascinating girl she has met in England!' (Beckson 1987: 50). While the idea of the suicide pact sounds dubious, it is evident that Olive knew of her friend's suicidal tendencies and that she was close enough to be taken into her confidence at the end.

Levy's poetry and prose bear witness to a gifted if still developing writer. Two of her three novels are particularly interesting for their portrayals of women. In *The Romance of a Shop* four orphaned sisters set up in business as professional photographers – an act of declared sexual independence: 'But a business – that is so different. It is progressive; a creature capable of growth; the very qualities in which women's work is dreadfully lacking' (1888a: 10). In the end, however, the business fails and the women marry. *Reuben Sachs: A Sketch* is a love story set in the Jewish community of London, where the different snobberies of wealth, race, culture and class are sharply evoked and mocked. The real centre of the novel is not Reuben, however, but Judith, who, in spite of her intelligence and capabilities, is fated to remain, in words echoing Augusta Webster, one of the 'vast crowd of girls awaiting their promotion by marriage' (1888b: 35). When she is snubbed by the self-seeking Reuben and accepts a proposal of marriage elsewhere, Judith recalls a friend's warning 'that marriage was an opiate' (244), and the story ends with one of Levy's characteristically gloomy pronouncements on the inherent contradictions of life: 'It seemed to her as she sat there in the fading light, that this is the bitter lesson of existence: that the sacred serves only to teach the full meaning of sacrilege; the beautiful of the hideous; modesty of outrage; joy of sorrow; life of death' (266). Such paradoxes recur throughout her poetry. It may be that the disapproval Levy incurred from the Jewish community after the publication of *Reuben Sachs* had more to do with this underlying confusion of values in it than with its declared criticisms of the provincialism and materialism of Jewish life. Her third novel, *Miss Meredith* (1889), is, by comparison, a rather slight and unconvincing romance about a governess in Italy.

Levy's poetry at first seems milder than her prose and more straightforwardly plaintive and lyrical. But even here the strain of dissent shows through. Her melancholy, far from being a cultivated Romantic manner, edges on idiosyncratic, wry cynicism (see 'Epitaph'), and her pessimism, far from being personal and lovelorn, is an almost cool, philosophical attitude in the face of a morally senseless world. Her poem 'Magdalen' hints at this difference. Although it fits the popular genre of the 'fallen woman' poem, it is ultimately neither a work of social protest nor of emotional betrayal. Compared with Rossetti's 'The Convent Threshold', Procter's 'A Legend of Provence', Webster's 'A Castaway' or Greenwell's 'Christina', this Magdalen is no longer fighting against the moral injustices of the world or passionately declaring her own feelings, but wearily and grimly accepting her fate: 'And good is evil, evil good: Nothing is known or understood/Save only Pain.' Pain, which is the only residue from moral anarchy, is one of the keynotes of Levy's work, expressing her vision of a world which is unredeemed by faith, love or social change. The extraordinary *Ballad of Religion and Marriage*, which was privately printed after Levy's death in an edition of only twelve copies, veers recklessly from disapprobation to triumph at the thought of a future in which religion and marriage have been abolished, and women freed to live as 'neither pairs nor odd'.

If the fine dramatic monologue, 'A Minor Poet', is Levy's most autobiographical work, evoking her own garret above the roofs of London and foretelling her suicide, it suggests that one other cause of her early death might have been dissatisfaction with her art. Doomed to remain a 'minor poet' by reason of her sex (as she might have thought), she chose death instead. In a memorable passage from *Reuben Sachs*, one character writes in her prayer book: 'Cursed art Thou, O Lord my God, Who hast had the cruelty to make me a woman', and adds, darkly: 'I have gone on saying that prayer all my life – the only one' (1888b: 193). Levy's life and work are a sad reminder that the odds against which women were struggling at this time, in spite of so many opportunities gained, could still be too great for them.

A.L.

Levy, Amy (1881) *Xantippe and Other Verse*, Cambridge.
—— (1884) *A Minor Poet And Other Verse*, London.
—— (1888a) *The Romance of a Shop*, London.
—— (1888b) *Reuben Sachs: A Sketch*, London.
—— (1889) *Miss Meredith*, London.
—— (1889) *A London Plane-Tree and Other Verse*, London.
—— (1915) *A Ballad of Religion and Marriage*, privately printed, London.

Beckson, Karl (1987) *Arthur Symons: A Life*, Oxford, Clarendon Press.
Schreiner, Olive (1924) *Letters*, ed. S. C. Cronwright-Schreiner, London, Fisher Unwin.

Xantippe

(A Fragment)

What, have I waked again? I never thought
To see the rosy dawn, or ev'n this grey,
Dull, solemn stillness, ere the dawn has come.

The lamp burns low; low burns the lamp of life:
The still morn stays expectant, and my soul,   5
All weighted with a passive wonderment,
Waiteth and watcheth, waiteth for the dawn.
Come hither, maids; too soundly have ye slept
That should have watched me; nay, I would not chide –
Oft have I chidden, yet I would not chide   10
In this last hour; – now all should be at peace,
I have been dreaming in a troubled sleep
Of weary days I thought not to recall;
Of stormy days, whose storms are hushed long since;
Of gladsome days, of sunny days; alas   15
In dreaming, all their sunshine seem'd so sad,
As though the current of the dark To-Be
Had flow'd, prophetic, through the happy hours.
And yet, full well, I know it was not thus;
I mind me sweetly of the summer days,   20
When, leaning from the lattice, I have caught
The fair, far glimpses of a shining sea;
And, nearer, of tall ships which thronged the bay,
And stood out blackly from a tender sky
All flecked with sulphur, azure, and bright gold;   25
And in the still, clear air have heard the hum
Of distant voices; and me thinks there rose
No darker fount to mar or stain the joy
Which sprang ecstatic in my maiden breast
Than just those vague desires, those hopes and fears,   30
Those eager longings, strong, though undefined,
Whose very sadness makes them seem so sweet.
What cared I for the merry mockeries
Of other maidens sitting at the loom?
Or for sharp voices, bidding me return   35
To maiden labour? Were we not apart –
I and my high thoughts, and my golden dreams,
My soul which yearned for knowledge, for a tongue
That should proclaim the stately mysteries
Of this fair world, and of the holy gods?   40
Then followed days of sadness, as I grew
To learn my woman-mind had gone astray,
And I was sinning in those very thoughts –
For maidens, mark, such are not woman's thoughts –
(And yet, 'tis strange, the gods who fashion us   45
Have given us such promptings)....
                                        Fled the years,
Till seventeen had found me tall and strong,
And fairer, runs it, than Athenian maids
Are wont to seem; I had not learnt it well –
My lesson of dumb patience – and I stood   50

At Life's great threshold with a beating heart,
And soul resolved to conquer and attain. . . .
Once, walking 'thwart the crowded market-place,
With other maidens, bearing in the twigs
White doves for Aphrodite's sacrifice,   55
I saw him, all ungainly and uncouth,
Yet many gathered round to hear his words,
Tall youths and stranger-maidens – Sokrates –
I saw his face and marked it, half with awe,
Half with a quick repulsion at the shape. . . .   60
The richest gem lies hidden furthest down,
And is the dearer for the weary search;
We grasp the shining shells which strew the shore,
Yet swift we fling them from us; but the gem
We keep for aye and cherish. So a soul,   65
Found after weary searching in the flesh
Which half repelled our senses, is more dear,
For that same seeking, than the sunny mind
Which lavish Nature marks with thousand hints
Upon a brow of beauty. We are prone   70
To overweigh such subtle hints, then deem,
In after disappointment, we are fooled. . . .
And when, at length, my father told me all,
That I should wed me with great Sokrates,
I, foolish, wept to see at once cast down   75
The maiden image of a future love,
Where perfect body matched the perfect soul.
But slowly, softly did I cease to weep;
Slowly I 'gan to mark the magic flash
Leap to the eyes, to watch the sudden smile   80
Break round the mouth, and linger in the eyes;
To listen for the voice's lightest tone –
Great voice, whose cunning modulations seemed
Like to the notes of some sweet instrument.
So did I reach and strain, until at last   85
I caught the soul athwart the grosser flesh.
Again of thee, sweet Hope, my spirit dreamed!
I, guided by his wisdom and his love,
Led by his words, and counselled by his care,
Should lift the shrouding veil from things which be,   90
And at the flowing fountain of his soul
Refresh my thirsting spirit. . . .
                              And indeed,
In those long days which followed that strange day
When rites and song, and sacrifice and flow'rs,
Proclaimed that we were wedded, did I learn,   95
In sooth, a-many lessons; bitter ones
Which sorrow taught me, and not love inspired,

Which deeper knowledge of my kind impressed
With dark insistence on reluctant brain; –
But that great wisdom, deeper, which dispels   100
Narrowed conclusions of a half-grown mind,
And sees athwart the littleness of life
Nature's divineness and her harmony,
Was never poor Xantippe's. . . .
                           I would pause
And would recall no more, no more of life,   105
Than just the incomplete, imperfect dream
Of early summers, with their light and shade,
Their blossom-hopes, whose fruit was never ripe;
But something strong within me, some sad chord
Which loudly echoes to the later life,   110
Me to unfold the after-misery
Urges, with plaintive wailing in my heart.
Yet, maidens, mark; I would not that ye thought
I blame my lord departed, for he meant
No evil, so I take it, to his wife.   115
'Twas only that the high philosopher,
Pregnant with noble theories and great thoughts,
Deigned not to stoop to touch so slight a thing
As the fine fabric of a woman's brain –
So subtle as a passionate woman's soul.   120
I think, if he had stooped a little, and cared,
I might have risen nearer to his height,
And not lain shattered, neither fit for use
As goodly household vessel, nor for that
Far finer thing which I had hoped to be. . . .   125
Death, holding high his retrospective lamp,
Shows me those first, far years of wedded life,
Ere I had learnt to grasp the barren shape
Of what the Fates had destined for my life
Then, as all youthful spirits are, was I   130
Wholly incredulous that Nature meant
So little, who had promised me so much.
At first I fought my fate with gentle words,
With high endeavours after greater things;
Striving to win the soul of Sokrates,   135
Like some slight bird, who sings her burning love
To human master, till at length she finds
Her tender language wholly misconceived,
And that same hand whose kind caress she sought,
With fingers flippant flings the careless corn. . . .   140
I do remember how, one summer's eve,
He, seated in an arbour's leafy shade,
Had bade me bring fresh wine-skins. . . .
                              As I stood

Ling'ring upon the threshold, half concealed
By tender foliage, and my spirit light   145
With draughts of sunny weather, did I mark
An instant the gay group before mine eyes.
Deepest in shade, and facing where I stood,
Sat Plato, with his calm face and low brows
Which met above the narrow Grecian eyes,   150
The pale, thin lips just parted to the smile,
Which dimpled that smooth olive of his cheek.
His head a little bent, sat Sokrates,
With one swart finger raised admonishing,
And on the air were borne his changing tones.   155
Low lounging at his feet, one fair arm thrown
Around his knee (the other, high in air
Brandish'd a brazen amphor, which yet rained
Bright drops of ruby on the golden locks
And temples with their fillets of the vine),   160
Lay Alkibiades the beautiful.
And thus, with solemn tone, spake Sokrates:
'This fair Aspasia, which our Perikles
Hath brought from realms afar, and set on high
In our Athenian city, hath a mind,   165
I doubt not, of a strength beyond her race;
And makes employ of it, beyond the way
Of women nobly gifted: woman's frail –
Her body rarely stands the test of soul;
She grows intoxicate with knowledge; throws   170
The laws of custom, order, 'neath her feet,
Feasting at life's great banquet with wide throat.'
Then sudden, stepping from my leafy screen,
Holding the swelling wine-skin o'er my head,
With breast that heaved, and eyes and cheeks aflame,   175
Lit by a fury and a thought, I spake:
'By all great powers around us! can it be
That we poor women are empirical?
That gods who fashioned us did strive to make
Beings too fine, too subtly delicate,   180
With sense that thrilled response to ev'ry touch
Of nature's, and their task is not complete?
That they have sent their half-completed work
To bleed and quiver here upon the earth?
To bleed and quiver, and to weep and weep,   185
To beat its soul against the marble walls
Of men's cold hearts, and then at last to sin!'
I ceased, the first hot passion stayed and stemmed
And frighted by the silence: I could see,
Framed by the arbour foliage, which the sun   190
In setting softly gilded with rich gold,

Those upturned faces, and those placid limbs;
Saw Plato's narrow eyes and niggard mouth,
Which half did smile and half did criticise,
One hand held up, the shapely fingers framed   195
To gesture of entreaty – 'Hush, I pray,
Do not disturb her; let us hear the rest;
Follow her mood, for here's another phase
Of your black-browed Xantippe. . . .'
                          Then I saw
Young Alkibiades, with laughing lips   200
And half-shut eyes, contemptuous shrugging up
Soft, snowy shoulders, till he brought the gold
Of flowing ringlets round about his breasts.
But Sokrates, all slow and solemnly,
Raised, calm, his face to mine, and sudden spake: 205
'I thank thee for the wisdom which thy lips
Have thus let fall among us: prythee tell
From what high source, from what philosophies
Didst cull the sapient notion of thy words?'
Then stood I straight and silent for a breath,   210
Dumb, crushed with all that weight of cold contempt;
But swiftly in my bosom there uprose
A sudden flame, a merciful fury sent
To save me; with both angry hands I flung
The skin upon the marble, where it lay   215
Spouting red rills and fountains on the white;
Then, all unheeding faces, voices, eyes,
I fled across the threshold, hair unbound –
White garment stained to redness – beating heart
Flooded with all the flowing tide of hopes   220
Which once had gushed out golden, now sent back
Swift to their sources, never more to rise. . . .
I think I could have borne the weary life,
The narrow life within the narrow walls,
If he had loved me; but he kept his love   225
For this Athenian city and her sons;
And, haply, for some stranger-woman, bold
With freedom, thought, and glib philosophy. . . .
Ah me! the long, long weeping through the nights,
The weary watching for the pale-eyed dawn   230
Which only brought fresh grieving: then I grew
Fiercer, and cursed from out my inmost heart
The Fates which marked me an Athenian maid.
Then faded that vain fury; hope died out;
A huge despair was stealing on my soul,   235
A sort of fierce acceptance of my fate, –
He wished a household vessel – well 'twas good,
For he should have it! He should have no more

The yearning treasure of a woman's love,
But just the baser treasure which he sought.   240
I called my maidens, ordered out the loom,
And spun unceasing from the morn till eve;
Watching all keenly over warp and woof,
Weighing the white wool with a jealous hand.
I spun until, methinks, I spun away   245
The soul from out my body, the high thoughts
From out my spirit; till at last I grew
As ye have known me, – eye exact to mark
The texture of the spinning; ear all keen
For aimless talking when the moon is up,   250
And ye should be a-sleeping; tongue to cut
With quick incision, 'thwart the merry words
Of idle maidens....
                    Only yesterday
My hands did cease from spinning; I have wrought
My dreary duties, patient till the last.   255
The gods reward me! Nay, I will not tell
The after years of sorrow; wretched strife
With grimmest foes – sad Want and Poverty; –
Nor yet the time of horror, when they bore
My husband from the threshold; nay, nor when   260
The subtle weed had wrought its deadly work.
Alas! alas! I was not there to soothe
The last great moment; never any thought
Of her that loved him – save at least the charge,
All earthly, that her body should not starve....   265
You weep, you weep; I would not that ye wept;
Such tears are idle; with the young, such grief
Soon grows to gratulation, as, 'her love
Was withered by misfortune; mine shall grow
All nurtured by the loving,' or, 'her life   270
Was wrecked and shattered – mine shall smoothly sail.'
Enough, enough. In vain, in vain, in vain!
The gods forgive me! Sorely have I sinned
In all my life. A fairer fate befall
You all that stand there....
                              Ha! the dawn has come;   275
I see a rosy glimmer – nay! it grows dark;
Why stand ye so in silence? throw it wide,
The casement, quick; why tarry? – give me air –
O fling it wide, I say, and give me light!

A Minor Poet

What should such fellows as I do,
Crawling between earth and heaven?

Here is the phial; here I turn the key
  Sharp in the lock. Click! – there's no doubt it turned.
This is the third time; there is luck in threes –
Queen Luck, that rules the world, befriend me now
And freely I'll forgive you many wrongs!   5
Just as the draught began to work, first time,
Tom Leigh, my friend (as friends go in the world),
Burst in, and drew the phial from my hand,
(Ah, Tom! ah, Tom! that was a sorry turn!)
And lectured me a lecture, all compact   10
Of neatest, newest phrases, freshly culled
From works of newest culture: 'common good;'
'The world's great harmonies;' 'must be content
With knowing God works all things for the best,
And Nature never stumbles.' Then again,   15
'The common good,' and still, 'the common, good;'
And what a small thing was our joy or grief
When weigh'd with that of thousands. Gentle Tom,
But you might wag your philosophic tongue
From morn till eve, and still the thing's the same;   20
I am myself, as each man is himself –
Feels his own pain, joys his own joy, and loves
With his own love, no other's. Friend, the world
Is but one man; one man is but the world.
And I am I, and you are Tom, that bleeds   25
When needles prick your flesh (mark, yours, not mine).
I must confess it; I can feel the pulse
A-beating at my heart, yet never knew
The throb of cosmic pulses. I lament
The death of youth's ideal in my heart;   30
And, to be honest, never yet rejoiced
In the world's progress – scarce, indeed, discerned;
(For still it seems that God's a Sisyphus
With the world for stone).
                  You shake your head. I'm base,
Ignoble? Who is noble – you or I?   35
I was not once thus? Ah, my friend, we are
As the Fates make us.
                This time is the third;
The second time the flask fell from my hand,
Its drowsy juices spilt upon the board;
And there my face fell flat, and all the life   40

Crept from my limbs, and hand and foot were bound
With mighty chains, subtle, intangible;
While still the mind held to its wonted use,
Or rather grew intense and keen with dread,
An awful dread – I thought I was in Hell.   45
In Hell, in Hell! Was ever Hell conceived
By mortal brain, by brain Divine devised,
Darker, more fraught with torment, than the world
For such as I? A creature maimed and marr'd
From very birth. A blot, a blur, a note   50
All out of tune in this world's instrument.
A base thing, yet not knowing to fulfil
Base functions. A high thing, yet all unmeet
For work that's high. A dweller on the earth,
Yet not content to dig with other men   55
Because of certain sudden sights and sounds
(Bars of broke music; furtive, fleeting glimpse
Of angel faces 'thwart the grating seen)
Perceived in Heaven. Yet when I approach
To catch the sound's completeness, to absorb   60
The faces' full perfection, Heaven's gate,
Which then had stood ajar, sudden falls to,
And I, a-shiver in the dark and cold,
Scarce hear afar the mocking tones of men:
'He would not dig, forsooth; but he must strive   65
For higher fruits than what our tillage yields;
Behold what comes, my brothers, of vain pride!'
Why play with figures? trifle prettily
With this my grief which very simply 's said,
'There is no place for me in all the world'?   70
The world's a rock, and I will beat no more
A breast of flesh and blood against a rock....
A stride across the planks for old time's sake.
Ah, bare, small room that I have sorrowed in;
Ay, and on sunny days, haply, rejoiced;   75
We know some things together, you and I!
Hold there, you rangèd row of books! In vain
You beckon from your shelf. You've stood my friends
Where all things else were foes; yet now I'll turn
My back upon you, even as the world   80
Turns it on me. And yet – farewell, farewell!
You, lofty Shakespeare, with the tattered leaves
And fathomless great heart, your binding 's bruised
Yet did I love you less? Goethe, farewell;
Farewell, triumphant smile and tragic eyes,   85
And pitiless world-wisdom!
                    For all men
These two. And 'tis farewell with you, my friends,

More dear because more near: Theokritus;
Heine that stings and smiles; Prometheus' bard;
(I've grown too coarse for Shelley latterly:)   90
And one wild singer of to-day, whose song
Is all aflame with passionate bard's blood
Lash'd into foam by pain and the world's wrong.
At least, he has a voice to cry his pain;
For him, no silent writhing in the dark,   95
No muttering of mute lips, no straining out
Of a weak throat a-choke with pent-up sound,
A-throb with pent-up passion...
                                  Ah, my sun!
That's you, then, at the window, looking in
To beam farewell on one who's loved you long   100
And very truly. Up, you creaking thing,
You squinting, cobwebbed casement!
                                  So, at last,
I can drink in the sunlight. How it falls
Across that endless sea of London roofs,
Weaving such golden wonders on the grey,   105
That almost, for the moment, we forget
The world of woe beneath them.
                                  Underneath,
For all the sunset glory, Pain is king.
Yet, the sun's there, and very sweet withal;
And I'll not grumble that it's only sun,   110
But open wide my lips – thus – drink it in;
Turn up my face to the sweet evening sky
(What royal wealth of scarlet on the blue
So tender toned, you'd almost think it green)
And stretch my hands out – so – to grasp it tight.   115
Ha, ha! 'tis sweet awhile to cheat the Fates,
And be as happy as another man.
The sun works in my veins like wine, like wine!
'Tis a fair world: if dark, indeed, with woe,
Yet having hope and hint of such a joy,   120
That a man, winning, well might turn aside,
Careless of Heaven...
                                  O enough; I turn
From the sun's light, or haply I shall hope.
I have hoped enough; I would not hope again:
'Tis hope that is most cruel.
                                  Tom, my friend,   125
You very sorry philosophic fool;
'Tis you, I think, that bid me be resign'd,
Trust, and be thankful.
                                  Out on you! Resign'd?
I'm not resign'd, not patient, not school'd in

To take my starveling's portion and pretend 130
I'm grateful for it. I want all, all, all;
I've appetite for all. I want the best:
Love, beauty, sunlight, nameless joy of life.
There's too much patience in the world, I think.
We have grown base with crooking of the knee. 135
Mankind – say – God has bidden to a feast;
The board is spread, and groans with cates and drinks;
In troop the guests; each man with appetite
Keen-whetted with expectance.
                In they troop,
Struggle for seats, jostle and push and seize. 140
What's this? what's this? There are not seats for all!
Some men must stand without the gates; and some
Must linger by the table, ill-supplied
With broken meats. One man gets meat for two,
The while another hungers. If I stand 145
Without the portals, seeing others eat
Where I had thought to satiate the pangs
Of mine own hunger; shall I then come forth
When all is done, and drink my Lord's good health
In my Lord's water? Shall I not rather turn 150
And curse him, curse him for a niggard host?
O, I have hungered, hungered, through the years,
Till appetite grows craving, then disease;
I am starved, wither'd, shrivelled.
                Peace, O peace!
This rage is idle; what avails to curse 155
The nameless forces, the vast silences
That work in all things.
              This time is the third,
I wrought before in heat, stung mad with pain,
Blind, scarcely understanding; now I know
What thing I do.
            There was a woman once; 160
Deep eyes she had, white hands, a subtle smile,
Soft speaking tones: she did not break my heart,
Yet haply had her heart been otherwise
Mine had not now been broken. Yet, who knows?
My life was jarring discord from the first: 165
Tho' here and there brief hints of melody,
Of melody unutterable, clove the air.
From this bleak world, into the heart of night,
The dim, deep bosom of the universe,
I cast myself. I only crave for rest; 170
Too heavy is the load. I fling it down.

Epilogue

We knocked and knocked; at last, burst in the door,
And found him as you know – the outstretched arms
Propping the hidden face. The sun had set,
And all the place was dim with lurking shade. 175
There was no written word to say farewell,
Or make more clear the deed.
                   I search'd and search'd;
The room held little: just a row of books
Much scrawl'd and noted; sketches on the wall,
Done rough in charcoal; the old instrument 180
(A violin, no Stradivarius)
He played so ill on; in the table drawer
Large schemes of undone work. Poems half-writ;
Wild drafts of symphonies; big plans of fugues;
Some scraps of writing in a woman's hand: 185
No more – the scattered pages of a tale,
A sorry tale that no man cared to read.
Alas, my friend, I lov'd him well, tho' he
Held me a cold and stagnant-blooded fool,
Because I am content to watch, and wait 190
With a calm mind the issue of all things.
Certain it is my blood's no turbid stream;
Yet, for all that, haply I understood
More than he ever deem'd; nor held so light
The poet in him. Nay, I sometimes doubt 195
If they have not, indeed, the better part –
These poets, who get drunk with sun, and weep
Because the night or a woman's face is fair.
Meantime there is much talk about my friend.
The women say, of course, he died for love; 200
The men, for lack of gold, or cavilling
Of carping critics. I, Tom Leigh, his friend
I have no word at all to say of this.
Nay, I had deem'd him more philosopher;
For did he think by this one paltry deed 205
To cut the knot of circumstance, and snap
The chain which binds all being?

Magdalen

All things I can endure, save one.
The bare, blank room where is no sun;
The parcelled hours; the pallet hard;
The dreary faces here within;
The outer women's cold regard; 5

The Pastor's iterated 'sin'; –
These things could I endure, and count
No overstrain'd, unjust amount;
No undue payment for such bliss –
Yea, all things bear, save only this: 10
That you, who knew what thing would be,
Have wrought this evil unto me.
It is so strange to think on still –
That you, that *you* should do me ill!
Not as one ignorant or blind,   15
But seeing clearly in your mind
How this must be which now has been,
Nothing aghast at what was seen.
Now that the tale is told and done,
It is so strange to think upon.   20
You were so tender with me, too!
One summer's night a cold blast blew,
Closer about my throat you drew
The half-slipt shawl of dusky blue.
And once my hand, on a summer's morn,   25
I stretched to pluck a rose; a thorn
Struck through the flesh and made it bleed
(A little drop of blood indeed!)
Pale grew your cheek; you stoopt and bound
Your handkerchief about the wound;   30
Your voice came with a broken sound;
With the deep breath your breast was riven;
I wonder, did God laugh in Heaven?

How strange, that *you* should work my woe!
How strange! I wonder, do you know   35
How gladly, gladly I had died
(And life was very sweet that tide)
To save you from the least, light ill?
How gladly I had borne your pain.
With one great pulse we seem'd to thrill, –   40
Nay, but we thrill'd with pulses twain.

Even if one had told me this,
'A poison lurks within your kiss,
Gall that shall turn to night his day:'
Thereon I straight had turned away –   45
Ay, tho' my heart had crack'd with pain –
And never kiss'd your lips again.

At night, or when the daylight nears,
I hear the other women weep;
My own heart's anguish lies too deep   50

For the soft rain and pain of tears.
I think my heart has turn'd to stone,
A dull, dead weight that hurts my breast;
Here, on my pallet-bed alone,
I keep apart from all the rest.   55
Wide-eyed I lie upon my bed,
I often cannot sleep all night;
The future and the past are dead,
There is no thought can bring delight.
All night I lie and think and think;   60
If my heart were not made of stone,
But flesh and blood, it needs must shrink
Before such thoughts. Was ever known
A woman with a heart of stone?

The doctor says that I shall die.   65
It may be so, yet what care I?
Endless reposing from the strife?
Death do I trust no more than life
For one thing is like one arrayed,
And there is neither false nor true;   70
But in a hideous masquerade
All things dance on, the ages through.
And good is evil, evil good;
Nothing is known or understood
Save only Pain. I have no faith   75
In God or Devil, Life or Death.

The doctor says that I shall die.
You, that I knew in days gone by,
I fain would see your face once more,
Con well its features o'er and o'er;   80
And touch your hand and feel your kiss,
Look in your eyes and tell you this:
That all is done, that I am free;
That you, through all eternity,
Have neither part nor lot in me.   85

A Cross-Road Epitaph

Am Kreuzweg wird begraben
Wer selber brachte sich um.[1]

When first the world grew dark to me
I call'd on God, yet came not he.

---

[1] Those who committ suicide will be buried at the
crossroads.

Whereon, as wearier wax'd my lot,
On Love I call'd, but Love came not.
When a worse evil did befall,   5
Death, on thee only did I call.

Epitaph (On a Commonplace Person who Died in Bed)

This is the end of him, here he lies:
The dust in his throat, the worm in his eyes,
The mould in his mouth, the turf on his breast;
This is the end of him, this is best.
He will never lie on his couch awake,   5
Wide-eyed, tearless, till dim daybreak.
Never again will he smile and smile
When his heart is breaking all the while.
He will never stretch out his hands in vain
Groping and groping – never again.   10
Never ask for bread, get a stone instead,
Never pretend that the stone is bread.
Never sway and sway 'twixt the false and true,
Weighing and noting the long hours through.
Never ache and ache with the chok'd-up sighs;   15
This is the end of him, here he lies.

A March Day in London

The east wind blows in the street to-day;
The sky is blue, yet the town looks grey.
'Tis the wind of ice, the wind of fire,
Of cold despair and of hot desire,
Which chills the flesh to aches and pains,   5
And sends a fever through all the veins.

From end to end, with aimless feet,
All day long have I paced the street.
My limbs are weary, but in my breast
Stirs the goad of a mad unrest.   10
I would give anything to stay
The little wheel that turns in my brain;
The little wheel that turns all day,
That turns all night with might and main.

What is the thing I fear, and why?   15
Nay, but the world is all awry –
The wind's in the east, the sun's in the sky.
The gas-lamps gleam in a golden line;

The ruby lights of the hansoms shine,
Glance, and flicker like fire-flies bright;   20
The wind has fallen with the night,
And once again the town seems fair
Thwart the mist that hangs i' the air.

And o'er, at last, my spirit steals
A weary peace; peace that conceals   25
Within its inner depths the grain
Of hopes that yet shall flower again.

Straw in the Street

Straw in the street where I pass to-day
Dulls the sound of the wheels and feet.
'Tis for a failing life they lay
        Straw in the street.

Here, where the pulses of London beat,
Someone strives with the Presence grey;   5
Ah, is it victory or defeat?

The hurrying people go their way,
Pause and jostle and pass and greet;
For life, for death, are they treading, say,
        Straw in the street?

A Reminiscence

It is so long gone by, and yet
  How clearly now I see it all!
The glimmer of your cigarette,
  The little chamber, narrow and tall.

Perseus; your picture in its frame;   5
  (How near they seem and yet how far!)
The blaze of kindled logs; the flame
  Of tulips in a mighty jar.

Florence and spring-time: surely each
  Glad things unto the spirit saith.   10
Why did you lead me in your speech
  To these dark mysteries of death?

The Sequel to 'A Reminiscence'

Not in the street and not in the square,
   The street and square where you went and came;
With shuttered casement your house stands bare,
   Men hush their voice when they speak your name.

I, too, can play at the vain pretence,   5
   Can feign you dead; while a voice sounds clear
In the inmost depths of my heart: Go hence,
   Go, find your friend who is far from here.

Not here, but somewhere where I can reach!
   Can a man with motion, hearing and sight,   10
And a thought that answered my thought and speech,
   Be utterly lost and vanished quite?

Whose hand was warm in my hand last week? . . .
   My heart beat fast as I neared the gate –
Was it this I had come to seek,   15
   'A stone that stared with your name and date;'

A hideous, turfless, fresh-made mound;
   A silence more cold than the wind that blew?
What had I lost, and what had I found?
   My flowers that mocked me fell to the ground –   20
Then, and then only, my spirit knew.

Twilight

So Mary died last night! To-day
   The news has travelled here.
And Robert died at Michaelmas,
   And Walter died last year.

I went at sunset up the lane,   5
   I lingered by the stile;
I saw the dusky fields that stretched
   Before me many a mile.

I leaned against the stile, and thought
   Of her whose soul had fled. –   10
I knew that years on years must pass
   Or e'er I should be dead.

The Old House

In through the porch and up the silent stair;
  Little is changed, I know so well the ways; –
Here, the dead came to meet me; it was there
  The dream was dreamed in unforgotten days.

But who is this that hurries on before,   5
  A flitting shade the brooding shades among? –
She turned, – I saw her face, – O God, it wore
  The face I used to wear when I was young!

I thought my spirit and my heart were tamed
  To deadness; dead the pangs that agonise.   10
The old grief springs to choke me, – I am shamed
  Before that little ghost with eager eyes.

O turn away, let her not see, not know!
  How should she bear it, how should understand?
O hasten down the stairway, haste and go,   15
  And leave her dreaming in the silent land.

Felo de Se[1]

With Apologies to Mr Swinburne

For repose I have sighed and have struggled; have sigh'd and have struggled in vain;
I am held in the Circle of Being and caught in the Circle of Pain.
I was wan and weary with life; my sick soul yearned for death;
I was weary of women and war and the sea and the wind's wild breath;
I cull'd sweet poppies and crush'd them, the blood ran rich and red: –   5
And I cast it in crystal chalice and drank of it till I was dead.
And the mould of the man was mute, pulseless in ev'ry part,
The long limbs lay on the sand with an eagle eating the heart.
Repose for the rotting head and peace for the putrid breast,
But for that which is 'I' indeed the gods have decreed no rest;   10
No rest but an endless aching, a sorrow which grows amain: –
I am caught in the Circle of Being and held in the Circle of Pain.
Bitter indeed is Life, and bitter of Life the breath,
But give me life and its ways and its men, if this be Death.
Wearied I once of the Sun and the voices which clamour'd around: 15
Give them me back – in the sightless depths there is neither light nor sound.
Sick is my soul, and sad and feeble and faint as it felt
When (far, dim day) in the fair flesh-fane of the body it dwelt.

[1 A suicide]

But then I could run to the shore, weeping and weary and weak;
See the waves' blue sheen and feel the breath of the breeze on my cheek: 20
Could wail with the wailing wind; strike sharply the hands in despair;
Could shriek with the shrieking blast, grow frenzied and tear the hair;
Could fight fierce fights with the foe or clutch at a human hand;
And weary could lie at length on the soft, sweet, saffron sand....
I have neither a voice nor hands, nor any friend nor a foe;   25
I am I – just a Pulse of Pain – I am I, that is all I know.
For Life, and the sickness of Life, and Death and desire to die; –
They have passed away like the smoke, here is nothing but Pain and I.

To Vernon Lee

On Bellosguardo, when the year was young,
We wandered, seeking for the daffodil
And dark anemone, whose purples fill
The peasant's plot, between the corn-shoots sprung.

Over the grey, low wall the olive flung   5
Her deeper greyness; far off, hill on hill
Sloped to the sky, which, pearly-pale and still,
Above the large and luminous landscape hung.

A snowy blackthorn flowered beyond my reach;
You broke a branch and gave it to me there;   10
I found for you a scarlet blossom rare.

Thereby ran on of Art and Life our speech;
And of the gifts the gods had given to each –
Hope unto you, and unto me Despair.

A Ballad of Religion and Marriage

Swept into limbo is the host
   Of heavenly angels, row on row;
The Father, Son, and Holy Ghost,
   Pale and defeated rise and go.
The great Jehovah is laid low,   5
   Vanished his burning bush and rod –
Say, are we doomed to deeper woe?
   Shall marriage go the way of God?

Monogamous, still at our post,
   Reluctantly we undergo   10
Domestic round of boiled and roast,
   Yet deem the whole proceeding slow.

Daily the secret murmurs grow;
    We are no more content to plod
Along the beaten paths – and so   15
    Marriage must go the way of God.

Soon, before all men, each shall toast
    The seven strings unto his bow,
Like beacon fires along the coast,
    The flames of love shall glance and glow.   20
Nor let nor hindrance man shall know,
    From natal bath to funeral sod;
Perennial shall his pleasures flow
    When marriage goes the way of God.

Grant in a million years at most,   25
    Folk shall be neither pairs nor odd –
Alas! we sha'n't be there to boast
    'Marriage has gone the way of God!'

Mary E. Coleridge (1861–1907)

Mary Elizabeth Coleridge was the great-great niece of Samuel Taylor Coleridge. She was born in London and lived all her life, with one sister, in her parents' home. Her father was Clerk of the Assize and, like her mother, an amateur musician and keen supporter of the arts. Tennyson, Browning, Ruskin and Fanny Kemble were regular visitors to the house, though Mary on these occasions was usually shy and retiring. She was educated at home under the tutorship of William Cory, a scholar and poet who had resigned as classics master at Eton after a scandal involving an intimate letter to a pupil. 'Like Socrates', one commentator wrote, 'he adored the beauty of youth, which filled him with a protective yearning, at times sentimental' (1954: 35). He subsequently became tutor to a circle of young girls, which included Mary, and which met regularly to discuss literature, history and the classics. Cory not only made available to them, by default, some of the education otherwise reserved for boys, he may also have passed on to them some of his own idealistic-erotic platonism. Mary almost certainly knew his anonymously published volume *Ionica* (1891), which contains several love poems to boys as well as verses recognizing the intellectual and artistic advances of girls:

Into the breach our daughters press,
Brave patriots in unwarlike dress,
Adepts at thought-in-idleness,
Sweet devotees of freedom (1891: 194).

The strain of homoerotic aestheticism in Cory is matched by something similar, but more covert, in Coleridge.

Mary went on several trips to Germany with her family, and later visited Italy with some friends. This was, familiarly, a gender-specific homecoming: 'I feel as if I'd come not to a Fatherland but to a Motherland that I had always longed for and never known' (1910: 35). Otherwise, her life was outwardly uneventful. She gathered round her a circle of close women friends who shared her intellectual and literary interests. Many of Coleridge's poems ('Gone', 'Mortal Combat', 'Friends', 'Broken Friendship', 'Shadow') are about friendship – its failure and anguish as well as its delights. 'Marriage', which is addressed to one who has deserted the circle of her 'merry sisters', thus relinquishing the 'Wantonly free' state of maidenhood, is reminiscent of one of Sappho's gently reproachful nuptial songs to her girls. Very often in Coleridge the thrill of sexual desire, the 'kissing and dancing', is associated with the company of women rather than of men.

In the 1890s, influenced by her reading of Tolstoy (who was by then writing Christian-Anarchist tracts), Mary started to give lessons in English literature to working girls at her own home, and then, in 1895, became a teacher at the Working Women's College. It was at about this time that Robert Bridges picked up a manuscript of her poems in the house of a friend and promptly offered to assist in their publication. He entered into a correspondence with the poet, suggesting improvements and alterations, not all of which she accepted. In 1896 she published a volume under the pseudonym 'Anodos', 'the wanderer', or strictly, 'on no road'. A second volume appeared in the following year, but most of Coleridge's poetry was not collected and published until after her death. During her lifetime she was known mainly by her five, rather loosely constructed novels, some short stories and a volume of essays. When her mother died in 1898, Mary, her sister and her father drew ever closer together. Then, on one of the family's yearly trips to Harrogate, she suffered an attack of appendicitis and died shortly after the operation. Her family followed her instructions and destroyed most of her private papers. Robert Bridges, in a discreet obituary, recalled her 'superabundant' sense of humour and a streak of the quirkily enigmatic in her writing (*Cornhill*, 137 (1907), 595), while Walter de la Mare praised her verses' 'delicate, fearless irony' (*The Guardian*, 11 September 1907, 13.)

With two poets of the same name preceding her, it is perhaps not surprising that Coleridge was shy of publication. She seems to have written poetry continuously throughout her life, but mainly for the private readership of her friends and family. In one of her essays she recalls an exchange with the elderly Fanny Kemble, who peremptorily asked to see something she had written. Mary became 'flustered' (1900: 183) and refused. Her interlocutor's reply may have had more than a grain of truth to it: 'There is a kind of modesty that comes dangerously near self-love' (184), she ranted, and changed the subject of conversation to the untidy state of Mary's dress.

Coleridge's essays and published diary extracts contain hints of her literary tastes and opinions. She admires Sara Coleridge's 'Phantasmion', Darwin's *Descent of Man* and Yeats's early poems: 'I am afraid of boring people with them, they seem to me so beautiful with the pathetic, tremulous beauty of Irish airs' (1910: 266). She tries to read d'Annunzio, but gets 'tired of his being so tired of everything' (264), while Euripides' Medea bemuses her: 'How are you to be seriously interested in a woman who has murdered her mother and boiled her father-in-law before the play begins?' 'Medea', she summarizes, 'is thoroughly *fin de siècle*; says she would rather go into battle three times than have a baby once, pitches into men like anything' (235). Her feelings about Ibsen's *Ghosts* were more ambiguous. The play disturbed her and she wondered if it were 'very nasty' (228), but also acknowledged that 'a man that thoroughly understands a woman was a very great man indeed' (227).

On the whole she seems to have participated very little in the feminist debates of the day. 'Woman with a big W bores me supremely' (234), she once declared. However, on the subject of sexual, and by implication literary, difference she is adamant: 'I don't think we are separate only in body and in mind, I think we are separate in soul too, and that a woman's prayer is as different from a man's as a woman's thought or a woman's hand. I cannot think of souls that are not masculine or feminine . . . If we do not retain sex I don't see how we can retain identity' (233). Certainly her own poetry, although it is rarely written from a confessional standpoint, assumes and promotes an almost separatist female perspective. Works like 'The Other Side of a Mirror', 'A Day-dream', 'The Witch', 'The Witches' Wood' and 'The White Women' all conjure up an alternative world of women, riddled with risky secret knowledge, sexual power and hidden, white-hot passion. The speaker of 'A Day-dream', with its mummified dead kings and triumphantly living maids and crones, is haunted by a lost, 'true', matrilineal music. The idea of a sexualized maiden landscape – the white women desire and reproduce parthenogenically – runs through Coleridge's poems like the 'white ink' of another, enigmatic script of desire.

Some of her poems also arrestingly rewrite earlier texts. In particular, as Gilbert and Gubar have suggested, 'The Other Side of a Mirror' seems, whether consciously or not, to acknowledge Bertha Mason as the female self's monstrous doppelgänger, while 'The Witch' is evidently S. T. Coleridge's 'Christabel', written in another voice ('the voice that women have') and re-imagined as a love poem rather than a poem of supernatural fear. The two 'I's of Mary's work, who may or may not be Christabel and Geraldine (the same fire flickers in both poems), urgently and knowingly converge, until that movement of desire is abruptly stopped, or possibly censored, in the last lines. Whether or not it is true, as her editor cautiously asserts, that 'No one so feminine can ever have longed more to be a man' (1954: 50), it is certainly the case that many of Coleridge's poems evoke a lesbian subtext which cannot be entirely 'whitened' out. She once wrote to a friend: 'I don't feel sure of the sun, but there is not the faintest doubt that that moon was once a woman, she is the most human thing in creation . . . Somebody treated her very badly, depend upon it' (1910: 9–10). Women are so often white in her poems, not because they are pure, pining maidens, dying for love, but because their desires have another, secret source which lies always on the other side of her printed words. The secretive quality of Coleridge's poetry comes from its quietly ironic minimalism, its sense of holding back, of figuring an emotional event in an empty, contextless space, which seems sometimes altogether outside history and ideology.

Edith Sichel, who knew Mary and many of her friends, quotes with audible relief the poet's last words of faith in God, because, she warily acknowledges, 'her poems have sometimes given a wrong impression' (1910: 40). It is that element of fantasy and daring, disguised by the easy sonority of her verse, which makes Coleridge so original and even brilliant a poet. She catches an idea, like the blue bird of 'L'Oiseau Bleu', in an atmosphere which is beyond moral or sentimental gloss. In this, as in her gifted handling of metres and studied *effects* of simplicity, she is comparable to Rossetti. The difference between them lies in the nature of the desire which they evoke: Rossetti's is sexually oppositional and death-dealing, Coleridge's is communal, girlish and defiant. Her speakers may grieve for wasted or lost love, but they do not die.

A.L.

Coleridge, Mary E. (1908) *Poems*, London, Elkin Matthews.
—— (1954) *Collected Poems*, ed. Theresa Whistler, London, Rupert Hart-Davis.
—— (1900) *Non Sequitur*, London.
—— (1910) *Gathered Leaves from the Prose of Mary E. Coleridge*, with a Memoir by Edith Sichel, London, Constable.

Cory, William Johnson (1891) *Ionica*, London.
Gilbert, Sandra M. and Gubar, Susan (1979) *The Madwoman in the Attic*, New Haven and London, Yale University Press.

The Other Side of a Mirror

I sat before my glass one day,
   And conjured up a vision bare,
Unlike the aspects glad and gay,
   That erst were found reflected there –
The vision of a woman, wild   5
   With more than womanly despair.

Her hair stood back on either side
   A face bereft of loveliness.
It had no envy now to hide
   What once no man on earth could guess.   10
It formed the thorny aureole
   Of hard unsanctified distress.

Her lips were open – not a sound
   Came through the parted lines of red.
Whate'er it was, the hideous wound   15
   In silence and in secret bled.
No sigh relieved her speechless woe,
   She had no voice to speak her dread.

And in her lurid eyes there shone
   The dying flame of life's desire,   20
Made mad because its hope was gone,
   And kindled at the leaping fire
Of jealousy, and fierce revenge,
   And strength that could not change nor tire.

Shade of a shadow in the glass,   25
   O set the crystal surface free!
Pass – as the fairer visions pass –
   Nor ever more return, to be
The ghost of a distracted hour,
   That heard me whisper, 'I am she!'   30

A Clever Woman

You thought I had the strength of men,
  Because with men I dared to speak,
And courted Science now and then,
  And studied Latin for a week;
But woman's woman, even when   5
  She reads her Ethics in the Greek.

You thought me wiser than my kind;
  You thought me 'more than common tall;'
You thought because I had a mind,
  That I could have no heart at all;   10
But woman's woman you will find,
  Whether she be great or small.

And then you needs must die – ah, well!
  I knew you not, you loved not me.
'Twas not because that darkness fell,   15
  You saw not what there was to see.
But I that saw and could not tell –
  O evil Angel, set me free!

Impromptu

Gorgeous grew the common walls about me,
Floor and ceiling very Heaven became,
Music all within me and about me,
Brain on fire and heart aflame;
Yet I could not speak for shame,   5
And I stammered when I tried to speak the name.

Gone the light and vanished all the glory,
Clasping, grasping Fancy strives in vain;
None can sing the song or tell the story,
Walls are only walls again,   10
Now the stammering tongue speaks plain.
O, the ache of dreary dullness worse than pain.

Solo

Leave me alone! my tears would make you laugh,
Or kindly turn away to hide a smile.
My brimming granaries cover many a mile;
How should you know that all my corn is chaff?
Leave me alone! my tears would make you laugh.   5

Leave me alone! my mirth would make you weep.
I only smile at all that you hold dear;
I only laugh at that which most you fear;
I see the shallows where you sound the deep.
Leave me alone! my mirth would make you weep.   10

'I envy not the dead that rest'

I envy not the dead that rest,
  The souls that sing and fly;
Not for the sake of all the Blest,
  Am I content to die.

If ever men were laid in earth,   5
  And might in earth repose,
Where spirits have no second birth –
  Those, those, I envy, those.

My being would I gladly give,
  Rejoicing to be freed;   10
But if for ever I must live,
  Then let me live indeed.

What peace could ever be to me
  The joy that strives with strife?
What blissful immortality   15
  So sweet as struggling life?

Gone

About the little chambers of my heart
Friends have been coming – going – many a year.
  The doors stand open there.
Some, lightly stepping, enter; some depart.

Freely they come and freely go, at will.   5
The walls give back their laughter; all day long
  They fill the house with song.
One door alone is shut, one chamber still.

'True to myself am I, and false to all'

To thine own self be true,
And it must follow, as the night the day,
Thou canst not then be false to any man.

True to myself am I, and false to all.
  Fear, sorrow, love, constrain us till we die.
  But when the lips betray the spirit's cry,
The will, that should be sovereign, is a thrall.
Therefore let terror slay me, ere I call   5
  For aid of men. Let grief begrudge a sigh.
  'Are you afraid?' – 'unhappy?' 'No!'
    The lie
About the shrinking truth stands like a wall.
'And have you loved?' 'No, never!' All the while,   10
  The heart within my flesh is turned to stone.
Yea, none the less that I account it vile,
  The heart within my heart makes speechless moan,
  And when they see one face, one face alone,
The stern eyes of the soul are moved to smile.   15

Mortal Combat

It is because you were my friend,
  I fought you as the devil fights.
Whatever fortune God may send,
  For once I set the world to rights.

And that was when I thrust you down,   5
  And stabbed you twice and twice again,
Because you dared take off your crown,
  And be a man like other men.

Friends – With a Difference

O, one I need to love me,
  And one to understand,
And one to soar above me,
  And one to clasp my hand,

And one to make me slumber,   5
  And one to bid me strive,
But seven's the sacred number
  That keeps the soul alive.

And first and last of seven,
    And all the world and more,   10
Is she I need in Heaven,
    And may not need before.

Master and Guest

There came a man across the moor,
    Fell and foul of face was he.
    He left the path by the cross-roads three,
And stood in the shadow of the door.

I asked him in to bed and board.   5
    I never hated any man so.
    He said he could not say me No.
He sat in the seat of my own dear lord.

'Now sit you by my side!' he said,
    'Else may I neither eat nor drink.   10
    You would not have me starve, I think.'
He ate the offerings of the dead.

'I'll light you to your bed,' quoth I.
    'My bed is yours — but light the way!'
    I might not turn aside nor stay;   15
I showed him where we twain did lie.

The cock was trumpeting the morn.
    He said: 'Sweet love, a long farewell!
    You have kissed a citizen of Hell,
And a soul was doomed when you were born.   20

'Mourn, mourn no longer for your dear!
    Him may you never meet above.
    The gifts that Love hath given to Love,
Love gives away again to Fear.'

Gifts

I tossed my friend a wreath of roses, wet
    With early dew, the garland of the morn.
He lifted it — and on his brow he set
        A crackling crown of thorn.

Against my foe I hurled a murderous dart.   5
    He caught it in his hand — I heard him laugh —

I saw the thing that should have pierced his heart
    Turn to a golden staff.

The Witch

I have walked a great while over the snow,
And I am not tall nor strong.
My clothes are wet, and my teeth are set,
And the way was hard and long.
I have wandered over the fruitful earth,   5
But I never came here before.
Oh, lift me over the threshold, and let me in at the door!

The cutting wind is a cruel foe.
I dare not stand in the blast.
My hands are stone, and my voice a groan,   10
And the worst of death is past.
I am but a little maiden still,
My little white feet are sore.
Oh, lift me over the threshold, and let me in at the door!

Her voice was the voice that women have,   15
Who plead for their heart's desire.
She came — she came — and the quivering flame
Sank and died in the fire.
It never was lit again on my hearth
Since I hurried across the floor,   20
To lift her over the threshold, and let her in at the door.

The Contents of an Ink-bottle

Well of blackness, all defiling,
Full of flattery and reviling,
Ah, what mischief hast thou wrought
Out of what was airy thought,
What beginnings and what ends,   5
Making and dividing friends!

Colours of the rainbow lie
In thy tint of ebony;
Many a fancy have I found
Bright upon that sombre ground;   10
Cupid plays along the edge,
Skimming o'er it like a midge;
Niobe in turn appears,
Thinning it with crystal tears.

False abuse and falser praise,   15
Falsest lays and roundelays!
One thing, one alone, I think,
Never yet was found in ink; –
Truth lies not, the truth to tell,
At the bottom of this well!   20

L'Oiseau Bleu

The lake lay blue below the hill.
  O'er it, as I looked, there flew
Across the waters, cold and still,
  A bird whose wings were palest blue.

The sky above was blue at last,   5
  The sky beneath me blue in blue.
A moment, ere the bird had passed,
  It caught his image as he flew.

In London Town

It was a bird of Paradise,
  Over the roofs he flew.
All the children, in a trice,
Clapped their hands and cried, 'How nice!'
  'Look – his wings are blue!'   5

His body was of ruby red,
  His eyes were burning gold.
All the grown-up people said,
'What a pity the creature is not dead,
  For then it could be sold!'   10

One was braver than the rest.
  He took a loaded gun;
Aiming at the emerald crest,
He shot the creature through the breast.
  Down it fell in the sun.   15

It was not heavy, it was not fat,
  And folk began to stare.
'We cannot eat it, that is flat!
And such outlandish feathers as that
  Why, who could ever wear?'   20

They flung it into the river brown.
  'A pity the creature died!'

With a smile and with a frown,
Thus they did in London town;
   But all the children cried.   25

The Witches' Wood

There was a wood, a witches' wood,
   All the trees therein were pale.
They bore no branches green and good,
   But as it were a gray nun's veil.

They talked and chattered in the wind   5
   From morning dawn to set of sun,
Like men and women that have sinned,
   Whose thousand evil tongues are one.

Their roots were like the hands of men,
   Grown hard and brown with clutching gold.   10
Their foliage women's tresses when
   The hair is withered, thin, and old.

There never did a sweet bird sing
   For happy love about his nest.
The clustered bats on evil wing   15
   Each hollow trunk and bough possessed.

And in the midst a pool there lay
   Of water white, as tho' a scare
Had frightened off the eye of day
   And kept the Moon reflected there.   20

An Insincere Wish Addressed to a Beggar

We are not near enough to love,
   I can but pity all your woe;
For wealth has lifted me above,
   And falsehood set you down below.

If you were true, we still might be   5
   Brothers in something more than name;
And were I poor, your love to me
   Would make our differing bonds the same.

But golden gates between us stretch,
   Truth opens her forbidding eyes;   10
You can't forget that I am rich,
   Nor I that you are telling lies.

Love never comes but at love's call,
  And pity asks for him in vain;
Because I cannot give you all,   15
  You give me nothing back again.

And you are right with all your wrong,
  For less than all is nothing too;
May Heaven beggar me ere long,
  And Truth reveal herself to you!   20

A Day-dream

The murmur of the city sounded on
  Below the plaintive murmur of a hymn
That Sabbath day; the edge of life was gone,
  A veil of smoke made all the houses dim.
My eyes forgot to see — and lo, they saw   5
A sight that filled my shaken soul with awe!

For I was in the land where all lay clear
  Betwixt the sunshine and the shining sand.
And nothing far there was and nothing near —
  You might have touched the mountains with your hand —   10
And yet I looked upon them o'er a plain
Vast as the vastness of the untravelled main.

Tall rows of pillars — stems of flowering stone
  Sprang up around me in their ordered growth.
Here sat a maid, and there an ancient crone —   15
  The straight, bright shafts of light illumined both.
No shadow was there and no sound — the hum
Of brooding silence kept the temple dumb.

Three tombs of Kings, each with his corners three,
  Shut out three spaces of the golden sky.   20
Clear, flat, and bright, they hid no mystery,
  But painted mummies, of a scarlet dye,
That lay embalmed there many a long term,
Safe from unkindly damp and creeping worm.

Deep set beneath a sibyl's wrinkled brow,   25
  The ancient woman's eyes were full of song.
They held the voice of Time; and even now
  I mind me how the burden rolled along;
For I forgot the music of the birds,
And music's self, and music knit to words.   30

Then did I turn me to the maiden's eyes,
  And they were as the sea, brimming and deep.
Within them lay the secret of the skies,
  The rhythmical tranquillity of sleep.
They were more quiet than a windless calm   35
Among the isles of spices and of balm.

Now music is an echo in mine ear,
  And common stillness but the lack of noise;
For the true music I shall never hear,
  Nor the true silence, mother of all joys.   40
They dwell apart on that enchanted ground
Where not a shadow falls and not a sound.

Unwelcome

We were young, we were merry, we were very very wise,
  And the door stood open at our feast,
When there passed us a woman with the West in her eyes,
  And a man with his back to the East.

O, still grew the hearts that were beating so fast,   5
  The loudest voice was still.
The jest died away on our lips as they passed,
  And the rays of July struck chill.

The cups of red wine turned pale on the board,
  The white bread black as soot.   10
The hound forgot the hand of her lord,
  She fell down at his foot.

Low let me lie, where the dead dog lies,
  Ere I sit me down again at a feast,
When there passes a woman with the West in her eyes,   15
  And a man with his back to the East.

Wilderspin

In the little red house by the river,
  When the short night fell,
Beside his web sat the weaver,
  Weaving a twisted spell.
Mary and the Saints deliver   5
  My soul from the nethermost Hell!

In the little red house by the rushes
  It grew not dark at all,

For day dawned over the bushes
  Before the night could fall.   10
Where now a torrent rushes,
  The brook ran thin and small.

In the little red house a chamber
  Was set with jewels fair;
There did a vine clamber   15
  Along the clambering stair,
And grapes that shone like amber
  Hung at the windows there.

Will the loom not cease whirring?
  Will the house never be still?   20
Is never a horseman stirring
  Out and about on the hill?
Was it the cat purring?
  Did some one knock at the sill?

To the little red house a rider   25
  Was bound to come that night.
A cup of sheeny cider
  Stood ready for his delight.
And like a great black spider,
  The weaver watched on the right.   30

To the little red house by the river
  I came when the short night fell.
I broke the web for ever,
  I broke my heart as well.
Michael and the Saints deliver   35
  My soul from the nethermost Hell!

The Lady of Trees

By a lake below the mountain
  Hangs the birch, as if, in glee,
The lake had flung the moon a fountain,
  She had turned it to a tree.

Therefore do her dull leaves glimmer   5
  Like the waves that mothered them.
Therefore flits a moony shimmer
  Always round her curvèd stem.

Broken Friendship

Give me no gift! Less than thyself were nought.
It was thyself, alas! not thine I sought.
Once reigned I as a monarch in this heart,
Now from the doors a stranger I depart.

Shadow

Child of my love! though thou be bright as day,
  Though all the sons of joy laugh and adore thee,
Thou canst not throw thy shadow self away.
  Where thou dost come, the earth is darker for thee.

When thou dost pass, a flower that saw the sun   5
  Sees him no longer.
The hosts of darkness are, thou radiant one,
  Through thee made stronger!

The White Women[1]

Where dwell the lovely, wild white women folk,
    Mortal to man?
They never bowed their necks beneath the yoke,
They dwelt alone when the first morning broke
    And Time began.   5

Taller are they than man, and very fair,
    Their cheeks are pale,
At sight of them the tiger in his lair,
The falcon hanging in the azure air,
    The eagles quail.   10

The deadly shafts their nervous hands let fly
    Are stronger than our strongest – in their form
Larger, more beauteous, carved amazingly,
And when they fight, the wild white women cry
    The war-cry of the storm.   15

Their words are not as ours. If man might go
    Among the waves of Ocean when they break
And hear them – hear the language of the snow
Falling on torrents – he might also know
    The tongue they speak.   20

---

[1] From a legend of Malay, told by Hugh Clifford.

Pure are they as the light; they never sinned,
But when the rays of the eternal fire
Kindle the West, their tresses they unbind
And fling their girdles to the Western wind,
Swept by desire.   25

Lo, maidens to the maidens then are born,
Strong children of the maidens and the breeze,
Dreams are not – in the glory of the morn,
Seen through the gates of ivory and horn –
More fair than these.   30

And none may find their dwelling. In the shade
Primeval of the forest oaks they hide.
One of our race, lost in an awful glade,
Saw with his human eyes a wild white maid,
And gazing, died.   35

Marriage

No more alone sleeping, no more alone waking,
Thy dreams divided, thy prayers in twain;
Thy merry sisters to-night forsaking,
Never shall we see thee, maiden, again.

Never shall we see thee, thine eyes glancing,   5
Flashing with laughter and wild in glee,
Under the mistletoe kissing and dancing,
Wantonly free.

There shall come a matron walking sedately,
Low-voiced, gentle, wise in reply.   10
Tell me, O tell me, can I love her greatly?
All for her sake must the maiden die!

'But in that Sleep of Death what Dreams may Come?'

O grant me darkness! Let no gleam
Recall the visionary ray!
Give me to sleep without a dream.
Too often have I dreamt by day.
The dreams of day are all too strong;   5
Give me undreaming sleep, and long.

If blackest night be of the stuff
Whereof sun-woven days are made,

I that have dreamed, and dreamed enough
   Tremble, of dreamier dreams afraid.   10
Give to the heart Thy dreams have blest
The dark unconsciousness of rest!

'The fire, the lamp, and I, were alone together'

The fire, the lamp, and I, were alone together.
Out in the street it was wild and windy weather.

The fire said, 'Once I lived, and now I shine.
I was a wood once, and the wind was mine.'

The lamp said, 'Once I lived and was the Sun.   5
The fire and I, in those old days, were one.'

The fire said, 'Once I lived and saw the Spring.
I die in smoke to warm this mortal thing.'

The lamp said, 'I was once alive and free.
In smoke I die to let this mortal see.'   10

Then I remembered all the beasts that died
That I might eat and might be satisfied.

Then I remembered how my feet were shod,
Thought of the myriad lives on which I trod,

And sighed to feel that as I went my way,   15
I was a murderer ninety times a day.

'Only a little shall we speak of thee'

ONLY a little shall we speak of thee,
   And not the thoughts we think;
There, where thou art – and art not – words would be
   As stones that sink.

We shall not see each other for thy face,   5
   Nor know the silly things we talk upon.
Only the heart says, 'She was in this place,
   And she is gone.'

May Kendall (1861–*c.* 1931)

May Kendall was the only woman writer whose work A. H. Miles included in the selection of 'Humorous Verse' which makes up volume 10 of *The Poets and the Poetry of the Century*. He writes of her there: 'Miss Kendall's poetic work shows a grip of intellect and a depth of feeling not always found together, and a sense of humour rarely found in the verse of women' (Miles 1897: 10, 113). Kendall's work can be funny, but so is that of Dufferin, or Naden, Probyn or Fane, so why accord her this accolade? The answer lies partly with Miles's own limited reading list, but it also rests with his need to defuse some of her more ironic and critical poems.

Born Emma Goldworth Kendall, May was the daughter of Eliza Level and James Kendall, a Wesleyan minister in Bridlington, Yorkshire. She seems to have had some independent means and to have lived most of her life in the north of England, in Liverpool and Birmingham. Her first publication was a collaboration with Andrew Lang, the classical scholar best remembered now for his books of fairy tales. In 1885 when *That Very Mab* was published Andrew was an established man of letters and May an unknown young woman. She acknowledged him as joint author in the dedication to a later novel, but most of the work in this book seems to be hers. It consists of biting verse, and essays of fierce social satire written in a dry and brittle tone which is both amusing and painful.

During the 1880s her verses were published in many magazines and two volumes of poetry appeared in 1887 and 1894. She also wrote three novels and a book of short stories called *Turkish Bonds* (1898) which takes up the Armenian cause at a time when they were being massacred by the Turks. Her story may be fiction she says, but, 'Armenian suffering and Armenian heroism are neither invented nor exaggerated'.

Given the militant tone of many of her poems and stories, it seems clear that May was interested in women's politics. Her poem 'Woman's Future' is a rousing call to action, and one of the stories in *Turkish Bonds* has a heroine who is the despair of the old-fashioned hero: '... he could not make Marjorie adapt herself to the role of a rescued heroine. She was more like a knight errant. He was persuaded she would not faint in an emergency, though she might demand a revolver' (Kendall 1898: 67). Her main interests, however, lay with social reform and work among the poor. After 1898 May gave up publishing to concentrate on this, though she did later publish stories and poems in the *Cornhill* from 1927 to 1931. May was an 'other-worldly person' who 'would not accept a salary and always gave loyal devoted service' (Lancelyn Green 1946: 65). She worked with B. Seebohm Rowntree on *How the Labourer Lives* (1913). Her job was to use her 'gift for homely anecdote' to make his articles and books 'more readable' (Briggs 1961: 83–4). Her services were required again in 1918 when Seebohm Rowntree compiled a book on the minimum wage, *The Human Needs of Labour*. May's name, however, does not appear on the title page of this volume nor in other books where she is presumed to have assisted. The date of her death is unknown. No will was probated for her between 1931 and 1953.

Kendall's poems address contemporary issues with a sceptical tone which is telling. One of her techniques is to create a first-person speaker, usually male, usually self-satisfied, whose complacent platitudes are radically undercut by the voice of a criticizing other. The joke comes out of the disparity of status and the fact that the real wisdom comes from the underling. So the jelly-fish is a better thinker than the philanthropist ('The Philanthropist and the Jelly-fish'), and the lowly porter is more discerning than the gentleman ('Underground'). 'Lay of the Trilobite' is another of these didactic poems, and its situation, where man, the highly organized creature, encounters the fossil of a simpler life form, may owe something to the scene of Knight's fall in Thomas Hardy's *A Pair of Blue Eyes* (1873). Its rollicking style, however, takes the portentous subjects of evolution and science into the realm of nonsense and nursery poems. Like Rossetti's verses for children, Kendall's poems are cheeky satires for adults. In the manner of Lewis Carroll, the poems tease the reader by using grand scientific terms for the sake of their sound and often entirely without regard to sense.

In taking science as a subject for poetry, Kendall along with writers such as Naden and Blind, is working with new themes. In 'Woman's Future' Kendall embraces the theory of evolution. At first, it looks as if she has misinterpreted Darwin and equates the evolutionary process with a progressist model; 'The laws of the universe these are our friends. Our talents shall rise in a mighty crescendo,/ We trust Evolution to make us amends!' But the following verses, where she exhorts her 'sisters' to 'rouse to a lifework – do something worth doing', suggest that she knows well that it is only a change in environment and condition that will bring about the selection process necessary to allow 'our brains' to 'expand'. 'A Pure Hypothesis' is a poem which, like Robinson's 'The Idea', questions the established systems of the physical and social world by attempting to imagine a metaphysical scene without them.

If Kendall is keen on new ways of thinking, she is severely critical of the old. In 'Education's Martyr' the unfeeling pedant can categorize but cannot appreciate. In 'The Vision of Noah' the nation's factions are reviewed in their various 'arks' of laissez-faire, philosophical romance, arrogant isolationism and socialist indiscrimination. In 'A Fossil' the complacent churchman is depicted, fired not by faith, but by smouldering memories of youth. In this poem, as in others, Kendall tackles serious issues with gusto so that she never sounds preachy. Her ear for the rhythms of colloquial speech is sure, and where she bends it to fit elaborate rhyme schemes (in 'Education's Martyr' for instance), the effect is one of confident panache.

Her poems on the suffering of the poor and the oppressed labouring classes exhibit her capacity for creating a distinctive voice like that of the child in 'Legend of the Crossing Sweeper'. As Kendall gave up writing for reforming work, her address to the poet in 'Failures' suggests a personal discomfort with the 'mood aesthetic' which her verses so wittily reproduce even while they satirize.

M. R.

Kendall, May (1885) *That Very Mab*, with Andrew Lang, London.
—— (1887) *Dreams to Sell*, London.
—— (1894) *Songs from Dreamland*, London.
Miles, A. H. ed. (1891–7) *The Poets and the Poetry of the Century*, 10 vols, London.

Briggs, Asa (1961) *Social Thought and Social Action: A Study of the Work of B. Seebohm Rowntree*, London, Longmans.
Green, Roger Lancelyn (1946) *Andrew Lang*, Leicester, E. Ward.

A Fossil

He had his Thirty-nine Articles,
    And his Nicene Creed.
And his Athanasian. Nothing else
    He appeared to need.
He looked like a walking dogma, pent   5
    Neath a shovel brim;
If he never knew what the dogma meant,
    'Twas small blame to him.

He did not hazard a single guess,
    That might lead to twain,   10
Whose answers never would coalesce
    In a peaceful brain!
He seemed pure fossil: yet I protest
    That across the aisle
I one day saw him of life possessed   15
    For a little while!

'And streams in the desert,' sang the choir.
    What a strange surmise
Just then awoke, like a smouldering fire,
    In his weary eyes!   20
That never came from the Nicene Creed –
    'Twas a dream, I know,
Of some fair day when he lived indeed,
    In the long ago!

Legend of the Crossing-Sweeper

The boarders look so good and new,
    A saint it would annoy!
To squirt upon them two by two
    Would be my greatest joy.
The boarders think – I know it's true,   5
    I am a wicked boy.

Save one – I've never known *her* stare
    As if I were a wall
That had no business to be there,
    Or anywhere at all;   10
And once – to stop she didn't dare –
    She let a sixpence fall.

She smiled to show she couldn't wait,
    And gently said, 'Good-night.'

You bet I pulled my cap off straight,   15
    I nodded all my might;
But now she seldom comes: I hate
    To see her look so white.

There is a place – *she'll* go some day,
    Right up above the sky.   20
It is uncommon bright and gay,
    Swells live there when they die.
Some tell us any fellow may,
    But that is all my eye.

They stand with harps and crowns in rows,   25
    For doing all they should;
But I should miss her, I suppose,
    I'd save her if I could –
Only a boy that never goes
    To Sunday school's no good.   30

And I'm the worst boy in the town,
    I lark, I fight, I swear,
I knock the other fellows down
    And lick them. I don't care.
They'll give her such a harp and crown,   35
    But I shall not be there.

Those crowns – if one could hang about
    The gate, till all was done –
She'll stand in a white gown, no doubt,
    With gold hair like the sun.   40
I'd like to see them given out,
    I'd never ask for one.

Lay of the Trilobite

A mountain's giddy height I sought,
    Because I could not find
Sufficient vague and mighty thought
    To fill my mighty mind;
And as I wandered ill at case,   5
    There chanced upon my sight
A native of Silurian seas,
    An ancient Trilobite.

So calm, so peacefully he lay,
    I watched him even with tears: 10
I thought of Monads far away
    In the forgotten years.

How wonderful it seemed and right,
    The providential plan,
That he should be a Trilobite,   15
    And I should be a Man!

And then, quite natural and free
    Out of his rocky bed,
That Trilobite he spoke to me,
    And this is what he said: 20
'I don't know how the thing was done,
    Although I cannot doubt it;
But Huxley – he if anyone
    Can tell you all about it;

'How all your faiths are ghosts and dreams,   25
    How in the silent sea
Your ancestors were Monotremes –
    Whatever these may be;
How you evolved your shining lights
    Of wisdom and perfection   30
From Jelly-fish and Trilobites
    By Natural Selection.

'You've Kant to make your brains go round,
    Hegel you have to clear them,
You've Mr. Browning to confound,   35
    And Mr. Punch to cheer them!
The native of an alien land
    You call a man and brother,
And greet with hymn-book in one hand
    And pistol in the other!   40

'You've Politics to make you fight
    As if you were possessed:
You've cannon and you've dynamite
    To give the nations rest:
The side that makes the loudest din   45
    Is surest to be right,
And oh, a pretty fix you're in!'
    Remarked the Trilobite.

'But gentle, stupid, free from woe
    I lived among my nation,   50
I didn't care – I didn't know
    That I was a Crustacean.'[1]

---

[1] He was not a Crustacean. He has since discovered   says it does not matter. He says they told him wrong
that he was an Arachnid, or something similar. But he   once, and they may again.

I didn't grumble, didn't steal,
  I *never* took to rhyme:
Salt water was my frugal meal,   55
  And carbonate of lime.'

Reluctantly I turned away,
  No other word he said;
An ancient Trilobite, he lay
  Within his rocky bed.   60
I did not answer him, for that
  Would have annoyed my pride:
I merely bowed, and raised my hat,
  But in my heart I cried: —

'I wish our brains were not so good,   65
  I wish our skulls were thicker,
I wish that Evolution could
  Have stopped a little quicker;
For oh, it was a happy plight,
  Of liberty and ease,   70
To be a simple Trilobite
  In the Silurian seas!'

Woman's Future

Complacent they tell us, hard hearts and derisive,
  In vain is our ardour: in vain are our sighs:
Our intellects, bound by a limit decisive,
  To the level of Homer's may never arise.
We heed not the falsehood, the base innuendo,   5
  The laws of the universe, these are our friends,
Our talents shall rise in a mighty crescendo,
  We trust Evolution to make us amends!

But ah, when I ask you for food that is mental,
  My sisters, you offer me ices and tea!   10
You cherish the fleeting, the mere accidental,
  At cost of the True, the Intrinsic, the Free.
Your feelings, compressed in Society's mangle,
  Are vapid and frivolous, pallid and mean.
To slander you love; but you don't care to wrangle;   15
  You bow to Decorum, and cherish Routine.

Alas, is it woolwork you take for your mission,
  Or Art that your fingers so gaily attack?
Can patchwork atone for the mind's inanition?
  Can the soul, oh my sisters, be fed on a *plaque*?   20

Is this your vocation? My goal is another,
   And empty and vain is the end you pursue.
In antimacassars the world you may smother;
   But intellect marches o'er them and o'er you.

On Fashion's vagaries your energies strewing,   25
   Devoting your days to a rug or a screen,
Oh, rouse to a lifework – do something worth doing!
   Invent a new planet, a flying-machine.
Mere charms superficial, mere feminine graces,
   That fade or that flourish, no more you may prize;   30
But the knowledge of Newton will beam from your faces,
   The soul of a Spencer will shine in your eyes.

Envoy

Though jealous exclusion may tremble to own us,
   Oh, wait for the time when our brains shall expand!
When once we're enthroned, you shall never dethrone us –
   The poets, the sages, the seers of the land!

Underground

The Porter Speaks

A quarter of an hour to wait,
   And quite sufficient too,
Since your remarks on Bishopsgate
   Impress the mind as true,
Unless you work here soon and late,   5
   Till 'tis like home to you.

You see, a chap stands what he must,
   He'll hang on anywhere;
He'll learn to live on smoke and dust,
   Though 'tisn't healthy fare.   10
We're used to breathing grime in, just
   Like you to breathing air.

And yet 'tis odd to think these trains,
   In half an hour, maybe,
Will be right out among green lanes,   15
   Where the air is pure and free.
Well, sir, there's Bishopsgate remains
   For us, and here are we!

Your train. First class, sir. That's your style!
   In future, I'll be bound,   20

You'll stick to hansoms, since you'd spile
    Here in the Underground.
I've got to wait a little while
    Before *my* train comes round.

A Pure Hypothesis

A Lover, in Four-dimensioned Space, describes a Dream

Ah, love, the teacher we decried,
    That erudite professor grim,
In mathematics drenched and dyed,
    Too hastily we scouted him.
He said: 'The bounds of Time and Space,   5
    The categories we revere,
May be in quite another case
    In quite another sphere.'

He told us: 'Science can conceive
    A race whose feeble comprehension   10
Can't be persuaded to believe
    That there exists our Fourth Dimension,
Whom Time and Space for ever baulk;
    But of these beings incomplete,
Whether upon their heads they walk   15
    Or stand upon their feet –

We cannot tell, we do not know,
    Imagination stops confounded;
We can but say "It *may* be so,"
    To every theory propounded.'   20
Too glad were we in this our scheme
    Of things, his notions to embrace, –
But – I have dreamed an awful dream
    Of *Three-dimensioned* Space!

I dreamed – the horror seemed to stun   25
    My logical perception strong,
That everything beneath the sun
    Was *so unutterably wrong.*
I thought – what words can I command? –
    That nothing ever did come right.   30
No wonder *you* can't understand:
    I could not, till last night!

I would not, if I could, recall
    The horror of those novel heavens,

Where Present, Past, and Future all   35
  Appeared at sixes and at sevens,
Where Capital and Labour fought,
  And, in the nightmare of the mind,
No contradictories were thought
  As truthfully combined!   40

Nay, in that dream-distorted clime,
  These fatal wilds I wandered through,
The boundaries of Space and Time
  Had got most frightfully askew.
  'What *is* "askew"?' my love, you cry;   45
  I cannot answer, can't portray;
The sense of Everything awry
  No language can convey.

I can't tell what my words denote,
  I know not what my phrases mean: 50
Inexplicable terrors float
  Before this spirit once screne.
Ah, what if on some lurid star
  There should exist a hapless race,
Who live and love, who think and are,   55
  In Three-dimensioned Space!

Education's Martyr

He loved peculiar plants and rare,
For any plant he did not care
  That he had seen before;
Primroses by the river's brim
Dicotyledons were to him,   5
  And they were nothing more.

The mighty cliffs we bade him scan,
He banned them for Laurentian,
  With sad, dejected mien.
'Than all this bleak Azoic rock,'   10
He said, 'I'd sooner have a block –
  Ah me! – of Pleistocene!'

His eyes were bent upon the sand;
He owned the *scenery* was grand,
  In a reproachful voice;   15
But if a centipede he found,
He'd fall before it on the ground,
  And worship and rejoice.

We spoke of Poets dead and gone,
Of that Maeonian who shone
  O'er Hellas like a star:
We talked about the King of Men, –
'Observe,' he said, 'the force of κεν,
  And note the use of γαρ!'   20

Yes, all that has been or may be,
States, beauties, battles, land, and sea,
  The matin songs of larks,
With glacier, earthquake, avalanche,
To him were each a separate 'branch,'
  And stuff for scoring marks!   30

Ah! happier he who does not know
The power that makes the Planets go,
  The slaves of Kepler's Laws;
Who finds not glands in joy or grief,
Nor, in the blossom and the leaf,   35
  Seeks for the secret Cause!

The Philanthropist and the Jelly-fish

Her beauty, passive in despair,
  Through sand and seaweed shone,
The fairest jelly-fish I e'er
  Had set mine eyes upon.

It would have made a stone abuse   5
  The callousness of fate,
This creature of prismatic hues,
  Stranded and desolate!

Musing I said: 'My mind's unstrung,
  Joy, hope, are in their grave: 10
Yet ere I perish all unsung
  One jelly-fish I'll save!'

And yet I fancied I had dreamed
  Of somewhere having known
Or met, a jelly-fish that seemed   15
  As utterly alone.

But ah, if ever out to sea
  That jelly-fish I bore,
Immediately awaited me
  A level hundred more!   20

I knew that it would be in vain
  To try to float them all;
And though my nature is humane,
  I *felt* that it would pall.

Yet this one jelly-fish,' I cried,   25
  I'll rescue if I may.
I'll wade out with her through the tide
  And leave her in the bay.'

I paused, my feelings to control,
  To wipe away a tear –   30
It seemed to me a murmur stole
  Out of the crystal sphere.

She said: 'Your culture's incomplete,
  Though your intention's kind;
The sand, the seaweed, and the heat   35
  I do not really mind.

'To wander through the briny deep
  I own I do not care;
I somehow seem to go to sleep
  Here, there, or anywhere.   40

'When wild waves tossed me to and fro,
  I never felt put out;
I never got depressed and low,
  Or paralysed by doubt.

''Twas not the ocean's soothing balm.   45
  Ah no, 'twas something more!
I'm just as peaceful and as calm
  Here shrivelling on the shore.

'It does not matter what may come,
  I'm dead to woe or bliss: 50
I haven't a Sensorium,
  And that is how it is.'

The Vision of Noah

The rising deluge he descried.
He saw upon the foaming tide
The nation's arks at random ride.

One ark came slow and heavily,
By toiling swimmers on the sea   5
Supported, as most arks must be.

It seemed unconscious of the flood,
There sat within a multitude
Discoursing on the public good.

No ark had some, nor aught unsound.   10
Serenely upon higher ground
They stood and waited to be drowned.

With pensive scrutiny remote
They criticised each kind of boat,
Remarking how it would not float.   15

Drowning was safer, they averred;
In peaceful minor keys he heard
Them murmur, drowning they preferred.

There braved the foaming flood's expanse,
There took the waves with sprightly dance –   20
The philosophical romance.

'If I might venture a remark,'
He said, 'a very pretty bark!
But which is flood, and which is ark?'

Others, avoiding more and more   25
All the weak points of arks of yore,
Had built an ark without a door.

They clung to it in calm austere,
Remarking: 'It is very clear,
The flood can never enter here!'   30

They passed him, fading into mist,
There floated near him ere he wist
The vessel of the Socialist.

A goodly, but confusing bark,
A vision on the waters dark   35
Of many doors without an ark.

Hard by a lurid vessel shone,
That even as he looked thereon
Swiftly exploded, and was gone!

A tear for memory he shed,   40
He shook his patriarchal head,
And 'Give *me* gopherwood!' he said.

The Lower Life

It might seem matter for regret
That Evolution has not yet
  Fulfilled our wishes.
The birds soar higher far than we,
The fish outswim us in the sea,   5
  The simple fishes.

But, evolutionists reflect,
We have the pull in intellect,
  And that's undoubted:
Yet still we cry: 'Can this atone   10
For fins or pinions of our own,
  Not to be scouted?'

We hold that Evolution's plan,
To give as little as she can,
  Is sometimes trying.   15
Fair share of brains, indeed, we win;
But why not throw the swimming in,
  Why not the flying?

But ah, she gives not more or less.
We pay for all that we possess,   20
  We weep and waver,
While Evolution, still the same,
With knights or pawns pursues the game,
  And shows no favour.

As onward yet life's currents roll,   25
The gaining of a higher goal
  Increaseth sorrow;
And what we win at its own cost
We win; and what we lose is lost,
  Nor can we borrow.   30

If we have freedom, we lose peace.
If self-renunciation, cease
  To care for pleasure.
If we have Truth – important prize!
We wholly must away with lies,   35
  Or in a measure.

Is wisdom, then, the only test,
Of lot superlatively blest?
  There have been others.

Our aeon too will pass, and then   40
Are monads so much less than men?
  Alas, my brothers!

This higher life is curious stuff,
Too high, yet not quite high enough,
  A mingled vial!   45
This higher life is sold too dear —
Would I could give a lower sphere
  An equal trial!

Ah, could I be a fish indeed,
Of lucky horoscope, and creed   50
  Utilitarian,
'Mong blissful waves to glide or rest,
I'd choose the lot I found the best,
  Or fish or Aryan!

Or could I be a bird and fly   55
Through forests all unhaunted by
  The shooting season,
I'd tell you which I voted for,
The flight of airy pinions, or
  The March of Reason!   60

Failures

And you have failed, O Poet? Sad!
  Yet failures are a commonplace.
Boast not as though you only had
  Secured a failure in the race.
You see them thick on every hand   5
  As blackberries; but you, you say,
Because your nature was so grand,
  Have failed in a peculiar way.

You weep: 'I had such lofty aims.
  My soul had yearnings truly great.   10
Than broken altars, dying flames,
  I had deserved a better fate.
And others gain my heart's desire
  They win the prize I vainly crave;
And they will set the Thames on fire   15
  When I am mouldering in my grave.'

What matter, yet? The years of blight
  The fair and laughing seasons bring —

And if you flee or if you fight,
　　It is a very little thing.　　　　　　　　　　　　　　20
Small anguish have *you* undergone,
　　Poor fool, to write, with careful art,
Your melancholy sonnets on,
　　When some, to fail, would break the heart!

Go, look into some dingy street　　　　　　　　　　25
　　Your mood æsthetic scorns to pace.
Mark well the throng; you will not meet
　　One happy or one careless face.
Have these not failed, on whom the rain
　　Strikes cheerless from the sky of grey?　　　　30
No lurking comfort in their pain
　　Of subtle self-esteem have they.

They live their wasted lives, and die,
　　Nor much their destiny bewail,
While you to all the world must cry:　　　　　　　35
　　'Alas, but see how *I* can fail!
Compassionate my fruitless tears,
　　Peruse the volumes of my woes,
The burden of my blighted years,
　　In metre some, and some in prose!'　　　　　　40

You fail? Then take it at the worst.
　　Shall some not gloriously succeed?
Ah, waive awhile your lot accurst,
　　To triumph in a noble deed!
Nay, but you grudge the victory,　　　　　　　　45
　　Nor heed how the hard fight prevailed.
Through Time's exulting harmony
　　You shriek, 'Alas, *but I have failed*!'

Dora Sigerson (1866–1918)

Dora Sigerson was the elder of two daughters born into an artistic, staunchly Republican family in Dublin. Her mother, Hester Varian, was a novelist and poet, and her father, George Sigerson, was a surgeon and also a poet. Dora was educated at home, and soon became a keen painter, sculptor and poet as well. Katharine Tynan, who was to become a lifelong friend, recalled her first meeting with the Sigersons in 1887, at a dinner with the Yeats's. Dora, she recalled, was naturally gifted, and was generally to be found 'painting or writing or doing sculpture' (1918: ix). She was also passionately fond of animals, and would pick up stray dogs in the Dublin Streets, much to the amusement of passers-by, and take them to the dog home. At this time the Sigersons' house in Clare Street was a centre of artistic and Republican activity. In

1888, the Pan Celtic Society was founded, its nationalist but non-sectarian aims finding support amongst members of all three families. Later, Katharine and Dora became Parnellites, attending Parnell's meetings and siding with him when it came to the split with the Church.

Dora published her first collection of poems in 1893. Three years later, after a last, carefree holiday with Katharine in Ireland, she married Clement Shorter, editor of the *Illustrated London News*, and moved to London. There she became active in English literary circles, meeting Hardy, Swinburne, and Meredith who wrote introductions to her poems. She also remained friendly with Yeats, who was frequently a guest at their house and offered Dora advice about her poetry. Tynan's comment that 'No one will say she was not happy in her English life' (1918: xi) hints loudly at the opposite. Certainly, the failure of the Easter Uprising in 1916 left her depressed and disappointed, and it is possible that the event hastened her relatively early death. Her memorial sculpture to the patriots of 1916 is in the Dublin cemetery.

The strength of Sigerson's nationalism comes through in her poetry. Much of it, particularly the ballads for which she was highly praised, depicts Irish life and recounts traditional Irish legends. These tales of the supernatural show a keen, if not very original, sense of ghostliness and melodrama. Her domestic poems, by contrast, seem more contemporary in their concerns, probing as they often do the claustrophobic unhappiness of family life. 'The Skeleton in the Cupboard' hints at the emotional destructiveness of the Victorian home, with its rattling secrets in the cupboard – secrets which the poem does not spell out. 'The Mother', on the other hand, catches, with powerful drama and sentiment, the horror of child mortality in an age when it was still a common fact of life.

A.L.

Sigerson (Shorter), Dora (1907) *Collected Poems*, introduction by George Meredith, London, Hodder and Stoughton.
—— (1918) *The Sad Years, and Other Poems*, with a tribute and memories by Katharine Tynan, London, Constable

Yeats, W. B. (1986) *Collected Letters*, vol. I, 1865–1895, eds John Kelly and Eric Domville, Oxford, Clarendon Press.

The Skeleton in the Cupboard

Just this one day in all the year
Let all be one, let all be dear;
Wife, husband, child in fond embrace,
And thrust the phantom from its place.
No bitter words, no frowning brow,   5
Disturb the Christmas festal, now
The skeleton's behind the door.

Nor let the child, with looks askance,
Find out its sad inheritance
From souls that held no happiness   10
Of home, where love is seldom guest;

But in his coming years retain
This one sweet night that had no pain;
The skeleton's behind the door.

In vain you raise the wassail bowl,   15
And pledge your passion, soul to soul
You hear the sweet bells ring in rhyme,
You wreathe the room for Christmas-time
In vain. The solemn silence falls,
The death-watch ticks within the walls;   20
The skeleton taps on the door.
Then let him back into his place,
Let us sit out the old disgrace;
Nor seek the phantom now to lay
That haunted us through every day;   25
For plainer is the ghost; useless
Is this pretence of happiness;
The skeleton taps on the door.

The Mother

'Ho!' said the child, 'how fine the horses go,
With nodding plumes, with measured step and slow
Who rides within this coach, is he not great?
Some King, I think, for see, he rides in state!'

I turned, and saw a little coffin lie   5
Half-hid in flowers as the slow steeds went by,
So small a woman's arms might hold it pressed
As some rare jewel-casket to her breast;

Or like Pandora's box with pulsing lid
Where throbbing thoughts must lie for ever hid.   10
'Why this? Why this?' comes forth the panting breath,
'And was I born to taste of nought save death?'

'Ho!' said the child, 'how the proud horses shake
Their silver harness till they music make.
Who drives abroad with all this majesty?   15
Is it some Prince who fain his world would see?'

And as I looked I saw through the dim glass
Of one sad coach that all so slow did pass
A woman's face – a mother's eyes ablaze
Seize on the child in fierce and famished gaze.   20

'Death drives,' I said, and drew him in alarm
Within the shelter of my circling arm.

So in my heart cried out a thousand fears,
'A King goes past.' He wondered at my tears.

Charlotte Mew (1869–1928)

Charlotte Mew's life was a sad one. She was the third of seven children born to Frederick Mew, an architect who moved to London from the Isle of Wight, and Anna Maria, who was for much of her life an invalid. Three of her four brothers died in childhood, two of them, aged five and one, in the same year. The memory of childhood mortality haunts Mew's poetry, as does the idea of the mother left empty-handed. When she was ten, Charlotte was sent to Gower Street School for girls, run by the inspirational teacher and suffragist Lucy Harrison, whose passion for women's poetry was remembered by many of her pupils. These school years, broken by holidays on the Isle of Wight, were probably the happiest of her life.

By the late 1880s, however, tragedy struck again. Henry, the oldest son, then in his early twenties, began to show signs of mental breakdown. He was confined in Peckham hospital, where he died of pneumonia some ten years later. Then the youngest daughter, Freda, showed similar symptoms, and was confined for life to an asylum on the Isle of Wight. The social stigma of mental illness at this time, exacerbated by the new theories of eugenics which dwelt on the 'ghosts' of inherited disease and warned against procreation by the unfit, may explain some of Charlotte's wary attitudes to sexuality as well as her lifelong silence about these siblings. Her poetry, however, returns guiltily and tormentedly to the strange-familiar world of the mad. 'Ken', which was rejected by one editor because it seems to question the necessity of confinement, and 'On the Asylum Road', both play on the otherness and yet brotherliness of the insane. When, in 1898, their father also died, Charlotte and her younger sister Anne were left, with their invalid mother, as sole survivors of this devastated family.

There were some compensations, however. In 1901 the two sisters went on a holiday to Brittany with four other women, Charlotte dancing a can-can for them on the boat in her silk knickers. They stayed at the convent of St Gildas de Rhuys, a place which inspired several poems and stories, in particular 'At the Convent Gate', recalling Rossetti's 'The Convent Threshold'. This was the first of many trips to France. Freed from the constraints of her Victorian background, Charlotte revelled in the 'open road' of travel (see 'The Forest Road'). She attended plays, had a whirl at the Casino, took impromptu buses into the countryside, made friends with market women and fishermen. Back in London, she started contributing stories and poems to *The Yellow Book*, some of them under the pseudonym Charles Catty.

It is possible that at this time Charlotte fell in love with Ella D'Arcy, another *Yellow Book* contributer. In 1902 she visited Ella in Paris and, it has been suggested, made a rash and perhaps immediately regretted declaration of love (Fitzgerald 1984: 82–7). At any rate, it seems that she was rebuffed, and returned home, as usual, empty-handed. The situation repeated itself some years later when, so rumour had it, Charlotte fell in love with May Sinclair. The story, as it was crudely reported, was that May was chased upstairs by her ardent pursuer and had 'to leap the bed five times!' (133). This unlikely spriteliness in two middle-aged women suggests some rhetorical elaboration, but the underlying fact of Charlotte's unrequited love remains audible through it. The highly-charged and ambiguously gendered dramatic monologues, 'The Farmer's Bride' and 'The Forest Road', both express a yearning eroticism as well as a fear of possession and responsibility.

Charlotte was forty-seven when her first volume of poems, *The Farmer's Bride* (1916), was published. Harold and Alida Monro of the Poetry Bookshop had come to know the reclusive spinster, and they invited her to read at one of their poetry evenings, an occasion which was probably the source of the poem 'Fame'. It was they who published her first, slim volume, overcoming the obstacles of a compositor who refused to set 'Madeleine in Church' because he thought it blasphemous, and Charlotte's own insistence that its long lines should not be broken up. In spite of these problems, not to mention the war, the volume came out, and Alida was occasionally invited to visit Charlotte and Anne at home. It was she who, when the sisters' nerve failed them, administered chloroform to their ferocious old parrot, Wek, wringing the bird's neck as a final resort. Alida remembered how Charlotte, as she sat talking and smoking, would insouciantly make spills from what she claimed were manuscripts of her poems, while vaguely referring to 'stacks of MSS salted away in trunks' (Monro 1953: xx). None of these was ever found, though Alida remembered poems which never appeared in print.

One consequence of the publication of *The Farmer's Bride* was that Charlotte was invited to visit Max Gate. Hardy had been greatly impressed by the volume and thought her the best living woman poet. Unfortunately, whether through nervousness or pent-up loneliness, Charlotte chattered incessantly for the two days of her visit, exhausting her hosts. Her public manner, often out of step with her private self, could seem gauche or garrulous. None the less, a friendship with Florence Hardy survived the visit and the two women continued to meet in London. Another friend of her later years was Sydney Cockerell, director of the Fitzwilliam Museum in Cambridge. He would take Charlotte out for lunch when he was in London, and once organized a dinner so that she could meet Walter de la Mare, who was struck by her vivid story-telling. In 1920, she finally agreed to a long-standing invitation to Cambridge. There, she met Kate Cockerell, the illustrator, who was now a crippled invalid. Once again, Charlotte struck up the stronger friendship with the woman, Kate's shyness and infirmity touching a chord of sympathy in her. She was also shown one of Sydney's treasured possessions: a lock of Lizzie Siddal's hair, still, in the 1920s, an object of legendary fascination. In 1923, the year that old Mrs Mew died and the lease on the family home ran out, Charlotte received a Civil List pension, which at least afforded some security in her last years.

By 1926 it became clear that Anne was ailing. She was diagnosed as having cancer of the liver, and died in June 1927. After this, all Charlotte's thin defences seemed to crack. She started to imagine that Anne had been buried alive (that old claustrophobic imagery of Victorian women's lives returning to haunt her) and left instructions in her will that her own arteries be cut before burial. Then she imagined that Anne had been infected by black specks which appeared in the studio. A doctor tried to persuade her to enter an asylum, but that, understandably, was a prospect too full of old horror for her. Eventually she entered a small nursing home. One of her last letters was to Kate Cockerell, declaring her gratitude and love, but also telling of her immense loneliness. On 24 March she went out and bought a bottle of Lysol, a household disinfectant, and drank the contents. She died after a struggle, and was buried next to her sister.

In spite of the slimness of her output (two volumes of poems and a handful of stories), Charlotte Mew is one of the great original voices in poetry. Neither a Georgian nor an Imagist, her imaginative loyalties lie ultimately with the nineteenth century, and particularly with the tradition of women poets, Rossetti, Emily Brontë and Alice Meynell, whom she read at school. Mew's great innovation, however, lies in the dramatic monologue. This form, explored rather stiffly in the historical monologues of Hemans, and then developed by Webster as a medium for social criticism, becomes, in her hands, a sinuous and flexible form through which to convey the movements of erotic fantasy. Hers is a sure and brilliant ear for metre. She can stretch the rhythms of her lines from short to long, to match the yearning or blocking mechanisms of desire. In 'Madeleine in Church' some lines run to as many as fourteen feet, as if the speaking voice were pushing out the boundaries of poetry almost into prose, at least until the surprise of a rhyme at the end. This work is a tour de force of emotional permission and restraint, license and control, as if the form of the poem touched on the two extremes of Mew's own temperament: its sexual longing and its rigid self-denial. This, like 'Ne Me Tangito', is one of the last 'fallen woman' poems of the Victorian era. It has all the lush, supercharged eroticism of a still forbidden topic, though its cross-purpose of religious and physical desire is, by now, almost out of date.

Other monologues, like 'Fame', 'The Forest Road', 'Ken' and 'The Farmer's Bride' all play on the idea of missed communication, of speech which cannot overcome misunderstanding, difference, fear. The very form of the monologue becomes a sign of that alienation, that inner loneliness, which characterizes Mew's writing. These speakers are talking to themselves, though longing for a listener. Like the twig which Ken leaves on the doorstep, the poem is merely a token symbol of a vision which belongs to other, stranger countries of the mind. Even Mew's love poems end by affirming, not love, but the bleak, cold freedoms of lovelessness: the 'dead, new-born lamb' of art rather than the 'tossed bed' ('Fame') of sexual pleasure, the free road of the soul rather than the bright hair and hands of desire ('The Forest Road'). In a sense her eroticism, for all its Nineties extravagance, remains cold at the core.

Mew marks what is practically the end of the road of Victorian women's poetry. All the old motifs of desire, guilt, death, prostitution and sainthood are still present, but in a new, agnostic form. Ultimately, her vision does not lead to the pearly gates of heaven, though she is still haunted by them, but 'winds to silence and a space of sleep' ('Not for That City'). Her tragically few but exquisitely fine poems close the chapter of Victorianism once and for all, while opening up in the direction of the new, experimental possibilities of modernism.

A.L.

Mew, Charlotte (1916) The Farmer's Bride, London, Poetry Bookshop.
—— (1929) The Rambling Sailor, London, Poetry Bookshop.
—— (1953) Collected Poems of Charlotte Mew, with a Memoir by Alida Monro, London, Duckworth.
—— (1981) Collected Poems and Prose, ed. Val Warner, Manchester, Carcanet with Virago Press.

Fitzgerald, Penelope (1984) Charlotte Mew and her Friends, London, Collins.
Leighton, Angela (1992) Victorian Women Poets, Hemel Hempstead, Harvester, pp. 266–98.

At the Convent Gate

'Why do you shrink away, and start and stare?
Life frowns to see you leaning at death's gate –
    Not back, but on. Ah! sweet, it is too late:
You cannot cast these kisses from your hair.
Will God's cold breath blow kindly anywhere   5
    Upon such burning gold? Oh! lips worn white
    With waiting! Love will blossom in a night
And you shall wake to find the roses there!'

'Oh hush! He seems to stir, He lifts His Head.
He smiles. Look where He hangs against the sky.   10
He never smiled nor stirred, that God of pain
With tired eyes and limbs above my bed –
But loose me, this is death, I will not die –
Not while He smiles. Oh! Christ, Thine own again!'

The Farmer's Bride

Three Summers since I chose a maid,
    Too young maybe – but more's to do
At harvest-time than bide and woo.
    When us was wed she turned afraid
Of love and me and all things human;   5
Like the shut of a winter's day.
Her smile went out, and 'twasn't a woman –
    More like a little frightened fay.
        One night, in the Fall, she runned away.

'Out 'mong the sheep, her be,' they said,   10
'Should properly have been abed;
But sure enough she wasn't there
Lying awake with her wide brown stare.
So over seven-acre field and up-along across the down
    We chased her, flying like a hare   15
Before our lanterns. To Church-Town
    All in a shiver and a scare
We caught her, fetched her home at last
    And turned the key upon her, fast.

She does the work about the house   20
As well as most, but like a mouse:
    Happy enough to chat and play
    With birds and rabbits and such as they,
So long as men-folk keep away.

'Not near, not near!' her eyes beseech   5
When one of us comes within reach.
   The women say that beasts in stall
   Look round like children at her call.
   I've hardly heard her speak at all.

Shy as a leveret, swift as he,   30
Straight and slight as a young larch tree,
Sweet as the first wild violets, she,
To her wild self. But what to me?
The short days shorten and the oaks are brown,
   The blue smoke rises to the low grey sky,   35
One leaf in the still air falls slowly down,
   A magpie's spotted feathers lie
On the black earth spread white with rime,
The berries redden up to Christmas-time.
   What's Christmas-time without there be   40
   Some other in the house than we!

She sleeps up in the attic there
   Alone, poor maid. 'Tis but a stair
Betwixt us. Oh! my God! the down,
   The soft young down of her, the brown,   45
The brown of her – her eyes, her hair, her hair!

Fame

Sometimes in the over-heated house, but not for long,
   Smirking and speaking rather loud,
  I see myself among the crowd,
Where no one fits the singer to his song,
Or sifts the unpainted from the painted faces   5
Of the people who are always on my stair;
They were not with me when I walked in heavenly places;
   But could I spare
In the blind Earth's great silence and spaces,
  The din, the scuffle, the long stare   10
  If I went back and it was not there?
Back to the old known things that are the new,
The folded glory of the gorse, the sweet-briar air,
To the larks that cannot praise us, knowing nothing of what we do
  And the divine, wise trees that do not care   15
Yet, to leave Fame, still with such eyes and that bright hair!
God! If I might! And before I go hence
   Take in her stead
   To our tossed bed,
One little dream, no matter how small, how wild.   20

Just now, I think I found it in a field, under a fence –
A frail, dead, new-born lamb, ghostly and pitiful and white,
    A blot upon the night,
    The moon's dropped child!

Ken

The town is old and very steep,
    A place of bells and cloisters and grey towers,
And black-clad people walking in their sleep –
    A nun, a priest, a woman taking flowers
      To her new grave; and watched from end to end   5
      By the great Church above, through the still hours:
      But in the morning and the early dark
The children wake to dart from doors and call
Down the wide, crooked street, where, at the bend,
    Before it climbs up to the park,   10
Ken's is the gabled house facing the Castle wall.

When first I came upon him there
Suddenly, on the half-lit stair,
I think I hardly found a trace
Of likeness to a human face   15
  In his. And I said then
If in His image God made men,
Some other must have made poor Ken –
But for his eyes which looked at you
As two red, wounded stars might do.   20

He scarcely spoke, you scarcely heard,
  His voice broke off in little jars
To tear sometimes. An uncouth bird
  He seemed as he ploughed up the street,
Groping, with knarred, high-lifted feet   25
  And arms thrust out as if to beat
    Always against a threat of bars.

  And oftener than not there'd be
  A child just higher than his knee
Trotting beside him. Through his dim   30
  Long twilight this, at least, shone clear,
  That all the children and the deer,
    Whom every day he went to see
Out in the park, belonged to him.

    'God help the folk that next him sits   35
    He fidgets so, with his poor wits.'
The neighbours said on Sunday nights

When he would go to Church to 'see the lights!'
  Although for these he used to fix
  His eyes upon a crucifix
In a dark corner, staring on   40
Till everybody else had gone.
And sometimes, in his evil fits,
You could not move him from his chair –
You did not look at him as he sat there,   45
  Biting his rosary to bits.
While pointing to the Christ he tried to say
  'Take it away.'

    Nothing was dead:
He said 'a bird' if he picked up a broken wing,   50
  A perished leaf or any such thing
  Was just 'a rose'; and once when I had said
He must not stand and knock there any more,
He left a twig on the mat outside my door.

    Not long ago   55
The last thrush stiffened in the snow,
  While black against a sullen sky
  The sighing pines stood by.
But now the wind has left our rattled pane
To flutter the hedge-sparrow's wing,   60
The birches in the wood are red again
  And only yesterday
The larks went up a little way to sing
  What lovers say
  Who loiter in the lanes to-day;   65
  The buds begin to talk of May
  With learned rooks on city trees,
    And if God please
    With all of these
We too, shall see another Spring.   70

But in that red brick barn upon the hill
  I wonder – can one own the deer,
And does one walk with children still
    As one did here –
    Do roses grow   75
Beneath those twenty windows in a row –
    And if some night
When you have not seen any light
They cannot move you from your chair
    What happens there?   80
    I do not know.

So, when they took
Ken to that place, I did not look
After he called and turned on me
His eyes. These I shall see –   85

A Quoi Bon Dire

Seventeen years ago you said
    Something that sounded like Good-bye;
    And everybody thinks that you are dead,
        But I.

  So I, as I grow stiff and cold   5
To this and that say Good-bye too;
    And everybody sees that I am old
        But you.

  And one fine morning in a sunny lane
Some boy and girl will meet and kiss and swear   10
    That nobody can love their way again
        While over there
You will have smiled, I shall have tossed your hair.

On the Asylum Road

Theirs is the house whose windows – every pane –
    Are made of darkly stained or clouded glass:
Sometimes you come upon them in the lane,
    The saddest crowd that you will ever pass.

But still we merry town or village folk   5
    Throw to their scattered stare a kindly grin,
And think no shame to stop and crack a joke
    With the incarnate wages of man's sin.

None but ourselves in our long gallery we meet,
    The moor-hen stepping from her reeds with dainty feet,   10
        The hare-bell bowing on his stem,
Dance not with us; their pulses beat
    To fainter music; nor do we to them
        Make their life sweet.

The gayest crowd that they will ever pass   15
    Are we to brother-shadows in the lane:
Our windows, too, are clouded glass
    To them, yes, every pane!

The Forest Road

The forest road,
The infinite straight road stretching away
World without end: the breathless road between the walls
Of the black listening trees: the hushed, grey road
Beyond the window that you shut to-night   5
Crying that you would look at it by day –
There is a shadow there that sings and calls
But not for you. Oh! hidden eyes that plead in sleep
Against the lonely dark, if I could touch the fear
And leave it kissed away on quiet lids –   10
If I could hush these hands that are half-awake,
Groping for me in sleep I could go free.
I wish that God would take them out of mine
And fold them like the wings of frightened birds
Shot cruelly down, but fluttering into quietness so soon,   15
Broken, forgotten things; there is no grief for them in the green Spring
When the new birds fly back to the old trees.
But it shall not be so with you. I will look back. I wish I knew that God would stand
Smiling and looking down on you when morning comes,
To hold you, when you wake, closer than I,   20
So gently though: and not with famished lips or hungry arms:
He does not hurt the frailest, dearest things
As we do in the dark. See, dear, your hair –
I must unloose this hair that sleeps and dreams
About my face, and clings like the brown weed   25
To drowned, delivered things, tossed by the tired sea
Back to the beaches. Oh! your hair! If you had lain
A long time dead on the rough, glistening ledge
Of some black cliff, forgotten by the tide,
The raving winds would tear, the dripping brine would rust away   30
Fold after fold of all the loveliness
That wraps you round, and makes you, lying here,
The passionate fragrance that the roses are.
But death would spare the glory of your head
In the long sweetness of the hair that does not die: 35
The spray would leap to it in every storm,
The scent of the unsilenced sea would linger on
In these dark waves, and round the silence that was you –
Only the nesting gulls would hear – but there would still be whispers in your hair;
Keep them for me; keep them for me. What *is* this singing on the road   40
That makes all other music like the music in a dream –
Dumb to the dancing and the marching feet; you know, in dreams, you see
Old pipers playing that you cannot hear,
And ghostly drums that only seem to beat. This seems to climb: 45
Is it the music of a larger place? It makes our room too small: it is like a stair,

A calling stair that climbs up to a smile you scarcely see,
Dim but so waited for; and *you* know what a smile is, how it calls,
How, if I smiled you always ran to me.
Now you must sleep forgetfully, as children do.   50
There is a Spirit sits by us in sleep
Nearer than those who walk with us in the bright day.
I think he has a tranquil, saving face: I think he came
Straight from the hills: he may have suffered there in time gone by,
And once, from those forsaken heights, looked down,   55
Lonely himself, on all the lonely sorrows of the earth.
It is his kingdom – Sleep. If I could leave you there –
If, without waking you, I could get up and reach the door –!
We used to go together. – Shut, scared eyes,
Poor, desolate, desperate hands, it is not I   60
Who thrust you off. No, take your hands away –
I cannot strike your lonely hands. Yes, I have struck your heart,
It did not come so near. Then lie you there
Dear and wild heart behind this quivering snow
With two red stains on it: and I will strike and tear   65
Mine out, and scatter it to yours. Oh! throbbing dust,
You that were life, our little wind-blown hearts!
        The road! the road!
There is a shadow there: I see my soul,
I hear my soul, singing among the trees!   70

Madeleine in Church

Here, in the darkness, where this plaster saint
  Stands nearer than God stands to our distress,
And one small candle shines, but not so faint
  As the far lights of everlastingness
I'd rather kneel than over there, in open day   5
  Where Christ is hanging, rather pray
    To something more like my own clay,
      Not too divine;
    For, once, perhaps my little saint
    Before he got his niche and crown,   10
  Had one short stroll about the town;
  It brings him closer, just that taint
    And anyone can wash the paint
  Off our poor faces, his and mine!

Is that why I see Monty now? equal to any saint, poor boy, as good as gold,   15
But still, with just the proper trace
Of earthliness on his shining wedding face;
And then gone suddenly blank and old
The hateful day of the divorce:

Stuart got his, hands down, of course   20
Crowing like twenty cocks and grinning like a horse:
But Monty took it hard. All said and done I liked him best, —
He was the first, he stands out clearer than the rest.
        It seems too funny all we other rips
  Should have immortal souls; Monty and Redge quite damnably   25
  Keep theirs afloat while we go down like scuttled ships. —
       It's funny too, how easily we sink,
        One might put up a monument, I think
  To half the world and cut across it 'Lost at Sea!'
I should drown Jim, poor little sparrow, if I netted him to-night —   30
    No, it's no use this penny light —
  Or my poor saint with his tin-pot crown —
  The trees of Calvary are where they were,
    When we are sure that we can spare
  The tallest, let us go and strike it down   35
And leave the other two still standing there.
    I, too, would ask Him to remember me
If there were any Paradise beyond this earth that I could see.

    Oh! quiet Christ who never knew
    The poisonous fangs that bite us through   40
     And make us do the things we do,
    See how we suffer and fight and die,
     How helpless and how low we lie,
    God holds You, and You hang so high,
    Though no one looking long at You,   45
     Can think You do not suffer too,
But, up there, from your still, star-lighted tree
  What can You know, what can You really see
   Of this dark ditch, the soul of me!

    We are what we are: when I was half a child I could not sit   50
Watching black shadows on green lawns and red carnations burning in the sun,
       Without paying so heavily for it
That joy and pain, like any mother and her unborn child were almost one.
       I could hardly bear
  The dreams upon the eyes of white geraniums in the dusk,   55
     The thick, close voice of musk,
   The jessamine music on the thin night air,
Or, sometimes, my own hands about me anywhere —
The sight of my own face (for it was lovely then) even the scent of my own hair,
  Oh! there was nothing, nothing that did not sweep to the high seat   60
   Of laughing gods, and then blow down and beat
My soul into the highway dust, as hoofs do the dropped roses of the street.
     I think my body was my soul,
     And when we are made thus
      Who shall control   65

Our hands, our eyes, the wandering passion of our feet,
    Who shall teach us
To thrust the world out of our heart; to say, till perhaps in death,
      When the race is run,
And it is forced from us with our last breath   70
    'Thy will be done'?
If it is Your will that we should be content with the tame, bloodless things.
  As pale as angels smirking by, with folded wings.
    Oh! I know Virtue, and the peace it brings!
        The temperate, well-worn smile   75
The one man gives you, when you are evermore his own:
  And afterwards the child's, for a little while,
    With its unknowing and all-seeing eyes
     So soon to change, and make you feel how quick
The clock goes round. If one had learned the trick –   80
     (How does one though?) quite early on,
Of long green pastures under placid skies,
One might be walking now with patient truth.
What did we ever care for it, who have asked for youth,
  When, oh! my God! this is going or has gone?   85

   There is a portrait of my mother, at nineteen,
  With the black spaniel, standing by the garden seat,
  The dainty head held high against the painted green
And throwing out the youngest smile, shy, but half haughty and half sweet.
  Her picture then: but simply Youth, or simply Spring   90
    To me to-day: a radiance on the wall,
    So exquisite, so heart-breaking a thing
  Beside the mask that I remember, shrunk and small,
    Sapless and lined like a dead leaf,
All that was left of oh! the loveliest face, by time and grief!   95

And in the glass, last night, I saw a ghost behind my chair –
Yet why remember it, when one can still go moderately gay – ?
  Or could – with any one of the old crew,
    But oh! these boys! the solemn way
They take you and the things they say –   100
This 'I have only as long as you'
When you remind them you are not precisely twenty-two –
  Although at heart perhaps – God! if it were
    Only the face, only the hair!
    If Jim had written to me as he did to-day   105
    A year ago – and now it leaves me cold –
    I know what this means, old, old, *old*!
    Et avec ça – mais on a vécu, tout se paie.

That is not always true: there was my Mother – (well at least the dead are free!)
  Yoked to the man that Father was; yoked to the woman I am, Monty too; 110

The little portress at the Convent School, stewing in hell so patiently;
The poor, fair boy who shot himself at Aix. And what of me – and what of me?
But I, I paid for what I had, and they for nothing. No, one cannot see
How it shall be made up to them in some serene eternity.
If there were fifty heavens God could not give us back the child who went
or never came;   115
Here, on our little patch of this great earth, the sun of any darkened day,
Not one of all the starry buds hung on the hawthorn trees of last year's May,
No shadow from the sloping fields of yesterday;
For every hour they slant across the hedge a different way,
The shadows are never the same.   120

'Find rest in Him!' One knows the parsons' tags –
Back to the fold, across the evening fields, like any flock of baa-ing sheep:
Yes, it may be, when He has shorn, led us to slaughter, torn the bleating soul in
us to rags,
For so He giveth His belovèd sleep.
Oh! He will take us stripped and done,   125
Driven into His heart. So we are won:
Then safe, safe are we? in the shelter of His everlasting wings –
I do not envy Him his victories, His arms are full of broken things.

But I shall not be in them. Let Him take
The finer ones, the easier to break.   130
And they are not gone, yet, for me, the lights, the colours, the perfumes,
Though now they speak rather in sumptuous rooms,
In silks and in gem-like wines;
Here, even, in this corner where my little candle shines
And overhead the lancet-window glows   135
With golds and crimsons you could almost drink
To know how jewels taste, just as I used to think
There was the scent in every red and yellow rose
Of all the sunsets. But this place is grey,
And much too quiet. No one here,   140
Why, this is awful, this is fear!
Nothing to see, no face,
Nothing to hear except your heart beating in space
As if the world was ended. Dead at last!
Dead soul, dead body, tied together fast.   145
These to go on with and alone, to the slow end:
No one to sit with, really, or to speak to, friend to friend:
Out of the long procession, black or white or red
Not one left now to say 'Still I am here, then see you, dear, lay here your head.'
Only the doll's house looking on the Park   150
To-night, all nights, I know, when the man puts the lights out, very dark.
With, upstairs, in the blue and gold box of a room, just the maids' footsteps
overhead,
Then utter silence and the empty world – the room – the bed –

The corpse! No, not quite dead, while this cries out in me,
    But nearly: very soon to be 155
    A handful of forgotten dust –
There must be someone. Christ! there must,
    Tell me there *will* be some one. Who?
If there were no one else, could it be You?

    How old was Mary out of whom you cast 160
  So many devils? Was she young or perhaps for years
She had sat staring, with dry eyes, at this and that man going past
    Till suddenly she saw You on the steps of Simeon's house
    And stood and looked at You through tears.
      I think she must have known by those 165
The thing, for what it was that had come to her.
For some of us there is a passion, I suppose
So far from earthly cares and earthly fears
That in its stillness you can hardly stir
    Or in its nearness, lift your hand, 170
So great that you have simply got to stand
Looking at it through tears, through tears.
Then straight from these there broke the kiss,
    I think You must have known by this
The thing, for what it was, that had come to You: 75
    She did not love You like the rest,
  It was in her own way, but at the worst, the best,
    She gave you something altogether new.
    And through it all, from her, no word,
      She scarcely saw You, scarcely heard: 180
Surely You knew when she so touched You with her hair,
    Or by the wet cheek lying there,
And while her perfume clung to You from head to feet all through the day
    That You can change the things for which we care,
    But even You, unless You kill us, not the way. 185

    This, then was peace for her, but passion too.
    I wonder was it like a kiss that once I knew,
      The only one that I would care to take
Into the grave with me, to which if there were afterwards, to wake.
    Almost as happy as the carven dead 190
    In some dim chancel lying head by head
We slept with it, but face to face, the whole night through –
One breath, one throbbing quietness, as if the thing behind our lips was
    endless life,
  Lost, as I woke, to hear in the strange earthly dawn, his 'Are you there?'
    And lie still, listening to the wind outside, among the firs. 195

So Mary chose the dream of Him for what was left to her of night and day,
It is the only truth: it is the dream in us that neither life nor death nor any other
    thing can take away:

But if she had not touched Him in the doorway of the dream could she have
      cared so much?
She was a sinner, we are what we are: the spirit afterwards, but first, the touch.

And He has never shared with me my haunted house beneath the trees   200
Of Eden and Calvary, with its ghosts that have not any eyes for tears,
And the happier guests who would not see, or if they did, remember these,
      Though they lived there a thousand years.
      Outside, too gravely looking at me, He seems to stand,
      And looking at Him, if my forgotten spirit came   205
      Unwillingly back, what could it claim
      Of those calm eyes, that quiet speech,
      Breaking like a slow tide upon the beach,
      The scarred, not quite human hand? –
Unwillingly back to the burden of old imaginings   210
When it has learned so long not to think, not to be,
Again, again it would speak as it has spoken to me of things
      That I shall not see!

      I cannot bear to look at this divinely bent and gracious head:
When I was small I never quite believed that He was dead: 215
      And at the Convent school I used to lie awake in bed
      Thinking about His hands. It did not matter what they said,
He was alive to me, so hurt, so hurt! And most of all in Holy Week
      When there was no one else to see
      I used to think it would not hurt me too, so terribly,   220
      If He had ever seemed to notice me
      Of, if, for once, He would only speak.

Not for That City

Not for that city of the level sun,
Its golden streets and glittering gates ablaze –
  The shadeless, sleepless city of white days,
White nights, or nights and days that are as one –
We weary, when all is said, all thought, all done.   5
  We strain our eyes beyond this dusk to see
  What, from the threshold of eternity
We shall step into. No, I think we shun
The splendour of that everlasting glare,
  The clamour of that never-ending song.   10
  And if for anything we greatly long,
It is for some remote and quiet stair
  Which winds to silence and a space of sleep
  Too sound for waking and for dreams too deep.

Ne Me Tangito

This man . . . would have known who and what manner of woman this is: for she is, a sinner.
S. Luke vii 39

Odd, *You* should fear the touch,
The first that I was ever ready to let go,
I, that have not cared much
For any toy I could not break and throw
To the four winds when I had done with it. You need not fear the touch,   5
Blindest of all the things that I have cared for very much
In the whole gay, unbearable, amazing show.

True – for a moment – no, dull heart, you were too small,
Thinking to hide the ugly doubt behind that hurried puzzled little smile:
Only the shade, was it, you saw? but still the shade of something vile: 10
        Oddest of all!
So I will tell you this. Last night, in sleep,
Walking through April fields I heard the far-off bleat of sheep
And from the trees about the farm, not very high,
A flight of pigeons fluttered up into an early evening mackerel sky.   15
        Someone stood by and it was you:
        About us both a great wind blew.
        My breast was bared
        But sheltered by my hair
        I found you, suddenly, lying there,   20
Tugging with tiny fingers at my heart, no more afraid:
        The weakest thing, the most divine
        That ever yet was mine,
        Something that I had strangely made,
        So then it seemed –   25
The child for which I had not looked or ever cared,
        Of whom, before, I had never dreamed.

The Trees are Down

– and he cried with a loud voice:
Hurt not the earth, neither the sea, nor the trees –
Revelation

They are cutting down the great plane-trees at the end of the gardens.
   For days there has been the grate of the saw, the swish of the branches as
     they fall,
The crash of trunks, the rustle of trodden leaves,
With the 'Whoops' and the 'Whoas,' the loud common talk, the loud common
   laughs of the men, above it all.

I remember one evening of a long past Spring   5
Turning in at a gate, getting out of a cart, and finding a large dead rat in the
    mud of the drive.
I remember thinking: alive or dead, a rat was a god-forsaken thing,
But at least, in May, that even a rat should be alive.

The week's work here is as good as done. There is just one bough
  On the roped bole, in the fine grey rain,   10
        Green and high
        And lonely against the sky.
          (Down now! –)
        And but for that,
        If an old dead rat   15
Did once, for a moment, unmake the Spring, I might never have thought of
    him again.

It is not for a moment the Spring is unmade to-day;
These were great trees, it was them from root to stem:
When the men with the 'Whoops' and the 'Whoas' have carted the whole
    of the whispering loveliness away
Half the Spring, for me, will have gone with them.   20

It is going now, and my heart has been struck with the hearts of the planes;
Half my life it has beat with these, in the sun, in the rains,
    In the March wind, the May breeze,
In the great gales that came over to them across the roofs from the great seas.
    There was only a quiet rain when they were dying;   25
    They must have heard the sparrows flying,
And the small creeping creatures in the earth where they were lying –
    But I, all day, I heard an angel crying:
        'Hurt not the trees.'

Selected Bibliography of Poets' Works

Alexander, Cecil Frances (1818–1895)

1846   *Verses for Holy Seasons; with questions for examination*, Francis & John Rivington: London
1848   *The Lord of the Forest and his Vassals. An Allegory*, London
1852   *Hymns for Little Children*, Joseph Masters: London
1879   *Short Points for daily meditation*, W. Knott: London
1896   *Poems* edited with a Preface by William Alexander, London

Barrett Browning, Elizabeth (1806–1861)

1820   *The Battle of Marathon*, privately printed
1826   *An Essay on Mind with other Poems*, London
1833   *Prometheus Bound: Translated from the Greek of Aeschylus and Miscellaneous Poems*, London
1838   *The Seraphim and Other Poems*, London
1842   'Some Account of the Greek Christian Poets' and 'The Book of the Poets', *The Athenaeum*, London
1844   *Poems* by Elizabeth Barrett Barrett, 2 vols, London
1850   *Poems*, revised and selected (includes *Sonnets from the Portuguese*), London
1851   *Casa Guidi Windows: A Poem*, London
1857   (1856) *Aurora Leigh*, London
1860   *Poems Before Congress*, London
1862   *Last Poems*, London
1897   *The Letters of Elizabeth Barrett Browning*, 2 vols, ed. Frederic G. Kenyon, London
1900   *The Complete Works of Elizabeth Barrett Browning*, 6 vols, ed. Charlotte Porter and Helen A. Clarke, Crowell: New York, reprinted 1973, AMS Press: New York
1914   *New Poems by Robert Browning and Elizabeth Barrett Browning*, ed. Frederic G. Kenyon, London.
1929   *Elizabeth Barrett Browning: Letters to her Sister, 1846–1859*, ed. Leonard Huxley, John Murray: London
1955   *Elizabeth Barrett to Mr. Boyd: Unpublished Letters of Elizabeth Barrett and Hugh Stuart Boyd*, ed. Barbara P. McCarthy, John Murray: London
1958   *Letters of the Brownings to George Barrett*, ed. Paul Landis, assisted by Ronald E. Freeman, University of Illinois Press: Urbana
1969   *The Letters of Robert Browning and Elizabeth Barrett Barrett, 1845–1846*, ed. Elvan Kintner, Harvard University Press: Cambridge, Mass.
1969   *Diary by E.B.B.: The Unpublished Diary of Elizabeth Barrett Barrett, 1831–1832*, eds Philip Kelley and Ronald Hudson, Ohio University Press, Athens, Ohio
1974   *Elizabeth Barrett Browning's Letters to Mrs. David Ogilvy, 1849–1861*, eds Peter N. Heydon and Philip Kelley, John Murray: London
1977   *Casa Guidi Windows*, ed. Julia Markus, The Browning Institute: New York
1983   *The Letters of Elizabeth Barrett Browning and Mary Russell Mitford, 1836–1854*, eds Meredith B. Raymond and Mary Rose Sullivan, Wedgestone Press: Winfield, Kan
1984   *The Brownings' Correspondence*, eds Philip Kelley and Ronald Hudson, later, Philip Kelley and Scott Lewis, Wedgestone Press: Winfield, Kan., 10 vols and continuing
1992   *Aurora Leigh*, ed. Margaret Reynolds, Ohio University Press: Athens, Ohio

Bevington, L. S. (1845–1895)

1879   *Keynotes*, C. Kegan Paul: London
1882   *Poems, Lyrics and Sonnets*, Elliot Stock: London
1895   *Liberty Lyrics*, James Tochatti's 'Liberty' Press: London

Blagden, Isa (1816?–1873)

1861   *Agnes Tremorne*, [A Novel], Smith, Elder & Co: London
1863   *The Cost of a Secret*, [A Novel], Chapman & Hall: London
1865   *The Woman I Loved and the Woman Who Loved Me*, [Stories], London
1867   *Nora and Archibald Lee. A Novel*, London
1869   *The Crown of Life*, [A Novel], Hurst & Blackett: London
1873   *Poems by Isa Blagden*, with a memoir by Alfred Austin, W. Blackwood & Sons: Edinburgh
    & London

Blind, Mathilde (1841–1896)

1867   *Poems*, London [published under the pseudonym of Claude Lake]
1872   *Percy Bysshe Shelley: A Biography*, London
1881   *The Prophecy of Saint Oran and Other Poems*, Newman & Co: London
1883   *George Eliot*, [A Biography], in the Eminent Women series, W. H. Allen & Co.
1885   *Tarantella. A Romance*, T. Fisher Unwin: London
1886   *The Heather on Fire. A Tale of the Highland Clearances*, [In verse], Walter Scott: London
1886   *Madame Roland*, [A Biography], in the Eminent Women series, W. H. Allen & Co: London
1886   *Shelley's View of Nature contrasted with Darwin's*, Privately Printed: London
1890   *Journal of Marie Bashkirtseff*, [A Translation], 2 vols, London
1891   *Dramas in Miniature*, Chatto & Windus: London
1895   *Birds of Passage. Songs of the Orient and Occident*, Chatto & Windus: London
1889   *The Ascent of Man*, Chatto & Windus: London
1897   *A Selection from the Poems of Mathilde Blind*, T. Fisher Unwin: London
1900   *The Poetical Works of Mathilde Blind*, with a memoir by Richard Garnett, A. Symons ed., T.
    F. Unwin: London

Brontë Anne (1820–1849)

1846   *Poems by Currer, Ellis and Acton Bell* [i.e. Charlotte, Emily and Anne Brontë]: Aylott &
    Jones: London
1847   *Agnes Grey*, Thomas Newby: London
1848   *The Tenant of Wildfell Hall*, Thomas Newby: London
1979   *The Poems of Anne Brontë: A New Text and Commentary*, ed. Edward Chitham, Macmillan:
    London

Brontë, Charlotte (1816–1855)

1846   *Poems by Currer, Ellis and Acton Bell* [i.e. Charlotte, Emily and Anne Brontë], Aylott &
    Jones: London

1847   *Jane Eyre. An Autobiography*, Smith, Elder & Co: London
1849   *Shirley. A Tale*, Smith, Elder & Co: London
1855   *Villette*, Smith, Elder & Co: London
1857   *The Professor. A Tale*, Smith, Elder & Co: London

Brontë, Emily (1818–1848)

1846   *Poems by Currer, Ellis and Acton Bell* [i.e. Charlotte, Emily and Anne Brontë], Aylott &
         Jones: London
1847   *Wuthering Heights. A Novel by Ellis Bell*, Thomas Newby: London
1992   *The Poems of Emily Brontë*, ed. Barbara Lloyd-Evans, Batsford: London

Brown(e), Frances (1816–1879)

1844   *The Star of Attéghéi: The Vision of Schwartz and Other Poems*, Edward Moxon: London
1848   *Lyrics and Miscellaneous Poems*, Sutherland & Knox: Edinburgh
1852   *The Ericksons. The Clever Boy; or Consider Another*, Paton & Richie: Edinburgh
1856   *Pictures and Songs of Home*, T. Nelson & Sons: London
1857   *Granny's Wonderful Chair and its Tales of Fairy Times*, Griffith & Farrar: London
1859   *Our Uncle the Traveller's Stories*, W. Kent & Co: London
1861   *My Share of the World: An Autobiography*, Hurst & Blackett: London
1862   *The Castleford Case*, Hurst & Blackett: London
1864   *The Young Foresters*, Groombridge & Sons: London
1866   *The Hidden Sin. A Novel*, London
1869   *The Exiles Trust; a Tale of the French Revolution and Other Stories*, Leisure Hour: London
1875   *The Nearest Neighbour and Other Stories*, R. T. S: London

Clive, Caroline ('V') (1801–1873)

1841   *IX Poems by V*, Saunders & Otley: London
1842   *I Watched the Heavens. A Poem*, London
1847   *The Queen's Ball. A Poem*, London
1853   *The Morlas. A Poem*, London
1855   *Paul Ferroll. A Tale*, London
1858   *Year after Year. A Tale*, London
1872   *Poems by V, the Author of 'Paul Ferroll'*, London
1949   *Caroline Clive. From the Diary and Family Papers of Mrs. Archer Clive 1801–1873*, ed. Mary Clive,
         Bodley Head: London

Coleridge, Mary E. (1861–1907)

1893   *The Seven Sleepers of Ephesus*, [A novel], Chatto & Windus: London
1896   *Fancy's Following*, Oxford [published under the pseudonym Anodos]
1897   *Fancy's Guerdon*, London [published under the pseudonym Anodos]
1899   *The Garland of New Poetry by Various Writers*, London
1900   *Non Sequitur*, London
1908   *Poems*, ed. Henry Newbolt, Elkin Matthews: London.

1910   *Gathered Leaves from the prose of Mary E. Coleridge*, with a Memoir by Edith Sichel, Constable: London
1954   *The Collected Poems of Mary E. Coleridge*, ed. Theresa Whistler, Rupert Hart-Davis: London

Coleridge, Sara (1802–1852)

1834   *Pretty Lessons in Verse for Good Children*, John W. Parker: London
1837   *Phantasmion*, W. Pickering: London
1873   *Memoirs and Letters*, 2 vols, ed. by her daughter, London

Cook, Eliza (1817–1889)

1835   *Lays of a Wild Harp, A Collection of Metrical Pieces*, John Bennett; E. Spettigue: London
1838   *Melaia and Other Poems*, R. J. Wood: London
1845   *Poems*, Simpkin, Marshall & Co: London
1845–54   *Eliza Cook's Journal*, London
1850   *Song of the Haymakers*, Ryle & Co: London
1860   *Jottings from my Journal*, Routledge, Warne & Routledge: London
1864   *New Echoes and Other Poems*, Routledge, Warne & Routledge: London
1865   *Diamond Dust [A Collection of Aphorisms]*, F. Pitman: London
1874   *The Poetical Works of Eliza Cook, Complete Edition*, Frederick Warne & Co: London

Dufferin, Helen (1807–1867)

1835   *The Charming Woman*, [published anonymously] London
1840   *The Irish Emigrant*, London
1855   *Terence's Farewell*, London
1861   *Helen's Tower, Clandeboye* a souvenir of the completion of the tower, consisting of two poems, 'To my Dear Son on his 21st Birthday', by H. S. Hay and 'Helen's Tower', by A. Tennyson
1863   *Lispings from Low Latitudes, or Extracts from the Journal of the Hon. Impulsia Gushington*, [published under the pseudonym of Impulsia Gushington], London
n.d.   *The Fine Young English Gentleman and Other Songs and Poems*, London.
1863   *Finesse, or Spy and Counter Spy*, London
1894   *Songs, Poems and Verses, edited with a memoir and some Account of the Sheridan family*, by her son, The Marquess of Dufferin and Ava, John Murray: London.

Eliot, George (1819–1880)

1859   *Adam Bede*, William Blackwood & Sons: London & Edinburgh
1860   *The Mill on the Floss*, William Blackwood & Sons: London & Edinburgh
1863   *Romola*, Smith, Elder & Co: London
1866   *Felix Holt, the Radical*, William Blackwood & Sons: London & Edinburgh
1868   *The Spanish Gypsy. A Poem*, William Blackwood & Sons: London & Edinburgh
1869   *Agatha*, Trübner & Co: London
1871   *Middlemarch. A Study of Provincial Life*, William Blackwood & Sons: London & Edinburgh
1874   *The Legend of Jubal and Other Poems*, William Blackwood & Sons: London & Edinburgh

1876   *Daniel Deronda*, William Blackwood & Sons: London & Edinburgh
1985   *Selections from George Eliot's Letters*, ed. Gordon S. Haight, New Haven and London

'Fane, Violet' (1843–1905)

1872   *From Dawn to Noon*, London
1875   *Denzil Place: A Story in Verse*, London
1876   *The Queen of the Fairies and Other Poems*, London
1877   *Anthony Babington: A Drama in Five Acts and in Prose and Verse*, London
1880   *Collected Verses*, Smith, Elder & Co: London
1889   *Autumn Songs*, Chapman & Hall: London
1892   *Margaret de Valois. Queen Consort of Henry IV. King of France. Memoirs*, Violet Fane
       (introduction & notes), J. C. Nimmo: London
1896   *Under Cross and Crescent; Poems*, J. C. Nimmo: London
1900   *Betwixt Two Seas, Poems and Ballads Written at Constantinople and Therapia*, J. C. Nimmo:
       London

Field, Michael (Katherine Bradley (1846–1914) and Edith Cooper (1862–1913))

1889   *Long Ago*, G. Bell & Sons: London
1892   *Sight and Song*, Elkin Matthews & John Lane: London
1893   *Underneath the Bough. A Book of Verses*, G. Bell & Sons: London
1908   *Wild Honey from Various Thyme*, T. Fisher Unwin: London
1912   *Poems of Adoration*, Sands & Co: London & Edinburgh
1913   *Mystic Trees*, Eveleigh Nash: London
1914   *Dedicated: An Early Work of Michael Field*, G. Bell & Sons: London
1914   *Whym Chow: Flame of Love*, privately printed at the Eragny Press: London
1923   *A Selection from the Poems of Michael Field*, Poetry Bookshop: London
1930   *The Wattlefold: Unpublished Poems by Michael Field*, collected by Emily C. Fortey, Basil
       Blackwell: Oxford
1933   *Works and Days: From the Journal of Michael Field*, eds T. and D. C. Sturge Moore, John
       Murray: London

Greenwell, Dora (1821–1882)

1848   *Poems*, London
1850   *Stories that might be true, with other poems*, London
1861   *Poems*, London
1866   *Essays*, London
1867   *Poems*, London
1869   *Carmina Crucis*, H. R. Allenson: London
1869   *On the Education of the Imbecile*, London
1875   *Liber Humanitatis. A Series of Essays on Various Aspects of Spiritual and Social Life*, London
1876   *Camera Obscura*, London
1889   *Poems, selected with introduction by W. Dorling*, London

Havergal, Frances Ridley (1836–1879)

1880   *Memorials*, by M. V. G. Havergal, London
1884   *The Poetical Works of F. R. Havergal*, ed. M. V. G. Havergal, J. Nisbet & Co: London
1885   *Letters of Frances Ridley Havergal* ed. by her Sister, London

Hemans, Felicia (1793–1835)

1808   *Poems*, T. Cadell: London
1812   *The Domestic Affections and other Poems*, T. Cadell: London
1816   *The Restoration of the Works of Art to Italy. A Poem*, J. Ebers: London
1819   *Tales and Historic Scenes, in verse*, John Murray: London
1820   *The Sceptic, a poem. Stanzas to the Memory of the late King*, John Murray: London
1825   *The Forest Sanctuary, and other Poems*, John Murray: London
1828   *Records of Women, with other Poems*, Blackwood: Edinburgh
1830   *Songs of the Affections with other Poems*, William Blackwood: Edinburgh; T. Cadell: London
1839   *The Works of Mrs. Hemans. With a Memoir of her Life by her Sister*, 7 vols, Blackwood: Edinburgh

Hickey, Emily (1845–1924)

1881   *A Sculptor and Other Poems*, Kegan Paul & Co: London
1889   *Verse-Tales, Lyrics and Translations*, W. & J. Arnold: Liverpool
1891   *Michael Villiers, Idealist, and Other Poems*, Smith & Elder: London
1898   *Ancilla Domini. Thoughts in Verse on the Life of the Blessed Virgin Mary*, London
1906   *Thoughts for Creedless Women*, Catholic Truth Society: London
1913   *Later Poems*, Grant Richards: London
1922   *Devotional Poems*, Elliot Stock: London
1924   *Jesukin, and other Christmastide Poems*, Burns, Oates & Co: London

Howitt, Mary (1799–1888)

1823   *The Forest Minstrel and Other Poems*, in conjunction with William Howitt, London
1834   *Sketches of Natural History*, Effingham Wilson: London
1836   *Tales in Prose*, William Darton & Son: London
1836   *Tales in Verse*, William Darton & Son: London
1839   *Hymns and Verses*, London
1845   *Fireside Verses*, London
1847   *Ballads and Other Poems*, London
1855   *Birds and Flowers and Other Country Things*, London
1856   *Mary Howitt's Tales in Verse for the Young. The Little Mariner and Other Poems*, Darton & Co: London
1859   *Marion's Pilgrimage, a Fire-Side Story and Other Poems*, London
1889   *Mary Howitt. An Autobiography*, ed. Margaret Howitt W. Isbister: London
1900   *The Cry of the Animals. A Poem*, Church Extension Association: London

Ingelow, Jean (1820–1897)

1863 *Poems*, London
1865 *Home Thoughts and Home Scenes*, London
1869 *Mopsa the Fairy*, London
1871 *The High Tide on the Coast of Lincolnshire*, Roberts Bros.: Boston
1872 *Off the Skelligs*, (a novel), 4 vols, London
1874 *Poems*, Second Series, Longmans: London
1885 *Poems*, Third Series, Longmans: London
1895 *Lyrical and Other Poems*, Longmans & Green: London and New York
1898 *The Poetic Works of Jean Ingelow*, Longmans & Co: London
1921 *Poems*, Oxford University Press: London

Jewsbury, Maria (1800–1833)

1825 *Phantasmagoria, or Sketches of Life and Literature*, Hurst Robinson and Co: London
1828 *Letters to the Young*, J. Hatchard and Son: London
1829 *Lays of Leisure Hours*, J. Hatchard and Son: London
1830 *The Three Histories. The History of an Enthusiast. The History of a Nonchalant. The History of a Realist*, F. Westley & Co: London
1932 *Occasional Papers, selected with a Memoir* by Eric Gillett, Oxford University Press, London

Johnston, Ellen (1835–1873)

1867 *Autobiography, Poems and Songs*, Glasgow
1869 *Autobiography, Poems and Songs*, Glasgow [Second edition with Shortened *Autobiography* and additional poems.]

Kemble, Frances Anne (1809–1893)

1832 *Francis the First, an Historical Drama*, London
1844 *Poems*, John Penington: Philadelphia
1847 *A Year of Consolation*, [Travels in Italy], 2 vols, London
1863 *Journal of a Residence on a Georgian Plantation in 1838–1839*, Philadelphia
1866 *Poems*, E. Moxon & Co: London
1878 *Record of a Girlhood*. An Autobiography, 3 vols, London
1882 *Records of Later Life*, 3 vols, Bentley and Son: London
1883 *Poems*, Bentley & Son: London
1891 *Further records, 1848–1883*, 2 vols, Bentley and Son: London

Kendall, May (1861–c.1931)

1885 *That Very Mab*, with Andrew Lang
1887 *Dreams to Sell*. [In Verse], Longmans & Co: London
1887 *From a Garret*. [A Novel], Longmans & Co: London
1889 *Such is Life*. [A Novel], Longmans & Co: London
1893 *White Poppies*. [A Novel], Ward & Lock: London

Songs from Dreamland, Longmans & Co: London
Turkish Bonds [Short Stories], C. A. Pearson: London
How the Labourer Lives. A Study of the Rural Labour Problem, with B. Seebohm Rowntree, Thomas Nelson & Sons: London

King, Harriet Hamilton (1840–1920)

1869 *Aspromonte and Other Poems,* Macmillan & Co: London
1873 *The Disciples,* [In Verse], London
1883 *A Book of Dreams,* [In Verse], Kegan Paul & Co: London
1889 *Ballads of the North and Other Poems,* Kegan Paul & Co: London
1895 *The Prophecy of Westminster and Other Poems. In honour of Henry Edward, Cardinal Manning,* Whittingham & Co: London
1902 *The Hours of the Passion and Other Poems,* Grant Richards: London

Landon, Letitia Elizabeth (L.E.L.) (1802–1832)

1821 *The Fate of Adelaide, a Swiss romantic tale and other poems,* London
1824 *The Improvisatrice; and other poems,* Hurst, Robinson & Co: London
1825 *The Troubadour; Catalogue of Pictures and Historical Sketches,* London
1827 *The Golden Violet, and other poems,* London
1829 *The Venetian Bracelet, the Lost Pleiad, a History of the Lyre, and other poems,* London
1831 *Romance and Reality* (a novel), London
1835 *The Vow of the Peacock and other poems,* London
1837 *Ethel Churchill; or, The Two Brides* (a novel), London
1839 *The Poetical Works of Lelitia Elizabeth Landon,* 4 vols, London
1841 *Life and Literary Remains of L.E.L.,* 2 vols, Laman Blanchard: London
1873 *The Poetical Works,* ed. William B. Scott, London

Levy, Amy (1861–1889)

1881 *Xantippe and other Verse,* E. Johnson: Cambridge
1884 *A Minor Poet and other Verse,* T. Fisher Unwin: London
1888 *The Romance of a Shop,* T. Fisher Unwin: London
1888 *Reuben Sachs. A Sketch,* Macmillan & Co: London
1889 *Miss Meredith,* Hodder & Stoughton: London
1889 *A London Plane-Tree and other Verse,* The Cameo Series: London
1915 *A Ballad of Religion and Marriage,* privately printed: London
1993 *Selected Writings of Amy Levy, 1861–1889,* ed. Melvyn New University Press of Florida: Gainsville

Lindsay, Caroline (1844–1912)

1889 *Caroline,* [A Novel], Bentley & Son: London
1889 *About Robins. Songs, facts, and legends collected and illustrated by Caroline Lindsay,* G. Routledge & Sons: London
1890 *Lyrics and Other Poems,* Kegan Paul & Co: London
1892 *A String of Beads,* London

1894   The King's Last Vigil and Other Poems, Kegan Paul & Co: London
1896   The Flower Seller and Other Poems, Longmans & Co: London
1898   The Christmas of the Sorrowful. [A Poem], Kegan Paul & Sons: London
1899   The Apostle of the Ardennes, Kegan Paul & Co: London
1899   The Art of Poetry with Regard to Women Writers, Hatchards: London
1900   For England. [A Poem], Messrs. Hatchard: London
1900   The Prayer of St. Scholastica and Other Poems, Kegan & Co: London
1903   From a Venetian Balcony and Other Poems of Venice and the Near Lands, Kegan Paul & Co:
        London
1905   Godfrey's Quest: a fantastic poem, Kegan & Co: London
1907   Lays and Lyrics, S. Rosen: Venice
1907   Poems of Love and Death, Kegan Paul & Co: London
1908   From A Venetian Calle. [Poems], Kegan Paul & Co: London
1910   Within Hospital Walls, London

Mew, Charlotte (1869–1928)

1916   The Farmer's Bride, Poetry Bookshop: London
1929   The Rambling Sailor, Poetry Bookshop: London
1953   Collected Poems of Charlotte Mew, with a Memoir by Alida Monro, Gerald Duckworth:
        London
1981   Collected Poems and Prose, ed. Val Warner, Carcanet with Virago: Manchester

Meynell, Alice (1847–1922)

1875   Preludes, Henry S. King & Co: London
1896   Other Poems, London, privately printed
1913   Collected Poems, Bumes & Oates: London
1915   Ten Poems 1913–1915, Romney Street Press: London
1917   A Father of Women and other poems, Burns Oates & Washbourne: London
1923   Poems. Complete Edition, Burnes Oates & Washbourne: London
1940   Poems, Oxford University Press: London
1947   The Poems of Alice Meynell. A Centenary Edition, Hollis & Carter: London
1947   Prose and Poetry, introduction by V. Sackville-West, Jonathan Cape: London

Naden, Constance (1858–1889)

1881   Songs and Sonnets of Springtime, Kegan Paul & Co: London
1883   What is Religion? A Vindication of Freethought, London.
1887   A Modern Apostle, the Elixir of Life and Other Poems, Kegan Paul & Co: London
1893   Selections from the Philosophical and Poetical Works of Constance C. W. Naden, compiled by
        Emily and Edith Hughes, Bickers and Sons: London
1894   The Complete Poetical Works of Constance Naden, with a foreward by Robert Lewins, Bickers
        and Sons: London

Nesbit, E. (1858–1924)

1886   Lays and Legends, Longmans, Green & Co: London
1888   Leaves of Life, Longmans, Green & Co: London and New York

1895   *A Pomander of Verse*, John Lane: London
1898   *Songs of Love and Empire*, London
1902   *Five Children and It*, T. Fisher Unwin: London
1904   *The New Treasure Seekers*, T. Fisher Unwin: London
1904   *The Phoenix and the Carpet*, George Newnes: London
1905   *The Rainbow and the Rose*, Longmans, Green & Co: London
1906   *The Railway Children*, Wells Gardner & Co: London
1907   *The Enchanted Castle*, T. Fisher Unwin: London
1908   *Ballads and Lyrics of Socialism 1883–1908,* Fabian Society; A. C. Fifield: London
1911   *Ballads and Verses of the Spiritual Life*, Elkin Matthews: London
1922   *Many Voices*, Hutchinson & Co: London

Norton, Caroline (1808–1877)

1829   *The Sorrows of Rosalie. A Tale with Other Poems*, London
1830   *The Undying One and Other Poems*, London
1833   *Poems*, Boston (Mass.)
1836   *A Voice from the Factories in serious verse*, London
1839   *A Plain Letter to the Lord Chancellor on the Infant Custody Bill*, London
1840   *The Dream, and Other Poems*, Henry Colburn: London
1845   *A Child of the Islands. A Poem*, London
1854   *English Laws for Women in the Nineteenth Century*, Privately Printed: London
1855   *A Letter to the Queen on Lord Chancellor Cranworth's Marriage and Divorce Bill*, London
1861   *The Lady of La Garaye. A Poem*, Cambridge
1865   *Home Thoughts and Home Scenes. In original poems by J. I. etc.*, London
1978   *Selected Writings of Caroline Norton*, facsimile reproduction, Hoge, J. & Marcus, J. eds, Scholar's Facsimiles and Reprints: Delaware New York

Ogilvy, Eliza (1822–1912)

1845   *Rose Leaves*, privately printed
1846   *A Book of Highland Minstrelsy*, London
1851   *Traditions of Tuscany. In Verse*, London
1856   *Poems of Ten Years (1846–1855)*, London
1867   *Sunday Acrostics. Selected from Names or Words in the Bible*, London

Parkes, Bessie Rayner (1829–1925)

1852   *Poems*, London
1854   *Remarks on the Education of Girls*, London
1854   *Summer Sketches and Other Poems*, London
1856   *Gabriel, [A Poem]*, London
1856   *The History of Our Cat Aspasia*, London
1863   *Ballads and Songs*, London
1865   *Essays on Woman's Work*, London
1868   *La Belle France*, London
1895   *In a Walled Garden*, [Miscellaneous Essays published under the name of Belloc], Ward & Downey: London
1898   *Historic Nuns*, Duckworth & Co: London
1904   *In Fifty Years*, [Poems], London

Pfeiffer, Emily (1827–90)

1861 *Margaret, or The Motherless. A Poem*, Hurst & Blackett: London
1873 *Gerard's Monument and Other Poems*, London
1876 *Poems*, London
1877 *Glân-Alarch, his silence and his song. A Poem*, London
1879 *Quarterman's Grace and Other Poems*, London
1880 *Sonnets & Songs*, C. Kegan Paul & Co: London
1881 *The Wynnes of Wynhavod. A Drama of Modern Life. In Four Acts and in Verse*
1884 *The Rhyme of the Lady of the Rock, and how it grew. Prose and Verse*, Kegan Paul & Co: London
1885 *Flying Leaves from East and West*, [A Travel Book], London
1888 *Women and Work: An Essay Treating on the Relation to Health and Physical Development of the Higher Education of Girls . . . .* Trübner & Co: London
1889 *Flowers of the Night*, Trübner & Co: London
1882 *Under the Aspens: Lyrical and Dramatic*, London

Probyn, May (dates unknown)

1878 *Once! Twice! Thrice! And Away!* [A Novel], London
1880 'Robert Tresilian. A Story' in *The Seaside Annual for 1880*
1880 *Who Killed Cock Robin?* [A Story], Literary Production Committee: London
1881 *Poems*, W. Satchell & Co: London
1883 *A Ballad of the Road and Other Poems*, W. Satchell & Co: London
1895 *Pansies. A Book of Poems*, E. Matthews: London

Procter, Adelaide Anne (1825–64)

1858 *Legends & Lyrics. A Book of Verses*, Bell & Daldy: London
1861 *The Victoria Regia: a volume of original contributions of poetry and prose*, ed. A. A. Procter, London
1861 *A Chaplet of Verses*, London

Robinson, Agnes Mary, F. (1857–1944)

1878 *A Handful of Honeysuckle*; [In Verse], London
1881 *The Crowned Hippolytus*, Kegan Paul & Co: London
1883 *Arden* [A Novel], Longmans & Co: London
1883 *Emily Brontë* [A biography] in the Eminent Women series, W. H. Allen & Co: London
1884 *The New Arcadia and Other Poems*, Ellis & White: London
1886 *An Italian Garden. A Book of Songs*, T. F. Unwin: London
1888 *Songs, Ballads and a Garden Play*, T. Fisher Unwin: London
1893 *Retrospect and Other Poems*, The Cameo Series, London
1902 *The Collected Poems, Lyrical and Narrative of Mary F. Robinson (Madame Duclaux)*, T. Fisher Unwin: London
1903 *Fields of France: Little Essays in Descriptive Sociology*, Chapman & Hall: London
1904 *The Return to Nature: Songs and Symbols*, Chapman & Hall: London
1923 *Images & Meditations: Poems*, T. Fisher Unwin: London

Christina Rossetti (1830–1894)

1842 *To My Mother on the Anniversary of her Birth, April 27, 1842*, privately printed at G. Polidori's: London

1862 *Goblin Market and Other Poems*, with two designs by D. G. Rossetti, Cambridge

1866 *The Princ's Progress and Other Poems*, with two designs by D. G. Rossetti, London

1870 *Commonplace, and Other Short Stories*, London

1872 *Sing-Song, A Nursery Rhyme Book*, Routledge and Sons: London

1874 *Speaking Likenesses* (stories), Macmillan: London

1881 *A Pageant and Other Poems*, Macmillan: London

1885 *Time Flies: A Reading Diary*, London

1890 *Poems, New and Enlarged Edition*, Macmillan: London and New York.

1892 *The Face of the Deep: A Devotional Commentary on the Apocalypse*, London

1896 *New Poems, Hitherto Unpublished or Uncollected*, ed. W. M. Rossetti, Macmillan: London and New York

1897 *Maude: A Story for Girls*, introduced by W. M. Rossetti, J. Bowden: London

1904 *Poetical Works*, with Memoir and Notes by W. M. Rossetti, Macmillan: London

1908 *Family Letters*, ed. W. M. Rossetti, Brown, Langham: London

1979–90 *The Complete Poems of Christina Rossetti: A Variorum Edition*, 3 vols ed. R. W. Crump, Louisiana State University Press: Baton Rouge and London

Siddal, Elizabeth (1829–62)

1899 in Rossetti, William Michael, *Ruskin: Rossetti: Preraphaelitism: Papers 1854 to 1862*, London

1906 in Rossetti, William Michael, *Some Reminiscences of William Michael Rossetti*, vol 2., London

1978 *Poems and Drawings*, eds Roger C. Lewis and Mark S. Lasner, The Wombat Press: Wolfville, Nova Scotia

Dora Sigerson (Shorter) (1866–1918)

1899 *Ballads and Poems*, J. Bowden: London

1893 *Verses*, E. Stock: London

1907 *Collected Poems*, introduction by George Meredith, Hodder & Stoughton: London

1912 *New Poems*, Maunsel & Co.: Dublin and London

1916 *Love of Ireland: Poems and Ballads*, Maunsel & Co.: Dublin and London

1918 *The Sad Years, and other Poems*, with a tribute and memories by Katharine Tynan, Constable & Co.: London

Smedley, Menella Bute (1820–1877)

1849 *The Maiden Aunt*, [A Novel], London

1849 'A Very Woman' in *Seven Tales by Seven Authors*, M. B. Smedley ed., London

1852 *The Use of Sunshine: a Christmas Narrative by S. M.*, London

1853 *Nina. A Tale for the Twilight*, London

1856 *Lays & Ballads from English History*, London

1863 *The Story of Queen Isabel and Other Verses*, London

1868 *Poems*, London

1868 *Poems Written for a Child* by Two Friends, (in conjunction with E. A. Hart), Wells Gardner & Co: London

1869   *Child World*, Strahan & Co: London
1869   *Other Folks Lives*, London
1874   *Two Dramatic Poems. Blind Love: a dramatic poem. Cyril: Four Scenes From a Life*, London

Tindal, Henrietta (1818–1879)

1850   *Lines and Leaves*, London
1879   *Rhymes and Legends*, R. Bentley & Son: London
1856   *The Heirs of Blackridge Manor. A Tale of the Past and Present*, Chapman & Hall: London

Watson, Rosamond Marriott (Graham R. Johnson) (1860–1911)

1889   *The Bird-Bride: A Volume of Ballads and Sonnets*, Longmans: London
1891   *A Summer Night, and other Poems*, Methuen: London
1912   *Poems*, John Lane The Bodley Head: London

Webster, Augusta (1837–1894)

1860   *Blanche Lisle, and other Poems*, Cambridge [published under the pseudonym of Cecil Home]
1864   *Lesley's Guardians*, London & Cambridge
1864   *Lilian Gray*, London
1866   *Dramatic Studies*, London and Cambridge
1867   *A Woman Sold, and Other Poems*, London
1878   *Parliamentary Franchise for Women Ratepayers*, London
1879   *Disguises. A Drama*, C. Kegan Paul & Co: London
1879   *A Housewife's Opinions*, London
1881   *A Book of Rhyme*, Macmillan & Co: London
1882   *In a Day. A Drama*, Kegan Paul, Trench & Co: London
1884   *Daffodil and the Croaexaxicans. A Romance History*, Macmillan & Co: London
1887   *The Sentence. A Drama*, T. Fisher Unwin: London
1893   *Selections from The Verse of Augusta Webster*, Macmillan & Co: London
1895   *Mother & Daughter: An Uncompleted Sonnet-Sequence*, introduced by W. M. Rossetti, London

Wilde, Jane Francesca (Speranza) (1821–1896)

1857   *Hugo Bassi. A Tale of the Italian Revolution*, London
1864   *Poems by Speranza*, James Duffy: Dublin
1866   *Poems, Second series, Translations*, Dublin
1871   *Poems*, Cameron and Ferguson: Glasgow
1888   *Ancient Legends, Mystic Charms and Superstitions of Ireland*, Ward and Downey: London
1890   *Ancient Cures, Charms and Usages of Ireland. Contributions to Irish Lore*, Ward and Downey: London
1891   *Notes on Men, Women and Books*, Ward and Downey: London
1893   *Social Studies*, Ward and Downey: London
1907   *Poems by Speranza*, M. H. Gill & Son: London

Selected Bibliography of Anthologies and Criticism

(Anthologies are asterisked)

Armstrong, Isobel (1993) *Victorian Poetry: Poetry, Poetics and Politics*, London and New York, Routledge.

*Bax, Clifford, and Stewart, Meum ed. (1949) *The Distaff Muse: An Anthology of Poetry Written by Women*, London, Hollis & Carter.

*Bernikow, Louise ed. (1979) *The World Split Open: Four Centuries of Women Poets in England and America, 1552–1950*, London, Women's Press.

*Bethune, Geo W. ed. (1848) *The British Female Poets: with Biographical and Critical Notices*, Philadelphia.

Blake, Kathleen (1983) *Love and the Woman Question in Victorian Literature: The Art of Self-Postponement*, Hemel Hempstead, Harvester.

*Breen, Jennifer ed. (1994) *Victorian Women Poets 1830–1901: An Anthology*, London, Everyman, Dent.

Bristow, Joseph ed. (1995) *Victorian Women Poets*, New Casebook, Basingstoke, Macmillan.

Christ, Carol T. (1987) 'The Feminine Subject in Victorian Poetry', *English Literary History*, 54 (1987), 385–401.

DeJean, Joan (1989) *Fictions of Sappho, 1546–1937*, Chicago, Chicago University Press.

De Shazer, Mary K. (1986) *Inspiring Women: Re-Imagining the Muse*, Elmsford New York and Oxford, Pergamon Press.

Diehl, Joanne Feit (1978) ' "Come Slowly – Eden": An Exploration of Women Poets and Their Muse', *Signs*, 3 (1978), 572–87.

Elston, Mary Ann (1987) 'Women and Anti-vivisection in Victorian England, 1870–1900' in *Vivisection in Historial Perspective*, ed. Nicolaas A. Rupke, London, Croom Helm.

Faderman, Lillian (1981; 1985) *Surpassing the Love of Men*, London, Women's Press.

Flint, Kate (1993) *The Woman Reader 1837–1914*, Oxford, Clarendon Press.

Gilbert, Sandra M. and Gubar, Susan (1979) *The Madwoman in the Attic*, New Haven, Yale University Press.

—— eds (1979) *Shakespeare's Sisters: Feminist Essays on Women Poets*, Bloomington and London, Indiana University Press.

Gilmour, Robin (1993) *The Victorian Period: The Intellectual and Cultural Context of English Literature, 1830–1890*, London, Longman.

Gubar, Susan (1984) 'Sapphistries', *Signs*, 10 (1984), 43–62.

Hickok, Kathleen (1984) *Representations of Women: Nineteenth-Century British Women's Poetry*, Westport, Conn., Greenwood Press.

—— (1995) ' "Intimate Egoism": Reading and Evaluating Noncanonical Poetry by Women', *Victorian Poetry*, 33 (1995).

Homans, Margaret (1980) *Women Writers and Poetic Identity: Dorothy Wordsworth, Emily Brontë, and Emily Dickinson*, Princeton, N.J., Princeton University Press.

Hughes, Linda K. ed. (1995) *Victorian Poetry* (Special issue on women poets), 33 (1995).

*Kaplan, Cora ed. (1975) *Salt and Bitter and Good: Three Centuries of English and American Women Poets*, New York and London, Paddington Press.

—— (1986) 'Language and Gender' in *Sea Changes: Essays on Culture and Feminism*, London, Verso.

Lecercle, Jean-Jacques (1994) *Philosophy of Nonsense: The Intuitions of Victorian Nonsense Literature*, London, Routledge.

Leder, Sharon, with Abbott, Andrea (1987) *The Language of Exclusion: The Poetry of Emily Dickinson and Christina Rossetti*, New York, Greenwood Press.

Leighton, Angela (1989) '"Because men made the laws": The Fallen Woman and the Woman Poet', *Victorian Poetry*, 27 (1989), 109–27.

—— (1992) *Victorian Women Poets: Writing Against the Heart*, Hemel Hempstead, Harvester.

Lipking, Lawrence (1983) 'Aristotle's Sister: A Poetics of Abandonment' in *Critical Inquiry* Vol. 10, No. 1, 61–81.

*May, Caroline (1848) *The American Female Poets*, Philadelphia.

Mermin, Dorothy (1986) 'The Damsel, the Knight, and the Victorian Woman Poet', *Critical Inquiry*, 13 (1986), 64–80.

—— (1993) *Godiva's Ride: Women of Letters in England, 1830–1880*, Bloomington and Indianapolis, Indiana University Press.

Michie, Elsie B. (1993) *Outside the Pale: Cultural Exclusion, Gender Difference, and the Victorian Woman Writer*, Ithaca, New York, Cornell University Press.

*Miles, Alfred H. ed. (1891–7) *The Poets and the Poetry of the Century*, 10 vols, London.

Moers, Ellen (1963; 1978) *Literary Women*, London, The Women's Press.

Montefiore, Jan (1987) *Feminism and Poetry*, London, Pandora.

Ostriker, Alicia (1982) 'The Thieves of Language: Women Poets and Revisionist Mythmaking', *Signs*, 8, 68–90.

Pearce, Lynne (1991) *Woman/Image/Text: Readings in Pre-Raphaelite Art and Literature*, Hemel Hempstead, Harvester.

Robertson, Eric S. (1883) *English Poetesses: A Series of Critical Biographies, with Illustrative Extracts*, London.

*Rowton, Frederic ed. (1848; 1853) *The Female Poets of Great Britain*, Facsimile edition, with an introduction by Marilyn L. Williamson, Detroit, Wayne State University Press.

*Scott, Diana (1982) ed. *Bread and Roses: An Anthology of Nineteenth- and Twentieth-Century Poetry By Women Writers*, London, Virago.

*Sharp, Elizabeth A. ed. (1887) *Women's Voices: An Anthology of the Most Characteristic Poems by English, Scotch, and Irish Women*, London.

*Stanford, Ann ed. (1972) *The Women Poets in English: An Anthology*, New York, Herder.

Stodart, Mary Ann (1842) *Female Writers: Thoughts on Their Proper Sphere and on Their Powers of Usefulness*, London.

Index to the Notes

Index of Titles and First Lines